Microservices with Sp and Spring Cloud

Second Edition

Build resilient and scalable microservices using Spring Cloud, Istio, and Kubernetes

Magnus Larsson

BIRMINGHAM – MUMBAI

Microservices with Spring Boot and Spring Cloud

Second Edition

Producer: Caitlin Meadows
Acquisition Editor – Peer Reviews: Saby Dsilva
Project Editor: Rianna Rodrigues
Content Development Editor: Lucy Wan
Copy Editor: Safis Editing
Technical Editor: Aniket Shetty
Proofreader: Safis Editing
Indexer: Pratik Shirodkar
Presentation Designer: Ganesh Bhadwalkar

First published: September 2019

Second edition: July 2021

Production reference: 1270721

Published by Packt Publishing Ltd.
Livery Place
35 Livery Street
Birmingham
B3 2PB, UK.

ISBN 978-1-80107-297-7

www.packt.com

Contributors

About the author

Magnus Larsson has been in the IT industry for 35 years, working as a consultant for large companies in Sweden such as Volvo, Ericsson, and AstraZeneca. In the past, he struggled with the challenges associated with distributed systems. Today, these challenges can be handled with open source tools such as Spring Cloud, Kubernetes, and Istio. Over the last years, Magnus has been helping customers use these tools and has also given several presentations and written blog posts on the subject.

I would like to thank the following people:

Caitlin Meadows, Lucy Wan, Rianna Rodrigues, and Aniket Shetty from Packt Publishing for their support.

To my wife, Maria, thank you for all of your support and understanding throughout the process of writing this book.

About the reviewer

Kirill Merkushev is an engineer with a wide background in server-side development, infrastructure, and test automation. Starting off as an intern in Personal Services at Yandex, he quickly became a team lead, helping others to automate any kind of development process. He worked on a number of internal projects with amazing people who really love their job! In that kind of environment, it was incredibly easy for him to learn new approaches, frameworks, and languages. Given the size of Yandex and its services, it was a great chance to try out things at scale. For example, early reactive libraries in Java, the freshly released Spring Boot, the rock-solid Apache Camel, and golang.

During that time he became an open source expert, maintaining several projects including the Jenkins GitHub plugin, Aerokube Selenoid, and dozens of small libraries. After 7 years at Yandex, an opportunity to work in Germany in a small but quite promising health-tech startup called Vivy brought him to Berlin, where new challenges emerged, like how to build an event-sourced system, use encryption for good, and operate an internal Apache Pulsar cluster.

Now he is a happy power user of Testcontainers, father of two kids, Brompton rider, and a reviewer of this book!

I'd like to thank Sergei Egorov, who has shared tons of knowledge with me; Andrei Andryashin, who helped me with my first server-side development issues; Artem Eroshenko, who taught me how to give my first public talks; obviously, my wife, who makes it possible for me to code and review books in a comfortable environment any time of day; and my sons, who can already understand that daddy is actually working when he sits all day long in front of a PC!

Table of Contents

Preface

This book is about building production-ready microservices using Spring Boot and Spring Cloud. Eight years ago, when I began to explore microservices, I was looking for a book like this.

This book has been developed after I learned about, and mastered, open source software used for developing, testing, deploying, and managing landscapes of cooperating microservices.

This book primarily covers Spring Boot, Spring Cloud, Docker, Kubernetes, Istio, the EFK stack, Prometheus, and Grafana. Each of these open source tools works great by itself, but it can be challenging to understand how to use them together in an advantageous way. In some areas, they complement each other, but in other areas they overlap, and it is not obvious which one to choose for a particular situation.

This is a hands-on book that describes step by step how to use these open source tools together. This is the book I was looking for eight years ago when I started to learn about microservices, but with updated versions of the open source tools it covers.

Who this book is for

This book is for Java and Spring developers and architects who want to learn how to build microservice landscapes from the ground up and deploy them either on-premises or in the cloud, using Kubernetes as a container orchestrator and Istio as a service mesh. No familiarity with microservices architecture is required to get started with this book.

What this book covers

Chapter 1, Introduction to Microservices, will help you understand the basic premise of the book - microservices - along with the essential concepts and design patterns that go along with them.

Chapter 2, Introduction to Spring Boot, will get you introduced to Spring Boot and the other open source projects that will be used in the first part of the book: Spring WebFlux for developing RESTful APIs, springdoc-openapi for producing OpenAPI-based documentation for the APIs, Spring Data for storing data in SQL and NoSQL databases, Spring Cloud Stream for message-based microservices, and Docker to run the microservices as containers.

Chapter 3, Creating a Set of Cooperating Microservices, will teach you how to create a set of cooperating microservices from scratch. You will use Spring Initializr to create skeleton projects based on Spring Framework 5.3 and Spring Boot 2.5. The idea is to create three core services (that will handle their own resources) and one composite service that uses the three core services to aggregate a composite result. Toward the end of the chapter, you will learn how to add very basic RESTful APIs based on Spring WebFlux. In the next chapters, more and more functionality will be added to these microservices.

Chapter 4, Deploying Our Microservices Using Docker, will teach you how to deploy microservices using Docker. You will learn how to add Dockerfiles and docker-compose files in order to start up the whole microservice landscape with a single command. Then, you will learn how to use multiple Spring profiles to handle configurations with and without Docker.

Chapter 5, Adding an API Description Using OpenAPI, will get you up to speed with documenting the APIs exposed by a microservice using OpenAPI. You will use the `springdoc-openapi` tool to annotate the services to create OpenAPI-based API documentation on the fly. The key highlight will be how the APIs can be tested in a web browser using Swagger UI.

Chapter 6, Adding Persistence, will show you how to add persistence to the microservices' data. You will use Spring Data to set up and access data in a MongoDB document database for two of the core microservices and access data in a MySQL relational database for the remaining microservice. Testcontainers will be used to start up databases when running integration tests.

Chapter 7, Developing Reactive Microservices, will teach you why and when a reactive approach is of importance and how to develop end-to-end reactive services. You will learn how to develop and test both non-blocking synchronous RESTful APIs and asynchronous event-driven services.

You will also learn how to use the reactive non-blocking driver for MongoDB and use conventional blocking code for MySQL.

Chapter 8, Introduction to Spring Cloud, will introduce you to Spring Cloud and the components of Spring Cloud that will be used in this book.

Chapter 9, Adding Service Discovery Using Netflix Eureka, will show you how to use Netflix Eureka in Spring Cloud to add service discovery capabilities. This will be achieved by adding a Netflix Eureka-based service discovery server to the system landscape. You will then configure the microservices to use Spring Cloud LoadBalancer to find other microservices. You will understand how microservices are registered automatically and how traffic through Spring Cloud LoadBalancer is automatically load balanced to new instances when they become available.

Chapter 10, Using Spring Cloud Gateway to Hide Microservices behind an Edge Server, will guide you through how to hide the microservices behind an edge server using Spring Cloud Gateway and only expose select APIs to external consumers. You will also learn how to hide the internal complexity of the microservices from external consumers. This will be achieved by adding a Spring Cloud Gateway-based edge server to the system landscape and configuring it to only expose the public APIs.

Chapter 11, Securing Access to APIs, will explain how to protect exposed APIs using OAuth 2.0 and OpenID Connect. You will learn how to add an OAuth 2.0 authorization server based on Spring Authorization Server to the system landscape, and how to configure the edge server and the composite service to require valid access tokens issued by that authorization server. You will learn how to expose the authorization server through the edge server and secure its communication with external consumers using HTTPS. Finally, you will learn how to replace the internal OAuth 2.0 authorization server with an external OpenID Connect provider from Auth0.

Chapter 12, Centralized Configuration, will deal with how to collect the configuration files from all the microservices in one central repository and use the configuration server to distribute the configuration to the microservices at runtime. You will also learn how to add a Spring Cloud Config Server to the system landscape and configure all microservices to use the Spring Config Server to get its configuration.

Chapter 13, Improving Resilience Using Resilience4j, will explain how to use the capabilities of Resilience4j to prevent, for example, the "chain of failure" anti-pattern. You will learn how to add a retry mechanism and a circuit breaker to the composite service, how to configure the circuit breaker to fail fast when the circuit is open, and how to utilize a fallback method to create a best-effort response.

Chapter 14, Understanding Distributed Tracing, will show you how to use Zipkin to collect and visualize tracing information. You will also use Spring Cloud Sleuth to add trace IDs to requests so that request chains between cooperating microservices can be visualized.

Chapter 15, Introduction to Kubernetes, will explain the core concepts of Kubernetes and how to perform a sample deployment. You will also learn how to set up Kubernetes locally for development and testing purposes using Minikube.

Chapter 16, Deploying Our Microservices to Kubernetes, will show how to deploy microservices on Kubernetes. You will also learn how to use Helm to package and configure microservices for deployment in Kubernetes. Helm will be used to deploy the microservices for different runtime environments, such as test and production environments. Finally, you will learn how to replace Netflix Eureka with the built-in support in Kubernetes for service discovery, based on Kubernetes Service objects and the kube-proxy runtime component.

Chapter 17, Implementing Kubernetes Features to Simplify the System Landscape, will explain how to use Kubernetes features as an alternative to the Spring Cloud services introduced in the previous chapters. You will learn why and how to replace Spring Cloud Config Server with Kubernetes Secrets and ConfigMaps. You will also learn why and how to replace Spring Cloud Gateway with Kubernetes Ingress objects and how to add cert-manager to automatically provision and rotate certificates for external HTTPS endpoints.

Chapter 18, Using a Service Mesh to Improve Observability and Management, will introduce the concept of a service mesh and explain how to use Istio to implement a service mesh at runtime using Kubernetes. You will learn how to use a service mesh to further improve the resilience, security, traffic management, and observability of the microservice landscape.

Chapter 19, Centralized Logging with the EFK Stack, will explain how to use Elasticsearch, Fluentd, and Kibana (the EFK stack) to collect, store, and visualize log streams from microservices. You will learn how to deploy the EFK stack in Minikube and how to use it to analyze collected log records and find log output from all microservices involved in the processing of a request that spans several microservices. You will also learn how to perform root cause analysis using the EFK stack.

Chapter 20, Monitoring Microservices, will show you how to monitor the microservices deployed in Kubernetes using Prometheus and Grafana. You will learn how to use existing dashboards in Grafana to monitor different types of metrics, and you will also learn how to create your own dashboards. Finally, you will learn how to create alerts in Grafana that will be used to send emails with alerts when configured thresholds are passed for selected metrics.

Chapter 21, Installation Instructions for macOS, will show you how to install the tools used in this book on a Mac.

Chapter 22, Installation Instructions for Microsoft Windows with WSL 2 and Ubuntu, will show you how to install the tools used in this book on a Windows PC using Windows Subsystem for Linux 2.

Chapter 23, Native Compiled Java Microservices, will show you how to use the recently announced beta of Spring Native and the underlying GraalVM Native Image builder to create Spring-based microservices that are compiled to native code. Compared to using the regular Java Virtual Machine, this will result in microservices that can start up almost instantly.

At the end of every chapter, you'll find some straightforward questions that will help you to recap some of the content covered in the chapter. *Assessments* is a file that can be found in the GitHub repository containing the answers to these questions.

To get the most out of this book

A basic understanding of Java and Spring is recommended.

To be able to run all content in the book, you are required to have a Mac or PC with at least 16 GB of memory, though it is recommended you have at least 24 GB, as the microservice landscape becomes more complex and resource-demanding toward the end of the book.

For a full list of software requirements and detailed instructions for setting up your environment to be able to follow along with this book, head over to *Chapter 21* (for macOS) and *Chapter 22* (for Windows).

Download the example code files

The code bundle for the book is hosted on GitHub at `https://github.com/PacktPublishing/Microservices-with-Spring-Boot-and-Spring-Cloud-2E`. We also have other code bundles from our rich catalog of books and videos available at `https://github.com/PacktPublishing/`. Check them out!

Download the color images

We also provide a PDF file that has color images of the screenshots/diagrams used in this book. You can download it here: `https://static.packt-cdn.com/downloads/9781801072977_ColorImages.pdf`.

Conventions used

There are a number of text conventions used throughout this book.

`CodeInText`: Indicates code words in text, database table names, folder names, filenames, file extensions, pathnames, dummy URLs, user input, and Twitter handles. For example; "The test class, `PersistenceTests`, declares a method, `setupDb()`, annotated with `@BeforeEach`, which is executed before each test method."

A block of code is set as follows:

```
public interface ReviewRepository extends CrudRepository<ReviewEntity,
Integer> {
    @Transactional(readOnly = true)
    List<ReviewEntity> findByProductId(int productId);
}
```

When we wish to draw your attention to a particular part of a code block, the relevant lines or items are highlighted:

```
public interface ReviewRepository extends CrudRepository<ReviewEntity,
Integer> {
    @Transactional(readOnly = true)
    List<ReviewEntity> findByProductId(int productId);
}
```

Any command-line input or output is written as follows:

```
kubectl config get-contexts
```

Bold: Indicates a new term, an important word, or words that you see on the screen, for example, in menus or dialog boxes, also appear in the text like this. For example: "The two core concepts of the programming model in Spring Data are **entities** and **repositories**."

Warnings or important notes appear like this.

Tips and tricks appear like this.

Get in touch

Feedback from our readers is always welcome.

General feedback: Email `feedback@packtpub.com`, and mention the book's title in the subject of your message. If you have questions about any aspect of this book, please email us at `questions@packtpub.com`.

Errata: Although we have taken every care to ensure the accuracy of our content, mistakes do happen. If you have found a mistake in this book we would be grateful if you would report this to us. Please visit `http://www.packtpub.com/submit-errata`, select your book, click on the Errata Submission Form link, and enter the details.

Piracy: If you come across any illegal copies of our works in any form on the Internet, we would be grateful if you would provide us with the location address or website name. Please contact us at `copyright@packtpub.com` with a link to the material.

If you are interested in becoming an author: If there is a topic that you have expertise in and you are interested in either writing or contributing to a book, please visit `http://authors.packtpub.com`.

Share your thoughts

Once you've read *Microservices with Spring Boot and Spring Cloud, Second Edition*, we'd love to hear your thoughts! Scan the QR code below to go straight to the Amazon review page for this book and share your feedback.

https://packt.link/r/1-801-07297-3

Your review is important to us and the tech community and will help us make sure we're delivering excellent quality content.

Part I

Getting Started with Microservice Development Using Spring Boot

In this part, you will learn how to use some of the most important features of Spring Boot to develop microservices.

This part includes the following chapters:

- *Chapter 1, Introduction to Microservices*
- *Chapter 2, Introduction to Spring Boot*
- *Chapter 3, Creating a Set of Cooperating Microservices*
- *Chapter 4, Deploying Our Microservices Using Docker*
- *Chapter 5, Adding an API Description Using OpenAPI*
- *Chapter 6, Adding Persistence*
- *Chapter 7, Developing Reactive Microservices*

1

Introduction to Microservices

This book does not blindly praise microservices. Instead, it's about how we can use their benefits while being able to handle the challenges of building scalable, resilient, and manageable microservices.

As an introduction to this book, the following topics will be covered in this chapter:

- How I learned about microservices and what experience I have of their benefits and challenges
- What is a microservice-based architecture?
- Challenges with microservices
- Design patterns for handling challenges
- Software enablers that can help us handle these challenges
- Other important considerations that aren't covered in this book

Technical requirements

No installations are required for this chapter. However, you may be interested in taking a look at the C4 model conventions, `https://c4model.com`, since the illustrations in this chapter are inspired by the C4 model.

This chapter does not contain any source code.

My way into microservices

When I first learned about the concept of microservices back in 2014, I realized that I had been developing microservices (well, kind of) for a number of years without knowing it was microservices I was dealing with. I was involved in a project that started in 2009 where we developed a platform based on a set of separated features. The platform was delivered to a number of customers that deployed it on-premises. To make it easy for customers to pick and choose what features they wanted to use from the platform, each feature was developed as an **autonomous software component**; that is, it had its own persistent data and only communicated with other components using well-defined APIs.

Since I can't discuss specific features in this project's platform, I have generalized the names of the components, which are labeled from **Component A** to **Component F**. The **composition** of the platform into a set of components is illustrated as follows:

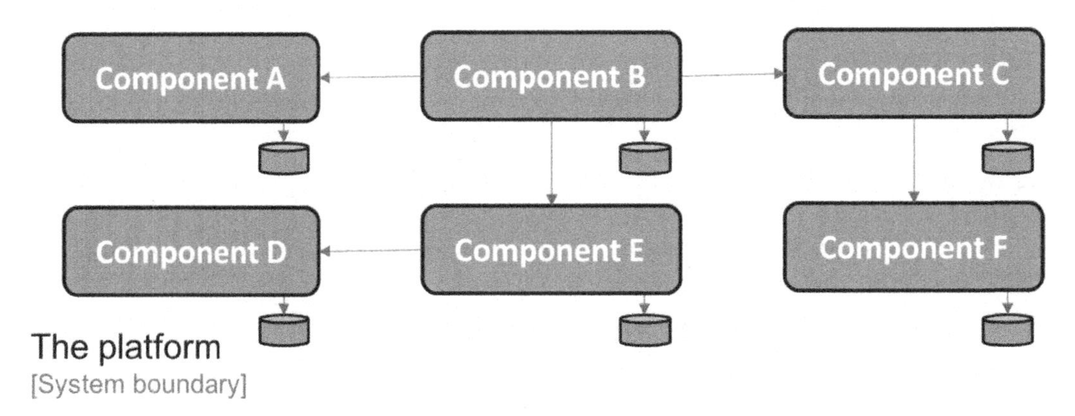

Figure 1.1: The composition of the platform

From the illustration, we can also see that each component has its own storage for persistent data, and is not sharing databases with other components.

Each component is developed using Java and the Spring Framework, packaged as a WAR file and deployed as a web app in a Java EE web container, for example, Apache Tomcat. Depending on the customer's specific requirements, the platform can be deployed on single or multiple servers. A two-node deployment may look as follows:

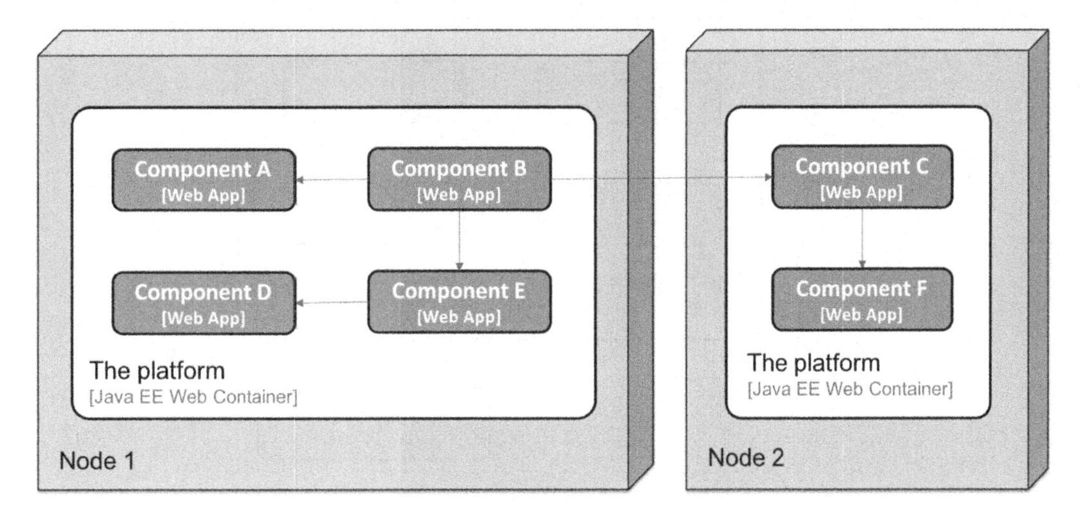

Figure 1.2: A two-node deployment scenario

Benefits of autonomous software components

From this project, I learned that decomposing the platform's functionality into a set of autonomous software components provides a number of benefits:

- A customer can deploy parts of the platform in its own system landscape, integrating it with its existing systems using its well-defined APIs.

  The following is an example where one customer decided to deploy **Component A**, **Component B**, **Component D**, and **Component E** from the platform and integrate them with two existing systems in the customer's system landscape, **System A** and **System B**:

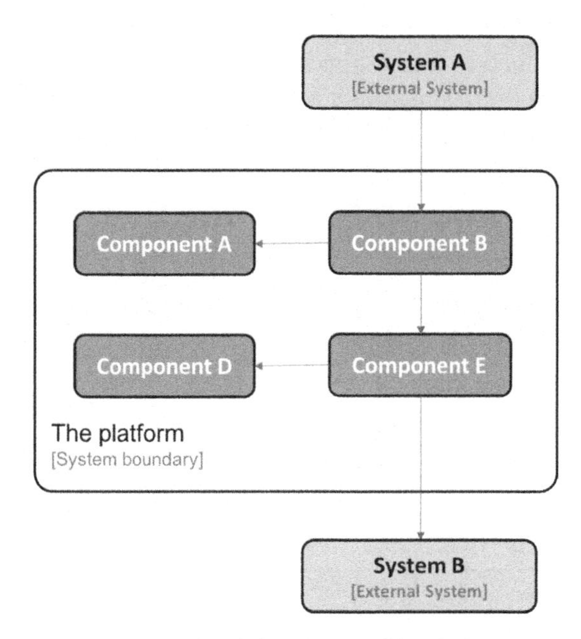

Figure 1.3: Partial deployment of the platform

- Another customer can choose to replace parts of the platform's functionality with implementations that already exist in the customer's system landscape, potentially requiring some adoption of the existing functionality in the platform's APIs. The following is an example where a customer has replaced **Component C** and **Component F** in the platform with their own implementation:

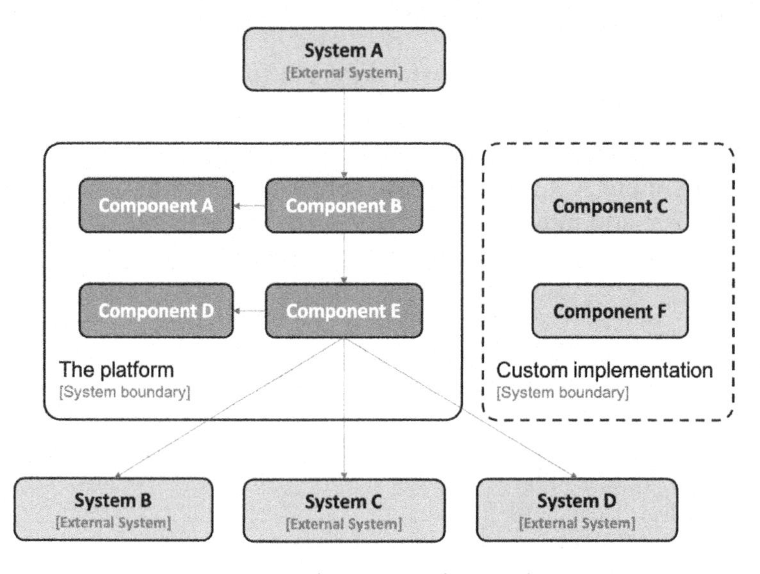

Figure 1.4: Replacing parts of the platform

- Each component in the platform can be delivered and upgraded separately. Thanks to the use of well-defined APIs, one component can be upgraded to a new version without being dependent on the life cycle of the other components.

  The following is an example where **Component A** has been upgraded from version **v1.1** to **v1.2. Component B**, which calls **Component A**, does not need to be upgraded since it uses a well-defined API; that is, it's still the same after the upgrade (or it's at least backward-compatible):

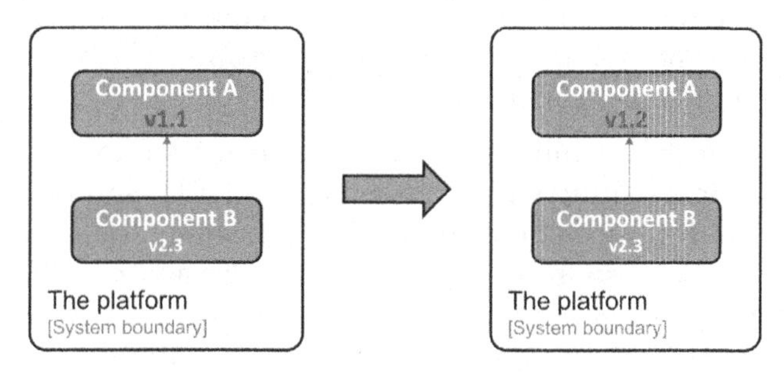

Figure 1.5: Upgrading a specific component

- Thanks to the use of well-defined APIs, each component in the platform can also be scaled out to multiple servers independently of the other components. Scaling can be done either to meet high availability requirements or to handle higher volumes of requests. In this specific project, it was achieved by *manually* setting up load balancers in front of a number of servers, each running a Java EE web container. An example where **Component A** has been scaled out to three instances looks as follows:

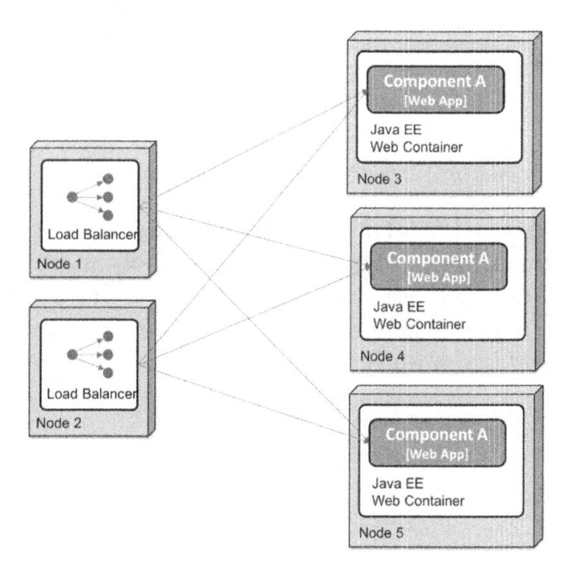

Figure 1.6: Scaling out the platform

Challenges with autonomous software components

My team also learned that decomposing the platform introduced a number of new challenges that we were not exposed to (at least not to the same degree) when developing more traditional, monolithic applications:

- Adding new instances to a component required manually configuring load balancers and manually setting up new nodes. This work was both time-consuming and error-prone.
- The platform was initially prone to errors caused by the other systems it was communicating with. If a system stopped responding to requests that were sent from the platform in a timely fashion, the platform quickly ran out of crucial resources, for example, OS threads, specifically when exposed to a large number of concurrent requests. This caused components in the platform to hang or even crash. Since most of the communication in the platform is based on synchronous communication, one component crashing can lead to cascading failures; that is, clients of the crashing components could also crash after a while. This is known as a **chain of failures**.
- Keeping the configuration in all the instances of the components consistent and up to date quickly became a problem, causing a lot of manual and repetitive work. This led to quality problems from time to time.
- Monitoring the state of the platform in terms of latency issues and hardware usage (for example, usage of CPU, memory, disks, and the network) was more complicated compared to monitoring a single instance of a monolithic application.
- Collecting log files from a number of distributed components and correlating related log events from the components was also difficult, but feasible since the number of components was fixed and known in advance.

Over time, we addressed most of the challenges that were mentioned in the preceding list with a mix of in-house-developed tools and well-documented instructions for handling these challenges manually. The scale of the operation was, in general, at a level where manual procedures for releasing new versions of the components and handling runtime issues were acceptable, even though they were not desirable.

Enter microservices

Learning about microservice-based architectures in 2014 made me realize that other projects had also been struggling with similar challenges (partly for other reasons than the ones I described earlier, for example, the large cloud service providers meeting web-scale requirements). Many microservice pioneers had published details of lessons they'd learned. It was very interesting to learn from these lessons.

Many of the pioneers initially developed monolithic applications that made them very successful from a business perspective. But over time, these monolithic applications became more and more difficult to maintain and evolve. They also became challenging to scale beyond the capabilities of the largest machines available (also known as **vertical scaling**). Eventually, the pioneers started to find ways to split monolithic applications into smaller components that could be released and scaled independently of each other. Scaling small components can be done using **horizontal scaling**, that is, deploying a component on a number of smaller servers and placing a load balancer in front of it. If done in the cloud, the scaling capability is potentially endless – it is just a matter of how many virtual servers you bring in (given that your component can scale out on a huge number of instances, but more on that later on).

In 2014, I also learned about a number of new open source projects that delivered tools and frameworks that simplified the development of microservices and could be used to handle the challenges that come with a microservice-based architecture. Some of these are as follows:

- Pivotal released **Spring Cloud**, which wraps parts of the **Netflix OSS** in order to provide capabilities such as dynamic service discovery, configuration management, distributed tracing, circuit breaking, and more.
- I also learned about **Docker** and the container revolution, which is great for minimizing the gap between development and production. Being able to package a component not only as a deployable runtime artifact (for example, a Java `war` or `jar` file) but as a complete image, ready to be launched as a container on a server running Docker, was a great step forward for development and testing.

For now, think of a container as an isolated process. We will learn more about containers in *Chapter 4, Deploying Our Microservices Using Docker.*

- A container engine, such as Docker, is not enough to be able to use containers in a production environment. Something is needed that can ensure that all the containers are up and running and that can scale out containers on a number of servers, thereby providing high availability and increased compute resources.

- These types of product became known as **container orchestrators**. A number of products have evolved over the last few years, such as Apache Mesos, Docker in Swarm mode, Amazon ECS, HashiCorp Nomad, and **Kubernetes**. Kubernetes was initially developed by Google. When Google released v1.0 in 2015, they also donated Kubernetes to **CNCF** (`https://www.cncf.io/`). During 2018, Kubernetes became kind of a de facto standard, available both pre-packaged for on-premises use and as a service from most of the major cloud providers.

> As explained in `https://kubernetes.io/blog/2015/04/borg-predecessor-to-kubernetes/`, Kubernetes is actually an open source-based rewrite of an internal container orchestrator, named **Borg**, used by Google for more than a decade before the Kubernetes project was founded.

- In 2018, I started to learn about the concept of a **service mesh** and how a service mesh can complement a container orchestrator to further offload microservices from responsibilities to make them manageable and resilient.

A sample microservice landscape

Since this book can't cover all aspects of the technologies I just mentioned, I will focus on the parts that have proven to be useful in customer projects I have been involved in since 2014. I will describe how they can be used together to create cooperating microservices that are manageable, scalable, and resilient.

Each chapter in this book will address a specific concern. To demonstrate how things fit together, I will use a small set of cooperating microservices that we will evolve throughout this book. The microservice landscape will be described in *Chapter 3, Creating a Set of Cooperating Microservices*; for now, it is sufficient to know that it looks like this:

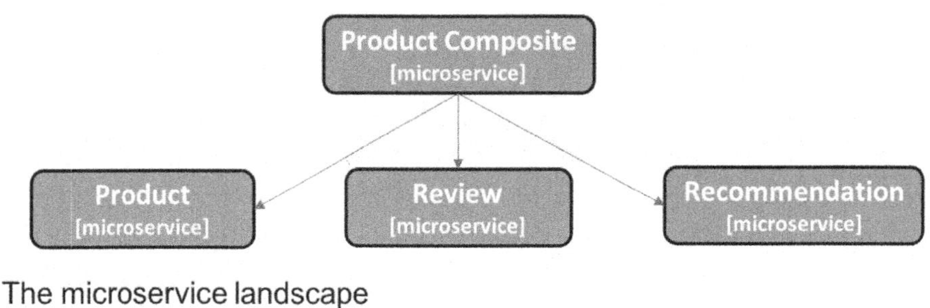

Figure 1.7: The microservice-based system landscape used in the book

Note that this is a very small system landscape of cooperating microservices. The surrounding support services that we will add in the coming chapters might look overwhelmingly complex for these few microservices. But keep in mind that the solutions presented in this book aim to support a much larger system landscape.

Now that we have been introduced to the potential benefits and challenges of microservices, let's start to look into how a microservice can be defined.

Defining a microservice

A microservice architecture is about splitting up monolithic applications into smaller components, which achieves two major goals:

- Faster development, enabling continuous deployments
- Easier to scale, manually or automatically

A microservice is essentially an autonomous software component that is independently upgradeable, replaceable, and scalable. To be able to act as an autonomous component, it must fulfill certain criteria, as follows:

- It must conform to a shared-nothing architecture; that is, microservices don't share data in databases with each other!
- It must only communicate through well-defined interfaces, either using APIs and synchronous services or preferably by sending messages asynchronously. The APIs and message formats used must be stable, well-documented, and evolve by following a defined versioning strategy.
- It must be deployed as separate runtime processes. Each instance of a microservice runs in a separate runtime process, for example, a Docker container.
- Microservice instances are stateless so that incoming requests to a microservice can be handled by any of its instances.

Using a set of cooperating microservices, we can deploy to a number of smaller servers instead of being forced to deploy to a single big server, like we have to do when deploying a monolithic application.

Given that the preceding criteria have been fulfilled, it is easier to scale up a single microservice into more instances (for example, using more virtual servers) compared to scaling up a big monolithic application.

Utilizing autoscaling capabilities that are available in the cloud is also a possibility, but is not typically feasible for a big monolithic application. It's also easier to upgrade or even replace a single microservice compared to upgrading a big monolithic application.

This is illustrated by the following diagram, where a monolithic application has been divided into six microservices, all of which have been deployed into separate servers. Some of the microservices have also been scaled up independently of the others:

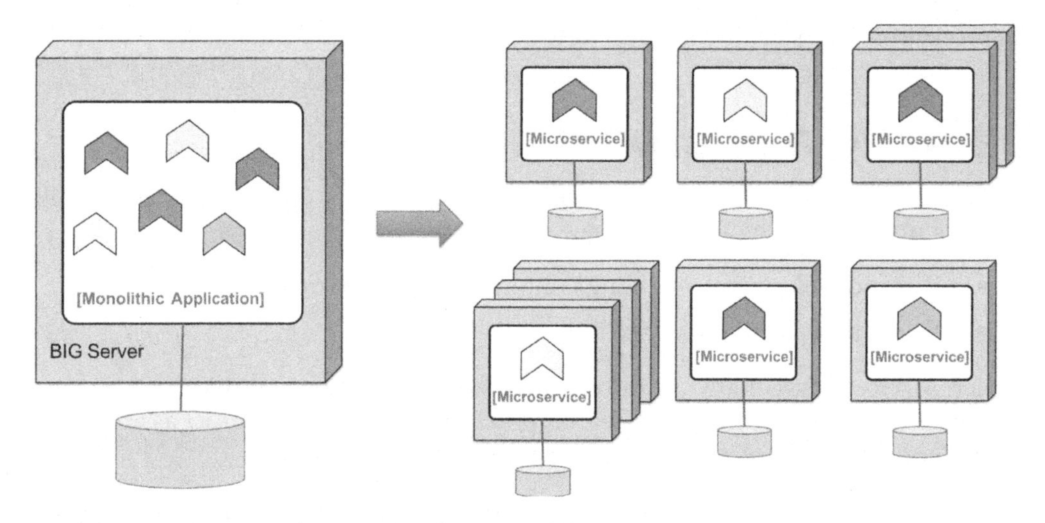

Figure 1.8: Dividing a monolith into microservices

A very frequent question I receive from customers is:

> *How big should a microservice be?*

I try to use the following rules of thumb:

- Small enough to fit in the head of a developer
- Big enough to not jeopardize performance (that is, latency) and/or data consistency (SQL foreign keys between data that's stored in different microservices are no longer something you can take for granted)

So, to summarize, a microservice architecture is, in essence, an architectural style where we decompose a monolithic application into a group of cooperating autonomous software components. The motivation is to enable faster development and to make it easier to scale the application.

With a better understanding of how to define a microservice, we can move on and detail the challenges that come with a system landscape of microservices.

Challenges with microservices

In the *Challenges with autonomous software components* section, we have already seen some of the challenges that autonomous software components can bring (and they all apply to microservices as well) as follows:

- Many small components that use synchronous communication can cause *a chain of failure* problem, especially under high load
- Keeping the configuration up to date for many small components can be challenging
- It's hard to track a request that's being processed and involves many components, for example, when performing root cause analysis, where each component stores log records locally
- Analyzing the usage of hardware resources on a component level can be challenging as well
- Manual configuration and management of many small components can become costly and error-prone

Another downside (but not always obvious initially) of decomposing an application into a group of autonomous components is that they form a **distributed system**. Distributed systems are known to be, by their nature, very hard to deal with. This has been known for many years (but in many cases neglected until proven differently). My favorite quote to establish this fact is from Peter Deutsch who, back in 1994, stated the following:

> **The 8 fallacies of distributed computing**: *Essentially everyone, when they first build a distributed application, makes the following eight assumptions. All prove to be false in the long run and all cause big trouble and painful learning experiences:*
>
> 1. *The network is reliable*
> 2. *Latency is zero*
> 3. *Bandwidth is infinite*
> 4. *The network is secure*
> 5. *Topology doesn't change*
> 6. *There is one administrator*
> 7. *Transport cost is zero*
> 8. *The network is homogeneous*
>
> *– Peter Deutsch, 1994*

In general, building microservices based on these false assumptions leads to solutions that are prone to both temporary network glitches and problems that occur in other microservice instances. When the number of microservices in a system landscape increases, the likelihood of problems also goes up. A good rule of thumb is to design your microservice architecture based on the assumption that there is always something going wrong in the system landscape. The microservice architecture needs to be designed to handle this, in terms of detecting problems and restarting failed components. Also, on the client side, ensure that requests are not sent to failed microservice instances. When problems are corrected, requests to the previously failing microservice should be resumed; that is, microservice clients need to be resilient. All of this needs, of course, to be fully automated. With a large number of microservices, it is not feasible for operators to handle this manually!

The scope of this is large, but we will limit ourselves for now and move on to learn about design patterns for microservices.

Design patterns for microservices

This topic will cover the use of design patterns to mitigate challenges with microservices, as described in the preceding section. Later in this book, we will see how we can implement these design patterns using Spring Boot, Spring Cloud, Kubernetes, and Istio.

The concept of design patterns is actually quite old; it was invented by Christopher Alexander back in 1977. In essence, a design pattern is about describing a reusable solution to a problem when given a specific context. Using a tried and tested solution from a design pattern can save a lot of time and increase the quality of the implementation compared to spending time on inventing the solution ourselves.

The design patterns we will cover are as follows:

- Service discovery
- Edge server
- Reactive microservices
- Central configuration
- Centralized log analysis
- Distributed tracing
- Circuit breaker
- Control loop
- Centralized monitoring and alarms

This list is not intended to be comprehensive; instead, it's a minimal list of design patterns that are required to handle the challenges we described previously.

We will use a lightweight approach to describing design patterns, and focus on the following:

- The problem
- A solution
- Requirements for the solution

Throughout in this book, we will delve more deeply into how to apply these design patterns. The context for these design patterns is a system landscape of cooperating microservices where the microservices communicate with each other using either synchronous requests (for example, using HTTP) or by sending asynchronous messages (for example, using a message broker).

Service discovery

The service discovery pattern has the following problem, solution, and solution requirements.

Problem

How can clients find microservices and their instances?

Microservices instances are typically assigned dynamically allocated IP addresses when they start up, for example, when running in containers. This makes it difficult for a client to make a request to a microservice that, for example, exposes a REST API over HTTP. Consider the following diagram:

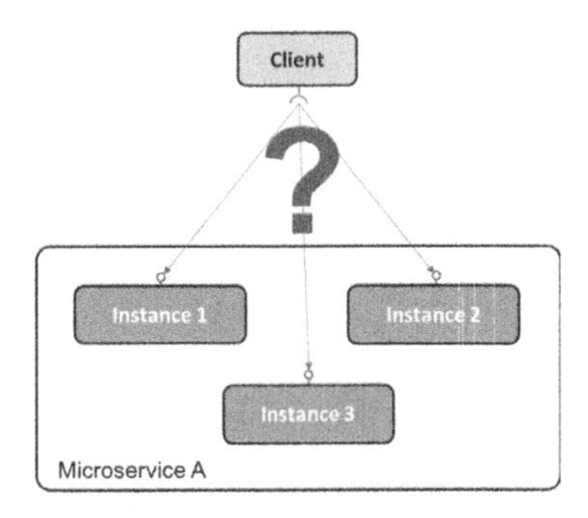

Figure 1.9: The service discovery issue

Solution

Add a new component - a **service discovery** service - to the system landscape, which keeps track of currently available microservices and the IP addresses of its instances.

Solution requirements

Some solution requirements are as follows:

- Automatically register/unregister microservices and their instances as they come and go.
- The client must be able to make a request to a logical endpoint for the microservice. The request will be routed to one of the available microservice instances.
- Requests to a microservice must be load-balanced over the available instances.
- We must be able to detect instances that currently are unhealthy, so that requests will not be routed to them.

Implementation notes: As we will see, in *Chapter 9, Adding Service Discovery Using Netflix Eureka*, *Chapter 15, Introduction to Kubernetes*, and *Chapter 16, Deploying Our Microservices to Kubernetes*, this design pattern can be implemented using two different strategies:

- **Client-side routing**: The client uses a library that communicates with the service discovery service to find out the proper instances to send the requests to.
- **Server-side routing**: The infrastructure of the service discovery service also exposes a reverse proxy that all requests are sent to. The reverse proxy forwards the requests to a proper microservice instance on behalf of the client.

Edge server

The edge server pattern has the following problem, solution, and solution requirements.

Problem

In a system landscape of microservices, it is in many cases desirable to expose some of the microservices to the outside of the system landscape and hide the remaining microservices from external access. The exposed microservices must be protected against requests from malicious clients.

Solution

Add a new component, an **edge server**, to the system landscape that all incoming requests will go through:

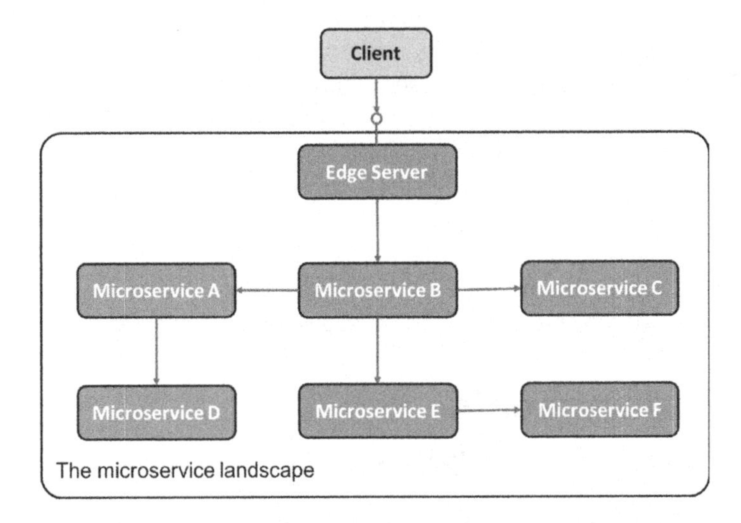

Figure 1.10: The edge server design pattern

Implementation notes: An edge server typically behaves like a reverse proxy and can be integrated with a discovery service to provide dynamic load-balancing capabilities.

Solution requirements

Some solution requirements are as follows:

- Hide internal services that should not be exposed outside their context; that is, only route requests to microservices that are configured to allow external requests
- Expose external services and protect them from malicious requests; that is, use standard protocols and best practices such as OAuth, OIDC, JWT tokens, and API keys to ensure that the clients are trustworthy

Reactive microservices

The reactive microservice pattern has the following problem, solution, and solution requirements.

Problem

Traditionally, as Java developers, we are used to implementing synchronous communication using blocking I/O, for example, a RESTful JSON API over HTTP. Using a blocking I/O means that a thread is allocated from the operating system for the length of the request. If the number of concurrent requests goes up, a server might run out of available threads in the operating system, causing problems ranging from longer response times to crashing servers. Using a microservice architecture typically makes this problem even worse, where typically a chain of cooperating microservices is used to serve a request. The more microservices involved in serving a request, the faster the available threads will be drained.

Solution

Use non-blocking I/O to ensure that no threads are allocated while waiting for processing to occur in another service, that is, a database or another microservice.

Solution requirements

Some solution requirements are as follows:

- Whenever feasible, use an asynchronous programming model, sending messages without waiting for the receiver to process them.
- If a synchronous programming model is preferred, use reactive frameworks that can execute synchronous requests using non-blocking I/O, without allocating a thread while waiting for a response. This will make the microservices easier to scale in order to handle an increased workload.
- Microservices must also be designed to be resilient and self-healing. Resilient meaning being capable of producing a response even if one of the services it depends on fails; self-healing meaning that once the failing service is operational again, the microservice must be able to resume using it.

In 2013, key principles for designing reactive systems were established in **The Reactive Manifesto** (`https://www.reactivemanifesto.org/`).

According to the manifesto, the foundation for reactive systems is that they are message-driven; they use asynchronous communication. This allows them to be elastic, that is, scalable, and resilient, that is, tolerant to failures. Elasticity and resilience together enable a reactive system to always respond in a timely fashion.

Central configuration

The central configuration pattern has the following problem, solution, and solution requirements.

Problem

An application is, traditionally, deployed together with its configuration, for example, a set of environment variables and/or files containing configuration information. Given a system landscape based on a microservice architecture, that is, with a large number of deployed microservice instances, some queries arise:

- How do I get a complete picture of the configuration that is in place for all the running microservice instances?
- How do I update the configuration and make sure that all the affected microservice instances are updated correctly?

Solution

Add a new component, a **configuration server**, to the system landscape to store the configuration of all the microservices, as illustrated by the following diagram:

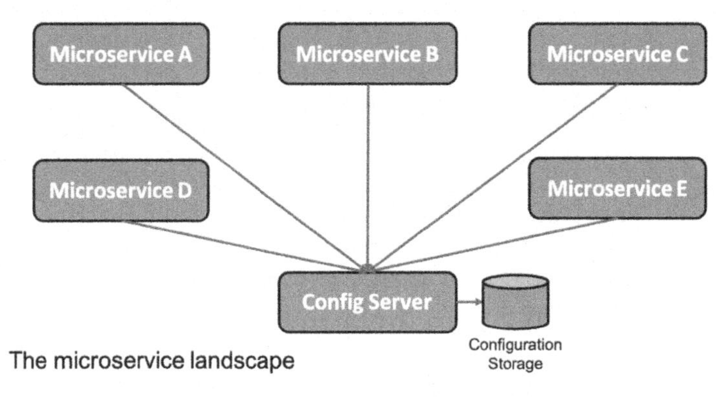

Figure 1.11: The central configuration design pattern

Solution requirements

Make it possible to store configuration information for a group of microservices in one place, with different settings for different environments (for example, **dev**, **test**, **qa**, and **prod**).

Centralized log analysis

Centralized log analysis has the following problem, solution, and solution requirements.

Problem

Traditionally, an application writes log events to log files that are stored in the local filesystem of the server that the application runs on. Given a system landscape based on a microservice architecture, that is, with a large number of deployed microservice instances on a large number of smaller servers, we can ask the following questions:

- How do I get an overview of what is going on in the system landscape when each microservice instance writes to its own local log file?
- How do I find out if any of the microservice instances get into trouble and start writing error messages to their log files?

- If end users start to report problems, how can I find related log messages; that is, how can I identify which microservice instance is the root cause of the problem? The following diagram illustrates the problem:

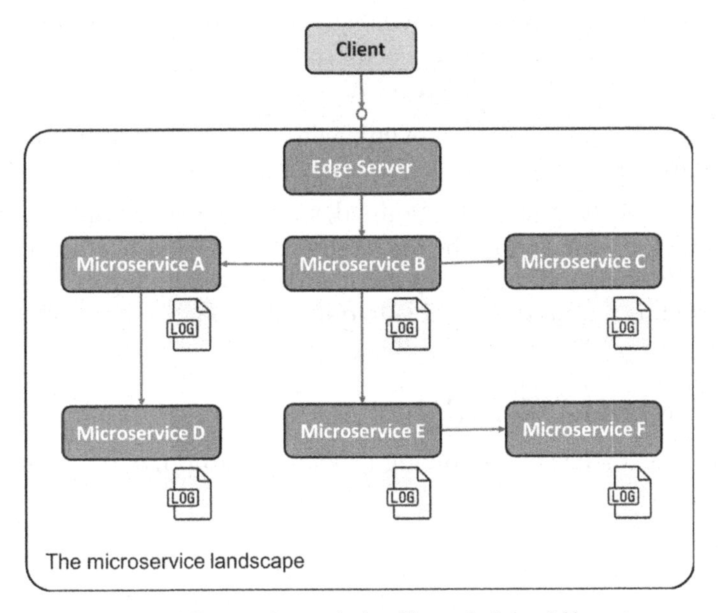

Figure 1.12: Microservices write log files to their local file system

Solution

Add a new component that can manage **centralized logging** and is capable of the following:

- Detecting new microservice instances and collecting log events from them
- Interpreting and storing log events in a structured and searchable way in a central database
- Providing APIs and graphical tools for querying and analyzing log events

Solution requirements

Some solution requirements are as follows:

- Microservices stream log events to standard system output, `stdout`. This makes it easier for a log collector to find the log events compared to when log events are written to microservice-specific logfiles.
- Microservices tag the log events with the correlation ID described in the next section regarding the *Distributed tracing* design pattern.
- A canonical log format is defined, so that log collectors can transform log events collected from the microservices to a canonical log format before log events are stored in the central database. Storing log events in a canonical log format is required to be able to query and analyze the collected log events.

Distributed tracing

Distributed tracing has the following problem, solution, and solution requirements.

Problem

It must be possible to track requests and messages that flow between microservices while processing an external request to the system landscape.

Some examples of fault scenarios are as follows:

- If end users start to file support cases regarding a specific failure, how can we identify the microservice that caused the problem, that is, the root cause?
- If one support case mentions problems related to a specific entity, for example, a specific order number, how can we find log messages related to processing this specific order – for example, log messages from all microservices that were involved in processing it?
- If end users start to file support cases regarding an unacceptably long response time, how can we identify which microservice in a call chain is causing the delay?

The following diagram depicts this:

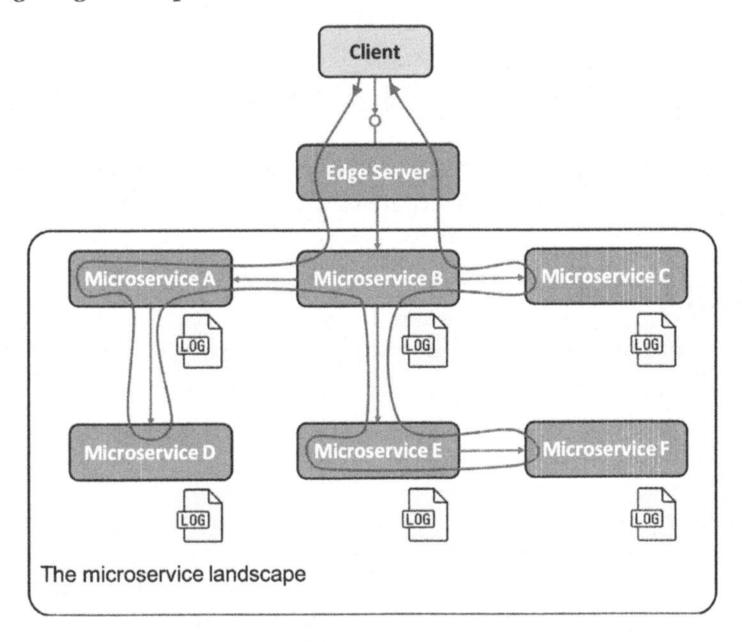

Figure 1.13: The distributed tracing issue

Solution

To track the processing between cooperating microservices, we need to ensure that all related requests and messages are marked with a common **correlation ID** and that the correlation ID is part of all log events. Based on a correlation ID, we can use the centralized logging service to find all related log events. If one of the log events also includes information about a business-related identifier, for example, the ID of a customer, product, or order, we can find all related log events for that business identifier using the correlation ID.

To be able to analyze delays in a call chain of cooperating microservices, we must be able to collect timestamps for when requests, responses, and messages enter and exit each microservice.

Solution requirements

The solution requirements are as follows:

- Assign unique correlation IDs to all incoming or new requests and events in a well-known place, such as a header with a standardized name

- When a microservice makes an outgoing request or sends a message, it must add the correlation ID to the request and message
- All log events must include the correlation ID in a predefined format so that the centralized logging service can extract the correlation ID from the log event and make it searchable
- Trace records must be created for when requests, responses, and messages both enter or exit a microservice instance

Circuit breaker

The circuit breaker pattern has the following problem, solution, and solution requirements.

Problem

A system landscape of microservices that uses synchronous intercommunication can be exposed to a **chain of failures**. If one microservice stops responding, its clients might get into problems as well and stop responding to requests from their clients. The problem can propagate recursively throughout a system landscape and take out major parts of it.

This is especially common in cases where synchronous requests are executed using blocking I/O, that is, blocking a thread from the underlying operating system while a request is being processed. Combined with a large number of concurrent requests and a service that starts to respond unexpectedly slowly, thread pools can quickly become drained, causing the caller to hang and/or crash. This failure can spread unpleasantly quickly to the caller's caller, and so on.

Solution

Add a **circuit breaker** that prevents new outgoing requests from a caller if it detects a problem with the service it calls.

Solution requirements

The solution requirements are as follows:

- **Open** the circuit and fail fast (without waiting for a timeout) if problems with the service are detected.
- Probe for failure correction (also known as a **half-open** circuit); that is, allow a single request to go through on a regular basis to see whether the service is operating normally again.

- **Close** the circuit if the probe detects that the service is operating normally again. This capability is very important since it makes the system landscape resilient to these kinds of problems; in other words, it self-heals.

The following diagram illustrates a scenario where all synchronous communication within the system landscape of microservices goes through circuit breakers. All the circuit breakers are closed; they allow traffic, except for one circuit breaker (for **Microservice E**) that has detected problems in the service the requests go to. Therefore, this circuit breaker is open and utilizes fast-fail logic; that is, it does not call the failing service and waits for a timeout to occur. Instead, **Microservice E** can immediately return a response, optionally applying some fallback logic before responding:

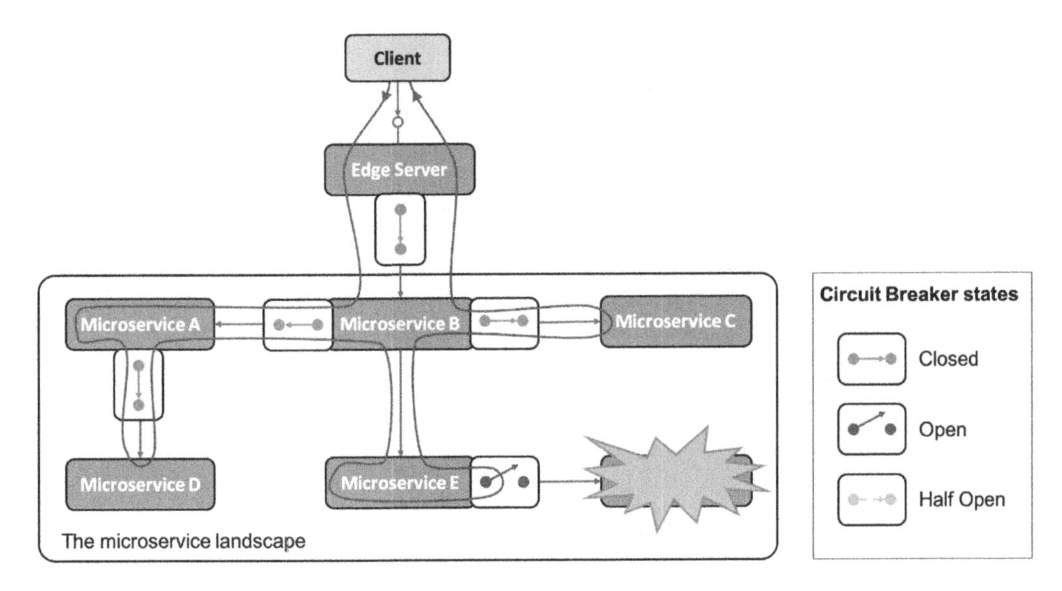

Figure 1.14: The circuit breaker design pattern

Control loop

The control loop pattern has the following problem, solution, and solution requirements.

Problem

In a system landscape with a large number of microservice instances spread out over a number of servers, it is very difficult to manually detect and correct problems such as crashed or hung microservice instances.

Solution

Add a new component, a **control loop**, to the system landscape. This process is illustrated as follows:

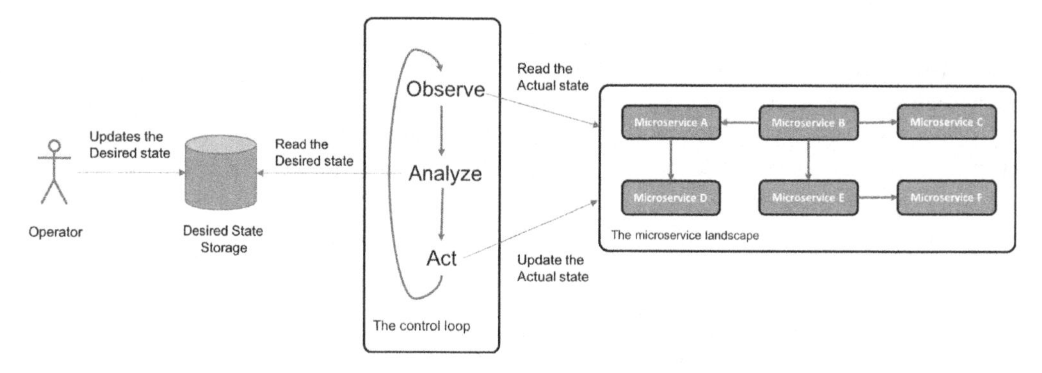

Figure 1.15: The control loop design pattern

Solution requirements

The control loop will constantly observe the **actual state** of the system landscape, comparing it with a **desired state**, as specified by the operators. If the two states differ, it will take actions to make the actual state equal to the desired state.

Implementation notes: In the world of containers, a *container orchestrator* such as Kubernetes is typically used to implement this pattern. We will learn more about Kubernetes in *Chapter 15, Introduction to Kubernetes*.

Centralized monitoring and alarms

For this pattern, we have the following problem, solution, and solution requirements.

Problem

If observed response times and/or the usage of hardware resources become unacceptably high, it can be very hard to discover the root cause of the problem. For example, we need to be able to analyze hardware resource consumption per microservice.

Solution

To curb this, we add a new component, a **monitor service**, to the system landscape, which is capable of collecting metrics about hardware resource usage for each microservice instance level.

Solution requirements

The solution requirements are as follows:

- It must be able to collect metrics from all the servers that are used by the system landscape, which includes autoscaling servers
- It must be able to detect new microservice instances as they are launched on the available servers and start to collect metrics from them
- It must be able to provide APIs and graphical tools for querying and analyzing the collected metrics
- It must be possible to define alerts that are triggered when a specified metric exceeds a specified threshold value

The following screenshot shows Grafana, which visualizes metrics from Prometheus, a monitoring tool that we will look at in *Chapter 20, Monitoring Microservices*:

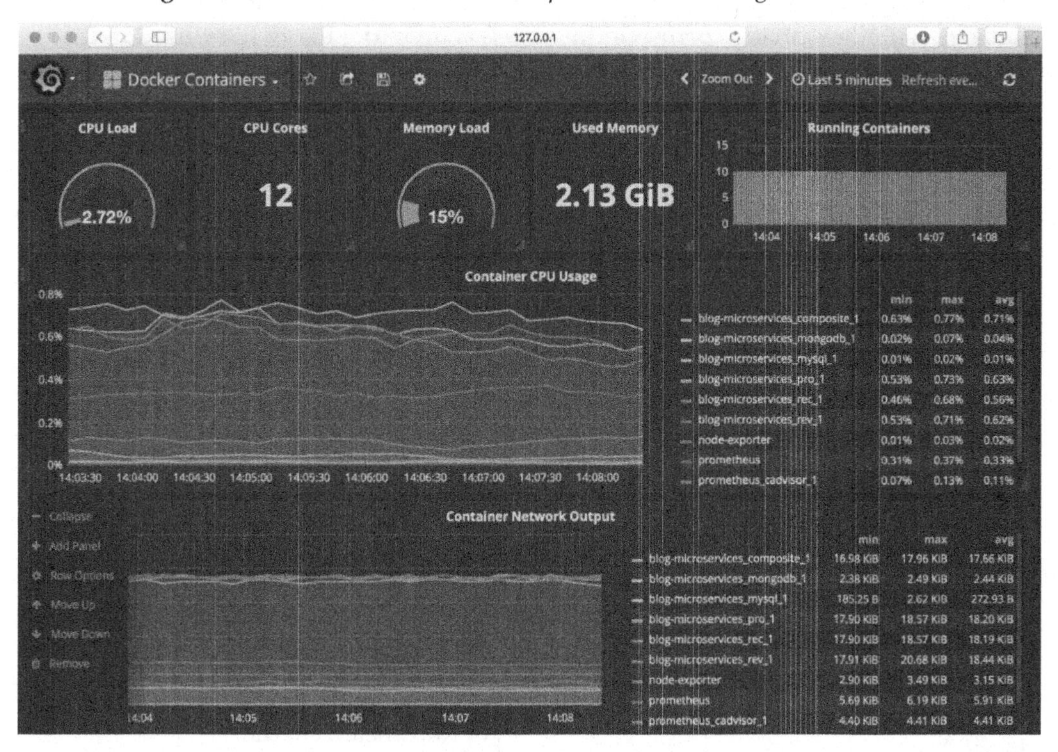

Figure 1.16: Monitoring with Grafana

That was an extensive list! I am sure these design patterns helped you to understand the challenges with microservices better. Next, we will move on to learning about software enablers.

Software enablers

As we've already mentioned, we have a number of very good open source tools that can help us both meet our expectations of microservices and, most importantly, handle the new challenges that come with them:

- **Spring Boot**, an application framework
- **Spring Cloud/Netflix OSS**, a mix of application framework and ready-to-use services
- **Docker**, a tool for running containers in a single server
- **Kubernetes**, a container orchestrator that manages a cluster of servers that run containers
- **Istio**, a service mesh implementation

The following table maps the design patterns we will need to handle these challenges, along with the corresponding open source tool that will be used in this book to implement the design patterns:

Design Pattern	Spring Boot	Spring Cloud	Kubernetes	Istio
Service discovery		Netflix Eureka and Spring Cloud LoadBalancer	Kubernetes `kube-proxy` and service resources	
Edge server		Spring Cloud and Spring Security OAuth	Kubernetes Ingress controller	Istio ingress gateway
Reactive microservices	Project Reactor and Spring WebFlux			
Central configuration		Spring Config Server	Kubernetes `ConfigMaps` and Secrets	
Centralized log analysis			Elasticsearch, Fluentd, and Kibana Note: Actually not part of Kubernetes, but can easily be deployed and configured together with Kubernetes	

Distributed tracing		Spring Cloud Sleuth and Zipkin		Jaeger
Circuit breaker		Resilience4j		Outlier detection
Control loop			Kubernetes controller managers	
Centralized monitoring and alarms				Kiali, Grafana, and Prometheus

Please note that any of Spring Cloud, Kubernetes, or Istio can be used to implement some design patterns, such as service discovery, edge server, and central configuration. We will discuss the pros and cons of using these alternatives later in this book.

With the design patterns and tools that we will use in the book introduced, we will wrap up this chapter by going through some related areas that are also important, but not covered in this text.

Other important considerations

To be successful when it comes to implementing a microservice architecture, there are a number of related areas to consider as well. I will not cover these areas in this book; instead, I'll just briefly mention them here as follows:

- **Importance of DevOps**: One of the benefits of a microservice architecture is that it enables shorter delivery times and, in extreme cases, allows *continuous delivery* of new versions. To be able to deliver that fast, you need to establish an organization where dev and ops work together under the mantra *you built it, you run it*. This means that developers are no longer allowed to simply pass new versions of the software over to the operations team. Instead, the dev and ops organizations need to work much more closely together, organized into teams that have full responsibility for the end-to-end life cycle of one microservice (or a group of related microservices). Besides the organizational part of dev/ops, the teams also need to automate the delivery chain, that is, the steps for building, testing, packaging, and deploying the microservices to the various deployment environments. This is known as setting up a *delivery pipeline*.

- **Organizational aspects and Conway's law**: Another interesting aspect of how a microservice architecture might affect the organization is *Conway's law*, which states the following:

  > *"Any organization that designs a system (defined broadly) will produce a design whose structure is a copy of the organization's communication structure."*
  >
  > *- Melvyn Conway, 1967*

  This means that the traditional approach of organizing IT teams for large applications based on their technology expertise (for example, UX, business logic, and database teams) will lead to a big three-tier application - typically, a big monolithic application with a separately deployable unit for the UI, one for processing the business logic, and one for the big database. To successfully deliver an application based on a microservice architecture, the organization needs to be changed into teams that work with one or a group of related microservices. The team must have the skills that are required for those microservices, for example, languages and frameworks for the business logic and database technologies for persisting its data.

- **Decomposing a monolithic application into microservices**: One of the most difficult decisions (and expensive if done wrong) is how to decompose a monolithic application into a set of cooperating microservices. If this is done in the wrong way, you will end up with problems such as the following:
  - **Slow delivery**: Changes in the business requirements will affect too many of the microservices, resulting in extra work.
  - **Bad performance**: To be able to perform a specific business function, a lot of requests have to be passed between various microservices, resulting in long response times.
  - **Inconsistent data**: Since related data is separated into different microservices, inconsistencies can appear over time in data that's managed by different microservices.

  A good approach to finding proper boundaries for microservices is to apply **domain-driven design** and its concept of **bounded contexts**. According to Eric Evans, a *bounded context* is:

  > *"A description of a boundary (typically a subsystem, or the work of a particular team) within which a particular model is defined and applicable."*

  This means that a microservice defined by a bounded context will have a well-defined model of its own data.

- **Importance of API design**: If a group of microservices exposes a common, externally available API, it is important that the API is easy to understand and adheres to the following guidelines:
    - If the same concept is used in multiple APIs, it should have the same description in terms of the naming and data types used.
    - It is of great importance that APIs are allowed to evolve in an independent but controlled manner. This typically requires applying a proper versioning schema for the APIs, for example, `https://semver.org/`. This implies supporting multiple major versions of an API over a specific period of time, allowing clients of the API to migrate to new major versions at their own pace.
- **Migration paths from on-premises to the cloud**: Many companies today run their workload on-premises, but are searching for ways to move parts of their workload to the cloud. Since most cloud providers today offer *Kubernetes as a Service*, an appealing migration approach can be to first move the workload into Kubernetes on-premises (as microservices or not) and then redeploy it on a Kubernetes as a Service offering provided by a preferred cloud provider.
- **Good design principles for microservices, the 12-factor app**: The 12-factor app (`https://12factor.net`) is a set of design principles for building software that can be deployed in the cloud. Most of these design principles are applicable to building microservices independently of where and how they will be deployed, that is, in the cloud or on-premises. Some of these principles will be covered in this book, such as config, processes, and logs, but not all.

That's it for the first chapter! I hope this gave you a good basic idea of microservices and the challenges that come with it, as well as an overview of what we will cover in this book.

Summary

In this introductory chapter, I described my own way into microservices and delved into a bit of their history. We defined what a microservice is - a kind of autonomous distributed component with some specific requirements. We also went through the good and challenging aspects of a microservice-based architecture.

To handle these challenges, we defined a set of design patterns and briefly mapped the capabilities of open source products such as Spring Boot, Spring Cloud, Kubernetes, and Istio to the design patterns.

You're eager to develop your first microservice now, right? In the next chapter, we will be introduced to Spring Boot and complementary open source tools that we will use to develop our first microservices.

2

Introduction to Spring Boot

In this chapter, we will be introduced to how to build a set of cooperating microservices using Spring Boot, focusing on how to develop functionality that delivers business value. The challenges with microservices that we pointed out in the previous chapter will be considered only to some degree, but they will be addressed to their full extent in later chapters.

We will develop microservices that contain business logic based on plain **Spring Beans** and expose REST APIs using **Spring WebFlux**. The APIs will be documented based on the OpenAPI specification using **springdoc-openapi**. To make the data processed by the microservices persistent, we will use **Spring Data** to store data in both SQL and NoSQL databases.

Since Spring Boot v2.0 was released in March 2018, it has become much easier to develop reactive microservices, including non-blocking synchronous REST APIs. To develop message-based asynchronous services we will use **Spring Cloud Stream**. Refer to *Chapter 1, Introduction to Microservices*, the *Reactive microservices* section, for more information.

Finally, we will use **Docker** to run our microservices as containers. This will allow us to start and stop our microservice landscape, including database servers and a message broker, with a single command.

That's a lot of technologies and frameworks, so let's go through each of them briefly to see what they are about!

In this chapter, we will introduce the following open source projects:

- Spring Boot
- Spring WebFlux
- springdoc-openapi
- Spring Data
- Spring Cloud Stream
- Docker

More details about each product will be provided in upcoming chapters.

Technical requirements

This chapter does not contain any source code that can be downloaded, nor does it require any tools to be installed.

Spring Boot

Spring Boot, and the Spring Framework that Spring Boot is based on, is a great framework for developing microservices in Java.

When the Spring Framework was released in v1.0 back in 2004, one of its main goals was to address the overly complex **J2EE** standard (short for **Java 2 Platforms, Enterprise Edition**) with its infamous and heavyweight deployment descriptors. The Spring Framework provided a much more lightweight development model based on the concept of **dependency injection**. The Spring Framework also used far more lightweight XML configuration files compared to the deployment descriptors in J2EE.

To make things even worse with the J2EE standard, the heavyweight deployment descriptors actually came in two types:

- Standard deployment descriptors, describing the configuration in a standardized way
- Vendor-specific deployment descriptors, mapping the configuration to vendor-specific features in the vendor's application server

In 2006, J2EE was renamed **Java EE**, short for **Java Platform, Enterprise Edition**. In 2017, Oracle submitted Java EE to the Eclipse foundation. In February 2018, Java EE was renamed Jakarta EE.

Over the years, while the Spring Framework gained increasing popularity, the functionality in the Spring Framework grew significantly. Slowly, the burden of setting up a Spring application using the no-longer-so-lightweight XML configuration file became a problem.

In 2014, Spring Boot v1.0 was released, addressing these problems!

Convention over configuration and fat JAR files

Spring Boot targets the fast development of production-ready Spring applications by being strongly opinionated about how to set up both core modules from the Spring Framework and third-party products, such as libraries that are used for logging or connecting to a database. Spring Boot does that by applying a number of conventions by default, minimizing the need for configuration. Whenever required, each convention can be overridden by writing some configuration, case by case. This design pattern is known as **convention over configuration** and minimizes the need for initial configuration.

Configuration, when required, is in my opinion written best using Java and annotations. The good old XML-based configuration files can still be used, although they are significantly smaller than before Spring Boot was introduced.

Added to the usage of convention over configuration, Spring Boot also favors a runtime model based on a standalone JAR file, also known as a **fat JAR file**. Before Spring Boot, the most common way to run a Spring application was to deploy it as a WAR file on a Java EE web server, such as Apache Tomcat. WAR file deployment is still supported by Spring Boot.

A fat JAR file contains not only the classes and resource files of the application itself, but also all the JAR files the application depends on. This means that the fat JAR file is the only JAR file required to run the application; that is, we only need to transfer one JAR file to an environment where we want to run the application instead of transferring the application's JAR file along with all the JAR files the application depends on.

Starting a fat JAR requires no separately installed Java EE web server, such as Apache Tomcat. Instead, it can be started with a simple command such as `java -jar app.jar`, making it a perfect choice for running in a Docker container! If the Spring Boot application, for example, uses HTTP to expose a REST API, it will also contain an embedded web server.

Code examples for setting up a Spring Boot application

To better understand what this means, let's look at some source code examples.

We will only look at some small fragments of code here to point out the main features. For a fully working example, you'll have to wait until the next chapter!

The magic @SpringBootApplication annotation

The convention-based autoconfiguration mechanism can be initiated by annotating the application class, that is, the class that contains the static `main` method, with the `@SpringBootApplication` annotation. The following code shows this:

```
@SpringBootApplication
public class MyApplication {

  public static void main(String[] args) {
```

```
    SpringApplication.run(MyApplication.class, args);
  }
}
```

The following functionality will be provided by this annotation:

- It enables component scanning, that is, looking for Spring components and configuration classes in the package of the application class and all its sub-packages.
- The application class itself becomes a configuration class.
- It enables autoconfiguration, where Spring Boot looks for JAR files in the classpath that it can configure automatically. For example, if you have Tomcat in the classpath, Spring Boot will automatically configure Tomcat as an embedded web server.

Component scanning

Let's assume we have the following Spring component in the package of the application class (or in one of its sub-packages):

```
@Component
public class MyComponentImpl implements MyComponent { ...
```

Another component in the application can get this component automatically injected, also known as **auto-wiring**, using the `@Autowired` annotation:

```
public class AnotherComponent {

  private final MyComponent myComponent;

  @Autowired
  public AnotherComponent(MyComponent myComponent) {
    this.myComponent = myComponent;
  }
```

I prefer using constructor injection (over field and setter injection) to keep the state in my components immutable. An immutable state is important if you want to be able to run the component in a multithreaded runtime environment.

If we want to use components that are declared in a package outside the application's package, for example, a utility component shared by multiple Spring Boot applications, we can complement the `@SpringBootApplication` annotation in the application class with a `@ComponentScan` annotation:

```
package se.magnus.myapp;

@SpringBootApplication
@ComponentScan({"se.magnus.myapp","se.magnus.utils"})
public class MyApplication {
```

We can now auto-wire components from the `se.magnus.util` package in the application code, for example, a utility component named `MyUtility`, as follows:

```
package se.magnus.utils;

@Component
public class MyUtility { ...
```

This utility component can be auto-wired in an application component like so:

```
package se.magnus.myapp.services;

public class AnotherComponent {

 private final MyUtility myUtility;

 @Autowired
 public AnotherComponent(MyUtility myUtility) {
   this.myUtility = myUtility;
 }
```

Java-based configuration

If we want to override Spring Boot's default configuration or if we want to add our own configuration, we can simply annotate a class with `@Configuration` and it will be picked up by the component scanning mechanism we described previously.

For example, if we want to set up a filter in the processing of HTTP requests (handled by Spring WebFlux, which is described in the following section) that writes a log message at the beginning and the end of the processing, we can configure a log filter, as follows:

```
@Configuration
public class SubscriberApplication {

  @Bean
  public Filter logFilter() {
    CommonsRequestLoggingFilter filter = new
        CommonsRequestLoggingFilter();
    filter.setIncludeQueryString(true);
    filter.setIncludePayload(true);
    filter.setMaxPayloadLength(5120);
    return filter;
  }
```

We can also place the configuration directly in the application class since the `@SpringBootApplication` annotation implies the `@Configuration` annotation.

Now that we have learned about Spring Boot, let's talk about Spring WebFlux.

Spring WebFlux

Spring Boot 2.0 is based on the Spring Framework 5.0, which came with built-in support for developing reactive applications. The Spring Framework uses **Project Reactor** as the base implementation of its reactive support, and also comes with a new web framework, **Spring WebFlux**, which supports the development of reactive, that is, non-blocking, HTTP clients and services.

Spring WebFlux supports two different programming models:

- An annotation-based imperative style, similar to the already existing web framework, Spring Web MVC, but with support for reactive services
- A new function-oriented model based on routers and handlers

In this book, we will use the annotation-based imperative style to demonstrate how easy it is to move REST services from Spring Web MVC to Spring WebFlux and then start to refactor the services so that they become fully reactive.

Spring WebFlux also provides a fully reactive HTTP client, `WebClient`, as a complement to the existing `RestTemplate` client.

Spring WebFlux supports running on a servlet container based on the Servlet specification v3.1 or higher, such as Apache Tomcat, but also supports reactive non-Servlet-based embedded web servers such as Netty (`https://netty.io/`).

The Servlet specification is a specification in the Java EE platform that standardizes how to develop Java applications that communicate using web protocols such as HTTP.

Code examples of setting up a REST service

Before we can create a REST service based on Spring WebFlux, we need to add Spring WebFlux (and the dependencies that Spring WebFlux requires) to the classpath for Spring Boot to be detected and configured during startup. Spring Boot provides a large number of convenient **starter dependencies** that bring in a specific feature, together with the dependencies each feature normally requires. So, let's use the starter dependency for Spring WebFlux and then see what a simple REST service looks like!

Starter dependencies

In this book, we will use Gradle as our build tool, so the Spring WebFlux starter dependency will be added to the `build.gradle` file. It looks like this:

```
implementation('org.springframework.boot:spring-boot-starter-webflux')
```

You might be wondering why we don't specify a version number. We will talk about that when we look at a complete example in *Chapter 3, Creating a Set of Cooperating Microservices*!

When the microservice is started up, Spring Boot will detect Spring WebFlux on the classpath and configure it, as well as other things such as starting up an embedded web server. Spring WebFlux uses Netty by default, which we can see from the log output:

```
2018-09-30 15:23:43.592 INFO 17429 --- [ main] o.s.b.web.embedded.
netty.NettyWebServer : Netty started on port(s): 8080
```

If we want to switch from Netty to Tomcat as our embedded web server, we can override the default configuration by excluding Netty from the starter dependency and adding the starter dependency for Tomcat:

```
implementation('org.springframework.boot:spring-boot-starter-webflux')
{
 exclude group: 'org.springframework.boot', module: 'spring-boot-
 starter-reactor-netty'
}
implementation('org.springframework.boot:spring-boot-starter-tomcat')
```

After restarting the microservice, we can see that Spring Boot picked Tomcat instead:

```
2018-09-30 18:23:44.182 INFO 17648 --- [ main] o.s.b.w.embedded.tomcat.
TomcatWebServer : Tomcat initialized with port(s): 8080 (http)
```

Property files

As you can see from the preceding examples, the web server is started up using port `8080`. If you want to change the port, you can override the default value using a property file. Spring Boot application property files can either be a `.properties` file or a `YAML` file. By default, they are named `application.properties` and `application.yml`, respectively.

In this book, we will use YAML files so that the HTTP port used by the embedded web server can be changed to, for example, `7001`. By doing this, we can avoid port collisions with other microservices running on the same server. To do this, we can add the following line to the `application.yml` file:

```
server.port: 7001
```

When we begin to develop our microservices as containers in *Chapter 4, Deploying Our Microservices Using Docker*, port collisions will no longer be a problem. Each container has its own hostname and port range, so all microservices can use, for example, port `8080` without colliding with each other.

Sample RestController

Now, with Spring WebFlux and an embedded web server of our choice in place, we can write a REST service in the same way as when using Spring MVC, that is, as a `RestController`:

```
@RestController
public class MyRestService {

  @GetMapping(value = "/my-resource", produces = "application/json")
  List<Resource> listResources() {
    ...
  }
```

The `@GetMapping` annotation on the `listResources()` method will map the Java method to an HTTP `GET` API on the `host:8080/myResource` URL. The return value of the `List<Resource>` type will be converted into JSON.

Now that we've talked about Spring WebFlux, let's see how we can document the APIs we develop using Spring WebFlux.

springdoc-openapi

One very important aspect of developing APIs, for example, RESTful services, is how to document them so that they are easy to use. The Swagger specification from SmartBear Software is one of the most widely used ways of documenting RESTful services. Many leading API gateways have native support for exposing the documentation of RESTful services using the Swagger specification.

In 2015, SmartBear Software donated the Swagger specification to the Linux Foundation under the **OpenAPI Initiative** and created the **OpenAPI Specification**. The name Swagger is still used for the tooling provided by SmartBear Software.

springdoc-openapi is an open-source project, separate from the Spring Framework, that can create OpenAPI-based API documentation at runtime. It does so by examining the application, for example, inspecting WebFlux and Swagger-based annotations.

We will look at full source code examples in upcoming chapters, but for now, the following condensed screenshot (removed parts are marked with "**...**") of a sample API documentation will do:

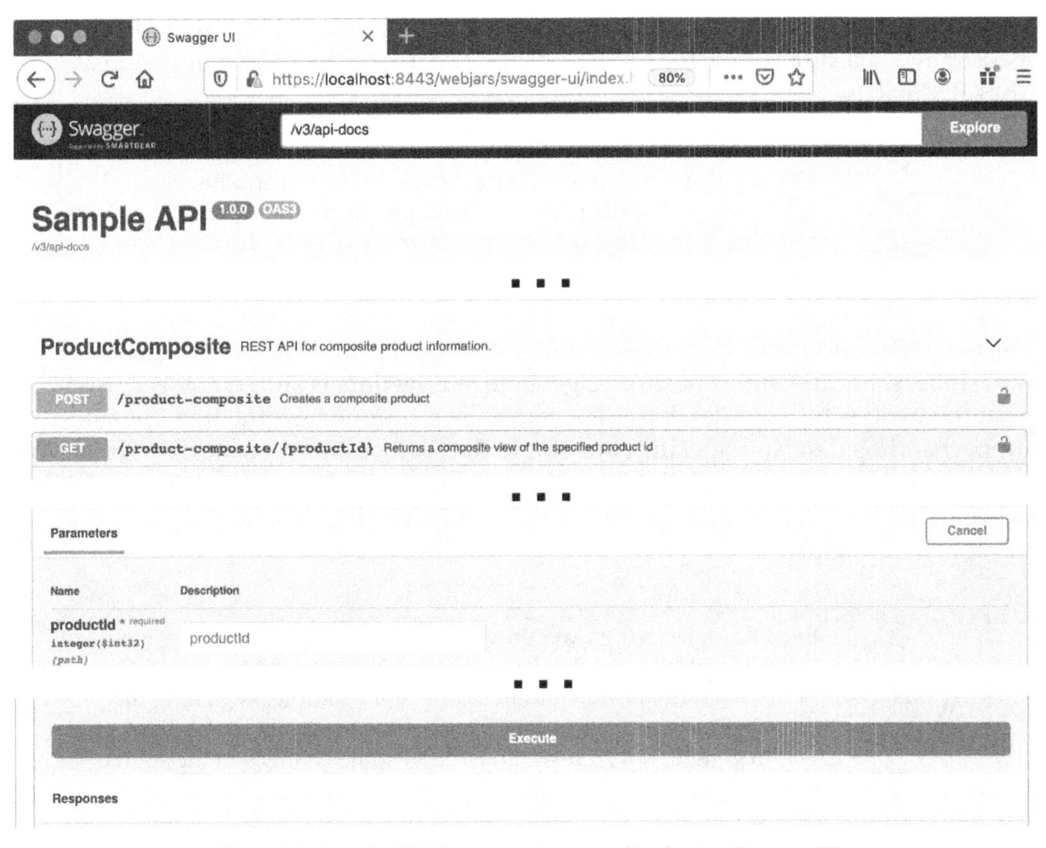

Figure 2.1: Sample API documentation visualized using Swagger UI

Note the big **Execute** button, which can be used to actually try out the API, not just read its documentation!

springdoc-openapi helps us to document the APIs exposed by our microservices. Now, let's move on to Spring Data.

Spring Data

Spring Data comes with a common programming model for persisting data in various types of database engine, ranging from traditional relational databases (SQL databases) to various types of NoSQL database engine, such as document databases (for example, MongoDB), key-value databases (for example, Redis), and graph databases (for example, Neo4J).

The Spring Data project is divided into several subprojects, and in this book we will use Spring Data subprojects for MongoDB and JPA that have been mapped to a MySQL database.

JPA stands for **Java Persistence API** and is a Java specification about how to handle relational data. Please go to `https://jcp.org/aboutJava/communityprocess/mrel/jsr338/index.html` for the latest specification, which is JPA 2.2 at the time of writing.

The two core concepts of the programming model in Spring Data are **entities** and **repositories**. Entities and repositories generalize how data is stored and accessed from the various types of database. They provide a common abstraction but still support adding database-specific behavior to the entities and repositories. These two core concepts are briefly explained together with some illustrative code examples as we proceed through this chapter. Remember that more details will be provided in the upcoming chapters!

Even though Spring Data provides a common programming model for different types of database, this doesn't mean that you will be able to write portable source code. For example, switching the database technology from a SQL database to a NoSQL database will in general not be possible without some changes in the source code!

Entity

An entity describes the data that will be stored by Spring Data. Entity classes are, in general, annotated with a mix of generic Spring Data annotations and annotations that are specific to each database technology.

For example, an entity that will be stored in a relational database can be annotated with JPA annotations such as the following:

```
import javax.persistence.Entity;
import javax.persistence.Id;
import javax.persistence.IdClass;
import javax.persistence.Table;

@Entity
```

```
@IdClass(ReviewEntityPK.class)
@Table(name = "review")
public class ReviewEntity {
 @Id private int productId;
 @Id private int reviewId;
 private String author;
 private String subject;
 private String content;
```

If an entity is to be stored in a MongoDB database, annotations from the Spring Data MongoDB subproject can be used together with generic Spring Data annotations. For example, consider the following code:

```
import org.springframework.data.annotation.Id;
import org.springframework.data.annotation.Version;
import org.springframework.data.mongodb.core.mapping.Document;

@Document
public class RecommendationEntity {

    @Id
    private String id;

    @Version
    private int version;

    private int productId;
    private int recommendationId;
    private String author;
    private int rate;
    private String content;
```

The `@Id` and `@Version` annotations are generic annotations, while the `@Document` annotation is specific to the Spring Data MongoDB subproject.

This can be revealed by studying the import statements; the import statements that contain `mongodb` come from the Spring Data MongoDB subproject.

Repositories

Repositories are used to store and access data from different types of database. In its most basic form, a repository can be declared as a Java interface, and Spring Data will generate its implementation on the fly using opinionated conventions. These conventions can be overridden and/or complemented by additional configuration and, if required, some Java code. Spring Data also comes with some base Java interfaces, for example, `CrudRepository`, to make the definition of a repository even simpler. The base interface, `CrudRepository`, provides us with standard methods for create, read, update, and delete operations.

To specify a repository for handling the JPA entity `ReviewEntity` we only need to declare the following:

```
import org.springframework.data.repository.CrudRepository;

public interface ReviewRepository extends
  CrudRepository<ReviewEntity, ReviewEntityPK> {

  Collection<ReviewEntity> findByProductId(int productId);
}
```

In this example we use a class, `ReviewEntityPK`, to describe a composite primary key. It looks as follows:

```
public class ReviewEntityPK implements Serializable {
    public int productId;
    public int reviewId;
}
```

We have also added an extra method, `findByProductId`, which allows us to look up `Review` entities based on `productid` – a field that is part of the primary key. The naming of the method follows a naming convention defined by Spring Data that allows Spring Data to generate the implementation of this method on the fly as well.

If we want to use the repository, we can simply inject it and then start to use it, for example:

```
private final ReviewRepository repository;

@Autowired
public ReviewService(ReviewRepository repository) {
 this.repository = repository;
}
```

```
public void someMethod() {
  repository.save(entity);
  repository.delete(entity);
  repository.findByProductId(productId);
```

Added to the `CrudRepository` interface, Spring Data also provides a reactive base interface, `ReactiveCrudRepository`, which enables reactive repositories. The methods in this interface do not return objects or collections of objects; instead, they return **Mono** and **Flux** objects. `Mono` and `Flux` objects are, as we will see in *Chapter 7, Developing Reactive Microservices*, reactive streams that are capable of returning either `0...1` or `0...m` entities as they become available on the stream. The reactive-based interface can only be used by Spring Data subprojects that support reactive database drivers; that is, they are based on non-blocking I/O. The Spring Data MongoDB subproject supports reactive repositories, while Spring Data JPA does not.

Specifying a reactive repository for handling the MongoDB entity, `RecommendationEntity`, as described previously, might look something like the following:

```
import org.springframework.data.repository.reactive.
ReactiveCrudRepository;
import reactor.core.publisher.Flux;

public interface RecommendationRepository extends ReactiveCrudRepositor
y<RecommendationEntity, String> {
    Flux<RecommendationEntity> findByProductId(int productId);
}
```

This concludes the section on Spring Data. Now let's see how we can use Spring Cloud Stream to develop message-based asynchronous services.

Spring Cloud Stream

We will not focus on Spring Cloud in this part; we will do that in *Part 2* of the book, from *Chapter 8, Introduction to Spring Cloud*, to *Chapter 14, Understanding Distributed Tracing*. However, we will bring in one of the modules that's part of Spring Cloud: **Spring Cloud Stream**. Spring Cloud Stream provides a streaming abstraction over messaging, based on the **publish and subscribe** integration pattern. Spring Cloud Stream currently comes with built-in support for Apache Kafka and RabbitMQ. A number of separate projects exist that provide integration with other popular messaging systems. See `https://github.com/spring-cloud?q=binder` for more details.

The core concepts in Spring Cloud Stream are as follows:

- **Message**: A data structure that's used to describe data sent to and received from a messaging system.
- **Publisher**: Sends messages to the messaging system, also known as a **Supplier**.
- **Subscriber**: Receives messages from the messaging system, also known as a **Consumer**.
- **Destination**: Used to communicate with the messaging system. Publishers use output destinations and subscribers use input destinations. Destinations are mapped by the specific binders to queues and topics in the underlying messaging system.
- **Binder**: A binder provides the actual integration with a specific messaging system, similar to what a JDBC driver does for a specific type of database.

The actual messaging system to be used is determined at runtime, depending on what is found on the classpath. Spring Cloud Stream comes with opinionated conventions on how to handle messaging. These conventions can be overridden by specifying a configuration for messaging features such as consumer groups, partitioning, persistence, durability, and error handling; for example, retries and dead letter queue handling.

Code examples for sending and receiving messages

To better understand how all this fits together, let's look at some source code examples.

Spring Cloud Stream comes with two programming models: one older and nowadays deprecated model based on the use of annotations (for example, `@EnableBinding`, `@Output`, and `@StreamListener`) and one newer model based on writing functions. In this book, we will use functional implementations.

To implement a publisher, we only need to implement the `java.util.function.Supplier` functional interface as a Spring Bean. For example, the following is a publisher that publishes messages as a String:

```
@Bean
public Supplier<String> myPublisher() {
   return () -> new Date().toString();
}
```

A subscriber is implemented as a Spring Bean implementing the `java.util.function.Consumer` functional interface. For example, the following is a subscriber that consumes messages as Strings:

```
@Bean
public Consumer<String> mySubscriber() {
   return s -> System.out.println("ML RECEIVED: " + s);
}
```

It is also possible to define a Spring Bean that processes messages, meaning that it both consumes and publishes messages. This can be done by implementing the `java.util.function.Function` functional interface. For example, a Spring Bean that consumes incoming messages and publishes a new message after some processing (both messages are Strings in this example):

```
@Bean
public Function<String, String> myProcessor() {
   return s -> "ML PROCESSED: " + s;
}
```

To make Spring Cloud Stream aware of these functions we need to declare them using the `spring.cloud.function.definition` configuration property. For example, for the three functions defined previously, this would look as follows:

```
spring.cloud.function:
  definition: myPublisher;myProcessor;mySubscriber
```

Finally, we need to tell Spring Cloud Stream what destination to use for each function. To connect our three functions so that our processor consumes messages from our publisher and our subscriber consumes messages from the processor, we can supply the following configuration:

```
spring.cloud.stream.bindings:
  myPublisher-out-0:
    destination: myProcessor-in
  myProcessor-in-0:
    destination: myProcessor-in
  myProcessor-out-0:
    destination: myProcessor-out
  mySubscriber-in-0:
    destination: myProcessor-out
```

This will result in the following message flow:

```
myPublisher → myProcessor → mySubscriber
```

A Supplier is triggered by Spring Cloud Stream by default every second, so we could expect output like the following if we start a Spring Boot application including the functions and configuration described previously:

```
ML RECEIVED: ML PROCESSED: Wed Jan 06 16:28:30 CET 2021
ML RECEIVED: ML PROCESSED: Wed Jan 06 16:28:31 CET 2021
ML RECEIVED: ML PROCESSED: Wed Jan 06 16:28:32 CET 2021
ML RECEIVED: ML PROCESSED: Wed Jan 06 16:28:33 CET 2021
```

In cases where the Supplier should be triggered by an external event instead of using a timer, the `StreamBridge` helper class can be used. For example, if a message should be published to the processor when a REST API, `sampleCreateAPI`, is called, the code could look like the following:

```
@Autowired
private StreamBridge streamBridge;

@PostMapping
void sampleCreateAPI(@RequestBody String body) {
  streamBridge.send("myProcessor-in-0", body);
}
```

Now that we understand the various Spring APIs, let's learn a bit about Docker and containers in the next section.

Docker

I assume that Docker and the concept of containers need no in-depth presentation. Docker made the concept of containers as a lightweight alternative to virtual machines very popular in 2013. A container is actually a process in a Linux host that uses Linux **namespaces** to provide isolation between different containers, in terms of their use of global system resources such as users, processes, filesystems, and networking. Linux **control groups** (also known as **cgroups**) are used to limit the amount of CPU and memory that a container is allowed to consume.

Compared to a virtual machine that uses a hypervisor to run a complete copy of an operating system in each virtual machine, the overhead in a container is a fraction of the overhead in a traditional virtual machine. This leads to much faster startup times and significantly lower overhead in terms of CPU and memory usage.

The isolation that's provided for a container is, however, not considered to be as secure as the isolation that's provided for a virtual machine. With the release of Windows Server 2016, Microsoft supports the use of Docker in Windows servers.

During the last few years, a lightweight form of virtual machines has evolved. It mixes the best of traditional virtual machines and containers, providing virtual machines with a footprint and startup time similar to containers and with the same level of secure isolation provided by traditional virtual machines. Some examples are Amazon Firecracker and Microsoft **Windows Subsystem for Linux v2** (**WSL2**). For more information, see `https://firecracker-microvm.github.io` and `https://docs.microsoft.com/en-us/windows/wsl/`.

Containers are very useful during both development and testing. Being able to start up a complete system landscape of cooperating microservices and resource managers (for example, database servers, messaging brokers, and so on) with a single command for testing is simply amazing.

For example, we can write scripts in order to automate end-to-end tests of our microservice landscape. A test script can start up the microservice landscape, run tests using the exposed APIs, and tear down the landscape. This type of automated test script is very useful, both for running locally on a developer PC before pushing code to a source code repository, and to be executed as a step in a delivery pipeline. A build server can run these types of test in its continuous integration and deployment process whenever a developer pushes code to the source repository.

For production usage, we need a container orchestrator such as Kubernetes. We will come back to container orchestrators and Kubernetes later in this book.

For most of the microservices we will look at in this book, a **Dockerfile** such as the following is all that is required to run the microservice as a Docker container:

```
FROM openjdk:16

MAINTAINER Magnus Larsson <magnus.larsson.ml@gmail.com>

EXPOSE 8080
ADD ./build/libs/*.jar app.jar
ENTRYPOINT ["java","-jar","/app.jar"]
```

If we want to start and stop many containers with one command, **Docker Compose** is the perfect tool. Docker Compose uses a YAML file to describe the containers to be managed. For our microservices, it might look something like the following:

```
product:
 build: microservices/product-service

recommendation:
 build: microservices/recommendation-service

review:
  build: microservices/review-service

composite:
  build: microservices/product-composite-service
  ports:
    - "8080:8080"
```

Let me explain the preceding source code a little:

- The `build` directive is used to specify which Dockerfile to use for each microservice. Docker Compose will use it to build a Docker image and then launch a Docker container based on that Docker image.
- The `ports` directive for the composite service is used to expose port `8080` on the server where Docker runs. On a developer's machine, this means that the port of the composite service can be reached simply by using `localhost:8080`!

All the containers in the YAML files can be managed with simple commands such as the following:

- `docker-compose up -d`: Starts all containers. `-d` means that the containers run in the background, not locking the terminal from where the command was executed.
- `docker-compose down`: Stops and removes all containers.
- `docker-compose logs -f --tail=0`: Prints out log messages from all containers. `-f` means that the command will not complete, and instead waits for new log messages. `--tail=0` means that we don't want to see any previous log messages, only new ones.

For a full list of Docker Compose commands, see `https://docs.docker.com/compose/reference/`.

This was a brief introduction to Docker. We will go into more detail about Docker starting with *Chapter 4, Deploying Our Microservices Using Docker*.

Summary

In this chapter, we have been introduced to Spring Boot and complementary open source tools that can be used to build cooperating microservices.

Spring Boot is used to simplify the development of Spring-based, production-ready applications, such as microservices. It is strongly opinionated in terms of how to set up both core modules from the Spring Framework and third-party tools. Using Spring WebFlux we can develop microservices that expose reactive, that is, non-blocking, REST services. To document these REST services we can use springdoc-openapi to create OpenAPI-based documentation for the APIs. If we need to persist data used by the microservices, we can use Spring Data, which provides an elegant abstraction for accessing and manipulating persistent data using entities and repositories. Spring Data's programming model is similar, but not fully portable between different types of database, for example, relational, document, key-value, and graph databases.

If we prefer sending messages asynchronously between our microservices, we can use Spring Cloud Stream, which provides a streaming abstraction over messaging. Spring Cloud Stream comes with out-of-the-box support for Apache Kafka and RabbitMQ but can be extended to support other messaging brokers using custom binders. Finally, Docker makes the concept of containers as a lightweight alternative to virtual machines easy to use. Based on Linux namespaces and control groups, containers provide isolation similar to what traditional virtual machines provide, but with a significantly lower overhead in terms of CPU and memory usage.

In the next chapter, we will take our first small steps, creating microservices with minimalistic functionality using Spring Boot and Spring WebFlux.

Questions

1. What is the purpose of the `@SpringBootApplication` annotation?
2. What are the main differences between the older Spring component for developing REST services, Spring Web MVC, and the new Spring WebFlux?
3. How does springdoc-openapi help a developer document REST APIs?
4. What is the function of a repository in Spring Data and what is the simplest possible implementation of a repository?
5. What is the purpose of a binder in Spring Cloud Stream?
6. What is the purpose of Docker Compose?

3

Creating a Set of Cooperating Microservices

In this chapter, we will build our first couple of microservices. We will learn how to create cooperating microservices with minimalistic functionality. In upcoming chapters, we will add more and more functionality to these microservices. By the end of this chapter, we will have a RESTful API exposed by a composite microservice. The composite microservice will call three other microservices using their RESTful APIs to create an aggregated response.

The following topics will be covered in this chapter:

- Introducing the microservice landscape
- Generating skeleton microservices
- Adding RESTful APIs
- Adding a composite microservice
- Adding error handling
- Testing the APIs manually
- Adding automated tests of microservices in isolation
- Adding semi-automated tests to a microservice landscape

Technical requirements

For instructions on how to install tools used in this book and how to access the source code for this book, see:

- *Chapter 21* for macOS
- *Chapter 22* for Windows

The code examples in this chapter all come from the source code in `$BOOK_HOME/Chapter03`.

With the tools and source code in place, we can start learning about the system landscape of microservices that we will create in this chapter.

Introducing the microservice landscape

In *Chapter 1, Introduction to Microservices*, we were briefly introduced to the microservice-based system landscape that we will use throughout this book:

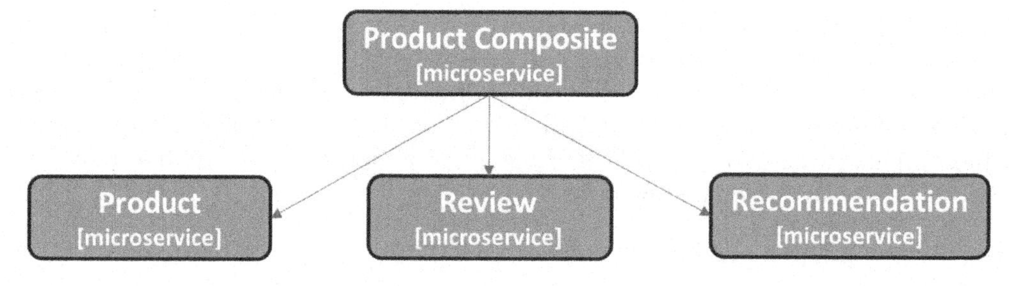

Figure 3.1: The microservice landscape

It consists of three core microservices, the **Product**, **Review**, and **Recommendation** services, all of which deal with one type of resource, and a composite microservice called the **Product Composite** service, which aggregates information from the three core services.

Information handled by the microservices

To keep the source code examples in this book easy to understand, they have a minimal amount of business logic. The information model for the business objects they process is kept minimal for the same reason. In this section, we will go through the information that's handled by each microservice, including infrastructure-related information.

Product service

The `product` service manages product information and describes each product with the following attributes:

- Product ID
- Name
- Weight

Review service

The `review` service manages product reviews and stores the following information about each review:

- Product ID
- Review ID
- Author
- Subject
- Content

Recommendation service

The `recommendation` service manages product recommendations and stores the following information about each recommendation:

- Product ID
- Recommendation ID
- Author
- Rate
- Content

Product composite service

The product composite service aggregates information from the three core services and presents information about a product as follows:

- Product information, as described in the `product` service
- A list of product reviews for the specified product, as described in the `review` service
- A list of product recommendations for the specified product, as described in the `recommendation` service

Infrastructure-related information

Once we start to run our microservices as containers that are managed by the infrastructure (first Docker and later on Kubernetes), it will be of interest to track which container actually responded to our requests. As a simple solution, a `serviceAddress` attribute has been added to all responses, formatted as `hostname/ip-address:port`.

In *Chapter 18, Using a Service Mesh to Improve Observability and Management*, and *Chapter 19, Centralized Logging with the EFK Stack*, we will learn about more powerful solutions to track requests that are processed by the microservices.

Temporarily replacing service discovery

Since, at this stage, we don't have any service discovery mechanism in place, we will run all microservices on `localhost` and use hardcoded port numbers for each microservice. We will use the following ports:

- Product composite service: `7000`
- Product service: `7001`
- Review service: `7002`
- Recommendation service: `7003`

We will get rid of the hardcoded ports later when we start using Docker and Kubernetes!

In this section, we have been introduced to the microservices we are going to create and the information that they will handle. In the next section, we will use Spring Initializr to create skeleton code for the microservices.

Generating skeleton microservices

Now it's time to see how we can create projects for our microservices. The final result for this topic can be found in the `$BOOK_HOME/Chapter03/1-spring-init` folder. To simplify setting up the projects, we will use **Spring Initializr** to generate a skeleton project for each microservice. A skeleton project contains the necessary files for building the project, along with an empty `main` class and test class for the microservice. After that, we will see how we can build all our microservices with one command using multi-project builds in the build tool that we will use, Gradle.

Using Spring Initializr to generate skeleton code

To get started with developing our microservices, we will use a tool called Spring Initializr to generate skeleton code for us. Spring Initializr is provided by the Spring team and can be used to configure and generate new Spring Boot applications. The tool helps developers to choose additional Spring modules to be used by the application and ensures that dependencies are configured to use compatible versions of the selected modules. The tool supports the use of either Maven or Gradle as a build system and can generate source code for either Java, Kotlin, or Groovy.

It can either be invoked from a web browser using the URL `https://start.spring.io/` or by a command-line tool, `spring init`. To make it easier to reproduce the creation of the microservices, we will use the command-line tool.

For each microservice, we will create a Spring Boot project that does the following:

- Uses Gradle as a build tool
- Generates code for Java 8
- Packages the project as a fat JAR file
- Brings in dependencies for the `Actuator` and `WebFlux` Spring modules
- Is based on Spring Boot v2.5.2 (which depends on Spring Framework v5.3.8)

Spring Boot Actuator enables a number of valuable endpoints for management and monitoring. We will see them in action later on. **Spring WebFlux** will be used here to create our RESTful APIs.

To create skeleton code for our microservices, we need to run the following command for `product-service`:

```
spring init \
--boot-version=2.5.2 \
--build=gradle \
--java-version=1.8 \
--packaging=jar \
--name=product-service \
--package-name=se.magnus.microservices.core.product \
--groupId=se.magnus.microservices.core.product \
--dependencies=actuator,webflux \
--version=1.0.0-SNAPSHOT \
product-service
```

If you want to learn more about the `spring init` CLI, you can run the `spring help init` command. To see what dependencies you can add, run the `spring init --list` command.

If you want to create the four projects on your own instead of using the source code in this book's GitHub repository, try out `$BOOK_HOME/Chapter03/1-spring-init/create-projects.bash`, as follows:

```
mkdir some-temp-folder
cd some-temp-folder
$BOOK_HOME/Chapter03/1-spring-init/create-projects.bash
```

After creating our four projects using `create-projects.bash`, we will have the following file structure:

```
microservices/
├── product-composite-service
├── product-service
├── recommendation-service
└── review-service
```

For each project, we can list the created files. Let's do this for the `product-service` project:

```
find microservices/product-service -type f
```

We will receive the following output:

```
$ find microservices/product-service -type f
microservices/product-service/gradle/wrapper/gradle-wrapper.jar
microservices/product-service/gradle/wrapper/gradle-wrapper.properties
microservices/product-service/gradlew
microservices/product-service/.gitignore
microservices/product-service/build.gradle
microservices/product-service/gradlew.bat
microservices/product-service/settings.gradle
microservices/product-service/src/test/java/se/magnus/microservices/core/product/ProductServiceApplicationTests.java
microservices/product-service/src/main/resources/application.properties
microservices/product-service/src/main/java/se/magnus/microservices/core/product/ProductServiceApplication.java
$
```

Figure 3.2: Listing the files we created for product-service

Spring Initializr created a number of files for Gradle, a `.gitignore` file, and three Spring Boot files:

- `ProductServiceApplication.java`, our main application class
- `application.properties`, an empty property file
- `ProductServiceApplicationTests.java`, a test class that's been configured to run tests on our Spring Boot application using JUnit

The `main` application class, `ProductServiceApplication.java`, looks as we'd expect based on the section *The magic @SpringBootApplication annotation* in the previous chapter:

```
package se.magnus.microservices.core.product;

@SpringBootApplication
public class ProductServiceApplication {

   public static void main(String[] args) {
      SpringApplication.run(ProductServiceApplication.class, args);
   }
}
```

The test class looks as follows:

```
package se.magnus.microservices.core.product;

@SpringBootTest
class ProductServiceApplicationTests {

   @Test
   void contextLoads() {
   }
}
```

The `@SpringBootTest` annotation will initialize our application in the same way that `@SpringBootApplication` does when running the application; that is, the Spring application context will be set up before the tests are executed using component scanning and auto-configuration, as described in the previous chapter.

Let's also look at the most important Gradle file, `build.gradle`. The content of this file describes how to build the project, for example, how to resolve dependencies and compile, test, and package the source code. The Gradle file starts by listing what plugins to apply:

```
plugins {
    id 'org.springframework.boot' version '2.5.2'
    id 'io.spring.dependency-management' version '1.0.11.RELEASE'
    id 'java'
}
```

The declared plugins are used as follows:

- The `java` plugin adds the Java compiler to the project.
- The plugins `org.springframework.boot` and `io.spring.dependency-management` are declared, which together ensure that Gradle will build a fat JAR file and that we don't need to specify any explicit version numbers on our Spring Boot starter dependencies. Instead, they are implied by the version of the `org.springframework.boot` plugin, that is, `2.5.2`.

In the rest of the build file, we basically declare a group name and version for our project, Java version, and its dependencies:

```
group = 'se.magnus.microservices.composite.product'
version = '1.0.0-SNAPSHOT'
sourceCompatibility = '1.8'

repositories {
    mavenCentral()
}

dependencies {
    implementation 'org.springframework.boot:spring-boot-starter-
actuator'
    implementation 'org.springframework.boot:spring-boot-starter-
webflux'
    testImplementation 'org.springframework.boot:spring-boot-starter-
test'
    testImplementation 'io.projectreactor:reactor-test'
}
```

```
test {
    useJUnitPlatform()
}
```

Some notes regarding the dependencies used and the final `test` declaration:

- Dependencies are, as with the preceding plugins, fetched from the central Maven repository.
- Dependencies are set up as specified in the `Actuator` and `WebFlux` modules, along with a couple of useful test dependencies.
- Finally, **JUnit** is configured to be used to run our tests in the Gradle builds.

We can build each microservice separately with the following command:

```
cd microservices/product-composite-service; ./gradlew build; cd -; \
cd microservices/product-service;           ./gradlew build; cd -; \
cd microservices/recommendation-service;    ./gradlew build; cd -; \
cd microservices/review-service;            ./gradlew build; cd -;
```

Note how we use the `gradlew` executables that are created by Spring Initializr; that is, we don't need to have Gradle installed!

The first time we run a command with `gradlew`, it will download Gradle automatically. The Gradle version that's used is determined by the `distributionUrl` property in the `gradle/wrapper/gradle-wrapper.properties` files.

Setting up multi-project builds in Gradle

To make it a bit simpler to build all the microservices with one command, we can set up a multi-project build in Gradle. The steps are as follows:

1. First, we create the `settings.gradle` file, which describes what projects Gradle should build:

```
cat <<EOF > settings.gradle
include ':microservices:product-service'
include ':microservices:review-service'
include ':microservices:recommendation-service'
include ':microservices:product-composite-service'
EOF
```

2. Next, we copy the Gradle executable files that were generated from one of the projects so that we can reuse them for the multi-project builds:

```
cp -r microservices/product-service/gradle .
cp microservices/product-service/gradlew .
cp microservices/product-service/gradlew.bat .
cp microservices/product-service/.gitignore .
```

3. We no longer need the generated Gradle executable files in each project, so we can remove them with the following commands:

```
find microservices -depth -name "gradle" -exec rm -rfv "{}" \;
find microservices -depth -name "gradlew*" -exec rm -fv "{}" \;
```

   The result should be similar to the code you can find in the folder `$BOOK_HOME/Chapter03/1-spring-init`.

4. Now, we can build all the microservices with one command:

```
./gradlew build
```

   If you haven't run the preceding commands, you can simply go to the book's source code and build it from there:

```
cd $BOOK_HOME/Chapter03/1-spring-init

./gradlew build
```

   This should result in the following output:

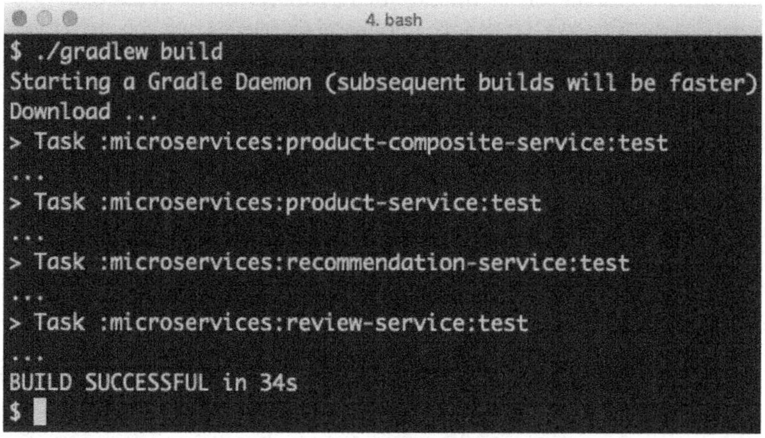

```
$ ./gradlew build
Starting a Gradle Daemon (subsequent builds will be faster)
Download ...
> Task :microservices:product-composite-service:test
...
> Task :microservices:product-service:test
...
> Task :microservices:recommendation-service:test
...
> Task :microservices:review-service:test
...
BUILD SUCCESSFUL in 34s
$ 
```

Figure 3.3: Output upon successful build

With skeleton projects for the microservices created using Spring Initializr and successfully built using Gradle, we are ready to add some code to the microservices in the next section.

From a DevOps perspective, a multi-project setup might not be preferred. Instead, to enable each microservice to have its own build and release cycle, setting up a separate build pipeline for each microservice project would probably be preferred. However, for the purposes of this book, we will use the multi-project setup to make it easier to build and deploy the whole system landscape with a single command.

Adding RESTful APIs

Now that we have projects set up for our microservices, let's add some RESTful APIs to our three core microservices!

The final result of this and the remaining topics in this chapter can be found in the `$BOOK_HOME/Chapter03/2-basic-rest-services` folder.

First, we will add two projects (`api` and `util`) that will contain code that is shared by the microservice projects, and then we will implement the RESTful APIs.

Adding an API and a util project

To add an `api` project, we need to do the following:

1. First, we will set up a separate Gradle project where we can place our API definitions. We will use Java interfaces in order to describe our RESTful APIs and model classes to describe the data that the API uses in its requests and responses. To describe what types of errors can be returned by the API, a number of exception classes are also defined. Describing a RESTful API in a Java interface instead of directly in the Java class is, to me, a good way of separating the API definition from its implementation. We will further extend this pattern later in this book when we add more API information in the Java interfaces to be exposed in an OpenAPI specification. See *Chapter 5, Adding an API Description Using OpenAPI*, for more information.

It is debatable whether it is good practice to store API definitions for a group of microservices in a common API module. It could potentially cause undesired dependencies between the microservices, resulting in monolithic characteristics, for example, causing a more complex and slow development process. To me, it is a good choice for microservices that are part of the same delivery organization, that is, whose releases are governed by the same organization (compare this to a **bounded context** in **domain-driven design**, where our microservices are placed in a single bounded context). As already discussed in *Chapter 1, Introduction to Microservices*, microservices within the same bounded context need to have API definitions that are based on a common information model, so storing these API definitions in the same API module doesn't add any undesired dependencies.

2. Next, we will create a `util` project that can hold some helper classes that are shared by our microservices, for example, for handling errors in a uniform way.

Again, from a DevOps perspective, it would be preferable to build all the projects in their own build pipeline and have version-controlled dependencies for the `api` and `util` projects in the microservice projects, that is, so that each microservice can choose what versions of the `api` and `util` projects to use. But to keep the build and deployment steps simple in the context of this book, we will make the `api` and `util` projects part of the multi-project build.

The API project

The `api` project will be packaged as a library; that is, it won't have its own `main` application class. Unfortunately, Spring Initializr doesn't support the creation of library projects. Instead, a library project has to be created manually from scratch. The source code for the API project is available at `$BOOK_HOME/Chapter03/2-basic-rest-services/api`.

The structure of a library project is the same as for an application project, except that we no longer have the `main` application class, as well as some minor differences in the `build.gradle` file. The Gradle plugin `org.springframework.boot` is replaced with an `implementation platform` section:

```
ext {
    springBootVersion = '2.5.2'
}
dependencies {
    implementation platform("org.springframework.boot:spring-boot-
dependencies:${springBootVersion}")
```

This allows us to retain Spring Boot dependency management while we are replacing the construction of a fat JAR in the build step with the creation of a normal JAR file that only contains the project's own classes and property files.

The Java files in the `api` project for our three core microservices are as follows:

```
$BOOK_HOME/Chapter03/2-basic-rest-services/api/src/main/java/se/magnus/
api/core
├── product
│   ├── Product.java
│   └── ProductService.java
├── recommendation
│   ├── Recommendation.java
│   └── RecommendationService.java
└── review
    ├── Review.java
    └── ReviewService.java
```

The structure of the Java classes looks very similar for the three core microservices, so we will only go through the source code for the `product` service.

First, we will look at the `ProductService.java` Java interface, as shown in the following code:

```
package se.magnus.api.core.product;

public interface ProductService {

    @GetMapping(
        value    = "/product/{productId}",
        produces = "application/json")
     Product getProduct(@PathVariable int productId);
}
```

The Java interface declaration works as follows:

- The `product` service only exposes one API method, `getProduct()` (we will extend the API later in this book in *Chapter 6, Adding Persistence*).
- To map the method to an HTTP `GET` request, we use the `@GetMapping` Spring annotation, where we specify what URL path the method will be mapped to (`/product/{productId}`) and what format the response will be in, in this case, JSON.
- The `{productId}` part of the path maps to a path variable named `productId`.
- The `productId` method parameter is annotated with `@PathVariable`, which will map the value that's passed in the HTTP request to the parameter. For example, an HTTP `GET` request to `/product/123` will result in the `getProduct()` method being called with the `productId` parameter set to `123`.

The method returns a `Product` object, a plain POJO-based model class with the member variables corresponding to attributes for `Product`, as described at the start of this chapter. `Product.java` looks as follows (with constructors and getter methods excluded):

```
public class Product {
  private final int productId;
  private final String name;
  private final int weight;
  private final String serviceAddress;
}
```

This type of POJO class is also known as a **Data Transfer Object** (**DTO**) as it is used to transfer data between the API implementation and the caller of the API. When we get to *Chapter 6, Adding Persistence*, we will look at another type of POJO that can be used to describe how data is stored in the databases, also known as entity objects.

The API project also contains the exception classes `InvalidInputException` and `NotFoundException`.

The util project

The `util` project will be packaged as a library in the same way as the `api` project. The source code for the `util` project is available at `$BOOK_HOME/Chapter03/2-basic-rest-services/util`. The project contains the following utility classes: `GlobalControllerExceptionHandler`, `HttpErrorInfo`, and `ServiceUtil`.

Except for the code in `ServiceUtil.java`, these classes are reusable utility classes that we can use to map Java exceptions to proper HTTP status codes, as described in the later section *Adding error handling*. The main purpose of `ServiceUtil.java` is to find out the hostname, IP address, and port used by the microservice. The class exposes a method, `getServiceAddress()`, that can be used by the microservices to find their hostname, IP address, and port, as described in the previous section, *Infrastructure-related information*.

Implementing our API

Now we can start to implement our APIs in the core microservices!

The implementation looks very similar for the three core microservices, so we will only go through the source code for the `product` service. You can find the other files in `$BOOK_HOME/Chapter03/2-basic-rest-services/microservices`. Let's see how we go about this:

1. We need to add the `api` and `util` projects as dependencies in our `build.gradle` file, in the `product-service` project:

   ```
   dependencies {
      implementation project(':api')
      implementation project(':util')
   ```

2. To enable Spring Boot's autoconfiguration feature to detect Spring Beans in the `api` and `util` projects, we also need to add a `@ComponentScan` annotation to the `main` application class, which includes the packages of the `api` and `util` projects:

   ```
   @SpringBootApplication
   @ComponentScan("se.magnus")
   public class ProductServiceApplication {
   ```

3. Next, we create our service implementation file, `ProductServiceImpl.java`, in order to implement the Java interface, `ProductService`, from the `api` project and annotate the class with `@RestController` so that Spring will call the methods in this class according to the mappings specified in the `Interface` class:

   ```
   package se.magnus.microservices.core.product.services;

   @RestController
   public class ProductServiceImpl implements ProductService {
   }
   ```

4. To be able to use the `ServiceUtil` class from the `util` project, we will inject it into the constructor, as follows:

   ```
   private final ServiceUtil serviceUtil;

   @Autowired
   public ProductServiceImpl(ServiceUtil serviceUtil) {
       this.serviceUtil = serviceUtil;
   }
   ```

5. Now, we can implement the API by overriding the `getProduct()` method from the interface in the `api` project:

   ```
   @Override
   public Product getProduct(int productId) {

    return new Product(productId, "name-" + productId, 123,
    serviceUtil.getServiceAddress());
   }
   ```

   Since we aren't currently using a database, we simply return a hardcoded response based on the input of `productId`, along with the service address supplied by the `ServiceUtil` class.

   For the final result, including logging and error handling, see `ProductServiceImpl.java`.

6. Finally, we also need to set up some runtime properties – what port to use and the desired level of logging. This is added to the property file `application.yml`:

   ```
   server.port: 7001

   logging:
     level:
       root: INFO
       se.magnus.microservices: DEBUG
   ```

Note that the empty `application.properties` file generated by Spring Initializr has been replaced by a YAML file, `application.yml`. YAML files provide better support for grouping related properties compared to `.properties` files. See the log level setting above as an example.

7. We can try out the `product` service on its own. Build and start the microservice with the following commands:

```
cd $BOOK_HOME/Chapter03/2-basic-rest-services
./gradlew build
java -jar microservices/product-service/build/libs/*.jar &
```

   Wait until the following is printed in the Terminal:

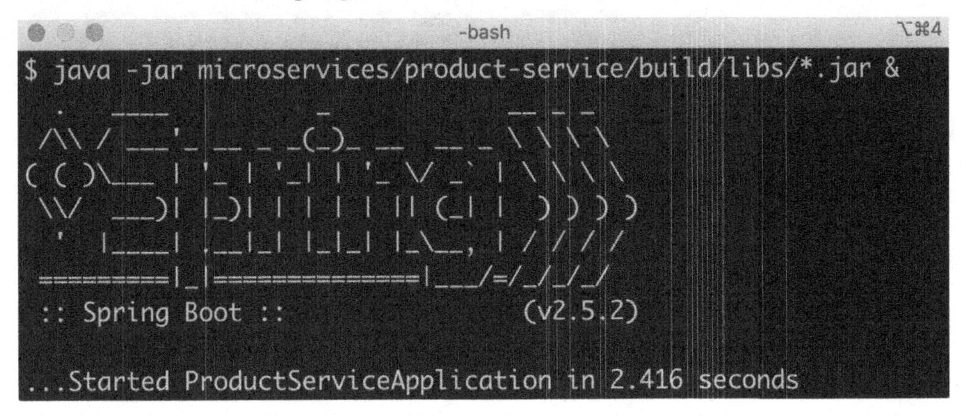

Figure 3.4: Starting ProductServiceApplication

8. Make a test call to the `product` service:

```
curl http://localhost:7001/product/123
```

   It should respond with something similar to the following:

```
$ curl http://localhost:7001/product/123
{"productId":123,"name":"name-123","weight":123,"serviceAddress":"Magnus-MBP32.local/192.168.1.185:7001"}
$
```

Figure 3.5: Expected response to test call

9. Finally, stop the `product` service:

```
kill $(jobs -p)
```

We have now built, run, and tested our first single microservice. In the next section, we will implement the composite microservice that will use the three core microservices we've created so far.

Starting with Spring Boot v2.5.0, two jar files are created when running the `./gradlew build` command: the ordinary jar file, plus a plain jar file containing only the class files resulting from compiling the Java files in the Spring Boot application. Since we don't need the new plain jar file, its creation has been disabled to make it possible to refer to the ordinary jar file using a wildcard when running the Spring Boot application, for example:

```
java -jar microservices/product-service/build/
libs/*.jar
```

The creation of the new plain jar file has been disabled by adding the following lines in the `build.gradle` file for each microservice:

```
jar {
    enabled = false
}
```

For further details, see `https://docs.spring.io/spring-boot/docs/2.5.2/gradle-plugin/reference/htmlsingle/#packaging-executable.and-plain-archives`.

Adding a composite microservice

Now, it's time to tie things together by adding the composite service that will call the three core services!

The implementation of the composite services is divided into two parts: an integration component that handles the outgoing HTTP requests to the core services and the composite service implementation itself. The main reason for this division of responsibility is that it simplifies automated unit and integration testing; we can test the service implementation in isolation by replacing the integration component with a mock.

As we will see later on in this book, this division of responsibility will also make it easier to introduce a circuit breaker!

Before we look into the source code of the two components, we need to take a look at the API classes that the composite microservices will use and also learn about how runtime properties are used to hold address information for the core microservices.

The full implementation of both the integration component and the implementation of the composite service can be found in the Java package `se.magnus.microservices.composite.product.services`.

API classes

In this section, we will take a look at the classes that describes the API of the composite component. They can be found in `$BOOK_HOME/Chapter03/2-basic-rest-services/api`. The following are the API classes:

```
$BOOK_HOME/Chapter03/2-basic-rest-services/api
└── src/main/java/se/magnus/api/composite
    └── product
        ├── ProductAggregate.java
        ├── ProductCompositeService.java
        ├── RecommendationSummary.java
        ├── ReviewSummary.java
        └── ServiceAddresses.java
```

The Java interface class, `ProductCompositeService.java`, follows the same pattern that's used by the core services and looks as follows:

```
package se.magnus.api.composite.product;

public interface ProductCompositeService {

    @GetMapping(
        value    = "/product-composite/{productId}",
        produces = "application/json")
    ProductAggregate getProduct(@PathVariable int productId);
}
```

The model class, `ProductAggregate.java`, is a bit more complex than the core models since it contains fields for lists of recommendations and reviews:

```
package se.magnus.api.composite.product;

public class ProductAggregate {
    private final int productId;
    private final String name;
    private final int weight;
    private final List<RecommendationSummary> recommendations;
    private final List<ReviewSummary> reviews;
    private final ServiceAddresses serviceAddresses;
```

The remaining API classes are plain POJO-based model objects and have the same structure as the model objects for the core APIs.

Properties

To avoid hardcoding the address information for the core services into the source code of the composite microservice, the latter uses a property file where information on how to find the core services is stored. The property file, `application.yml`, looks as follows:

```
server.port: 7000

app:
  product-service:
    host: localhost
    port: 7001
  recommendation-service:
    host: localhost
    port: 7002
  review-service:
    host: localhost
    port: 7003
```

This configuration will, as already noted, be replaced by a service discovery mechanism later on in this book.

Integration component

Let's look at the first part of the implementation of the composite microservice, the integration component, `ProductCompositeIntegration.java`. It is declared as a Spring Bean using the `@Component` annotation and implements the three core services' API interfaces:

```
package se.magnus.microservices.composite.product.services;

@Component
public class ProductCompositeIntegration implements ProductService,
RecommendationService, ReviewService {
```

The integration component uses a helper class in the Spring Framework, `RestTemplate`, to perform the actual HTTP requests to the core microservices. Before we can inject it into the integration component, we need to configure it. We do that in the `main` application class, `ProductCompositeServiceApplication.java`, as follows:

```
@Bean
RestTemplate restTemplate() {
   return new RestTemplate();
}
```

A `RestTemplate` object is highly configurable, but we leave it with its default values for now.

In the *Spring WebFlux* section in *Chapter 2, Introduction to Spring Boot,* we introduced the reactive HTTP client, `WebClient`. Using `WebClient` instead of `RestTemplate` in this chapter would require that all source code where `WebClient` is used is also reactive, including the declaration of the RESTful API in the API project and the source code in the composite microservice. In *Chapter 7, Developing Reactive Microservices,* we will learn how to change the implementation of our microservices to follow a reactive programming model. As one of the steps in that update, we will replace the `RestTemplate` helper class with the `WebClient` class. But until we have learned about reactive development in Spring, we will use the `RestTemplate` class.

We can now inject the `RestTemplate`, along with a JSON `mapper` that's used for accessing error messages in case of errors, and the configuration values that we have set up in the property file. Let's see how this is done:

1. The objects and configuration values are injected into the constructor as follows:

   ```
   private final RestTemplate restTemplate;
   private final ObjectMapper mapper;

   private final String productServiceUrl;
   private final String recommendationServiceUrl;
   private final String reviewServiceUrl;

   @Autowired
   public ProductCompositeIntegration(
     RestTemplate restTemplate,
     ObjectMapper mapper,

     @Value("${app.product-service.host}")
     String productServiceHost,

     @Value("${app.product-service.port}")
   ```

```
        int productServicePort,

        @Value("${app.recommendation-service.host}")
        String recommendationServiceHost,

        @Value("${app.recommendation-service.port}")
        int recommendationServicePort,

        @Value("${app.review-service.host}")
        String reviewServiceHost,

        @Value("${app.review-service.port}")
        int reviewServicePort
    )
```

2. The body of the constructor stores the injected objects and builds the URLs based on the injected values, as follows:

```
    {
      this.restTemplate = restTemplate;
      this.mapper = mapper;

      productServiceUrl = "http://" + productServiceHost + ":" +
      productServicePort + "/product/";
      recommendationServiceUrl = "http://" +
    recommendationServiceHost
      + ":" + recommendationServicePort + "/recommendation?
      productId="; reviewServiceUrl = "http://" + reviewServiceHost
    +
      ":" + reviewServicePort + "/review?productId=";
    }
```

3. Finally, the integration component implements the API methods for the three core services by using `RestTemplate` to make the actual outgoing calls:

```
    public Product getProduct(int productId) {
     String url = productServiceUrl + productId;
     Product product = restTemplate.getForObject(url, Product.
    class);
     return product;
    }
```

```
public List<Recommendation> getRecommendations(int productId) {
    String url = recommendationServiceUrl + productId;
    List<Recommendation> recommendations =
    restTemplate.exchange(url, GET, null, new
    ParameterizedTypeReference<List<Recommendation>>()
    {}).getBody();
    return recommendations;
}

public List<Review> getReviews(int productId) {
    String url = reviewServiceUrl + productId;
    List<Review> reviews = restTemplate.exchange(url, GET, null,
    new ParameterizedTypeReference<List<Review>>() {}).
getBody();
    return reviews;
}
```

Some interesting notes regarding the methods implementations:

1. For the `getProduct()` implementation, the `getForObject()` method can be used in `RestTemplate`. The expected response is a `Product` object. It can be expressed in the call to `getForObject()` by specifying the `Product.class` class that `RestTemplate` will map the JSON response to.
2. For the calls to `getRecommendations()` and `getReviews()`, a more advanced method, `exchange()`, has to be used. The reason for this is the automatic mapping from a JSON response to a model class that `RestTemplate` performs. The `getRecommendations()` and `getReviews()` methods expect a generic list in the responses, that is, `List<Recommendation>` and `List<Review>`. Since generics don't hold any type of information at runtime, we can't specify that the methods expect a generic list in their responses. Instead, we can use a helper class from the Spring Framework, `ParameterizedTypeReference`, that is designed to resolve this problem by holding the type information at runtime. This means that `RestTemplate` can figure out what class to map the JSON responses to. To utilize this helper class, we have to use the more involved `exchange()` method instead of the simpler `getForObject()` method on `RestTemplate`.

Composite API implementation

Finally, we will look at the last piece of the implementation of the composite microservice: the API implementation class `ProductCompositeServiceImpl.java`. Let's go through it step by step:

1. In the same way that we did for the core services, the composite service implements its API interface, `ProductCompositeService`, and is annotated with `@RestController` to mark it as a REST service:

   ```
   package se.magnus.microservices.composite.product.services;

   @RestController
   public class ProductCompositeServiceImpl implements
   ProductCompositeService {
   ```

2. The implementation class requires the `ServiceUtil` bean and its own integration component, so they are injected in its constructor:

   ```
   private final ServiceUtil serviceUtil;
   private ProductCompositeIntegration integration;

   @Autowired
   public ProductCompositeServiceImpl(ServiceUtil serviceUtil,
   ProductCompositeIntegration integration) {
       this.serviceUtil = serviceUtil;
       this.integration = integration;
   }
   ```

3. Finally, the API method is implemented as follows:

   ```
   @Override
   public ProductAggregate getProduct(int productId) {

     Product product = integration.getProduct(productId);
     List<Recommendation> recommendations =
     integration.getRecommendations(productId);
     List<Review> reviews = integration.getReviews(productId);

     return createProductAggregate(product, recommendations,
     reviews, serviceUtil.getServiceAddress());
   }
   ```

The integration component is used to call the three core services, and a helper method, `createProductAggregate()`, is used to create a response object of the `ProductAggregate` type based on the responses from the calls to the integration component.

The implementation of the helper method, `createProductAggregate()`, is quite lengthy and not very important and so has been omitted from this chapter; however, it can be found in this book's source code.

The full implementation of both the integration component and the composite service can be found in the Java package `se.magnus.microservices.composite.product.services`.

That completes the implementation of the composite microservice from a functional point of view. In the next section, we will see how we handle errors.

Adding error handling

Handling errors in a structured and well-thought-out way is essential in a microservice landscape where a large number of microservices communicate with each other using synchronous APIs, for example, using HTTP and JSON. It is also important to separate protocol-specific handling of errors, such as HTTP status codes, from the business logic.

It could be argued that a separate layer for the business logic should be added when implementing the microservices. This should ensure that business logic is separated from the protocol-specific code, making it easier both to test and reuse. To avoid unnecessary complexity in the examples provided in this book, we have left out a separate layer for business logic, so the microservices implement their business logic directly in the `@RestController` components.

I have created a set of Java exceptions in the `util` project that are used by both the API implementations and the API clients, initially `InvalidInputException` and `NotFoundException`. Look into the Java package `se.magnus.util.exceptions` for details.

The global REST controller exception handler

To separate protocol-specific error handling from the business logic in the REST controllers, that is, the API implementations, I have created a utility class, `GlobalControllerExceptionHandler.java`, in the `util` project that's annotated as `@RestControllerAdvice`.

For each Java exception that the API implementations throw, the utility class has an exception handler method that maps the Java exception to a proper HTTP response, that is, with a proper HTTP status and HTTP response body.

For example, if an API implementation class throws `InvalidInputException`, the utility class will map it to an HTTP response with the status code set to `422` (`UNPROCESSABLE_ENTITY`). The following code shows this:

```
@ResponseStatus(UNPROCESSABLE_ENTITY)
@ExceptionHandler(InvalidInputException.class)
public @ResponseBody HttpErrorInfo handleInvalidInputException(
    ServerHttpRequest request, InvalidInputException ex) {

    return createHttpErrorInfo(UNPROCESSABLE_ENTITY, request, ex);
}
```

In the same way, `NotFoundException` is mapped to a `404` (`NOT_FOUND`) HTTP status code.

Whenever a REST controller throws any of these exceptions, Spring will use the utility class to create an HTTP response.

Note that Spring itself returns the HTTP status code `400` (`BAD_REQUEST`) when it detects an invalid request, for example, if the request contains a non-numeric product ID (`productId` is specified as an integer in the API declaration).

For the full source code of the utility class, see `GlobalControllerExceptionHandler.java`.

Error handling in API implementations

API implementations use the exceptions in the `util` project to signal errors. They will be reported back to the REST client as HTTPS status codes indicating what went wrong. For example, the `Product` microservice implementation class, `ProductServiceImpl.java`, uses the `InvalidInputException` exception to return an error that indicates invalid input, as well as the `NotFoundException` exception to tell us that the product that was asked for does not exist. The code looks as follows:

```
if (productId < 1) throw new InvalidInputException("Invalid productId:
    " + productId);
if (productId == 13) throw new NotFoundException("No product found for
    productId: " + productId);
```

Since we currently aren't using a database, we have to simulate when to throw `NotFoundException`.

Error handling in the API client

The API client, that is, the integration component of the `Composite` microservice, does the reverse; it maps the `422` (`UNPROCESSABLE_ENTITY`) HTTP status code to `InvalidInputException` and the `404` (`NOT_FOUND`) HTTP status code to `NotFoundException`. See the `getProduct()` method in `ProductCompositeIntegration.java` for the implementation of this error handling logic. The source code looks as follows:

```
catch (HttpClientErrorException ex) {

    switch (ex.getStatusCode()) {

    case NOT_FOUND:
        throw new NotFoundException(getErrorMessage(ex));

    case UNPROCESSABLE_ENTITY:
        throw new InvalidInputException(getErrorMessage(ex));

    default:
        LOG.warn("Got an unexpected HTTP error: {}, will rethrow it",
        ex.getStatusCode());
        LOG.warn("Error body: {}", ex.getResponseBodyAsString());
        throw ex;
    }
}
```

The error handling for `getRecommendations()` and `getReviews()` in the integration component is a bit more relaxed – classed as best-effort, meaning that if it succeeds in getting product information but fails to get either recommendations or reviews, it is still considered to be okay. However, a warning is written to the log.

For details, see `ProductCompositeIntegration.java`.

That completes the implementation of both the code and composite microservices. In the next section, we will test the microservices and the API that they expose.

Testing APIs manually

That concludes the implementation of our microservices. Let's try them out by performing the following steps:

1. Build and start the microservices as background processes.
2. Use `curl` to call the composite API.
3. Stop them.

First, build and start up each microservice as a background process, as follows:

```
cd $BOOK_HOME/Chapter03/2-basic-rest-services/
./gradlew build
```

Once the build completes, we can launch our microservices as background processes to the Terminal process with the following code:

```
java -jar microservices/product-composite-service/build/libs/*.jar &
java -jar microservices/product-service/build/libs/*.jar &
java -jar microservices/recommendation-service/build/libs/*.jar &
java -jar microservices/review-service/build/libs/*.jar &
```

A lot of log messages will be written to the Terminal, but after a few seconds, things will calm down and we will find the following messages written to the log:

```
4. bash
...Started ProductCompositeServiceApplication...
...Started RecommendationServiceApplication...
...Started ProductServiceApplication...
...Started ReviewServiceApplication...
```

Figure 3.6: Log messages after applications start

This means that they are all ready to receive requests. Try this out with the following code:

```
curl http://localhost:7000/product-composite/1
```

After some log output, we will get a JSON response that looks something like the following:

```
4. bash
$ curl http://localhost:7000/product-composite/1
{"productId":1,"name":"name-1","weight":123,"recommendations":[{"recomm
endationId":1,"author":"Author 1","rate":1},{"recommendationId":2,"auth
or":"Author 2","rate":2},{"recommendationId":3,"author":"Author 3","rat
e":3}],"reviews":[{"reviewId":1,"author":"Author 1","subject":"Subject
1"},{"reviewId":2,"author":"Author 2","subject":"Subject 2"},{"reviewId
":3,"author":"Author 3","subject":"Subject 3"}],"serviceAddresses":{"cm
p":"Magnus-MBP32.lan/192.168.1.185:7000","pro":"Magnus-MBP32.lan/192.16
8.1.185:7001","rev":"Magnus-MBP32.lan/192.168.1.185:7003","rec":"Magnus
-MBP32.lan/192.168.1.185:7002"}}$
```

Figure 3.7: JSON response after request

To get the JSON response pretty-printed, you can use the `jq` tool:

```
curl http://localhost:7000/product-composite/1 -s | jq .
```

This results in the following output (some details have been replaced by `...` for increased readability):

```
-bash                                                        ⌥⌘1
$ curl http://localhost:7000/product-composite/1 -s | jq .
{
  "productId": 1,
  ...
  "recommendations": [ ... ],
  "reviews": [ ... ],
  "serviceAddresses": { ... }
}
$
```

Figure 3.8: Pretty-printed JSON response

If you want to, you can also try out the following commands to verify that the error handling works as expected:

```
# Verify that a 404 (Not Found) error is returned for a non-existing
productId (13)
curl http://localhost:7000/product-composite/13 -i
```

```
# Verify that no recommendations are returned for productId 113
curl http://localhost:7000/product-composite/113 -s | jq .

# Verify that no reviews are returned for productId 213
curl http://localhost:7000/product-composite/213 -s | jq .

# Verify that a 422 (Unprocessable Entity) error is returned for a
productId that is out of range (-1)
curl http://localhost:7000/product-composite/-1 -i

# Verify that a 400 (Bad Request) error is returned for a productId
that is not a number, i.e. invalid format
curl http://localhost:7000/product-composite/invalidProductId -i
```

Finally, you can shut down the microservices with the following command:

```
kill $(jobs -p)
```

If you are using an IDE such as Visual Studio Code, Spring Tool Suite, or IntelliJ IDEA Ultimate Edition, you can use their support for the Spring Boot Dashboard to start and stop your microservices with one click.

The following screenshot shows the use of the Spring Boot Dashboard in Visual Studio Code:

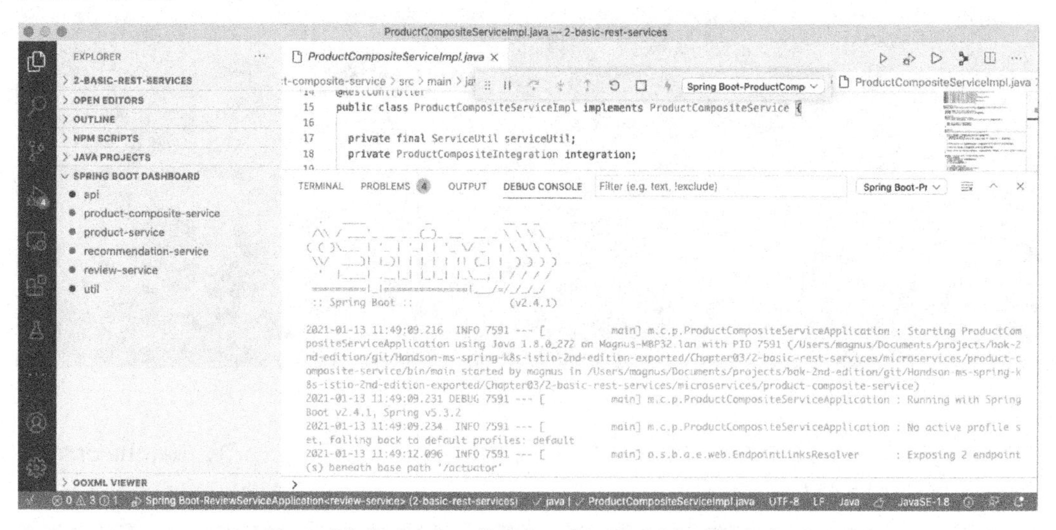

Figure 3.9: Spring Boot Dashboard in Visual Studio Code

The following screenshot shows the use of the Spring Boot Dashboard in Spring Tool Suite:

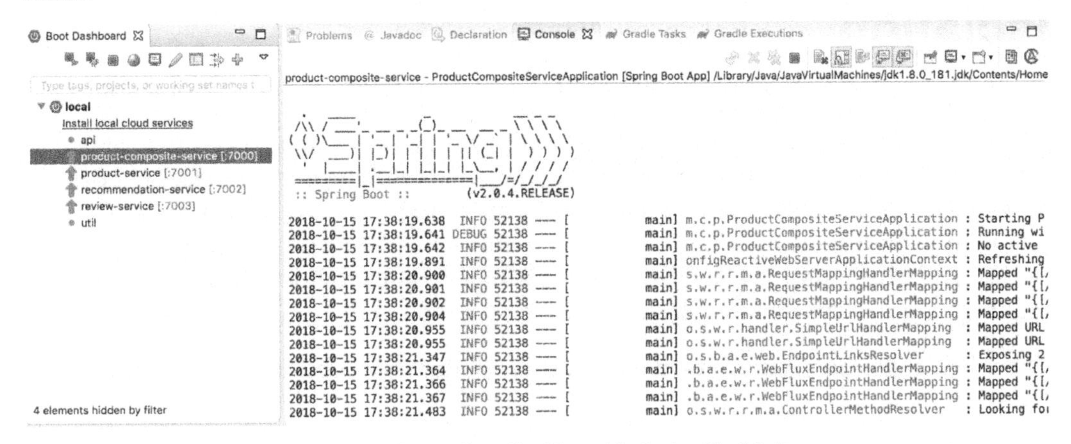

Figure 3.10: Spring Boot Dashboard in Spring Tool Suite

The following screenshot shows the use of the Spring Boot Dashboard in IntelliJ IDEA Ultimate Edition:

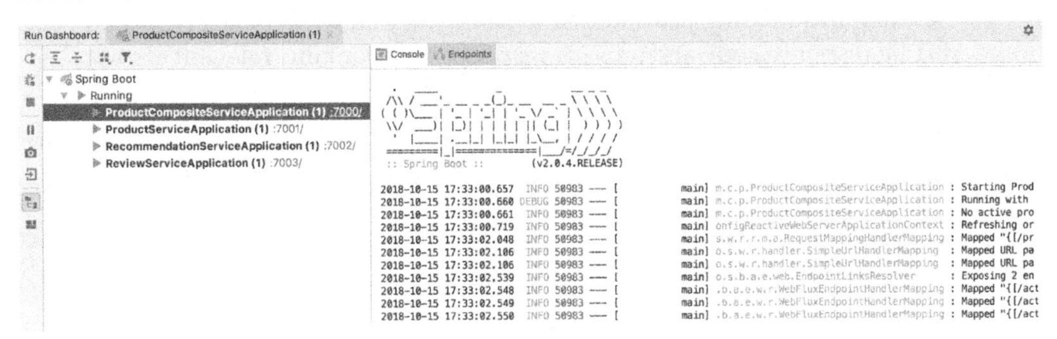

Figure 3.11: Spring Boot Dashboard in IntelliJ IDEA Ultimate Edition

In this section, we have learned how to manually start, test, and stop the system landscape of cooperating microservices. These types of tests are time-consuming, so they clearly need to be automated. In the next two sections, we will take our first steps toward learning how to automate testing, testing both a single microservice in isolation and a whole system landscape of cooperating microservices. Throughout this book, we will improve how we test our microservices.

Adding automated microservice tests in isolation

Before we wrap up the implementation, we also need to write some automated tests.

We don't have much business logic to test at this time, so we don't need to write any unit tests. Instead, we will focus on testing the APIs that our microservices expose; that is, we will start them up in integration tests with their embedded web server and then use a test client to perform HTTP requests and validate the responses. With Spring WebFlux comes a test client, `WebTestClient`, that provides a fluent API for making a request and then applying assertions on its result.

The following is an example where we test the composite product API by doing the following tests:

- Sending in `productId` for an existing product and asserting that we get back `200` as an HTTP response code and a JSON response that contains the requested `productId` along with one recommendation and one review
- Sending in a missing `productId` and asserting that we get back `404` as an HTTP response code and a JSON response that contains relevant error information

The implementation for these two tests is shown in the following code. The first test looks like this:

```
@Autowired
private WebTestClient client;

@Test
void getProductById() {
  client.get()
    .uri("/product-composite/" + PRODUCT_ID_OK)
    .accept(APPLICATION_JSON_UTF8)
    .exchange()
    .expectStatus().isOk()
    .expectHeader().contentType(APPLICATION_JSON_UTF8)
    .expectBody()
    .jsonPath("$.productId").isEqualTo(PRODUCT_ID_OK)
    .jsonPath("$.recommendations.length()").isEqualTo(1)
    .jsonPath("$.reviews.length()").isEqualTo(1);
}
```

The test code works like this:

- The test uses the fluent `WebTestClient` API to set up the URL to call `"/product-composite/" + PRODUCT_ID_OK` and specify the accepted response format, JSON.
- After executing the request using the `exchange()` method, the test verifies that the response status is `OK` (`200`) and that the response format actually is JSON (as requested).
- Finally, the test inspects the response body and verifies that it contains the expected information in terms of `productId` and the number of recommendations and reviews.

The second test looks as follows:

```
@Test
public void getProductNotFound() {
  client.get()
    .uri("/product-composite/" + PRODUCT_ID_NOT_FOUND)
    .accept(APPLICATION_JSON_UTF8)
    .exchange()
    .expectStatus().isNotFound()
    .expectHeader().contentType(APPLICATION_JSON_UTF8)
    .expectBody()
    .jsonPath("$.path").isEqualTo("/product-composite/" +
     PRODUCT_ID_NOT_FOUND)
    .jsonPath("$.message").isEqualTo("NOT FOUND: " +
     PRODUCT_ID_NOT_FOUND);
}
```

One important note regarding this test code is:

- This negative test is very similar to the preceding test in terms of its structure; the main difference is that it verifies that it got an error status code back, `Not Found` (`404`), and that the response body contains the expected error message.

To test the composite product API in isolation, we need to mock its dependencies, that is, the requests to the other three microservices that were performed by the integration component, `ProductCompositeIntegration`. We use **Mockito** to do this, as follows:

```
private static final int PRODUCT_ID_OK = 1;
private static final int PRODUCT_ID_NOT_FOUND = 2;
private static final int PRODUCT_ID_INVALID = 3;
```

```
@MockBean
private ProductCompositeIntegration compositeIntegration;

@BeforeEach
void setUp() {

  when(compositeIntegration.getProduct(PRODUCT_ID_OK)).
    thenReturn(new Product(PRODUCT_ID_OK, "name", 1, "mock-address"));
  when(compositeIntegration.getRecommendations(PRODUCT_ID_OK)).
    thenReturn(singletonList(new Recommendation(PRODUCT_ID_OK, 1,
    "author", 1, "content", "mock address")));
     when(compositeIntegration.getReviews(PRODUCT_ID_OK)).
    thenReturn(singletonList(new Review(PRODUCT_ID_OK, 1, "author",
    "subject", "content", "mock address")));

  when(compositeIntegration.getProduct(PRODUCT_ID_NOT_FOUND)).
    thenThrow(new NotFoundException("NOT FOUND: " +
    PRODUCT_ID_NOT_FOUND));

  when(compositeIntegration.getProduct(PRODUCT_ID_INVALID)).
    thenThrow(new InvalidInputException("INVALID: " +
    PRODUCT_ID_INVALID));
}
```

The mock implementation works as follows:

- First, we declare three constants that are used in the test class: `PRODUCT_ID_OK`, `PRODUCT_ID_NOT_FOUND`, and `PRODUCT_ID_INVALID`.
- Next, the annotation `@MockBean` is used to configure Mockito to set up a mock for the `ProductCompositeIntegration` interface.
- If the `getProduct()`, `getRecommendations()`, and `getReviews()` methods are called on the integration component, and `productId` is set to `PRODUCT_ID_OK`, the mock will return a normal response.
- If the `getProduct()` method is called with `productId` set to `PRODUCT_ID_NOT_FOUND`, the mock will throw `NotFoundException`.
- If the `getProduct()` method is called with `productId` set to `PRODUCT_ID_INVALID`, the mock will throw `InvalidInputException`.

The full source code for the automated integration tests on the composite product API can be found in the test class `ProductCompositeServiceApplicationTests.java`.

The automated integration tests on the API exposed by the three core microservices are similar, but simpler since they don't need to mock anything! The source code for the tests can be found in each microservice's `test` folder.

The tests are run automatically by Gradle when performing a build:

```
./gradlew build
```

You can, however, specify that you only want to run the tests (and not the rest of the build):

```
./gradlew test
```

This was an introduction to how to write automated tests for microservices in isolation. In the next section, we will learn how to write tests that automatically test a microservice landscape. In this chapter, these tests will only be semi-automated. In upcoming chapters, the tests will be fully automated, a significant improvement.

Adding semi-automated tests of a microservice landscape

Being able to automatically run unit and integration tests for each microservice in isolation using plain Java, JUnit, and Gradle is very useful during development, but insufficient when we move over to the operation side. In operation, we also need a way to automatically verify that a *system landscape* of cooperating microservices delivers what we expect. Being able to, at any time, run a script that verifies that a number of cooperating microservices all work as expected in operation is very valuable - the more microservices there are, the higher the value of such a verification script.

For this reason, I have written a simple `bash` script that can verify the functionality of a deployed system landscape by performing calls to the RESTful APIs exposed by the microservices. It is based on the `curl` commands we learned about and used above. The script verifies return codes and parts of the JSON responses using `jq`. The script contains two helper functions, `assertCurl()` and `assertEqual()`, to make the test code compact and easy to read.

For example, making a normal request and expecting `200` as the status code, as well as asserting that we get back a JSON response that returns the requested `productId` along with three recommendations and three reviews, looks like the following:

```
# Verify that a normal request works, expect three recommendations and
three reviews
assertCurl 200 "curl http://$HOST:${PORT}/product-composite/1 -s"
assertEqual 1 $(echo $RESPONSE | jq .productId)
assertEqual 3 $(echo $RESPONSE | jq ".recommendations | length")
assertEqual 3 $(echo $RESPONSE | jq ".reviews | length")
```

Verifying that we get `404 (Not Found)` back as an HTTP response code (when we try to look up a product that doesn't exist) looks as follows:

```
# Verify that a 404 (Not Found) error is returned for a non-existing
productId (13)
assertCurl 404 "curl http://$HOST:${PORT}/product-composite/13 -s"
```

The test script, `test-em-all.bash`, implements the manual tests that were described in the section *Testing APIs manually* and can be found in the top-level folder `$BOOK_HOME/Chapter03/2-basic-rest-services`. We will extend the functionality of the test script as we add more functionality to the system landscape in later chapters.

In *Chapter 20, Monitoring Microservices,* we will learn about complementary techniques for automatically keeping an eye on a system landscape in operation. Here we will learn about a monitoring tool that continuously monitors the state of the deployed microservices and how alarms can be raised if the collected metrics exceed configured thresholds, such as overuse of CPU or memory.

Trying out the test script

To try out the test script, perform the following steps:

1. First, start the microservices, as we did previously:

```
cd $BOOK_HOME/Chapter03/2-basic-rest-services
java -jar microservices/product-composite-service/build/libs/*.
jar &
java -jar microservices/product-service/build/libs/*.jar &
java -jar microservices/recommendation-service/build/libs/*.jar &
java -jar microservices/review-service/build/libs/*.jar &
```

2. Once they've all started up, run the test script:

```
./test-em-all.bash
```

Expect the output to look similar to the following:

```
$ ./test-em-all.bash
HOST=localhost
PORT=7000
Test OK (HTTP Code: 200)
Test OK (actual value: 1)
Test OK (actual value: 3)
Test OK (actual value: 3)
Test OK (HTTP Code: 404, {"timestamp":"2021-01-08T18:47:03.791+01:00","path":"/product-comp
osite/13","message":"No product found for productId: 13","error":"Not Found","status":404})
Test OK (actual value: No product found for productId: 13)
Test OK (HTTP Code: 200)
Test OK (actual value: 113)
Test OK (actual value: 0)
Test OK (actual value: 3)
Test OK (HTTP Code: 200)
Test OK (actual value: 213)
Test OK (actual value: 3)
Test OK (actual value: 0)
Test OK (HTTP Code: 422, {"timestamp":"2021-01-08T18:47:04.117+01:00","path":"/product-comp
osite/-1","message":"Invalid productId: -1","error":"Unprocessable Entity","status":422})
Test OK (actual value: "Invalid productId: -1")
Test OK (HTTP Code: 400, {"timestamp":"2021-01-08T17:47:04.172+00:00","path":"/product-comp
osite/invalidProductId","status":400,"error":"Bad Request","message":"Type mismatch.","requ
estId":"9c92dc8a-12"})
Test OK (actual value: "Type mismatch.")
End, all tests OK: Fri Jan 8 18:47:04 CET 2021
$
```

Figure 3.12: Output after running the test script

3. Wrap this up by shutting down the microservices with the following command:

```
kill $(jobs -p)
```

In this section, we have taken the first steps toward automating testing for a system landscape of cooperating microservices, all of which will be improved in upcoming chapters.

Summary

We have now built our first few microservices using Spring Boot. After being introduced to the microservice landscape that we will use throughout this book, we learned how to use Spring Initializr to create skeleton projects for each microservice.

Next, we learned how to add APIs using Spring WebFlux for the three core services and implemented a composite service that uses the three core services' APIs to create an aggregated view of the information in them. The composite service uses the `RestTemplate` class in the Spring Framework to perform HTTP requests to APIs that are exposed by the core services. After adding logic for error handling in the services, we ran some manual tests on the microservice landscape.

We wrapped this chapter up by learning how to add tests for microservices in isolation and when they work together as a system landscape. To provide controlled isolation for the composite service, we mocked its dependencies to the core services using Mockito. Testing the whole system landscape is performed by a Bash script that uses `curl` to perform calls to the API of the composite service.

With these skills in place, we are ready to take the next step, entering the world of Docker and containers in the next chapter! Among other things, we will learn how to use Docker to fully automate testing of a system landscape of cooperating microservices.

Questions

1. What is the command that lists available dependencies when you create a new Spring Boot project using the `spring init` Spring Initializr CLI tool?
2. How can you set up Gradle to build multiple related projects with one command?
3. What are the `@PathVariable` and `@RequestParam` annotations used for?
4. How can you separate protocol-specific error handling from the business logic in an API implementation class?
5. What is Mockito used for?

4

Deploying Our Microservices Using Docker

In this chapter, we will start using Docker and put our microservices into containers!

By the end of this chapter, we will have run fully automated tests of our microservice landscape that start all our microservices as Docker containers, requiring no infrastructure other than a Docker engine. We will have also run a number of tests to verify that the microservices work together as expected, and finally shut down all the microservices, leaving no traces of the tests we executed.

Being able to test a number of cooperating microservices in this way is very useful. As developers, we can verify that the microservices work on our local developer machines. We can also run exactly the same tests in a build server to automatically verify that changes to the source code won't break the tests at a system level. Additionally, we don't need to have a dedicated infrastructure allocated to run these types of tests. In the upcoming chapters, we will see how we can add databases and queue managers to our test landscape, all of which will run as Docker containers.

This does not, however, replace the need for automated unit and integration tests, which test individual microservices in isolation. They are as important as ever.

For production usage, as we mentioned earlier in this book, we need a container orchestrator such as Kubernetes. We will get back to container orchestrators and Kubernetes later in this book.

The following topics will be covered in this chapter:

- Introduction to Docker
- Docker and Java. Java hasn't been very friendly to containers historically, but that changed with Java 10. Let's see how Docker and Java fit together!
- Using Docker with one microservice
- Managing a landscape of microservices using Docker Compose
- Automating tests of cooperating microservices

Technical requirements

For instructions on how to install tools used in this book and how to access the source code for this book, see:

- *Chapter 21* for macOS
- *Chapter 22* for Windows

The code examples in this chapter all come from the source code in `$BOOK_HOME/Chapter04`.

If you want to see the changes that were applied to the source code in this chapter, that is, see what it took to add support for Docker, you can compare it with the source code for *Chapter 3, Creating a Set of Cooperating Microservices*. You can use your favorite `diff` tool and compare the two folders, `$BOOK_HOME/Chapter03/2-basic-rest-services` and `$BOOK_HOME/Chapter04`.

Introduction to Docker

As we already mentioned in *Chapter 2, Introduction to Spring Boot*, Docker made the concept of containers as a lightweight alternative to virtual machines very popular in 2013. To quickly recap: containers are actually processed in a Linux host that uses **Linux namespaces** to provide isolation between containers, and **Linux Control Groups (cgroups)** are used to limit the amount of CPU and memory that a container is allowed to consume.

Compared to a virtual machine that uses a hypervisor to run a complete copy of an operating system in each virtual machine, the overhead in a container is a fraction of the overhead in a virtual machine. This leads to much faster startup times and a significantly lower footprint. Containers are, however, not considered to be as secure as virtual machines. Take a look at the following diagram:

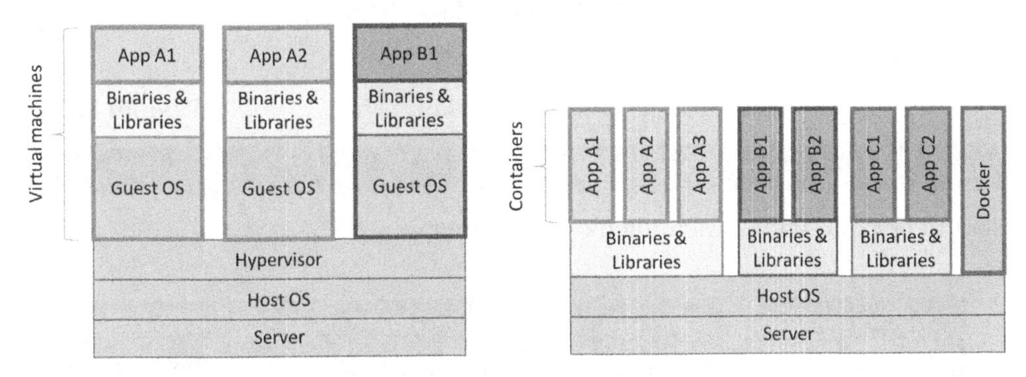

Figure 4.1: Virtual machines versus containers

The diagram illustrates the difference between the resource usage of virtual machines and containers, demonstrating that the same type of server can run significantly more containers than virtual machines. The main gain is that a container doesn't need to run its own instance of an operating system, as a virtual machine does.

Running our first Docker commands

Let's try to start a container by launching an Ubuntu server using Docker's `run` command:

```
docker run -it --rm ubuntu
```

With the preceding command, we ask Docker to create a container that runs Ubuntu, based on the latest version that's available of the official Docker image for Ubuntu. The `-it` option is used so that we can interact with the container using Terminal, and the `--rm` option tells Docker to remove the container once we exit the Terminal session; otherwise, the container will remain in the Docker engine with an `Exited` state.

The first time we use a Docker image that we haven't built ourselves, Docker will download it from a Docker registry, which is Docker Hub by default (`https://hub.docker.com`). This will take some time, but for subsequent usage of that Docker image, the container will start in just a few seconds!

Once the Docker image has been downloaded and the container has been started up, the Ubuntu server should respond with a prompt such as the following:

```
4. root@435dc56d39f6: / (docker)
$ docker run -it --rm ubuntu
root@435dc56d39f6:/#
```

Figure 4.2: Ubuntu server response

We can try out the container by, for example, asking what version of Ubuntu it runs:

```
cat /etc/os-release | grep 'VERSION='
```

It should respond with something like the following:

```
4. root@435dc56d39f6: / (docker)
root@435dc56d39f6:/# cat /etc/os-release | grep 'VERSION='
VERSION="18.04.3 LTS (Bionic Beaver)"
root@435dc56d39f6:/#
```

Figure 4.3: Ubuntu version response

We can leave the container with an `exit` command and verify that the Ubuntu container no longer exits with the `docker ps -a` command. We need to use the `-a` option to see stopped containers; otherwise, only running containers are displayed.

If you favor CentOS over Ubuntu, feel free to try the same with the `docker run --rm -it centos` command. Once the CentOS server has started running in its container you can, for example, ask what version of CentOS is running with the `cat /etc/redhat-release` command. It should respond with something like the following:

```
4. @700dd0df9ffe:/ (docker)
$ docker run --rm -it centos
[root@700dd0df9ffe /]# cat /etc/redhat-release
CentOS Linux release 7.6.1810 (Core)
[root@700dd0df9ffe /]#
```

Figure 4.4: CentOS version response

Leave the container with the `exit` command to remove it.

If, at some point, you find that you have a lot of unwanted containers in the Docker engine and you want to get a clean sheet, that is, get rid of them all, you can run the following command:

```
docker rm -f $(docker ps -aq)
```

The `docker rm -f` command stops and removes the containers whose container IDs are specified to the command. The `docker ps -aq` command lists the container IDs of all the running and stopped containers in the Docker engine. The `-q` option reduces the output from the `docker ps` command so that it only lists the container IDs.

Now we've understood what Docker is, we can move on to consider the problems we might face while running Java in Docker.

Challenges with running Java in Docker

Over the past few years, there have been a number of attempts to get Java working in Docker in a good way. Most importantly, Java hasn't historically been very good at respecting limits set for Docker containers when it comes to the use of memory and CPU.

Currently, the official Docker image for Java comes from the **OpenJDK** project: `https://hub.docker.com/_/openjdk/`. We will use an alternative Docker image from the **AdoptOpenJDK** project. It contains the same binaries from the OpenJDK project, but provides variants of the Docker images that meet our needs better than the Docker images from the OpenJDK project.

In this section, we will use a Docker image that contains the full **JDK** (**Java Development Kit**) with all its tools. When we start to package our microservices in Docker images in the *Using Docker with one microservice* section, we will use a more compact Docker image that is based on the **JRE** (**Java Runtime Environment**) only containing the Java tools required at runtime.

As already mentioned, earlier versions of Java have not been very good at honoring the quotas specified for a Docker container using Linux cgroups; they simply ignored these settings. So, instead of allocating memory inside the JVM in relation to the memory available in the container, Java allocated memory as if it had access to all the memory in the Docker host. When trying to allocate more memory than allowed, the Java container was killed by the host with an "out of memory" error message. In the same way, Java allocated CPU-related resources such as thread pools in relation to the total number of available CPU cores in the Docker host, instead of the number of CPU cores that were made available for the container JVM was running in.

In Java SE 9, initial support for container-based CPU and memory constraints was provided, much improved in Java SE 10.

Let's look at how Java SE 16 responds to limits we set on a container it runs in!

In the following tests, we will run the Docker engine inside a virtual machine on a MacBook Pro, acting as the Docker host. The Docker host is configured to use **12 CPU** cores and **16 GB of memory**.

We will start by seeing how we can limit the number of available CPUs to a container that runs Java. After that, we will do the same with limiting memory.

Limiting available CPUs

Let's start by finding out how many available processors, that is CPU cores, Java sees without applying any constraints. We can do this by sending the Java statement `Runtime.getRuntime().availableprocessors()` to the Java CLI tool `jshell`. We will run `jshell` in a container using the Docker image that contains the full Java 16 JDK. The Docker tag for this image is `adoptopenjdk:16`. The command looks like:

```
echo 'Runtime.getRuntime().availableProcessors()' | docker run --rm -i
adoptopenjdk:16 jshell -q
```

This command will send the string `Runtime.getRuntime().availableProcessors()` to the Docker container that will process the string using `jshell`. We will get the following response:

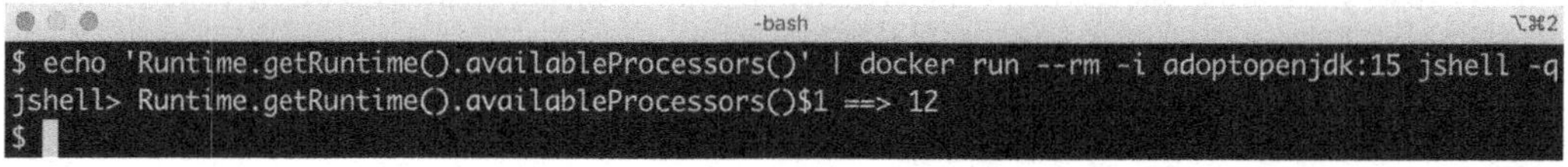

```
-bash                                                                        ⌥⌘2
$ echo 'Runtime.getRuntime().availableProcessors()' | docker run --rm -i adoptopenjdk:15 jshell -q
jshell> Runtime.getRuntime().availableProcessors()$1 ==> 12
$
```

Figure 4.5: Response showing number of CPU cores available

The response of `12` cores is as expected, since the Docker host was configured to use 12 CPU cores. Let's move on and restrict the Docker container to only be allowed to use three CPU cores using the `--cpus 3` Docker option, then ask the JVM about how many available processors it sees:

```
echo 'Runtime.getRuntime().availableProcessors()' | docker run --rm -i
--cpus=3 adoptopenjdk:16 jshell -q
```

The JVM now responds with `Runtime.getRuntime().availableProcessors()$1 ==> 3`, that is, Java SE 16 honors the settings in the container and will, therefore, be able to configure CPU-related resources such as thread pools correctly!

Limiting available memory

In terms of the amount of available memory, let's ask the JVM for the maximum size that it thinks it can allocate for the heap. We can achieve this by asking the JVM for extra runtime information using the `-XX:+PrintFlagsFinal` Java option and then using the `grep` command to filter out the `MaxHeapSize` parameter, like so:

```
docker run -it --rm adoptopenjdk:16 java -XX:+PrintFlagsFinal | grep
"size_t MaxHeapSize"
```

With 16 GB of memory allocated to the Docker host, we will get the following response:

```
$ docker run -it --rm adoptopenjdk:15 java -XX:+PrintFlagsFinal -version | grep "size_t MaxHeapSize"
   size_t MaxHeapSize = 4198498304
$
```

Figure 4.6: Response showing MaxHeapSize

With no JVM memory constraints, that is not using the JVM parameter `-Xmx`, Java will allocate one-quarter of the memory available to the container for its heap. So, we expect it to allocate up to 4 GB to its heap. From the preceding screenshot, we can see that the response was 4,198,498,304 bytes. That equals $4{,}198{,}498{,}304 / 1024^2$ = 4004 MB, which is close to the expected 4 GB.

If we constrain the Docker container to only use up to 1 GB of memory using the Docker option `-m=1024M`, we expect to see a lower max memory allocation. Running the command:

```
docker run -it --rm -m=1024M adoptopenjdk:16 java -XX:+PrintFlagsFinal
| grep "size_t MaxHeapSize"
```

Will result in the response 268,435,456 bytes, which equals $268{,}435{,}456 / 1024^2$ = 256 MB. 256 MB is one-quarter of 1 GB, so again, this is as expected.

We can, as usual, set the max heap size on the JVM ourselves. For example, if we want to allow the JVM to use 600 MB of the total 1 GB we have for its heap, we can specify that using the JVM option `-Xmx600m` like:

```
docker run -it --rm -m=1024M adoptopenjdk:16 java -Xmx600m
-XX:+PrintFlagsFinal -version | grep "size_t MaxHeapSize"
```

The JVM will respond with 629,145,600 bytes = $600 * 1024^2$ = 600 MB, again as expected.

Let's conclude with an "out of memory" test to ensure that this really works!

We'll allocate some memory using `jshell` in a JVM that runs in a container that has been given 1 GB of memory; that is, it has a max heap size of 256 MB.

First, try to allocate a byte array of 100 MB:

```
echo 'new byte[100_000_000]' | docker run -i --rm -m=1024M
adoptopenjdk:16 jshell -q
```

The command will respond with `$1 ==>`, meaning that it worked fine!

Normally, `jshell` will print out the value resulting from the command, but 100 MB of bytes all set to zero is a bit too much to print, and so we get nothing.

Now, let's try to allocate a byte array that is larger than the max heap size, for example, 500 MB:

```
echo 'new byte[500_000_000]' | docker run -i --rm -m=1024M
adoptopenjdk:16 jshell -q
```

The JVM sees that it can't perform the action since it honors the container settings of max memory and responds immediately with
`Exception java.lang.OutOfMemoryError: Java heap space`. Great!

So, to summarize, we have now seen how Java honors the settings of available CPUs and the memory of its container. Let's move on and build our first Docker images for one of the microservices!

Using Docker with one microservice

Now that we understand how Java works in a container, we can start using Docker with one of our microservices. Before we can run our microservice as a Docker container, we need to package it in a Docker image. To build a Docker image, we need a Dockerfile, so we will start with that. Next, we need a Docker-specific configuration for our microservice. Since a microservice that runs in a container is isolated from other microservices – it has its own IP address, hostname, and ports – it needs a different configuration compared to when it's running on the same host with other microservices.

For example, since the other microservices no longer run on the same host, no port conflicts will occur. When running in Docker, we can use the default port `8080` for all our microservices without any risk of port conflicts. On the other hand, if we need to talk to the other microservices, we can no longer use `localhost` like we could when we ran them on the same host.

The source code in the microservices will not be affected by running the microservices in containers, only their configuration!

To handle the different configurations that are required when running locally without Docker and when running the microservices as Docker containers, we will use Spring profiles. Since *Chapter 3, Creating a Set of Cooperating Microservices,* we have been using the default Spring profile for running locally without Docker. Now, we will create a new Spring profile named `docker` to be used when we run our microservices as containers in Docker.

Changes in source code

We will start with the `product` microservice, which can be found in the source code at `$BOOK_HOME/Chapter04/microservices/product-service/`. In the next section, we will apply this to the other microservices as well.

First, we add the Spring profile for Docker at the end of the property file `application.yml`:

```
---
spring.config.activate.on-profile: docker

server.port: 8080
```

Spring profiles can be used to specify environment-specific configuration, which in this case is a configuration that is only to be used when running the microservice in a Docker container. Other examples are configurations that are specific to `dev`, `test`, and `production` environments. Values in a profile override values from the default profile. Using `yaml` files, multiple Spring profiles can be placed in the same file, separated by `---`.

The only parameter we change for now is the port that's being used; we will use the default port `8080` when running the microservice in a container.

Next, we will create the Dockerfile that we will use to build the Docker image. As mentioned in *Chapter 2, Introduction to Spring Boot*, a Dockerfile can be as straightforward as:

```
FROM openjdk:16

EXPOSE 8080

ADD ./build/libs/*.jar app.jar

ENTRYPOINT ["java","-jar","/app.jar"]
```

Some things to take note of are:

- The Docker images will be based on the official Docker image for OpenJDK and use version 16.
- Port `8080` will be exposed to other Docker containers.
- The fat-jar file will be added to the Docker image from the Gradle build library, `build/libs`.
- The command used by Docker to start a container based on this Docker image is `java -jar /app.jar`.

This simple approach has a couple of disadvantages:

1. We are using the full JDK of Java SE 16, including compilers and other development tools. That makes the Docker images unnecessarily large and from a security perspective, we don't want to bring more tools into the image than necessary. Therefore, we would prefer to use a base image for the Java SE 16 JRE, Java Runtime Environment, that only contains programs and libraries required to run a Java program. Unfortunately, the OpenJDK project does not provide a Docker image for Java SE 16 JRE.
2. The fat-jar file takes time to unpackage when the Docker container starts up. A better approach is to instead unpackage the fat-jar when the Docker image is built.
3. The fat-jar file is very big, as we will see below, some 20 MB. If we want to make repeatable changes to the application code in the Docker images during development, this will result in suboptimal usage of the Docker build command. Since Docker images are built in layers, we will get one very big layer that needs to be replaced each time, even in the case where only a single Java class is changed in the application code.

> A better approach is to divide the content into different layers, where files that do not change so frequently are added in the first layer and files that change the most are placed in the last layer. This will result in good use of Docker's caching mechanism for layers. For the first stable layers that are not changed when some application code is changed, Docker will simply use the cache instead of rebuilding them. This will result in faster builds of the microservices' Docker images.

Regarding the lack of a Docker image for Java SE 16 JRE from the OpenJDK project, there are other open source projects that package the OpenJDK binaries into Docker images. One of the most widely used projects is **AdoptOpenJDK** (`https://adoptopenjdk.net`). In June 2020, the AdoptOpenJDK project decided to join the Eclipse Foundation. AdoptOpenJDK provides both full JDK editions and minimized JRE editions of their Docker images.

When it comes to handling the suboptimal packaging of fat-jar files in Docker images, Spring Boot addressed this issue in v2.3.0, making it possible to extract the content of a fat-jar file into a number of folders. By default, Spring Boot creates the following folders after extracting a fat-jar file:

1. `dependencies`, containing all dependencies as jar-files
2. `spring-boot-loader`, containing Spring Boot classes that know how to start a Spring Boot application
3. `snapshot-dependencies`, containing snapshot dependencies, if any
4. `application`, containing application class files and resources

The Spring Boot documentation recommends creating one Docker layer for each folder in the order listed above. After replacing the JDK-based Docker image with a JRE-based image and adding instructions for exploding the fat-jar file into proper layers in the Docker image, the Dockerfile looks like:

```
FROM adoptopenjdk:16_36-jre-hotspot as builder
WORKDIR extracted
ADD ./build/libs/*.jar app.jar
RUN java -Djarmode=layertools -jar app.jar extract

FROM adoptopenjdk:16_36-jre-hotspot
WORKDIR application
COPY --from=builder extracted/dependencies/ ./
COPY --from=builder extracted/spring-boot-loader/ ./
COPY --from=builder extracted/snapshot-dependencies/ ./
COPY --from=builder extracted/application/ ./
```

```
EXPOSE 8080

ENTRYPOINT ["java", "org.springframework.boot.loader.JarLauncher"]
```

To handle the extraction of the fat-jar file in the Dockerfile we use a **multi-stage build**, meaning that there is a first step, named `builder`, that handles the extraction. The second stage builds the actual Docker image that will be used at runtime, picking the files as required from the first stage. Using this technique, we can handle all packaging logic in the Dockerfile but at the same time keep the size of the final Docker image to a minimum:

1. The first stage starts with the line:

   ```
   FROM adoptopenjdk:16_36-jre-hotspot as builder
   ```

   From this line, we can see that a Docker image from the AdoptOpenJDK project is used and that it contains Java SE JRE for v16_36. We can also see that the stage is named `builder`.
2. The `builder` stage sets the working directory to `extracted` and adds the fat-jar file from the Gradle build library, `build/libs`, to that folder.
3. The `builder` stage then runs the command `java -Djarmode=layertools -jar app.jar extract`, which will perform the extraction of the fat-jar file into its working directory, the `extracted` folder.
4. The next and final stage starts with the line:

   ```
   FROM adoptopenjdk:16_36-jre-hotspot
   ```

   It uses the same base Docker image as in the first stage, and the folder `application` as its working directory. It copies the exploded files from the `builder` stage, folder by folder, into the `application` folder. This creates one layer per folder as described above. The parameter `--from=builder` is used to instruct Docker to pick the files from the file system in the `builder` stage.
5. After exposing the proper ports, `8080` in this case, the Dockerfile wraps up by telling Docker what Java class to run to start the microservice in the exploded format, that is, `org.springframework.boot.loader.JarLauncher`.

After learning about the required changes in source code, we are ready to build our first Docker image.

Building a Docker image

To build the Docker image, we first need to build our deployment artifact, that is, the fat-jar-file, for `product-service`:

```
cd $BOOK_HOME/Chapter04
./gradlew :microservices:product-service:build
```

Since we only want to build `product-service` and the projects it depends on (the `api` and `util projects`), we don't use the normal `build` command, which builds all the microservices. Instead, we use a variant that tells Gradle to only build the `product-service` project: `:microservices:product-service:build`.

We can find the fat-jar file in the Gradle build library, `build/libs`. The command `ls -l microservices/product-service/build/libs` will report something like the following:

```
6. @b394afed9384:/ (bash)
$ ls -l microservices/product-service/build/libs
-rw-r--r--  1 magnus  staff  19618829 Aug 30 18:59 product-service-1.0.0-SNAPSHOT.jar
$
```

Figure 4.7: Viewing the fat-jar file details

As you can see, the JAR file is close to 20 MB in size – no wonder they are called fat-jar files!

If you are curious about its actual content, you can view it by using the command `unzip -l microservices/product-service/build/libs/product-service-1.0.0-SNAPSHOT.jar`.

Next, we will build the Docker image and name it `product-service`, as follows:

```
cd microservices/product-service
docker build -t product-service .
```

Docker will use the Dockerfile in the current directory to build the Docker image. The image will be tagged with the name `product-service` and stored locally inside the Docker engine.

Verify that we got a Docker image, as expected, by using the following command:

```
docker images | grep product-service
```

The expected output is as follows:

```
$ docker images | grep product-service
product-service  latest  61e051e29627  6 seconds ago  309MB
$
```

Figure 4.8: Verifying we built our Docker image

So now that we have built the image, let's see how we can start the service.

Starting up the service

Let's start up the `product` microservice as a container by using the following command:

```
docker run --rm -p8080:8080 -e "SPRING_PROFILES_ACTIVE=docker" product-service
```

This is what we can infer from the command:

1. `docker run`: The `docker run` command will start the container and display log output in the Terminal. The Terminal will be locked as long as the container runs.
2. We have seen the `--rm` option already; it will tell Docker to clean up the container once we stop the execution from the Terminal using *Ctrl* + *C*.
3. The `-p8080:8080` option maps port `8080` in the container to port `8080` in the Docker host, which makes it possible to call it from the outside. In the case of Docker Desktop for Mac, which runs Docker in a local Linux virtual machine, the port will also be port-forwarded to macOS, which is made available on `localhost`. Remember that we can only have one container mapping to a specific port in the Docker host!
4. With the `-e` option, we can specify environment variables for the container, which in this case is `SPRING_PROFILES_ACTIVE=docker`. The `SPRING_PROFILES_ACTIVE` environment variable is used to tell Spring what profiles to use. In our case, we want Spring to use the `docker` profile.
5. Finally, we have `product-service`, which is the name of the Docker image we built above and that Docker will use to start the container.

The expected output is as follows:

```
$ docker run --rm -p8080:8080 -e "SPRING_PROFILES_ACTIVE=docker" product-service

  .   ____          _            __ _ _
 /\\ / ___'_ __ _ _(_)_ __  __ _ \ \ \ \
( ( )\___ | '_ | '_| | '_ \/ _` | \ \ \ \
 \\/  ___)| |_)| | | | | || (_| |  ) ) ) )
  '  |____| .__|_| |_|_| |_\__, | / / / /
 =========|_|==============|___/=/_/_/_/
 :: Spring Boot ::                (v2.4.3)

2021-03-11 09:39:11.454  INFO ... Starting ProductServiceApplication using Java 15.0.1 on baf8ee2a623f with PID 1 (/application/BOOT-INF/classes started by root in /application)
2021-03-11 09:39:11.458 DEBUG ... Running with Spring Boot v2.4.3, Spring v5.3.4
2021-03-11 09:39:11.459  INFO ... The following profiles are active: docker
2021-03-11 09:39:13.524  INFO ... Exposing 2 endpoint(s) beneath base path '/actuator'
2021-03-11 09:39:14.189  INFO ... Netty started on port 8080
2021-03-11 09:39:14.214  INFO ... Started ProductServiceApplication in 4.562 seconds (JVM running for 5.225)
```

Figure 4.9: Output after starting up the product microservice

From the preceding screenshot we can see:

- The profile that's used by Spring is `docker`. Look for `The following profiles are active: docker` in the output to verify this.
- The port that's allocated by the container is `8080`. Look for `Netty started on port(s): 8080` in the output to verify this.
- The microservice is ready to accept requests once the log message `Started ProductServiceApplication` has been written!

We can use port `8080` on localhost to communicate with the microservice, as explained previously. Try out the following command in another Terminal window:

```
curl localhost:8080/product/3
```

The following is the expected output:

```
$ curl localhost:8080/product/3
{"productId":3,"name":"name-3","weight":123,"serviceAddress":"9dc086e4a88b/172.17.0.2:8080"}
$
```

Figure 4.10: Requesting information on product 3

This is similar to the output we received from the previous chapter, but with one major difference: we now have the content of `"service Address":"9dc086e4a88b/172.17.0.2:8080"`, the port is `8080`, as expected, and the IP address, `172.17.0.2`, is the IP address that's been allocated to the container from an internal network in Docker - but where did the hostname, `9dc086e4a88b`, come from?

Ask Docker for all the running containers:

```
docker ps
```

We will see something like the following:

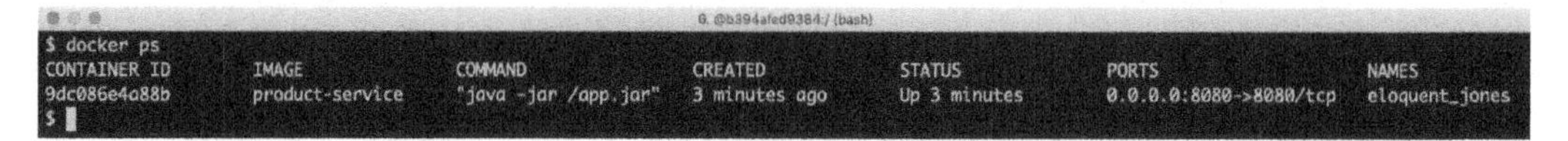

Figure 4.11: All running containers

As we can see from the preceding output, the hostname is equivalent to the ID of the container, which is good to know if you want to understand which container actually responded to your request!

Wrap this up by stopping the container in Terminal with the *Ctrl* + *C* command. With this done, we can now move on to running the container detached.

Running the container detached

Okay, that was great, but what if we don't want to lock the Terminal from where we started the container? In most cases, it is inconvenient to have a Terminal session locked for each running container. It's time to learn how to start the container **detached** – running the container without locking the Terminal!

We can do this by adding the `-d` option and at the same time giving it a name using the `--name` option. Giving it a name is optional, and Docker will generate a name if we don't, but it makes it easier to send commands to the detached container using a name that we have decided. The `--rm` option is no longer required since we will stop and remove the container explicitly when we are done with it:

```
docker run -d -p8080:8080 -e "SPRING_PROFILES_ACTIVE=docker" --name my-prd-srv product-service
```

If we run the `docker ps` command again, we will see our new container, called `my-prd-srv`:

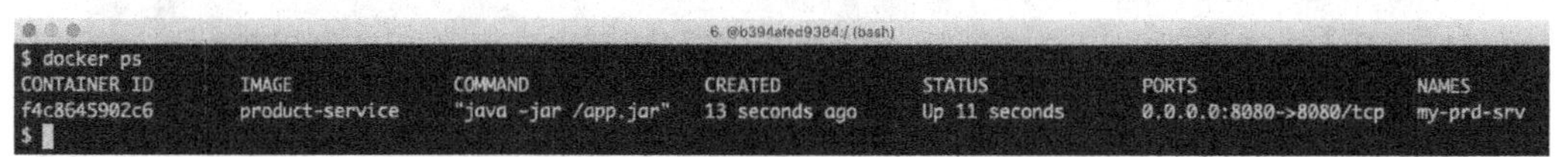

Figure 4.12: Starting the container as detached

But how do we get the log output from our container?

Meet the `docker logs` command:

```
docker logs my-prd-srv -f
```

The `-f` option tells the command to follow the log output, that is, not end the command when all the current log output has been written to the Terminal, but also wait for more output. If you expect a lot of old log messages that you don't want to see, you can also add the `--tail 0` option so that you only see new log messages. Alternatively, you can use the `--since` option and specify either an absolute timestamp or a relative time, for example, `--since 5m`, to see log messages that are at most five minutes old.

Try this out with a new `curl` request. You should see that a new log message has been written to the log output in the Terminal.

Wrap this up by stopping and removing the container:

```
docker rm -f my-prd-srv
```

The `-f` option forces Docker to remove the container, even if it is running. Docker will automatically stop the container before it removes it.

Now that we know how to use Docker with a microservice, we can see how to manage a microservice landscape with the help of Docker Compose.

Managing a landscape of microservices using Docker Compose

We've already seen how we can run a single microservice as a Docker container, but what about managing a whole system landscape of microservices?

As we mentioned earlier, this is the purpose of `docker-compose`. By using single commands, we can build, start, log, and stop a group of cooperating microservices running as Docker containers.

Changes in the source code

To be able to use Docker Compose, we need to create a configuration file, `docker-compose.yml`, that describes the microservices Docker Compose will manage for us. We also need to set up Dockerfiles for the remaining microservices and add a Docker-specific Spring profile to each of them. All four microservices have their own Dockerfile, but they all look the same as the preceding one.

When it comes to the Spring profiles, the three core services, `product-`, `recommendation-`, and `review-service`, have the same `docker` profile, which only specifies that the default port `8080` should be used when running as a container.

For the `product-composite-service`, things are a bit more complicated since it needs to know where to find the core services. When we ran all the services on localhost, it was configured to use localhost and individual port numbers, `7001-7003`, for each core service. When running in Docker, each service will have its own hostname but will be accessible on the same port number, `8080`. Here, the `docker` profile for `product-composite-service` looks as follows:

```
---
spring.config.activate.on-profile: docker

server.port: 8080

app:
  product-service:
    host: product
    port: 8080
  recommendation-service:
    host: recommendation
    port: 8080
  review-service:
    host: review
    port: 8080
```

This configuration is stored in the property file, `application.yml`.

Where did the hostnames, `product`, `recommendation`, and `review` come from?

These are specified in the `docker-compose.yml` file, which is located in the `$BOOK_HOME/Chapter04` folder. It looks like this:

```
version: '2.1'

services:
  product:
    build: microservices/product-service
    mem_limit: 512m
    environment:
      - SPRING_PROFILES_ACTIVE=docker

  recommendation:
    build: microservices/recommendation-service
    mem_limit: 512m
```

```
    environment:
      - SPRING_PROFILES_ACTIVE=docker

  review:
    build: microservices/review-service
    mem_limit: 512m
    environment:
      - SPRING_PROFILES_ACTIVE=docker

  product-composite:
    build: microservices/product-composite-service
    mem_limit: 512m
    ports:
      - "8080:8080"
    environment:
      - SPRING_PROFILES_ACTIVE=docker
```

For each microservice, we specify the following:

- The name of the microservice. This will also be the hostname of the container in the internal Docker network.
- A build directive that specifies where to find the Dockerfile that was used to build the Docker image.
- A memory limit of 512 MB. 512 MB should be sufficient for all our microservices for the scope of this book. For this chapter, it could be set to a lower value, but as we add more capabilities in the microservices in the coming chapters, their memory requirements will increase.
- The environment variables that will be set up for the container. In our case, we used these to specify which Spring profile to use.

For the `product-composite` service, we will also specify port mappings - we will expose its port so it can be reached from outside Docker. The other microservices will not be accessible from the outside. Next, we will see how to start up a microservice landscape.

In *Chapter 10, Using Spring Cloud Gateway to Hide Microservices behind an Edge Server*, and *Chapter 11, Securing Access to APIs*, we will learn more about how to lock down and secure external access to a system landscape of microservices.

Starting up the microservice landscape

With all the necessary code changes in place, we can build our Docker images, start up the microservice landscape, and run some tests to verify that it works as expected. For this, we need to do the following:

1. First, we build our deployment artifacts with Gradle and then the Docker images with Docker Compose:

```
cd $BOOK_HOME/Chapter04
./gradlew build
docker-compose build
```

2. Then, we need to verify that we can see our Docker images, as follows:

```
docker images | grep chapter04
```

We should see the following output:

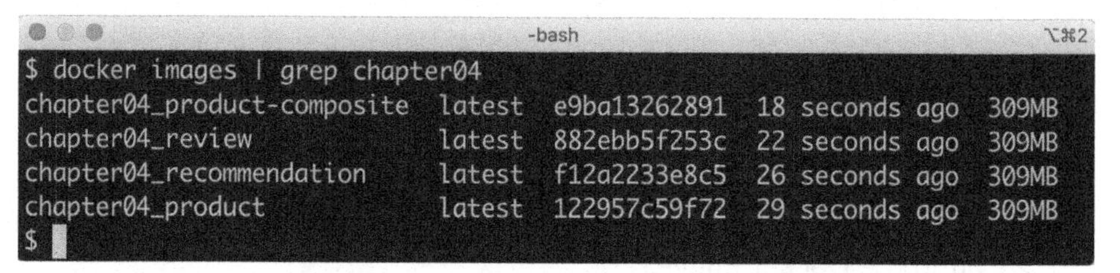

Figure 4.13: Verifying our Docker images

3. Start up the microservices landscape with the following command:

```
docker-compose up -d
```

The `-d` option will make Docker Compose run the containers in detached mode, the same as for Docker.

We can follow the startup by monitoring the output that's written to each container log with the following command:

```
docker-compose logs -f
```

The `docker compose logs` command supports the same `-f` and `--tail` options as `docker logs`, as described earlier.

The Docker Compose `logs` command also supports restricting the log output to a group of containers. Simply add the names of the containers you want to see the log output of after the `logs` command. For example, to only see log output from the `product` and `review` services, use `docker-compose logs -f product review`.

When all four microservices have reported that they have started up, we are ready to try out the microservices landscape. Look for the following:

```
6. @b394afed9384:/ (bash)
$ docker-compose logs -f
...
review_1 | 2018-11-04 09:22:03.618 INFO 1 --- [ main] s.m.m.c.review.ReviewServiceApplication
 : Started ReviewServiceApplication in 6.051 seconds (JVM running for 6.952)
...
product-composite_1 | 2018-11-04 09:22:03.151 INFO 1 --- [ main] m.c.p.ProductCompositeServic
eApplication : Started ProductCompositeServiceApplication in 6.414 seconds (JVM running for 6
.936)
...
recommendation_1 | 2018-11-04 09:22:03.542 INFO 1 --- [ main] m.m.c.r.RecommendationServiceAp
plication : Started RecommendationServiceApplication in 6.199 seconds (JVM running for 7.131)
...
product_1 | 2018-11-04 09:22:04.250  INFO 1 --- [ main] s.m.m.c.p.ProductServiceApplication :
 Started ProductServiceApplication in 6.212 seconds (JVM running for 7.614)
```

Figure 4.14: Starting up all four microservices

Note that each log message is prefixed with the name of the container that produced the output!

Now, we are ready to run some tests to verify that this works as expected. The port number is the only change we need to make when calling the composite service in Docker compared to when we ran it directly on the localhost, as we did in the previous chapter. We now use port `8080`:

```
curl localhost:8080/product-composite/123 -s | jq .
```

We will get the same type of response:

```
6. @b394afed9384:/ (bash)
$ curl localhost:8080/product-composite/123 -s | jq .
{
  "productId": 123,
  ...
  "recommendations": [ ... ],
  "reviews": [ ... ],
  "serviceAddresses": { ... }
}
$
```

Figure 4.15: Calling the composite service

However, there's one big difference – the hostnames and ports reported by `serviceAddresses` in the response:

```
6. @b394afed9384:/ (bash)
"serviceAddresses": {
  "cmp": "98059be902bf/172.21.0.2:8080",
  "pro": "99774d9be7b8/172.21.0.4:8080",
  "rev": "a89da16763d9/172.21.0.5:8080",
  "rec": "2a846794a1d0/172.21.0.3:8080"
}
```

Figure 4.16: Viewing the serviceAddresses

Here, we can see the hostnames and IP addresses that have been allocated to each of the Docker containers.

We're done; now only one step is left:

```
docker-compose down
```

The preceding command will shut down the microservices landscape. So far, we have seen how we can test the cooperating microservices running bash commands by hand. In the next section, we will see how we can enhance our test script to automate these manual steps.

Automating tests of cooperating microservices

Docker Compose is really helpful when it comes to manually managing a group of microservices. In this section, we will take this one step further and integrate Docker Compose into our test script, `test-em-all.bash`. The test script will automatically start up the microservice landscape, run all the required tests to verify that the microservice landscape works as expected, and finally tear it down, leaving no traces behind.

The test script can be found at `$BOOK_HOME/Chapter04/test-em-all.bash`.

Before the test script runs the test suite, it will check for the presence of a `start` argument in the invocation of the test script. If found, it will restart the containers with the following code:

```
if [[ $@ == *"start"* ]]
then
    echo "Restarting the test environment..."
    echo "$ docker-compose down --remove-orphans"
    docker-compose down --remove-orphans
    echo "$ docker-compose up -d"
    docker-compose up -d
fi
```

After that, the test script will wait for the `product-composite` service to respond with OK:

```
waitForService http://$HOST:${PORT}/product-composite/1
```

The `waitForService` bash function is implemented as:

```
function testUrl() {
    url=$@
    if curl $url -ks -f -o /dev/null
    then
          return 0
    else
          return 1
    fi;
}

function waitForService() {
    url=$@
```

```
    echo -n "Wait for: $url... "
    n=0
    until testUrl $url
    do
        n=$((n + 1))
        if [[ $n == 100 ]]
        then
            echo " Give up"
            exit 1
        else
            sleep 3
            echo -n ", retry #$n "
        fi
    done
    echo "DONE, continues..."
}
```

The `waitForService` function sends HTTP requests to the supplied URL using `curl`. Requests are sent repeatedly until `curl` responds that it got a successful response back from the request. The function waits `3` seconds between each attempt and gives up after `100` attempts, stopping the script with a failure.

Next, all the tests are executed like they were previously. Afterward, the script will tear down the landscape if it finds the `stop` argument in the invocation parameters:

```
if [[ $@ == *"stop"* ]]
then
    echo "We are done, stopping the test environment..."
    echo "$ docker-compose down"
    docker-compose down
fi
```

Note that the test script will not tear down the landscape if some tests fail; it will simply stop, leaving the landscape up for error analysis!

The test script has also changed the default port from `7000`, which we used when we ran the microservices without Docker, to `8080`, which is used by our Docker containers.

Let's try it out! To start the landscape, run the tests, and tear it down afterward, run the command:

```
./test-em-all.bash start stop
```

The following is some sample output from a test run focusing on the startup and shutdown phases. Output from the actual tests have been removed (they are the same as in the previous chapter):

```
$ ./test-em-all.bash start stop
Start Tests: Fri Jan 15 09:43:26 CET 2021
HOST=localhost
PORT=8080
Restarting the test environment...
$ docker-compose down
Removing network chapter04_default
WARNING: Network chapter04_default not found.
$ docker-compose up -d
Creating network "chapter04_default" with the default driver
Creating chapter04_product-composite_1 ... done
Creating chapter04_product_1           ... done
Creating chapter04_recommendation_1    ... done
Creating chapter04_review_1            ... done
Wait for: curl http://localhost:8080/product-composite/1... ,
retry #1 , retry #2 , retry #3 , retry #4 DONE, continues...
...Tests OK...
We are done, stopping the test environment...
$ docker-compose down
Stopping chapter04_review_1            ... done
Stopping chapter04_recommendation_1    ... done
Stopping chapter04_product_1           ... done
Stopping chapter04_product-composite_1 ... done
Removing chapter04_review_1            ... done
Removing chapter04_recommendation_1    ... done
Removing chapter04_product_1           ... done
Removing chapter04_product-composite_1 ... done
Removing network chapter04_default
End, all tests OK: Fri Jan 15 09:43:46 CET 2021
$
```

Figure 4.17: Sample output from a test run

After running these tests, we can move on to see how to troubleshoot tests that fail.

Troubleshooting a test run

If the tests that were running `./test-em-all.bash start stop` fail, following these steps can help you identify the problem and resume the tests once the problem has been fixed:

1. First, check the status of the running microservices with the following command:

   ```
   docker-compose ps
   ```

   If all the microservices are up and running and healthy, you will receive the following output:

   ```
   Chapter04 $ docker-compose ps
               Name                       Command          State           Ports
   -------------------------------------------------------------------------------------------
   chapter04_product-composite_1   java -jar /app.jar   Up      0.0.0.0:8080->8080/tcp
   chapter04_product_1             java -jar /app.jar   Up      8080/tcp
   chapter04_recommendation_1      java -jar /app.jar   Up      8080/tcp
   chapter04_review_1              java -jar /app.jar   Up      8080/tcp
   Chapter04 $
   ```

   Figure 4.18: Checking the status of running microservices

2. If any of the microservices do not have a status of `Up`, check their log output for any errors by using the `docker-compose logs` command. For example, you would use the following command if you wanted to check the log output for the `product` service:

   ```
   docker-compose logs product
   ```

   At this stage, it is not easy to cause an error to be logged, since the microservices are so simple. Instead, here is a sample error log from the `product` microservice in *Chapter 6, Adding Persistence*. Assume that the following is found in its log output:

   ```
   $ docker-compose logs product
   ...
   product_1          | 2021-03-11 11:48:15.552  INFO [product,,] 1 --- []-mongodb:27017]
                      : Exception in monitor thread while connecting to server mongodb:27017
   product_1          |
   product_1          | com.mongodb.MongoSocketException: mongodb: Name or service not known
   product_1          |  at com.mongodb.ServerAddress.getSocketAddresses(ServerAddress.java:211)
   ...
   ```

   Figure 4.19: Sample error information in the log output

From reading the above log output, it is quite clear that the `product` microservice can't reach its MongoDB database. Given that the database also runs as a Docker container managed by the same Docker Compose file, the `docker-compose logs` command can be used to see what's wrong with the database.

If required, you can restart a failed container with the `docker-compose restart` command. For example, you would use the following command if you wanted to restart the `product` microservice:

```
docker-compose restart product
```

If a container is missing, for example, due to a crash, you start it up with the `docker-compose up -d --scale` command. For example, you would use the following command for the `product` microservice:

```
docker-compose up -d --scale product=1
```

If errors in the log output indicate that Docker is running out of disk space, parts of it can be reclaimed with the following command:

```
docker system prune -f --volumes
```

3. Once all the microservices are up and running and healthy, run the test script again, but without starting the microservices:

```
./test-em-all.bash
```

The tests should now run fine!

4. When you are done with the testing, remember to tear down the system landscape:

```
docker-compose down
```

Finally, a tip about a combined command that builds runtime artifacts and Docker images from source and then executes all tests in Docker:

```
./gradlew clean build && docker-compose build &&
./test-em-all.bash start stop
```

This is perfect if you want to check that everything works before you push new code to your Git repository or as part of a build pipeline in your build server!

Summary

In this chapter, we have seen how Docker can be used to simplify testing a landscape of cooperating microservices.

We learned how Java SE, since v10, honors constraints that we put on containers regarding how much CPU and memory they are allowed to use. We have also seen how little it takes to make it possible to run a Java-based microservice as a Docker container. Thanks to Spring profiles, we can run the microservice in Docker without having to make any code changes.

Finally, we have seen how Docker Compose can help us manage a landscape of cooperating microservices with single commands, either manually or, even better, automatically, when integrated with a test script such as `test-em-all.bash`.

In the next chapter, we will study how we can add some documentation of the API using OpenAPI/Swagger descriptions.

Questions

1. What are the major differences between a virtual machine and a Docker container?
2. What is the purpose of namespaces and cgroups in Docker?
3. What happens with a Java application that doesn't honor the max memory settings in a container and allocates more memory than it is allowed to?
4. How can we make a Spring-based application run as a Docker container without requiring modifications of its source code?
5. Why will the following Docker Compose code snippet not work?

```
review:
  build: microservices/review-service
  ports:
    - "8080:8080"
  environment:
    - SPRING_PROFILES_ACTIVE=docker

product-composite:
  build: microservices/product-composite-service
  ports:
    - "8080:8080"
  environment:
    - SPRING_PROFILES_ACTIVE=docker
```

5

Adding an API Description Using OpenAPI

The value of an API, such as a RESTful service, depends to a large extent on how easy it is to consume. Good and easily accessible documentation is an important part of whether an API is useful. In this chapter, we will learn how we can use the **OpenAPI Specification** to document APIs that we can make externally accessible from a microservice landscape.

As we mentioned in *Chapter 2, Introduction to Spring Boot*, the OpenAPI Specification, previously known as the Swagger specification, is one of the most commonly used specifications when it comes to documenting RESTful services. Many of the leading API gateways have native support for the OpenAPI Specification. We will learn how to use the open source project **springdoc-openapi** to produce such documentation. We will also learn how to embed an API documentation viewer, **Swagger UI viewer**, which can be used both to inspect the API documentation and also to make requests to the API.

By the end of this chapter, we will have OpenAPI-based API documentation for the external API that's exposed by the `product-composite-service` microservice. The microservice will also expose a Swagger UI viewer that we can use to both visualize and test the API.

The following topics will be covered in this chapter:

- Introduction to using springdoc-openapi
- Adding springdoc-openapi to the source code
- Building and starting the microservice landscape
- Trying out the OpenAPI documentation

Technical requirements

For instructions on how to install tools used in this book and how to access the source code for this book, refer to:

- *Chapter 21* for macOS
- *Chapter 22* for Windows

The code examples in this chapter all come from the source code in `$BOOK_HOME/Chapter05`.

If you want to view the changes that were applied to the source code in this chapter, that is, see what it took to create OpenAPI-based API documentation using springdoc-openapi, you can compare it with the source code for *Chapter 4, Deploying Our Microservices Using Docker*. You can use your favorite `diff` tool and compare the two folders, that is, `$BOOK_HOME/Chapter04` and `$BOOK_HOME/Chapter05`.

Introduction to using springdoc-openapi

springdoc-openapi makes it possible to keep the documentation of the API together with the source code that implements the API. springdoc-openapi can create the API documentation on the fly at runtime by inspecting Java annotations in the code. To me, this is an important feature. If the API documentation is maintained in a separate life cycle from the Java source code, they will diverge from each other over time. In many cases, this will happen sooner than expected (based on my own experience).

Before springdoc-openapi was created, another open source project, **SpringFox** (`http://springfox.github.io/springfox/`), provided similar features. Over recent years, the SpringFox project has not been actively maintained and, as a reaction to that, the springdoc-openapi project was created. A migration guide for SpringFox users can be found at `https://springdoc.org/#migrating-from-springfox`.

As always, it is important to separate the interface of a component from its implementation. In terms of documenting a RESTful API, we should add the API documentation to the Java interface that describes the API, and not to the Java class that implements the API. To simplify updating the textual parts of the API documentation (for example, longer descriptions), we can place the descriptions in property files instead of in the Java code directly.

Added to creating the API specification on the fly, springdoc-openapi also comes with an embedded API viewer called Swagger UI. We will configure the `product-composite-service` service to expose Swagger UI for its API.

Even though Swagger UI is very useful during development and test phases, it is typically not exposed in public for APIs in a production environment, for security reasons. In many cases, APIs are exposed publicly using an API Gateway. Today, most API Gateway products support exposing API documentation based on a OpenAPI document. So instead of exposing Swagger UI, the API's OpenAPI document, generated by springdoc-openapi, is exported to an API Gateway that can publish the API documentation in a secure way.

If APIs are expected to be consumed by third-party developers, a developer portal can be set up containing documentation and tools, used for self-registration, for example. Swagger UI can be used in a developer portal to allow developers to learn about the API by reading the documentation and also trying out the APIs using a test instance.

In *Chapter 11, Securing Access to APIs,* we will learn how to lock down access to APIs using OAuth 2.1. We will also learn how to configure the Swagger UI component to acquire OAuth 2.1 access tokens and use them when the user tries out the APIs through Swagger UI.

The following screenshot is an example of what Swagger UI will look like:

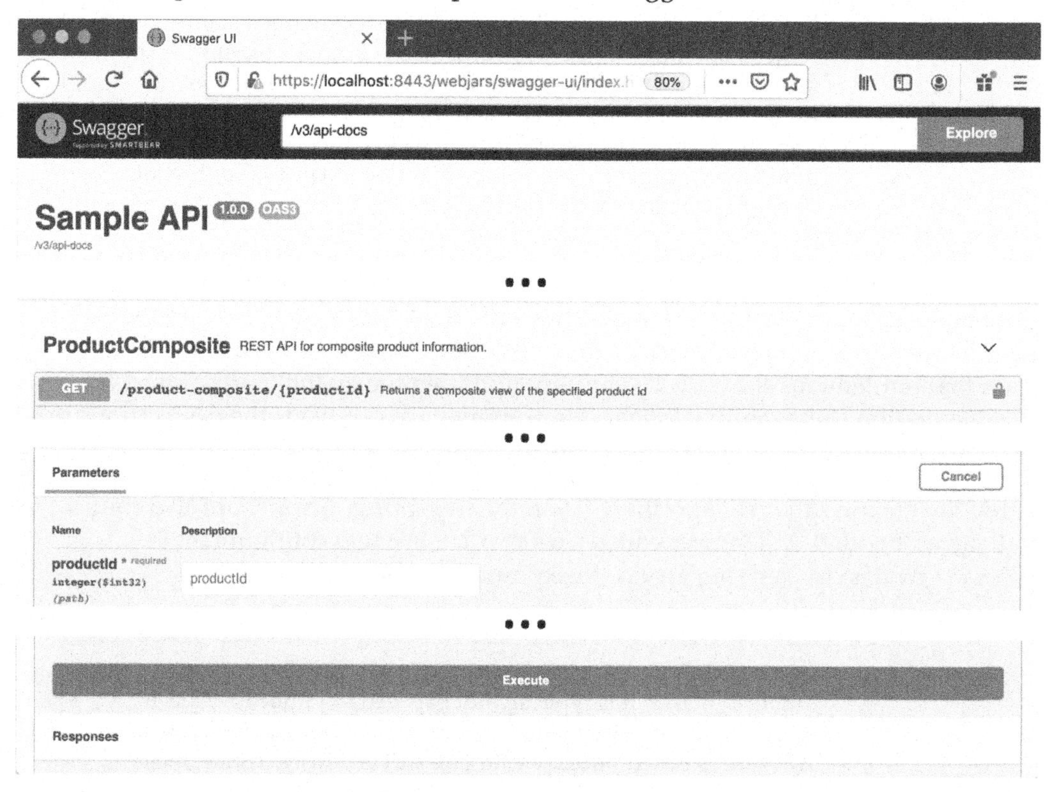

Figure 5.1: Swagger UI example

Some, for now, unimportant parts of the screenshot have been replaced by "..." in the preceding figure. We will get back to these details later on in this chapter.

To enable springdoc-openapi to create the API documentation, we need to add some dependencies to our build files and add some annotations to the Java interfaces that define the RESTful services. As mentioned above, we will also place the descriptive parts of the API documentation in a property file.

If parts of the documentation have been placed in property files to simplify updating the API documentation, it is important that the property files are handled in the same life cycle and under the same version control as the source code. Otherwise, there is a risk that they will start to diverge from the implementation, that is, become out of date.

With springdoc-openapi introduced, let's see how we can start using it by making the required changes in the source code.

Adding springdoc-openapi to the source code

To add OpenAPI-based documentation regarding the external API that's exposed by the `product-composite-service` microservice, we need to change the source code in two projects:

- `product-composite-service`: Here, we will set up a configuration of springdoc-openapi in the Java application class, `ProductCompositeServiceApplication`, and describe general information pertaining to the API.
- `api`: Here, we will add annotations to the Java interface, `ProductCompositeService`, describing each RESTful service and its operations. At this stage, we only have one RESTful service with one operation, accepting HTTP GET requests to `/product-composite/{productId}`, which is used for requesting composite information regarding a specific product.

The actual texts that are used to describe the API operation will be placed in the default property file, `application.yml`, in the `product-composite-service` project.

Before we can start using springdoc-openapi, we need to add it as a dependency in the Gradle build files. So, let's start with that!

Adding dependencies to the Gradle build files

The springdoc-openapi project is divided into a number of modules. For the `api` project we only need the module that contains the annotations we will use to document the API. We can add it to the `api` project's build file, `build.gradle`, as follows:

```
implementation 'org.springdoc:springdoc-openapi-common:1.5.9'
```

The `product-composite-service` project requires a more fully featured module that contains both the Swagger UI viewer and support for Spring WebFlux. We can add the dependency to the build file, `build.gradle`, as follows:

```
implementation 'org.springdoc:springdoc-openapi-webflux-ui:1.5.9'
```

That is all the dependencies that need to be added; now for the configuration.

Adding OpenAPI configuration and general API documentation to the ProductCompositeService

To enable springdoc-openapi in the `product-composite-service` microservice, we have to add some configuration. To keep the source code compact, we will add it directly to the application class, `ProductCompositeServiceApplication.java`.

If you prefer, you can place the configuration of springdoc-openapi in a separate Spring configuration class.

First, we need to define a Spring Bean that returns an `OpenAPI` bean. The source code looks like this:

```
@Bean
public OpenAPI getOpenApiDocumentation() {
  return new OpenAPI()
    .info(new Info().title(apiTitle)
      .description(apiDescription)
      .version(apiVersion)
      .contact(new Contact()
        .name(apiContactName)
        .url(apiContactUrl)
        .email(apiContactEmail))
      .termsOfService(apiTermsOfService)
      .license(new License()
        .name(apiLicense)
        .url(apiLicenseUrl)))
    .externalDocs(new ExternalDocumentation()
      .description(apiExternalDocDesc)
      .url(apiExternalDocUrl));
}
```

From the preceding code, we can see that the configuration contains general descriptive information about the API, such as:

- The name, description, version, and contact information for the API
- Terms of usage and license information

- Links to external information regarding the API, if any

The `api*` variables that are used to configure the `OpenAPI` bean are initialized from the property file using Spring `@Value` annotations. These are as follows:

```
@Value("${api.common.version}")         String apiVersion;
@Value("${api.common.title}")           String apiTitle;
@Value("${api.common.description}")     String apiDescription;
@Value("${api.common.termsOfService}")  String apiTermsOfService;
@Value("${api.common.license}")         String apiLicense;
@Value("${api.common.licenseUrl}")      String apiLicenseUrl;
@Value("${api.common.externalDocDesc}") String apiExternalDocDesc;
@Value("${api.common.externalDocUrl}")  String apiExternalDocUrl;
@Value("${api.common.contact.name}")    String apiContactName;
@Value("${api.common.contact.url}")     String apiContactUrl;
@Value("${api.common.contact.email}")   String apiContactEmail;
```

The actual values are set in the property file, `application.yml`, as follows:

```
api:
  common:
    version: 1.0.0
    title: Sample API
    description: Description of the API...
    termsOfService: MY TERMS OF SERVICE
    license: MY LICENSE
    licenseUrl: MY LICENSE URL

    externalDocDesc: MY WIKI PAGE
    externalDocUrl: MY WIKI URL
    contact:
      name: NAME OF CONTACT
      url: URL TO CONTACT
      email: contact@mail.com
```

The property file also contains some configuration for springdoc-openapi:

```
springdoc:
  swagger-ui.path: /openapi/swagger-ui.html
  api-docs.path: /openapi/v3/api-docs
  packagesToScan: se.magnus.microservices.composite.product
  pathsToMatch: /**
```

The configuration parameters have the following purposes:

- `springdoc.swagger-ui.path` and `springdoc.api-docs.path` are used to specify that the URLs used by the embedded Swagger UI viewer are available under the path `/openapi`. Later on in this book, when we add different types of edge servers in front and address security challenges, this will simplify the configuration of the edge servers used. Refer to the following chapters for more information:
    - *Chapter 10, Using Spring Cloud Gateway to Hide Microservices behind an Edge Server*
    - *Chapter 11, Securing Access to APIs*
    - *Chapter 17, Implementing Kubernetes Features to Simplify the System Landscape*, the *Replacing the Spring Cloud Gateway* section
    - *Chapter 18, Using a Service Mesh to Improve Observability and Management*, the *Replacing Kubernetes Ingress controller with Istio Ingress Gateway* section
- `springdoc.packagesToScan` and `springdoc.pathsToMatch` control where in the code base springdoc-openapi will search for annotations. The narrower the scope we can give springdoc-openapi, the faster the scan will be performed.

For details, refer to the application class `ProductCompositeServiceApplication.java` and the `application.yml` property file in the `product-composite-service` project. We can now proceed to see how to add API-specific documentation to the Java interface `ProductCompositeService.java` in the `api` project.

Adding API-specific documentation to the ProductCompositeService interface

To document the actual API and its RESTful operations, we will add an `@Tag` annotation to the Java interface declaration in `ProductCompositeService.java` in the `api` project. For each RESTful operation in the API, we will add an `@Operation` annotation, along with `@ApiResponse` annotations on the corresponding Java method, to describe the operation and its expected responses. We will describe both successful and error responses.

Added to reading these annotations at runtime, springdoc-openapi will also inspect Spring annotations, such as the `@GetMapping` annotation, to understand what input arguments the operation takes and what the response will look like if a successful response is produced. To understand the structure of potential error responses, springdoc-openapi will look for `@RestControllerAdvice` and `@ExceptionHandler` annotations. In *Chapter 3, Creating a Set of Cooperating Microservices*, we added a utility class, `GlobalControllerExceptionHandler.java`, in the `util` project.

This class is annotated with `@RestControllerAdvice`. See the *The global REST controller exception handler* section for details. The exception handler takes care of `404` (`NOT_FOUND`) and `422` (`UNPROCESSABLE_ENTITY`) errors. To allow springdoc-openapi to also correctly document `400` (`BAD_REQUEST`) errors that Spring WebFlux generates when it discovers incorrect input arguments in a request, we have also added an `@ExceptionHandler` for `400` (`BAD_REQUEST`) errors in `GlobalControllerExceptionHandler.java`.

The documentation of the API on the resource level, corresponding to the Java interface declaration, looks as follows:

```
@Tag(name = "ProductComposite", description =
  "REST API for composite product information.")
public interface ProductCompositeService {
```

For the API operation, we have extracted the actual text used in the `@Operation` and `@ApiResponse` annotations to the property file. The annotations contain property placeholders, like `${name-of-the-property}`, that springdoc-openapi will use to look up the actual text from the property file at runtime. The API operation is documented as follows:

```
@Operation(
  summary =
    "${api.product-composite.get-composite-product.description}",
  description =
    "${api.product-composite.get-composite-product.notes}")
@ApiResponses(value = {
  @ApiResponse(responseCode = "200", description =
    "${api.responseCodes.ok.description}"),
  @ApiResponse(responseCode = "400", description =
    "${api.responseCodes.badRequest.description}"),
  @ApiResponse(responseCode = "404", description =
    "${api.responseCodes.notFound.description}"),
  @ApiResponse(responseCode = "422", description =
    "${api.responseCodes.unprocessableEntity.description}")
})
@GetMapping(
  value = "/product-composite/{productId}",
  produces = "application/json")
ProductAggregate getProduct(@PathVariable int productId);
```

springdoc-openapi will be able to extract the following information about the operation from the preceding source code:

- The operation accepts HTTP GET requests to the URL `/product-composite/{productid}`, where the last part of the URL, `{productid}`, is used as an input parameter to the request.
- A successful response will produce a JSON structure corresponding to the Java class, `ProductAggregate`.
- In the event of an error, either an HTTP error code `400`, `404`, or `422` will be returned together with error information in the body, as described by `@ExceptionHandler` in the Java class `GlobalControllerExceptionHandler.java` in the `util` project, as described above.

For the values specified in the `@Operation` and `@ApiResponse` annotations, we can use property placeholders directly, without using Spring `@Value` annotations. The actual values are set in the property file, `application.yml`, like this:

```
api:
  responseCodes:
    ok.description: OK
    badRequest.description: Bad Request, invalid format of the request. See response message for more information
    notFound.description: Not found, the specified id does not exist
    unprocessableEntity.description: Unprocessable entity, input parameters caused the processing to fail. See response message for more information

  product-composite:

    get-composite-product:
      description: Returns a composite view of the specified product id
      notes: |
        # Normal response
        If the requested product id is found the method will return information regarding:
        1. Base product information
        1. Reviews
        1. Recommendations
        1. Service Addresses\n(technical information regarding the addresses of the microservices that created the response)
```

```
        # Expected partial and error responses
        In the following cases, only a partial response be created
(used to simplify testing of error conditions)

        ## Product id 113
        200 - Ok, but no recommendations will be returned

        ## Product id 213
        200 - Ok, but no reviews will be returned

        ## Non-numerical product id
        400 - A **Bad Request** error will be returned

        ## Product id 13
        404 - A **Not Found** error will be returned

        ## Negative product ids
        422 - An **Unprocessable Entity** error will be returned
```

From the preceding configuration, we can learn the following:

- A property placeholder such as `${api.responseCodes.ok.description}` will be translated to `OK`. Note the hierarchical structure of the YAML-based property file:

  ```
  api:
    responseCodes:
      ok.description: OK
  ```

- A multi-line value starts with | like the one for the property `api.get-composite-product.description.notes`. Also note that springdoc-openapi supports the provision of a multi-line description using **Markdown** syntax.

For details, see the service interface class `ProductCompositeService.java` in the `api` project and the property file, `application.yml`, in the `product-composite-service` project.

If you want to find out more about how a YAML file is constructed, view the specification: `https://yaml.org/spec/1.2/spec.html`.

Building and starting the microservice landscape

Before we can try out the OpenAPI documentation, we need to build and start the microservice landscape!

This can be done with the following commands:

```
cd $BOOK_HOME/Chapter05
./gradlew build && docker-compose build && docker-compose up -d
```

You may run into an error message regarding port `8080` already being allocated. This will look as follows:

```
ERROR: for product-composite Cannot start service
product-composite: driver failed programming external
connectivity on endpoint chapter05_product-composite_1
(0138d46f2a3055ed1b90b3b3daca92330919a1e7fec20351728633222db5e737):
Bind for 0.0.0.0:8080 failed: port is already allocated
```

If this is the case, you might have forgotten to bring down the microservice landscape from the previous chapter. To find out the names of the executing containers, run the following command:

```
docker ps --format {{.Names}}
```

A sample response when a microservice landscape from the previous chapter is still running is as follows:

```
chapter05_review_1
chapter05_product_1
chapter05_recommendation_1
chapter04_review_1
chapter04_product-composite_1
chapter04_product_1
chapter04_recommendation_1
```

If you find containers from other chapters in the output from the command, for example, from *Chapter 4, Deploying Our Microservices Using Docker*, as in the preceding example, you need to jump over to the source code folder for that chapter and bring down its containers:

```
cd ../Chapter04
docker-compose down
```

Now, you can bring up the missing container for this chapter:

```
cd ../Chapter05
docker-compose up -d
```

Note that only the missing container, `product-composite`, is started by the command since the other ones were already started successfully:

```
Starting chapter05_product-composite_1 ... done
```

To wait for the microservice landscape to start up and verify that it works, you can run the following command:

```
./test-em-all.bash
```

With the successful startup of the microservices, we can move on and try out the OpenAPI documentation exposed by the `product-composite` microservice using its embedded Swagger UI viewer.

Trying out the OpenAPI documentation

To browse the OpenAPI documentation, we will use the embedded Swagger UI viewer. If we open the `http://localhost:8080/openapi/swagger-ui.html` URL in a web browser, we will see a web page that looks something like the following screenshot:

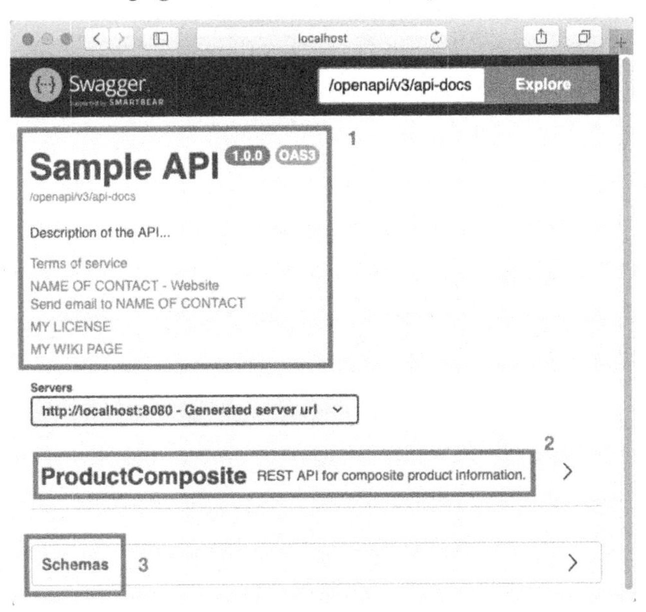

Figure 5.2: OpenAPI documentation with the Swagger UI viewer

Here, we can ascertain the following:

1. The general information we specified in the springdoc-openapi `OpenAPI` bean and a link to the actual OpenAPI document, **/openapi/v3/api-docs**, pointing to `http://localhost:8080/openapi/v3/api-docs`.

Note that this is the link to the OpenAPI document that can be exported to an API Gateway, as discussed in the *Introduction to using springdoc-openapi* section above.

2. A list of API resources; in our case, the **ProductComposite** API.
3. At the bottom of the page, there is a section where we can inspect the schemas used in the API.

Proceed with the examination of the API documentation as follows:

1. Click on the **ProductComposite** API resource to expand it. You will get a list of operations that are available on the resource. You will only see one operation, **/product-composite/{productId}**.
2. Click on it to expand it. You will see the documentation of the operation that we specified in the `ProductCompositeService` Java interface:

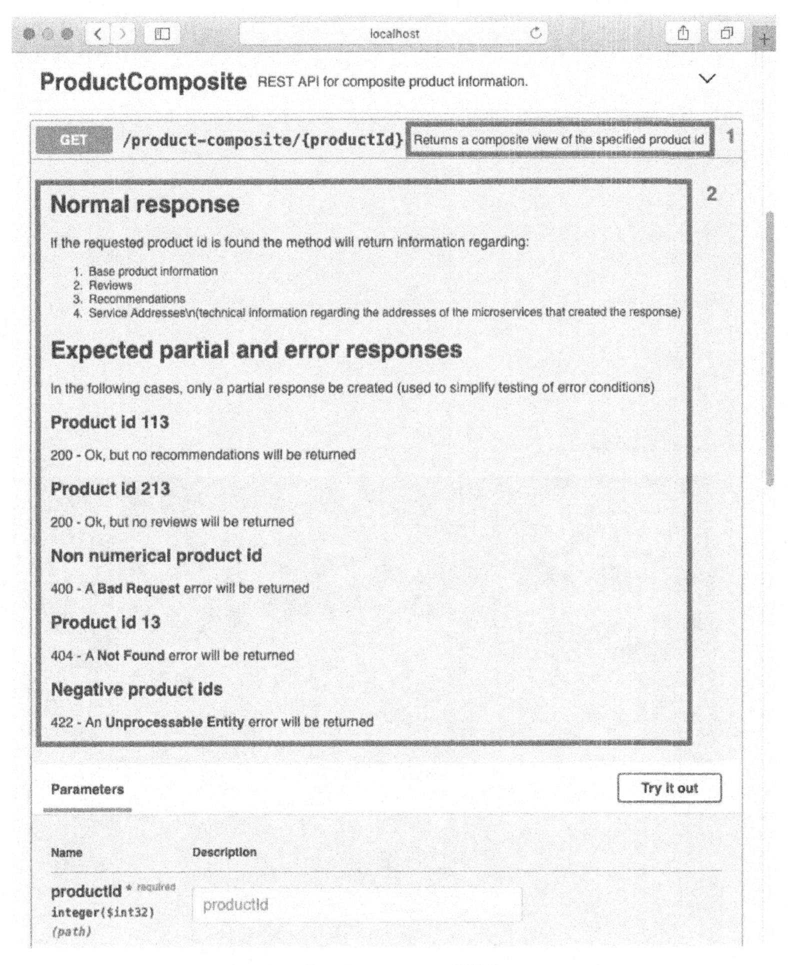

Figure 5.3: ProductComposite API documentation

Here, we can see the following:

- The one-line description of the operation.
- A section with details regarding the operation, including the input parameters it supports. Note how the Markdown syntax from the `notes` field in the `@ApiOperation` annotation has been nicely rendered!

If you scroll down the web page, you will also find documentation regarding the expected responses and their structure, both for a normal **200 (OK)** response…

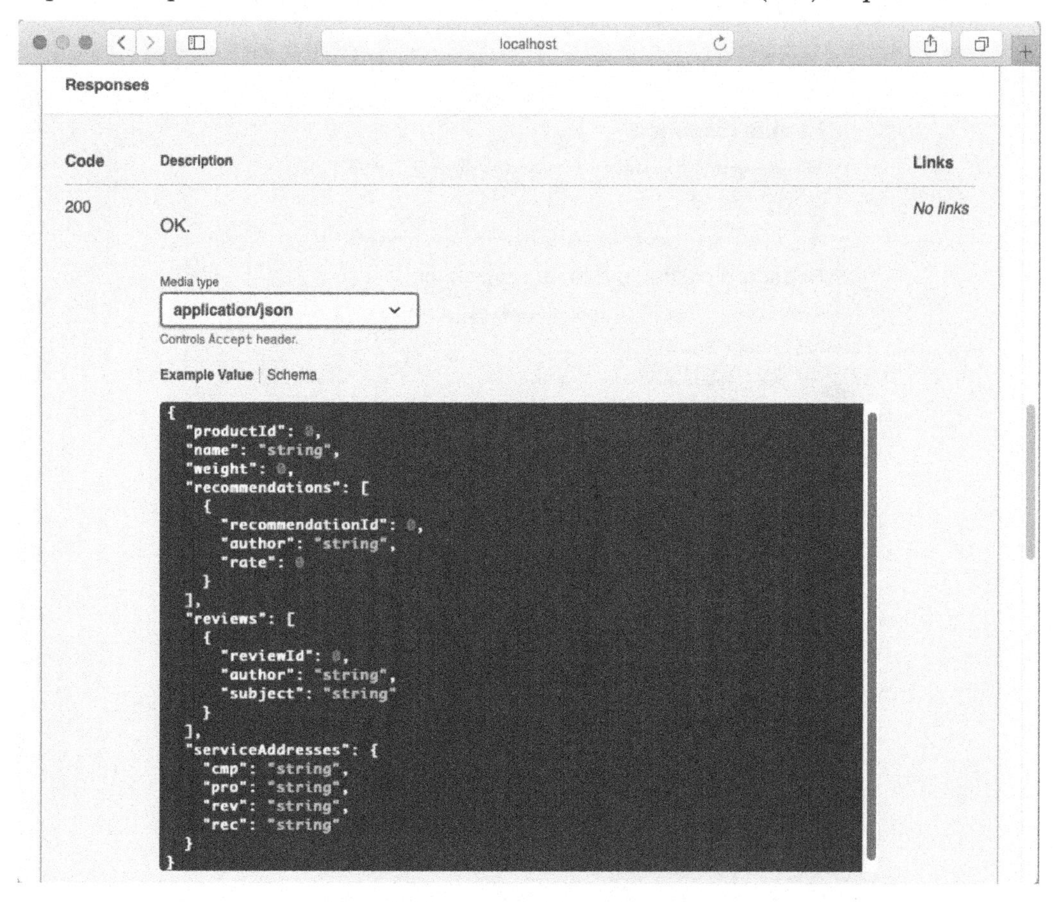

Figure 5.4: Documentation for 200 response

…and the various 4xx error responses we defined earlier, as shown in the following screenshot:

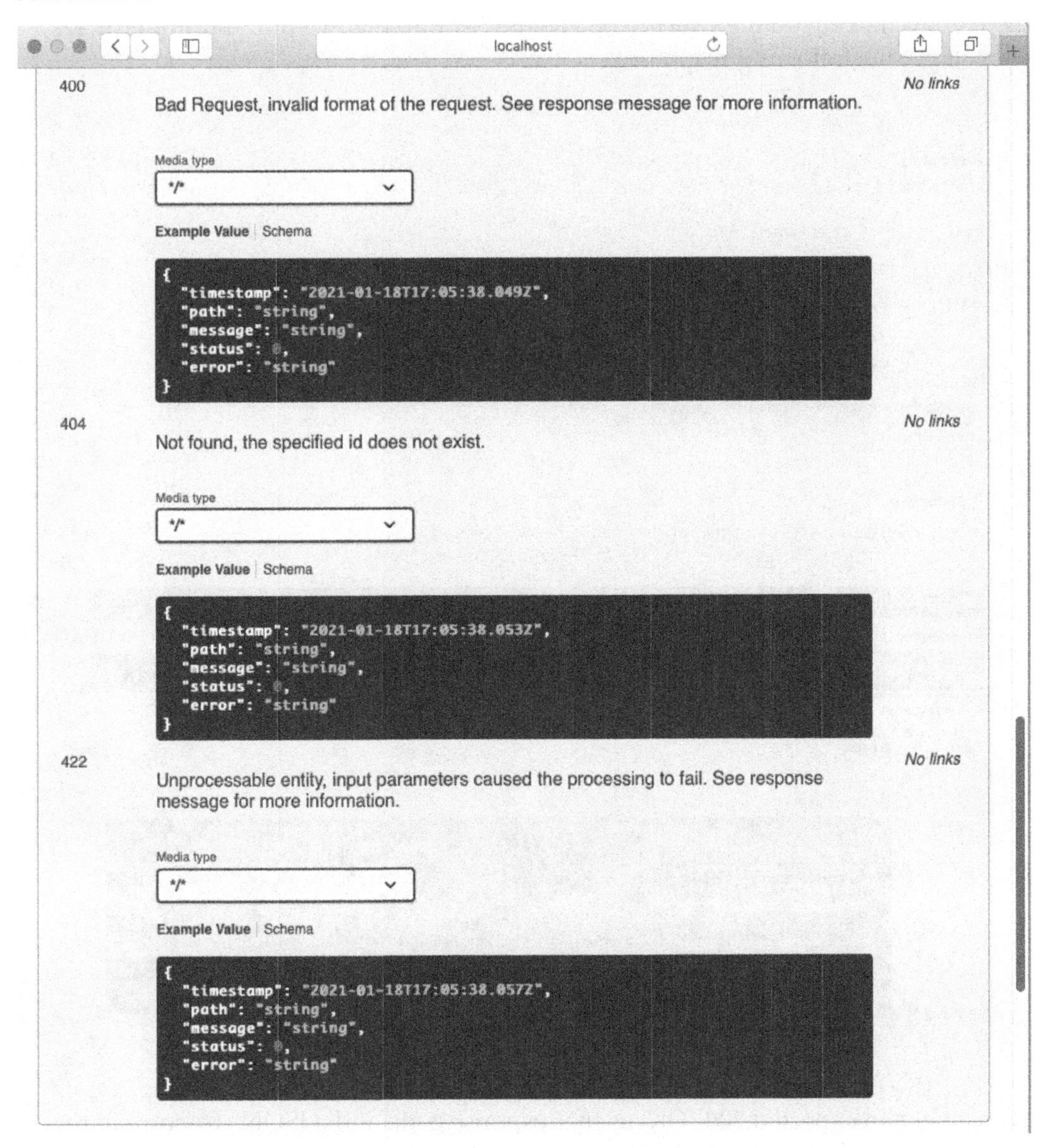

Figure 5.5: Documentation for 4xx responses

For each documented potential error response, we can learn about its meaning and the structure of the response body.

If we scroll back up to the parameter description, we will find the **Try it out** button. If we click on the button, we can fill in actual parameter values and send a request to the API by clicking on the **Execute** button. For example, if we put in **productId** `123`, we will get the following response:

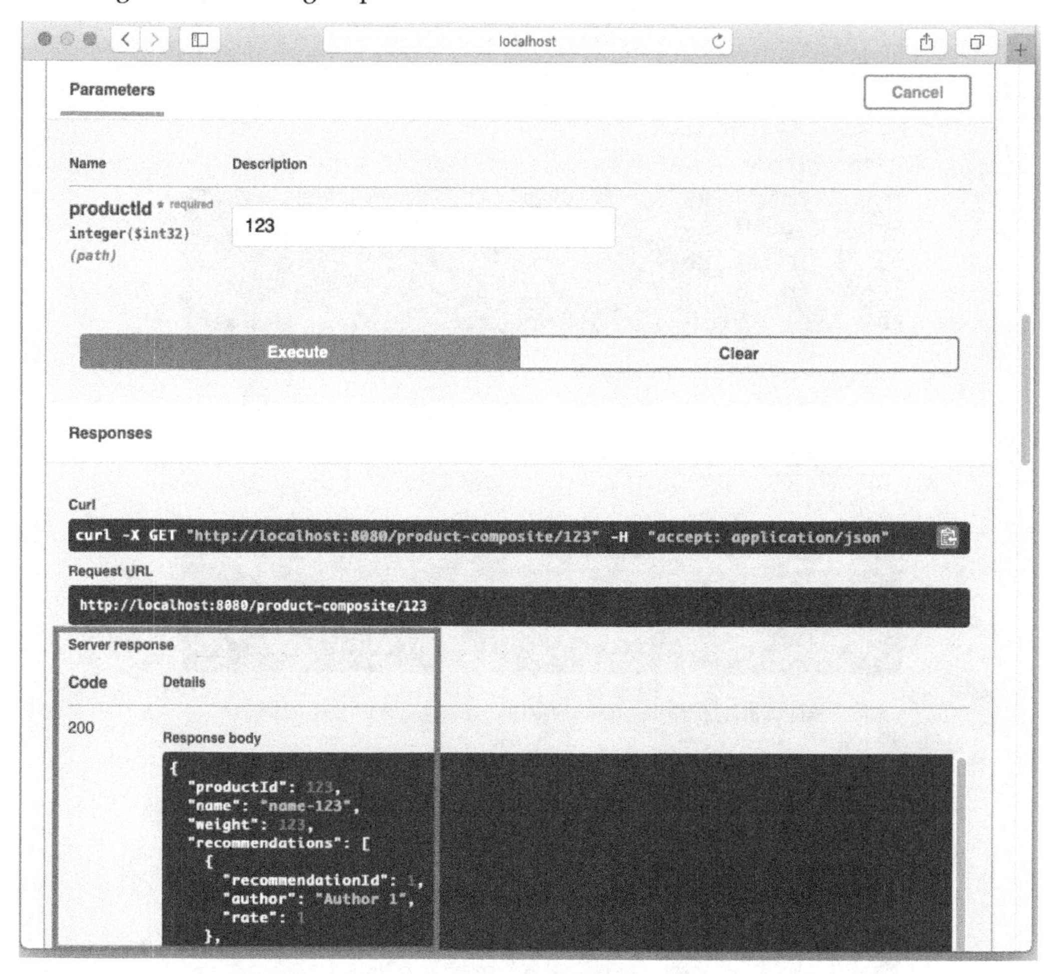

Figure 5.6: Response after sending a request for an existing product

We will get an expected **200** (OK) as the response code and a JSON structure in the response body that we are already familiar with!

If we enter an incorrect input, such as `-1`, we will get a proper error code as the response code, **422**, and a corresponding JSON-based error description in the response body:

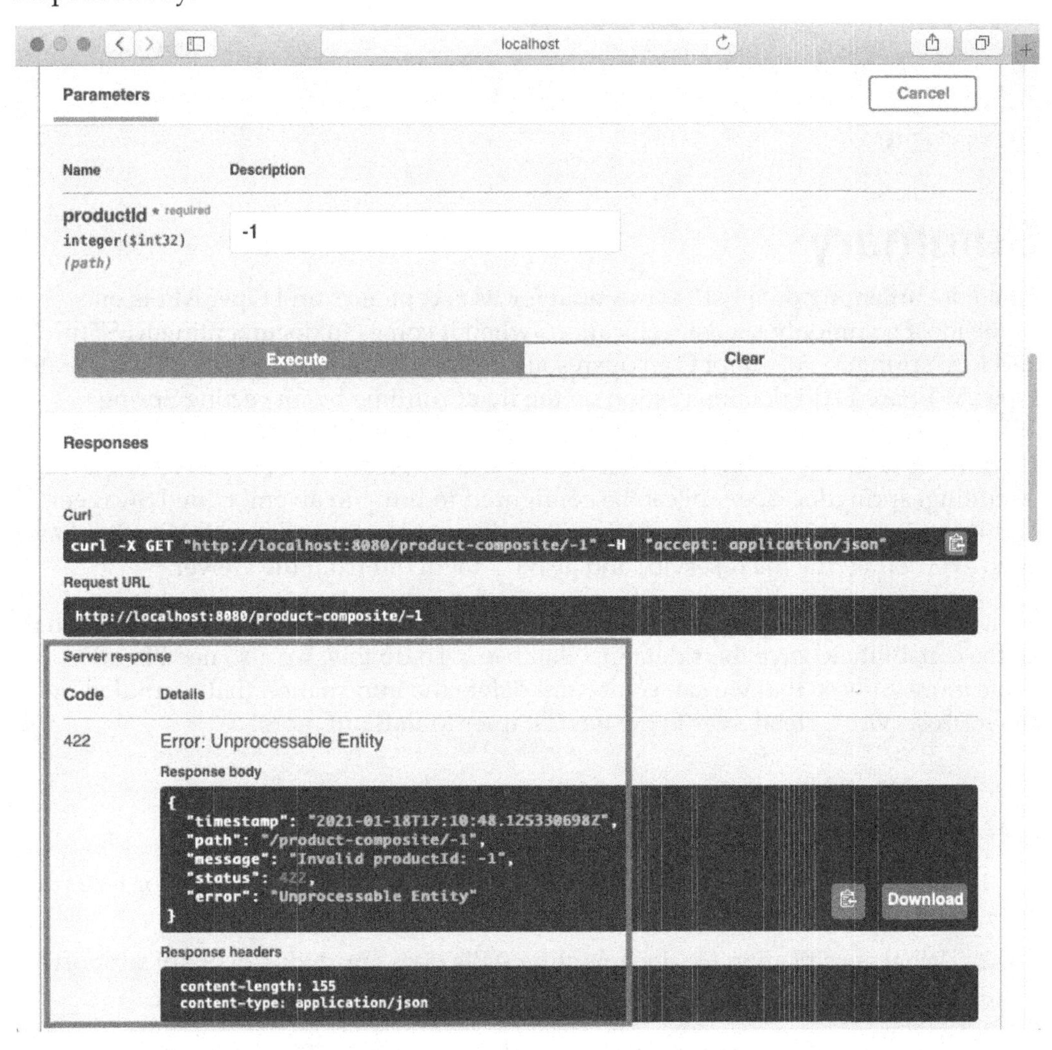

Figure 5.7: Response after sending a request with invalid input

Note that the **message** field in the response body clearly points out the problem: **"Invalid productid: -1"**.

If you want to try calling the API without using the Swagger UI viewer, you can copy the corresponding `curl` command from the **Responses** section and run it in a Terminal window, as shown in the preceding screenshot:

```
curl -X GET "http://localhost:8080/product-composite/123" -H "accept:
application/json"
```

Great, isn't it?

Summary

Good documenting of an API is essential for its acceptance, and OpenAPI is one of the most commonly used specifications when it comes to documenting RESTful services. springdoc-openapi is an open source project that makes it possible to create OpenAPI-based API documentation on the fly at runtime by inspecting Spring WebFlux and Swagger annotations. Textual descriptions of an API can be extracted from the annotations in the Java source code and be placed in a property file for ease of editing. springdoc-openapi can be configured to bring in an embedded Swagger UI viewer into a microservice, which makes it very easy to read about APIs that have been exposed by the microservice and also try them out from the viewer.

Now, what about bringing some life to our microservices by adding persistence, that is, the capability to save their data in a database? To do this, we also need to add some more APIs so that we can create and delete the information that's handled by the microservices. Head over to the next chapter to find out more!

Questions

1. How does springdoc-openapi help us create API documentation for RESTful services?
2. What specification for documenting APIs does springdoc-openapi support?
3. What is the purpose of the springdoc-openapi `OpenAPI` bean?
4. Name some annotations that springdoc-openapi reads at runtime to create the API documentation on the fly.
5. What does the code `": |"` mean in a YAML file?
6. How can you repeat a call to an API that was performed using the embedded Swagger UI viewer without using the viewer again?

6
Adding Persistence

In this chapter, we will learn how to persist data that a microservice is using. As already mentioned in *Chapter 2, Introduction to Spring Boot*, we will use the Spring Data project to persist data to MongoDB and MySQL databases.

The `product` and `recommendation` microservices will use Spring Data for MongoDB and the `review` microservice will use Spring Data for the **JPA** (short for the **Java Persistence API**) to access a MySQL database. We will add operations to the RESTful APIs to be able to create and delete data in the databases. The existing APIs for reading data will be updated to access the databases. We will run the databases as Docker containers, managed by Docker Compose, that is, in the same way as we run our microservices.

The following topics will be covered in this chapter:

- Adding a persistence layer to the core microservices
- Writing automated tests that focus on persistence
- Using the persistence layer in the service layer
- Extending the composite service API
- Adding databases to the Docker Compose landscape
- Manual testing of the new APIs and the persistence layer
- Updating the automated tests of the microservice landscape

Technical requirements

For instructions on how to install the tools used in this book and how to access the source code for this book, see:

- *Chapter 21* for macOS
- *Chapter 22* for Windows

To access the databases manually, we will use the CLI tools provided in the Docker images used to run the databases. We will also expose the standard ports used for each database in Docker Compose, `3306` for MySQL and `27017` for MongoDB. This will enable us to use our favorite database tools for accessing the databases in the same way as if they were running locally on our computers.

The code examples in this chapter all come from the source code in `$BOOK_HOME/Chapter06`.

If you want to view the changes applied to the source code in this chapter, that is, see what it took to add persistence to the microservices using Spring Data, you can compare it with the source code for *Chapter 5, Adding an API Description Using OpenAPI*. You can use your favorite `diff` tool and compare the two folders, `$BOOK_HOME/Chapter05` and `$BOOK_HOME/Chapter06`.

Before going into details, let's see where we are heading.

Chapter objectives

By the end of this chapter, we will have layers inside our microservices that look like the following:

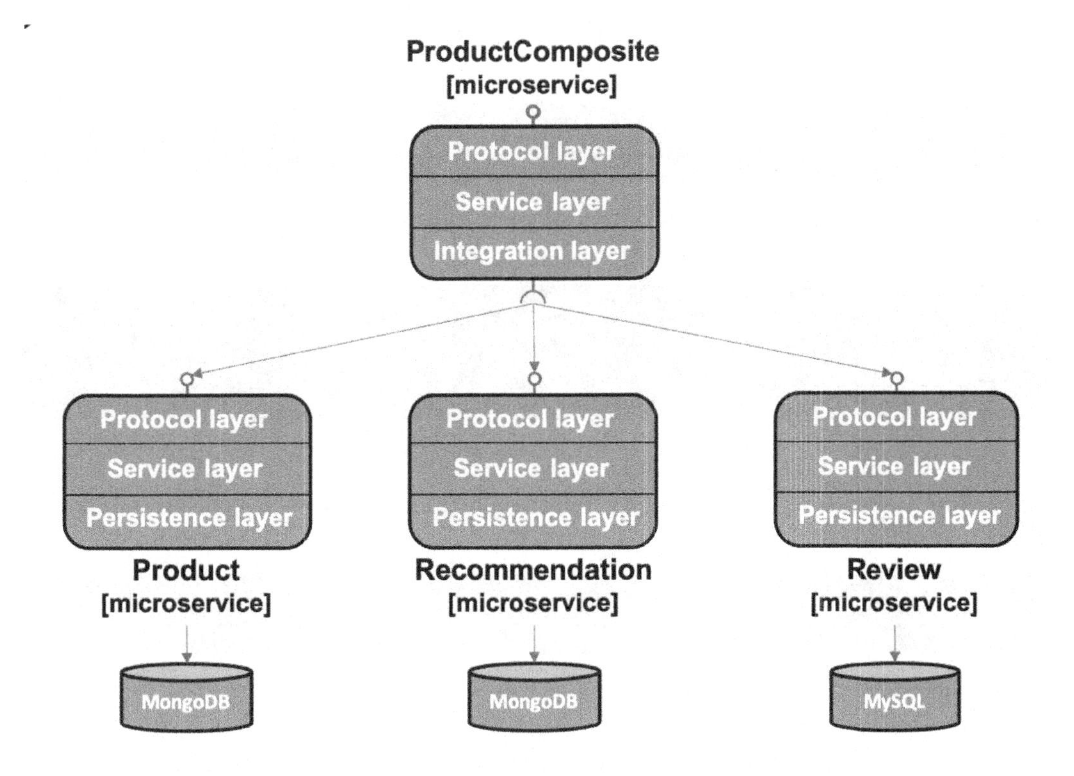

Figure 6.1: The microservice landscape we're aiming for

The **Protocol layer** handles protocol-specific logic. It is very thin, only consisting of the `RestController` annotations in the `api` project and the common `GlobalControllerExceptionHandler` in the `util` project. The main functionality of each microservice resides in the **Service layers**. The `product-composite` service contains an **Integration layer** used to handle the communication with the three core microservices. The core microservices will all have a **Persistence layer** used for communicating with their databases.

We will be able to access data stored in MongoDB with a command like the following:

```
docker-compose exec mongodb mongo product-db --quiet --eval "db.
products.find()"
```

The result of the command should look like the following:

```
2. bash
{ "_id" : ..., "productId" : 1, "name" : "product 1", "weight" : 1 }
{ "_id" : ..., "productId" : 113, "name" : "product 113", "weight" : 113 }
{ "_id" : ..., "productId" : 213, "name" : "product 213", "weight" : 213 }
$
```

Figure 6.2: Accessing data stored in MongoDB

Regarding data stored in MySQL, we will be able to access it with a command like this:

```
docker-compose exec mysql mysql -uuser -p review-db -e "select * from
reviews"
```

The result of the command should look as follows:

```
2. bash
+----+----------+-----------+------------+-----------+
| id | author   | content   | product_id | review_id |
+----+----------+-----------+------------+-----------+
|  1 | author 1 | content 1 |          1 |         1 |
|  2 | author 2 | content 2 |          1 |         2 |
+----+----------+-----------+------------+-----------+
$
```

Figure 6.3: Accessing data stored in MySQL

The output from the `mongo` and `mysql` commands has been shortened for improved readability.

Let's see how to implement this. We will start with adding persistence functionality to our core microservices!

Adding a persistence layer to the core microservices

Let's start with adding a persistence layer to the core microservices. Besides using Spring Data, we will also use a Java bean mapping tool, **MapStruct**, that makes it easy to transform between Spring Data entity objects and the API model classes. For further details, see `http://mapstruct.org/`.

First, we need to add dependencies to MapStruct, Spring Data, and the JDBC drivers for the databases we intend to use. After that, we can define our Spring Data entity classes and repositories. The Spring Data entity classes and repositories will be placed in their own Java package, `persistence`. For example, for the product microservice, they will be placed in the Java package `se.magnus.microservices.core.product.persistence`.

Adding dependencies

We will use MapStruct v1.3.1, so we start by defining a variable holding the version information in the build file for each core microservice, `build.gradle`:

```
ext {
  mapstructVersion = "1.3.1"
}
```

Next, we declare a dependency on MapStruct:

```
implementation "org.mapstruct:mapstruct:${mapstructVersion}"
```

Since MapStruct generates the implementation of the bean mappings at compile time by processing MapStruct annotations, we need to add an `annotationProcessor` and a `testAnnotationProcessor` dependency:

```
annotationProcessor "org.mapstruct:mapstruct-
processor:${mapstructVersion}"
testAnnotationProcessor "org.mapstruct:mapstruct-
processor:${mapstructVersion}"
```

To make the compile-time generation work in popular IDEs such as IntelliJ IDEA, we also need to add the following dependency:

```
compileOnly "org.mapstruct:mapstruct-processor:${mapstructVersion}"
```

If you are using IntelliJ IDEA, you also need to ensure that support for annotation processing is enabled. Open **Preferences** and navigate to **Build, Execute, Deployment | Compiler | Annotations Processors**. Verify that the checkbox named **Enable annotation processing** is selected!

For the `product` and `recommendation` microservices, we declare the following dependencies to Spring Data for MongoDB:

```
implementation 'org.springframework.boot:spring-boot-starter-data-
mongodb'
```

For the `review` microservice, we declare a dependency to Spring Data for JPA and a JDBC driver for MySQL like this:

```
implementation 'org.springframework.boot:spring-boot-starter-data-jpa'
implementation 'mysql:mysql-connector-java'
```

To enable the use of MongoDB and MySQL when running automated integration tests, we will use **Testcontainers** and its support for JUnit 5, MongoDB, and MySQL. For the `product` and `recommendation` microservices, we declare the following test dependencies:

```
implementation platform('org.testcontainers:testcontainers-bom:1.15.2')
testImplementation 'org.testcontainers:testcontainers'
testImplementation 'org.testcontainers:junit-jupiter'
testImplementation 'org.testcontainers:mongodb'
```

For the `review` microservices, we declare the following test dependencies:

```
implementation platform('org.testcontainers:testcontainers-bom:1.15.2')
testImplementation 'org.testcontainers:testcontainers'
testImplementation 'org.testcontainers:junit-jupiter'
testImplementation 'org.testcontainers:mysql'
```

For more information on how Testcontainers is used in integration tests, see the *Writing automated tests that focus on persistence* section later on.

Storing data with entity classes

The entity classes are similar to the corresponding API model classes in terms of what fields they contain; see the Java package `se.magnus.api.core` in the `api` project. We will add two fields, `id` and `version`, in the entity classes compared to the API model classes.

The id field is used to hold the database identity of each stored entity, corresponding to the primary key when using a relational database. We will delegate the responsibility of generating unique values of the identity field to Spring Data. Depending on the database used, Spring Data can delegate this responsibility to the database engine or handle it on its own. In either case, the application code does not need to consider how a unique database id value is set. The id field is not exposed in the API, as a best practice from a security perspective. The fields in the model classes that identify an entity will be assigned a unique index in the corresponding entity class, to ensure consistency in the database from a business perspective.

The version field is used to implement optimistic locking, allowing Spring Data to verify that updates of an entity in the database do not overwrite a concurrent update. If the value of the version field stored in the database is higher than the value of the version field in an update request, it indicates that the update is performed on stale data—the information to be updated has been updated by someone else since it was read from the database. Attempts to perform updates based on stale data will be prevented by Spring Data. In the section on writing persistence tests, we will see tests verifying that the optimistic locking mechanism in Spring Data prevents updates performed on stale data. Since we only implement APIs for create, read, and delete operations, we will, however, not expose the version field in the API.

The most interesting parts of the product entity class, used for storing entities in MongoDB, look like this:

```
@Document(collection="products")
public class ProductEntity {

 @Id
 private String id;

 @Version
 private Integer version;

 @Indexed(unique = true)
 private int productId;

 private String name;
 private int weight;
```

Here are some observations from the preceding code:

- The @Document(collection = "products") annotation is used to mark the class as an entity class used for MongoDB, that is, mapped to a collection in MongoDB with the name products.

- The `@Id` and `@Version` annotations are used to mark the `id` and `version` fields to be used by Spring Data, as explained previously.
- The `@Indexed(unique = true)` annotation is used to get a unique index created for the business key, `productId`.

The most interesting parts of the `Recommendation` entity class, also used for storing entities in MongoDB, look like this:

```
@Document(collection="recommendations")
@CompoundIndex(name = "prod-rec-id", unique = true, def =
"{'productId': 1, 'recommendationId' : 1}")
public class RecommendationEntity {

    @Id
    private String id;

    @Version
    private Integer version;

    private int productId;
    private int recommendationId;
    private String author;
    private int rating;
    private String content;
```

Added to the explanations for the preceding product entity, we can see how a unique compound index is created using the `@CompoundIndex` annotation for the compound business key based on the `productId` and `recommendationId` fields.

Finally, the most interesting parts of the `Review` entity class, used for storing entities in a SQL database like MySQL, look like this:

```
@Entity
@Table(name = "reviews", indexes = { @Index(name = "reviews_unique_
idx", unique = true, columnList = "productId,reviewId") })
public class ReviewEntity {

    @Id @GeneratedValue
    private int id;

    @Version
```

```
    private int version;

    private int productId;
    private int reviewId;
    private String author;
    private String subject;
    private String content;
```

Notes from the preceding code:

- The `@Entity` and `@Table` annotations are used to mark the class as an entity class used for JPA—mapped to a table in a SQL database with the name `reviews`.
- The `@Table` annotation is also used to specify that a unique compound index will be created for the compound business key based on the `productId` and `reviewId` fields.
- The `@Id` and `@Version` annotations are used to mark the `id` and `version` fields to be used by Spring Data as explained previously. To direct Spring Data for JPA to automatically generate unique `id` values for the `id` field, we are using the `@GeneratedValue` annotation.

For the full source code of the entity classes, see the `persistence` package in each of the core microservice projects.

Defining repositories in Spring Data

Spring Data comes with a set of base classes for defining repositories. We will use the base classes `CrudRepository` and `PagingAndSortingRepository`:

- The `CrudRepository` base class provides standard methods for performing basic create, read, update, and delete operations on the data stored in the databases.
- The `PagingAndSortingRepository` base class adds support for paging and sorting to the `CrudRepository` base class.

We will use the `CrudRepository` class as the base class for the `Recommendation` and `Review` repositories and the `PagingAndSortingRepository` class as the base class for the `Product` repository.

We will also add a few extra query methods to our repositories for looking up entities using the business key, `productId`.

Spring Data supports defining extra query methods based on naming conventions for the signature of the method. For example, the `findByProductId(int productId)` method signature can be used to direct Spring Data to automatically create a query that returns entities from the underlying collection or table. In this case, it will return entities that have the `productId` field set to the value specified in the `productId` parameter. For more details on how to declare extra queries, see `https://docs.spring.io/spring-data/data-commons/docs/current/reference/html/#repositories.query-methods.query-creation`.

The `Product` repository class looks like this:

```
public interface ProductRepository extends PagingAndSortingRepository
<ProductEntity, String> {
    Optional<ProductEntity> findByProductId(int productId);
}
```

Since the `findByProductId` method might return zero or one product entity, the return value is marked to be optional by wrapping it in an `Optional` object.

The `Recommendation` repository class looks like this:

```
public interface RecommendationRepository extends CrudRepository
<RecommendationEntity, String> {
    List<RecommendationEntity> findByProductId(int productId);
}
```

In this case, the `findByProductId` method will return zero to many recommendation entities, so the return value is defined as a list.

Finally, the `Review` repository class looks like this:

```
public interface ReviewRepository extends CrudRepository<ReviewEntity,
Integer> {
    @Transactional(readOnly = true)
    List<ReviewEntity> findByProductId(int productId);
}
```

Since SQL databases are transactional, we have to specify the default transaction type—read-only in our case—for the query method, `findByProductId()`.

That's it—this is all it takes to establish a persistence layer for our core microservices.

For the full source code of the repository classes, see the `persistence` package in each of the core microservice projects.

Let's start using the persistence classes by writing some tests to verify that they work as intended.

Writing automated tests that focus on persistence

When writing persistence tests, we want to start a database when the tests begin and tear it down when the tests complete. However, we don't want the tests to wait for other resources to start up, for example, a web server such as Netty (which is required at runtime).

Spring Boot comes with two class-level annotations tailored for this specific requirement:

- `@DataMongoTest`: This annotation starts up a MongoDB database when the test starts.
- `@DataJpaTest`: This annotation starts up a SQL database when the test starts.
    - By default, Spring Boot configures the tests to roll back updates to the SQL database to minimize the risk of negative side effects on other tests. In our case, this behavior will cause some of the tests to fail. Therefore, automatic rollback is disabled with the class level annotation `@Transactional(propagation = NOT_SUPPORTED)`.

To handle the startup and tear down of databases during the execution of the integration tests, we will use Testcontainers. Before looking into how to write persistence tests, let's learn about how to use Testcontainers.

Using Testcontainers

Testcontainers (`https://www.testcontainers.org`) is a library that simplifies running automated integration tests by running resource managers like a database or a message broker as a Docker container. Testcontainers can be configured to automatically start up Docker containers when JUnit tests are started and tear down the containers when the tests are complete.

To enable Testcontainers in an existing test class for a Spring Boot application like the microservices in this book, we can add the `@Testcontainers` annotation to the test class. Using the `@Container` annotation, we can for example declare that the `Review` microservice's integration tests will use a Docker container running MySQL. The code looks like this:

```
@SpringBootTest
@Testcontainers
class SampleTests {
```

```
@Container
private static MySQLContainer database =
  new MySQLContainer("mysql:5.7.32");
```

The version specified for MySQL, 5.7.32, is copied from Docker Compose files to ensure that the same version is used.

A disadvantage of this approach is that each test class will use its own Docker container. Bringing up MySQL in a Docker container takes a few seconds, typically 10 seconds on my Mac. Running multiple test classes that use the same type of test container will add this latency for each test class. To avoid this extra latency, we can use the **Single Container Pattern** (see `https://www.testcontainers.org/test_framework_integration/manual_lifecycle_control/#singleton-containers`). Following this pattern, a base class is used to launch a single Docker container for MySQL. The base class, `MySqlTestBase`, used in the `Review` microservice looks like this:

```
public abstract class MySqlTestBase {

  private static MySQLContainer database =
    new MySQLContainer("mysql:5.7.32");

  static {
    database.start();
  }

  @DynamicPropertySource
  static void databaseProperties(DynamicPropertyRegistry registry) {
    registry.add("spring.datasource.url", database::getJdbcUrl);
    registry.add("spring.datasource.username", database::getUsername);
    registry.add("spring.datasource.password", database::getPassword);
  }
}
```

Explanations for the preceding source code:

- The `database` container is declared in the same way as in the preceding example.
- A `static` block is used to start the database container before any JUnit code is invoked.

- The database container will get some properties defined when started up, such as which port to use. To register these dynamically created properties in the application context, a static method `databaseProperties()` is defined. The method is annotated with `@DynamicPropertySource` to override the database configuration in the application context, such as the configuration from an `application.yml` file.

The test classes use the base class as follows:

```
class PersistenceTests extends MySqlTestBase {
class ReviewServiceApplicationTests extends MySqlTestBase {
```

For the `product` and `review` microservices, which use MongoDB, a corresponding base class, `MongoDbTestBase`, has been added.

By default, the log output from Testcontainers is rather extensive. A **Logback** configuration file can be placed in the `src/test/resource` folder to limit the amount of log output. Logback is a logging framework (`http://logback.qos.ch`), and it is included in the microservices by using the `spring-boot-starter-webflux` dependency. For details, see `https://www.testcontainers.org/supported_docker_environment/logging_config/`. The configuration file used in this chapter is named `src/test/resources/logback-test.xml` and looks like this:

```
<?xml version="1.0" encoding="UTF-8" ?>
<configuration>
    <include resource="org/springframework/boot/logging/logback/
defaults.xml"/>
    <include resource="org/springframework/boot/logging/logback/
console-appender.xml"/>

    <root level="INFO">
        <appender-ref ref="CONSOLE" />
    </root>
</configuration>
```

Some notes from the above `XML` file:

- The config file includes two config files provided by Spring Boot to get default values defined, and a log appender is configured that can write log events to the console.
- The config file limits log output to the `INFO` log level, discarding `DEBUG` and `TRACE` log records emitted by the Testcontainers library.

For details on Spring Boot support for logging and the use of Logback, see `https://docs.spring.io/spring-boot/docs/current/reference/html/howto.html#howto-configure-logback-for-logging`.

Finally, when using the `@DataMongoTest` and `@DataJpaTest` annotations instead of the `@SpringBootTest` annotation to only start up the MongoDB and SQL database during the integration test, there is one more thing to consider. The `@DataMongoTest` and `@DataJpaTest` annotations are designed to start an embedded database by default. Since we want to use a containerized database, we have to disable this feature. For the `@DataJpaTest` annotation, this can be done by using a `@AutoConfigureTestDatabase` annotation like this:

```
@DataJpaTest
@AutoConfigureTestDatabase(replace = AutoConfigureTestDatabase.Replace.
NONE)
class PersistenceTests extends MySqlTestBase {
```

For the `@DataMongoTest` annotation, this can be done by using the `excludeAutoConfiguration` parameter and specifying that the class `EmbeddedMongoAutoConfiguration` will be excluded. The code looks like this:

```
@DataMongoTest(
  excludeAutoConfiguration = EmbeddedMongoAutoConfiguration.class)
class PersistenceTests extends MongoDbTestBase {
```

With Testcontainers introduced, we are ready to see how persistence tests can be written.

Writing persistence tests

The persistence tests for the three core microservices are similar to each other, so we will only go through the persistence tests for the `product` microservice.

The test class, `PersistenceTests`, declares a method, `setupDb()`, annotated with `@BeforeEach`, which is executed before each test method. The setup method removes any entities from previous tests in the database and inserts an entity that the test methods can use as a base for their tests:

```
@DataMongoTest
class PersistenceTests {

    @Autowired
    private ProductRepository repository;
    private ProductEntity savedEntity;
```

```
    @BeforeEach
    void setupDb() {
        repository.deleteAll();
        ProductEntity entity = new ProductEntity(1, "n", 1);
        savedEntity = repository.save(entity);
        assertEqualsProduct(entity, savedEntity);
    }
```

Next come the various test methods. First out is a `create` test:

```
@Test
void create() {
    ProductEntity newEntity = new ProductEntity(2, "n", 2);
    repository.save(newEntity);

    ProductEntity foundEntity =
    repository.findById(newEntity.getId()).get();
    assertEqualsProduct(newEntity, foundEntity);

    assertEquals(2, repository.count());
}
```

This test creates a new entity, verifies that it can be found using the `findById()` method, and wraps up by asserting that there are two entities stored in the database, the one created by the `setup` method and the one created by the test itself.

The `update` test looks like this:

```
@Test
void update() {
    savedEntity.setName("n2");
    repository.save(savedEntity);

    ProductEntity foundEntity =
    repository.findById(savedEntity.getId()).get();
    assertEquals(1, (long)foundEntity.getVersion());
    assertEquals("n2", foundEntity.getName());
}
```

This test updates the entity created by the `setup` method, reads it again from the database using the standard `findById()` method, and asserts that it contains expected values for some of its fields. Note that, when an entity is created, its `version` field is set to `0` by Spring Data, so we expect it to be `1` after the update.

The `delete` test looks like this:

```
@Test
void delete() {
    repository.delete(savedEntity);
    assertFalse(repository.existsById(savedEntity.getId()));
}
```

This test deletes the entity created by the `setup` method and verifies that it no longer exists in the database.

The `read` test looks like this:

```
@Test
void getByProductId() {
    Optional<ProductEntity> entity =
    repository.findByProductId(savedEntity.getProductId());
    assertTrue(entity.isPresent());
    assertEqualsProduct(savedEntity, entity.get());
}
```

This test uses the `findByProductId()` method to get the entity created by the `setup` method, verifies that it was found, and then uses the local helper method, `assertEqualsProduct()`, to verify that the entity returned by `findByProductId()` looks the same as the entity stored by the `setup` method.

Next are two test methods that verify alternative flows—handling of error conditions. First is a test that verifies that duplicates are handled correctly:

```
@Test
void duplicateError() {
  assertThrows(DuplicateKeyException.class, () -> {
    ProductEntity entity = new ProductEntity(savedEntity.
getProductId(), "n", 1);
    repository.save(entity);
  });
}
```

The test tries to store an entity with the same business key as used by the entity created by the `setup` method. The test will fail if the save operation succeeds, or if the save fails with an exception other than the expected `DuplicateKeyException`.

The other negative test is, in my opinion, the most interesting test in the test class. It is a test that verifies a correct error handling in the case of updates of stale data—it verifies that the optimistic locking mechanism works. It looks like this:

```
@Test
void optimisticLockError() {

    // Store the saved entity in two separate entity objects
    ProductEntity entity1 =
    repository.findById(savedEntity.getId()).get();
    ProductEntity entity2 =
    repository.findById(savedEntity.getId()).get();

    // Update the entity using the first entity object
    entity1.setName("n1");
    repository.save(entity1);

    //  Update the entity using the second entity object.
    // This should fail since the second entity now holds an old version
    // number, that is, an Optimistic Lock Error
    assertThrows(OptimisticLockingFailureException.class, () -> {
      entity2.setName("n2");
      repository.save(entity2);
    });

    // Get the updated entity from the database and verify its new state
    ProductEntity updatedEntity =
    repository.findById(savedEntity.getId()).get();
    assertEquals(1, (int)updatedEntity.getVersion());
    assertEquals("n1", updatedEntity.getName());
}
```

The following is observed from the code:

1. First, the test reads the same entity twice and stores it in two different variables, `entity1` and `entity2`.
2. Next, it uses one of the variables, `entity1`, to update the entity. The update of the entity in the database will cause the version field of the entity to be increased automatically by Spring Data. The other variable, `entity2`, now contains stale data, manifested by its `version` field, which holds a lower value than the corresponding value in the database.
3. When the test tries to update the entity using the variable `entity2`, which contains stale data, it is expected to fail by throwing an `OptimisticLockingFailureException` exception.

4. The test wraps up by asserting that the entity in the database reflects the first update, that is, contains the name `"n1"`, and that the `version` field has the value `1`; only one update has been performed on the entity in the database.

Finally, the `product` service contains a test that demonstrates the usage of built-in support for sorting and paging in Spring Data:

```
@Test
void paging() {
    repository.deleteAll();
    List<ProductEntity> newProducts = rangeClosed(1001, 1010)
        .mapToObj(i -> new ProductEntity(i, "name " + i, i))
        .collect(Collectors.toList());
    repository.saveAll(newProducts);

    Pageable nextPage = PageRequest.of(0, 4, ASC, "productId");
    nextPage = testNextPage(nextPage, "[1001, 1002, 1003, 1004]",
    true);
    nextPage = testNextPage(nextPage, "[1005, 1006, 1007, 1008]",
    true);
    nextPage = testNextPage(nextPage, "[1009, 1010]", false);
}
```

Explanations for the preceding code:

1. The test starts with removing any existing data, then inserts 10 entities with the `productId` field ranging from `1001` to `1010`.
2. Next, it creates `PageRequest`, requesting a page count of `4` entities per page and a sort order based on `ProductId` in ascending order.
3. Finally, it uses a helper method, `testNextPage`, to read the expected three pages, verifying the expected product IDs in each page and verifying that Spring Data correctly reports back whether more pages exist or not.

The helper method `testNextPage` looks like this:

```
private Pageable testNextPage(Pageable nextPage, String
expectedProductIds, boolean expectsNextPage) {
    Page<ProductEntity> productPage = repository.findAll(nextPage);
    assertEquals(expectedProductIds, productPage.getContent()
    .stream().map(p -> p.getProductId()).collect(Collectors.
```

```
        toList()).toString());
    assertEquals(expectsNextPage, productPage.hasNext());
    return productPage.nextPageable();
}
```

The helper method uses the page request object, `nextPage`, to get the next page from the repository method, `findAll()`. Based on the result, it extracts the product IDs from the returned entities into a string and compares it to the expected list of product IDs. Finally, it returns the next page.

For the full source code of the persistence tests, see the test class `PersistenceTests` in each of the core microservice projects.

The persistence tests in the `product` microservice can be executed using Gradle with a command like this:

```
cd $BOOK_HOME/Chapter06
./gradlew microservices:product-service:test --tests PersistenceTests
```

After running the tests, it should respond with the following:

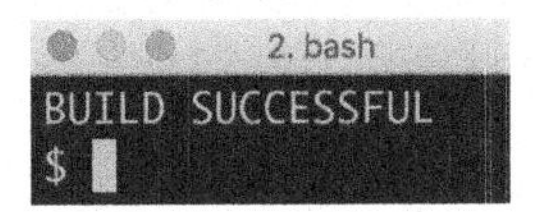

Figure 6.4: Build successful response

With a persistence layer in place, we can update the service layer in our core microservices to use the persistence layer.

Using the persistence layer in the service layer

In this section, we will learn how to use the persistence layer in the service layer to store and retrieve data from a database. We will go through the following steps:

1. Logging the database connection URL
2. Adding new APIs
3. Calling the persistence layer from the service layer
4. Declaring a Java bean mapper
5. Updating the service tests

Logging the database connection URL

When scaling up the number of microservices where each microservice connects to its own database, it can be hard to keep track of what database each microservice actually uses. To avoid this confusion, a good practice is to add a log statement directly after the startup of a microservice that logs connection information that is used to connect to the database.

For example, the startup code for the `product` service looks like this:

```
public class ProductServiceApplication {
  private static final Logger LOG =
  LoggerFactory.getLogger(ProductServiceApplication.class);

  public static void main(String[] args) {
    ConfigurableApplicationContext ctx =
    SpringApplication.run(ProductServiceApplication.class, args);
    String mongodDbHost =
    ctx.getEnvironment().getProperty("spring.data.mongodb.host");
    String mongodDbPort =
    ctx.getEnvironment().getProperty("spring.data.mongodb.port");
    LOG.info("Connected to MongoDb: " + mongodDbHost + ":" +
    mongodDbPort);
  }
}
```

The call to the `LOG.info` method will write something like the following to the log:

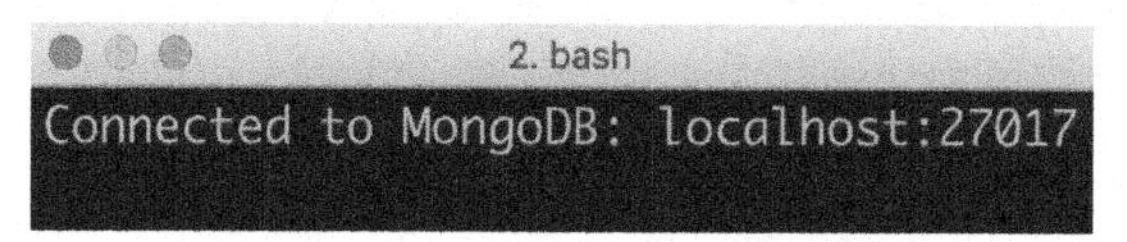

Figure 6.5: Expected log output

For the full source code, see the main application class in each of the core microservice projects, for example, `ProductServiceApplication` in the `product-service` project.

Adding new APIs

Before we can use the persistence layer for creating and deleting information in the database, we need to create the corresponding API operations in our core service APIs.

The API operations for creating and deleting a product entity look like this:

```
@PostMapping(
    value    = "/product",
    consumes = "application/json",
    produces = "application/json")
Product createProduct(@RequestBody Product body);

@DeleteMapping(value = "/product/{productId}")
void deleteProduct(@PathVariable int productId);
```

The implementation of the delete operation will be **idempotent**; that is, it will return the same result if called several times. This is a valuable characteristic in fault scenarios. For example, if a client experiences a network timeout during a call to a delete operation, it can simply call the delete operation again without worrying about varying responses, for example, OK (200) in response the first time and Not Found (404) in response to consecutive calls, or any unexpected side effects. This implies that the operation should return the status code OK (200) even though the entity no longer exists in the database.

The API operations for the `recommendation` and `review` entities look similar; however, note that when it comes to the delete operation for the `recommendation` and `review` entities, it will delete all `recommendations` and `reviews` for the specified `productId`.

For the full source code, see the interface declarations (`ProductService`, `RecommendationService`, and `ReviewService`) of the core microservices in the `api` project.

Calling the persistence layer from the service layer

The source code in the service layer for using the persistence layer is structured in the same way for all core microservices. Therefore, we will only go through the source code for the `product` microservice.

First, we need to inject the repository class from the persistence layer and a Java bean mapper class into the constructor:

```
private final ServiceUtil serviceUtil;
private final ProductRepository repository;
```

```
private final ProductMapper mapper;

@Autowired
public ProductServiceImpl(ProductRepository repository, ProductMapper
mapper, ServiceUtil serviceUtil) {
    this.repository = repository;
    this.mapper = mapper;
    this.serviceUtil = serviceUtil;
}
```

In the next section, we will see how the Java mapper class is defined.

Next, the `createProduct` method is implemented as follows:

```
public Product createProduct(Product body) {
    try {
        ProductEntity entity = mapper.apiToEntity(body);
        ProductEntity newEntity = repository.save(entity);
        return mapper.entityToApi(newEntity);
    } catch (DuplicateKeyException dke) {
        throw new InvalidInputException("Duplicate key, Product Id: " +
        body.getProductId());
    }
}
```

The `createProduct` method used the `save` method in the repository to store a new entity. It should be noted how the mapper class is used to convert Java beans between an API model class and an entity class using the two mapper methods, `apiToEntity()` and `entityToApi()`. The only error we handle for the `create` method is the `DuplicateKeyException` exception, which we convert into an `InvalidInputException` exception.

The `getProduct` method looks like this:

```
public Product getProduct(int productId) {
    if (productId < 1) throw new InvalidInputException("Invalid
    productId: " + productId);
    ProductEntity entity = repository.findByProductId(productId)
        .orElseThrow(() -> new NotFoundException("No product found for
         productId: " + productId));
    Product response = mapper.entityToApi(entity);
    response.setServiceAddress(serviceUtil.getServiceAddress());
    return response;
}
```

After some basic input validation (that is, ensuring that `productId` is not negative), the `findByProductId()` method in the repository is used to find the product entity. Since the repository method returns an `Optional` product, we can use the `orElseThrow()` method in the `Optional` class to conveniently throw a `NotFoundException` exception if no product entity is found. Before the product information is returned, the `serviceUtil` object is used to fill in the currently used address of the microservice.

Finally, let's see the `deleteProduct` method:

```
public void deleteProduct(int productId) {
    repository.findByProductId(productId).ifPresent(e ->
    repository.delete(e));
}
```

The `delete` method also uses the `findByProductId()` method in the repository and uses the `ifPresent()` method in the `Optional` class to conveniently delete the entity only if it exists. Note that the implementation is idempotent; it will not report any failure if the entity is not found.

For the full source code, see the service implementation class in each of the core microservice projects, for example, `ProductServiceImpl` in the `product-service` project.

Declaring a Java bean mapper

So, what about the magic Java bean mapper?

As already mentioned, MapStruct is used to declare our mapper classes. The use of MapStruct is similar in all three core microservices, so we will only go through the source code for the mapper object in the `product` microservice.

The mapper class for the `product` service looks like this:

```
@Mapper(componentModel = "spring")
public interface ProductMapper {

    @Mappings({
        @Mapping(target = "serviceAddress", ignore = true)
    })
    Product entityToApi(ProductEntity entity);

    @Mappings({
        @Mapping(target = "id", ignore = true),
```

```
        @Mapping(target = "version", ignore = true)
    })
    ProductEntity apiToEntity(Product api);
}
```

The following can be noted from the code:

- The `entityToApi()` method maps entity objects to the API model object. Since the entity class does not have a field for `serviceAddress`, the `entityToApi()` method is annotated to ignore the `serviceAddress` field in the API model object.
- The `apiToEntity()` method maps API model objects to entity objects. In the same way, the `apiToEntity()` method is annotated to ignore the `id` and `version` fields that are missing in the API model class.

Not only does MapStruct support mapping fields by name, but it can also be directed to map fields with different names. In the mapper class for the `recommendation` service, the `rating` entity field is mapped to the API model field, `rate`, using the following annotations:

```
@Mapping(target = "rate", source="entity.rating"),
Recommendation entityToApi(RecommendationEntity entity);

@Mapping(target = "rating", source="api.rate"),
RecommendationEntity apiToEntity(Recommendation api);
```

After a successful Gradle build, the generated mapping implementation can be found in the `build/classes` folder for each project. For example, `ProductMapperImpl.java` in the `product-service` project.

For the full source code, see the mapper class in each of the core microservice projects, for example, `ProductMapper` in the `product-service` project.

Updating the service tests

The tests of the APIs exposed by the core microservices have been updated since the previous chapter with tests covering the create and delete API operations.

The added tests are similar in all three core microservices, so we will only go through the source code for the service tests in the `product` microservice.

To ensure a known state for each test, a setup method, `setupDb()`, is declared and annotated with `@BeforeEach`, so it is executed before each test. The setup method removes any previously created entities:

```
@Autowired
private ProductRepository repository;

@BeforeEach
void setupDb() {
   repository.deleteAll();
}
```

The test method for the create API verifies that a product entity can be retrieved after it has been created and that creating another product entity with the same `productId` results in an expected error, `UNPROCESSABLE_ENTITY`, in the response to the API request:

```
@Test
void duplicateError() {
   int productId = 1;
   postAndVerifyProduct(productId, OK);
   assertTrue(repository.findByProductId(productId).isPresent());

   postAndVerifyProduct(productId, UNPROCESSABLE_ENTITY)
      .jsonPath("$.path").isEqualTo("/product")
      .jsonPath("$.message").isEqualTo("Duplicate key, Product Id: " +
       productId);
}
```

The test method for the delete API verifies that a product entity can be deleted and that a second delete request is idempotent—it also returns the status code OK, even though the entity no longer exists in the database:

```
@Test
void deleteProduct() {
   int productId = 1;
   postAndVerifyProduct(productId, OK);
   assertTrue(repository.findByProductId(productId).isPresent());

   deleteAndVerifyProduct(productId, OK);
   assertFalse(repository.findByProductId(productId).isPresent());

   deleteAndVerifyProduct(productId, OK);
}
```

To simplify sending the create, read, and delete requests to the API and verify the response status, three helper methods have been created:

- `postAndVerifyProduct()`
- `getAndVerifyProduct()`
- `deleteAndVerifyProduct()`

The `postAndVerifyProduct()` method looks like this:

```
private WebTestClient.BodyContentSpec postAndVerifyProduct(int
productId, HttpStatus expectedStatus) {
   Product product = new Product(productId, "Name " + productId,
   productId, "SA");
   return client.post()
      .uri("/product")
      .body(just(product), Product.class)
      .accept(APPLICATION_JSON)
      .exchange()
      .expectStatus().isEqualTo(expectedStatus)
      .expectHeader().contentType(APPLICATION_JSON)
      .expectBody();
}
```

The helper method performs the actual HTTP request and verifies the response code and content type of the response body. Added to that, the helper method also returns the body of the response for further investigations by the caller, if required. The other two helper methods for read and delete requests are similar.

The source code for the three service test classes can be found in each of the core microservice projects, for example, `ProductServiceApplicationTests` in the `product-service` project.

Now, let's move on to see how we extend a composite service API.

Extending the composite service API

In this section, we will see how we can extend the composite API with operations for creating and deleting composite entities. We will go through the following steps:

1. Adding new operations in the composite service API
2. Adding methods in the integration layer
3. Implementing the new composite API operations
4. Updating the composite service tests

Adding new operations in the composite service API

The composite versions of creating and deleting entities and handling aggregated entities are similar to the create and delete operations in the core service APIs. The major difference is that they have annotations added for OpenAPI-based documentation. For an explanation of the usage of the OpenAPI annotations `@Operation` and `@ApiResponse`, refer to *Chapter 5, Adding an API Description Using OpenAPI*, specifically the *Adding API-specific documentation to the ProductCompositeService interface* section.

The API operation for creating a composite product entity is declared as follows:

```
@Operation(
  summary = "${api.product-composite.create-composite-product.
description}",
  description = "${api.product-composite.create-composite-product.
notes}")
@ApiResponses(value = {
  @ApiResponse(responseCode = "400", description = "${api.
responseCodes.badRequest.description}"),
  @ApiResponse(responseCode = "422", description = "${api.
responseCodes.unprocessableEntity.description}")
  })
@PostMapping(
  value    = "/product-composite",
  consumes = "application/json")
void createProduct(@RequestBody ProductAggregate body);
```

The API operation for deleting a composite product entity is declared as follows:

```
@Operation(
  summary = "${api.product-composite.delete-composite-product.
description}",
  description = "${api.product-composite.delete-composite-product.
notes}")
@ApiResponses(value = {
  @ApiResponse(responseCode = "400", description = "${api.
responseCodes.badRequest.description}"),
  @ApiResponse(responseCode = "422", description = "${api.
responseCodes.unprocessableEntity.description}")
})
@DeleteMapping(value = "/product-composite/{productId}")
void deleteProduct(@PathVariable int productId);
```

For the full source code, see the Java interface `ProductCompositeService` in the `api` project.

We also need to, as before, add the descriptive text of the API documentation to the property file, `application.yml`, in the `product-composite` project:

```
create-composite-product:
  description: Creates a composite product
  notes: |
    # Normal response
    The composite product information posted to the API will be
    split up and stored as separate product-info, recommendation
    and review entities.

    # Expected error responses
    1. If a product with the same productId as specified in the
    posted information already exists, an **422 - Unprocessable
    Entity** error with a "duplicate key" error message will be
    Returned

delete-composite-product:
  description: Deletes a product composite
  notes: |
    # Normal response
    Entities for product information, recommendations and reviews
    related to the specified productId will be deleted.
    The implementation of the delete method is idempotent, that is,
    it can be called several times with the same response.
    This means that a delete request of a non-existing product will
    return **200 Ok**.
```

Using the Swagger UI viewer, the updated OpenAPI documentation will look like this:

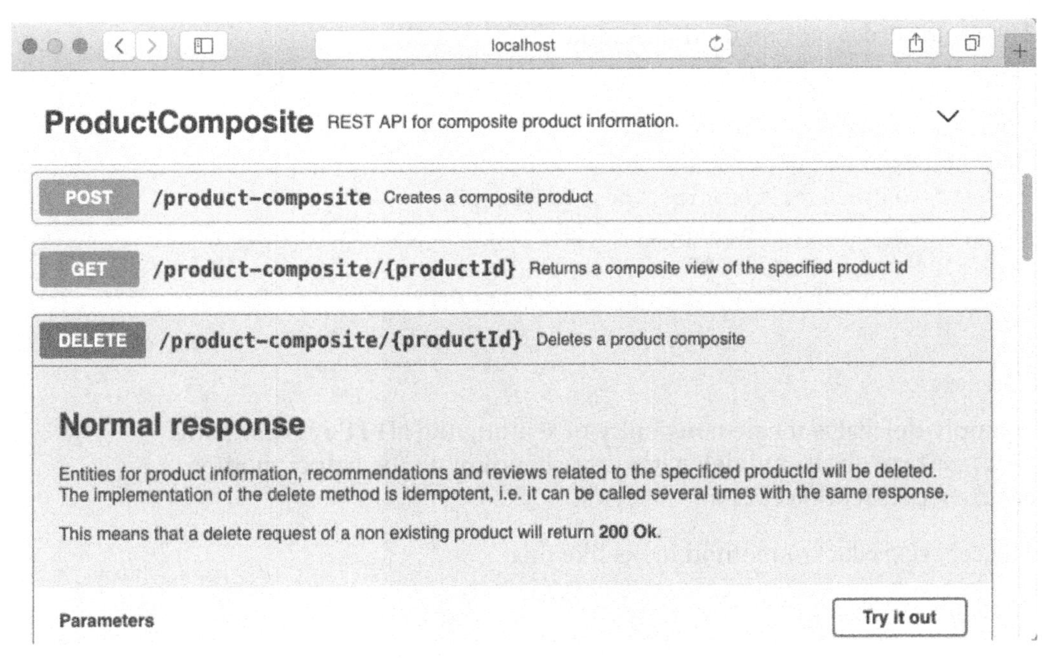

Figure 6.6: Updated OpenAPI documentation

Later on in this chapter, we will use the Swagger UI viewer to try out the new composite API operations.

Adding methods in the integration layer

Before we can implement the new create and delete APIs in the composite services, we need to extend the integration layer so it can call the underlying create and delete operations in the APIs of the core microservices.

The methods in the integration layer for calling the create and delete operations in the three core microservices are straightforward and similar to each other, so we will only go through the source code for the methods that call the `product` microservice.

The `createProduct()` method looks like this:

```
@Override
public Product createProduct(Product body) {
    try {
        return restTemplate.postForObject(
                    productServiceUrl, body, Product.class);
    } catch (HttpClientErrorException ex) {
        throw handleHttpClientException(ex);
    }
}
```

It simply delegates the responsibility of sending the HTTP request to the `RestTemplate` object and delegates error handling to the helper method, `handleHttpClientException`.

The `deleteProduct()` method looks like this:

```
@Override
public void deleteProduct(int productId) {
    try {
        restTemplate.delete(productServiceUrl + "/" + productId);
    } catch (HttpClientErrorException ex) {
        throw handleHttpClientException(ex);
    }
}
```

It is implemented in the same way as for the create method, but performs an HTTP delete request instead.

The full source code for the integration layer can be found in the `ProductCompositeIntegration` class in the `product-composite` project.

Implementing the new composite API operations

Now, we can implement the composite create and delete methods!

The composite's create method will split up the aggregate product object into discrete objects for `product`, `recommendation`, and `review` and call the corresponding create methods in the integration layer:

```
@Override
public void createProduct(ProductAggregate body) {
    try {
        Product product = new Product(body.getProductId(),
        body.getName(), body.getWeight(), null);
        integration.createProduct(product);

        if (body.getRecommendations() != null) {
            body.getRecommendations().forEach(r -> {
                Recommendation recommendation = new
                Recommendation(body.getProductId(),
                r.getRecommendationId(), r.getAuthor(), r.getRate(),
                r.getContent(), null);
                integration.createRecommendation(recommendation);
            });
        }

        if (body.getReviews() != null) {
            body.getReviews().forEach(r -> {
                Review review = new Review(body.getProductId(),
                r.getReviewId(), r.getAuthor(), r.getSubject(),
                r.getContent(), null);
                integration.createReview(review);
            });
        }
    } catch (RuntimeException re) {
        LOG.warn("createCompositeProduct failed", re);
        throw re;
    }
}
```

The composite's delete method simply calls the three delete methods in the integration layer to delete the corresponding entities in the underlying databases:

```
@Override
public void deleteProduct(int productId) {
    integration.deleteProduct(productId);
    integration.deleteRecommendations(productId);
    integration.deleteReviews(productId);
}
```

The full source code for the service implementation can be found in the `ProductCompositeServiceImpl` class in the `product-composite` project.

For happy day scenarios, this implementation will work fine, but if we consider various error scenarios we see that this implementation will cause trouble!

What if, for example, one of the underlying core microservices is temporarily not available, for instance, due to internal, network, or database problems?

This might result in partly created or deleted composite products. For the delete operation, this can be fixed if the requester simply calls the composite's delete method until it succeeds. However, if the underlying problem remains for a while, the requester will probably give up, resulting in an inconsistent state of the composite product—not acceptable in most cases!

In the next chapter, *Chapter 7, Developing Reactive Microservices*, we will see how we can address these types of shortcomings with synchronous APIs as a RESTful API.

For now, let's move on with this fragile design in mind.

Updating the composite service tests

Testing composite services, as already mentioned in *Chapter 3, Creating a Set of Cooperating Microservices* (refer to the *Adding automated microservice tests in isolation* section), are limited to using simple mock components instead of the actual core services. This restricts us from testing more complex scenarios, for example, error handling when trying to create duplicates in the underlying databases. The tests of the composite create and delete API operations are therefore relatively simple:

```
@Test
void createCompositeProduct1() {
   ProductAggregate compositeProduct = new ProductAggregate(1, "name",
   1, null, null, null);
   postAndVerifyProduct(compositeProduct, OK);
}

@Test
void createCompositeProduct2() {
    ProductAggregate compositeProduct = new ProductAggregate(1, "name",
        1, singletonList(new RecommendationSummary(1, "a", 1, "c")),
        singletonList(new ReviewSummary(1, "a", "s", "c")), null);
    postAndVerifyProduct(compositeProduct, OK);
}
```

```
@Test
void deleteCompositeProduct() {
    ProductAggregate compositeProduct = new ProductAggregate(1, "name",
        1,singletonList(new RecommendationSummary(1, "a", 1, "c")),
        singletonList(new ReviewSummary(1, "a", "s", "c")), null);
    postAndVerifyProduct(compositeProduct, OK);
    deleteAndVerifyProduct(compositeProduct.getProductId(), OK);
    deleteAndVerifyProduct(compositeProduct.getProductId(), OK);
}
```

The full source code for the service test can be found in the `ProductCompositeServiceApplicationTests` class in the `product-composite` project.

These are all the changes required in the source code. Before we can test the microservices together, we must learn how to add databases to the system landscape managed by Docker Compose.

Adding databases to the Docker Compose landscape

Now, we have all of the source code in place. Before we can start up the microservice landscape and try out the new APIs together with the new persistence layer, we must start up some databases.

We will bring MongoDB and MySQL into the system landscape controlled by Docker Compose and add configuration to our microservices so that they can find their databases when running.

The Docker Compose configuration

MongoDB and MySQL are declared as follows in the Docker Compose configuration file, `docker-compose.yml`:

```
  mongodb:
    image: mongo:4.4.2
    mem_limit: 512m
    ports:
      - "27017:27017"
    command: mongod
    healthcheck:
      test: "mongo --eval 'db.stats().ok'"
      interval: 5s
```

```
      timeout: 2s
      retries: 60

  mysql:
    image: mysql:5.7.32
    mem_limit: 512m
    ports:
      - "3306:3306"
    environment:
      - MYSQL_ROOT_PASSWORD=rootpwd
      - MYSQL_DATABASE=review-db
      - MYSQL_USER=user
      - MYSQL_PASSWORD=pwd
    healthcheck:
      test: "/usr/bin/mysql --user=user --password=pwd --execute \"SHOW DATABASES;\""
      interval: 5s
      timeout: 2s
      retries: 60
```

Notes from the preceding code:

1. We will use the official Docker image for MongoDB v4.4.2 and MySQL 5.7.32 and forward their default ports `27017` and `3306` to the Docker host, also made available on `localhost` when using Docker Desktop for Mac.
2. For MySQL, we also declare some environment variables, defining the following:
    - The root password
    - The name of the database that will be created on container startup
    - A username and password for a user that is set up for the database on container startup
3. We also declare a health check that Docker will run to determine the status of the MongoDB and MySQL database.

To avoid problems with microservices that try to connect to their databases before the database is up and running, the `product` and `recommendation` services are declared dependent on the MongoDB database, as follows:

```
depends_on:
  mongodb:
    condition: service_healthy
```

For the same reason, the review service is declared dependent on the mysql database:

```
depends_on:
  mysql:
    condition: service_healthy
```

This means that Docker Compose will not start up the microservice containers until the database containers are launched and reported healthy by their health checks.

Database connection configuration

With the database in place, we now need to set up the configuration for the core microservices so they know how to connect to their databases. This is set up in each core microservice's configuration file, `application.yml`, in the `product-service`, `recommendation-service`, and `review-service` projects.

The configuration for the `product` and `recommendation` services are similar, so we will only look into the configuration of the `product` service. The following part of the configuration is of interest:

```
spring.data.mongodb:
  host: localhost
  port: 27017
  database: product-db

logging:
 level:
 org.springframework.data.mongodb.core.MongoTemplate: DEBUG

---
spring.config.activate.on-profile: docker

spring.data.mongodb.host: mongodb
```

Important parts of the preceding code:

1. When running without Docker using the default Spring profile, the database is expected to be reachable on `localhost:27017`.
2. Setting the log level for `MongoTemplate` to `DEBUG` will allow us to see which MongoDB statements are executed in the log.
3. When running inside Docker using the Spring profile, `docker`, the database is expected to be reachable on `mongodb:27017`.

The configuration for the `review` service, which affects how it connects to its SQL database, looks like the following:

```
spring.jpa.hibernate.ddl-auto: update

spring.datasource:
  url: jdbc:mysql://localhost/review-db
  username: user
  password: pwd

spring.datasource.hikari.initializationFailTimeout: 60000

logging:
 level:
 org.hibernate.SQL: DEBUG
 org.hibernate.type.descriptor.sql.BasicBinder: TRACE

---
spring.config.activate.on-profile: docker

spring.datasource:
 url: jdbc:mysql://mysql/review-db
```

Explanations for the preceding code:

1. By default, Hibernate will be used by Spring Data JPA as the JPA Entity Manager.
2. The `spring.jpa.hibernate.ddl-auto` property is used to tell Spring Data JPA to create new or update existing SQL tables during startup.

Note: It is strongly recommended to set the `spring.jpa.hibernate.ddl-auto` property to `none` or `validate` in a production environment—this prevents Spring Data JPA from manipulating the structure of the SQL tables. For more information, see `https://docs.spring.io/spring-boot/docs/current/reference/htmlsingle/#howto-database-initialization`.

3. When running without Docker, using the default Spring profile, the database is expected to be reachable on `localhost` using the default port `3306`.

4. By default, HikariCP is used by Spring Data JPA as the JDBC connection pool. To minimize startup problems on computers with limited hardware resources, the `initializationFailTimeout` parameter is set to 60 seconds. This means that the Spring Boot application will wait for up to 60 seconds during startup to establish a database connection.
5. The log level settings for Hibernate will cause Hibernate to print the SQL statements used and the actual values used. Please note that when used in a production environment, writing the actual values to the log should be avoided for privacy reasons.
6. When running inside Docker using the Spring profile, `docker`, the database is expected to be reachable on the `mysql` hostname using the default port `3306`.

With this configuration in place, we are ready to start up the system landscape. But before we do that, let's learn how we can run database CLI tools.

The MongoDB and MySQL CLI tools

Once we have started to run some tests with the microservices, it will be interesting to see what data is actually stored in the microservices' databases. Each database Docker container comes with CLI-based tools that can be used to query the database tables and collections. To be able to run the database CLI tools, the Docker Compose `exec` command can be used.

The commands described in this section will be used when we get to the manual tests in the next section. Don't try to run them now; they will fail since we have no databases up and running yet!

To start the MongoDB CLI tool, `mongo`, inside the `mongodb` container, run the following command:

```
docker-compose exec mongodb mongo --quiet
>
```

Enter `exit` to leave the `mongo` CLI.

To start the MySQL CLI tool, `mysql`, inside the `mysql` container and log in to `review-db` using the user created at startup, run the following command:

```
docker-compose exec mysql mysql -uuser -p review-db
mysql>
```

The `mysql` CLI tool will prompt you for a password; you can find it in the `docker-compose.yml` file. Look for the value of the environment variable `MYSQL_PASSWORD`.

Enter `exit` to leave the `mysql` CLI.

We will see the usage of these tools in the next section.

If you prefer graphical database tools, you can run them locally as well, since both the MongoDB and the MySQL containers expose their standard ports on localhost.

Manual tests of the new APIs and the persistence layer

Now, we have everything in place to test the microservices together. We will build new Docker images and start up the system landscape using Docker Compose based on the Docker images. Next, we will use the Swagger UI viewer to run some manual tests. Finally, we will use the database CLI tools to see what data was inserted into the databases.

Build and start the system landscape with the following command:

```
cd $BOOK_HOME/Chapter06
./gradlew build && docker-compose build && docker-compose up
```

Open Swagger UI in a web browser, `http://localhost:8080/openapi/swagger-ui.html`, and perform the following steps on the web page:

1. Click on the **ProductComposite** service and the **POST** method to expand them
2. Click on the **Try it out** button and go down to the body field
3. Replace the default value, `0`, of the `productId` field with `123456`
4. Scroll down to the **Execute** button and click on it
5. Verify that the returned response code is **200**

The following is a sample screenshot after hitting the **Execute** button:

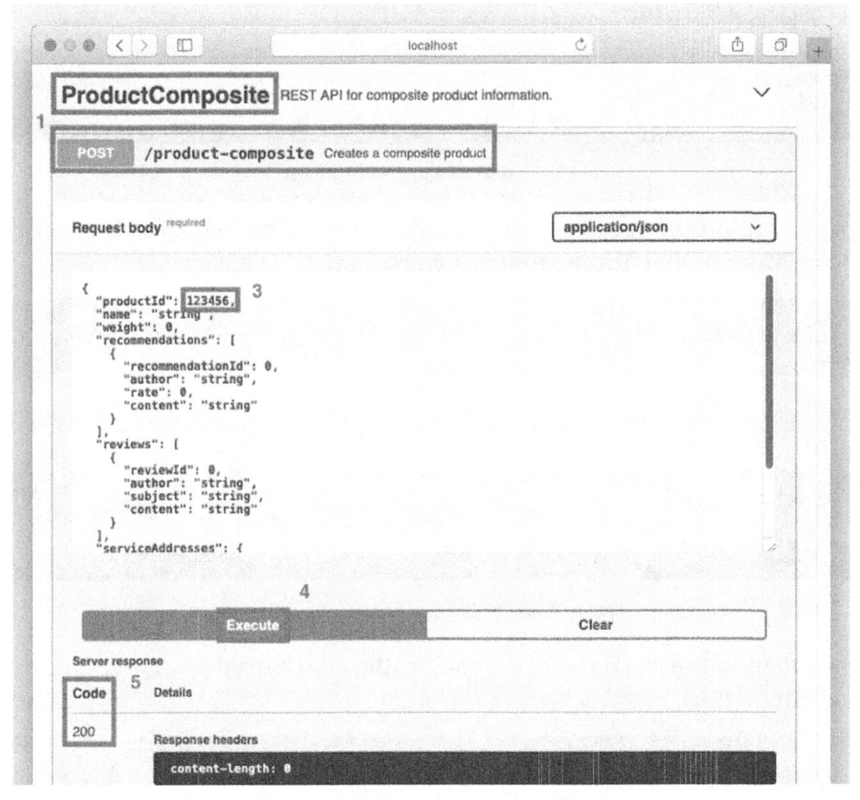

Figure 6.7: Testing the server response

In the log output from the `docker-compose up` command, we should be able to see output like the following (abbreviated for increased readability):

```
product-composite_1 | ... createCompositeProduct: creates a new composite entity for productId: 123456
product_1 | ... createProduct: entity created for productId: 123456
recommendation_1 | ... createRecommendation: created a recommendation entity: 123456/0
review_1 | ... createReview: created a review entity: 123456/0
```

Figure 6.8: Log output from docker-compose up

We can also use the database CLI tools to see the actual content in the different databases.

Look up content in the `product` service, that is, the `products` collection in MongoDB, with the following command:

```
docker-compose exec mongodb mongo product-db --quiet --eval "db.
products.find()"
```

Expect a response like this:

```
2. bash
{ "_id" : ObjectId("5c04ed370e8e3d000102ef94"), "version" : 0, "productId" : 123456, "name" : "string",
  "weight" : 0, "_class" : "se.magnus.microservices.core.product.persistence.ProductEntity" }
$
```

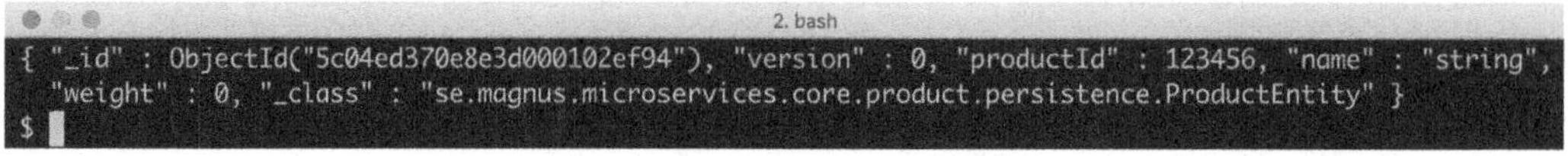

Figure 6.9: Looking up products

Look up content in the `recommendation` service, that is, the `recommendations` collection in MongoDB, with the following command:

```
docker-compose exec mongodb mongo recommendation-db --quiet --eval "db.
recommendations.find()"
```

Expect a response like this:

```
2. bash
{ "_id" : ObjectId("5c04ed378b87bc000133c349"), "version" : 0, "productId" : 123456,
  "recommendationId" : 0, "author" : "string", "rating" : 0, "content" : "string",
  "_class" : "se.magnus.microservices.core.recommendation.persistence.RecommendationEntity" }
$
```

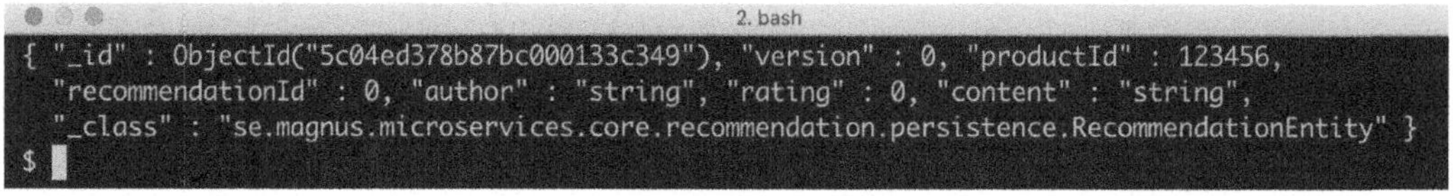

Figure 6.10: Looking up recommendations

Look up content in the `review` service, that is, the `reviews` table in MySQL, with the following command:

```
docker-compose exec mysql mysql -uuser -p review-db -e "select * from
reviews"
```

The `mysql` CLI tool will prompt you for a password; you can find it in the `docker-compose.yml` file. Look for the value of the environment variable `MYSQL_PASSWORD`. Expect a response like the following:

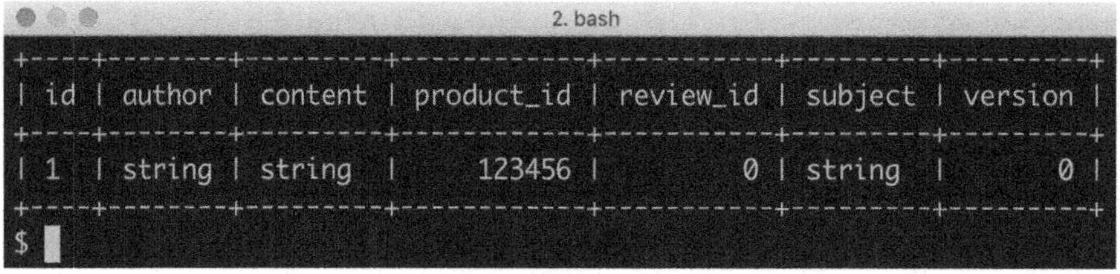

```
2. bash
+----+--------+---------+------------+-----------+---------+---------+
| id | author | content | product_id | review_id | subject | version |
+----+--------+---------+------------+-----------+---------+---------+
| 1  | string | string  |     123456 |         0 | string  |       0 |
+----+--------+---------+------------+-----------+---------+---------+
$
```

Figure 6.11: Looking up reviews

Bring down the system landscape by interrupting the `docker-compose up` command with *Ctrl* + *C*, followed by the command `docker-compose down`. After this, let us see how to update the automated tests in a microservice landscape.

Updating the automated tests of the microservice landscape

The automated tests of the microservice landscape, `test-em-all.bash`, need to be updated so that they ensure that the database of each microservice has a known state before it runs the tests.

The script is extended with a setup function, `setupTestdata()`, which uses the composite's create and delete APIs to set up test data used by the tests.

The `setupTestdata` function looks like this:

```
function setupTestdata() {

    body=\
    '{"productId":1,"name":"product 1","weight":1, "recommendations":[
        {"recommendationId":1,"author":"author
         1","rate":1,"content":"content 1"},
        {"recommendationId":2,"author":"author
         2","rate":2,"content":"content 2"},
        {"recommendationId":3,"author":"author
         3","rate":3,"content":"content 3"}
    ], "reviews":[
        {"reviewId":1,"author":"author 1","subject":"subject
         1","content":"content 1"},
        {"reviewId":2,"author":"author 2","subject":"subject
         2","content":"content 2"},
        {"reviewId":3,"author":"author 3","subject":"subject
         3","content":"content 3"}
    ]}'
    recreateComposite 1 "$body"

    body=\
    '{"productId":113,"name":"product 113","weight":113, "reviews":[
    {"reviewId":1,"author":"author 1","subject":"subject
     1","content":"content 1"},
    {"reviewId":2,"author":"author 2","subject":"subject
     2","content":"content 2"},
    {"reviewId":3,"author":"author 3","subject":"subject
     3","content":"content 3"}
]}'
    recreateComposite 113 "$body"
```

```
    body=\
    '{"productId":213,"name":"product 213","weight":213,
    "recommendations":[
        {"recommendationId":1,"author":"author
          1","rate":1,"content":"content 1"},
        {"recommendationId":2,"author":"author
         2","rate":2,"content":"content 2"},
        {"recommendationId":3,"author":"author
         3","rate":3,"content":"content 3"}
]}'
    recreateComposite 213 "$body"

}
```

It uses a helper function, `recreateComposite()`, to perform the actual requests to the delete and create APIs:

```
function recreateComposite() {
    local productId=$1
    local composite=$2

    assertCurl 200 "curl -X DELETE http://$HOST:$PORT/product-
    composite/${productId} -s"
    curl -X POST http://$HOST:$PORT/product-composite -H "Content-Type:
    application/json" --data "$composite"
}
```

The `setupTestdata` function is called directly after the `waitForService` function:

```
waitForService curl -X DELETE http://$HOST:$PORT/product-composite/13

setupTestdata
```

The main purpose of the `waitForService` function is to verify that all microservices are up and running. In the previous chapter, the get API on the composite product service was used. In this chapter, the delete API is used instead. When using the get API, only the `product` core microservice is called if the entity is not found; the `recommendation` and `review` services will not be called to verify that they are up and running. The call to the delete API will also ensure that the *Not Found* test on `productId 13` will succeed. In the next chapter, we will see how we can define specific APIs for checking the health state of a microservice landscape.

Execute the updated test script with the following command:

```
cd $BOOK_HOME/Chapter06
./test-em-all.bash start stop
```

The execution should end by writing a log message like this:

```
2. bash
End: Wed Dec 5 06:48:20 CET 2018
$
```

Figure 6.12: Log message at the end of test execution

This concludes the updates on the automated tests of the microservice landscape.

Summary

In this chapter, we have seen how we can use Spring Data to add a persistence layer to the core microservices. We used the core concepts of Spring Data, repositories, and entities to store data in both MongoDB and MySQL. The programming model is similar for a NoSQL database such as MongoDB and a SQL database such as MySQL, even though it's not fully portable. We have also seen how Spring Boot's annotations, `@DataMongoTest` and `@DataJpaTest`, can be used to conveniently set up tests targeted for persistence; this is where a database is started automatically before the test runs, but no other infrastructure that the microservice will need at runtime, for example, a web server such as Netty, is started up. To handle the startup and teardown of databases, we have used Testcontainers, which runs the databases in Docker containers. This results in persistence tests that are easy to set up and that start with minimum overhead.

We have also seen how the persistence layer can be used by the service layer and how we can add APIs for creating and deleting entities, both core and composite.

Finally, we learned how convenient it is to start up databases such as MongoDB and MySQL at runtime using Docker Compose and how to use the new create and delete APIs to set up test data before running automated tests of the microservice-based system landscape.

However, one major concern was identified in this chapter. Updating (creating or deleting) a composite entity—an entity whose parts are stored in a number of microservices—using synchronous APIs can lead to inconsistencies, if not all involved microservices are updated successfully. This is, in general, not acceptable. This leads us into the next chapter, where we will look into why and how to build reactive microservices, that is, microservices that are scalable and robust.

Questions

1. Spring Data, a common programming model based on entities and repositories, can be used for different types of database engines. From the source code examples in this chapter, what are the most important differences in the persistence code for MySQL and MongoDB?
2. What is required to implement optimistic locking using Spring Data?
3. What is MapStruct used for?
4. What does it mean if an operation is idempotent and why is that useful?
5. How can we access the data that is stored in the MySQL and MongoDB databases without using the API?

7

Developing Reactive Microservices

In this chapter, we will learn how to develop reactive microservices, that is, how to develop non-blocking synchronous REST APIs and asynchronous event-driven services. We will also learn about how to choose between these two alternatives. Finally, we will see how to create and run manual and automated tests of a reactive microservice landscape.

As already described in *Chapter 1, Introduction to Microservices*, the foundation for reactive systems is that they are message-driven—they use asynchronous communication. This enables them to be elastic, in other words, scalable and resilient, meaning that they will be tolerant of failures. Elasticity and resilience together will enable a reactive system to be responsive.

The following topics will be covered in this chapter:

- Choosing between non-blocking synchronous APIs and event-driven asynchronous services
- Developing non-blocking synchronous REST APIs
- Developing event-driven asynchronous services
- Running manual tests of the reactive microservice landscape
- Running automated tests of the reactive microservice landscape

Technical requirements

For instructions on how to install tools used in this book and how to access the source code for this book, see:

- *Chapter 21* for macOS
- *Chapter 22* for Windows

The code examples in this chapter all come from the source code in `$BOOK_HOME/Chapter07`.

If you want to view the changes applied to the source code in this chapter, that is, see what it takes to make the microservices reactive, you can compare it with the source code for *Chapter 6, Adding Persistence*. You can use your favorite `diff` tool and compare the two folders, that is, `$BOOK_HOME/Chapter06` and `$BOOK_HOME/Chapter07`.

Choosing between non-blocking synchronous APIs and event-driven asynchronous services

When developing reactive microservices, it is not always obvious when to use non-blocking synchronous APIs and when to use event-driven asynchronous services. In general, to make a microservice robust and scalable, it is important to make it as autonomous as possible, for example, by minimizing its runtime dependencies. This is also known as **loose coupling**. Therefore, asynchronous message passing of events is preferable over synchronous APIs. This is because the microservice will only depend on access to the messaging system at runtime, instead of being dependent on synchronous access to a number of other microservices.

There are, however, a number of cases where synchronous APIs could be favorable. For example:

- For read operations where an end user is waiting for a response
- Where the client platforms are more suitable for consuming synchronous APIs, for example, mobile apps or SPA web applications
- Where the clients will connect to the service from other organizations – where it might be hard to agree on a common messaging system to use across organizations

For the system landscape in this book, we will use the following:

- The create, read, and delete services exposed by the product composite microservice will be based on non-blocking synchronous APIs. The composite microservice is assumed to have clients on both web and mobile platforms, as well as clients coming from other organizations rather than the ones that operate the system landscape. Therefore, synchronous APIs seem like a natural match.
- The read services provided by the core microservices will also be developed as non-blocking synchronous APIs since there is an end user waiting for their responses.
- The create and delete services provided by the core microservices will be developed as event-driven asynchronous services, meaning that they will listen for create and delete events on topics dedicated to each microservice.
- The synchronous APIs provided by the composite microservices to create and delete aggregated product information will publish create and delete events on these topics. If the publish operation succeeds, it will return with a 202 (Accepted) response, otherwise an error response will be returned. The 202 response differs from a normal 200 (OK) response - it indicates that the request has been accepted, but not fully processed. Instead, the processing will be completed asynchronously and independently of the 202 response.

This is illustrated by the following diagram:

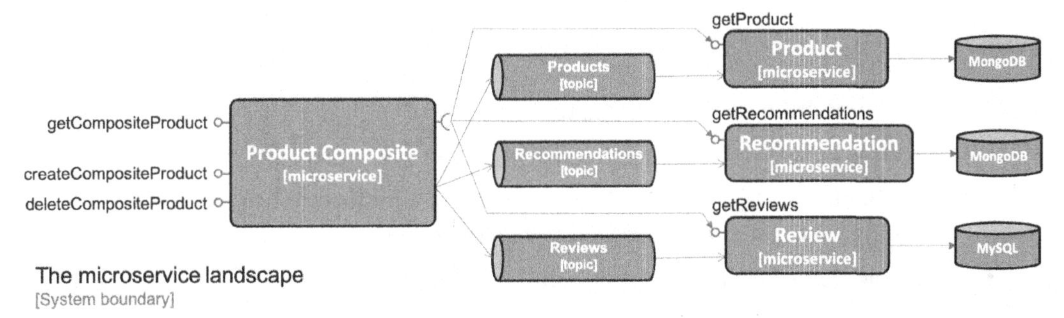

Figure 7.1: The microservice landscape

First, let's learn how we can develop non-blocking synchronous REST APIs, and thereafter, we will look at how to develop event-driven asynchronous services.

Developing non-blocking synchronous REST APIs

In this section, we will learn how to develop non-blocking versions of the read APIs. The composite service will make reactive, that is, non-blocking, calls in parallel to the three core services. When the composite service has received responses from all of the core services, it will create a composite response and send it back to the caller. This is illustrated in the following diagram:

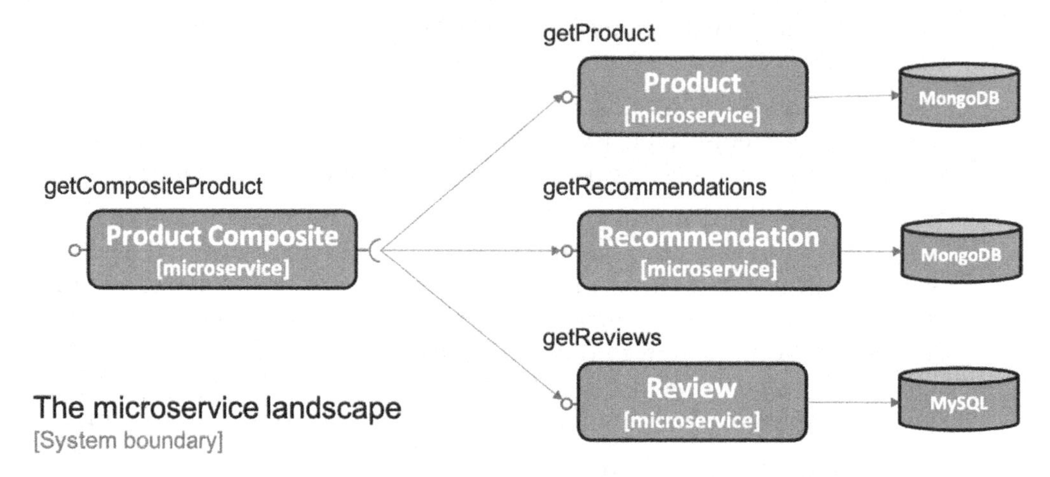

Figure 7.2: The getCompositeProduct part of the landscape

In this section, we will cover the following:

- An introduction to Project Reactor
- Non-blocking persistence using Spring Data for MongoDB
- Non-blocking REST APIs in the core services, including how to handle blocking code for the JPA-based persistence layer
- Non-blocking REST APIs in the composite service

An introduction to Project Reactor

As we mentioned in the *Spring WebFlux* section in *Chapter 2, Introduction to Spring Boot*, the reactive support in Spring 5 is based on **Project Reactor** (`https://projectreactor.io`). Project Reactor is based on the *Reactive Streams specification* (`http://www.reactive-streams.org`), a standard for building reactive applications. Project Reactor is fundamental – it is what Spring WebFlux, Spring WebClient, and Spring Data rely on to provide their reactive and non-blocking features.

The programming model is based on processing streams of data, and the core data types in Project Reactor are **Flux** and **Mono**. A `Flux` object is used to process a stream of *0...n* elements and a `Mono` object is used to process a stream that either is empty or returns at most one element. We will see numerous examples of their usage in this chapter. As a short introduction, let's look at the following test:

```
@Test
void testFlux() {

  List<Integer> list = Flux.just(1, 2, 3, 4)
    .filter(n -> n % 2 == 0)
    .map(n -> n * 2)
    .log()
    .collectList().block();

  assertThat(list).containsExactly(4, 8);
}
```

Here is an explanation of the preceding source code:

1. We initiate the stream with the integers `1`, `2`, `3`, and `4` using the static helper method `Flux.just()`.
2. Next, we `filter` out the odd numbers – we only allow even numbers to proceed through the stream. In this test, these are `2` and `4`.
3. Next, we transform (or `map`) the values in the stream by multiplying them by `2`, so they become `4` and `8`.
4. Then, we `log` the data that flows through the stream after the `map` operation.
5. We use the `collectList` method to collect all items from the stream into a `List`, emitted once the stream completes.
6. So far, we have only declared the processing of a stream. To actually get the stream processed, we need someone to subscribe to it. The final call to the `block` method will register a subscriber that waits for the processing to complete.
7. The resulting list is saved in a member variable named `list`.
8. We can now wrap up the test by using the `assertThat` method to assert that `list` after the processing of the stream contains the expected result – the integers `4` and `8`.

The log output will look like the following:

```
20:01:45.714 [main] INFO reactor.Flux.MapFuseable.1 - | onSubscribe([Fuseable] FluxMapFuseable.MapFuseableSubscriber)
20:01:45.716 [main] INFO reactor.Flux.MapFuseable.1 - | request(unbounded)
20:01:45.716 [main] INFO reactor.Flux.MapFuseable.1 - | onNext(4)
20:01:45.717 [main] INFO reactor.Flux.MapFuseable.1 - | onNext(8)
20:01:45.717 [main] INFO reactor.Flux.MapFuseable.1 - | onComplete()
```

Figure 7.3: Log output for the code above

From the preceding log output, we can see that:

1. The processing of the stream is started by a subscriber that subscribes to the stream and requests its content.
2. Next, the integers `4` and `8` pass through the `log` operation.
3. The processing concludes with a call to the `onComplete` method on the subscriber, notifying it that the stream has come to an end.

For the full source code, see the `ReactorTests` test class in the `util` project.

Normally, we don't initiate the processing of the stream. Instead, we only define how it will be processed, and it will be the responsibility of an infrastructure component to initiate the processing. For example, Spring WebFlux will do this as a response to an incoming HTTP request. An exception to this rule of thumb is the case where blocking code needs a response from a reactive stream. In these cases, the blocking code can call the `block()` method on the `Flux` or `Mono` object to get the response in a blocking way.

Non-blocking persistence using Spring Data for MongoDB

Making the MongoDB-based repositories for the `product` and `recommendation` services reactive is very simple:

- Change the base class for the repositories to `ReactiveCrudRepository`
- Change the custom finder methods to return either a `Mono` or a `Flux` object

`ProductRepository` and `RecommendationRepository` look like the following after the change:

```
public interface ProductRepository extends ReactiveCrudRepository
<ProductEntity, String> {
    Mono<ProductEntity> findByProductId(int productId);
}

public interface RecommendationRepository extends ReactiveCrudRepository
<RecommendationEntity, String> {
    Flux<RecommendationEntity> findByProductId(int productId);
}
```

No changes are applied to the persistence code for the `review` service; it will remain blocking using the JPA repository. See the following section *Dealing with blocking code* for how to handle the blocking code in the persistence layer of the `review` service.

For the full source code, take a look at the following classes:

- `ProductRepository` in the `product` project
- `RecommendationRepository` in the `recommendation` project

Changes in the test code

When it comes to testing the persistence layer, we have to make some changes. Since our persistence methods now return a `Mono` or `Flux` object, the test methods have to wait for the response to be available in the returned reactive objects. The test methods can either use an explicit call to the `block()` method on the `Mono`/`Flux` object to wait until a response is available, or they can use the `StepVerifier` helper class from Project Reactor to declare a verifiable sequence of asynchronous events.

Let's see how we can change the following test code to work for the reactive version of the repository:

```
ProductEntity foundEntity = repository.findById(newEntity.getId()).get();
assertEqualsProduct(newEntity, foundEntity);
```

We can use the `block()` method on the `Mono` object returned by the `repository.findById()` method and keep the imperative programming style, as shown here:

```
ProductEntity foundEntity = repository.findById(newEntity.getId()).
block();
assertEqualsProduct(newEntity, foundEntity);
```

Alternatively, we can use the `StepVerifier` class to set up a sequence of processing steps that both executes the repository find operation and also verifies the result. The sequence is initialized by the final call to the `verifyComplete()` method like this:

```
StepVerifier.create(repository.findById(newEntity.getId()))
  .expectNextMatches(foundEntity -> areProductEqual(newEntity, 
foundEntity))
  .verifyComplete();
```

For examples of tests that use the `StepVerifier` class, see the `PersistenceTests` test class in the `product` project.

For corresponding examples of tests that use the `block()` method, see the `PersistenceTests` test class in the `recommendation` project.

Non-blocking REST APIs in the core services

With a non-blocking persistence layer in place, it's time to make the APIs in the core services non-blocking as well. We need to make the following changes:

- Change the APIs so that they only return reactive data types
- Change the service implementations so they don't contain any blocking code
- Change our tests so that they can test the reactive services
- Deal with blocking code – isolate the code that still needs to be blocking from the non-blocking code

Changes in the APIs

To make the APIs of the core services reactive, we need to update their methods so that they return either a `Mono` or `Flux` object.

For example, `getProduct()` in the `product` service now returns `Mono<Product>` instead of a `Product` object:

```
Mono<Product> getProduct(@PathVariable int productId);
```

For the full source code, take a look at the following `core` interfaces in the `api` project:

- `ProductService`
- `RecommendationService`
- `ReviewService`

Changes in the service implementations

For the implementations of the services in the `product` and `recommendation` projects, which use a reactive persistence layer, we can use the fluent API in Project Reactor. For example, the implementation of the `getProduct()` method looks like the following code:

```
public Mono<Product> getProduct(int productId) {

    if (productId < 1) {
      throw new InvalidInputException("Invalid productId: " + productId);
    }

    return repository.findByProductId(productId)
        .switchIfEmpty(Mono.error(new NotFoundException("No product found
         for productId: " + productId)))
        .log(LOG.getName(), FINE)
        .map(e -> mapper.entityToApi(e))
        .map(e -> setServiceAddress(e));
}
```

Let's examine what the code does:

1. The method will return a `Mono` object; the processing is only declared here. The processing is triggered by the web framework, Spring WebFlux, subscribing to the `Mono` object once it receives a request to this service!
2. A product will be retrieved using its `productId` from the underlying database using the `findByProductId()` method in the persistence repository.
3. If no product is found for the given `productId`, a `NotFoundException` will be thrown.
4. The `log` method will produce log output.
5. The `mapper.entityToApi()` method will be called to transform the returned entity from the persistence layer to an API model object.
6. The final `map` method will use a helper method, `setServiceAddress()`, to set the DNS name and IP address of the microservices that processed the request in the `serviceAddress` field of the model object.

Some sample log output for a successful processing is as follows:

```
-bash
2021-01-30 10:09:47.006 INFO 62314 --- [ctor-http-nio-2] reactor.Mono.SwitchIfEmpty.1 : onSubscribe(FluxSwitchIfEmpty
.SwitchIfEmptySubscriber)
2021-01-30 10:09:47.007 INFO 62314 --- [ctor-http-nio-2] reactor.Mono.SwitchIfEmpty.1 : request(unbounded)
2021-01-30 10:09:47.034 INFO 62314 --- [ntLoopGroup-2-2] reactor.Mono.SwitchIfEmpty.1 : onNext(ProductEntity: 1)
2021-01-30 10:09:47.048 INFO 62314 --- [ntLoopGroup-2-2] reactor.Mono.SwitchIfEmpty.1 : onComplete()
```

Figure 7.4: Log output when processing is successful

The following is a sample log output of a failed processing (throwing a `NotFoundException`):

```
-bash
2021-01-30 10:09:52.643 INFO 62314 --- [ctor-http-nio-3] reactor.Mono.SwitchIfEmpty.2 : onSubscribe(FluxSwitchIfEmpty.SwitchIfEmptySubscriber)
2021-01-30 10:09:52.643 INFO 62314 --- [ctor-http-nio-3] reactor.Mono.SwitchIfEmpty.2 : request(unbounded)
2021-01-30 10:09:52.648 ERROR 62314 --- [ntLoopGroup-2-2] reactor.Mono.SwitchIfEmpty.2 : onError(se.magnus.util.exceptions.NotFoundException:
No product found for productId: 2)
2021-01-30 10:09:52.654 ERROR 62314 --- [ntLoopGroup-2-2] reactor.Mono.SwitchIfEmpty.2 :

se.magnus.util.exceptions.NotFoundException: No product found for productId: 2
  at se.magnus.microservices.core.product.services.ProductServiceImpl.getProduct(ProductServiceImpl.java:58) ~[classes/:na]
    ...
```

Figure 7.5: Log output when processing fails

For the full source code, see the following classes:

- `ProductServiceImpl` in the `product` project
- `RecommendationServiceImpl` in the `recommendation` project

Changes in the test code

The test code for service implementations has been changed in the same way as the tests for the persistence layer we described previously. To handle the asynchronous behavior of the reactive return types, `Mono` and `Flux`, the tests use a mix of calling the `block()` method and using the `StepVerifier` helper class.

For the full source code, see the following test classes:

- `ProductServiceApplicationTests` in the `product` project
- `RecommendationServiceApplicationTests` in the `recommendation` project

Dealing with blocking code

In the case of the `review` service, which uses JPA to access its data in a relational database, we don't have support for a non-blocking programming model. Instead, we can run the blocking code using a `Scheduler`, which is capable of running the blocking code on a thread from a dedicated thread pool with a limited number of threads. Using a thread pool for the blocking code avoids draining the available threads in the microservice and avoids affecting concurrent non-blocking processing in the microservice, if there is any.

Let's see how this can be set up in the following steps:

1. First, we configure a scheduler bean and its thread pool in the main class `ReviewServiceApplication`, as follows:

   ```
   @Autowired
   public ReviewServiceApplication(
     @Value("${app.threadPoolSize:10}") Integer threadPoolSize,
     @Value("${app.taskQueueSize:100}") Integer taskQueueSize
   ) {
     this.threadPoolSize = threadPoolSize;
     this.taskQueueSize = taskQueueSize;
   }

   @Bean
   public Scheduler jdbcScheduler() {
     return Schedulers.newBoundedElastic(threadPoolSize,
       taskQueueSize, "jdbc-pool");
   }
   ```

   From the preceding code we can see that the scheduler bean is named `jdbcScheduler` and that we can configure its thread pool using the following properties:

   - `app.threadPoolSize`, specifying the max number of threads in the pool; defaults to `10`
   - `app.taskQueueSize`, specifying the max number of tasks that are allowed to be placed in a queue waiting for available threads; defaults to `100`

2. Next, we inject the scheduler named `jdbcScheduler` into the `review` service implementation class, as shown here:

   ```
   @RestController
   public class ReviewServiceImpl implements ReviewService {

     private final Scheduler jdbcScheduler;

     @Autowired
     public ReviewServiceImpl(
       @Qualifier("jdbcScheduler")
       Scheduler jdbcScheduler, ...) {
       this.jdbcScheduler = jdbcScheduler;
     }
   ```

3. Finally, we use the scheduler's thread pool in the reactive implementation of the `getReviews()` method, like so:

```
@Override
public Flux<Review> getReviews(int productId) {

  if (productId < 1) {
    throw new InvalidInputException("Invalid productId: " +
      productId);
  }

  LOG.info("Will get reviews for product with id={}",
    productId);

  return Mono.fromCallable(() -> internalGetReviews(productId))
    .flatMapMany(Flux::fromIterable)
    .log(LOG.getName(), FINE)
    .subscribeOn(jdbcScheduler);
}

private List<Review> internalGetReviews(int productId) {

  List<ReviewEntity> entityList = repository.
    findByProductId(productId);
  List<Review> list = mapper.entityListToApiList(entityList);
  list.forEach(e -> e.setServiceAddress(serviceUtil.
    getServiceAddress()));

  LOG.debug("Response size: {}", list.size());

  return list;
}
```

Here, the blocking code is placed in the `internalGetReviews()` method and is wrapped in a `Mono` object using the `Mono.fromCallable()` method. The `getReviews()` method uses the `subscribeOn()` method to run the blocking code in a thread from the thread pool of `jdbcScheduler`.

When we run tests later on in this chapter, we can look in the log output from the `review` service and see proofs that SQL statements are run in threads from the scheduler's dedicated pool. We will be able to see log output like this:

```
2021-04-05 09:24:13.376  INFO --- [ctor-http-nio-4] s.m.m.c.r.services.ReviewServiceImpl:
  Will get reviews for product with id=1
2021-04-05 09:24:13.423 DEBUG --- [    jdbc-pool-1] org.hibernate.SQL                   :
  select ... from reviews reviewenti0_ where reviewenti0_.product_id=?
```

Figure 7.6: Log output from the review service

From the preceding log output, we can see the following:

- The first log output is from the `LOG.info()` call in the `getReviews()` method and it is executed on an HTTP thread, named `ctor-http-nio-4`, a thread used by WebFlux.
- In the second log output, we can see the SQL statement generated by Spring Data JPA, using Hibernate under the hood. The SQL statement corresponds to the method call `repository.findByProductId()`. It is executed on a thread named `jdbc-pool-1`, meaning it is executed in a thread from the dedicated thread pool for blocking code, as expected!

For the full source code, see the `ReviewServiceApplication` and `ReviewServiceImpl` classes in the `review` project.

With the logic for handling blocking code in place, we are done with implementing the non-blocking REST APIs in the core services. Let's move on and see how to also make the REST APIs in the composite services non-blocking.

Non-blocking REST APIs in the composite services

To make our REST API in the composite service non-blocking, we need to do the following:

- Change the API so that its operations only return reactive datatypes
- Change the service implementation so it calls the core services' APIs in parallel and in a non-blocking way
- Change the integration layer so it uses a non-blocking HTTP client
- Change our tests so that they can test the reactive service

Changes in the API

To make the API of the composite service reactive, we need to apply the same type of change that we applied for the APIs of the core services we described previously. This means that the return type of the `getProduct()` method, `ProductAggregate`, needs to be replaced with `Mono<ProductAggregate>`. The `createProduct()` and `deleteProduct()` methods need to be updated to return a `Mono<Void>` instead of a `void`, otherwise we can't propagate any error responses back to the callers of the API.

For the full source code, see the `ProductCompositeService` interface in the `api` project.

Changes in the service implementation

To be able to call the three APIs in parallel, the service implementation uses the static `zip()` method on the `Mono` class. The `zip` method is capable of handling a number of parallel reactive requests and zipping them together once they all are complete. The code looks like this:

```
@Override
public Mono<ProductAggregate> getProduct(int productId) {
  return Mono.zip(

    values -> createProductAggregate(
      (Product) values[0],
      (List<Recommendation>) values[1],
      (List<Review>) values[2],
      serviceUtil.getServiceAddress()),

    integration.getProduct(productId),
    integration.getRecommendations(productId).collectList(),
    integration.getReviews(productId).collectList())

    .doOnError(ex ->
      LOG.warn("getCompositeProduct failed: {}",
      ex.toString()))
    .log(LOG.getName(), FINE);
}
```

Let's take a closer look:

- The first parameter of the `zip` method is a lambda function that will receive the responses in an array, named `values`. The array will contain a product, a list of recommendations, and a list of reviews. The actual aggregation of the responses from the three API calls is handled by the same helper method as before, `createProductAggregate()`, without any changes.

- The parameters after the lambda function are a list of the requests that the `zip` method will call in parallel, one `Mono` object per request. In our case, we send in three `Mono` objects that were created by the methods in the integration class, one for each request that is sent to each core microservice.

For the full source code, see the `ProductCompositeServiceImpl` class in the `product-composite` project.

For information on how the `createProduct` and `deleteProduct` API operations are implemented in the `product-composite` service, see the *Publishing events in the composite service* section later on.

Changes in the integration layer

In the `ProductCompositeIntegration` integration class, we have replaced the blocking HTTP client, `RestTemplate`, with a non-blocking HTTP client, `WebClient`, that comes with Spring 5.

To create a `WebClient` instance, a **builder pattern** is used. If customization is required, for example, setting up common headers or filters, it can be done using the builder. For the available configuration options, see `https://docs.spring.io/spring/docs/current/spring-framework-reference/web-reactive.html#webflux-client-builder`.

The `WebClient` is used as follows:

1. In the constructor, the `WebClient` is auto-injected. We build the `WebClient` instance without any configuration:

```
public class ProductCompositeIntegration implements
ProductService, RecommendationService, ReviewService {

    private final WebClient webClient;

    @Autowired
    public ProductCompositeIntegration(
        WebClient.Builder webClient, ...
    ) {
        this.webClient = webClient.build();
    }
```

2. Next, we use the `webClient` instance to make our non-blocking requests for calling the `product` service:

```
@Override
public Mono<Product> getProduct(int productId) {
  String url = productServiceUrl + "/product/" + productId;

  return webClient.get().uri(url).retrieve()
    .bodyToMono(Product.class)
    .log(LOG.getName(), FINE)
    .onErrorMap(WebClientResponseException.class,
      ex -> handleException(ex)
    );
}
```

If the API call to the `product` service fails with an HTTP error response, the whole API request will fail. The `onErrorMap()` method in `WebClient` will call our `handleException(ex)` method, which maps the HTTP exceptions thrown by the HTTP layer to our own exceptions, for example, a `NotFoundException` or a `InvalidInputException`.

However, if calls to the `product` service succeed but the call to either the `recommendation` or `review` API fails, we don't want to let the whole request fail. Instead, we want to return as much information as is available back to the caller. Therefore, instead of propagating an exception in these cases, we will instead return an empty list of recommendations or reviews. To suppress the error, we will make the call `onErrorResume(error -> empty())`. For this, the code looks like the following:

```
@Override
public Flux<Recommendation> getRecommendations(int productId) {

  String url = recommendationServiceUrl + "/recommendation?
  productId=" + productId;

  // Return an empty result if something goes wrong to make it
  // possible for the composite service to return partial responses
  return webClient.get().uri(url).retrieve()
    .bodyToFlux(Recommendation.class)
    .log(LOG.getName(), FINE)
    .onErrorResume(error -> empty());
}
```

The `GlobalControllerExceptionHandler` class, from the `util` project, will as previously catch exceptions and transform them to proper HTTP error responses that are sent back to the caller of the composite API. This way we can decide if a specific HTTP error response from the underlying API calls will result in an HTTP error response or just a partly empty response.

For the full source code, see the `ProductCompositeIntegration` class in the `product-composite` project.

Changes in the test code

The only change that's required in the test classes is to update the setup of Mockito and its mock of the integration class. The mock needs to return `Mono` and `Flux` objects. The `setup()` method uses the helper methods `Mono.just()` and `Flux.fromIterable()`, as shown in the following code:

```
class ProductCompositeServiceApplicationTests {

    @BeforeEach
    void setUp() {

        when(compositeIntegration.getProduct(PRODUCT_ID_OK)).
            thenReturn(Mono.just(new Product(PRODUCT_ID_OK, "name", 1,
             "mock-address")));

        when(compositeIntegration.getRecommendations(PRODUCT_ID_OK)).
            thenReturn(Flux.fromIterable(singletonList(new
             Recommendation(PRODUCT_ID_OK, 1, "author", 1, "content",
             "mock address"))));

        when(compositeIntegration.getReviews(PRODUCT_ID_OK)).
            thenReturn(Flux.fromIterable(singletonList(new
             Review(PRODUCT_ID_OK, 1, "author", "subject", "content",
             "mock address"))));
```

For the full source code, see the `ProductCompositeServiceApplicationTests` test class in the `product-composite` project.

This completes the implementation of our non-blocking synchronous REST APIs. Now it is time to develop our event-driven asynchronous services.

Developing event-driven asynchronous services

In this section, we will learn how to develop event-driven and asynchronous versions of the create and delete services. The composite service will publish create and delete events on each core service topic and then return an OK response back to the caller without waiting for processing to take place in the core services. This is illustrated in the following diagram:

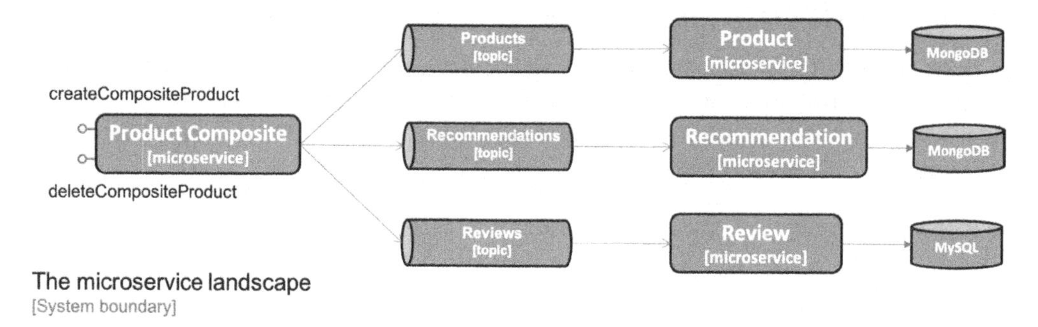

Figure 7.7: The createCompositeProduct and deleteCompositeProduct parts of the landscape

We will cover the following topics:

- Handling challenges with messaging
- Defining topics and events
- Changes in Gradle build files
- Consuming events in the core services
- Publishing events in the composite service

Handling challenges with messaging

To implement the event-driven create and delete services, we will use Spring Cloud Stream. In *Chapter 2, Introduction to Spring Boot*, we have already seen how easy it is to publish and consume messages on a topic using Spring Cloud Stream. The programming model is based on a functional paradigm, where functions implementing one of the functional interfaces `Supplier`, `Function`, or `Consumer` in the package `java.util.function` can be chained together to perform decoupled event-based processing. To trigger such functional-based processing externally, from non-functional code, the helper class `StreamBridge` can be used.

For example, to publish the body of an HTTP request to a topic, we only have to write the following:

```
@Autowired
private StreamBridge streamBridge;

@PostMapping
void sampleCreateAPI(@RequestBody String body) {
  streamBridge.send("topic", body);
}
```

The helper class `StreamBridge` is used to trigger the processing. It will publish a message on a topic. A function that consumes events from a topic (not creating new events) can be defined by implementing the functional interface `java.util.function.Consumer` as:

```
@Bean
public Consumer<String> mySubscriber() {
   return s -> System.out.println("ML RECEIVED: " + s);
}
```

To tie the various functions together, we use configuration. We will see examples of such configuration below in the sections *Adding configuration for publishing events* and *Adding configuration for consuming events*.

This programming model can be used independently of the messaging system used, for example, RabbitMQ or Apache Kafka!

Even though sending asynchronous messages is preferred over synchronous API calls, it comes with challenges of its own. We will see how we can use Spring Cloud Stream to handle some of them. The following features in Spring Cloud Stream will be covered:

- Consumer groups
- Retries and dead-letter queues
- Guaranteed orders and partitions

We'll study each of these in the following sections.

Consumer groups

The problem here is, if we scale up the number of instances of a message consumer, for example, if we start two instances of the `product` microservice, both instances of the `product` microservice will consume the same messages, as illustrated by the following diagram:

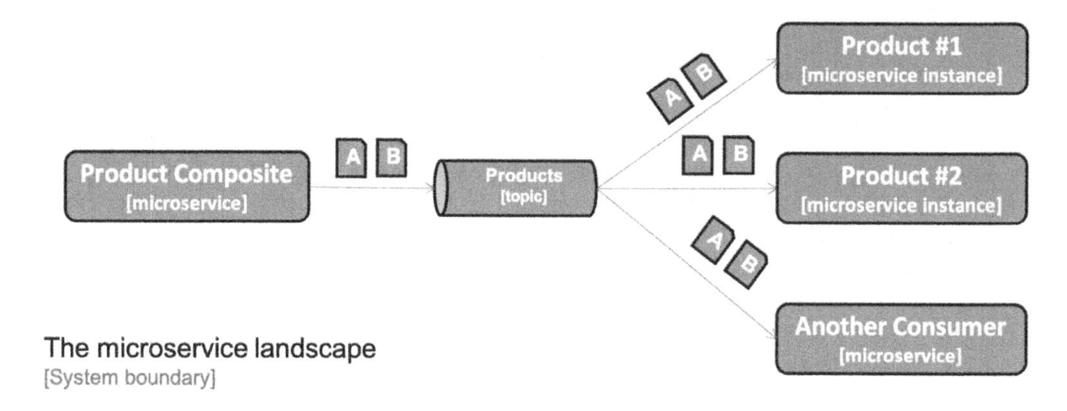

Figure 7.8: Products #1 and #2 consuming the same messages

This could result in one message being processed two times, potentially leading to duplicates or other undesired inconsistencies in the database. Therefore, we only want one instance per consumer to process each message. This can be solved by introducing a **consumer group**, as illustrated by the following diagram:

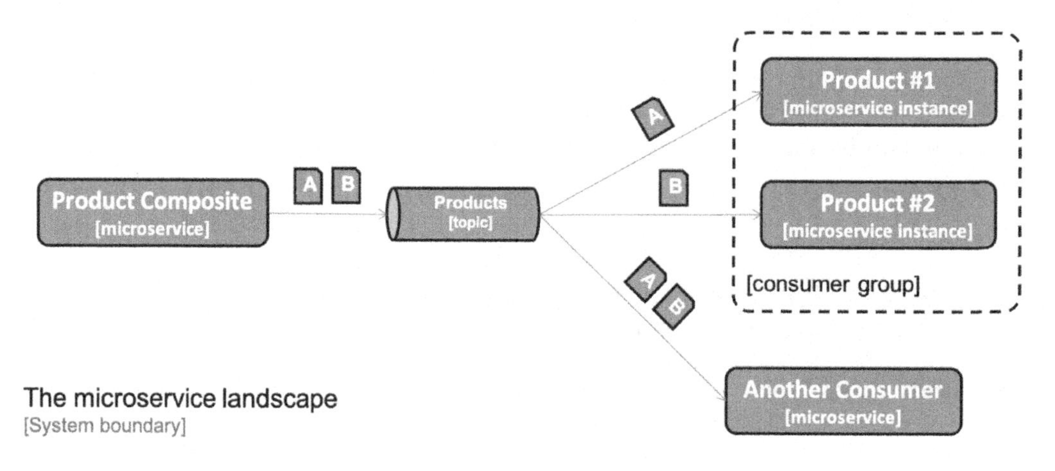

Figure 7.9: Consumer group

In Spring Cloud Stream, a consumer group can be configured on the consumer side. For example, for the `product` microservice it will look like this:

```
spring.cloud.stream:
  bindings.messageProcessor-in-0:
    destination: products
    group: productsGroup
```

From this configuration, we can learn the following:

- Spring Cloud Stream applies, by default, a naming convention for binding a configuration to a function. For messages sent to a function, the binding name is `<functionName>-in-<index>`:
    - `functionName` being the name of the function, `messageProcessor` in the preceding example.
    - `index` being set to `0`, unless the function requires multiple input or output arguments. We will not use multi-argument functions, so `index` will always be set to `0` in our examples.
    - For outgoing messages, the binding name convention is `<functionName>-out-<index>`.
- The `destination` property specifies the name of the topic that messages will be consumed from, `products` in this case.
- The `group` property specifies what consumer group to add instances of the `product` microservice to, `productsGroup` in this example. This means that messages sent to the `products` topic will only be delivered by Spring Cloud Stream to one of the instances of the `product` microservice.

Retries and dead-letter queues

If a consumer fails to process a message, it may be requeued for the failing consumer until it is successfully processed. If the content of the message is invalid, also known as a **poisoned message**, the message will block the consumer from processing other messages until it is manually removed. If the failure is due to a temporary problem, for example, the database can't be reached due to a temporary network error, the processing will probably succeed after a number of retries.

It must be possible to specify the number of retries until a message is moved to another storage for fault analysis and correction. A failing message is typically moved to a dedicated queue called a dead-letter queue. To avoid overloading the infrastructure during temporary failure, for example, a network error, it must be possible to configure how often retries are performed, preferably with an increasing length of time between each retry.

In Spring Cloud Stream, this can be configured on the consumer side, for example, for the `product` microservice, as shown here:

```
spring.cloud.stream.bindings.messageProcessor-in-0.consumer:
  maxAttempts: 3
  backOffInitialInterval: 500
  backOffMaxInterval: 1000
  backOffMultiplier: 2.0

spring.cloud.stream.rabbit.bindings.messageProcessor-in-0.consumer:
  autoBindDlq: true
  republishToDlq: true

spring.cloud.stream.kafka.bindings.messageProcessor-in-0.consumer:
  enableDlq: true
```

In the preceding example, we specify that Spring Cloud Stream should perform `3` retries before placing a message on the dead-letter queue. The first retry will be attempted after `500` ms and the two other attempts after `1000` ms.

Enabling the use of dead-letter queues is binding-specific; therefore, we have one configuration for RabbitMQ and one for Kafka.

Guaranteed order and partitions

If the business logic requires that messages are consumed and processed in the same order as they were sent, we cannot use multiple instances per consumer to increase processing performance; for example, we cannot use consumer groups. This might, in some cases, lead to an unacceptable latency in the processing of incoming messages.

We can use **partitions** to ensure that messages are delivered in the same order as they were sent but without losing performance and scalability.

In most cases, strict order in the processing of messages is only required for messages that affect the same business entities. For example, messages affecting the product with product ID `1` can, in many cases, be processed independently of messages that affect the product with product ID `2`. This means that the order only needs to be guaranteed for messages that have the same product ID.

The solution to this is to make it possible to specify a **key** for each message, which the messaging system can use to guarantee that the order is kept between messages with the same key. This can be solved by introducing sub-topics, also known as **partitions**, in a topic. The messaging system places messages in a specific partition based on its key.

Messages with the same key are always placed in the same partition. The messaging system only needs to guarantee the delivery order for messages in the same partition. To ensure the order of the messages, we configure one consumer instance per partition within a consumer group. By increasing the number of partitions, we can allow a consumer to increase its number of instances. This increases its message processing performance without losing the delivery order. This is illustrated in the following diagram:

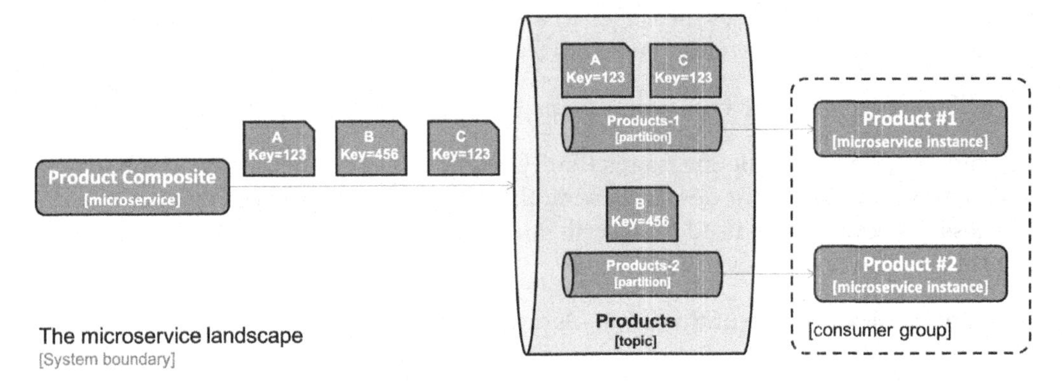

Figure 7.10: Specifying keys for messages

As seen in the preceding diagram, all messages with the `Key` set to `123` always go to the partition `Products-1`, while messages with the `Key` set to `456` go to the partition `Products-2`.

In Spring Cloud Stream, this needs to be configured on both the publisher and consumer sides. On the publisher side, the key and number of partitions must be specified. For example, for the `product-composite` service, we have the following:

```
spring.cloud.stream.bindings.products-out-0.producer:
  partition-key-expression: headers['partitionKey']
  partition-count: 2
```

This configuration means that the key will be taken from the message header with the name `partitionKey` and that two partitions will be used.

Each consumer can specify which partition it wants to consume messages from. For example, for the `product` microservice, we have the following:

```
spring.cloud.stream.bindings.messageProcessor-in-0:
  destination: products
  group:productsGroup
  consumer:
    partitioned: true
    instance-index: 0
```

This configuration tells Spring Cloud Stream that this consumer will only consume messages from partition number `0`, that is, the first partition.

Defining topics and events

As we already mentioned in the *Spring Cloud Stream* section in *Chapter 2, Introduction to Spring Boot*, Spring Cloud Stream is based on the publish and subscribe pattern, where a publisher publishes messages to topics and subscribers subscribe to topics they are interested in receiving messages from.

We will use one **topic** per type of entity: `products`, `recommendations`, and `reviews`.

Messaging systems handle **messages** that typically consist of headers and a body. An **event** is a message that describes something that has happened. For events, the message body can be used to describe the type of event, the event data, and a timestamp for when the event occurred.

An event is, for the scope of this book, defined by the following:

- The **type** of event, for example, a create or delete event
- A **key** that identifies the data, for example, a product ID
- A **data** element, that is, the actual data in the event
- A **timestamp**, which describes when the event occurred

The event class we will use looks as follows:

```
public class Event<K, T> {

    public enum Type {CREATE, DELETE}

    private Event.Type eventType;
    private K key;
    private T data;
    private ZonedDateTime eventCreatedAt;

    public Event() {
        this.eventType = null;
        this.key = null;
        this.data = null;
```

```
        this.eventCreatedAt = null;
    }

    public Event(Type eventType, K key, T data) {
        this.eventType = eventType;
        this.key = key;
        this.data = data;
        this.eventCreatedAt = now();
    }

    public Type getEventType() {
        return eventType;
    }

    public K getKey() {
        return key;
    }

    public T getData() {
        return data;
    }

    public ZonedDateTime getEventCreatedAt() {
        return eventCreatedAt;
    }
}
```

Let's explain the preceding source code in detail:

- The `Event` class is a generic class parameterized over the types of its `key` and `data` fields, `K` and `T`
- The event type is declared as an enumerator with the allowed values, that is, `CREATE` and `DELETE`
- The class defines two constructors, one empty and one that can be used to initialize the type, key, and value members
- Finally, the class defines getter methods for its member variables

For the full source code, see the `Event` class in the `api` project.

Changes in the Gradle build files

To bring in Spring Cloud Stream and its binders for RabbitMQ and Kafka, we need to add the two starter dependencies known as `spring-cloud-starter-stream-rabbit` and `spring-cloud-starter-stream-kafka`. We also need a test dependency in the `product-composite` project, `spring-cloud-stream::test-binder`, to bring in test support. The following code shows this:

```
dependencies {
  implementation 'org.springframework.cloud:spring-cloud-starter-stream-rabbit'
  implementation 'org.springframework.cloud:spring-cloud-starter-stream-kafka'
  testImplementation 'org.springframework.cloud:spring-cloud-stream::test-binder'
}
```

To specify what version of Spring Cloud we want to use, we first declare a variable for the version:

```
ext {
    springCloudVersion = "2020.0.3"
}
```

Next, we use the variable to set up dependency management for the specified Spring Cloud version, as seen here:

```
dependencyManagement {
    imports {
        mavenBom "org.springframework.cloud:spring-cloud-
        dependencies:${springCloudVersion}"
    }
}
```

For the full source code, see the `build.gradle` build file in each of the microservices projects.

With the required dependencies added to the Gradle build files, we can start to learn how to consume events in the core services.

Consuming events in the core services

To be able to consume events in the core services, we need to do the following:

- Declare message processors that consume events published on the core service's topic
- Change our service implementations to use the reactive persistence layer
- Add configuration required for consuming events
- Change our tests so that they can test the asynchronous processing of the events

The source code for consuming events is structured in the same way in all three core services, so we will only go through the source code for the `product` service.

Declaring message processors

The REST APIs for creating and deleting entities have been replaced with a **message processor** in each core microservice that consumes create and delete events on each entity's topic. To be able to consume messages that have been published to a topic, we need to declare a Spring Bean that implements the functional interface `java.util.function.Consumer`.

The message processor for the `product` service is declared as:

```
@Configuration
public class MessageProcessorConfig {

  private final ProductService productService;

  @Autowired
  public MessageProcessorConfig(ProductService productService)
  {
    this.productService = productService;
  }

  @Bean
  public Consumer<Event<Integer,Product>> messageProcessor() {
    ...
```

From the preceding code, we can see that:

- The class is annotated with `@Configuration`, telling Spring to look for Spring beans in the class.
- We inject an implementation of the `ProductService` interface in the constructor. The `productService` bean contains the business logic to perform the actual creation and deletions of the product entities.
- We declare the message processor as a Spring bean that implements the functional interface `Consumer`, accepting an event as an input parameter of type `Event<Integer,Product>`.

The implementation of the `Consumer` function looks like this:

```
return event -> {

  switch (event.getEventType()) {

    case CREATE:
      Product product = event.getData();
      productService.createProduct(product).block();
      break;

    case DELETE:
      int productId = event.getKey();
      productService.deleteProduct(productId).block();
      break;

    default:
      String errorMessage = "Incorrect event type: " +
        event.getEventType() +
        ", expected a CREATE or DELETE event";
      throw new EventProcessingException(errorMessage);
  }

};
```

The preceding implementation does the following:

- It takes an event of type `Event<Integer,Product>` as an input parameter
- Using a `switch` statement, based on the event type, it will either create or delete a product entity
- It uses the injected `productService` bean to perform the actual create and delete operation

- If the event type is neither create nor delete, an exception will be thrown

To ensure that we can propagate exceptions thrown by the `productService` bean back to the messaging system, we call the `block()` method on the responses we get back from the `productService` bean. This ensures that the message processor waits for the `productService` bean to complete its creation or deletion in the underlying database. Without calling the `block()` method, we would not be able to propagate exceptions and the messaging system would not be able to re-queue a failed attempt or possibly move the message to a dead-letter queue; instead, the message would silently be dropped.

Calling a `block()` method is, in general, considered a bad practice from a performance and scalability perspective. But in this case, we will only handle a few incoming messages in parallel, one per partition as described above. This means that we will only have a few threads blocked concurrently, which will not negatively impact the performance or the scalability.

For the full source code, see the `MessageProcessorConfig` classes in the `product`, `recommendation`, and `review` projects.

Changes in the service implementations

The service implementations of the create and delete methods for the `product` and `recommendation` service have been rewritten to use the non-blocking reactive persistence layer for MongoDB. For example, creating product entities is done as follows:

```
@Override
public Mono<Product> createProduct(Product body) {

  if (body.getProductId() < 1) {
    throw new InvalidInputException("Invalid productId: " +
      body.getProductId());
  }

  ProductEntity entity = mapper.apiToEntity(body);
  Mono<Product> newEntity = repository.save(entity)
    .log(LOG.getName(), FINE)
    .onErrorMap(
      DuplicateKeyException.class,
      ex -> new InvalidInputException
```

```
        ("Duplicate key, Product Id: " + body.getProductId()))
    .map(e -> mapper.entityToApi(e));

  return newEntity;
}
```

Note from the preceding code that the `onErrorMap()` method is used to map the `DuplicateKeyException` persistence exception to our own `InvalidInputException` exception.

For the `review` service, which uses the blocking persistence layer for JPA, the create and delete methods have been updated in the same way as described in the section *Dealing with blocking code*.

For the full source code, see the following classes:

- `ProductServiceImpl` in the `product` project
- `RecommendationServiceImpl` in the `recommendation` project
- `ReviewServiceImpl` in the `review` project

Adding configuration for consuming events

We also need to set up a configuration for the messaging system to be able to consume events. To do this, we need to complete the following steps:

1. We declare that RabbitMQ is the default messaging system and that the default content type is JSON:

```
spring.cloud.stream:
  defaultBinder: rabbit
  default.contentType: application/json
```

2. Next, we bind the input to the message processors to specific topic names, as follows:

```
spring.cloud.stream:
  bindings.messageProcessor-in-0:
    destination: products
```

3. Finally, we declare connectivity information for both Kafka and RabbitMQ:

```
spring.cloud.stream.kafka.binder:
  brokers: 127.0.0.1
```

```
      defaultBrokerPort: 9092

    spring.rabbitmq:
      host: 127.0.0.1
      port: 5672
      username: guest
      password: guest

    ---
    spring.config.activate.on-profile: docker

    spring.rabbitmq.host: rabbitmq
    spring.cloud.stream.kafka.binder.brokers: kafka
```

In the default Spring profile, we specify hostnames to be used when we run our system landscape without Docker on `localhost` with the IP address `127.0.0.1`. In the `docker` Spring profile, we specify the hostnames we will use when running in Docker and using Docker Compose, that is, `rabbitmq` and `kafka`.

Added to this configuration, the consumer configuration also specifies consumer groups, retry handling, dead-letter queues, and partitions as they were described earlier in the *Handling challenges with messaging* section.

For the full source code, see the `application.yml` configuration files in the `product`, `recommendation`, and `review` projects.

Changes in the test code

Since the core services now receive events for creating and deleting their entities, the tests need to be updated so that they send events instead of calling REST APIs, as they did in the previous chapters. To be able to call the message processor from the test class, we inject the message processor bean into a member variable:

```
@SpringBootTest
class ProductServiceApplicationTests {

  @Autowired
  @Qualifier("messageProcessor")
  private Consumer<Event<Integer, Product>> messageProcessor;
```

From the preceding code, we can see that we not only inject any `Consumer` function but use the `@Qualifier` annotation to specify that we want to inject the `Consumer` function that has the name `messageProcessor`.

To send create and delete events to the message processor, we add two helper methods, `sendCreateProductEvent` and `sendDeleteProductEvent`, in the test class:

```
  private void sendCreateProductEvent(int productId) {
    Product product = new Product(productId, "Name " + productId,
productId, "SA");
    Event<Integer, Product> event = new Event(CREATE, productId,
product);
    messageProcessor.accept(event);
  }

  private void sendDeleteProductEvent(int productId) {
    Event<Integer, Product> event = new Event(DELETE, productId, null);
    messageProcessor.accept(event);
  }
```

Note that we use the `accept()` method in the `Consumer` function interface declaration to invoke the message processor. This means that we shortcut the messaging system in the tests and call the message processor directly.

The tests for creating and deleting entities are updated to use these helper methods.

For the full source code, see the following test classes:

- `ProductServiceApplicationTests` in the `product` project
- `RecommendationServiceApplicationTests` in the `recommendation` project
- `ReviewServiceApplicationTests` in the `review` project

We have seen what is required to consume events in the core microservices. Now let's see how we can publish events in the composite microservice.

Publishing events in the composite service

When the composite service receives HTTP requests for the creation and deletion of composite products, it will publish the corresponding events to the core services on their topics. To be able to publish events in the composite service, we need to perform the following steps:

1. Publish events in the integration layer
2. Add configuration for publishing events
3. Change tests so that they can test the publishing of events

Note that no changes are required in the composite service implementation class – it is taken care of by the integration layer!

Publishing events in the integration layer

To publish an event in the integration layer, we need to:

1. Create an `Event` object based on the body in the HTTP request
2. Create a `Message` object where the `Event` object is used as the payload and the key field in the `Event` object is used as the partition key in the header
3. Use the helper class `StreamBridge` to publish the event on the desired topic

The code for sending create product events looks like:

```
@Override
public Mono<Product> createProduct(Product body) {

  return Mono.fromCallable(() -> {
    sendMessage("products-out-0",
      new Event(CREATE, body.getProductId(), body));
    return body;
  }).subscribeOn(publishEventScheduler);
}

private void sendMessage(String bindingName, Event event) {
  Message message = MessageBuilder.withPayload(event)
    .setHeader("partitionKey", event.getKey())
    .build();
  streamBridge.send(bindingName, message);
}
```

In the preceding code, we can see:

- The integration layer implements the `createProduct()` method in the `ProductService` interface by using a helper method, `sendMessage()`. The helper method takes the name of an output binding and an event object. The binding name `products-out-0` will be bound to the topic of the `product` service in the configuration below.

- Since the `sendMessage()` uses blocking code, when calling `streamBridge`, it is executed on a thread provided by a dedicated scheduler, `publishEventScheduler`. This is the same approach as for handling blocking JPA code in the `review` microservice. See the section on *Dealing with blocking code* for details.
- The helper method, `sendMessage()`, creates a `Message` object and sets the `payload` and the `partitionKey` header as described above. Finally, it uses the `streamBridge` object to send the event to the messaging system, which will publish it on the topic defined in the configuration.

For the full source code, see the `ProductCompositeIntegration` class in the `product-composite` project.

Adding configuration for publishing events

We also need to set up the configuration for the messaging system, to be able to publish events; this is similar to what we did for the consumers. Declaring RabbitMQ as the default messaging system, JSON as the default content type, and Kafka and RabbitMQ for connectivity information is the same as for the consumers.

To declare what topics to be used for the output binding names used, we have the following configuration:

```
spring.cloud.stream:
  bindings:
    products-out-0:
      destination: products
    recommendations-out-0:
      destination: recommendations
    reviews-out-0:
      destination: reviews
```

When using partitions, we also need to specify the partition key and the number of partitions that will be used:

```
spring.cloud.stream.bindings.products-out-0.producer:
  partition-key-expression: headers['partitionKey']
  partition-count: 2
```

In the preceding configuration, we can see that:

- The configuration applies for the binding name `products-out-0`
- The partition key used will be taken from the message header `partitionKey`

- Two partitions will be used

For the full source code, see the `application.yml` configuration file in the `product-composite` project.

Changes in the test code

Testing asynchronous event-driven microservices is, by its nature, difficult. Tests typically need to synchronize on the asynchronous background processing in some way to be able to verify the result. Spring Cloud Stream comes with support, in the form of a test binder, that can be used to verify what messages have been sent without using any messaging system during the tests!

See the *Changes in the Gradle build files* section earlier for how the test support is included in the `product-composite` project.

The test support includes an `OutputDestination` helper class that can be used to get the messages that were sent during a test. A new test class, `MessagingTests`, has been added to run tests that verify that the expected messages are sent. Let's go through the most important parts of the test class:

1. To be able to inject an `OutputDestination` bean in the test class, we also need to bring in its configuration from the class `TestChannelBinderConfiguration`. This is done with the following code:

   ```
   @SpringBootTest
   @Import({TestChannelBinderConfiguration.class})
   class MessagingTests {

     @Autowired
     private OutputDestination target;
   ```

2. Next, we declare a couple of helper methods for reading messages and also to be able to purge a topic. The code looks like:

   ```
   private void purgeMessages(String bindingName) {
     getMessages(bindingName);
   }

   private List<String> getMessages(String bindingName){
     List<String> messages = new ArrayList<>();
   ```

```
    boolean anyMoreMessages = true;

    while (anyMoreMessages) {
      Message<byte[]> message =
        getMessage(bindingName);

      if (message == null) {
        anyMoreMessages = false;

      } else {
        messages.add(new String(message.getPayload()));
      }
    }
    return messages;
  }

  private Message<byte[]> getMessage(String bindingName){
    try {
      return target.receive(0, bindingName);
    } catch (NullPointerException npe) {
      LOG.error("getMessage() received a NPE with binding = {}",
  bindingName);
      return null;
    }
  }
```

From the preceding code, we can see that:

- The `getMessage()` method returns a message from a specified topic using the `OutputDestination` bean, named `target`
- The `getMessages()` method uses the `getMessage()` method to return all messages in a topic
- The `purgeMessages()` method uses the `getMessages()` method to purge a topic from all current messages

3. Each test starts with purging all topics involved in the tests using a `setup()` method annotated with `@BeforeEach`:

```
@BeforeEach
void setUp() {
  purgeMessages("products");
  purgeMessages("recommendations");
  purgeMessages("reviews");
}
```

4. An actual test can verify the messages in a topic using the `getMessages()` method. For example, see the following test for the creation of a composite product:

```
@Test
void createCompositeProduct1() {

  ProductAggregate composite = new ProductAggregate(1, "name",
1, null, null, null);
  postAndVerifyProduct(composite, ACCEPTED);

  final List<String> productMessages = getMessages("products");
  final List<String> recommendationMessages =
getMessages("recommendations");
  final List<String> reviewMessages = getMessages("reviews");

  // Assert one expected new product event queued up
  assertEquals(1, productMessages.size());

  Event<Integer, Product> expectedEvent =
    new Event(CREATE, composite.getProductId(), new
Product(composite.getProductId(), composite.getName(),
composite.getWeight(), null));
  assertThat(productMessages.get(0), is(sameEventExceptCreatedAt
(expectedEvent)));

  // Assert no recommendation and review events
  assertEquals(0, recommendationMessages.size());
  assertEquals(0, reviewMessages.size());
}
```

From the preceding code, we can see an example where a test:

1. First makes an HTTP POST request, requesting the creation of a composite product.
2. Next, gets all messages from the three topics, one for each underlying core service.
3. For these tests, the specific timestamp for when an event was created is irrelevant. To be able to compare an actual event with an expected event, ignoring differences in the field `eventCreatedAt`, a helper class called `IsSameEvent` can be used. The `sameEventExceptCreatedAt()` method is a static method in the `IsSameEvent` class that compares `Event` objects and treats them as equal if all the fields are equal, except for the `eventCreatedAt` field.

4. Finally, it verifies that the expected events can be found, and no others.

For the full source code, see the test classes `MessagingTests` and `IsSameEvent` in the `product-composite` project.

Running manual tests of the reactive microservice landscape

Now, we have fully reactive microservices, both in terms of non-blocking synchronous REST APIs and event-driven asynchronous services. Let's try them out!

We will learn how to run tests using both RabbitMQ and Kafka as the message broker. Since RabbitMQ can be used both with and without partitions, we will test both cases. Three different configurations will be used, each defined in a separate Docker Compose file:

- Using RabbitMQ without the use of partitions
- Using RabbitMQ with two partitions per topic
- Using Kafka with two partitions per topic

However, before testing these three configurations, we need to add two features to be able to test the asynchronous processing:

- Saving events for later inspection when using RabbitMQ
- A health API that can be used to monitor the state of the microservice landscape

Saving events

After running some tests on event-driven asynchronous services, it might be of interest to see what events were actually sent. When using Spring Cloud Stream with Kafka, events are retained in the topics, even after consumers have processed them. However, when using Spring Cloud Stream with RabbitMQ, the events are removed after they have been processed successfully.

To be able to see what events have been published on each topic, Spring Cloud Stream is configured to save published events in a separate consumer group, `auditGroup`, per topic. For the `products` topic, the configuration looks like the following:

```
spring.cloud.stream:
  bindings:
    products-out-0:
      destination: products
      producer:
        required-groups: auditGroup
```

When using RabbitMQ, this will result in extra queues being created where the events are stored for later inspection.

For the full source code, see the `application.yml` configuration file in the `product-composite` project.

Adding a health API

Testing a system landscape of microservices that uses a combination of synchronous APIs and asynchronous messaging is challenging. For example, how do we know when a newly started landscape of microservices, together with their databases and messaging system, are ready to process requests and messages?

To make it easier to know when all the microservices are ready, we have added health APIs to the microservices. The health APIs are based on the support for **health endpoints** that comes with the Spring Boot module **Actuator**. By default, an Actuator-based health endpoint answers `UP` (and gives 200 as the HTTP return status) if the microservice itself and all the dependencies Spring Boot knows about are available. Dependencies Spring Boot knows about include, for example, databases and messaging systems. If the microservice itself or any of its dependencies are not available, the health endpoint answers `DOWN` (and returns 500 as the HTTP return status).

We can also extend health endpoints to cover dependencies that Spring Boot is not aware of. We will use this feature to extend to the product composite's `health` endpoint, so it also includes the health of the three core services. This means that the product composite `health` endpoint will only respond with `UP` if itself and the three core microservices are healthy. This can be used either manually or automatically by the `test-em-all.bash` script to find out when all the microservices and their dependencies are up and running.

In the `ProductCompositeIntegration` class, we have added helper methods for checking the health of the three core microservices, as follows:

```
public Mono<Health> getProductHealth() {
    return getHealth(productServiceUrl);
}

public Mono<Health> getRecommendationHealth() {
    return getHealth(recommendationServiceUrl);
}

public Mono<Health> getReviewHealth() {
    return getHealth(reviewServiceUrl);
}

private Mono<Health> getHealth(String url) {
    url += "/actuator/health";
    LOG.debug("Will call the Health API on URL: {}", url);
    return webClient.get().uri(url).retrieve().bodyToMono(String.class)
        .map(s -> new Health.Builder().up().build())
        .onErrorResume(ex -> Mono.just(new
         Health.Builder().down(ex).build()))
        .log(LOG.getName(), FINE);
}
```

This code is similar to the code we used previously to call the core services to read APIs. Note that the health endpoint is, by default, set to `/actuator/health`.

For the full source code, see the `ProductCompositeIntegration` class in the `product-composite` project.

In the main application class, `ProductCompositeServiceApplication`, we use these helper methods to register a composite health check using the Spring Actuator class `CompositeReactiveHealthContributor`:

```
@Autowired
ProductCompositeIntegration integration;

@Bean
ReactiveHealthContributor coreServices() {

  final Map<String, ReactiveHealthIndicator> registry = new
LinkedHashMap<>();
```

```
    registry.put("product", () -> integration.getProductHealth());
    registry.put("recommendation", () -> integration.
  getRecommendationHealth());
    registry.put("review", () -> integration.getReviewHealth());

    return CompositeReactiveHealthContributor.fromMap(registry);
  }
```

For the full source code, see the `ProductCompositeServiceApplication` class in the `product-composite` project.

Finally, in the `application.yml` configuration file of all four microservices, we configure the Spring Boot Actuator so that it does the following:

- Shows details about the state of health, which not only includes `UP` or `DOWN`, but also information about its dependencies
- Exposes all its endpoints over HTTP

The configuration for these two settings looks as follows:

```
management.endpoint.health.show-details: "ALWAYS"
management.endpoints.web.exposure.include: "*"
```

For an example of the full source code, see the `application.yml` configuration file in the `product-composite` project.

WARNING: These configuration settings are helpful during development, but it can be a security issue to reveal too much information in actuator endpoints in production systems. Therefore, plan to minimize the information exposed by the actuator endpoints in production!

This can be done by replacing `"*"` with, for example, `health,info` in the setting of the `management.endpoints.web.exposure.include` property above.

For details regarding the endpoints that are exposed by Spring Boot Actuator, see `https://docs.spring.io/spring-boot/docs/current/reference/html/production-ready-endpoints.html`.

The health endpoint can be used manually with the following command (don't try it yet, wait until we have started up the microservice landscape below!):

```
curl localhost:8080/actuator/health -s | jq .
```

This will result in a response containing:

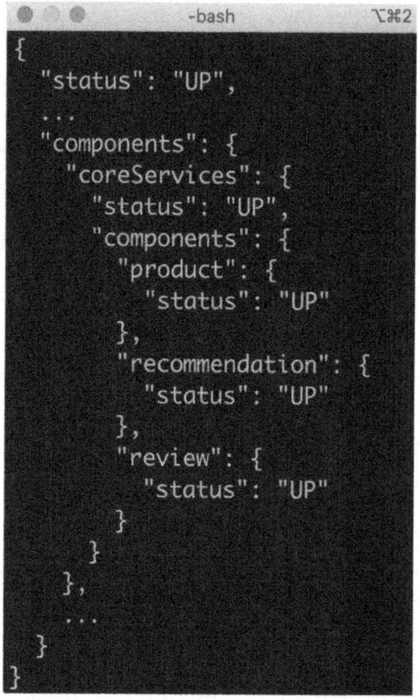

```
-bash                                    ⌥⌘2
{
  "status": "UP",
  ...
  "components": {
    "coreServices": {
      "status": "UP",
      "components": {
        "product": {
          "status": "UP"
        },
        "recommendation": {
          "status": "UP"
        },
        "review": {
          "status": "UP"
        }
      }
    },
    ...
  }
}
```

Figure 7.11: Health endpoint response

In the preceding output, we can see that the composite service reports that it is healthy, that is, its status is `UP`. At the end of the response, we can see that all three core microservices are also reported as healthy.

With a health API in place, we are ready to test our reactive microservices.

Using RabbitMQ without using partitions

In this section, we will test the reactive microservices together with RabbitMQ but without using partitions.

The default `docker-compose.yml` Docker Compose file is used for this configuration. The following changes have been added to the file:

- RabbitMQ has been added, as shown here:

```
rabbitmq:
  image: rabbitmq:3.8.11-management
  mem_limit: 512m
  ports:
    - 5672:5672
```

```
    - 15672:15672
  healthcheck:
    test: ["CMD", "rabbitmqctl", "status"]
    interval: 5s
    timeout: 2s
    retries: 60
```

From the declaration of RabbitMQ above, we can see that:

- We use a Docker image for RabbitMQ v3.8.11 including the management plugin and Admin Web UI
- We expose the standard ports for connecting to RabbitMQ and the Admin Web UI, `5672` and `15672`
- We add a health check so that Docker can find out when RabbitMQ is ready to accept connections

- The microservices now have a dependency declared on the RabbitMQ service. This means that Docker will not start the microservice containers until the RabbitMQ service is reported to be healthy:

```
depends_on:
  rabbitmq:
    condition: service_healthy
```

To run manual tests, perform the following steps:

1. Build and start the system landscape with the following commands:

```
cd $BOOK_HOME/Chapter07
./gradlew build && docker-compose build && docker-compose up -d
```

2. Now, we have to wait for the microservice landscape to be up and running. Try running the following command a few times:

```
curl -s localhost:8080/actuator/health | jq -r .status
```

When it returns `UP`, we are ready to run our tests!

3. First, create a composite product with the following commands:

```
body='{"productId":1,"name":"product name C","weight":300,
"recommendations":[
{"recommendationId":1,"author":"author
1","rate":1,"content":"content 1"},
 {"recommendationId":2,"author":"author
2","rate":2,"content":"content 2"},
 {"recommendationId":3,"author":"author
```

```
3","rate":3,"content":"content 3"}
], "reviews":[
 {"reviewId":1,"author":"author 1","subject":"subject
1","content":"content 1"},
 {"reviewId":2,"author":"author 2","subject":"subject
2","content":"content 2"},
 {"reviewId":3,"author":"author 3","subject":"subject
3","content":"content 3"}
]}'

curl -X POST localhost:8080/product-composite -H "Content-Type:
application/json" --data "$body"
```

When using Spring Cloud Stream together with RabbitMQ, it will create one RabbitMQ exchange per topic and a set of queues, depending on our configuration. Let's see what queues Spring Cloud Stream has created for us!

4. Open the following URL in a web browser: `http://localhost:15672/#/queues`. Log in with the default username/password `guest/guest`. You should see the following queues:

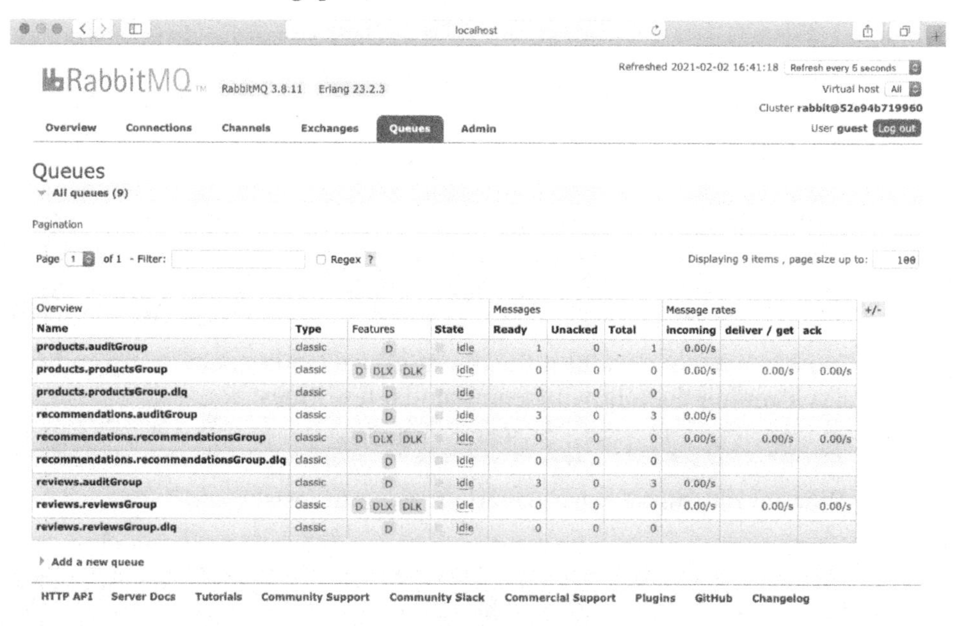

Figure 7.12: List of queues

For each topic, we can see one queue for the **auditGroup**, one queue for the consumer group that's used by the corresponding core microservice, and one dead-letter queue. We can also see that the **auditGroup** queues contain messages, as expected!

5. Click on the **products.auditGroup** queue and scroll down to the **Get messages** section, expand it, and click on the button named **Get Message(s)** to see the message in the queue:

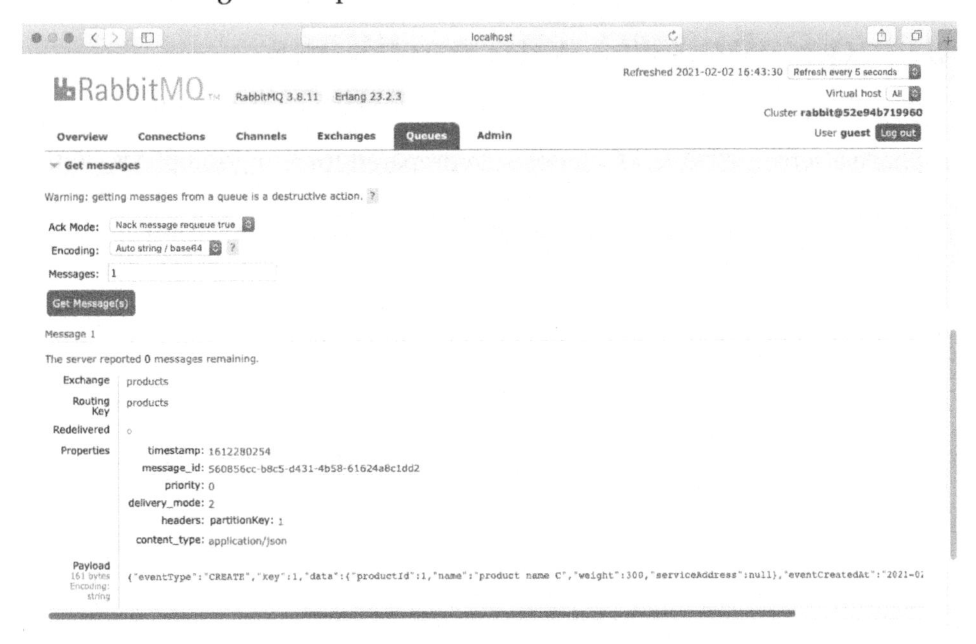

Figure 7.13: Viewing the message in the queue

From the preceding screenshot, note the **Payload** but also the header **partitionKey**, which we will use in the next section where we try out RabbitMQ with partitions.

6. Next, try to get the product composite using the following code:

```
curl -s localhost:8080/product-composite/1 | jq
```

7. Finally, delete it with the following command:

```
curl -X DELETE localhost:8080/product-composite/1
```

8. Try to get the deleted product again. It should result in a `404 - "NotFound"` response!
9. If you look in the RabbitMQ audit queues again, you should be able to find new messages containing delete events.
10. Wrap up the test by bringing down the microservice landscape with the following command:

```
docker-compose down
```

This completes the tests where we use RabbitMQ without partitions. Now, let's move on and test RabbitMQ with partitions.

Using RabbitMQ with partitions

Now, let's try out the partitioning support in Spring Cloud Stream!

We have a separate Docker Compose file prepared for using RabbitMQ with two partitions per topic: `docker-compose-partitions.yml`. It will also start two instances per core microservice, one for each partition. For example, a second `product` instance is configured as follows:

```
  product-p1:
    build: microservices/product-service
    mem_limit: 512m
    environment:
      - SPRING_PROFILES_ACTIVE=docker,streaming_partitioned,
streaming_instance_1
    depends_on:
      mongodb:
        condition: service_healthy
      rabbitmq:
        condition: service_healthy
```

Here is an explanation of the preceding configuration:

- We use the same source code and Dockerfile that we did for the first `product` instance but configure them differently.
- To make all microservice instances aware that they will use partitions, we have added the Spring profile `streaming_partitioned` to their environment variable `SPRING_PROFILES_ACTIVE`.
- We assign the two `product` instances to different partitions using different Spring profiles. The Spring profile `streaming_instance_0` is used by the first product instance and `streaming_instance_1` is used by the second instance, `product-p1`.
- The second `product` instance will only process asynchronous events; it will not respond to API calls. Since it has a different name, `product-p1` (also used as its DNS name), it will not respond to calls to a URL starting with `http://product:8080`.

Start up the microservice landscape with the following command:

```
export COMPOSE_FILE=docker-compose-partitions.yml
docker-compose build && docker-compose up -d
```

Create a composite product in the same way as for the tests in the previous section but also create a composite product with the product ID set to `2`. If you take a look at the queues set up by Spring Cloud Stream, you will see one queue per partition and that the product audit queues now contain one message each; the event for product ID `1` was placed in one partition and the event for product ID `2` was placed in the other partition. If you go back to `http://localhost:15672/#/queues` in your web browser, you should see something like the following:

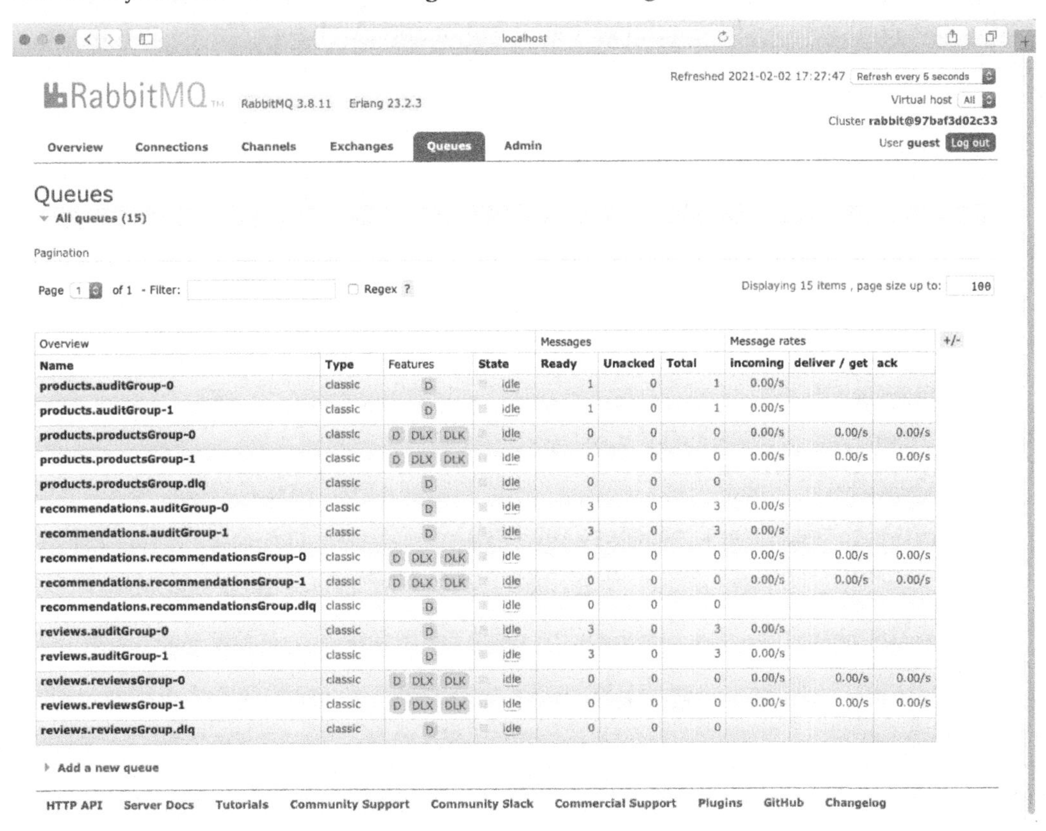

Figure 7.14: List of queues

To end the test with RabbitMQ using partitions, bring down the microservice landscape with the following command:

```
docker-compose down
unset COMPOSE_FILE
```

We are now done with tests using RabbitMQ, both with and without partitions. The final test configuration we shall try out is testing the microservices together with Kafka.

Using Kafka with two partitions per topic

Now, we shall try out a very cool feature of Spring Cloud Stream: changing the messaging system from RabbitMQ to Apache Kafka!

This can be done simply by changing the value of the `spring.cloud.stream.defaultBinder` property from `rabbit` to `kafka`. This is handled by the `docker-compose-kafka.yml` Docker Compose file that has also replaced RabbitMQ with Kafka and ZooKeeper. The configuration of Kafka and ZooKeeper looks as follows:

```
kafka:
  image: wurstmeister/kafka:2.12-2.5.0
  mem_limit: 512m
  ports:
    - "9092:9092"
  environment:
    - KAFKA_ADVERTISED_HOST_NAME=kafka
    - KAFKA_ADVERTISED_PORT=9092
    - KAFKA_ZOOKEEPER_CONNECT=zookeeper:2181
  depends_on:
    - zookeeper

zookeeper:
  image: wurstmeister/zookeeper:3.4.6
  mem_limit: 512m
  ports:
    - "2181:2181"
  environment:
    - KAFKA_ADVERTISED_HOST_NAME=zookeeper
```

Kafka is also configured to use two partitions per topic, and like before, we start up two instances per core microservice, one for each partition. See the Docker Compose file, `docker-compose-kafka.yml`, for details!

Start up the microservice landscape with the following command:

```
export COMPOSE_FILE=docker-compose-kafka.yml
docker-compose build && docker-compose up -d
```

Repeat the tests from the previous section: create two products, one with the product ID set to `1` and one with the product ID set to `2`.

Unfortunately, Kafka doesn't come with any graphical tools that can be used to inspect topics, partitions, and the messages that are placed within them. Instead, we can run CLI commands in the Kafka Docker container.

To see a list of topics, run the following command:

```
docker-compose exec kafka /opt/kafka/bin/kafka-topics.sh --zookeeper
zookeeper --list
```

Expect an output like the one shown here:

```
2. @700dd0df9ffe:/ (bash)
error.products.productsGroup
error.recommendations.recommendationsGroup
error.reviews.reviewsGroup
products
recommendations
reviews
$
```

Figure 7.15: Viewing a list of topics

Here is what we see in the preceding output:

- The topics prefixed with `error` are the topics corresponding to dead-letter queues.
- You will not find any `auditGroup` as in the case of RabbitMQ. Since events are retained in the topics by Kafka, even after consumers have processed them, there is no need for an extra `auditGroup`.

To see the partitions in a specific topic, for example, the `products` topic, run the following command:

```
docker-compose exec kafka /opt/kafka/bin/kafka-topics.sh --describe
--zookeeper zookeeper --topic products
```

Expect an output like the one shown here:

```
2. @700dd0df9ffe:/ (bash)
Topic:products PartitionCount:2 ReplicationFactor:1 Configs:
  Topic: products Partition: 0 Leader: 1001 Replicas: 1001 Isr: 1001
  Topic: products Partition: 1 Leader: 1001 Replicas: 1001 Isr: 1001
$
```

Figure 7.16: Viewing partitions in the products topic

To see all the messages in a specific topic, for example, the `products` topic, run the following command:

```
docker-compose exec kafka /opt/kafka/bin/kafka-console-consumer.sh
--bootstrap-server localhost:9092 --topic products --from-beginning
--timeout-ms 1000
```

Expect an output like the one shown here:

```
2. @700dd0df9ffe:/ (bash)
{"eventType":"CREATE","key":2,"data":{"productId":2,"name":"product name C","weight":300,
"serviceAddress":null},"eventCreatedAt":"2019-02-09T07:21:09.014259"}
{"eventType":"DELETE","key":2,"data":null,"eventCreatedAt":"2019-02-09T07:23:04.017709"}
{"eventType":"CREATE","key":1,"data":{"productId":1,"name":"product name C","weight":300,
"serviceAddress":null},"eventCreatedAt":"2019-02-09T07:18:11.600382"}
{"eventType":"DELETE","key":1,"data":null,"eventCreatedAt":"2019-02-09T07:23:02.359117"}
$
```

Figure 7.17: Viewing all messages in the products topic

To see all the messages in a specific partition, for example, partition `1` in the `products` topic, run the following command:

```
docker-compose exec kafka /opt/kafka/bin/kafka-console-consumer.sh
--bootstrap-server localhost:9092 --topic products --from-beginning
--timeout-ms 1000 --partition 1
```

Expect an output like the one shown here:

```
2. @700dd0df9ffe:/ (bash)
{"eventType":"CREATE","key":1,"data":{"productId":1,"name":"product name C","weight":300,
"serviceAddress":null},"eventCreatedAt":"2019-02-09T07:18:11.600382"}
{"eventType":"DELETE","key":1,"data":null,"eventCreatedAt":"2019-02-09T07:23:02.359117"}
$
```

Figure 7.18: Viewing all messages in partition 1 in the products topic

The output will end with a timeout exception since we stop the command by specifying a timeout for the command of `1000` ms.

Bring down the microservice landscape with the following command:

```
docker-compose down
unset COMPOSE_FILE
```

Now, we have learned how Spring Cloud Stream can be used to switch a message broker from RabbitMQ to Kafka without requiring any changes in the source code. It just requires a few changes in the Docker Compose file.

Let's move on to the last section of this chapter, learning how to run these tests automatically!

Running automated tests of the reactive microservice landscape

To be able to run tests of the reactive microservice landscape automatically instead of manually, the automated `test-em-all.bash` test script has been enhanced. The most important changes are as follows:

- The script uses the new `health` endpoint to know when the microservice landscape is operational, as shown here:

  ```
  waitForService curl http://$HOST:$PORT/actuator/health
  ```

- The script has a new `waitForMessageProcessing()` function, which is called after the test data is set up. Its purpose is simply to wait for the creation of the test data to be completed by the asynchronous create services.

To use the test script to automatically run the tests with RabbitMQ and Kafka, perform the following steps:

1. Run the tests using the default Docker Compose file, that is, with RabbitMQ without partitions, with the following commands:

   ```
   unset COMPOSE_FILE
   ./test-em-all.bash start stop
   ```

2. Run the tests for RabbitMQ with two partitions per topic using the Docker Compose `docker-compose-partitions.yml` file with the following commands:

   ```
   export COMPOSE_FILE=docker-compose-partitions.yml
   ./test-em-all.bash start stop
   unset COMPOSE_FILE
   ```

3. Finally, run the tests with Kafka and two partitions per topic using the Docker Compose `docker-compose-kafka.yml` file with the following commands:

```
export COMPOSE_FILE=docker-compose-kafka.yml
./test-em-all.bash start stop
unset COMPOSE_FILE
```

In this section, we have learned how to use the `test-em-all.bash` test script to automatically run tests of the reactive microservice landscape that has been configured to use either RabbitMQ or Kafka as its message broker.

Summary

In this chapter, we have seen how we can develop reactive microservices!

Using Spring WebFlux and Spring WebClient, we can develop non-blocking synchronous APIs that can handle incoming HTTP requests and send outgoing HTTP requests without blocking any threads. Using Spring Data's reactive support for MongoDB, we can also access MongoDB databases in a non-blocking way, that is, without blocking any threads while waiting for responses from the database. Spring WebFlux, Spring WebClient, and Spring Data rely on Project Reactor to provide their reactive and non-blocking features. When we must use blocking code, for example, when using Spring Data for JPA, we can encapsulate the processing of the blocking code by scheduling the processing of it in a dedicated thread pool.

We have also seen how Spring Data Stream can be used to develop event-driven asynchronous services that work on both RabbitMQ and Kafka as messaging systems without requiring any changes in the code. By doing some configuration, we can use features in Spring Cloud Stream such as consumer groups, retries, dead-letter queues, and partitions to handle the various challenges of asynchronous messaging.

We have also learned how to manually and automatically test a system landscape consisting of reactive microservices.

This was the final chapter on how to use fundamental features in Spring Boot and Spring Framework.

Next up is an introduction to Spring Cloud and how it can be used to make our services production-ready, scalable, robust, configurable, secure, and resilient!

Questions

1. Why is it important to know how to develop reactive microservices?
2. How do you choose between non-blocking synchronous APIs and event/message-driven asynchronous services?
3. What makes an event different from a message?
4. Name some challenges with message-driven asynchronous services. How do we handle them?
5. Why is the following test not failing?

    ```
    @Test
    void testStepVerifier() {

      StepVerifier.create(Flux.just(1, 2, 3, 4)
        .filter(n -> n % 2 == 0)
        .map(n -> n * 2)
        .log())
        .expectNext(4, 8, 12);
    }
    ```

    First, ensure that the test fails. Next, correct the test so that it succeeds.
6. What are the challenges of writing tests with reactive code using JUnit, and how can we handle them?

Part II

Leveraging Spring Cloud to Manage Microservices

In this part, you'll gain an understanding of how Spring Cloud can be used to manage the challenges faced when developing microservices (that is, building a distributed system).

This part includes the following chapters:

- *Chapter 8, Introduction to Spring Cloud*
- *Chapter 9, Adding Service Discovery Using Netflix Eureka*
- *Chapter 10, Using Spring Cloud Gateway to Hide Microservices behind an Edge Server*
- *Chapter 11, Securing Access to APIs*
- *Chapter 12, Centralized Configuration*
- *Chapter 13, Improving Resilience Using Resilience4j*
- *Chapter 14, Understanding Distributed Tracing*

8

Introduction to Spring Cloud

So far, we have seen how we can use Spring Boot to build microservices with well-documented APIs, along with Spring WebFlux and `springdoc-openapi`; persist data in MongoDB and SQL databases using Spring Data for MongoDB and JPA; build reactive microservices either as non-blocking APIs using Project Reactor or as event-driven asynchronous services using Spring Cloud Stream with RabbitMQ or Kafka, together with Docker; and manage and test a system landscape consisting of microservices, databases, and messaging systems.

Now, it's time to see how we can use **Spring Cloud** to make our services production-ready; that is scalable, robust, configurable, secure, and resilient.

In this chapter, we will introduce you to how Spring Cloud can be used to implement the following design patterns from *Chapter 1, Introduction to Microservices*, in the *Design patterns for microservices* section:

- Service discovery
- Edge server
- Centralized configuration
- Circuit breaker
- Distributed tracing

Technical requirements

This chapter does not contain any source code, and so no tools need to be installed.

The evolution of Spring Cloud

In its initial 1.0 release in March 2015, Spring Cloud was mainly a wrapper around tools from Netflix OSS, which are as follows:

- Netflix Eureka, a discovery server
- Netflix Ribbon, a client-side load balancer
- Netflix Zuul, an edge server
- Netflix Hystrix, a circuit breaker

The initial release of Spring Cloud also contained a configuration server and integration with Spring Security that provided OAuth 2.0 protected APIs. In May 2016, the Brixton release (v1.1) of Spring Cloud was made generally available. With the Brixton release, Spring Cloud got support for distributed tracing based on Spring Cloud Sleuth and Zipkin, which originated from Twitter. These initial Spring Cloud components could be used to implement the preceding design patterns. For more details, see `https://spring.io/blog/2015/03/04/spring-cloud-1-0-0-available-now` and `https://spring.io/blog/2016/05/11/spring-cloud-brixton-release-is-available`.

Since its inception, Spring Cloud has grown considerably over the years and has added support for the following, among others:

- Service discovery and centralized configuration based on HashiCorp Consul and Apache Zookeeper
- Event-driven microservices using Spring Cloud Stream
- Cloud providers such as Microsoft Azure, Amazon Web Services, and Google Cloud Platform

See `https://spring.io/projects/spring-cloud` for a complete list of tools.

Since the release of Spring Cloud Greenwich (v2.1) in January 2019, some of the Netflix tools mentioned previously have been placed in maintenance mode in Spring Cloud.

The reason for this is a mixture of Netflix no longer adding new features to some of the tools and Spring Cloud adding better alternatives. The following replacements are recommended by the Spring Cloud project:

Current component	Replaced by
Netflix Hystrix	Resilience4j
Netflix Hystrix Dashboard/Netflix Turbine	Micrometer and monitoring system
Netflix Ribbon	Spring Cloud LoadBalancer
Netflix Zuul	Spring Cloud Gateway

For more details, see:

- `https://spring.io/blog/2019/01/23/spring-cloud-greenwich-release-is-now-available`
- `https://github.com/Netflix/Hystrix#hystrix-status`
- `https://github.com/Netflix/ribbon#project-status-on-maintenance`

With the release of Spring Cloud Ilford (v2020.0.0) in December 2020, the only remaining Netflix component in Spring Cloud is Netflix Eureka.

In this book, we will use the replacement alternatives to implement the design patterns mentioned previously. The following table maps each design pattern to the software components that will be used to implement it:

Design pattern	Software component
Service discovery	Netflix Eureka and Spring Cloud LoadBalancer
Edge server	Spring Cloud Gateway and Spring Security OAuth
Centralized configuration	Spring Cloud Configuration Server
Circuit breaker	Resilience4j
Distributed tracing	Spring Cloud Sleuth and Zipkin

Now, let's go through the design patterns and introduce the software components that will be used to implement them!

Using Netflix Eureka for service discovery

Service discovery is probably the most important support function required to make a landscape of cooperating microservices production ready. As we already described in *Chapter 1, Introduction to Microservices*, in the *Service discovery* section, a service discovery service (or a *discovery service* as an abbreviation) can be used to keep track of existing microservices and their instances.

The first discovery service that Spring Cloud supported was *Netflix Eureka*.

We will use this in *Chapter 9, Adding Service Discovery Using Netflix Eureka*, along with a load balancer based on Spring Cloud LoadBalancer.

We will see how easy it is to register microservices with Netflix Eureka when using Spring Cloud. We will also learn how a client can send HTTP requests, such as a call to a RESTful API, to one of the instances registered in Netflix Eureka. In addition, the chapter will cover how to scale up the number of instances of a microservice, and how requests to a microservice will be load-balanced over its available instances (based on, by default, round-robin scheduling).

The following screenshot demonstrates the web UI from Eureka, where we can see what microservices we have registered:

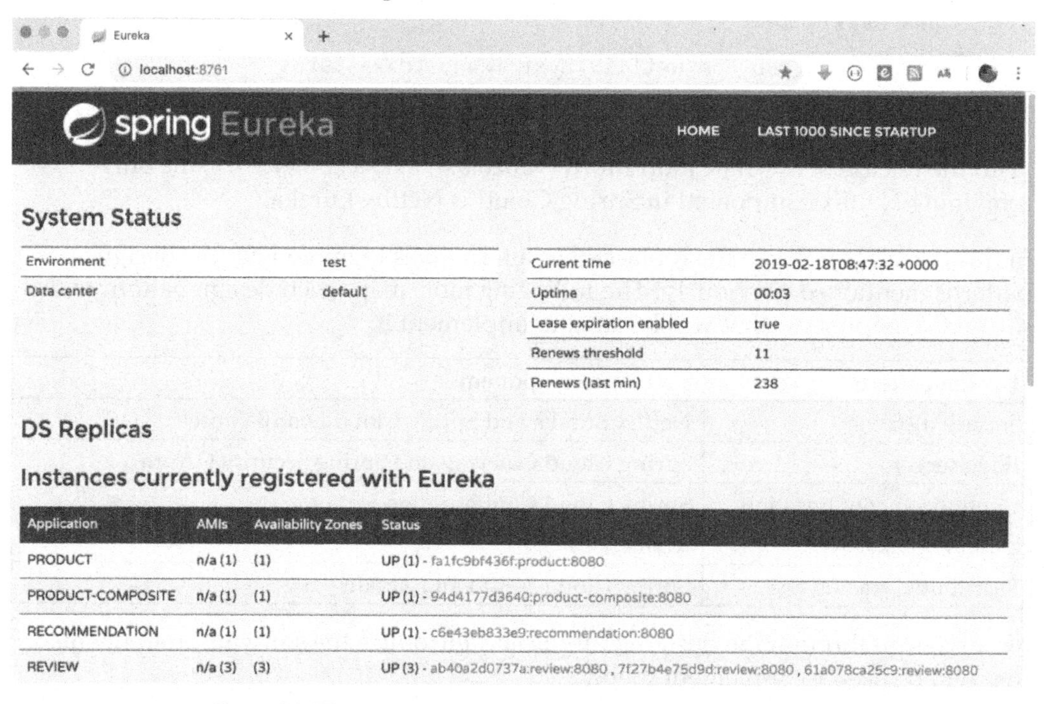

Figure 8.1: Viewing microservices currently registered with Eureka

From the preceding screenshot, we can see that the review service has three instances available, while the other three services only have one instance each.

With Netflix Eureka introduced, let's introduce how Spring Cloud can help to protect a microservices system landscape using an edge server.

Using Spring Cloud Gateway as an edge server

Another very important support function is an edge server. As we already described in *Chapter 1*, *Introduction to Microservices*, in the *Edge server* section, it can be used to secure a microservice landscape, which involves hiding private services from external usage and protecting public services when they're used by external clients.

Initially, Spring Cloud used Netflix Zuul v1 as its edge server. Since the Spring Cloud Greenwich release, it's recommended to use **Spring Cloud Gateway** instead. Spring Cloud Gateway comes with similar support for critical features, such as URL path-based routing and the protection of endpoints via the use of **OAuth 2.0** and **OpenID Connect** (OIDC).

One important difference between Netflix Zuul v1 and Spring Cloud Gateway is that Spring Cloud Gateway is based on non-blocking APIs that use Spring 5, Project Reactor, and Spring Boot 2, while Netflix Zuul v1 is based on blocking APIs. This means that Spring Cloud Gateway should be able to handle larger numbers of concurrent requests than Netflix Zuul v1, which is important for an edge server that all external traffic goes through.

The following diagram shows how all requests from external clients go through Spring Cloud Gateway as an edge server. Based on URL paths, it routes requests to the intended microservice:

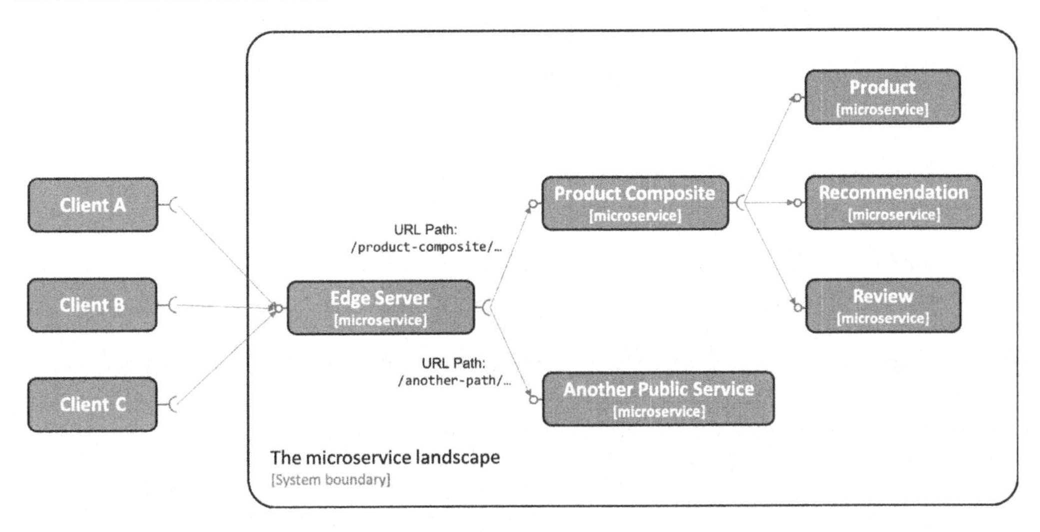

Figure 8.2: Requests being routed through an edge server

In the preceding diagram, we can see how the edge server will send external requests that have a URL path that starts with `/product-composite/` to the **Product Composite** microservice. The core services **Product**, **Recommendation**, and **Review** are not reachable from external clients.

In *Chapter 10, Using Spring Cloud Gateway to Hide Microservices Behind an Edge Server*, we will look at how to set up Spring Cloud Gateway with our microservices.

In *Chapter 11, Securing Access to APIs*, we will see how we can use Spring Cloud Gateway together with Spring Security OAuth2 to protect access to the edge server using OAuth 2.0 and OIDC. We will also see how Spring Cloud Gateway can propagate identity information of the caller down to our microservices, for example, the username or email address of the caller.

With Spring Cloud Gateway introduced, let's see how Spring Cloud can help to manage the configuration of a system landscape of microservices.

Using Spring Cloud Config for centralized configuration

To manage the configuration of a system landscape of microservices, Spring Cloud contains Spring Cloud Config, which provides the centralized management of configuration files according to the requirements described in *Chapter 1, Introduction to Microservices*, in the *Central configuration* section.

Spring Cloud Config supports storing configuration files in a number of different backends, such as the following:

- A Git repository, for example, on GitHub or Bitbucket
- A local filesystem
- HashiCorp Vault
- A JDBC database

Spring Cloud Config allows us to handle configuration in a hierarchical structure; for example, we can place common parts of the configuration in a common file and microservice-specific settings in separate configuration files.

Spring Cloud Config also supports detecting changes in the configuration and pushing notifications to the affected microservices. It uses **Spring Cloud Bus** to transport the notifications. Spring Cloud Bus is an abstraction on top of Spring Cloud Stream that we are already familiar with; that is, it supports the use of either RabbitMQ or Kafka as the messaging system for transporting notifications out of the box.

The following diagram illustrates the cooperation between Spring Cloud Config, its clients, a Git repository, and Spring Cloud Bus:

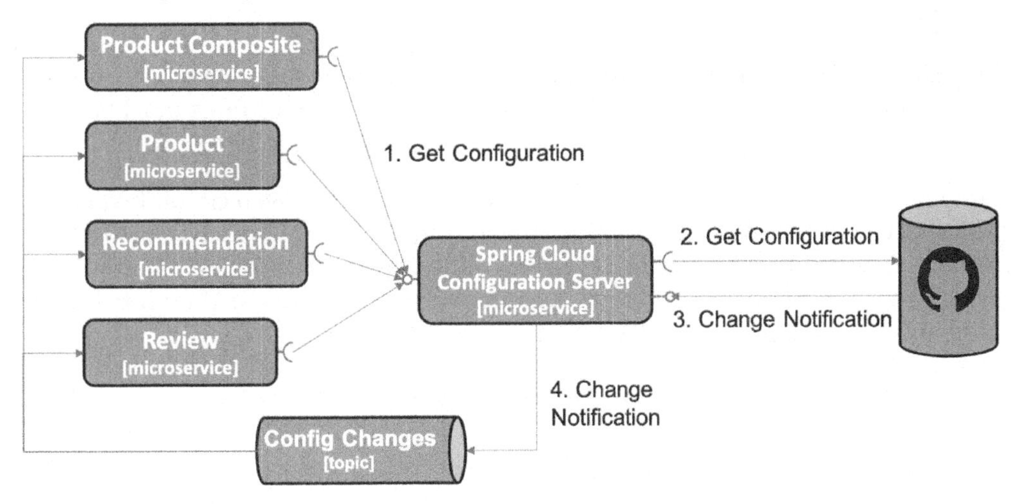

Figure 8.3: How Spring Cloud Config fits into the microservice landscape

The diagram shows the following:

1. When the microservices start up, they ask the configuration server for its configuration.
2. The configuration server gets the configuration from, in this case, a Git repository.
3. Optionally, the Git repository can be configured to send notifications to the configuration server when Git commits are pushed to the Git repository.
4. The configuration server will publish change events using Spring Cloud Bus. The microservices that are affected by the change will react and retrieve its updated configuration from the configuration server.

Finally, Spring Cloud Config also supports the encryption of sensitive information in the configuration, such as credentials.

We will learn about Spring Cloud Config in *Chapter 12, Centralized Configuration.*

With Spring Cloud Config introduced, let's see how Spring Cloud can help make microservices more resilient to failures that happen from time to time in a system landscape.

Using Resilience4j for improved resilience

In a fairly large-scaled system landscape of cooperating microservices, we must assume that there is something going wrong all of the time. Failures must be seen as a normal state, and the system landscape must be designed to handle it!

Initially, Spring Cloud came with Netflix Hystrix, a well-proven circuit breaker. But as already mentioned above, since the Spring Cloud Greenwich release, it is recommended to replace Netflix Hystrix with **Resilience4j**. Resilience4j is an open source-based fault tolerance library. It comes with a larger range of fault tolerance mechanisms compared to Netflix Hystrix:

- **Circuit breaker** is used to prevent a chain of failure reaction if a remote service stops responding.
- **Rate limiter** is used to limit the number of requests to a service during a specified time period.
- **Bulkhead** is used to limit the number of concurrent requests to a service.
- **Retries** are used to handle random errors that might happen from time to time.
- **Time limiter** is used to avoid waiting too long for a response from a slow or not responding service.

You can discover more about Resilience4j at `https://github.com/resilience4j/resilience4j`.

In *Chapter 13, Improving Resilience Using Resilience4j*, we will focus on the circuit breaker in Resilience4j. It follows the classic design of a circuit breaker, as illustrated in the following state diagram:

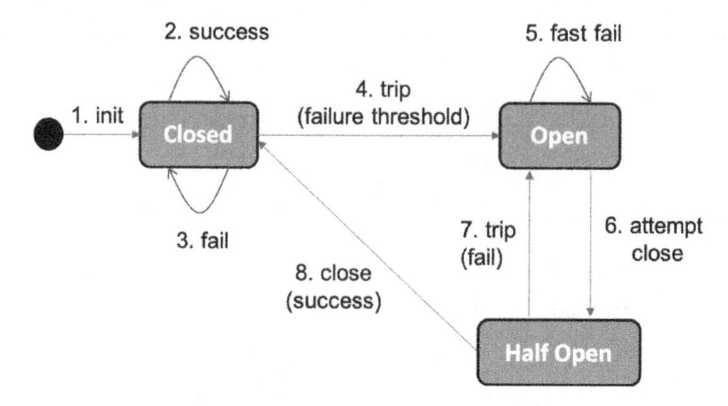

Figure 8.4: Circuit breaker state diagram

Let's take a look at the state diagram in more detail:

1. A circuit breaker starts as **Closed**, allowing requests to be processed.
2. As long as the requests are processed successfully, it stays in the **Closed** state.
3. If failures start to happen, a counter starts to count up.
4. If a threshold of failures is reached within a specified period of time, the circuit breaker will **trip**, that is, go to the **Open** state, not allowing further requests to be processed. Both the threshold of failures and the period of time are configurable.
5. Instead, a request will **Fast Fail**, meaning it will return immediately with an exception.
6. After a configurable period of time, the circuit breaker will enter a **Half Open** state and allow one request to go through, as a probe, to see whether the failure has been resolved.
7. If the probe request fails, the circuit breaker goes back to the **Open** state.
8. If the probe request succeeds, the circuit breaker goes to the initial **Closed** state, allowing new requests to be processed.

Sample usage of the circuit breaker in Resilience4j

Let's assume we have a REST service, called `myService`, that is protected by a circuit breaker using Resilience4j.

If the service starts to produce internal errors, for example, because it can't reach a service it depends on, we might get a response from the service such as `500 Internal Server Error`. After a number of configurable attempts, the circuit will open and we will get a fast failure that returns an error message such as `CircuitBreaker 'myService' is open`. When the error is resolved and we make a new attempt (after the configurable wait time), the circuit breaker will allow a new attempt as a probe. If the call succeeds, the circuit breaker will be closed again; that is, operating normally.

When using Resilience4j together with Spring Boot, we will be able to monitor the state of the circuit breakers in a microservice using its Spring Boot Actuator `health` endpoint. We can, for example, use `curl` to see the state of the circuit breaker, `myService`:

```
curl $HOST:$PORT/actuator/health -s | jq .components.circuitBreakers
```

If it operates normally, that is, the circuit is **closed**, it will respond with something such as the following:

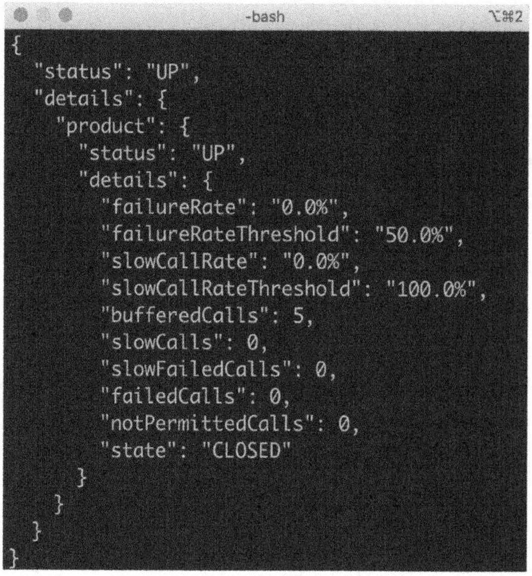

```
-bash                                                    ⌥⌘2
{
  "status": "UP",
  "details": {
    "product": {
      "status": "UP",
      "details": {
        "failureRate": "0.0%",
        "failureRateThreshold": "50.0%",
        "slowCallRate": "0.0%",
        "slowCallRateThreshold": "100.0%",
        "bufferedCalls": 5,
        "slowCalls": 0,
        "slowFailedCalls": 0,
        "failedCalls": 0,
        "notPermittedCalls": 0,
        "state": "CLOSED"
      }
    }
  }
}
```

Figure 8.5: Closed circuit response

If something is wrong and the circuit is **open**, it will respond with something such as the following:

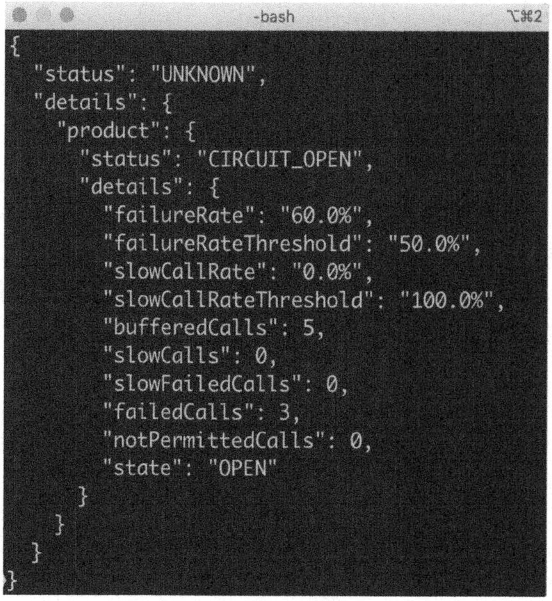

```
-bash                                                    ⌥⌘2
{
  "status": "UNKNOWN",
  "details": {
    "product": {
      "status": "CIRCUIT_OPEN",
      "details": {
        "failureRate": "60.0%",
        "failureRateThreshold": "50.0%",
        "slowCallRate": "0.0%",
        "slowCallRateThreshold": "100.0%",
        "bufferedCalls": 5,
        "slowCalls": 0,
        "slowFailedCalls": 0,
        "failedCalls": 3,
        "notPermittedCalls": 0,
        "state": "OPEN"
      }
    }
  }
}
```

Figure 8.6: Open circuit response

With Resilience4j introduced, we have seen an example of how the circuit breaker can be used to handle errors for a REST client. Let's wrap up this chapter with an introduction to how Spring Cloud can be used for distributed tracing.

Using Spring Cloud Sleuth and Zipkin for distributed tracing

To understand what is going on in a distributed system such as a system landscape of cooperating microservices, it is crucial to be able to track and visualize how requests and messages flow between microservices when processing an external call to the system landscape.

Refer to *Chapter 1*, *Introduction to Microservices*, in the *Distributed tracing* section, for more information on this subject.

Spring Cloud comes with **Spring Cloud Sleuth**, which can mark requests and messages/events that are part of the same processing flow with a common **correlation ID**.

Spring Cloud Sleuth can also decorate log records with correlation IDs to make it easier to track log records from different microservices that come from the same processing flow. **Zipkin** is a distributed tracing system (`http://zipkin.io`) that Spring Cloud Sleuth can send tracing data to for storage and visualization. Later on, in *Chapter 19*, *Centralized Logging with the EFK Stack*, we will learn how to find and visualize log records from one and the same processing flow using the correlation ID.

The infrastructure for handling distributed tracing information in Spring Cloud Sleuth and Zipkin is based on Google Dapper (`https://ai.google/research/pubs/pub36356`). In Dapper, the tracing information from a complete workflow is called a **trace tree**, and subparts of the tree, such as the basic units of work, are called **spans**. Spans can, in turn, consist of sub-spans, which form the trace tree. A correlation ID is called **TraceId**, and a span is identified by its own unique **SpanId**, along with the **TraceId** of the trace tree it belongs to.

A short history lesson regarding the evolution of standards (or at least commons efforts on establishing open de facto standards) for implementing distributed tracing:

Google published the paper on Dapper back in 2010, after using it internally since 2005.

In 2016, the **OpenTracing** project joined **CNCF**. OpenTracing is heavily influenced by Dapper and provides vendor-neutral APIs and language-specific libraries for instrumenting distributed tracing.

In 2019, the OpenTracing project merged with the **OpenCensus** project, forming a new CNCF project, **OpenTelemetry**. The OpenCensus project delivers a set of libraries for collecting metrics and distributed traces.

Suggested URLs for further reading:

- `https://opentracing.io`
- `https://opentelemetry.io`
- `https://opencensus.io`

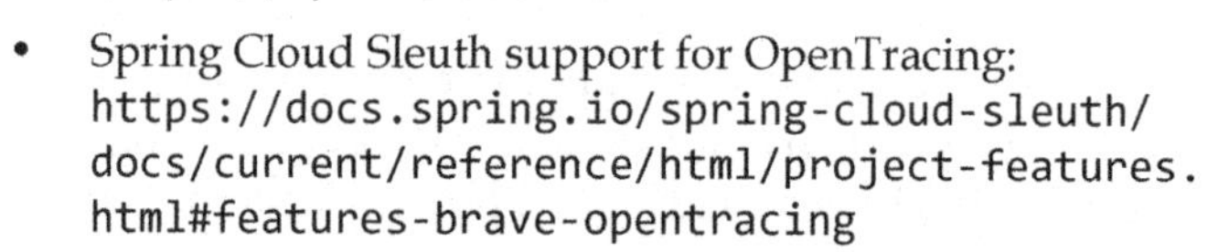

- Spring Cloud Sleuth support for OpenTracing: `https://docs.spring.io/spring-cloud-sleuth/docs/current/reference/html/project-features.html#features-brave-opentracing`

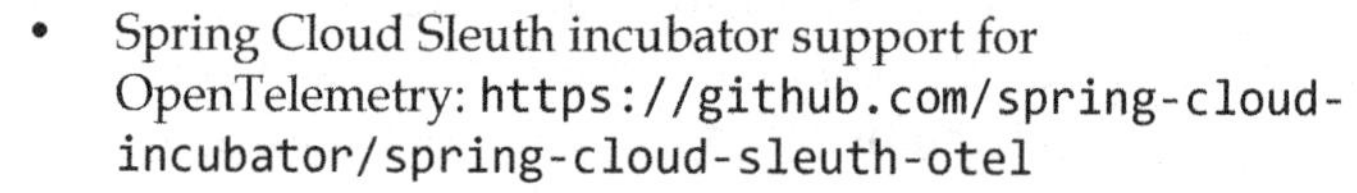

- Spring Cloud Sleuth incubator support for OpenTelemetry: `https://github.com/spring-cloud-incubator/spring-cloud-sleuth-otel`

For the scope of this book, we will use the direct integration between Spring Cloud Sleuth and Zipkin.

Spring Cloud Sleuth can send requests to Zipkin either synchronously over HTTP or asynchronously using either RabbitMQ or Kafka. To avoid creating runtime dependencies on the Zipkin server from our microservices, we prefer sending trace information to Zipkin asynchronously using either RabbitMQ or Kafka. This is illustrated by the following diagram:

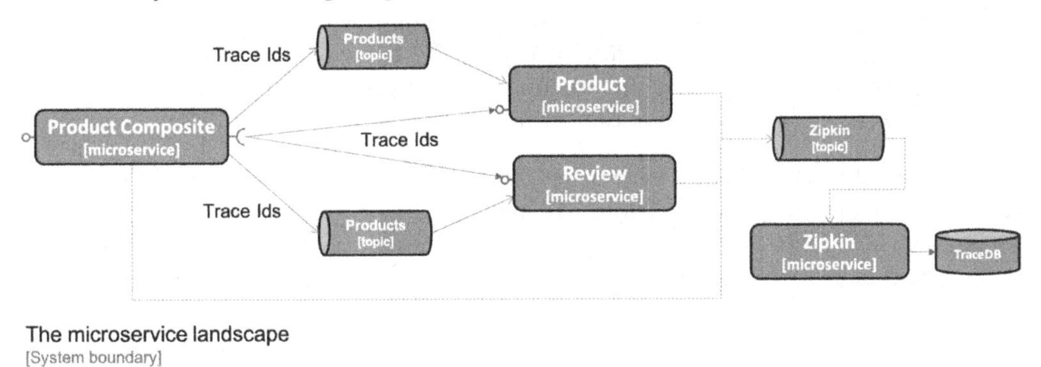

Figure 8.7: Sending trace information to Zipkin asynchronously

In *Chapter 14, Understanding Distributed Tracing*, we will see how we can use Spring Cloud Sleuth and Zipkin to trace the processing that goes on in our microservice landscape. The following is a screenshot from the Zipkin UI, which visualizes the trace tree that was created as a result of processing the creation of an aggregated product:

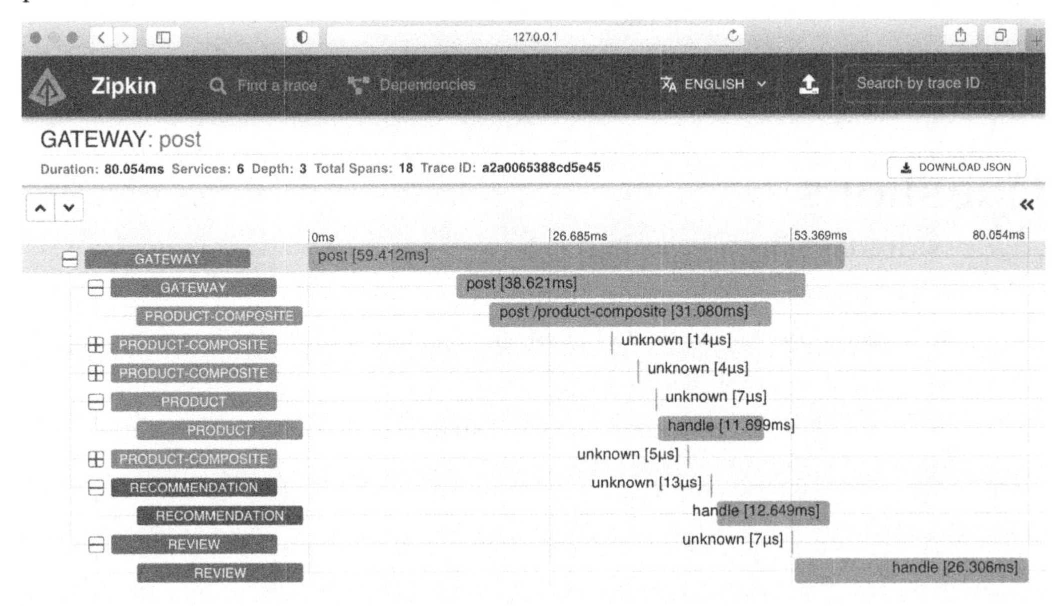

Figure 8.8: Trace tree in Zipkin

From the preceding screenshot, we can see that an HTTP `POST` request is sent to the **product-composite** service through the gateway (our edge server) and it responds by publishing create events to the topics for products, recommendations, and reviews. These events are consumed by the three core microservices in parallel and asynchronously, meaning that the **product-composite** service does not wait for the core microservices to complete their work. The data in the create events are stored in each microservice's database. A number of very short-lived spans named **unknown** are also shown in the preceding screenshot. They represent the interaction with the message broker, either publishing or consuming an event.

With Spring Cloud Sleuth and Zipkin for distributed tracing being introduced, we have seen an example of distributed tracing of the processing of an external synchronous HTTP request that includes asynchronous passing of events between the involved microservices.

Summary

In this chapter, we have seen how Spring Cloud has evolved from being rather Netflix OSS-centric to having a much larger scope as of today. We also introduced how components from the latest release of Spring Cloud Greenwich can be used to implement some of the design patterns we described in *Chapter 1, Introduction to Microservices*, in the *Design patterns for microservices* section. These design patterns are required to make a landscape of cooperating microservices production ready.

Head over to the next chapter to see how we can implement service discovery using Netflix Eureka and Spring Cloud LoadBalancer!

Questions

1. What is the purpose of Netflix Eureka?
2. What are the main features of Spring Cloud Gateway?
3. What backends are supported by Spring Cloud Config?
4. What are the capabilities that Resilience4j provides?
5. What are the concepts of trace tree and span used for in distributed tracing, and what is the paper called that defined them?

9
Adding Service Discovery Using Netflix Eureka

In this chapter, we will learn how to use Netflix Eureka as a discovery service for microservices based on Spring Boot. To allow our microservices to communicate with Netflix Eureka, we will use the Spring Cloud module for Netflix Eureka clients. Before we delve into the details, we will elaborate on why a discovery service is needed and why a DNS server isn't sufficient.

The following topics will be covered in this chapter:

- Introduction to service discovery
- Setting up a Netflix Eureka server
- Connecting microservices to a Netflix Eureka server
- Setting up the configuration for development use
- Trying out Netflix Eureka as a discovery service

Technical requirements

For instructions on how to install tools used in this book and how to access the source code for this book see:

- *Chapter 21* for macOS
- *Chapter 22* for Windows

The code examples in this chapter all come from the source code in `$BOOK_HOME/Chapter09`.

If you want to view the changes applied to the source code in this chapter, that is, see what it took to add Netflix Eureka as a discovery service to the microservices landscape, you can compare it with the source code for *Chapter 7, Developing Reactive Microservices*. You can use your favorite `diff` tool and compare the two folders, that is, `$BOOK_HOME/Chapter07` and `$BOOK_HOME/Chapter09`.

Introducing service discovery

Service discovery is probably the most important support function required to make a landscape of cooperating microservices production-ready. Netflix Eureka was the first discovery server supported by Spring Cloud.

We are strictly speaking about a *service* for *service discovery*, but instead of referring to it as a *service discovery service*, it will simply be referred to as a *discovery service*. When referring to an actual implementation of *service discovery*, like Netflix Eureka, the term *discovery server* will be used.

We will see how easy it is to register microservices with Netflix Eureka when using Spring Cloud. We will also learn how a client can use Spring Cloud LoadBalancer to send HTTP requests to one of the instances registered in Netflix Eureka. Finally, we will try scaling the microservices up and down, together with running some disruptive tests to see how Netflix Eureka can handle different types of fault scenarios.

Before we jump into the implementation details, we will look at the following topics:

- The problem with DNS-based service discovery
- Challenges with service discovery
- Service discovery with Netflix Eureka in Spring Cloud

The problem with DNS-based service discovery

Why can't we simply start new instances of a microservice and rely on round-robin DNS?

The idea behind round-robin DNS is that each instance of a microservice registers its IP address under the same name in a DNS server. When a client asks for IP addresses for the DNS name, the DNS server will return a list of IP addresses for the registered instances. The client can use this list of IP addresses to send requests to the microservice instances in a round-robin fashion, using the IP addresses one after another.

Let's try it out and see what happens! Follow these steps:

1. Assuming that you have followed the instructions from *Chapter 7, Developing Reactive Microservices*, start the system landscape and insert some test data with the following command:

```
cd $BOOK_HOME/Chapter07
./test-em-all.bash start
```

2. Scale up the `review` microservice to two instances:

```
docker-compose up -d --scale review=2
```

3. Ask the composite product service for the IP addresses it finds for the `review` microservice:

```
docker-compose exec product-composite getent hosts review
```

   Expect an answer like the following:

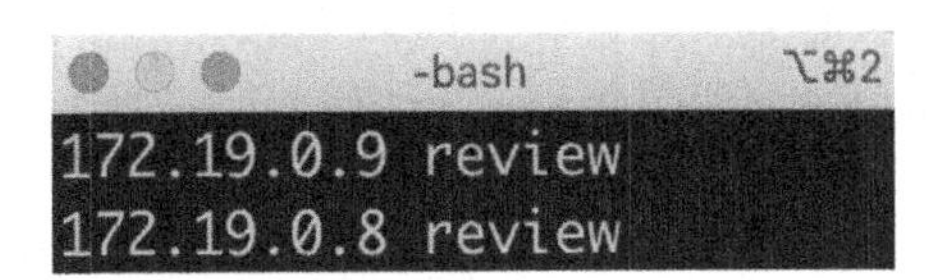

Figure 9.1: Review microservice IP addresses

   Great, the composite product service sees two IP addresses – in my case, `172.19.0.8` and `172.19.0.9` – one for each instance of the `review` microservice!

4. If you want to, you can verify that these are the correct IP addresses by using the following commands. The commands ask each instance of the `review` microservice for its IP address:

```
docker-compose exec --index=1 review cat /etc/hosts
docker-compose exec --index=2 review cat /etc/hosts
```

The last line in the output from each command should contain one of the IP addresses, as shown in the preceding code. For example:

Figure 9.2: IP address output

5. Now, let's try out a couple of calls to the `product-composite` service and see whether it uses both instances of the `review` microservice:

```
curl localhost:8080/product-composite/1 -s | jq -r
.serviceAddresses.rev
```

Unfortunately, we will only get responses from one of the microservice instances, as in this example:

Figure 9.3: Response from one review instance only

That was disappointing!

Okay, so what is going on here?

A DNS client asks a DNS server to resolve a DNS name and receives a list of IP addresses. Next, the DNS client tries out the received IP addresses one by one until it finds one that works, in most cases the first one in the list. A DNS client typically holds on to a working IP address; it does not apply a round-robin approach per request. Added to this, neither a typical DNS server implementation nor the DNS protocol itself is well suited for handling volatile microservice instances that come and go all the time. Because of this, even though DNS-based round robin is appealing in theory, it is not very practical to use for service discovery of microservice instances.

Before we move on and learn how to handle service discovery in a better way, let's shut down the system landscape:

```
docker-compose down
```

Challenges with service discovery

So, we need something a bit more powerful than a plain DNS to keep track of available microservice instances!

We must take the following into consideration when we're keeping track of many small moving parts, that is, microservice instances:

- New instances can start up at any point in time
- Existing instances can stop responding and eventually crash at any point in time
- Some of the failing instances might be okay after a while and should start to receive traffic again, while others will not and should be removed from the service registry
- Some microservice instances might take some time to start up; that is, just because they can receive HTTP requests doesn't mean that traffic should be routed to them
- Unintended network partitioning and other network-related errors can occur at any time

Building a robust and resilient discovery server is not an easy task, to say the least. Let's see how we can use Netflix Eureka to handle these challenges!

Service discovery with Netflix Eureka in Spring Cloud

Netflix Eureka implements client-side service discovery, meaning that the clients run software that talks to the discovery server, Netflix Eureka, to get information about the available microservice instances. This is illustrated in the following diagram:

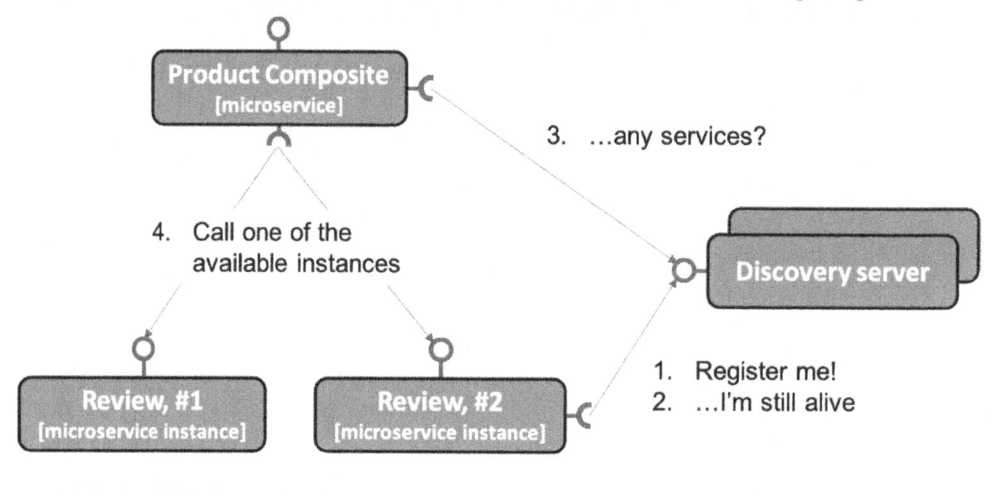

Figure 9.4: Discovery server diagram

The process is as follows:

1. Whenever a microservice instance starts up - for example, the **Review** service - it registers itself to one of the Eureka servers.
2. On a regular basis, each microservice instance sends a heartbeat message to the Eureka server, telling it that the microservice instance is okay and is ready to receive requests.
3. Clients - for example, the **Product Composite** service - use a client library that regularly asks the Eureka service for information about available services.
4. When the client needs to send a request to another microservice, it already has a list of available instances in its client library and can pick one of them without asking the discovery server. Typically, available instances are chosen in a round-robin fashion; that is, they are called one after another before the first one is called once more.

In *Chapter 17, Implementing Kubernetes Features to Simplify the System Landscape*, we will look at an alternative approach to providing a discovery service using a **server-side service** concept in Kubernetes.

Spring Cloud comes with an abstraction of how to communicate with a discovery service such as Netflix Eureka and provides an interface called `DiscoveryClient`. This can be used to interact with a discovery service to get information regarding available services and instances. Implementations of the `DiscoveryClient` interface are also capable of automatically registering a Spring Boot application with the discovery server.

Spring Boot can find implementations of the `DiscoveryClient` interface automatically during startup, so we only need to bring in a dependency on the corresponding implementation to connect to a discovery server. In the case of Netflix Eureka, the dependency that's used by our microservices is `spring-cloud-starter-netflix-eureka-client`.

Spring Cloud also has `DiscoveryClient` implementations that support the use of either Apache ZooKeeper or HashiCorp Consul as a discovery server.

Spring Cloud also comes with an abstraction - the `LoadBalancerClient` interface - for clients that want to make requests through a load balancer to registered instances in the discovery service. The standard reactive HTTP client, `WebClient`, can be configured to use the `LoadBalancerClient` implementation. By adding the `@LoadBalanced` annotation to a `@Bean` declaration that returns a `WebClient.Builder` object, a `LoadBalancerClient` implementation will be injected into the `Builder` instance as an `ExchangeFilterFunction`. Later in this chapter, in the *Connecting microservices to a Netflix Eureka server* section, we will look at some source code examples of how this can be used.

In summary, Spring Cloud makes it very easy to use Netflix Eureka as a discovery service. With this introduction to service discovery, and its challenges, and how Netflix Eureka can be used together with Spring Cloud, we are ready to learn how to set up a Netflix Eureka server.

Setting up a Netflix Eureka server

In this section, we will learn how to set up a Netflix Eureka server for service discovery. Setting up a Netflix Eureka server using Spring Cloud is really easy – just follow these steps:

1. Create a Spring Boot project using Spring Initializr, as described in *Chapter 3, Creating a Set of Cooperating Microservices*, in the *Using Spring Initializr to generate skeleton code* section.
2. Add a dependency to `spring-cloud-starter-netflix-eureka-server`.
3. Add the `@EnableEurekaServer` annotation to the application class.
4. Add a Dockerfile, similar to the Dockerfiles that are used for our microservices, with the exception that we export the default Eureka port, `8761`, instead of the default port for our microservices, `8080`.
5. Add the Eureka server to our three Docker Compose files, that is, `docker-compose.yml`, `docker-compose-partitions.yml`, and `docker-compose-kafka.yml`, like this:

   ```
   eureka:
     build: spring-cloud/eureka-server
     mem_limit: 512m
     ports:
       - "8761:8761"
   ```

6. Finally, add some configuration. Please see the *Setting up configuration for development use* section in this chapter, where we will go through the configuration for both the Eureka server and our microservices.

That's all it takes!

You can find the source code for the Eureka server in the `$BOOK_HOME/Chapter09/spring-cloud/eureka-server` folder.

Now we have set up a Netflix Eureka server for service discovery, we are ready to learn how to connect microservices to it.

Connecting microservices to a Netflix Eureka server

In this section, we will learn how to connect microservice instances to a Netflix Eureka server. We will learn both how microservices instances register themselves to the Eureka server during their startup and how clients can use the Eureka server to find the microservice instances they want to call.

To be able to register a microservice instance in the Eureka server, we need to do the following:

1. Add a dependency to `spring-cloud-starter-netflix-eureka-client` in the build file, `build.gradle`:

   ```
   Implementation 'org.springframework.cloud:spring-cloud-starter-
   netflix-eureka-client'
   ```

2. When running tests on a single microservice, we don't want to depend on having the Eureka server up and running. Therefore, we will disable the use of Netflix Eureka in all Spring Boot tests, that is, JUnit tests annotated with `@SpringBootTest`. This can be done by adding the `eureka.client.enabled` property and setting it to `false` in the annotation, like so:

   ```
   @SpringBootTest(webEnvironment=RANDOM_PORT, properties =
   {"eureka.client.enabled=false"})
   ```

3. Finally, add some configuration. Please go to the *Setting up configuration for development use* section, where we will go through the configuration for both the Eureka server and our microservices.

There is one property in the configuration that is extra important: `spring.application.name`. It is used to give each microservice a virtual hostname, a name used by the Eureka service to identify each microservice. Eureka clients will use this virtual hostname in the URLs that are used to make HTTP calls to the microservice, as we will see as we proceed.

To be able to look up available microservices instances through the Eureka server in the `product-composite` microservice, we also need to do the following:

1. Add a Spring bean in the main application class, `ProductCompositeServiceApplication`, that creates a load balancer-aware `WebClient`-builder:

   ```
   @Bean
   @LoadBalanced
   public WebClient.Builder loadBalancedWebClientBuilder() {
       return WebClient.builder();
   }
   ```

For more information on how to use a `WebClient` instance as a load balancer client, see `https://docs.spring.io/spring-cloud-commons/docs/current/reference/html/#webclinet-loadbalancer-client`.

2. The `WebClient`-builder bean can be used by the integration class, `ProductCompositeIntegration`, by injecting it into the constructor:

   ```
   private WebClient webClient;

   @Autowired
   public ProductCompositeIntegration(
     WebClient.Builder webClientBuilder,
     ...
   ) {
     this.webClient = webClientBuilder.build();
     ...
   }
   ```

   The constructor uses the injected builder to create the `webClient`.

   Once a `WebClient` is built, it is immutable. This means that it can be reused by concurrent requests without risking them stepping on each other's toes.

3. We can now get rid of our hardcoded configuration of available microservices in `application.yml`. It looks like this:

   ```
   app:
     product-service:
       host: localhost
       port: 7001
     recommendation-service:
       host: localhost
       port: 7002
     review-service:
       host: localhost
       port: 7003
   ```

4. The corresponding code in the integration class, `ProductCompositeIntegration`, that handled the hardcoded configuration is simplified and replaced by a declaration of the base URLs to the APIs of the core microservices. This is shown in the following code:

   ```
   private static final String PRODUCT_SERVICE_URL = "http://
   product";
   private static final String RECOMMENDATION_SERVICE_URL =
   "http://recommendation";
   private static final String REVIEW_SERVICE_URL = "http://
   review";
   ```

> The hostnames in the preceding URLs are not actual DNS names. Instead, they are the virtual hostnames that are used by the microservices when they register themselves to the Eureka server, in other words, the values of the `spring.application.name` property.

Now we've seen how to connect microservice instances to a Netflix Eureka server, we can move on and learn how to configure the Eureka server and the microservice instances that connect to it.

Setting up the configuration for development use

Now, it's time for the trickiest part of setting up Netflix Eureka as a discovery service: setting up a working configuration for both the Eureka server and its clients, our microservice instances.

Netflix Eureka is a highly configurable discovery server that can be set up for a number of different use cases, and it provides robust, resilient, and fault-tolerant runtime characteristics. One downside of this flexibility and robustness is that it has an almost overwhelming number of configuration options. Fortunately, Netflix Eureka comes with good default values for most of the configurable parameters - at least when it comes to using them in a production environment.

When it comes to using Netflix Eureka during development, the default values cause long startup times. For example, it can take a long time for a client to make an initial successful call to a microservices instance that is registered in the Eureka server.

Up to two minutes of wait time can be experienced when using the default configuration values. This wait time is added to the time it takes for the Eureka service and the microservices to start up. The reason for this wait time is that the involved processes need to synchronize registration information with each other. The microservices instances need to register with the Eureka server, and the client needs to gather information from the Eureka server. This communication is mainly based on heartbeats, which happen every 30 seconds by default. A couple of caches are also involved, which slows down the propagation of updates.

We will use a configuration that minimizes this wait time, which is useful during development. For use in production environments, the default values should be used as a starting point!

We will only use one Netflix Eureka server instance, which is okay in a development environment. In a production environment, you should always use two or more instances to ensure high availability for the Netflix Eureka server.

Let's start to learn what types of configuration parameters we need to know about.

Eureka configuration parameters

The configuration parameters for Eureka are divided into three groups:

- Parameters for the Eureka server, prefixed with `eureka.server`.
- Parameters for Eureka clients, prefixed with `eureka.client`. This is for clients who want to communicate with a Eureka server.
- Parameters for Eureka instances, prefixed with `eureka.instance`. This is for the microservices instances that want to register themselves in the Eureka server.

Some of the available parameters are described in the Spring Cloud Netflix documentation: `https://docs.spring.io/spring-cloud-netflix/docs/current/reference/html/`.

For an extensive list of available parameters, I recommend reading the source code:

- For Eureka server parameters, look at the `org.springframework.cloud.netflix.eureka.server.EurekaServerConfigBean` class for default values and the `com.netflix.eureka.EurekaServerConfig` interface for the relevant documentation
- For Eureka client parameters, look at the `org.springframework.cloud.netflix.eureka.EurekaClientConfigBean` class for the default values and documentation
- For Eureka instance parameters, look at the `org.springframework.cloud.netflix.eureka.EurekaInstanceConfigBean` class for default values and documentation

Let's start to learn about configuration parameters for the Eureka server.

Configuring the Eureka server

To configure the Eureka server for use in a development environment, the following configuration can be used:

```
server:
  port: 8761

eureka:
  instance:
    hostname: localhost
  client:
    registerWithEureka: false
    fetchRegistry: false
    serviceUrl:
      defaultZone: http://${eureka.instance.hostname}:${server.port}/
eureka/

  server:
    waitTimeInMsWhenSyncEmpty: 0
    response-cache-update-interval-ms: 5000
```

The first part of the configuration, for a Eureka `instance` and `client`, is a standard configuration for a standalone Eureka server. For details, see the Spring Cloud documentation that we referred to previously. The last two parameters used for the Eureka server, `waitTimeInMsWhenSyncEmpty` and `response-cache-update-interval-ms`, are used to minimize the startup time.

With the Eureka server configured, we are ready to see how clients to the Eureka server, that is, the microservice instances, can be configured.

Configuring clients to the Eureka server

To be able to connect to the Eureka server, the microservices have the following configuration:

```
eureka:
  client:
    serviceUrl:
      defaultZone: http://localhost:8761/eureka/
```

```
    initialInstanceInfoReplicationIntervalSeconds: 5
    registryFetchIntervalSeconds: 5
  instance:
    leaseRenewalIntervalInSeconds: 5
    leaseExpirationDurationInSeconds: 5

---
spring.config.activate.on-profile: docker

eureka.client.serviceUrl.defaultZone: http://eureka:8761/eureka/
```

The `eureka.client.serviceUrl.defaultZone` parameter is used to find the Eureka server, using the hostname `localhost` when running without Docker and the hostname `eureka` when running as containers in Docker. The other parameters are used to minimize the startup time and the time it takes to deregister a microservice instance that is stopped.

Now, we have everything in place that's required to actually try out the discovery service using the Netflix Eureka server together with our microservices.

Trying out the discovery service

With all of the details in place, we are ready to try out Netflix Eureka:

1. First, build the Docker images with the following commands:

   ```
   cd $BOOK_HOME/Chapter09
   ./gradlew build && docker-compose build
   ```

2. Next, start the system landscape and run the usual tests with the following command:

   ```
   ./test-em-all.bash start
   ```

   Expect output similar to what we have seen in previous chapters:

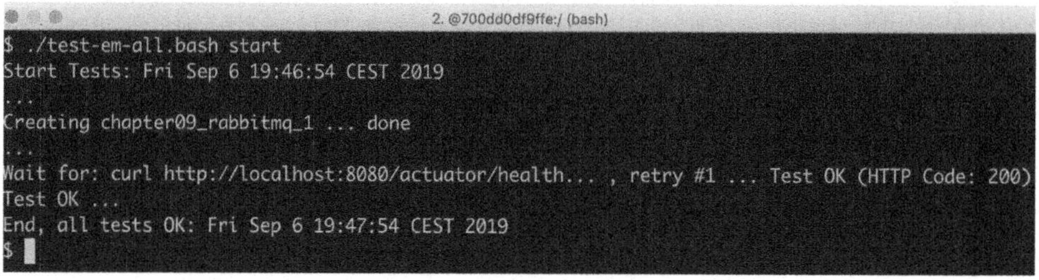

   ```
   2. @700dd0df9ffe:/ (bash)
   $ ./test-em-all.bash start
   Start Tests: Fri Sep 6 19:46:54 CEST 2019
   ...
   Creating chapter09_rabbitmq_1 ... done
   ...
   Wait for: curl http://localhost:8080/actuator/health... , retry #1 ... Test OK (HTTP Code: 200)
   Test OK ...
   End, all tests OK: Fri Sep 6 19:47:54 CEST 2019
   $
   ```

   Figure 9.5: Successful test output

With the system landscape up and running, we can start by testing how to scale up the number of instances for one of the microservices.

Scaling up

Run the following commands to try out scaling up a service:

1. Launch two extra `review` microservice instances:

```
docker-compose up -d --scale review=3
```

With the preceding command, we ask Docker Compose to run three instances of the `review` service. Since one instance is already running, two new instances will be started up.

2. Once the new instances are up and running, browse to `http://localhost:8761/` and expect something like the following:

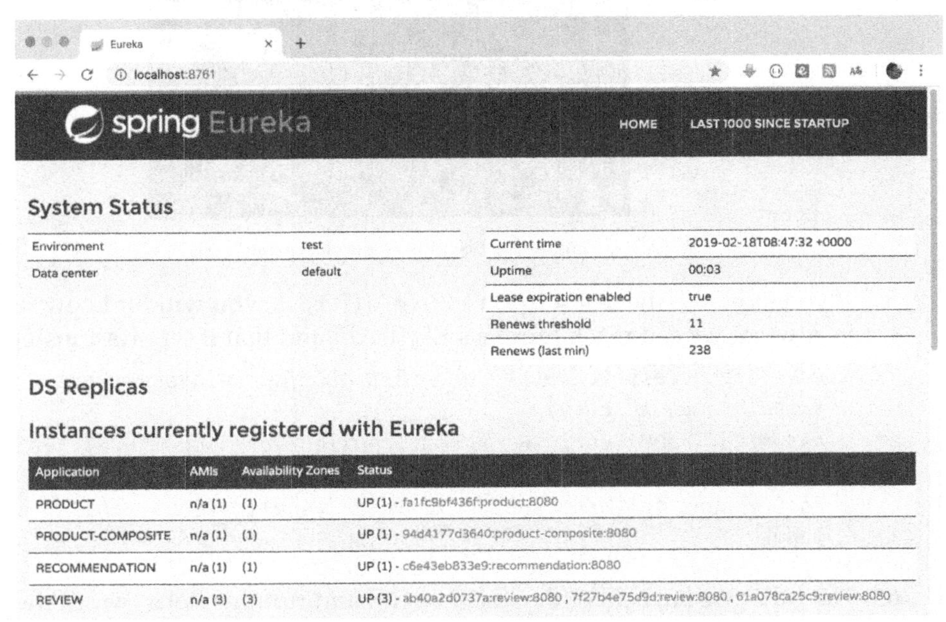

Figure 9.6: Viewing instances registered with Eureka

Verify that you can see three `review` instances in the Netflix Eureka web UI, as shown in the preceding screenshot.

3. One way of knowing when the new instances are up and running is to run this command:

```
docker-compose logs review | grep Started
```

Expect output that looks as follows:

```
2. @700dd0df9ffe:/ (bash)
review_2 | ... Started ReviewServiceApplication in 21.812 seconds (JVM running for 23.086)
review_3 | ... Started ReviewServiceApplication in 22.018 seconds (JVM running for 23.134)
```

Figure 9.7: New review instances

4. We can also use a REST API that the Eureka service exposes. To get a list of instance IDs, we can issue a `curl` command, like this:

```
curl -H "accept:application/json" localhost:8761/eureka/apps -s
| jq -r .applications.application[].instance[].instanceId
```

Expect a response that looks similar to the following:

2. @700dd0df9ffe:/ (bash)
3c7a676d8a5c:product-composite:8080
ac0a272e4488:product:8080
4034b100443e:review:8080
9599fead507d:review:8080
43d3788ce4e1:review:8080
f50156c9882a:recommendation:8080
$

Figure 9.8: List of microservice instance IDs

5. If you look into the test script, `test-em-all.bash`, you will find new tests that verify that we can reach Eureka's REST API and that it reports 4 instances:

```
# Verify access to Eureka and that all four microservices are
# registered in Eureka
assertCurl 200 "curl -H "accept:application/json" $HOST:8761/
eureka/apps -s"
assertEqual 4 $(echo $RESPONSE | jq ".applications.application |
length")
```

6. Now that we have all of the instances up and running, let's try out the client-side load balancer by making some requests and focusing on the address of the `review` service in the responses, as follows:

```
curl localhost:8080/product-composite/1 -s | jq -r
.serviceAddresses.rev
```

Expect responses similar to the following:

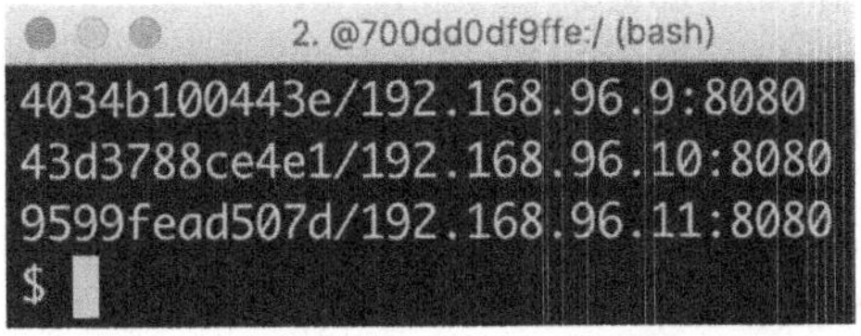
2. @700dd0df9ffe:/ (bash)
4034b100443e/192.168.96.9:8080
43d3788ce4e1/192.168.96.10:8080
9599fead507d/192.168.96.11:8080
$

Figure 9.9: Review service addresses

Note that the address of the `review` service changes in each response; the load balancer uses round-robin logic to call the available `review` instances, one at a time!

7. We can also take a look into the `review` instance's log records with the following command:

```
docker-compose logs review | grep getReviews
```

You will see output that looks similar to the following:

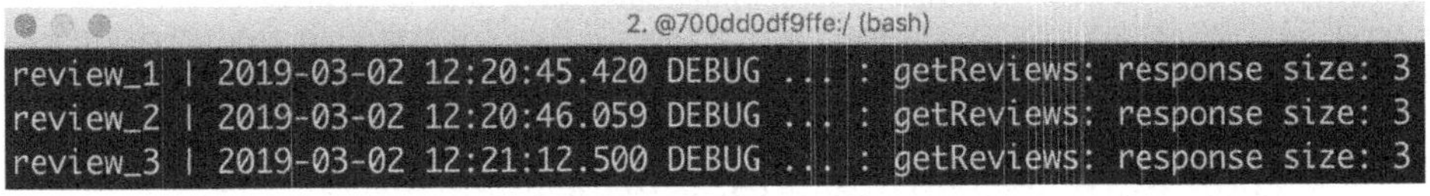
2. @700dd0df9ffe:/ (bash)
review_1 | 2019-03-02 12:20:45.420 DEBUG ... : getReviews: response size: 3
review_2 | 2019-03-02 12:20:46.059 DEBUG ... : getReviews: response size: 3
review_3 | 2019-03-02 12:21:12.500 DEBUG ... : getReviews: response size: 3

Figure 9.10: Review instance log records

In the preceding output, we can see how the three review microservice instances, `review_1`, `review_2`, and `review_3`, in turn, have responded to the requests.

We can also try to scale down the instances, which we will do next.

Scaling down

Let's also see what happens if we lose one instance of the `review` microservice. Run the following commands:

1. We can simulate one instance stopping unexpectedly by running the following command:

```
docker-compose up -d --scale review=2
```

2. After the shutdown of the `review` instance, there is a short time period during which calls to the API might fail. This is caused by the time it takes for information regarding the lost instance to propagate to the client, the `product-composite` service. During this time frame, the client-side load balancer might choose the instance that no longer exists. To prevent this from occurring, resilience mechanisms such as timeouts and retries can be used. In *Chapter 13, Improving Resilience Using Resilience4j*, we will see how this can be applied. For now, let's specify a timeout on our `curl` command, using the `-m 2` option to specify that we will wait no longer than 2 seconds for a response:

```
curl localhost:8080/product-composite/1 -m 2
```

If a timeout occurs, that is, the client-side load balancer tries to call an instance that no longer exists, the following response is expected from `curl`:

```
curl: (28) Operation timed out after 2003 milliseconds with 0 bytes received
$
```

Figure 9.11: Response from curl if a timeout occurs

3. Besides that, we should expect normal responses from the two remaining instances; that is, the `serviceAddresses.rev` field should contain the addresses of the two instances, as in the following:

```
"rev": "4034b100443e/192.168.96.9:8080"
"rev": "9599fead507d/192.168.96.11:8080"
```

Figure 9.12: Normal responses from remaining instances

In the preceding sample output, we can see that two different container names and IP addresses are reported. This means that the requests have been served by the two remaining microservice instances.

After trying out the scaling down of microservice instances, we can try out something that is a bit more disruptive: stopping the Eureka server and seeing what happens when the discovery server is temporarily unavailable.

Disruptive tests with the Eureka server

Let's bring some disorder to our Eureka server and see how the system landscape manages it!

To start with, what happens if we crash the Eureka server?

As long as clients have read the information regarding available microservice instances from the Eureka server before it is stopped, the clients will be fine since they cache the information locally. However, new instances will not be made available to clients, and they will not be notified if any running instances are terminated. So, calls to instances that are no longer running will cause failures.

Let's try this out!

Stopping the Eureka server

To simulate a Eureka server crash, follow these steps:

1. First, stop the Eureka server and keep the two `review` instances up and running:

```
docker-compose up -d --scale review=2 --scale eureka=0
```

2. Try a couple of calls to the API and extract the service address of the `review` service:

```
curl localhost:8080/product-composite/1 -s | jq -r
.serviceAddresses.rev
```

3. The response will – just like before we stopped the Eureka server – contain the addresses of the two `review` instances, like so:

```
2. @700dd0df9ffe:/ (bash)
4034b100443e/192.168.96.9:8080
9599fead507d/192.168.96.11:8080
```

Figure 9.13: Response with two review instance addresses

This shows that the client can make calls to existing instances, even though the Eureka server is no longer running.

Stopping a review instance

To further investigate what the effects are of a crashed Eureka server, let's also simulate the crash of one of the remaining `review` microservice instances:

1. Terminate one of the two `review` instances with the following command:

```
docker-compose up -d --scale review=1 --scale eureka=0
```

The client, that is, the `product-composite` service, will not be notified that one of the `review` instances has disappeared since no Eureka server is running. Due to this, it still thinks that there are two instances up and running. Every second call to the client will cause it to call a `review` instance that no longer exists, resulting in the response from the client not containing any information from the `review` service. The service address of the `review` service will be empty.

2. Try out the same `curl` command as before to verify that the service address of the `review` service will be empty every second time:

```
curl localhost:8080/product-composite/1 -s | jq -r
.serviceAddresses.rev
```

This can be prevented, as described previously, by using resilience mechanisms such as timeouts and retries.

Starting up an extra instance of the product service

As a final test of the effects of a crashed Eureka server, let's see what happens if we start up a new instance of the `product` microservice. Perform the following steps:

1. Let's try starting a new instance of the `product` service:

```
docker-compose up -d --scale review=1 --scale eureka=0 --scale
product=2
```

2. Call the API a couple of times and extract the address of the `product` service with the following command:

```
curl localhost:8080/product-composite/1 -s | jq -r
.serviceAddresses.pro
```

Since no Eureka server is running, the client will not be notified of the new `product` instance, and so all calls will go to the first instance, as in the following example:

Figure 9.14: Address of the first product instance only

We have seen some of the most important aspects of not having a Netflix Eureka server up and running. Let's conclude the section on disruptive tests by starting up the Netflix Eureka server again and seeing how the system landscape handles self-healing, that is, resilience.

Starting up the Eureka server again

In this section, we will wrap up the disruptive tests by starting up the Eureka server again. We will also verify that the system landscape self-heals, which means the new instance of the `product` microservice gets registered with the Netflix Eureka server and the client gets updated by the Eureka server. Perform the following steps:

1. Start the Eureka server with the following command:

```
docker-compose up -d --scale review=1 --scale eureka=1 --scale
product=2
```

2. Make the following call a couple of times to extract the addresses of the product and the `review` service:

```
curl localhost:8080/product-composite/1 -s | jq -r
.serviceAddresses
```

Verify that the following happens:

- All calls go to the remaining `review` instance, demonstrating that the client has detected that the second `review` instance is gone
- Calls to the `product` service are load-balanced over the two `product` instances, demonstrating the client has detected that there are two `product` instances available

The response should contain the same address for the `review` instance and two different addresses for the two `product` instances, as shown in the following two examples:

```
2. @700dd0df9ffe:/ (bash)
"pro": "cbfd07416ddc/192.168.128.3:8080",
"rev": "c5cc1f087afe/192.168.128.9:8080",
```

Figure 9.15: Product and review addresses

This is the second response:

```
2. @700dd0df9ffe:/ (bash)
"pro": "18d6e52267c2/192.168.128.7:8080",
"rev": "c5cc1f087afe/192.168.128.9:8080",
```

Figure 9.16: Product and review addresses

The IP addresses `192.168.128.3` and `192.168.128.7` belong to the two `product` instances. `192.168.128.9` is the IP address of the single remaining `review` instance.

To summarize, the Eureka server provides a very robust and resilient implementation of a discovery service. If even higher availability is desired, multiple Eureka servers can be launched and configured to communicate with each other. Details on how to set up multiple Eureka servers can be found in the Spring Cloud documentation: `https://docs.spring.io/spring-cloud-netflix/docs/current/reference/html/#spring-cloud-eureka-server-peer-awareness`.

3. Finally, shut down the system landscape with this command:

```
docker-compose down
```

This completes the tests of the discovery server, Netflix Eureka, where we have learned how to scale up and scale down microservice instances and what happens if a Netflix Eureka server crashes and later on comes back online.

Summary

In this chapter, we learned how to use Netflix Eureka for service discovery. First, we looked into the shortcomings of a simple DNS-based service discovery solution and the challenges that a robust and resilient service discovery solution must be able to handle.

Netflix Eureka is a very capable service discovery solution that provides robust, resilient, and fault-tolerant runtime characteristics. However, it can be challenging to configure correctly, especially for a smooth developer experience. With Spring Cloud, it becomes easy to set up a Netflix Eureka server and adapt Spring Boot-based microservices, both so that they can register themselves to Eureka during startup and, when acting as a client to other microservices, keep track of available microservice instances.

With a discovery server in place, it's time to see how we can handle external traffic using Spring Cloud Gateway as an edge server. Head over to the next chapter to find out how!

Questions

1. What is required to turn a Spring Boot application created with Spring Initializr into a fully fledged Netflix Eureka server?
2. What is required to make a Spring Boot-based microservice register itself automatically as a startup with Netflix Eureka?

3. What is required to make it possible for a Spring Boot-based microservice to call another microservice that is registered in a Netflix Eureka server?
4. Let's assume that you have a Netflix Eureka server up and running, along with one instance of microservice *A* and two instances of microservice *B*. All microservice instances register themselves with the Netflix Eureka server. Microservice *A* makes HTTP requests to microservice *B* based on the information it gets from the Eureka server. What will happen if, in turn, the following happens:
    - The Netflix Eureka server crashes
    - One of the instances of microservice *B* crashes
    - A new instance of microservice *A* starts up
    - A new instance of microservice *B* starts up
    - The Netflix Eureka server starts up again

10

Using Spring Cloud Gateway to Hide Microservices behind an Edge Server

In this chapter, we will learn how to use Spring Cloud Gateway as an edge server, to control what APIs are exposed from our microservices-based system landscape. We will see how microservices that have public APIs are made accessible from the outside through the edge server, while microservices that have private APIs are only accessible from the inside of the microservice landscape. In our system landscape, this means that the product composite service and the discovery server, Netflix Eureka, will be exposed through the edge server. The three core services, `product`, `recommendation`, and `review`, will be hidden from the outside.

The following topics will be covered in this chapter:

- Adding an edge server to our system landscape
- Setting up Spring Cloud Gateway, including configuring routing rules
- Trying out the edge server

Technical requirements

For instructions on how to install the tools used in this book and how to access the source code for this book, see:

- *Chapter 21* for macOS
- *Chapter 22* for Windows

The code examples in this chapter all come from the source code in `$BOOK_HOME/Chapter10`.

If you want to view the changes applied to the source code in this chapter, that is, see what it took to add Spring Cloud Gateway as an edge server to the microservices landscape, you can compare it with the source code for *Chapter 9, Adding Service Discovery Using Netflix Eureka*. You can use your favorite `diff` tool and compare the two folders, `$BOOK_HOME/Chapter09` and `$BOOK_HOME/Chapter10`.

Adding an edge server to our system landscape

In this section, we will see how the edge server is added to the system landscape and how it affects the way external clients access the public APIs that the microservices expose. All incoming requests will now be routed through the edge server, as illustrated by the following diagram:

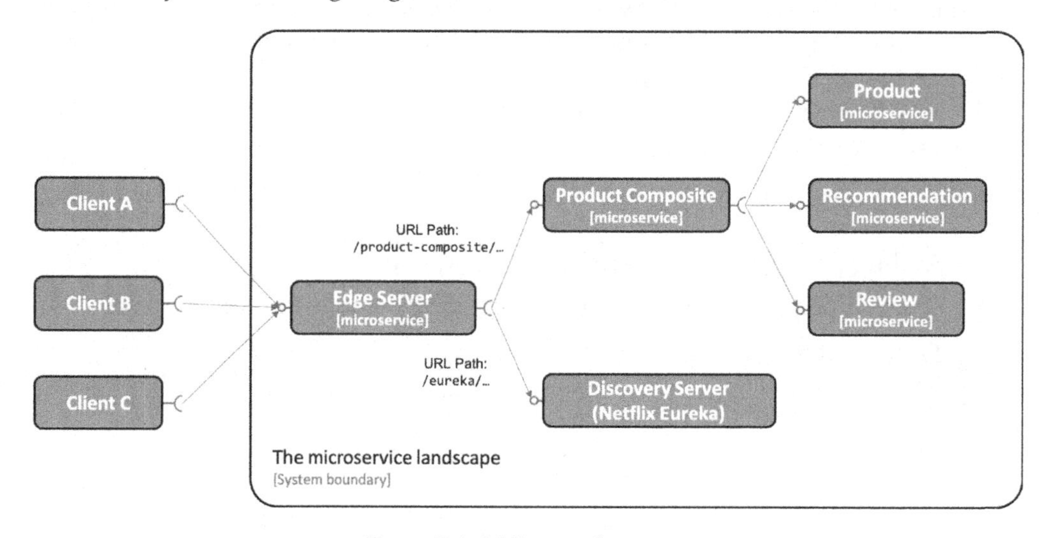

Figure 10.1: Adding an edge server

As we can see from the preceding diagram, external clients send all their requests to the edge server. The edge server can route the incoming requests based on the URL path. For example, requests with a URL that starts with `/product-composite/` are routed to the product composite microservice, and a request with a URL that starts with `/eureka/` is routed to the discovery server based on Netflix Eureka.

To make the discovery service work with Netflix Eureka, we don't need to expose it through the edge server. The internal services will communicate directly with Netflix Eureka. The reasons for exposing it are to make its web page and API accessible to an operator that needs to check the status of Netflix Eureka, and to see what instances are currently registered in the discovery service.

In *Chapter 9, Adding Service Discovery Using Netflix Eureka*, we exposed both the `product-composite` service and the discovery server, Netflix Eureka, to the outside. When we introduce the edge server in this chapter, this will no longer be the case. This is implemented by removing the following port declarations for the two services in the Docker Compose files:

```
product-composite:
  build: microservices/product-composite-service
  ports:
    - "8080:8080"

eureka:
  build: spring-cloud/eureka-server
  ports:
    - "8761:8761"
```

With the edge server introduced, we will learn how to set up an edge server based on Spring Cloud Gateway in the next section.

Setting up Spring Cloud Gateway

Setting up Spring Cloud Gateway as an edge server is straightforward and can be done with the following steps:

1. Create a Spring Boot project using Spring Initializr as described in *Chapter 3, Creating a Set of Cooperating Microservices* – refer to the *Using Spring Initializr to generate skeleton code* section.
2. Add a dependency on `spring-cloud-starter-gateway`.

3. To be able to locate microservice instances through Netflix Eureka, also add the `spring-cloud-starter-netflix-eureka-client` dependency.
4. Add the edge server project to the common build file, `settings.gradle`:
    ```
    include ':spring-cloud:gateway'
    ```
5. Add a `Dockerfile` with the same content as for the microservices; see `Dockerfile` content in the folder `$BOOK_HOME/Chapter10/microservices`.
6. Add the edge server to our three Docker Compose files:
    ```
    gateway:
      environment:
        - SPRING_PROFILES_ACTIVE=docker
      build: spring-cloud/gateway
      mem_limit: 512m
      ports:
        - "8080:8080"
    ```
    From the preceding code, we can see that the edge server exposes port `8080` to the outside of the Docker engine. To control how much memory is required, a memory limit of `512` MB is applied to the edge server, in the same way as we have done for the other microservices.
7. Since the edge server will handle all incoming traffic, we will move the composite health check from the product composite service to the edge server. This is described in the *Adding a composite health check* section next.
8. Add configuration for routing rules and more. Since there is a lot to configure, it is handled in a separate section below, *Configuring a Spring Cloud Gateway*.

You can find the source code for the Spring Cloud Gateway in `$BOOK_HOME/Chapter10/spring-cloud/gateway`.

Adding a composite health check

With an edge server in place, external health check requests also have to go through the edge server. Therefore, the composite health check that checks the status of all microservices has been moved from the `product-composite` service to the edge server. See *Chapter 7, Developing Reactive Microservices* – refer to the *Adding a health API* section for implementation details for the composite health check.

The following has been added to the edge server:

1. The `HealthCheckConfiguration` class has been added, which declares the reactive health contributor:

    ```
    @Bean
    ReactiveHealthContributor healthcheckMicroservices() {

      final Map<String, ReactiveHealthIndicator> registry =
        new LinkedHashMap<>();

      registry.put("product",           () ->
        getHealth("http://product"));
      registry.put("recommendation",    () ->
        getHealth("http://recommendation"));
      registry.put("review",            () ->
        getHealth("http://review"));
      registry.put("product-composite", () ->
        getHealth("http://product-composite"));

      return CompositeReactiveHealthContributor.fromMap(registry);
    }

    private Mono<Health> getHealth(String baseUrl) {
      String url = baseUrl + "/actuator/health";
      LOG.debug("Setting up a call to the Health API on URL: {}",
        url);
      return webClient.get().uri(url).retrieve()
        .bodyToMono(String.class)
        .map(s -> new Health.Builder().up().build())
        .onErrorResume(ex ->
        Mono.just(new Health.Builder().down(ex).build()))
        .log(LOG.getName(), FINE);
    }
    ```

    From the preceding code, we can see that a health check for the `product-composite` service has been added, instead of the health check used in *Chapter 7, Developing Reactive Microservices*!

2. The main application class, `GatewayApplication`, declares a `WebClient.Builder` bean to be used by the implementation of the health indicator as follows:

    ```
    @Bean
    @LoadBalanced
    public WebClient.Builder loadBalancedWebClientBuilder() {
      return WebClient.builder();
    }
    ```

    From the preceding source code, we see that `WebClient.builder` is annotated with `@LoadBalanced`, which makes it aware of microservice instances registered in the discovery server, Netflix Eureka. Refer to the *Service discovery with Netflix Eureka in Spring Cloud* section in *Chapter 9, Adding Service Discovery Using Netflix Eureka*, for details.

With a composite health check in place for the edge server, we are ready to look at the configuration that needs to be set up for the Spring Cloud Gateway.

Configuring a Spring Cloud Gateway

When it comes to configuring a Spring Cloud Gateway, the most important thing is setting up the routing rules. We also need to set up a few other things in the configuration:

1. Since Spring Cloud Gateway will use Netflix Eureka to find the microservices it will route traffic to, it must be configured as a Eureka client in the same way as described in *Chapter 9, Adding Service Discovery Using Netflix Eureka* – refer to the *Configuring clients to the Eureka server* section.
2. Configure Spring Boot Actuator for development usage as described in *Chapter 7, Developing Reactive Microservices* – refer to the *Adding a health API* section:

    ```
    management.endpoint.health.show-details: "ALWAYS"
    management.endpoints.web.exposure.include: "*"
    ```

3. Configure log levels so that we can see log messages from interesting parts of the internal processing in the Spring Cloud Gateway, for example, how it decides where to route incoming requests to:

    ```
    logging:
      level:
        root: INFO
        org.springframework.cloud.gateway.route.
            RouteDefinitionRouteLocator: INFO
        org.springframework.cloud.gateway: TRACE
    ```

For the full source code, refer to the configuration file, `src/main/resources/application.yml`.

Routing rules

Setting up routing rules can be done in two ways: programmatically, using a Java DSL, or by configuration. Using a Java DSL to set up routing rules programmatically can be useful in cases where the rules are stored in external storage, such as a database, or are given at runtime, for example, via a RESTful API or a message sent to the gateway. In more static use cases, I find it more convenient to declare the routes in the configuration file, `src/main/resources/application.yml`. Separating the routing rules from the Java code makes it possible to update the routing rules without having to deploy a new version of the microservice.

A **route** is defined by the following:

1. **Predicates**, which select a route based on information in the incoming HTTP request
2. **Filters**, which can modify both the request and/or the response
3. A **destination URI**, which describes where to send a request
4. An **ID**, that is, the name of the route

For a full list of available predicates and filters, refer to the reference documentation: `https://cloud.spring.io/spring-cloud-gateway/single/spring-cloud-gateway.html`.

Routing requests to the product-composite API

If we, for example, want to route incoming requests where the URL path starts with `/product-composite/` to our `product-composite` service, we can specify a routing rule like this:

```
spring.cloud.gateway.routes:
- id: product-composite
  uri: lb://product-composite
  predicates:
  - Path=/product-composite/**
```

Some points to note from the preceding code:

- `id: product-composite`: The name of the route is `product-composite`.

- `uri: lb://product-composite`: If the route is selected by its predicates, the request will be routed to the service that is named `product-composite` in the discovery service, Netflix Eureka. The protocol `lb://` is used to direct Spring Cloud Gateway to use the client-side load balancer to look up the destination in the discovery service.
- `predicates:`
  `- Path=/product-composite/**` is used to specify what requests this route should match. ** matches zero or more elements in the path.

To be able to route requests to the **Swagger UI** set up in *Chapter 5, Adding an API Description Using OpenAPI*, an extra route to the `product-composite` service is added:

```
- id: product-composite-swagger-ui
  uri: lb://product-composite
  predicates:
  - Path=/openapi/**
```

Requests sent to the edge server with a URI starting with `/openapi/` will be directed to the `product-composite` service.

When the Swagger UI is presented behind an edge server, it must be able to present an OpenAPI specification of the API that contains the correct server URL – the URL of the edge server instead of the URL of the `product-composite` service itself. To enable the `product-composite` service to produce a correct server URL in the OpenAPI specification, the following configuration has been added to the `product-composite` service:

```
server.forward-headers-strategy: framework
```

For details, see `https://springdoc.org/index.html#how-can-i-deploy-springdoc-openapi-ui-behind-a-reverse-proxy`.

To verify that the correct server URL is set in the OpenAPI specification, the following test has been added to the test script, `test-em-all.bash`:

```
assertCurl 200 "curl -s  http://$HOST:$PORT/
  openapi/v3/api-docs"
assertEqual "http://$HOST:$PORT" "$(echo $RESPONSE
  | jq -r .servers[].url)"
```

Routing requests to the Eureka server's API and web page

Eureka exposes both an API and a web page for its clients. To provide a clean separation between the API and the web page in Eureka, we will set up routes as follows:

- Requests sent to the edge server with the path starting with `/eureka/api/` should be handled as a call to the Eureka API
- Requests sent to the edge server with the path starting with `/eureka/web/` should be handled as a call to the Eureka web page

API requests will be routed to `http://${app.eureka-server}:8761/eureka`. The routing rule for the Eureka API looks like this:

```
- id: eureka-api
  uri: http://${app.eureka-server}:8761
  predicates:
  - Path=/eureka/api/{segment}
  filters:
  - SetPath=/eureka/{segment}
```

The `{segment}` part in the `Path` value matches zero or more elements in the path and will be used to replace the `{segment}` part in the `SetPath` value.

Web page requests will be routed to `http://${app.eureka-server}:8761`. The web page will load several web resources, such as `.js`, `.css`, and `.png` files. These requests will be routed to `http://${app.eureka-server}:8761/eureka`. The routing rules for the Eureka web page look like this:

```
- id: eureka-web-start
  uri: http://${app.eureka-server}:8761
  predicates:
  - Path=/eureka/web
  filters:
  - SetPath=/

- id: eureka-web-other
  uri: http://${app.eureka-server}:8761
  predicates:
  - Path=/eureka/**
```

From the preceding configuration, we can take the following notes. The `${app.eureka-server}` property is resolved by Spring's property mechanism depending on what Spring profile is activated:

1. When running the services on the same host without using Docker, for example, for debugging purposes, the property will be translated to `localhost` using the `default` profile.
2. When running the services as Docker containers, the Netflix Eureka server will run in a container with the DNS name `eureka`. Therefore, the property will be translated into `eureka` using the `docker` profile.

The relevant parts in the `application.yml` file that define this translation look like this:

```
app.eureka-server: localhost
---
spring.config.activate.on-profile: docker
app.eureka-server: eureka
```

Routing requests with predicates and filters

To learn a bit more about the routing capabilities in Spring Cloud Gateway, we will try out **host-based routing**, where Spring Cloud Gateway uses the hostname of the incoming request to determine where to route the request. We will use one of my favorite websites for testing HTTP codes: `http://httpstat.us/`.

A call to `http://httpstat.us/${CODE}` simply returns a response with the `${CODE}` HTTP code and a response body also containing the HTTP code and a corresponding descriptive text. For example, see the following `curl` command:

```
curl http://httpstat.us/200 -i
```

This will return the HTTP code `200`, and a response body with the text `200 OK`.

Let's assume that we want to route calls to `http://${hostname}:8080/headerrouting` as follows:

- Calls to the `i.feel.lucky` host should return `200 OK`
- Calls to the `im.a.teapot` host should return `418 I'm a teapot`
- Calls to all other hostnames should return `501 Not Implemented`

To implement these routing rules in Spring Cloud Gateway, we can use the `Host` route predicate to select requests with specific hostnames, and the `SetPath` filter to set the desired HTTP code in the request path. This can be done as follows:

1. To make calls to `http://i.feel.lucky:8080/headerrouting` return `200 OK`, we can set up the following route:

```
- id: host_route_200
  uri: http://httpstat.us
  predicates:
  - Host=i.feel.lucky:8080
  - Path=/headerrouting/**
  filters:
  - SetPath=/200
```

2. To make calls to `http://im.a.teapot:8080/headerrouting` return `418 I'm a teapot`, we can set up the following route:

```
- id: host_route_418
  uri: http://httpstat.us
  predicates:
  - Host=im.a.teapot:8080
  - Path=/headerrouting/**
  filters:
  - SetPath=/418
```

3. Finally, to make calls to all other hostnames return `501 Not Implemented`, we can set up the following route:

```
- id: host_route_501
  uri: http://httpstat.us
  predicates:
  - Path=/headerrouting/**
  filters:
  - SetPath=/501
```

Okay, that was quite a bit of configuration, so now let's try it out!

Trying out the edge server

To try out the edge server, we perform the following steps:

1. First, build the Docker images with the following commands:

```
cd $BOOK_HOME/Chapter10
./gradlew clean build && docker-compose build
```

2. Next, start the system landscape in Docker and run the usual tests with the following command:

```
./test-em-all.bash start
```

3. Expect output similar to what we have seen in previous chapters:

```
$ ./test-em-all.bash start
Start Tests: Fri Feb 19 14:46:54 CEST 2021
...
Creating chapter10_rabbitmq_1 ... done
...
Wait for: curl http://localhost:8080/actuator/health... , retry #1 ... Test OK (HTTP Code: 200)
...
Test OK (actual value: http://localhost:8080)
Test OK (HTTP Code: 200)
End, all tests OK: Fri Feb 19 14:47:54 CEST 2021
$
```

Figure 10.2: Output from test-em-all.bash

4. From the log output, note the second to last test result, `http://localhost:8080`. That is the output from the test that verifies that the server URL in Swagger UI's OpenAPI specification is correctly rewritten to be the URL of the edge server.

With the system landscape including the edge server up and running, let's explore the following topics:

- Examining what is exposed by the edge server outside of the system landscape running in the Docker engine
- Trying out some of the most frequently used routing rules as follows:
    - Use URL-based routing to call our APIs through the edge server
    - Use URL-based routing to call the Swagger UI through the edge server

- Use URL-based routing to call Netflix Eureka through the edge server, both using its API and web-based UI
- Use header-based routing to see how we can route requests based on the hostname in the request

Examining what is exposed outside the Docker engine

To understand what the edge server exposes to the outside of the system landscape, perform the following steps:

1. Use the `docker-compose ps` command to see which ports are exposed by our services:

```
docker-compose ps gateway eureka product-composite product recommendation review
```

2. As we can see in the following output, only the edge server (named `gateway`) exposes its port (`8080`) outside the Docker engine:

```
2. @700dd0df9ffe:/ (bash)
book-source-code_gateway_1            0.0.0.0:8080->8080/tcp
book-source-code_eureka_1             8761/tcp
book-source-code_product-composite_1  8080/tcp
book-source-code_product_1            8080/tcp
book-source-code_recommendation_1     8080/tcp
book-source-code_review_1             8080/tcp
$
```

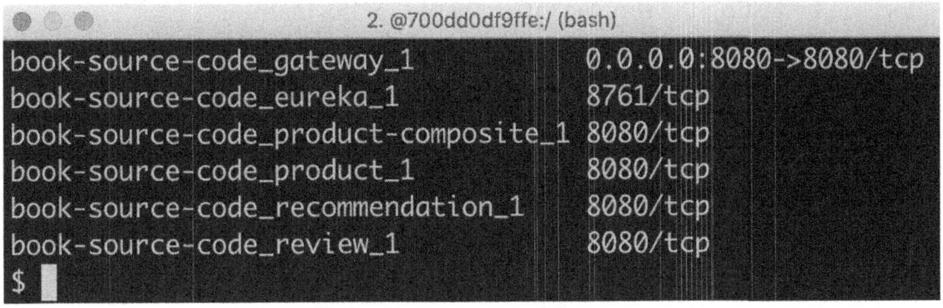

Figure 10.3: Output from docker-compose ps

3. If we want to see what routes the edge server has set up, we can use the `/actuator/gateway/routes` API. The response from this API is rather verbose. To limit the response to information we are interested in, we can apply a `jq` filter. In the following example, the `id` of the route and the `uri` the request will be routed to are selected:

```
curl localhost:8080/actuator/gateway/routes -s | jq '.[] | {"\(.route_id)": "\(.uri)"}' | grep -v '{\|}'
```

4. This command will respond with the following:

```
"product-composite": "lb://product-composite"
"product-composite-swagger-ui": "lb://product-composite"
"eureka-api": "http://eureka:8761"
"eureka-web-start": "http://eureka:8761"
"eureka-web-other": "http://eureka:8761"
"host_route_200": "http://httpstat.us:80"
"host_route_418": "http://httpstat.us:80"
"host_route_501": "http://httpstat.us:80"
```

Figure 10.4: Spring Cloud Gateway routing rules

This gives us a good overview of the actual routes configured in the edge server. Now, let's try out the routes!

Trying out the routing rules

In this section, we will try out the edge server and the routes it exposes to the outside of the system landscape. Let's start by calling the product composite API and its Swagger UI. Next, we'll call the Eureka API and visit its web page. Finally, we'll conclude by testing the routes that are based on hostnames.

Calling the product composite API through the edge server

Let's perform the following steps to call the product composite API through the edge server:

1. To be able to see what is going on in the edge server, we can follow its log output:

```
docker-compose logs -f --tail=0 gateway
```

2. Now, in a separate terminal window, make the call to the product composite API through the edge server:

```
curl http://localhost:8080/product-composite/1
```

3. Expect the normal type of response from the product composite API:

```
{"productId":1, ... "recommendations":[...],"reviews":[...],"serviceAddresses":{...}}
$
```

Figure 10.5: Output from retrieving the composite product with Product ID 1

4. We should be able to find the following information in the log output:

Figure 10.6: Log output from the edge server

5. From the log output, we can see the pattern matching based on the predicate we specified in the configuration, and we can see which microservice instance the edge server selected from the available instances in the discovery server – in this case, it forwards the request to `http://b8013440aea0:8080/product-composite/1`.

Calling the Swagger UI through the edge server

To verify that we can reach the Swagger UI introduced in *Chapter 5*, *Adding an API Description Using OpenAPI*, through the edge server, open the URL `http://localhost:8080/openapi/swagger-ui.html` in a web browser. The resulting Swagger UI page should look like this:

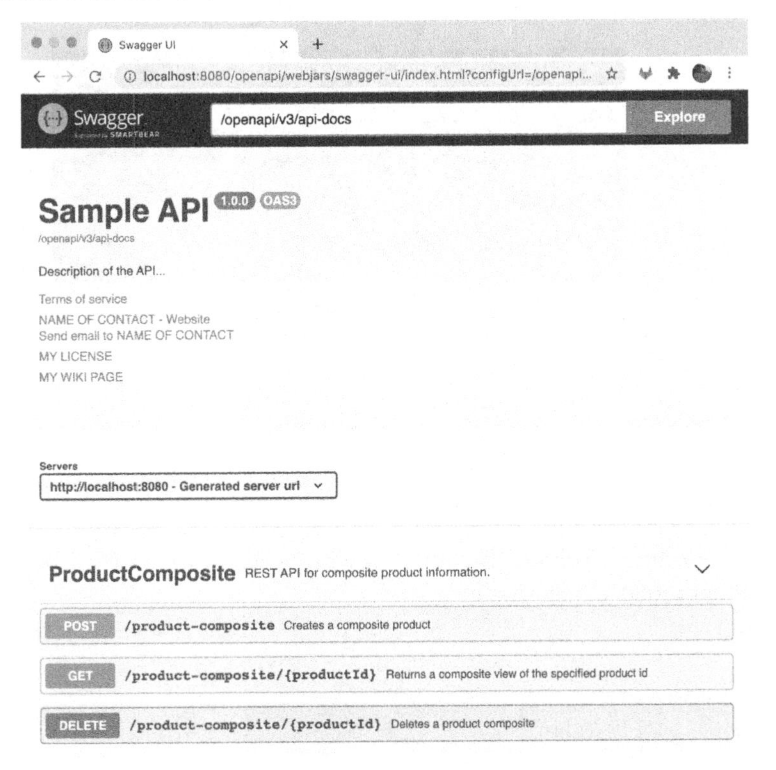

Figure 10.7: The Swagger UI through the edge server, gateway

Note the server URL: `http://localhost:8080`; this means that the `product-composite` API's own URL, `http://product-service:8080/` has been replaced in the OpenAPI specification returned by the Swagger UI.

If you want to, you can proceed and actually try out the `product-composite` API in the Swagger UI as we did back in *Chapter 5, Adding an API Description Using OpenAPI*!

Calling Eureka through the edge server

To call Eureka through an edge server, perform the following steps:

1. First, call the Eureka API through the edge server to see what instances are currently registered in the discovery server:

```
curl -H "accept:application/json"\
localhost:8080/eureka/api/apps -s | \
jq -r .applications.application[].instance[].instanceId
```

2. Expect a response along the lines of the following:

```
2. @700dd0df9ffe:/ (bash)
b91cde7148d9:gateway:8080
b8013440aea0:product-composite:8080
7c9a92146991:product:8080
21668e72a668:review:8080
ffcbdb9f32a4:recommendation:8080
$
```

Figure 10.8: Eureka listing the edge server, gateway, in REST call

Note that the edge server (named `gateway`) is also present in the response.

3. Next, open the Eureka web page in a web browser using the URL `http://localhost:8080/eureka/web`:

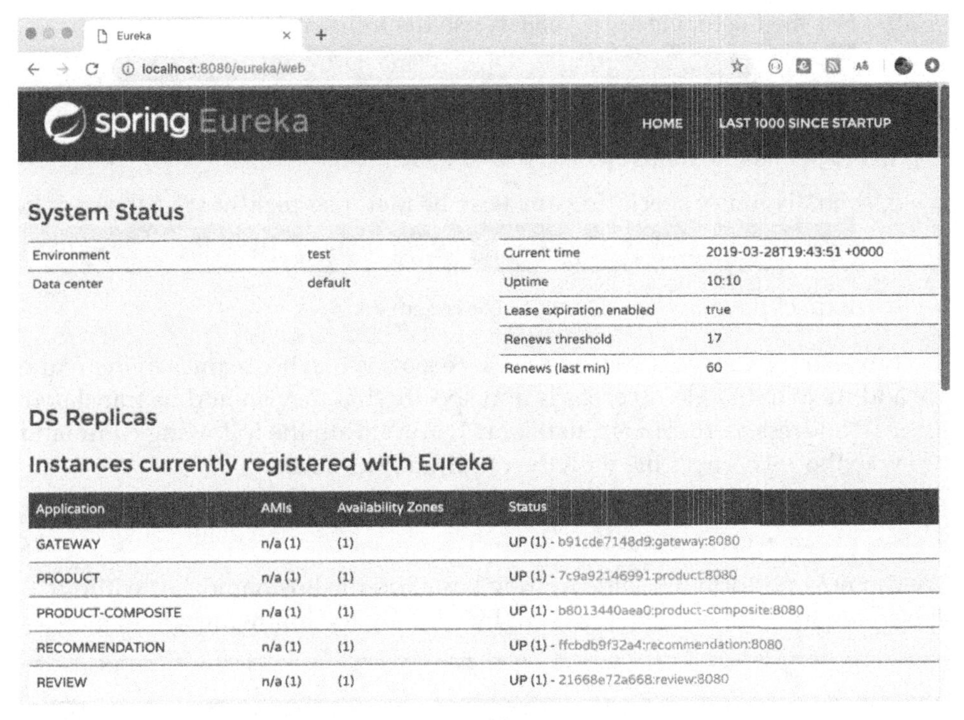

Figure 10.9: Eureka listing the edge server, gateway, in the web UI

4. From the preceding screenshot, we can see the Eureka web page reporting the same available instances as the API response in the previous step.

Routing based on the host header

Let's wrap up by testing the route configuration based on the hostname used in the requests!

Normally, the hostname in the request is set automatically in the `Host` header by the HTTP client. When testing the edge server locally, the hostname will be `localhost` – that is not so useful when testing hostname-based routing. But we can cheat by specifying another hostname in the `Host` header in the call to the API. Let's see how this can be done:

1. To call for the `i.feel.lucky` hostname, use this code:

```
curl http://localhost:8080/headerrouting -H "Host: i.feel.
lucky:8080"
```

2. Expect the response `200 OK`.

3. For the hostname `im.a.teapot`, use the following command:

```
curl http://localhost:8080/headerrouting -H "Host:
im.a.teapot:8080"
```

4. Expect the response `418 I'm a teapot`.
5. Finally, if not specifying any `Host` header, use `localhost` as the `Host` header:

```
curl http://localhost:8080/headerrouting
```

6. Expect the response `501 Not Implemented`.

We can also use `i.feel.lucky` and `im.a.teapot` as real hostnames in the requests if we add them to the file `/etc/hosts` and specify that they should be translated into the same IP address as `localhost`, that is, `127.0.0.1`. Run the following command to add a row to the `/etc/hosts` file with the required information:

```
sudo bash -c "echo '127.0.0.1 i.feel.lucky im.a.teapot' >> /etc/hosts"
```

We can now perform the same routing based on the hostname, but without specifying the `Host` header. Try it out by running the following commands:

```
curl http://i.feel.lucky:8080/headerrouting
curl http://im.a.teapot:8080/headerrouting
```

Expect the same responses as previously, `200 OK` and `418 I'm a teapot`.

Wrap up the tests by shutting down the system landscape with the following command:

```
docker-compose down
```

Also, clean up the `/etc/hosts` file from the DNS name translation we added for the hostnames, `i.feel.lucky` and `im.a.teapot`. Edit the `/etc/hosts` file and remove the line we added:

```
127.0.0.1 i.feel.lucky im.a.teapot
```

These tests of the routing capabilities in the edge server end the chapter.

Summary

In this chapter, we have seen how Spring Cloud Gateway can be used as an edge server to control what services are allowed to be called from outside of the system landscape. Based on predicates, filters, and destination URIs, we can define routing rules in a very flexible way. If we want to, we can configure Spring Cloud Gateway to use a discovery service such as Netflix Eureka to look up the target microservice instances.

One important question still unanswered is how we prevent unauthorized access to the APIs exposed by the edge server and how we can prevent third parties from intercepting traffic.

In the next chapter, we will see how we can secure access to the edge server using standard security mechanisms such as HTTPS, OAuth, and OpenID Connect.

Questions

1. What are the elements used to build a routing rule in Spring Cloud Gateway called?
2. What are they used for?
3. How can we instruct Spring Cloud Gateway to locate microservice instances through a discovery service such as Netflix Eureka?
4. In a Docker environment, how can we ensure that external HTTP requests to the Docker engine can only reach the edge server?
5. How do we change the routing rules so that the edge server accepts calls to the `product-composite` service on the `http://$HOST:$PORT/api/product` URL instead of the currently used `http://$HOST:$PORT/product-composite`?

11
Securing Access to APIs

In this chapter, we will see how we can secure access to the APIs and web pages exposed by the edge server introduced in the previous chapter. We will learn how to use HTTPS to protect against eavesdropping on external access to our APIs, and how to use OAuth 2.0 and OpenID Connect to authenticate and authorize users and client applications to access our APIs. Finally, we will use HTTP Basic authentication to secure access to the discovery server, Netflix Eureka.

The following topics will be covered in this chapter:

- An introduction to the OAuth 2.0 and OpenID Connect standards
- A general discussion on how to secure the system landscape
- Protecting external communication with HTTPS
- Securing access to the discovery server, Netflix Eureka
- Adding a local authorization server to our system landscape
- Authenticating and authorizing API access using OAuth 2.0 and OpenID Connect
- Testing with the local authorization server
- Testing with an external OpenID Connect provider, Auth0

Technical requirements

For instructions on how to install the tools used in this book and how to access the source code for this book, see:

- *Chapter 21* for macOS
- *Chapter 22* for Windows

The code examples in this chapter all come from the source code in `$BOOK_HOME/Chapter11`.

If you want to view the changes applied to the source code in this chapter, that is, see what it took to secure access to the APIs in the microservice landscape, you can compare it with the source code for *Chapter 10, Using Spring Cloud Gateway to Hide Microservices behind an Edge Server*. You can use your favorite `diff` tool and compare the two folders, `$BOOK_HOME/Chapter10` and `$BOOK_HOME/Chapter11`.

Introduction to OAuth 2.0 and OpenID Connect

Before introducing OAuth 2.0 and OpenID Connect, let's clarify what we mean by authentication and authorization. **Authentication** means identifying a user by validating credentials supplied by the user, such as a username and password. **Authorization** is about giving access to various parts of, in our case, an API to an authenticated user.

OAuth 2.0 is an open standard for **authorization delegation**, and **OpenID Connect** is an add-on to OAuth 2.0 that enables client applications to verify the identity of users based on the authentication performed by the authorization server. Let's look briefly at OAuth 2.0 and OpenID Connect separately to get an initial understanding of their purposes!

Introducing OAuth 2.0

OAuth 2.0 is a widely accepted open standard for authorization that enables a user to give consent for a third-party client application to access protected resources in the name of the user. Giving a third-party client application the right to act in the name of a user, for example, calling an API, is known as **authorization delegation**.

So, what does this mean?

Let's start by sorting out the concepts used:

- **Resource owner**: The end user.
- **Client**: The third-party client application, for example, a web app or a native mobile app, that wants to call some protected APIs in the name of the end user.
- **Resource server**: The server that exposes the APIs that we want to protect.
- **Authorization server**: The authorization server issues tokens to the client after the resource owner, that is, the end user, has been authenticated. The management of user information and the authentication of users are typically delegated, behind the scenes, to an **Identity Provider (IdP)**.

A client is registered in the authorization server and is given a **client ID** and a **client secret**. The client secret must be protected by the client, like a password. A client also gets registered with a set of allowed **redirect URIs** that the authorization server will use after a user has been authenticated to send **authorization codes** and **tokens** that have been issued back to the client application.

The following is an example by way of illustration. Let's say that a user accesses a third-party client application and the client application wants to call a protected API to serve the user. To be allowed to access these APIs, the client application needs a way to tell the APIs that it is acting in the name of the user. To avoid solutions where the user must share their credentials with the client application for authentication, an **access token** is issued by an authorization server that gives the client application limited access to a selected set of APIs in the name of the user.

This means that the user never has to reveal their credentials to the client application. The user can also give consent to the client application to access specific APIs on behalf of the user. An access token represents a time-constrained set of access rights, expressed as **scopes** in OAuth 2.0 terms. A **refresh token** can also be issued to a client application by the authorization server. A refresh token can be used by the client application to obtain new access tokens without having to involve the user.

The OAuth 2.0 specification defines four authorization grant flows for issuing access tokens, explained as follows:

- **Authorization code grant flow**: This is the safest, but also the most complex, grant flow. This grant flow requires that the user interacts with the authorization server using a web browser for authentication and giving consent to the client application, as illustrated by the following diagram:

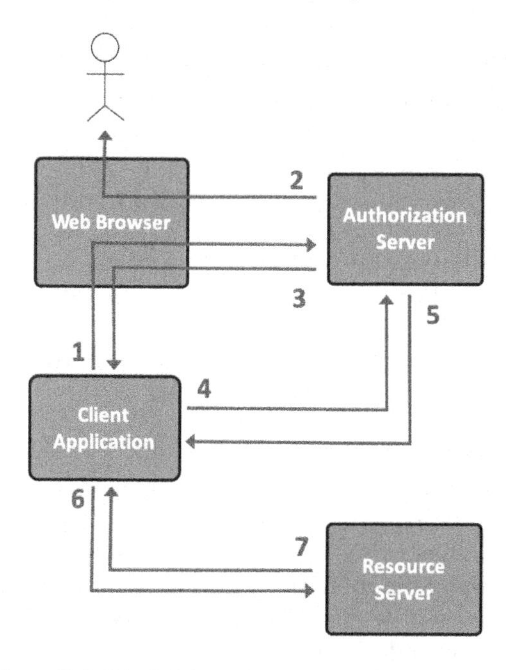

Figure 11.1: OAuth 2.0 – authorization code grant flow

Here's what's going on in this diagram:

1. The client application initiates the grant flow by sending the user to the authorization server in the web browser.
2. The authorization server will authenticate the user and ask for the user's consent.
3. The authorization server will redirect the user back to the client application with an authorization code. The authorization server will use a **redirect URI** specified by the client in *step 1* to know where to send the authorization code. Since the authorization code is passed back to the client application using the web browser, that is, to an unsecure environment where malicious JavaScript code can potentially pick up the authorization code, it is only allowed to be used once and only during a short time period.

4. To exchange the authorization code for an access token, the client application is expected to call the authorization server again. The client application must present its client ID and client secret together with the authorization code for the authorization server. Since the client secret is sensitive and must be protected, this call must be executed from server-side code.
5. The authorization server issues an access token and sends it back to the client application. The authorization server can also, optionally, issue and return a refresh token.
6. Using the access token, the client can send a request to the protected API exposed by the resource server.
7. The resource server validates the access token and serves the request in the event of a successful validation. *Steps 6* and *7* can be repeated as long as the access token is valid. When the lifetime of the access token has expired, the client can use their refresh token to acquire a new access token.

- **Implicit grant flow**: This flow is also web browser-based but intended for client applications that are not able to keep a client secret protected, for example, a single-page web application. The web browser gets an access token back from the authorization server instead of an authorization code. Since the implicit grant flow is less secure than the authorization code grant flow, the client can't request a refresh token.
- **Resource owner password credentials grant flow**: If a client application can't interact with a web browser, it can fall back on this grant flow. In this grant flow, the user must share their credentials with the client application and the client application will use these credentials to acquire an access token.
- **Client credentials grant flow**: In the case where a client application needs to call an API unrelated to a specific user, it can use this grant flow to acquire an access token using its own client ID and client secret.

The full specification can be found here: `https://tools.ietf.org/html/rfc6749`. There are also a number of additional specifications that detail various aspects of OAuth 2.0; for an overview, refer to `https://www.oauth.com/oauth2-servers/map-oauth-2-0-specs/`. One additional specification that is worth some extra attention is *RFC 7636 – Proof Key for Code Exchange by OAuth Public Clients* (PKCE), `https://tools.ietf.org/html/rfc7636`. This specification describes how an otherwise unsecure public client, such as a mobile native app or desktop application, can utilize the authorization code grant flow in a secure way by adding an extra layer of security.

The OAuth 2.0 specification was published in 2012, and over the years a lot of lessons have been learned about what works and what does not. In 2019, work began to establish OAuth 2.1, consolidating all the best practices and experiences from using OAuth 2.0. A draft version can be found here: `https://tools.ietf.org/html/draft-ietf-oauth-v2-1-01`.

In my opinion, the most important improvements in OAuth 2.1 are:

- PKCE is integrated in the authorization code grant flow. Use of PKCE will be required by public clients to improve their security, as described above. For confidential clients, where the authorization server can verify their credentials, the use of PKCE is not required, only recommended.
- The implicit grant flow is deprecated and omitted from the specification, due to its less secure nature.
- The resource owner password credentials grant flow is also deprecated and omitted from the specification, for the same reasons.

Given the direction in the upcoming OAuth 2.1 specification, we will only use the authorization code grant flow and the client credentials grant flow in this book.

When it comes to automating tests against APIs that are protected by OAuth 2.0, the client credentials grant flow is very handy since it doesn't require manual interaction using a web browser. We will use this grant flow later on in this chapter with our test script; see the *Changes in the test script* section.

Introducing OpenID Connect

OpenID Connect (abbreviated to **OIDC**) is, as has already been mentioned, an add-on to OAuth 2.0 that enables client applications to verify the identity of users. OIDC adds an extra token, an ID token, that the client application gets back from the authorization server after a completed grant flow.

The ID token is encoded as a **JSON Web Token** (**JWT**) and contains a number of claims, such as the ID and email address of the user. The ID token is digitally signed using JSON web signatures. This makes it possible for a client application to trust the information in the ID token by validating its digital signature using public keys from the authorization server.

Optionally, access tokens can also be encoded and signed in the same way as ID tokens, but it is not mandatory according to the specification. Also important, OIDC defines a **discovery endpoint**, which is a standardized way to establish URLs to important endpoints, such as requesting authorization codes and tokens or getting the public keys to verify a digitally signed JWT. Finally, it also defines a **user-info endpoint**, which can be used to get extra information about an authenticated user given an access token for that user.

For an overview of the available specifications, see `https://openid.net/developers/specs/`.

In this book, we will only use authorization servers that comply with the OpenID Connect specification. This will simplify the configuration of resource servers by the use of their discovery endpoints. We will also use the optional support for digitally signed JWT access tokens to simplify how resource servers can verify the authenticity of the access tokens. See the *Changes in both the edge server and the product-composite service* section below.

This concludes our introduction to the OAuth 2.0 and OpenID Connect standards. Later on in this chapter, we will learn more about how to use these standards. In the next section, we will get a high-level view of how the system landscape will be secured.

Securing the system landscape

To secure the system landscape as described in the introduction to this chapter, we will perform the following steps:

- Encrypt external requests and responses to and from our external API using HTTPS to protect against eavesdropping
- Authenticate and authorize users and client applications that access our APIs using OAuth 2.0 and OpenID Connect
- Secure access to the discovery server, Netflix Eureka, using HTTP basic authentication

We will only apply HTTPS for external communication to our edge server, using plain HTTP for communication inside our system landscape.

In the chapter on service meshes (*Chapter 18, Using a Service Mesh to Improve Observability and Management*) that will appear later in this book, we will see how we can get help from a service mesh product to automatically provision HTTPS to secure communication inside a system landscape.

For test purposes, we will add a local OAuth 2.0 authorization server to our system landscape. All external communication with the authorization server will be routed through the edge server. The edge server and the `product-composite` service will act as OAuth 2.0 resource servers; that is, they will require a valid OAuth 2.0 access token to allow access.

To minimize the overhead of validating access tokens, we will assume that they are encoded as signed JWTs and that the authorization server exposes an endpoint that the resource servers can use to access the public keys, also known as a **JSON Web Key Set** or **jwk-set** for short, required to validate the signing.

The system landscape will look like the following:

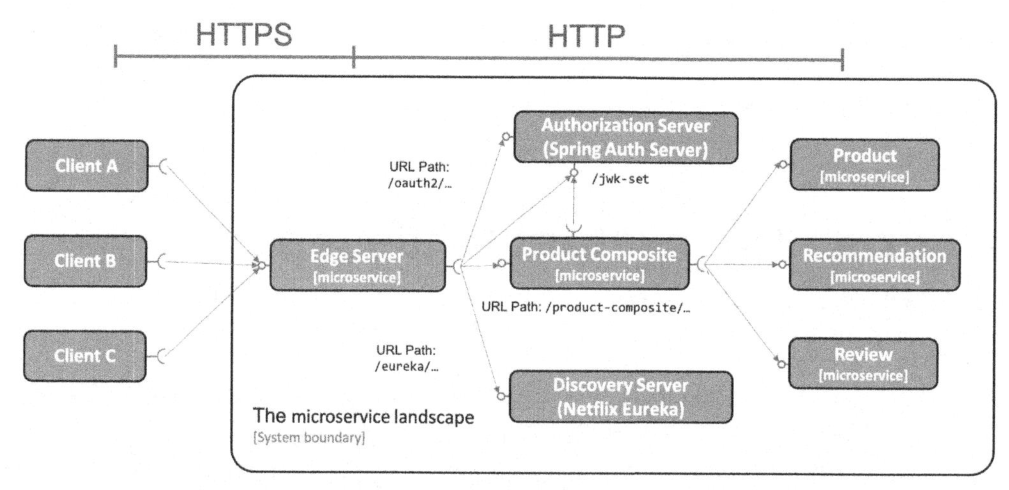

Figure 11.2: Adding an authorization server to the system landscape

From the preceding diagram, we can note that:

1. HTTPS is used for external communication, while plain text HTTP is used inside the system landscape
2. The local OAuth 2.0 authorization server will be accessed externally through the edge server
3. Both the edge server and the `product-composite` microservice will validate access tokens as signed JWTs

4. The edge server and the `product-composite` microservice will get the authorization server's public keys from its `jwk-set` endpoint and use them to validate the signature of the JWT-based access tokens

Note that we will focus on securing access to APIs over HTTP, not on covering general best practices for securing web applications, for example, managing web application security risks pointed out by the **OWASP Top Ten Project**. Refer to `https://owasp.org/www-project-top-ten/` for more information.

With this overview of how the system landscape will be secured, let's start to see how we can protect external communication from eavesdropping using HTTPS.

Protecting external communication with HTTPS

In this section, we will learn how to prevent eavesdropping on external communication, for example, from the internet, via the public APIs exposed by the edge server. We will use HTTPS to encrypt communication. To use HTTPS, we need to do the following:

- **Create a certificate**: We will create our own self-signed certificate, sufficient for development purposes
- **Configure the edge server**: It has to be configured to accept only HTTPS-based external traffic using the certificate

The self-signed certificate is created with the following command:

```
keytool -genkeypair -alias localhost -keyalg RSA -keysize 2048
-storetype PKCS12 -keystore edge.p12 -validity 3650
```

The source code comes with a sample certificate file, so you don't need to run this command to run the following examples.

The command will ask for a number of parameters. When asked for a password, I entered `password`. For the rest of the parameters, I simply entered an empty value to accept the default value. The certificate file created, `edge.p12`, is placed in the `gateway` projects folder, `src/main/resources/keystore`. This means that the certificate file will be placed in the `.jar` file when it is built and will be available on the classpath at runtime at `keystore/edge.p12`.

> Providing certificates using the classpath is sufficient during development, but not applicable to other environments, for example, a production environment. See the *Replacing a self-signed certificate at runtime* section below for how we can replace this certificate with an external certificate at runtime!

To configure the edge server to use the certificate and HTTPS, the following is added to `application.yml` in the `gateway` project:

```
server.port: 8443

server.ssl:
 key-store-type: PKCS12
 key-store: classpath:keystore/edge.p12
 key-store-password: password
 key-alias: localhost
```

Some notes from the preceding source code:

- The path to the certificate is specified in the `server.ssl.key-store` parameter, and is set to `classpath:keystore/edge.p12`. This means that the certificate will be picked up on the classpath from the location `keystore/edge.p12`.
- The password for the certificate is specified in the `server.ssl.key-store-password` parameter.
- To indicate that the edge server talks HTTPS and not HTTP, we also change the port from `8080` to `8443` in the `server.port` parameter.

In addition to these changes in the edge server, changes are also required in the following files to reflect the changes to the port and HTTP protocol, replacing `HTTP` with `HTTPS` and `8080` with `8443`:

- The three Docker Compose files, `docker-compose*.yml`
- The test script, `test-em-all.bash`

Providing certificates using the classpath is, as already mentioned previously, only sufficient during development. Let's see how we can replace this certificate with an external certificate at runtime.

Replacing a self-signed certificate at runtime

Placing a self-signed certificate in the `.jar` file is only useful for development. For a working solution in runtime environments, for example, for test or production, it must be possible to use certificates signed by authorized **CAs** (short for **Certificate Authorities**).

It must also be possible to specify the certificates to be used during runtime without the need to rebuild the `.jar` files and, when using Docker, the Docker image that contains the `.jar` file. When using Docker Compose to manage the Docker container, we can map a volume in the Docker container to a certificate that resides on the Docker host. We can also set up environment variables for the Docker container that points to the external certificate in the Docker volume.

In *Chapter 15, Introduction to Kubernetes*, we will learn about Kubernetes, where we will see more powerful solutions for how to handle secrets, such as certificates, that are suitable for running Docker containers in a cluster; that is, where containers are scheduled on a group of Docker hosts and not on a single Docker host.

The changes described in this topic have **not** been applied to the source code in the book's GitHub repository; you need to make them yourself to see them in action!

To replace the certificate packaged in the `.jar` file, perform the following steps:

1. Create a second certificate and set the password to `testtest`, when asked for it:

```
cd $BOOK_HOME/Chapter11
mkdir keystore

keytool -genkeypair -alias localhost -keyalg RSA -keysize 2048
-storetype PKCS12 -keystore keystore/edge-test.p12 -validity 3650
```

2. Update the Docker Compose file, `docker-compose.yml`, with environment variables for the location, the password for the new certificate, and a volume that maps to the folder where the new certificate is placed. The configuration of the edge server will look like the following after the change:

```
gateway:
  environment:
    - SPRING_PROFILES_ACTIVE=docker
    - SERVER_SSL_KEY_STORE=file:/keystore/edge-test.p12
    - SERVER_SSL_KEY_STORE_PASSWORD=testtest
  volumes:
    - $PWD/keystore:/keystore
  build: spring-cloud/gateway
  mem_limit: 512m
  ports:
    - "8443:8443"
```

3. If the edge server is up and running, it needs to be restarted with the following commands:

```
docker-compose up -d --scale gateway=0
docker-compose up -d --scale gateway=1
```

The command `docker-compose restart gateway` might look like a good candidate for restarting the gateway service, but it actually does not take changes in `docker-compose.yml` into consideration. Hence, it is not a useful command in this case.

The new certificate is now in use!

This concludes the section on how to protect external communication with HTTPS. In the next section, we will learn how to secure access to the discovery server, Netflix Eureka, using HTTP Basic authentication.

Securing access to the discovery server

Previously, we learned how to protect external communication with HTTPS. Now we will use HTTP Basic authentication to restrict access to the APIs and web pages on the discovery server, Netflix Eureka. This means that we will require a user to supply a username and password to get access. Changes are required both on the Eureka server and in the Eureka clients, described as follows.

Changes in the Eureka server

To protect the Eureka server, the following changes have been applied in the source code:

1. In `build.gradle`, a dependency has been added for Spring Security:

   ```
   implementation 'org.springframework.boot:spring-boot-starter-
   security'
   ```

2. Security configuration has been added to the `SecurityConfig` class:

   a. The user is defined as follows:

   ```
   public void configure(AuthenticationManagerBuilder auth)
   throws Exception {
     auth.inMemoryAuthentication()
      .passwordEncoder(NoOpPasswordEncoder.getInstance())
      .withUser(username).password(password)
      .authorities("USER");
   }
   ```

   b. The `username` and `password` are injected into the constructor from the configuration file:

   ```
   @Autowired
   public SecurityConfig(
     @Value("${app.eureka-username}") String username,
     @Value("${app.eureka-password}") String password
   ) {
     this.username = username;
     this.password = password;
   }
   ```

   c. All APIs and web pages are protected using HTTP Basic authentication by means of the following definition:

   ```
   protected void configure(HttpSecurity http) throws
   Exception {
     http
       .authorizeRequests()
         .anyRequest().authenticated()
         .and()
         .httpBasic();
   }
   ```

3. Credentials for the user are set up in the configuration file, `application.yml`:

   ```
   app:
    eureka-username: u
    eureka-password: p
   ```

4. Finally, the test class, `EurekaServerApplicationTests`, uses the credentials from the configuration file when testing the APIs of the Eureka server:

   ```
   @Value("${app.eureka-username}")
   private String username;

   @Value("${app.eureka-password}")
   private String password;

   @Autowired
   public void setTestRestTemplate(TestRestTemplate
   testRestTemplate) {
      this.testRestTemplate = testRestTemplate.
   withBasicAuth(username, password);
   }
   ```

The above are the steps required for restricting access to the APIs and web pages of the discovery server, Netflix Eureka. It will now use HTTP Basic authentication and require a user to supply a username and password to get access. The last step is to configure Netflix Eureka clients so that they pass credentials when accessing the Netflix Eureka server.

Changes in Eureka clients

For Eureka clients, the credentials can be specified in the connection URL for the Eureka server. This is specified in each client's configuration file, `application.yml`, as follows:

```
app:
  eureka-username: u
  eureka-password: p

eureka:
  client:
     serviceUrl:
       defaultZone: "http://${app.eureka-username}:${app.eureka-
                     password}@${app.eureka-server}:8761/eureka/"
```

This concludes the section on how to restrict access to the Netflix Eureka server. In the section *Testing the protected discovery server*, we will run tests to verify that the access is protected. In the next section, we will learn how to add a local authorization server to the system landscape.

Adding a local authorization server

To be able to run tests locally and fully automated with APIs that are secured using OAuth 2.0 and OpenID Connect, we will add an authorization server that is compliant with these specifications to our system landscape. Spring Security unfortunately does not provide an authorization server out of the box. But in April 2020, a community-driven project, **Spring Authorization Server**, led by the Spring Security team, was announced with the goal to deliver an authorization server. For more information, see `https://spring.io/blog/2020/04/15/announcing-the-spring-authorization-server`.

The Spring Authorization Server supports both the use of the OpenID Connect discovery endpoint and digital signing of access tokens. It also provides an endpoint that can be accessed using the discovery information to get keys for verifying the digital signature of a token. With support for these features, it can be used as the authorization server in local and automated tests that verify that the system landscape works as expected.

The authorization server in this book is based on the sample authorization server provided by the Spring Authorization Server project; see `https://github.com/spring-projects-experimental/spring-authorization-server/tree/master/samples/boot/oauth2-integration/authorizationserver`.

The following changes have been applied to the sample project:

- The build file has been updated to follow the structure of the other projects' build files in this book.
- The port is set to `9999`.
- A Dockerfile has been added with the same structure as for the other projects in this book.
- The authorization server has been integrated with Eureka for service discovery in the same way as the other projects in this book.
- Public access has been added to the actuator's endpoints.

WARNING: As already warned about in *Chapter 7, Developing Reactive Microservices*, allowing public access to the actuator's endpoints is very helpful during development, but it can be a security issue to reveal too much information in actuator endpoints in production systems. Therefore, plan for minimizing the information exposed by the actuator endpoints in production!

- Unit tests have been added that verify access to the most critical endpoints according to the OpenID Connect specification.
- The username and password for the single registered user are set to `"u"` and `"p"` respectively.
- Two OAuth clients are registered, `reader` and `writer`, where the `reader` client is granted a `product:read` scope and the `writer` client is granted both a `product:read` and `product:write` scope. Both clients are configured to have the client secret set to `secret`.
- Allowed redirect URIs for the clients are set to `https://my.redirect.uri` and `https://localhost:8443/webjars/swagger-ui/oauth2-redirect.html`. The first URL will be used in the tests described below and the second URL is used by the Swagger UI component.

The source code for the authorization server is available in `$BOOK_HOME/Chapter11/spring-cloud/authorization-server`.

To incorporate the authorization server in the system landscape, changes to the following files have been applied:

- The server has been added to the common build file, `settings.gradle`
- The server has been added to the three Docker Compose files, `docker-compose*.yml`
- The edge server, `spring-cloud/gateway`:
    - A health check has been added for the authorization server in `HealthCheckConfiguration`.
    - Routes to the authorization server for the URIs starting with `/oauth`, `/login`, and `/error` have been added in the configuration file `application.yml`. These URIs are used to issue tokens for clients, authenticate users, and show error messages.

- Since these three URIs need to be unprotected by the edge server, they are configured in the new class `SecurityConfig` to permit all requests.

Due to a regression in Spring Security 5.5, which is used by Spring Boot 2.5, the Spring Authorization Server can't be used with Spring Boot 2.5 at the time of writing this chapter. Instead, Spring Boot 2.4.4 and Spring Cloud 2020.0.2 are used. For details, see:

- `https://github.com/spring-projects-experimental/spring-authorization-server/issues/305`
- `https://github.com/spring-projects/spring-security/issues/9787`

With an understanding of how a local authorization server is added to the system landscape, let's move on and see how to use OAuth 2.0 and OpenID Connect to authenticate and authorize access to APIs.

Protecting APIs using OAuth 2.0 and OpenID Connect

With the authorization server in place, we can enhance the edge server and the `product-composite` service to become OAuth 2.0 resource servers, so that they will require a valid access token to allow access. The edge server will be configured to accept any access token it can validate using the digital signature provided by the authorization server. The `product-composite` service will also require the access token to contain valid OAuth 2.0 scopes:

- The `product:read` scope will be required for accessing the read-only APIs
- The `product:write` scope will be required for accessing the create and delete APIs

The `product-composite` service will also be enhanced with configuration that allows its Swagger UI component to interact with the authorization server to issue an access token. This will allow users of the Swagger UI web page to test the protected API.

We also need to enhance the test script, `test-em-all.bash`, so that it acquires access tokens and uses them when it performs the tests.

Changes in both the edge server and the product-composite service

The following changes have been applied in the source code to both the edge server and the `product-composite` service:

- Spring Security dependencies have been added to `build.gradle` to support OAuth 2.0 resource servers:

  ```
  implementation 'org.springframework.boot:spring-boot-starter-security'
  implementation 'org.springframework.security:spring-security-oauth2-resource-server'
  implementation 'org.springframework.security:spring-security-oauth2-jose'
  ```

- Security configurations have been added to new `SecurityConfig` classes in both projects:

  ```
  @EnableWebFluxSecurity
  public class SecurityConfig {

    @Bean
    SecurityWebFilterChain springSecurityFilterChain(
        ServerHttpSecurity http) {
      http
        .authorizeExchange()
          .pathMatchers("/actuator/**").permitAll()
          .anyExchange().authenticated()
          .and()
        .oauth2ResourceServer()
          .jwt();
      return http.build();
    }
  }
  ```

  Explanations for the preceding source code are as follows:

  - The annotation `@EnableWebFluxSecurity` enables Spring Security support for APIs based on Spring WebFlux.

    - `.pathMatchers("/actuator/**").permitAll()` is used to allow unrestricted access to URLs that should be unprotected, for example, the `actuator` endpoints in this case. Refer to the source code for URLs that are treated as unprotected. Be careful about which URLs are exposed unprotected. For example, the `actuator` endpoints should be protected before going to production.
    - `.anyExchange().authenticated()` ensures that the user is authenticated before being allowed access to all other URLs.
    - `.oauth2ResourceServer().jwt()` specifies that authorization will be based on OAuth 2.0 access tokens encoded as JWTs.

- The authorization server's OIDC discovery endpoint has been registered in the configuration file, `application.yml`:

```
app.auth-server: localhost

spring.security.oauth2.resourceserver.jwt.issuer-uri:
http://${app.auth-server}:9999

---
spring.config.activate.on-profile: docker

app.auth-server: auth-server
```

Later on in this chapter, when the system landscape is started up, you can test the discovery endpoint. You can, for example, find the endpoint that returns the keys required for verifying the digital signature of a token using the command:

```
docker-compose exec auth-server curl localhost:9999/.
well-known/openid-configuration -s | jq -r .jwks_uri
```

We also need to make some changes that only apply to the `product-composite` service.

Changes in the product-composite service only

In addition to the common changes applied in the previous section, the following changes have also been applied to the `product-composite` service:

- The security configuration in the `SecurityConfig` class has been refined by requiring OAuth 2.0 scopes in the access token in order to allow access:

  ```
  .pathMatchers(POST, "/product-composite/**")
    .hasAuthority("SCOPE_product:write")
  .pathMatchers(DELETE, "/product-composite/**")
    .hasAuthority("SCOPE_product:write")
  .pathMatchers(GET, "/product-composite/**")
    .hasAuthority("SCOPE_product:read")
  ```

By convention, OAuth 2.0 scopes need to be prefixed with `SCOPE_` when checked for authority using Spring Security.

- A method, `logAuthorizationInfo()`, has been added to log relevant parts from the JWT-encoded access token upon each call to the API. The access token can be acquired using the standard Spring Security, `SecurityContext`, which, in a reactive environment, can be acquired using the static helper method, `ReactiveSecurityContextHolder.getContext()`. Refer to the `ProductCompositeServiceImpl` class for details.
- The use of OAuth has been disabled when running Spring-based integration tests. To prevent the OAuth machinery from kicking in when we are running integration tests, we disable it as follows:
  - A security configuration, `TestSecurityConfig`, is added to be used during tests. It permits access to all resources:

    ```
    http.csrf().disable().authorizeExchange().anyExchange().
    permitAll();
    ```

  - In each Spring integration test class, we configure `TestSecurityConfig` to override the existing security configuration with the following:

    ```
    @SpringBootTest(
      classes = {TestSecurityConfig.class},
      properties = {"spring.main.allow-bean-definition-
        overriding=true"})
    ```

Changes to allow Swagger UI to acquire access tokens

To allow access to the protected APIs from the Swagger UI component, the following changes have been applied in the `product-composite` service:

- The web pages exposed by the Swagger UI component have been configured to be publicly available. The following line has been added to the `SecurityConfig` class:

```
.pathMatchers("/openapi/**").permitAll()
.pathMatchers("/webjars/**").permitAll()
```

- The OpenAPI Specification of the API has been enhanced to require that the security schema `security_auth` is applied.

  The following line has been added to the definition of the interface `ProductCompositeService` in the `API` project:

```
@SecurityRequirement(name = "security_auth")
```

- To define the semantics of the security schema `security_auth`, the class `OpenApiConfig` has been added to the `product-composite` project. It looks like this:

```
@SecurityScheme(
  name = "security_auth", type = SecuritySchemeType.OAUTH2,
  flows = @OAuthFlows(
    authorizationCode = @OAuthFlow(
      authorizationUrl = "${springdoc.oAuthFlow.
        authorizationUrl}",
      tokenUrl = "${springdoc.oAuthFlow.tokenUrl}",
      scopes = {
        @OAuthScope(name = "product:read", description =
          "read scope"),
        @OAuthScope(name = "product:write", description =
          "write scope")
      }
)))
public class OpenApiConfig {}
```

  From the preceding class definition, we can see:

  a. The security schema will be based on OAuth 2.0
  b. The authorization code grant flow will be used

c. The required URLs for acquiring an authorization code and access tokens will be supplied by the configuration using the parameters `springdoc.oAuthFlow.authorizationUrl` and `springdoc.oAuthFlow.tokenUrl`

d. A list of scopes (`product:read` and `product:write`) that Swagger UI will require to be able to call the APIs

- Finally, some configuration is added to `application.yml`:

```
swagger-ui:
  oauth2-redirect-url: https://localhost:8443/webjars/swagger-
ui/oauth2-redirect.html
  oauth:
    clientId: writer
    clientSecret: secret
    useBasicAuthenticationWithAccessCodeGrant: true
oAuthFlow:
  authorizationUrl: https://localhost:8443/oauth2/authorize
  tokenUrl: https://localhost:8443/oauth2/token
```

From the preceding configuration, we can see:

a. The redirect URL that Swagger UI will use to acquire the authorization code.

b. Its client ID and client secret.

c. It will use HTTP Basic Authentication when identifying itself for the authorization server.

d. The values of the `authorizationUrl` and `tokenUrl` parameters, used by the `OpenApiConfig` class described above. Note that these URLs are used by the web browser and not by the `product-composite` service itself. So they must be resolvable from the web browser.

To allow unprotected access to the Swagger UI web pages, the edge server has also been configured to allow unrestricted access to URLs that are routed to the Swagger UI component. The following is added to the edge server's `SecurityConfig` class:

```
.pathMatchers("/openapi/**").permitAll()
.pathMatchers("/webjars/**").permitAll()
```

With these changes in place, both the edge server and the `product-composite` service can act as OAuth 2.0 resource servers, and the Swagger UI component can act as an OAuth client. The last step we need to take to introduce the usage of OAuth 2.0 and OpenID Connect is to update the test script, so it acquires access tokens and uses them when running the tests.

Changes in the test script

To start with, we need to acquire an access token before we can call any of the APIs, except the health API. This is done, as already mentioned above, using the OAuth 2.0 client credentials flow. To be able to call the create and delete APIs, we acquire an access token as the `writer` client, as follows:

```
ACCESS_TOKEN=$(curl -k https://writer:secret@$HOST:$PORT/oauth2/
token -d grant_type=client_credentials -s | jq .access_token -r)
```

From the preceding command, we can see that it uses HTTP Basic authentication, passing its client ID and client secret as `writer:secret@` before the hostname.

To verify that the scope-based authorization works, two tests have been added to the test script:

```
# Verify that a request without access token fails on 401, Unauthorized
assertCurl 401 "curl -k https://$HOST:$PORT/product-composite/$PROD_ID_
REVS_RECS -s"

# Verify that the reader client with only read scope can call the read
API but not delete API
READER_ACCESS_TOKEN=$(curl -k https://reader:secret@$HOST:$PORT/oauth2/
token -d grant_type=client_credentials -s | jq .access_token -r)
READER_AUTH="-H \"Authorization: Bearer $READER_ACCESS_TOKEN\""

assertCurl 200 "curl -k https://$HOST:$PORT/product-composite/$PROD_ID_
REVS_RECS $READER_AUTH -s"
assertCurl 403 "curl -k https://$HOST:$PORT/product-composite/$PROD_ID_
REVS_RECS $READER_AUTH -X DELETE -s"
```

The test script uses the reader client's credentials to acquire an access token:

- The first test calls an API without supplying an access token. The API is expected to return the `401 Unauthorized` HTTP status.
- The second test verifies that the reader client can call a read-only API.
- The last test calls an updating API using the `reader` client, which is only granted a `read` scope. A request sent to the delete API is expected to return the `403 Forbidden` HTTP status.

For the full source code, see `test-em-all.bash`.

With the test script updated to acquire and use OAuth 2.0 access tokens, we are ready to try it out in the next section!

Testing with the local authorization server

In this section we will try out the secured system landscape; that is, we will test all the security components together. We will use the local authorization server to issue access tokens. The following tests will be performed:

1. First, we build from source and run the test script to ensure that everything fits together.
2. Next, we will test the protected discovery server's API and web page.
3. After that, we will learn how to acquire access tokens using OAuth 2.0 client credentials and authorization code grant flows.
4. With the issued access tokens, we will test the protected APIs. We will also verify that an access token issued for a reader client can't be used to call an updating API.
5. Finally, we will also verify that Swagger UI can issue access tokens and call the APIs.

Building and running the automated tests

To build and run automated tests, we perform the following steps:

1. First, build the Docker images from source with the following commands:
```
cd $BOOK_HOME/Chapter11
./gradlew build && docker-compose build
```
2. Next, start the system landscape in Docker and run the usual tests with the following command:
```
./test-em-all.bash start
```

Note the new negative tests at the end that verify that we get a `401 Unauthorized` code back when not authenticated, and `403 Forbidden` when not authorized.

Testing the protected discovery server

With the protected discovery server, Eureka, up and running, we have to supply valid credentials to be able to access its APIs and web pages.

For example, asking the Eureka server for registered instances can be done by means of the following `curl` command, where we supply the username and password directly in the URL:

```
curl -H "accept:application/json" https://u:p@localhost:8443/eureka/
api/apps -ks | jq -r .applications.application[].instance[].instanceId
```

A sample response is as follows:

```
2. @700dd0df9ffe:/ (bash)
abe7ee8d450c:gateway:8443
1fbb5fcd7864:auth-server:9999
6cdb02a5ad71:product-composite:8080
9975baef8ae7:product:8080
e7b8ac60ae6e:review:8080
d300f3e31c1f:recommendation:8080
$
```

Figure 11.3: Services registered in Eureka using an API call

When accessing the web page on `https://localhost:8443/eureka/web`, we first have to accept an unsecure connection, since our certificate is self-signed, and next we have to supply valid credentials, as specified in the configuration file (`u` as username and `p` as password):

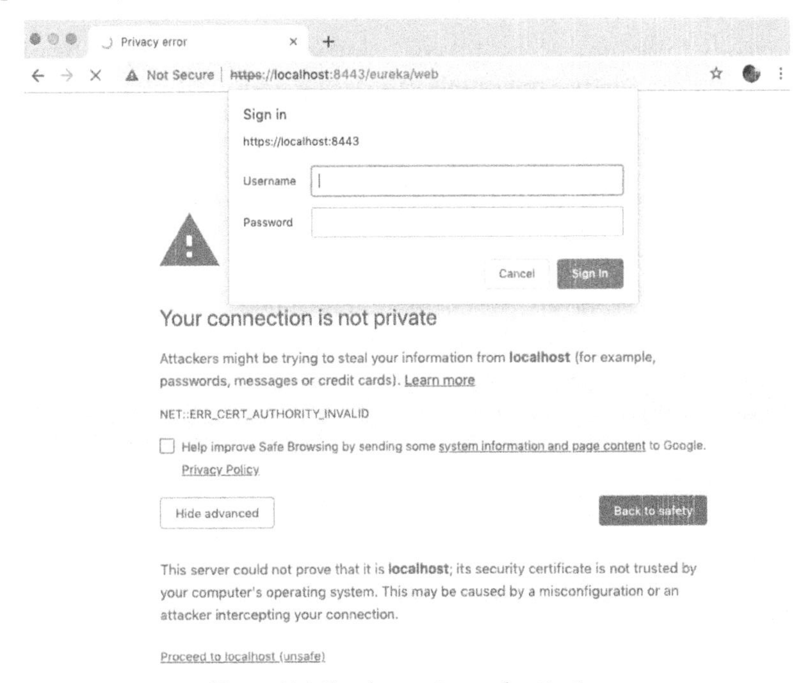

Figure 11.4: Eureka requires authentication

Following a successful login, we will see the familiar web page from the Eureka server:

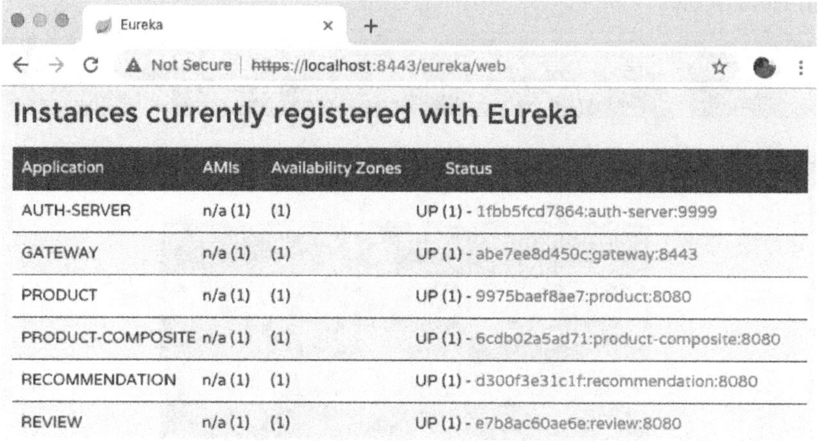
Eureka
Not Secure
https://localhost:8443/eureka/web
Instances currently registered with Eureka
Application
AMIs
Availability Zones
Status
AUTH-SERVER n/a (1) (1) UP (1) - 1fbb5fcd7864:auth-server:9999
GATEWAY n/a (1) (1) UP (1) - abe7ee8d450c:gateway:8443
PRODUCT n/a (1) (1) UP (1) - 9975baef8ae7:product:8080
PRODUCT-COMPOSITE n/a (1) (1) UP (1) - 6cdb02a5ad71:product-composite:8080
RECOMMENDATION n/a (1) (1) UP (1) - d300f3e31c1f:recommendation:8080
REVIEW n/a (1) (1) UP (1) - e7b8ac60ae6e:review:8080

Figure 11.5: Services registered in Eureka using the web page

After ensuring that access to the Eureka server is protected, we will learn how to issue OAuth access tokens.

Acquiring access tokens

Now we are ready to acquire access tokens using grant flows defined by OAuth 2.0. We will first try out the client credentials grant flow, followed by the authorization code grant flow.

Acquiring access tokens using the client credentials grant flow

To get an access token for the `writer` client, that is, with both the `product:read` and `product:write` scopes, issue the following command:

```
curl -k https://writer:secret@localhost:8443/oauth2/token -d grant_
type=client_credentials -s | jq .
```

The client identifies itself using HTTP Basic authentication, passing its client ID, `writer`, and its client secret, `secret`.

A sample response is as follows:

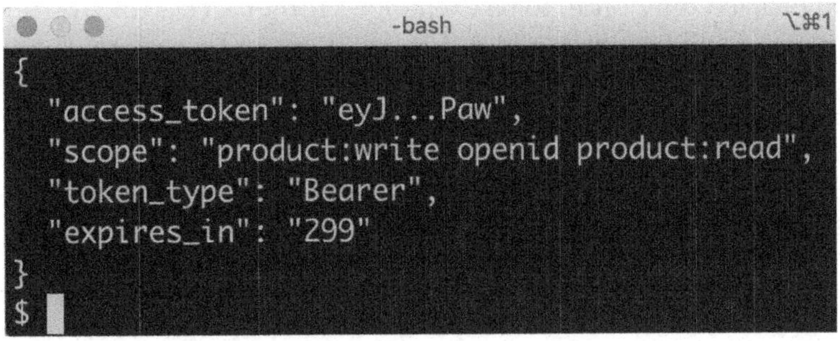

```
{
  "access_token": "eyJ...Paw",
  "scope": "product:write openid product:read",
  "token_type": "Bearer",
  "expires_in": "299"
}
$
```

Figure 11.6: Sample token response

From the screenshot we can see that we got the following information in the response:

- The access token itself.
- The scopes granted to the token. The `writer` client is granted both the `product:write` and `product:read` scope. It is also granted the `openid` scope, allowing access to information regarding the user's ID, such as an email address.
- The type of token we got; **Bearer** means that the bearer of this token should be given access according to the scopes granted to the token.
- The number of seconds that the access token is valid for, `299` seconds in this case.

To get an access token for the `reader` client, that is, with only the `product:read` scope, simply replace `writer` with `reader` in the preceding command, resulting in:

```
curl -k https://reader:secret@localhost:8443/oauth2/token -d grant_type=client_credentials -s | jq .
```

Acquiring access tokens using the authorization code grant flow

To acquire an access token using the authorization code grant flow, we need to involve a web browser. This grant flow is a bit more complicated in order to make it secure in an environment that is partly unsecure (the web browser).

In the first unsecure step, we will use the web browser to acquire an authorization code that can be used only once, to be exchanged for an access token. The authorization code will be passed from the web browser to a secure layer, for example, server-side code, which can make a new request to the authorization server to exchange the authorization code for an access token. In this secure exchange, the server has to supply a client secret to verify its identity.

Perform the following steps to execute the authorization code grant flow:

1. To get an authorization code for the `reader` client, use the following URL in a web browser that accepts the use of self-signed certificates, for example, Chrome: `https://localhost:8443/oauth2/authorize?response_type=code&client_id=reader&redirect_uri=https://my.redirect.uri&scope=product:read&state=35725`.
2. When asked to log in by the web browser, use the credentials specified in the configuration of the authorization server, `u` and `p`:

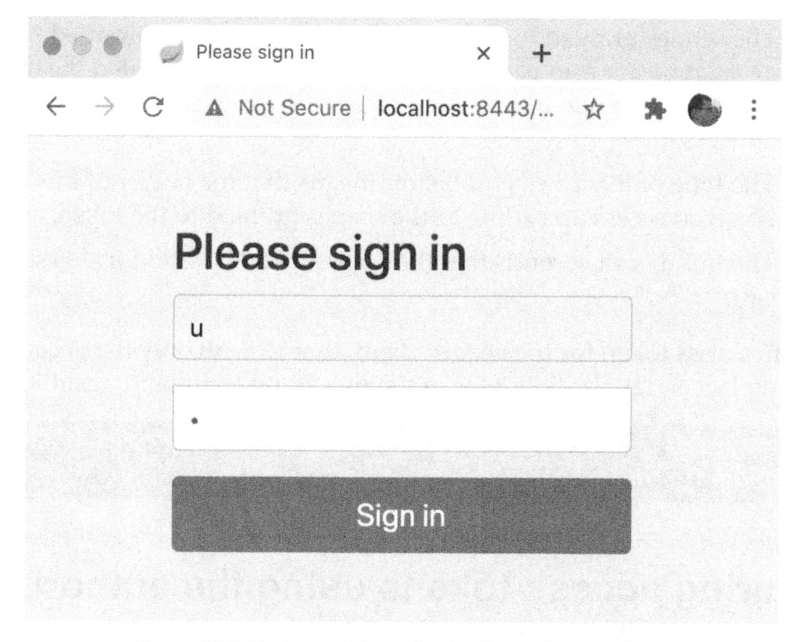

Figure 11.7: Trying out the authorization code grant flow

3. Next, we will be asked to give the `reader` client consent to call the APIs in our name:

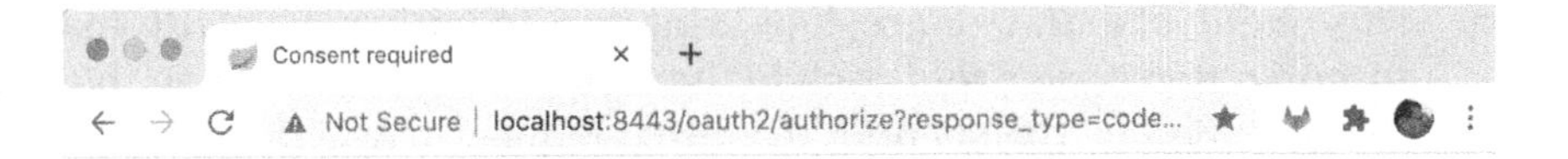
Consent required
Not Secure | localhost:8443/oauth2/authorize?response_type=code...

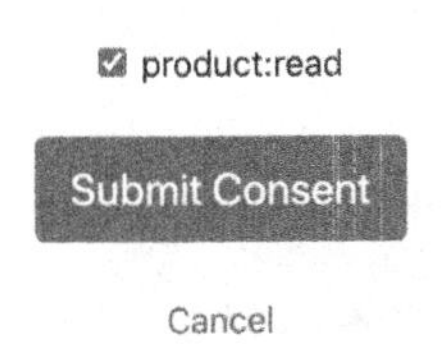
Consent required
reader wants to access your account u
The following permissions are requested by the above app.
Please review these and consent if you approve.
product:read
Submit Consent
Cancel
Your consent to provide access is required.
If you do not approve, click Cancel, in which case no information will be shared with the app.

Figure 11.8: Authorization code grant flow consent page

4. After clicking on the **Submit Consent** button, we will get the following response:

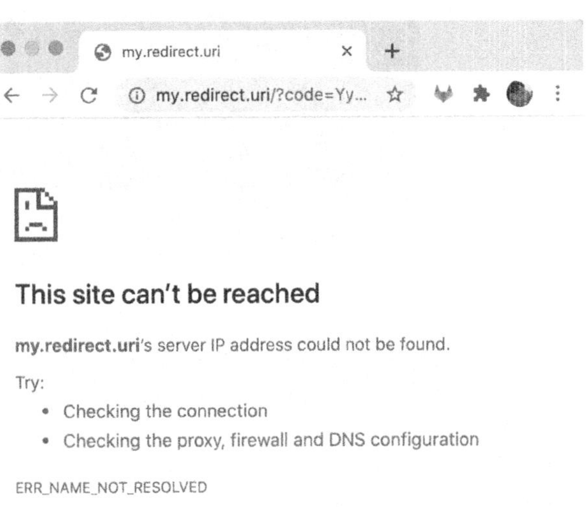
my.redirect.uri
my.redirect.uri/?code=Yy...
This site can't be reached
my.redirect.uri's server IP address could not be found.
Try:
Checking the connection
Checking the proxy, firewall and DNS configuration
ERR_NAME_NOT_RESOLVED
Details
Reload

Figure 11.9: Authorization code grant flow redirect page

5. This might, at a first glance, look a bit disappointing. The URL that the authorization server sent back to the web browser is based on the redirect URI specified by the client in the initial request. Copy the URL into a text editor and you will find something similar to the following:

   `https://my.redirect.uri/?code=Yyr...X0Q&state=35725`

   Great! We can find the authorization code in the redirect URL in the `code` request parameter. Extract the authorization code from the `code` parameter and define an environment variable, `CODE`, with its value:

   ```
   CODE=Yyr...X0Q
   ```

6. Next, pretend you are the backend server that exchanges the authorization code with an access token using the following `curl` command:

   ```
   curl -k https://reader:secret@localhost:8443/oauth2/token \
    -d grant_type=authorization_code \
    -d client_id=reader \
    -d redirect_uri=https://my.redirect.uri \
    -d code=$CODE -s | jq .
   ```

   A sample response is as follows:

   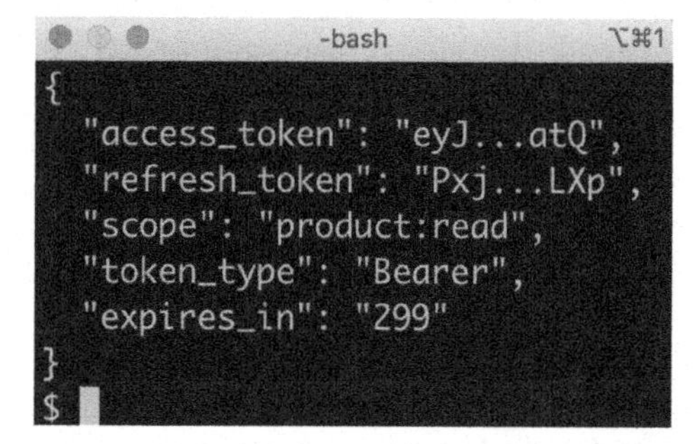

   Figure 11.10: Authorization code grant flow access token

   From the screenshot, we can see that we got similar information in the response as we got from the client credentials flow, with the following exceptions:

   - Since we used a more secure grant flow, we also got a `refresh token` issued
   - Since we asked for an access token for the `reader` client, we only got a `product:read` scope, no `product:write` scope

7. To get an authorization code for the `writer` client, use the following URL: `https://localhost:8443/oauth2/authorize?response_type=code&client_id=writer&redirect_uri=https://my.redirect.uri&scope=product:read+product:write&state=72489`.

8. To exchange the code for an access token for the `writer` client, run the following command:

```
curl -k https://writer:secret@localhost:8443/oauth2/token \
  -d grant_type=authorization_code \
  -d client_id=writer \
  -d redirect_uri=https://my.redirect.uri \
  -d code=$CODE -s | jq .
```

   Verify that the response now also contains the `product:write` scope!

Calling protected APIs using access tokens

Now, let's use the access tokens we have acquired to call the protected APIs.

An OAuth 2.0 access token is expected to be sent as a standard HTTP `authorization` header, where the access token is prefixed with `Bearer`.

Run the following commands to call the protected APIs:

1. First, call an API to retrieve a composite product without a valid access token:

```
ACCESS_TOKEN=an-invalid-token
curl https://localhost:8443/product-composite/1 -k -H
"Authorization: Bearer $ACCESS_TOKEN" -i
```

   It should return the following response:

```
2. @700dd0df9ffe:/ (bash)
HTTP/1.1 401 Unauthorized
WWW-Authenticate: Bearer error="invalid_token"
$
```

Figure 11.11: Invalid token results in a 401 Unauthorized response

   The error message clearly states that the access token is invalid!

2. Next, try using the API to retrieve a composite product using one of the access tokens acquired for the `reader` client from the previous section:

```
ACCESS_TOKEN={a-reader-access-token}
curl https://localhost:8443/product-composite/1 -k -H
"Authorization: Bearer $ACCESS_TOKEN" -i
```

Now we will get the `200 OK` status code and the expected response body will be returned:

```
HTTP/1.1 200 OK
...
{"productId":1, ...}
$
```

Figure 11.12: Valid access token results in a 200 OK response

3. If we try to access an updating API, for example, the delete API, with an access token acquired for the `reader` client, the call will fail:

```
ACCESS_TOKEN={a-reader-access-token}
curl https://localhost:8443/product-composite/999 -k -H
"Authorization: Bearer $ACCESS_TOKEN" -X DELETE -i
```

It will fail with a response similar to the following:

```
HTTP/1.1 403 Forbidden
WWW-Authenticate: Bearer error="insufficient_scope", error_description="The request requires higher privileges than provided by the access token.", error_uri="https://tools.ietf.org/html/rfc6750#section-3.1"
$
```

Figure 11.13: Insufficient scope results in a 403 Forbidden result

From the error response, it is clear that we are forbidden to call the API since the request requires higher privileges than what our access token is granted.

4. If we repeat the call to the delete API, but with an access token acquired for the `writer` client, the call will succeed with `200 OK` in the response.

The delete operation should return `200` even if the product with the specified product ID does not exist in the underlying database, since the delete operation is idempotent, as described in *Chapter 6, Adding Persistence*. Refer to the *Adding new APIs* section.

If you look into the log output using the `docker-compose logs -f product-composite` command, you should be able to find authorization information such as the following:

```
product-composite_1  ... Authorization info: Subject: u, scopes: ["product:write","product:read"], expires 2021-02-25T16:16:52Z: issuer: http://auth-server:9999, audience: [writer]
$
```

Figure 11.14: Authorization info in the log output

This information was extracted in the `product-composite` service from the JWT-encoded access token; the `product-composite` service did not need to communicate with the authorization server to get this information!

With these tests, we have seen how to acquire an access token with the client credentials and authorization code grant flows. We have also seen how scopes can be used to limit what a client can do with a specific access token, for example, only use it for reading operations.

Testing Swagger UI with OAuth 2.0

In this section, we will learn how to use the Swagger UI component to access the protected API. The configuration described in the *Changes in the product-composite service only* section above allows us to issue an access token for Swagger UI and use it when calling the APIs from Swagger UI.

To try it out, perform the following steps:

1. Open the Swagger UI start page by going to the following URL in a web browser: `https://localhost:8443/openapi/swagger-ui.html`.
2. On the start page we can now see a new button, next to the **Servers** drop-down list, with the text **Authorize**.
3. Click on the **Authorize** button to initiate an authorization code grant flow.
4. Swagger UI will present a list of scopes that it will ask the authorization server to get access to. Select all scopes by clicking on the link with the text **select all** and then clicking on the **Authorize** button:

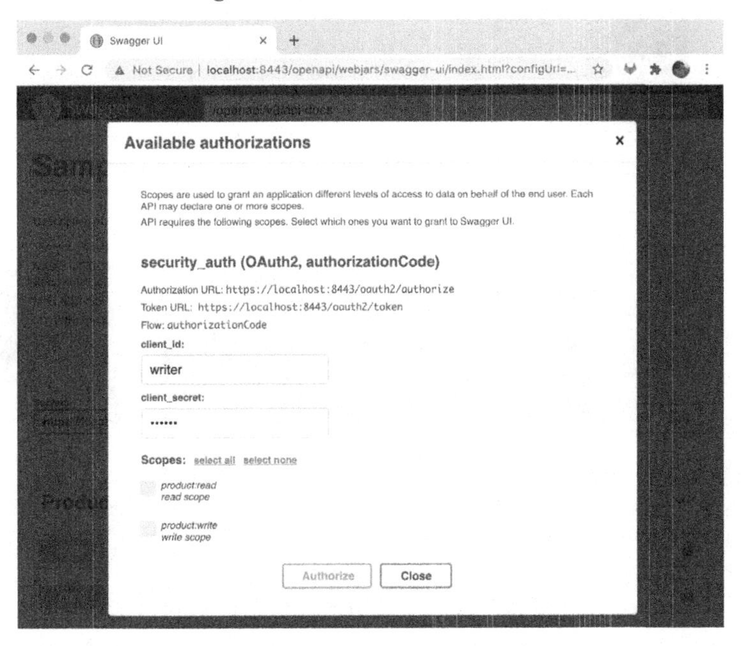

Figure 11.15: Swagger UI asking for OAuth scopes

You will then be redirected to the authorization server. If you are not already logged in from the web browser used, the authorization server will ask for your credentials as in the *Acquiring access tokens using the authorization code grant flow* section.

5. Log in with username `u` and password `p`.
6. Next, the authorization server will ask for your consent. Select both scopes and click on the **Submit Consent** button.
7. Swagger UI will complete the authorization process by showing information about the completed grant flow. Click on the **Close** button to get back to the start page:

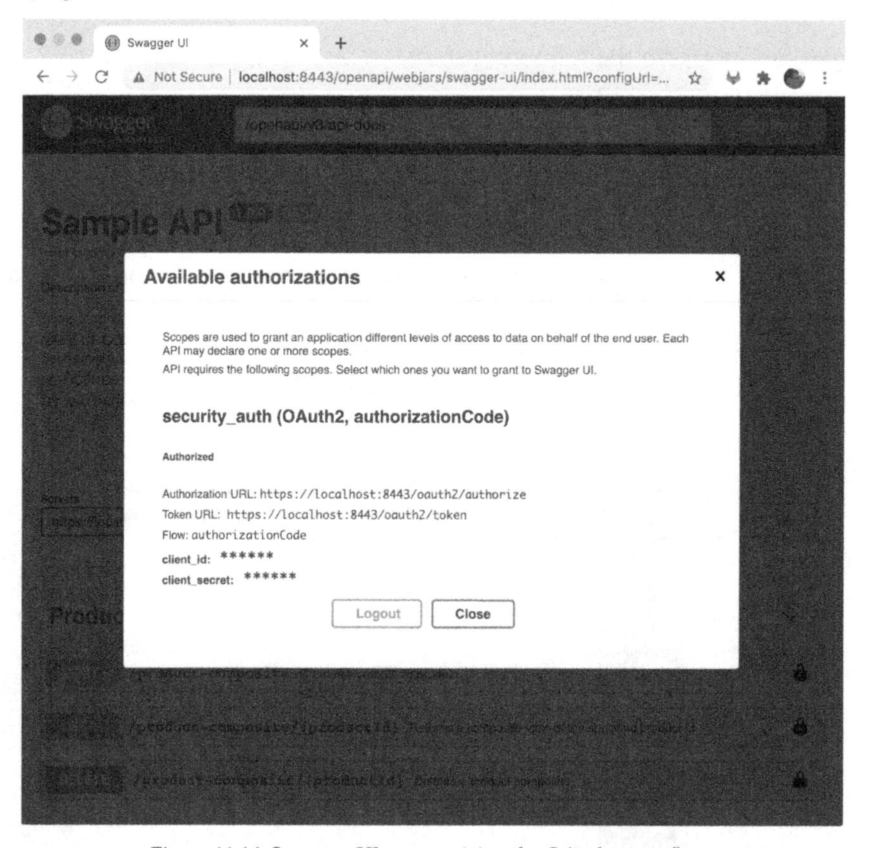

Figure 11.16: Swagger UI summarizing the OAuth grant flow

8. Now you can try out the APIs in the same way as described in *Chapter 5, Adding an API Description Using OpenAPI*. Swagger UI will add the access token to the requests. If you look closely in the **curl** command reported below the **Responses** header, you can find the access token.

This completes the tests we will perform with the local authorization server. In the next section, we will replace it with an external OpenID Connect-compliant provider.

Testing with an external OpenID Connect provider

So, the OAuth dance works fine with an authorization server we control ourselves. But what happens if we replace it with a certified OpenID Connect provider? In theory, it should work out of the box. Let's find out, shall we?

For a list of certified implementations of OpenID Connect, refer to `https://openid.net/developers/certified/`. We will use Auth0, `https://auth0.com/`, for our tests with an external OpenID provider. To be able to use Auth0 instead of our own authorization server, we will go through the following topics:

- Setting up an account with a reader and writer client and a user in Auth0
- Applying the changes required to use Auth0 as an OpenID provider
- Running the test script to verify that it is working
- Acquiring access tokens using the following grant flows:
    - Client credentials grant flow
    - Authorization code grant flow
- Calling protected APIs using the access tokens acquired from the grant flows
- Using the user info endpoint to get more information about a user

Let us go through each of them in the following sections.

Setting up and configuring an account in Auth0

Most of the configuration required in Auth0 will be taken care of by a script that uses Auth0's management API. But we must perform a few manual steps up to the point where Auth0 has created a client ID and client secret we can use to access the management API. Auth0's service is multi-tenant, allowing us to create our own domain of OAuth objects in terms of clients, resource owners, and resource servers.

Perform the following manual steps to sign up for a free account in Auth0 and create a client that we can use to access the management API:

1. Open the URL `https://auth0.com` in your browser.
2. Click on the **Sign up** button:
    a. Sign up with an email of your choice.
    b. After a successful sign-up, you will be asked to create a tenant domain. Enter the name of the tenant of your choice, in my case: `dev-ml.eu.auth0.com`.
    c. Fill in information about your account as requested.
    d. Also, look in your mailbox for an email with the subject *Please Verify Your Auth0 Account* and use the instructions in the email to verify your account.
3. Following sign-up, you will be directed to your dashboard with a **Getting Started** page.
4. In the menu to the left, click on **Applications** to get it expanded, then click on **APIs** to find the management API, **Auth0 Management API**. This API was created for you during the creation of your tenant. We will use this API to create the required definitions in the tenant.
5. Click on **Auth0 Management API** and select the **Test** tab.
6. A big button with the text **CREATE & AUTHORIZE TEST APPLICATION** will appear. Click on it to get a client created that can be used to access the management API.
7. Once created, a page is displayed with the header **Asking Auth0 for tokens from my application**. As a final step, we need to give the created client permission to use the management APIs.

8. Click on the tab **Machine to Machine Applications**, next to the **Test** tab.
9. Here we will find the test client, **Auth0 Management API (Test Application)**, and we can see that it is authorized to use the management API. If we click on the down arrow next to the **Authorized** toggle button, a large number of available privileges are revealed.
10. Click on the **All** choice and then on the **UPDATE** button. The screen should look similar to the following screenshot:

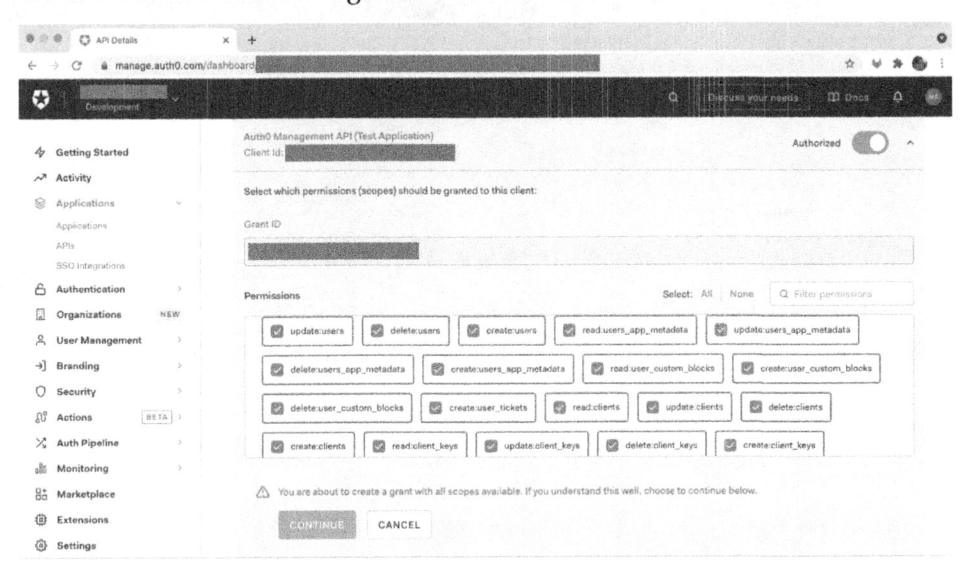

Figure 11.17: Auth0 management API client permissions

11. Press on the **CONTINUE** button after understanding that you now have a very powerful client with access to all management APIs within your tenant.

12. Now, we just need to collect the client ID and client secret of the created client. The easiest way to do that is to select **Applications** in the menu to the left (under the main menu choice **Applications**) and then select the application named **Auth0 Management API (Test Application)**. A screen similar to the following should be displayed:

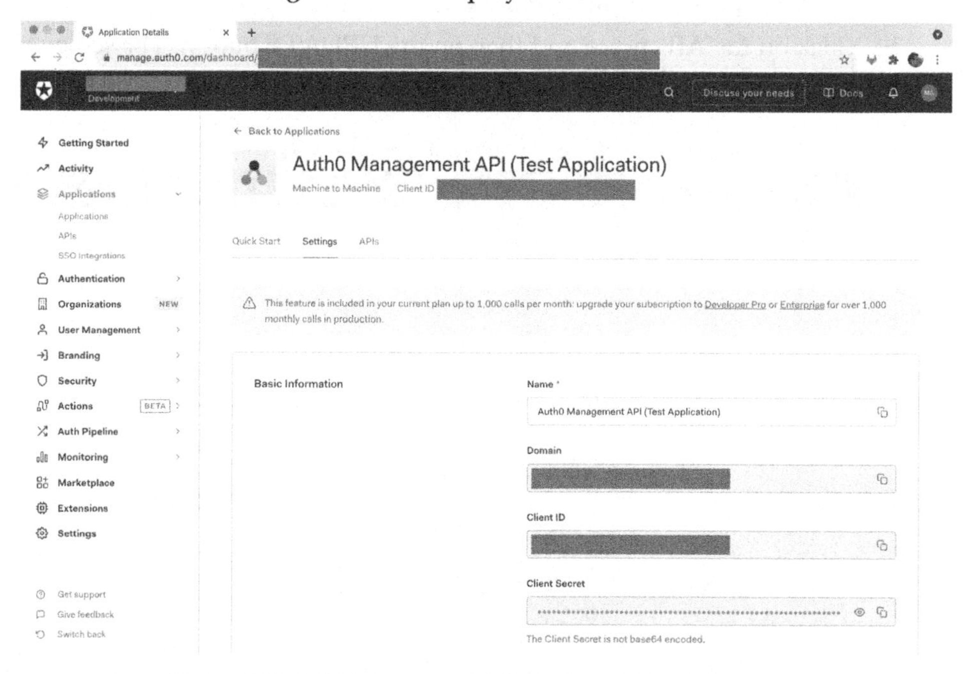

Figure 11.18: Auth0 management API client application information

13. Open the file `$BOOK_HOME/Chapter11/auth0/env.bash` and copy the following values from the screen above:
    a. **Domain** into the value of the variable `TENANT`
    b. **Client ID** into the value of the variable `MGM_CLIENT_ID`
    c. **Client Secret** into the value of the variable `MGM_CLIENT_SECRET`

14. Complete the values required in the `env.bash` file by specifying an email address and password, in the variables `USER_EMAIL` and `USER_PASSWORD`, of a test user that the script will create for us.

Specifying a password for a user like this is not considered best practice from a security perspective. Auth0 supports enrolling users who will be able to set the password themselves, but it is more involved to set up. For more information, see `https://auth0.com/docs/connections/database/password-change`. Since this is only used for test purposes, specifying a password like this is OK.

We can now run the script that will create the following definitions for us:

- Two applications, `reader` and `writer`, clients in OAuth terminology
- The `product-composite` API, a resource server in OAuth terminology, with the OAuth scopes `product:read` and `product:write`
- A user, a resource owner in OAuth terminology, that we will use to test the authorization code grant flow
- Finally, we will grant the `reader` application the scope `product:read`, and the `writer` application the scopes `product:read` and `product:write`

Run the following commands:

```
cd $BOOK_HOME/Chapter11/auth0
./setup-tenant.bash
```

Expect the following output (details removed from the output below):

```
Update the tenant, set its default connection to a user dictionary...
...
Creates reader client app...
...
Creates writer client app...
...
Creates API product-composite (https://localhost:8443/product-composite)...
...
Creates user with email NNN...
...
Create client grant for the reader app to access the product-composite API...
...
Create client grant for the writer app to access the product-composite API...
...
Auth0 - OAuth2 settings:

export TENANT=...
export WRITER_CLIENT_ID=...
export WRITER_CLIENT_SECRET=...
export READER_CLIENT_ID=...
export READER_CLIENT_SECRET=...
$
```

Figure 11.19: Output from setup-tenant.bash the first time it is executed

Save a copy of the `export` commands printed at the end of the output; we will use them multiple times later on in this chapter.

Also, look in your mailbox for the email specified for the test user. You will receive a mail with the subject *Verify your email*. Use the instructions in the email to verify the test user's email address.

Note that the script is idempotent, meaning it can be run multiple times without corrupting the configuration. If running the script again, it should respond with:

```
Update the tenant, set its default connection to a user dictionary...
...
Reader client app already exists
Writer client app already exists
API product-composite (https://localhost:8443/product-composite) already exists
User with email NNN already exists
Client grant for the reader app to access the product-composite API already exists
Client grant for the writer app to access the product-composite API already exists

Auth0 - OAuth2 settings:

export TENANT=...
export WRITER_CLIENT_ID=...
export WRITER_CLIENT_SECRET=...
export READER_CLIENT_ID=...
export READER_CLIENT_SECRET=...
$
```

Figure 11.20: Output from setup-tenant.bash the next time it is executed

It can be very handy to be able to run the script again, for example, to get access to the reader's and writer's client ID and client secret.

If you need to remove the objects created by `setup-tenant.bash`, you can run the script `reset-tenant.bash`.

With an Auth0 account created and configured, we can move on and apply the necessary configuration changes in the system landscape.

Applying the required changes to use Auth0 as an OpenID provider

In this section, we will learn what configuration changes are required to be able to replace the local authorization server with Auth0. We only need to change the configuration for the two services that act as OAuth resource servers, the `product-composite` and `gateway` services. We also need to change our test script a bit, so that it acquires the access tokens from Auth0 instead of acquiring them from our local authorization server. Let's start with the OAuth resource servers, the `product-composite` and `gateway` services.

The changes described in this topic have **not** been applied to the source code in the book's Git repository; you need to make them yourself to see them in action!

Changing the configuration in the OAuth resource servers

As already described, when using an OpenID Connect provider, we only have to configure the base URI to the standardized discovery endpoint in the OAuth resource servers.

In the `product-composite` and `gateway` projects, update the OIDC discovery endpoint to point to Auth0 instead of to our local authorization server. Make the following change to the `application.yml` file in both projects:

1. Locate the property `spring.security.oauth2.resourceserver.jwt.issuer-uri`.
2. Replace its value with `https://${TENANT}/`, where `${TENANT}` should be replaced with your tenant domain name; in my case, it is `dev-ml.eu.auth0.com`. Do **not** forget the trailing `/`!

In my case, the configuration of the OIDC discovery endpoint will look like this:

```
spring.security.oauth2.resourceserver.jwt.issuer-uri: https://dev-ml.eu.auth0.com/
```

If you are curious, you can see what's in the discovery document by running the following command:

```
curl https://${TENANT}/.well-known/openid-configuration -s | jq
```

Rebuild the `product-composite` and `gateway` services as follows:

```
cd $BOOK_HOME/Chapter11
./gradlew build && docker-compose up -d --build product-composite gateway
```

With the `product-composite` and `gateway` services updated, we can move on and also update the test script.

Changing the test script so it acquires access tokens from Auth0

We also need to update the test script so it acquires access tokens from the Auth0 OIDC provider. This is done by performing the following changes in `test-em-all.bash`:

1. Find the following command:

   ```
   ACCESS_TOKEN=$(curl -k https://writer:secret@$HOST:$PORT/oauth2/token -d grant_type=client_credentials -s | jq .access_token -r)
   ```

   Replace it with these commands:

   ```
   export TENANT=...
   export WRITER_CLIENT_ID=...
   export WRITER_CLIENT_SECRET=...

   ACCESS_TOKEN=$(curl -X POST https://$TENANT/oauth/token \
     -d grant_type=client_credentials \
     -d audience=https://localhost:8443/product-composite \
     -d scope=product:read+product:write \
     -d client_id=$WRITER_CLIENT_ID \
     -d client_secret=$WRITER_CLIENT_SECRET -s | jq -r .access_token)
   ```

Note from the preceding command that Auth0 requires us to specify the intended **audience** of the requested access token, as an extra layer of security. The audience is the API we plan to call using the access token. Given that an API implementation verifies the audience field, this would prevent the situation where someone tries to use an access token issued for another purpose to get access to an API.

2. Set the values for the environment variables `TENANT`, `WRITER_CLIENT_ID`, and `WRITER_CLIENT_SECRET` in the preceding commands with the values returned by the `setup-tenant.bash` script.

As mentioned above, you can run the script again to acquire these values without risking any negative side effects!

3. Next, find the following command:

```
READER_ACCESS_TOKEN=$(curl -k https://reader:secret@$HOST:$PORT/
oauth2/token -d grant_type=client_credentials -s | jq .access_
token -r)
```

Replace it with this command:

```
export READER_CLIENT_ID=...
export READER_CLIENT_SECRET=...

READER_ACCESS_TOKEN=$(curl -X POST https://$TENANT/oauth/token \
  -d grant_type=client_credentials \
  -d audience=https://localhost:8443/product-composite \
  -d scope=product:read \
  -d client_id=$READER_CLIENT_ID \
  -d client_secret=$READER_CLIENT_SECRET -s | jq -r .access_token)
```

Note that we only request the `product:read` scope and not the `product:write` scope here.

4. Set the values for the environment variables `READER_CLIENT_ID` and `READER_CLIENT_SECRET` in the preceding commands with the values returned by the `setup-tenant.bash` script.

Now the access tokens are issued by Auth0 instead of our local authorization server, and our API implementations can verify the access tokens using information from Auth0's discovery service configured in the `application.yml` files. The API implementations can, as before, use the scopes in the access tokens to authorize the client to perform the call to the API, or not.

With this, we have all the required changes in place. Let's run some tests to verify that we can acquire access tokens from Auth0.

Running the test script with Auth0 as the OpenID Connect provider

Now, we are ready to give Auth0 a try!

Run the usual tests, but this time using Auth0 as the OpenID Connect provider, with the following command:

```
./test-em-all.bash
```

In the logs, you will be able to find authorization information from the access tokens issued by Auth0. Run the command:

```
docker-compose logs product-composite | grep "Authorization info"
```

Expect the following outputs from the command:

1. From calls using an access token with both the `product:read` and `product:write` scopes, we will see both scopes listed as follows:

```
-bash                                                   ⌥⌘1
product-composite_1 ... Authorization info:
Subject: rFGXKLd8c6zM6P9KeQy67Qbv3QKtDh3S@clients,
scopes: product:read product:write,
expires 2021-02-28T14:07:56Z:
issuer: https://dev-ml.eu.auth0.com/,
audience: [https://localhost:8443/product-composite]
$
```

Figure 11.21: Authorization information for the writer client from Auth0 in the log output

2. From calls using an access token with only the `product:read` scope, we will see that only that scope is listed as follows:

Figure 11.22: Authorization information for the reader client from Auth0 in the log output

As we can see from the log output, we now also get information regarding the **intended audience** for this access token. To strengthen security, we could add a test to our service that verifies that its URL, `https://localhost:8443/product-composite` in this case, is part of the audience list. This would, as mentioned earlier, prevent the situation where someone tries to use an access token issued for another purpose than to get access to our API.

With the automated tests working together with Auth0, we can move on and learn how to acquire access tokens using the different types of grant flow. Let's start with the client credentials grant flow.

Acquiring access tokens using the client credentials grant flow

If you want to acquire an access token from Auth0 yourself, you can do so by running the following command, using the client credentials grant flow:

```
export TENANT=...
export WRITER_CLIENT_ID=...
export WRITER_CLIENT_SECRET=...
curl -X POST https://$TENANT/oauth/token \
  -d grant_type=client_credentials \
  -d audience=https://localhost:8443/product-composite \
  -d scope=product:read+product:write \
  -d client_id=$WRITER_CLIENT_ID \
  -d client_secret=$WRITER_CLIENT_SECRET
```

Set the values for the environment variables `TENANT`, `WRITER_CLIENT_ID`, and `WRITER_CLIENT_SECRET` in the preceding commands with the values returned by the `setup-tenant.bash` script.

Following the instructions in the *Calling protected APIs using access tokens* section, you should be able to call the APIs using the acquired access token.

Acquiring access tokens using the authorization code grant flow

In this section, we will learn how to acquire an access token from Auth0 using the authorization code grant flow. As already described above, we first need to acquire an authorization code using a web browser. Next, we can use server-side code to exchange the authorization code for an access token.

Perform the following steps to execute the authorization code grant flow with Auth0:

1. To get an authorization code for the default app client, use the following URL in the web browser: `https://${TENANT}/authorize?audience=https://localhost:8443/product-composite&scope=openid email product:read product:write&response_type=code&client_id=${WRITER_CLIENT_ID}&redirect_uri=https://my.redirect.uri&state=845361`.

   Replace `${TENANT}` and `${WRITER_CLIENT_ID}` in the preceding URL with the tenant domain name and writer client ID returned by the `setup-tenant.bash` script.

Auth0 should present the following login screen:

Figure 11.23: Authorization code grant flow with Auth0, login screen

2. Following a successful login, Auth0 will ask you to give the client application your consent:

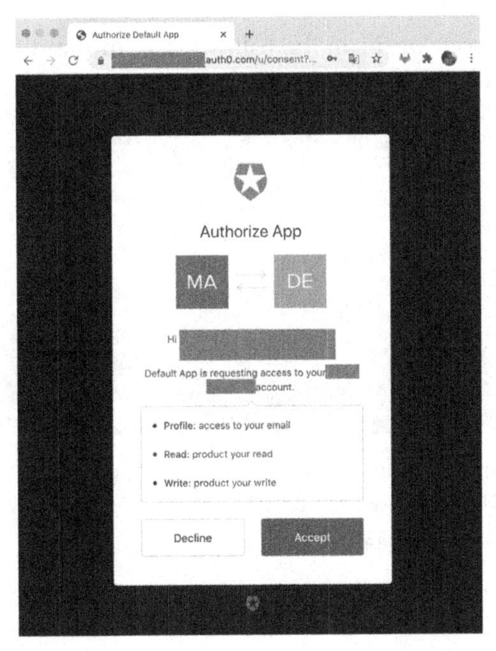

Figure 11.24: Authorization code grant flow with Auth0, consent screen

The authorization code is now in the URL in the browser, just like when we tried out the authorization code grant flow with our local authorization server:

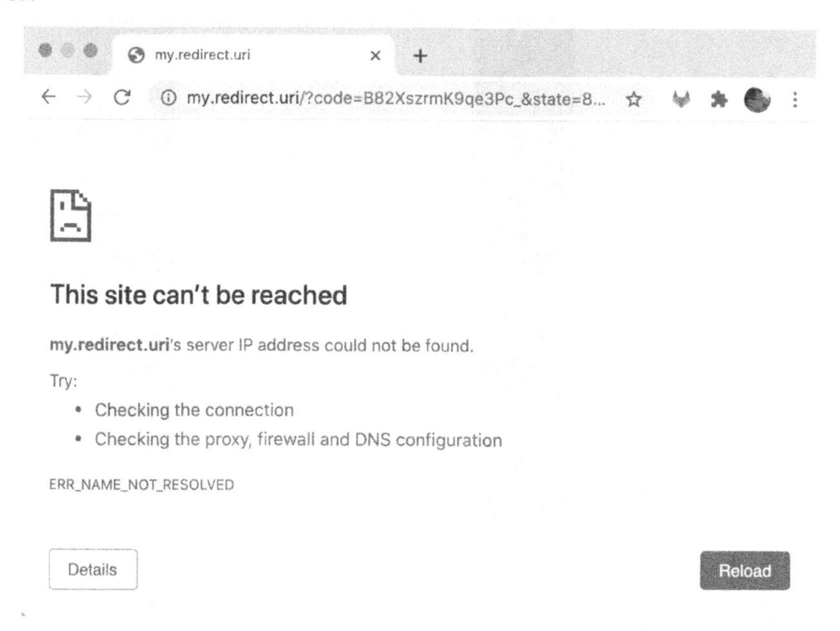

Figure 11.25: Authorization code grant flow with Auth0, access token

3. Extract the code and run the following command to get the access token:

```
CODE=...
export TENANT=...
export WRITER_CLIENT_ID=...
export WRITER_CLIENT_SECRET=...
curl -X POST https://$TENANT/oauth/token \
 -d grant_type=authorization_code \
 -d client_id=$WRITER_CLIENT_ID \
 -d client_secret=$WRITER_CLIENT_SECRET  \
 -d code=$CODE \
 -d redirect_uri=https://my.redirect.uri -s | jq .
```

   Set the values for the environment variables `TENANT`, `WRITER_CLIENT_ID`, and `WRITER_CLIENT_SECRET` in the preceding commands to the values returned by the `setup-tenant.bash` script.

Now that we have learned how to acquire access tokens using both grant flows, we are ready to try calling the external API using an access token acquired from Auth0 in the next section.

Calling protected APIs using the Auth0 access tokens

We can use access tokens issued by Auth0 to call our APIs, just like when we used access tokens issued by our local authorization server.

For a read-only API, execute the following command:

```
ACCESS_TOKEN=...
curl https://localhost:8443/product-composite/1 -k -H "Authorization: Bearer $ACCESS_TOKEN" -i
```

For an updating API, execute the following command:

```
ACCESS_TOKEN=...
curl https://localhost:8443/product-composite/999 -k -H "Authorization: Bearer $ACCESS_TOKEN" -X DELETE -i
```

Since we have requested both scopes, `product:read` and `product:write`, both the preceding API calls are expected to return `200 OK`.

Getting extra information about the user

From the log output in *Figures 11.21* and *11.22* in the section *Running the test script with Auth0 as the OpenID Connect provider*, we could not see any information about the user that initiated the API request. If you want your API implementation to know a bit more about the user, it can call Auth0's `userinfo_endpoint`. The URL of the user-info endpoint can be found in the response of a request to the OIDC discovery endpoint as described in the section *Changing the configuration in the OAuth resource servers*. To get user info related to an access token, make the following request:

```
Export TENANT=...
curl -H "Authorization: Bearer $ACCESS_TOKEN" https://$TENANT/userinfo -s | jq
```

Set the values for the `TENANT` environment variable in the preceding commands to the values returned by the `setup-tenant.bash` script.

Note that this command only applies to access tokens issued using the authorization code grant flow. Access tokens issued using the client credentials grant flow don't contain any user information and will result in an error response if tried.

A sample response is as follows:

```
2. @700dd0df9ffe:/ (bash)
{
 "sub": "auth0|...",
 "email": "...my email...",
 "email_verified": true
 }
$
```

Figure 11.26: Requesting extra user information from Auth0

This endpoint can also be used to verify that the user hasn't revoked the access token in Auth0.

Wrap up the tests by shutting down the system landscape with the following command:

```
docker-compose down
```

This concludes the section where we have learned how to replace the local OAuth 2.0 authorization server with an external alternative. We have also seen how to reconfigure the microservice landscape to validate access tokens using an external OIDC provider.

Summary

In this chapter, we have learned how to use Spring Security to protect our APIs.

We have seen how easy it is to enable HTTPS to prevent eavesdropping by third parties using Spring Security. With Spring Security, we have also learned that it is straightforward to restrict access to the discovery server, Netflix Eureka, using HTTP Basic authentication. Finally, we have seen how we can use Spring Security to simplify the use of OAuth 2.0 and OpenID Connect to allow third-party client applications to access our APIs in the name of a user, but without requiring that the user share credentials with the client applications. We have learned both how to set up a local OAuth 2.0 authorization server based on Spring Security and also how to change the configuration so that an external OpenID Connect provider, Auth0, can be used instead.

One concern, however, is how to manage the configuration required. Each microservice instance must be provided with its own configuration, making it hard to get a good overview of the current configuration. Updating configuration that concerns multiple microservices will also be challenging. Added to the scattered configuration is the fact that some of the configuration we have seen so far contains sensitive information, such as credentials or certificates. It seems like we need a better way to handle the configuration for a number of cooperating microservices and also a solution for how to handle sensitive parts of the configuration.

In the next chapter, we will explore the Spring Cloud Config Server and see how it can be used to handle these types of problems.

Questions

1. What are the benefits and shortcomings of using self-signed certificates?
2. What is the purpose of OAuth 2.0 authorization codes?
3. What is the purpose of OAuth 2.0 scopes?
4. What does it mean when a token is a JWT?
5. How can we trust the information that is stored in a JWT?
6. Is it suitable to use the OAuth 2.0 authorization code grant flow with a native mobile app?
7. What does OpenID Connect add to OAuth 2.0?

12

Centralized Configuration

In this chapter, we will learn how to use the Spring Cloud Configuration server to centralize managing the configuration of our microservices. As already described in *Chapter 1, Introduction to Microservices,* an increasing number of microservices typically come with an increasing number of configuration files that need to be managed and updated.

With the Spring Cloud Configuration server, we can place the configuration files for all our microservices in a central configuration repository that will make it much easier to handle them. Our microservices will be updated to retrieve their configuration from the configuration server at startup.

The following topics will be covered in this chapter:

- Introduction to the Spring Cloud Configuration server
- Setting up a config server
- Configuring clients of a config server
- Structuring the configuration repository
- Trying out the Spring Cloud Configuration server

Technical requirements

For instructions on how to install tools used in this book and how to access the source code for this book, see:

- *Chapter 21* for macOS
- *Chapter 22* for Windows

The code examples in this chapter all come from the source code in `$BOOK_HOME/Chapter12`.

If you want to view the changes applied to the source code in this chapter, that is, see what it took to add a configuration server to the microservice landscape, you can compare it with the source code for *Chapter 11, Securing Access to APIs*. You can use your favorite `diff` tool and compare the two folders, `$BOOK_HOME/Chapter11` and `$BOOK_HOME/Chapter12`.

Introduction to the Spring Cloud Configuration server

The Spring Cloud Configuration server (shortened to **config server**) will be added to the existing microservice landscape behind the edge server, in the same way as for the other microservices:

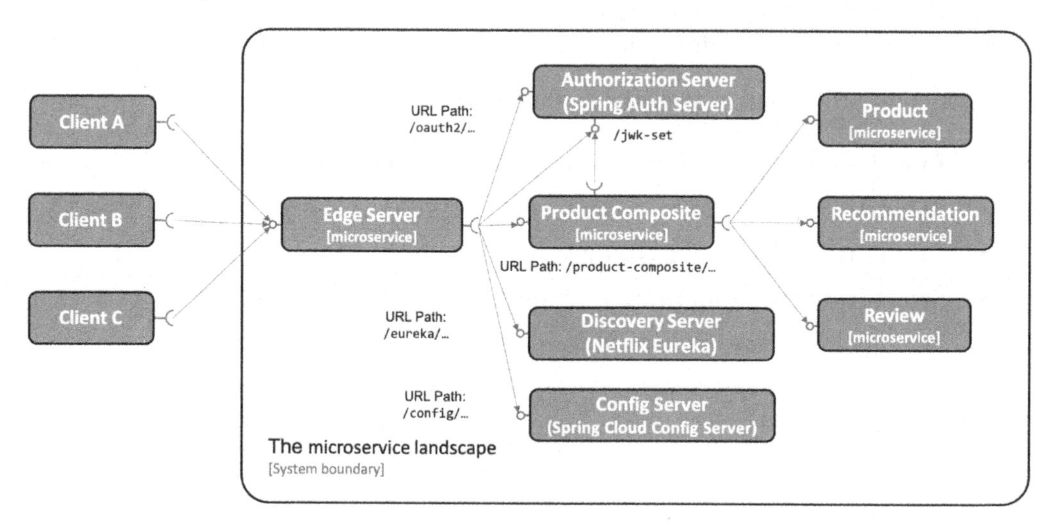

Figure 12.1: Adding a config server to the system landscape

When it comes to setting up a config server, there are a number of options to consider:

- Selecting a storage type for the configuration repository
- Deciding on the initial client connection, either to the config server or to the discovery server
- Securing the configuration, both against unauthorized access to the API and by avoiding storing sensitive information in plain text in the configuration repository

Let's go through each option one by one and also introduce the API exposed by the config server.

Selecting the storage type of the configuration repository

As already described in *Chapter 8, Introduction to Spring Cloud*, the config server supports the storing of configuration files in a number of different backends, for example:

- Git repository
- Local filesystem
- HashiCorp Vault
- JDBC database

For a full list of backends supported by the Spring Cloud Configuration Server project, see `https://cloud.spring.io/spring-cloud-config/reference/html/#_environment_repository`.

Other Spring projects have added extra backends for storing configuration, for example, the Spring Cloud AWS project, which has support for using either AWS Parameter Store or AWS Secrets Manager as backends. For details, see `https://docs.awspring.io/spring-cloud-aws/docs/current/reference/html/index.html`.

In this chapter, we will use a local filesystem. To use the local filesystem, the config server needs to be launched with the Spring profile, `native`, enabled. The location of the configuration repository is specified using the `spring.cloud.config.server.native.searchLocations` property.

Deciding on the initial client connection

By default, a client connects first to the config server to retrieve its configuration. Based on the configuration, it connects to the discovery server, Netflix Eureka in our case, to register itself. It is also possible to do this the other way around, that is, the client first connecting to the discovery server to find a config server instance and then connecting to the config server to get its configuration. There are pros and cons to both approaches.

In this chapter, the clients will first connect to the config server. With this approach, it will be possible to store the configuration of the discovery server in the config server.

To learn more about the other alternative, see `https://docs.spring.io/spring-cloud-config/docs/3.0.2/reference/html/#discovery-first-bootstrap`.

One concern with connecting to the config server first is that the config server can become a single point of failure. If the clients connect first to a discovery server, such as Netflix Eureka, there can be multiple config server instances registered so that a single point of failure can be avoided. When we learn about the service concept in Kubernetes later on in this book, starting with *Chapter 15, Introduction to Kubernetes*, we will see how we can avoid a single point of failure by running multiple containers, for example, config servers, behind each Kubernetes service.

Securing the configuration

Configuration information will, in general, be handled as sensitive information. This means that we need to secure the configuration information both in transit and at rest. From a runtime perspective, the config server does not need to be exposed to the outside through the edge server. During development, however, it is useful to be able to access the API of the config server to check the configuration. In production environments, it is recommended to lock down external access to the config server.

Securing the configuration in transit

When the configuration information is asked for by a microservice, or anyone using the API of the config server, it will be protected against eavesdropping by the edge server since it already uses HTTPS.

To ensure that the API user is a known client, we will use HTTP Basic authentication. We can set up HTTP Basic authentication by using Spring Security in the config server and specifying the environment variables, `SPRING_SECURITY_USER_NAME` and `SPRING_SECURITY_USER_PASSWORD`, with the permitted credentials.

Securing the configuration at rest

To avoid a situation where someone with access to the configuration repository can steal sensitive information, such as passwords, the config server supports the encryption of configuration information when stored on disk. The config server supports the use of both symmetric and asymmetric keys. Asymmetric keys are more secure but harder to manage.

In this chapter, we will use a symmetric key. The symmetric key is given to the config server at startup by specifying an environment variable, `ENCRYPT_KEY`. The encrypted key is just a plain text string that needs to be protected in the same way as any sensitive information.

To learn more about the use of asymmetric keys, see `https://docs.spring.io/spring-cloud-config/docs/3.0.2/reference/html/#_key_management`.

Introducing the config server API

The config server exposes a REST API that can be used by its clients to retrieve their configuration. In this chapter, we will use the following endpoints in the API:

- `/actuator`: The standard actuator endpoint exposed by all microservices. As always, these should be used with care. They are very useful during development but must be locked down before being used in production.
- `/encrypt` and `/decrypt`: Endpoints for encrypting and decrypting sensitive information. These must also be locked down before being used in production.
- `/{microservice}/{profile}`: Returns the configuration for the specified microservice and the specified Spring profile.

We will see some sample uses for the API when we try out the config server.

Setting up a config server

Setting up a config server on the basis of the decisions discussed is straightforward:

1. Create a Spring Boot project using Spring Initializr, as described in *Chapter 3, Creating a Set of Cooperating Microservices*. Refer to the *Using Spring Initializr to generate skeleton code* section.
2. Add the dependencies, `spring-cloud-config-server` and `spring-boot-starter-security`, to the Gradle build file, `build.gradle`.
3. Add the annotation `@EnableConfigServer` to the application class, `ConfigServerApplication`:

   ```
   @EnableConfigServer
   @SpringBootApplication
   public class ConfigServerApplication {
   ```

4. Add the configuration for the config server to the default property file, `application.yml`:

   ```
   server.port: 8888

   spring.cloud.config.server.native.searchLocations: file:${PWD}/
   config-repo

   management.endpoint.health.show-details: "ALWAYS"
   management.endpoints.web.exposure.include: "*"

   logging:
     level:
       root: info

   ---
   spring.config.activate.on-profile: docker
   spring.cloud.config.server.native.searchLocations: file:/config-
   repo
   ```

   The most important configuration is to specify where to find the configuration repository, indicated using the `spring.cloud.config.server.native.searchLocations` property.

5. Add a routing rule to the edge server to make the API of the config server accessible from outside the microservice landscape.
6. Add a Dockerfile and a definition of the config server to the three Docker Compose files.

7. Externalize sensitive configuration parameters to the standard Docker Compose environment file, `.env`. The parameters are described below, in the *Configuring the config server for use with Docker* section.
8. Add the config server to the common build file, `settings.gradle`:

```
include ':spring-cloud:config-server'
```

The source code for the Spring Cloud Configuration server can be found in `$BOOK_HOME/Chapter12/spring-cloud/config-server`.

Now, let's look into how to set up the routing rule referred to in *step 5* and how to configure the config server added in Docker Compose, as described in *steps 6* and *7*.

Setting up a routing rule in the edge server

To be able to access the API of the config server from outside the microservice landscape, we add a routing rule to the edge server. All requests to the edge server that begin with `/config` will be routed to the config server with the following routing rule:

```
- id: config-server
  uri: http://${app.config-server}:8888
 predicates:
 - Path=/config/**
 filters:
 - RewritePath=/config/(?&lt;segment&gt;.*), /$\{segment}
```

The `RewritePath` filter in the routing rule will remove the leading part, `/config`, from the incoming URL before it sends it to the config server.

The edge server is also configured to permit all requests to the config server, delegating the security checks to the config server. The following line is added to the `SecurityConfig` class in the edge server:

```
.pathMatchers("/config/**").permitAll()
```

With this routing rule in place, we can use the API of the config server; for example, run the following command to ask for the configuration of the `product` service when it uses the `docker` Spring profile:

```
curl https://dev-usr:dev-pwd@localhost:8443/config/product/docker -ks |
jq
```

We will run this command when we try out the config server later on.

Configuring the config server for use with Docker

The Dockerfile of the config server looks the same as for the other microservices, except for the fact that it exposes port 8888 instead of port 8080.

When it comes to adding the config server to the Docker Compose files, it looks a bit different from what we have seen for the other microservices:

```
config-server:
  build: spring-cloud/config-server
  mem_limit: 512m
  environment:
    - SPRING_PROFILES_ACTIVE=docker,native
    - ENCRYPT_KEY=${CONFIG_SERVER_ENCRYPT_KEY}
    - SPRING_SECURITY_USER_NAME=${CONFIG_SERVER_USR}
    - SPRING_SECURITY_USER_PASSWORD=${CONFIG_SERVER_PWD}
  volumes:
    - $PWD/config-repo:/config-repo
```

Here are the explanations for the preceding source code:

1. The Spring profile, `native`, is added to signal to the config server that the config repository is based on local files
2. The environment variable `ENCRYPT_KEY` is used to specify the symmetric encryption key that will be used by the config server to encrypt and decrypt sensitive configuration information
3. The environment variables `SPRING_SECURITY_USER_NAME` and `SPRING_SECURITY_USER_PASSWORD` are used to specify the credentials to be used for protecting the APIs using basic HTTP authentication
4. The volume declaration will make the `config-repo` folder accessible in the Docker container at `/config-repo`

The values of the three preceding environment variables, marked in the Docker Compose file with `${...}`, are fetched by Docker Compose from the `.env` file:

```
CONFIG_SERVER_ENCRYPT_KEY=my-very-secure-encrypt-key
CONFIG_SERVER_USR=dev-usr
CONFIG_SERVER_PWD=dev-pwd
```

The information stored in the `.env` file, that is, the username, password, and encryption key, is sensitive and must be protected if used for something other than development and testing. Also, note that losing the encryption key will lead to a situation where the encrypted information in the config repository cannot be decrypted!

Configuring clients of a config server

To be able to get their configurations from the config server, our microservices need to be updated. This can be done with the following steps:

1. Add the `spring-cloud-starter-config` and `spring-retry` dependencies to the Gradle build file, `build.gradle`.
2. Move the configuration file, `application.yml`, to the config repository and rename it with the name of the client as specified by the property `spring.application.name`.
3. Add a new `application.yml` file to the `src/main/resources` folder. This file will be used to hold the configuration required to connect to the config server. Refer to the following *Configuring connection information* section for an explanation of its content.
4. Add credentials for accessing the config server to the Docker Compose files, for example, the `product` service:

```
product:
  environment:
 - CONFIG_SERVER_USR=${CONFIG_SERVER_USR}
 - CONFIG_SERVER_PWD=${CONFIG_SERVER_PWD}
```

5. Disable the use of the config server when running Spring Boot-based automated tests. This is done by adding `spring.cloud.config.enabled=false` to the `@DataMongoTest`, `@DataJpaTest`, and `@SpringBootTest` annotations. They look like:

```
@DataMongoTest(properties = {"spring.cloud.config.
enabled=false"})

@DataJpaTest(properties = {"spring.cloud.config.enabled=false"})

@SpringBootTest(webEnvironment=RANDOM_PORT, properties
= {"eureka.client.enabled=false", "spring.cloud.config.
enabled=false"})
```

Starting with Spring Boot 2.4.0, the processing of multiple property files has changed rather radically. The most important changes, applied in this book, are:

- The order in which property files are loaded. Starting with Spring Boot 2.4.0, they are loaded in the order that they're defined.
- How property override works. Starting with Spring Boot 2.4.0, properties declared lower in a file will override those higher up.
- A new mechanism for loading additional property files, for example, property files from a config server, has been added. Starting with Spring Boot 2.4.0, the property `spring.config.import` can be used as a common mechanism for loading additional property files.

For more information and the reasons for making these changes, see `https://spring.io/blog/2020/08/14/config-file-processing-in-spring-boot-2-4`.

Spring Cloud Config v3.0.0, included in Spring Cloud 2020.0.0, supports the new mechanism for loading property files in Spring Boot 2.4.0. This is now the default mechanism for importing property files from a config repository. This means that the Spring Cloud Config-specific `bootstrap.yml` files are replaced by standard `application.yml` files, using a `spring.config.import` property to specify that additional configuration files will be imported from a config server. It is still possible to use the legacy bootstrap way of importing property files; for details, see `https://docs.spring.io/spring-cloud-config/docs/3.0.2/reference/html/#config-data-import`.

Configuring connection information

As mentioned previously, the `src/main/resources/application.yml` file now holds the client configuration that is required to connect to the config server. This file has the same content for all clients of the config server, except for the application name as specified by the `spring.application.name` property (in the following example, set to `product`):

```
spring.config.import: "configserver:"

spring:
```

```
  application.name: product
  cloud.config:
    failFast: true
    retry:
      initialInterval: 3000
      multiplier: 1.3
      maxInterval: 10000
      maxAttempts: 20
    uri: http://localhost:8888
    username: ${CONFIG_SERVER_USR}
    password: ${CONFIG_SERVER_PWD}

---
spring.config.activate.on-profile: docker

spring.cloud.config.uri: http://config-server:8888
```

This configuration will make the client do the following:

1. Connect to the config server using the `http://localhost:8888` URL when it runs outside Docker, and using the `http://config-server:8888` URL when running in a Docker container
2. Use HTTP Basic authentication, based on the value of the `CONFIG_SERVER_USR` and `CONFIG_SERVER_PWD` properties, as the client's username and password
3. Try to reconnect to the config server during startup up to 20 times, if required
4. If the connection attempt fails, the client will initially wait for 3 seconds before trying to reconnect
5. The wait time for subsequent retries will increase by a factor of 1.3
6. The maximum wait time between connection attempts will be 10 seconds
7. If the client can't connect to the config server after 20 attempts, its startup will fail

This configuration is generally good for resilience against temporary connectivity problems with the config server. It is especially useful when the whole landscape of microservices and its config server are started up at once, for example, when using the `docker-compose up` command. In this scenario, many of the clients will be trying to connect to the config server before it is ready, and the retry logic will make the clients connect to the config server successfully once it is up and running.

Structuring the configuration repository

After moving the configuration files from each client's source code to the configuration repository, we will have some common configuration in many of the configuration files, for example, for the configuration of actuator endpoints and how to connect to Eureka, RabbitMQ, and Kafka. The common parts have been placed in a common configuration file named `application.yml`. This file is shared by all clients. The configuration repository contains the following files:

```
config-repo/
├── application.yml
├── auth-server.yml
├── eureka-server.yml
├── gateway.yml
├── product-composite.yml
├── product.yml
├── recommendation.yml
└── review.yml
```

The configuration repository can be found in `$BOOK_HOME/Chapter12/config-repo`.

Trying out the Spring Cloud Configuration server

Now it is time to try out the config server:

1. First, we will build from source and run the test script to ensure that everything fits together
2. Next, we will try out the config server API to retrieve the configuration for our microservices
3. Finally, we will see how we can encrypt and decrypt sensitive information, for example, passwords

Building and running automated tests

So now we build and run verification tests of the system landscape, as follows:

1. First, build the Docker images with the following commands:

```
cd $BOOK_HOME/Chapter12
./gradlew build && docker-compose build
```

2. Next, start the system landscape in Docker and run the usual tests with the following command:

```
./test-em-all.bash start
```

Getting the configuration using the config server API

As already described previously, we can reach the API of the config server through the edge server by using the URL prefix, `/config`. We also have to supply credentials as specified in the `.env` file for HTTP Basic authentication. For example, to retrieve the configuration used for the `product` service when it runs as a Docker container, that is, having activated the Spring profile `docker`, run the following command:

```
curl https://dev-usr:dev-pwd@localhost:8443/config/product/docker -ks |
jq .
```

Expect a response with the following structure (many of the properties in the response are replaced by `...` to increase readability):

```
{
  "name": "product",
  "profiles": [
    "docker"
  ],
  ...
  "propertySources": [
    {
      "name": "...file [/config-repo/product.yml]...",
      "source": {
        "spring.config.activate.on-profile": "docker",
        "server.port": 8080,
        ...
      }
    },
    {
      "name": "...file [/config-repo/product.yml]...",
      "source": {
        "server.port": 7001,
        ...
      }
    },
```

```
    {
      "name": "...file [/config-repo/application.yml]...",
      "source": {
        "spring.config.activate.on-profile": "docker",
        ...
      }
    },
    {
      "name": "...file [/config-repo/application.yml]...",
      "source": {
        ...
        "app.eureka-password": "p",
        "spring.rabbitmq.password": "guest"
      }
    }
  ]
}
```

The explanations for this response are as follows:

- The response contains properties from a number of **property sources**, one per property file and Spring profile that matched the API request. The property sources are returned in priority order; if a property is specified in multiple property sources, the first property in the response takes precedence. The preceding sample response contains the following property sources, in the following priority order:
  - `/config-repo/product.yml`, for the `docker` Spring profile
  - `/config-repo/product.yml`, for the `default` Spring profile
  - `/config-repo/application.yml`, for the `docker` Spring profile
  - `/config-repo/application.yml`, for the `default` Spring profile

  For example, the port used will be `8080` and not `7001`, since `"server.port": 8080` is specified before `"server.port": 7001` in the preceding response.
- Sensitive information, such as the passwords to Eureka and RabbitMQ, are returned in plain text, for example, `"p"` and `"guest"`, but they are encrypted on disk. In the configuration file, `application.yml`, they are specified as follows:

  ```
  app:
    eureka-password:
  ```

```
'{cipher}
bf298f6d5f878b342f9e44bec08cb9ac00b4ce57e98316f030194a225
fac89fb'

spring.rabbitmq:
  password: '{cipher}17fcf0ae5b8c5cf87de6875b699be4a1746dd493a99
d926c7a26a68c422117ef'
```

Encrypting and decrypting sensitive information

Information can be encrypted and decrypted using the `/encrypt` and `/decrypt` endpoints exposed by the config server. The `/encrypt` endpoint can be used to create encrypted values to be placed in the property file in the config repository. Refer to the example in the previous section, where the passwords to Eureka and RabbitMQ are stored encrypted on disk. The `/decrypt` endpoint can be used to verify encrypted information that is stored on disk in the config repository.

To encrypt the `hello world` string, run the following command:

```
curl -k https://dev-usr:dev-pwd@localhost:8443/config/encrypt
--data-urlencode "hello world"
```

It is important to use the `--data-urlencode` flag when using `curl` to call the `/encrypt` endpoint, to ensure the correct handling of special characters such as `'+'`.

Expect a response along the lines of the following:

Figure 12.2: An encrypted value of a configuration parameter

To decrypt the encrypted value, run the following command:

```
curl -k https://dev-usr:dev-pwd@localhost:8443/config/decrypt -d
9eca39e823957f37f0f0f4d8b2c6c46cd49ef461d1cab20c65710823a8b412ce
```

Expect the `hello world` string as the response:

Figure 12.3: A decrypted value of a configuration parameter

If you want to use an encrypted value in a configuration file, you need to prefix it with `{cipher}` and wrap it in `''`. For example, to store the encrypted version of `hello world`, add the following line in a YAML-based configuration file:

```
my-secret:  '{cipher}9eca39e823957f37f0f0f4d8b2c6c46cd49ef461d1cab20c65
710823a8b412ce'
```

When the config server detects values in the format `'{cipher}...'`, it tries to decrypt them using its encryption key before sending them to a client.

These tests conclude the chapter on centralized configuration. Wrap it up by shutting down the system landscape:

```
docker-compose down
```

Summary

In this chapter, we have seen how we can use the Spring Cloud Configuration Server to centralize managing the configuration of our microservices. We can place the configuration files in a common configuration repository and share common configurations in a single configuration file, while keeping microservice-specific configuration in microservice-specific configuration files. The microservices have been updated to retrieve their configuration from the config server at startup and are configured to handle temporary outages while retrieving their configuration from the config server.

The config server can protect configuration information by requiring authenticated usage of its API with HTTP Basic authentication and can prevent eavesdropping by exposing its API externally through the edge server that uses HTTPS. To prevent intruders who obtained access to the configuration files on disk from gaining access to sensitive information such as passwords, we can use the config server `/encrypt` endpoint to encrypt the information and store it encrypted on disk.

While exposing the APIs from the config server externally is useful during development, they should be locked down before use in production.

In the next chapter, we will learn how we can use **Resilience4j** to mitigate the potential drawbacks of overusing synchronous communication between microservices.

Questions

1. What API call can we expect from a review service to the config server during startup to retrieve its configuration?
2. The review service was started up using the following command: `docker compose up -d`.

   What configuration information should we expect back from an API call to the config server using the following command?

   ```
   curl https://dev-usr:dev-pwd@localhost:8443/config/application/
   default -ks | jq
   ```
3. What types of repository backend does Spring Cloud Config support?
4. How can we encrypt sensitive information on disk using Spring Cloud Config?
5. How can we protect the config server API from misuse?
6. Mention some pros and cons for clients that first connect to the config server as opposed to those that first connect to the discovery server.

13

Improving Resilience Using Resilience4j

In this chapter, we will learn how to use Resilience4j to make our microservices more resilient, that is, how to mitigate and recover from errors. As we already discussed in *Chapter 1, Introduction to Microservices*, in the *Circuit breaker* section, and *Chapter 8, Introduction to Spring Cloud*, in the *Using Resilience4j for improved resilience* section, a circuit breaker can be used to minimize the damage that a slow or unresponsive downstream microservice can cause in a large-scale system landscape of synchronously communicating microservices. We will see how the circuit breaker in Resilience4j can be used together with a time limiter and retry mechanism to prevent two of the most common error situations:

- Microservices that start to respond slowly or not at all
- Requests that randomly fail from time to time, for example, due to temporary network problems

The following topics will be covered in this chapter:

- Introducing the three Resilience4j mechanisms: circuit breaker, time limiter, and retry
- Adding the mechanisms to the source code
- Trying out the mechanisms when deployed in the system landscape

Technical requirements

For instructions on how to install the tools used in this book and how to access the source code for this book, see:

- *Chapter 21* for macOS
- *Chapter 22* for Windows

The code examples in this chapter all come from the source code in `$BOOK_HOME/Chapter13`.

If you want to view the changes applied to the source code in this chapter, that is, see what it took to add resilience using Resilience4j, you can compare it with the source code for *Chapter 12, Centralized Configuration*. You can use your favorite `diff` tool and compare the two folders, `$BOOK_HOME/Chapter12` and `$BOOK_HOME/Chapter13`.

Introducing the Resilience4j resilience mechanisms

The circuit breaker, time limiter, and retry mechanisms are potentially useful in any synchronous communication between two software components, for example, microservices. In this chapter, we will apply these mechanisms in one place, in calls from the `product-composite` service to the `product` service. This is illustrated in the following figure:

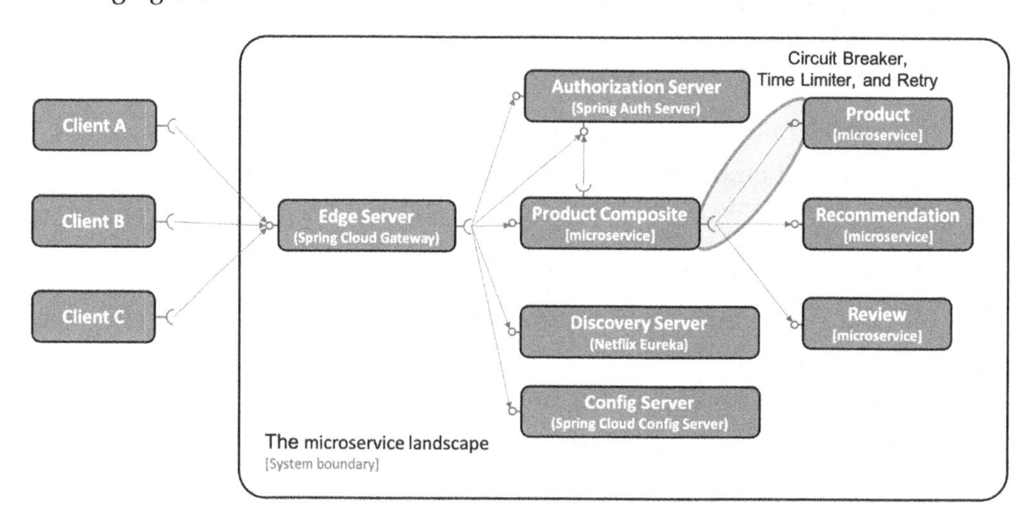

Figure 13.1: Adding resilience capabilities to the system landscape

Note that the synchronous calls to the discovery and config servers from the other microservices are not shown in the preceding diagram (to make it easier to read).

Recently, Spring Cloud added a project, **Spring Cloud Circuit Breaker**, that provides an abstraction layer for circuit breakers. Resilience4j can be configured to be used under the hood. This project does not provide other resilience mechanisms such as retries, time limiters, bulkheads, or rate limiters in an integrated way as the Resilience4j project does. For more information on the project, see `https://spring.io/projects/spring-cloud-circuitbreaker`.

A number of other alternatives exist as well. For example, the Reactor project comes with built-in support for retries and timeouts; see `Mono.retryWhen()` and `Mono.timeout()`. Spring also has a retry mechanism (see `https://github.com/spring-projects/spring-retry`), but it does not support a reactive programming model.

However, none of the alternatives provide such a cohesive and well-integrated approach to providing a set of resilience mechanisms as Resilience4j does, specifically, in a Spring Boot environment, where dependencies, annotations, and configuration are used in an elegant and consistent way. Finally, it is worth noting that the Resilience4j annotations work independently of the programming style used, be it reactive or imperative.

Introducing the circuit breaker

Let's quickly revisit the state diagram for a circuit breaker from *Chapter 8, Introduction to Spring Cloud*, in the *Using Resilience4j for improved resilience* section:

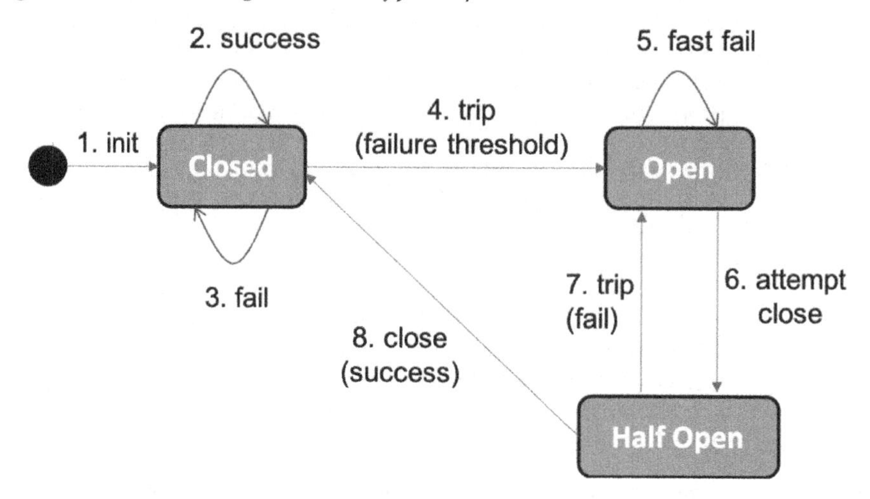

Figure 13.2: Circuit breaker state diagram

The key features of a circuit breaker are as follows:

- If a circuit breaker detects too many faults, it will open its circuit, that is, not allow new calls.
- When the circuit is open, a circuit breaker will perform fail-fast logic. This means that it doesn't wait for a new fault, for example, a timeout, to happen on subsequent calls. Instead, it directly redirects the call to a **fallback method**. The fallback method can apply various business logic to produce a best-effort response. For example, a fallback method can return data from a local cache or simply return an immediate error message. This will prevent a microservice from becoming unresponsive if the services it depends on stop responding normally. This is specifically useful under high load.
- After a while, the circuit breaker will be half-open, allowing new calls to see whether the issue that caused the failures is gone. If new failures are detected by the circuit breaker, it will open the circuit again and go back to the fail-fast logic. Otherwise, it will close the circuit and go back to normal operation. This makes a microservice resilient to faults, or self-healing, a capability that is indispensable in a system landscape of microservices that communicate synchronously with each other.

Resilience4j exposes information about circuit breakers at runtime in a number of ways:

- The current state of a circuit breaker can be monitored using the microservice's `actuator` `health` endpoint, `/actuator/health`.
- The circuit breaker also publishes events on an `actuator` endpoint, for example, state transitions, `/actuator/circuitbreakerevents`.
- Finally, circuit breakers are integrated with Spring Boot's metrics system and can use it to publish metrics to monitoring tools such as Prometheus.

We will try out the `health` and `event` endpoints in this chapter. In *Chapter 20, Monitoring Microservices*, we will see Prometheus in action and how it can collect metrics that are exposed by Spring Boot, for example, metrics from our circuit breaker.

To control the logic in a circuit breaker, Resilience4j can be configured using standard Spring Boot configuration files. We will use the following configuration parameters:

- `slidingWindowType`: To determine if a circuit breaker needs to be opened, Resilience4j uses a sliding window, counting the most recent events to make the decision. The sliding windows can either be based on a fixed number of calls or a fixed elapsed time. This parameter is used to configure what type of sliding window is used.

  We will use a count-based sliding window, setting this parameter to `COUNT_BASED`.
- `slidingWindowSize`: The number of calls in a closed state that are used to determine whether the circuit should be opened.

  We will set this parameter to `5`.
- `failureRateThreshold`: The threshold, in percent, for failed calls that will cause the circuit to be opened.

  We will set this parameter to `50%`. This setting, together with `slidingWindowSize` set to `5`, means that if three or more of the last five calls are faults, then the circuit will open.
- `automaticTransitionFromOpenToHalfOpenEnabled`: Determines whether the circuit breaker will automatically transition to the half-open state once the waiting period is over. Otherwise, it will wait for the first call after the waiting period is over until it transitions to the half-open state.

  We will set this parameter to `true`.
- `waitDurationInOpenState`: Specifies how long the circuit stays in an open state, that is, before it transitions to the half-open state.

We will set this parameter to `10000 ms`. This setting, together with enabling automatic transition to the half-open state, set by the previous parameter, means that the circuit breaker will keep the circuit open for 10 seconds and then transition to the half-open state.

- `permittedNumberOfCallsInHalfOpenState`: The number of calls in the half-open state that are used to determine whether the circuit will be opened again or go back to the normal, closed state.

  We will set this parameter to `3`, meaning that the circuit breaker will decide whether the circuit will be opened or closed based on the first three calls after the circuit has transitioned to the half-open state. Since the `failureRateThreshold` parameters are set to 50%, the circuit will be open again if two or all three calls fail. Otherwise, the circuit will be closed.

- `ignoreExceptions`: This can be used to specify exceptions that should not be counted as faults. Expected business exceptions such as `not found` or `invalid input` are typical exceptions that the circuit breaker should ignore; users who search for non-existing data or enter invalid input should not cause the circuit to open.

  We will set this parameter to a list containing the exceptions `NotFoundException` and `InvalidInputException`.

Finally, to configure Resilience4j to report the state of the circuit breaker in the `actuator` health endpoint in a correct way, the following parameters are set:

- `registerHealthIndicator = true` enables Resilience4j to fill in the health endpoint with information regarding the state of its circuit breakers.
- `allowHealthIndicatorToFail = false` tells Resilience4j not to affect the status of the health endpoint. This means that the health endpoint will still report `"UP"` even if one of the component's circuit breakers is in an open or half-open state. It is very important that the health state of the component is not reported as `"DOWN"` just because one of its circuit breakers is not in a closed state. This means that the component is still considered to be OK, even though one of the components it depends on is not.

This is actually the core value of a circuit breaker, so setting this value to `true` would more or less spoil the value of bringing in a circuit breaker. In earlier versions of Resilience4j, this was actually the behavior. In more recent versions, this has been corrected and `false` is actually the default value for this parameter. But since I consider it very important to understand the relation between the health state of the component and the state of its circuit breakers, I have added it to the configuration.

- Finally, we must also configure Spring Boot Actuator to add the circuit breaker health information that Resilience4j produces in the response to a request to its health endpoint:

  ```
  management.health.circuitbreakers.enabled: true
  ```

For a full list of available configuration parameters, see `https://resilience4j.readme.io/docs/circuitbreaker#create-and-configure-a-circuitbreaker`.

Introducing the time limiter

To help a circuit breaker handle slow or unresponsive services, a timeout mechanism can be helpful. Resilience4j's timeout mechanism, called a **TimeLimiter**, can be configured using standard Spring Boot configuration files. We will use the following configuration parameter:

- `timeoutDuration`: Specifies how long a `TimeLimiter` instance waits for a call to complete before it throws a timeout exception. We will set it to `2s`.

Introducing the retry mechanism

The **retry** mechanism is very useful for random and infrequent faults, such as temporary network glitches. The retry mechanism can simply retry a failed request a number of times with a configurable delay between the attempts. One very important restriction on the use of the retry mechanism is that the services that it retries must be **idempotent**, that is, calling the service one or many times with the same request parameters gives the same result. For example, reading information is idempotent, but creating information is typically not. You don't want a retry mechanism to accidentally create two orders just because the response from the first order's creation got lost in the network.

Resilience4j exposes retry information in the same way as it does for circuit breakers when it comes to events and metrics, but does not provide any health information. Retry events are accessible on the `actuator` endpoint, `/actuator/retryevents`. To control the retry logic, Resilience4j can be configured using standard Spring Boot configuration files. We will use the following configuration parameters:

- `maxAttempts`: The number of attempts before giving up, including the first call. We will set this parameter to `3`, allowing a maximum of two retry attempts after an initial failed call.
- `waitDuration`: The wait time before the next retry attempt. We will set this value to `1000` ms, meaning that we will wait 1 second between retries.

- `retryExceptions`: A list of exceptions that will trigger a retry. We will only trigger retries on `InternalServerError` exceptions, that is, when HTTP requests respond with a `500` status code.

> Be careful when configuring retry and circuit breaker settings so that, for example, the circuit breaker doesn't open the circuit before the intended number of retries have been completed!

For a full list of available configuration parameters, see `https://resilience4j.readme.io/docs/retry#create-and-configure-retry`.

With this introduction, we are ready to see how to add these resilience mechanisms to the source code in the `product-composite` service.

Adding the resilience mechanisms to the source code

Before we add the resilience mechanisms to the source code, we will add code that makes it possible to force an error to occur, either as a delay and/or as a random fault. Next, we will add a circuit breaker together with a time limiter to handle slow or unresponsive APIs, as well as a retry mechanism that can handle faults that happen randomly. Adding these features from Resilience4j follows the Spring Boot way, which we have been using in the previous chapters:

- Add a starter dependency on Resilience4j in the build file
- Add annotations in the source code where the resilience mechanisms will be applied
- Add configuration that controls the behavior of the resilience mechanisms

Handling resilience challenges is a responsibility for the integration layer; therefore, the resilience mechanisms will be placed in the `ProductCompositeIntegration` class. The source code in the business logic, implemented in the `ProductCompositeServiceImpl` class, will not be aware of the presence of the resilience mechanisms.

Once we have the mechanisms in place, we will finally extend our test script, `test-em-all.bash`, with tests that automatically verify that the circuit breaker works as expected when deployed in the system landscape.

Adding programmable delays and random errors

To be able to test our resilience mechanisms, we need a way to control when errors happen. A simple way to achieve this is by adding optional query parameters in the API used to retrieve a product and a composite product.

The code and API parameters added in this section to force delays and errors to occur should only be used during development and tests, not in production. When we learn about the concept of a service mesh in *Chapter 18, Using a Service Mesh to Improve Observability and Management*, we will learn about better methods that can be used in production to introduce delays and errors in a controlled way. Using a service mesh, we can introduce delays and errors, typically used for verifying resilience capabilities, without affecting the source code of the microservices.

The composite product API will simply pass on the parameters to the product API. The following query parameters have been added to the two APIs:

- `delay`: Causes the `getProduct` API on the `product` microservice to delay its response. The parameter is specified in seconds. For example, if the parameter is set to `3`, it will cause a delay of three seconds before the response is returned.
- `faultPercentage`: Causes the `getProduct` API on the `product` microservice to throw an exception randomly with the probability specified by the query parameter, from 0 to 100%. For example, if the parameter is set to `25`, it will cause every fourth call to the API, on average, to fail with an exception. It will return an HTTP error 500 (Internal Server Error) in these cases.

Changes in the API definitions

The two query parameters that we introduced above, `delay` and `faultPercentage`, have been defined in the `api` project in the following two Java interfaces:

- `ProductCompositeService`:

```
Mono<ProductAggregate> getProduct(
    @PathVariable int productId,
    @RequestParam(value = "delay", required = false, defaultValue =
    "0") int delay,
```

```
        @RequestParam(value = "faultPercent", required = false,
        defaultValue = "0") int faultPercent
    );
```

- `ProductService`:

```
    Mono<Product> getProduct(
         @PathVariable int productId,
         @RequestParam(value = "delay", required = false, defaultValue
         = "0") int delay,
         @RequestParam(value = "faultPercent", required = false,
         defaultValue = "0") int faultPercent
    );
```

The query parameters are declared optional with default values that disable the use of the error mechanisms. This means that if none of the query parameters are used in a request, neither a delay will be applied nor an error thrown.

Changes in the product-composite microservice

The `product-composite` microservice simply passes the parameters to the product API. The service implementation receives the API request and passes on the parameters to the integration component that makes the call to the product API:

- The call from the `ProductCompositeServiceImpl` class to the integration component looks like this:

```
public Mono<ProductAggregate> getProduct(int productId,
  int delay, int faultPercent) {
    return Mono.zip(
        ...
        integration.getProduct(productId, delay, faultPercent),
        ....
```

- The call from the `ProductCompositeIntegration` class to the product API looks like this:

```
public Mono<Product> getProduct(int productId, int delay,
  int faultPercent) {

    URI url = UriComponentsBuilder.fromUriString(
      PRODUCT_SERVICE_URL + "/product/{productId}?delay={delay}"
      + "&faultPercent={faultPercent}")
      .build(productId, delay, faultPercent);
```

```
    return webClient.get().uri(url).retrieve()...
```

Changes in the product microservice

The `product` microservice implements the actual delay and random error generator in the `ProductServiceImpl` class by extending the existing stream used to read product information from the MongoDB database. It looks like this:

```
public Mono<Product> getProduct(int productId, int delay,
  int faultPercent) {

  ...
  return repository.findByProductId(productId)
    .map(e -> throwErrorIfBadLuck(e, faultPercent))
    .delayElement(Duration.ofSeconds(delay))
    ...
}
```

When the stream returns a response from the Spring Data repository, it first applies the `throwErrorIfBadLuck` method to see whether an exception needs to be thrown. Next, it applies a delay using the `delayElement` function in the `Mono` class.

The random error generator, `throwErrorIfBadLuck()`, creates a random number between `1` and `100` and throws an exception if it is higher than, or equal to, the specified fault percentage. If no exception is thrown, the product entity is passed on in the stream. The source code looks like this:

```
private ProductEntity throwErrorIfBadLuck(
  ProductEntity entity, int faultPercent) {

  if (faultPercent == 0) {
    return entity;
  }

  int randomThreshold = getRandomNumber(1, 100);

  if (faultPercent < randomThreshold) {
    LOG.debug("We got lucky, no error occurred, {} < {}",
      faultPercent, randomThreshold);

  } else {
    LOG.debug("Bad luck, an error occurred, {} >= {}",
```

```
        faultPercent, randomThreshold);

      throw new RuntimeException("Something went wrong...");
    }

    return entity;
  }

  private final Random randomNumberGenerator = new Random();

  private int getRandomNumber(int min, int max) {

    if (max < min) {
      throw new IllegalArgumentException("Max must be greater than min");
    }

    return randomNumberGenerator.nextInt((max - min) + 1) + min;
  }
```

With the programmable delays and random error functions in place, we are ready to start adding the resilience mechanisms to the code. We will start with the circuit breaker and the time limiter.

Adding a circuit breaker and a time limiter

As we mentioned previously, we need to add dependencies, annotations, and configuration. We also need to add some code for implementing fallback logic for fail-fast scenarios. We will see how to do this in the following sections.

Adding dependencies to the build file

To add a circuit breaker and a time limiter, we have to add dependencies to the appropriate Resilience4j libraries in the build file, `build.gradle`. From the product documentation (`https://resilience4j.readme.io/docs/getting-started-3#setup`), we can learn that the following three dependencies need to be added. We will use the latest available version, `v1.7.0`, when this chapter was written:

```
  ext {
     resilience4jVersion = "1.7.0"
  }
  dependencies {
      implementation "io.github.resilience4j:resilience4j-spring-
```

```
boot2:${resilience4jVersion}"
    implementation "io.github.resilience4j:resilience4j-
reactor:${resilience4jVersion}"
    implementation 'org.springframework.boot:spring-boot-starter-aop'
    ...
```

To avoid Spring Cloud overriding the version used with the older version of Resilience4j that it bundles, we have to list all the sub-projects we also want to use and specify which version to use. We add this extra dependency in the `dependencyManagement` section to highlight that this is a workaround caused by the Spring Cloud dependency management:

```
dependencyManagement {
    imports {
        mavenBom "org.springframework.cloud:spring-cloud-dependencies:$
{springCloudVersion}"
    }
    dependencies {
        dependency "io.github.resilience4j:resilience4j-
spring:${resilience4jVersion}"
        ...
    }
}
```

Adding annotations in the source code

The circuit breaker can be applied by annotating the method it is expected to protect with `@CircuitBreaker(...)`, which in this case is the `getProduct()` method in the `ProductCompositeIntegration` class. The circuit breaker is triggered by an exception, not by a timeout itself. To be able to trigger the circuit breaker after a timeout, we will add a time limiter that can be applied with the annotation `@TimeLimiter(...)`. The source code looks as follows:

```
@TimeLimiter(name = "product")
@CircuitBreaker(
     name = "product", fallbackMethod = "getProductFallbackValue")

public Mono<Product> getProduct(
  int productId, int delay, int faultPercent) {
  ...
}
```

The name of the circuit breaker and the time limiter annotation, "product", is used to identify the configuration that will be applied. The fallbackMethod parameter in the circuit breaker annotation is used to specify what fallback method to call, getProductFallbackValue in this case, when the circuit breaker is open; see below for information on how it is used.

To activate the circuit breaker, the annotated method must be invoked as a Spring bean. In our case, it's the integration class that's injected by Spring into the service implementation class, ProductCompositeServiceImpl, and therefore used as a Spring bean:

```
private final ProductCompositeIntegration integration;

@Autowired
public ProductCompositeServiceImpl(... ProductCompositeIntegration
integration) {
  this.integration = integration;
}

public Mono<ProductAggregate> getProduct(int productId, int delay, int
faultPercent) {
  return Mono.zip(
    ...,
    integration.getProduct(productId, delay, faultPercent),
    ...
```

Adding fail-fast fallback logic

To be able to apply fallback logic when the circuit breaker is open, that is, when a request fails fast, we can specify a fallback method on the CircuitBreaker annotation as seen in the previous source code. The method must follow the signature of the method the circuit breaker is applied for and also have an extra last argument used for passing the exception that triggered the circuit breaker. In our case, the method signature for the fallback method looks like this:

```
private Mono<Product> getProductFallbackValue(int productId,
  int delay, int faultPercent, CallNotPermittedException ex) {
```

The last parameter specifies that we want to be able to handle exceptions of type CallNotPermittedException. We are only interested in exceptions that are thrown when the circuit breaker is in its open state, so that we can apply fail-fast logic. When the circuit breaker is open, it will not permit calls to the underlying method; instead, it will immediately throw a CallNotPermittedException exception. Therefore, we are only interested in catching CallNotPermittedException exceptions.

The fallback logic can look up information based on the `productId` from alternative sources, for example, an internal cache. In our case, we will return hardcoded values based on the `productId`, to simulate a hit in a cache. To simulate a miss in the cache, we will throw a `not found` exception in the case where the `productId` is `13`. The implementation of the fallback method looks like this:

```
private Mono<Product> getProductFallbackValue(int productId,
  int delay, int faultPercent, CallNotPermittedException ex) {

  if (productId == 13) {
    String errMsg = "Product Id: " + productId
      + " not found in fallback cache!";
    throw new NotFoundException(errMsg);
  }

  return Mono.just(new Product(productId, "Fallback product"
    + productId, productId, serviceUtil.getServiceAddress()));
}
```

Adding configuration

Finally, the configuration of the circuit breaker and time limiter is added to the `product-composite.yml` file in the config repository, as follows:

```
resilience4j.timelimiter:
  instances:
    product:
      timeoutDuration: 2s

management.health.circuitbreakers.enabled: true

resilience4j.circuitbreaker:
  instances:
    product:
      allowHealthIndicatorToFail: false
      registerHealthIndicator: true
      slidingWindowType: COUNT_BASED
      slidingWindowSize: 5
      failureRateThreshold: 50
      waitDurationInOpenState: 10000
      permittedNumberOfCallsInHalfOpenState: 3
      automaticTransitionFromOpenToHalfOpenEnabled: true
```

```
      ignoreExceptions:
        - se.magnus.api.exceptions.InvalidInputException
        - se.magnus.api.exceptions.NotFoundException
```

The values in the configuration have already been described in the previous sections, *Introducing the circuit breaker* and *Introducing the time limiter*.

Adding a retry mechanism

In the same way as for the circuit breaker, a retry mechanism is set up by adding dependencies, annotations, and configuration. The dependencies were added previously in the *Adding dependencies to the build file* section, so we only need to add the annotation and set up the configuration.

Adding the retry annotation

The retry mechanism can be applied to a method by annotating it with `@Retry(name="nnn")`, where `nnn` is the name of the configuration entry to be used for this method. See the following *Adding configuration* section for details on the configuration. The method, in our case, is the same as it is for the circuit breaker and time limiter, `getProduct()` in the `ProductCompositeIntegration` class:

```
@Retry(name = "product")
@TimeLimiter(name = "product")
@CircuitBreaker(name = "product", fallbackMethod =
  "getProductFallbackValue")
public Mono<Product> getProduct(int productId, int delay,
  int faultPercent) {
```

Adding configuration

Configuration for the retry mechanism is added in the same way as for the circuit breaker and time limiter in the `product-composite.yml` file in the config repository, like so:

```
resilience4j.retry:
  instances:
    product:
      maxAttempts: 3
      waitDuration: 1000
      retryExceptions:
      - org.springframework.web.reactive.function.client.WebClientResponse
Exception$InternalServerError
```

The actual values were discussed in the *Introducing the retry mechanism* section above.

That is all the dependencies, annotations, source code, and configuration required. Let's wrap up by extending the test script with tests that verify that the circuit breaker works as expected in a deployed system landscape.

Adding automated tests

Automated tests for the circuit breaker have been added to the `test-em-all.bash` test script in a separate function, `testCircuitBreaker()`:

```
...
function testCircuitBreaker() {
    echo "Start Circuit Breaker tests!"
    ...
}
...
testCircuitBreaker
...
echo "End, all tests OK:" `date`
```

To be able to perform some of the required verifications, we need to have access to the `actuator` endpoints of the `product-composite` microservice, which are not exposed through the edge server. Therefore, we will access the `actuator` endpoints by running a command in the `product-composite` microservice using the Docker Compose `exec` command. The base image used by the microservices, `adoptopenjdk`, bundles `curl`, so we can simply run a `curl` command in the `product-composite` container to get the information required. The command looks like this:

```
docker-compose exec -T product-composite curl -s http://product-
composite:8080/actuator/health
```

The `-T` argument is used to disable the use of a terminal for the `exec` command. This is important to make it possible to run the `test-em-all.bash` test script in an environment where no terminals exist, for example, in an automated build pipeline used for CI/CD.

To be able to extract the information we need for our tests, we can pipe the output to the `jq` tool. For example, to extract the actual state of the circuit breaker, we can run the following command:

```
docker-compose exec -T product-composite curl -s http://product-composite:8080/actuator/health | jq -r .components.circuitBreakers.details.product.details.state
```

It will return either `CLOSED`, `OPEN`, or `HALF_OPEN`, depending on the actual state.

The test starts by doing exactly this, that is, verifying that the circuit breaker is closed before the tests are executed:

```
assertEqual "CLOSED" "$(docker-compose exec -T product-composite curl -s http://product-composite:8080/actuator/health | jq -r .components.circuitBreakers.details.product.details.state)"
```

Next, the test will force the circuit breaker to open up by running three commands in a row, all of which will fail on a timeout caused by a slow response from the `product` service (the `delay` parameter is set to `3` seconds):

```
for ((n=0; n<3; n++))
do
    assertCurl 500 "curl -k https://$HOST:$PORT/product-composite/$PROD_ID_REVS_RECS?delay=3 $AUTH -s"
    message=$(echo $RESPONSE | jq -r .message)
    assertEqual "Did not observe any item or terminal signal within 2000ms" "${message:0:57}"
done
```

A quick reminder of the configuration: The timeout of the `product` service is set to two seconds so that a delay of three seconds will cause a timeout. The circuit breaker is configured to evaluate the last five calls when closed. The tests in the script that precede the circuit breaker-specific tests have already performed a couple of successful calls. The failure threshold is set to 50%; three calls with a three-second delay are enough to open the circuit.

With the circuit open, we expect a fail-fast behavior, that is, we won't need to wait for the timeout before we get a response. We also expect the `fallback` method to be called to return a best-effort response. This should also apply for a normal call, that is, without requesting a delay. This is verified with the following code:

```
assertEqual "OPEN" "$(docker-compose exec -T product-composite curl
-s http://product-composite:8080/actuator/health | jq -r .components.
circuitBreakers.details.product.details.state)"

assertCurl 200 "curl -k https://$HOST:$PORT/product-composite/$PROD_ID_
REVS_RECS?delay=3 $AUTH -s"
assertEqual "Fallback product$PROD_ID_REVS_RECS" "$(echo "$RESPONSE" |
jq -r .name)"

assertCurl 200 "curl -k https://$HOST:$PORT/product-composite/$PROD_ID_
REVS_RECS $AUTH -s"
assertEqual "Fallback product$PROD_ID_REVS_RECS" "$(echo "$RESPONSE" |
jq -r .name)"
```

The product ID `1` is stored in a variable, `$PROD_ID_REVS_RECS`, to make it easier to modify the script if required.

We can also verify that the simulated `not found` error logic works as expected in the fallback method, that is, the fallback method returns `404, NOT_FOUND` for product ID `13`:

```
assertCurl 404 "curl -k https://$HOST:$PORT/product-composite/$PROD_ID_
NOT_FOUND $AUTH -s"
assertEqual "Product Id: $PROD_ID_NOT_FOUND not found in fallback
cache!" "$(echo $RESPONSE | jq -r .message)"
```

The product ID `13` is stored in a variable, `$PROD_ID_NOT_FOUND`.

As configured, the circuit breaker will change its state to half-open after `10` seconds. To be able to verify that, the test waits for `10` seconds:

```
echo "Will sleep for 10 sec waiting for the CB to go Half Open..."
sleep 10
```

After verifying the expected state (half-open), the test runs three normal requests to make the circuit breaker go back to its normal state, which is also verified:

```
assertEqual "HALF_OPEN" "$(docker-compose exec -T product-composite
curl -s http://product-composite:8080/actuator/health | jq -r
.components.circuitBreakers.details.product.details.state)"

for ((n=0; n<3; n++))
do
    assertCurl 200 "curl -k https://$HOST:$PORT/product-
composite/$PROD_ID_REVS_RECS $AUTH -s"
    assertEqual "product name C" "$(echo "$RESPONSE" | jq -r .name)"
done

assertEqual "CLOSED" "$(docker-compose exec -T product-composite curl
-s http://product-composite:8080/actuator/health | jq -r .components.
circuitBreakers.details.product.details.state)"
```

The test code also verifies that it got a response with data from the underlying database. It does that by comparing the returned product name with the value stored in the database. For the product with product ID `1`, the name is `"product name C"`.

A quick reminder of the configuration: The circuit breaker is configured to evaluate the first three calls when in the half-open state. Therefore, we need to run three requests where more than 50% are successful before the circuit is closed.

The test wraps up by using the `/actuator/circuitbreakerevents` actuator API, which is exposed by the circuit breaker to reveal internal events. It is used to find out what state transitions the circuit breaker has performed. We expect the last three state transitions to be as follows:

- First state transition: Closed to open
- Next state transition: Open to half-open
- Last state transition: Half-open to closed

This is verified by the following code:

```
assertEqual "CLOSED_TO_OPEN"      "$(docker-compose exec -T
product-composite curl -s http://product-composite:8080/actuator/
circuitbreakerevents/product/STATE_TRANSITION | jq -r
```

```
.circuitBreakerEvents[-3].stateTransition)"

assertEqual "OPEN_TO_HALF_OPEN"    "$(docker-compose exec -T
product-composite curl -s http://product-composite:8080/
actuator/circuitbreakerevents/product/STATE_TRANSITION | jq -r
.circuitBreakerEvents[-2].stateTransition)"

assertEqual "HALF_OPEN_TO_CLOSED" "$(docker-compose exec -T
product-composite curl -s http://product-composite:8080/
actuator/circuitbreakerevents/product/STATE_TRANSITION | jq -r
.circuitBreakerEvents[-1].stateTransition)"
```

The `jq` expression, `circuitBreakerEvents[-1]`, means the last entry in the array of circuit breaker events, `[-2]` is the second to last event, while `[-3]` is the third to last event. Together, they are the three latest events, the ones we are interested in.

We added quite a lot of steps to the test script, but with this, we can automatically verify that the expected basic behavior of our circuit breaker is in place. In the next section, we will try it out. We will run tests both automatically by running the test script and manually by running the commands in the test script by hand.

Trying out the circuit breaker and retry mechanism

Now, it's time to try out the circuit breaker and retry mechanism. We will start, as usual, by building the Docker images and running the test script, `test-em-all.bash`. After that, we will manually run through the tests we described previously to ensure that we understand what's going on! We will perform the following manual tests:

- Happy days tests of the circuit breaker, to verify that the circuit is closed under normal operations
- Negative tests of the circuit breaker, to verify that the circuit opens up when things start to go wrong
- Going back to normal operation, to verify that the circuit goes back to its closed state once the problems are resolved
- Trying out the retry mechanism with random errors

Building and running the automated tests

To build and run the automated tests, we need to do the following:

1. First, build the Docker images with the following commands:

```
cd $BOOK_HOME/Chapter13
./gradlew build && docker-compose build
```

2. Next, start the system landscape in Docker and run the usual tests with the following command:

```
./test-em-all.bash start
```

When the test script prints out **Start Circuit Breaker tests!**, the tests we described previously have been executed!

Verifying that the circuit is closed under normal operations

Before we can call the API, we need an access token. Run the following commands to acquire an access token:

```
unset ACCESS_TOKEN
ACCESS_TOKEN=$(curl -k https://writer:secret@localhost:8443/oauth2/
token -d grant_type=client_credentials -s | jq -r .access_token)
echo $ACCESS_TOKEN
```

An access token issued by the authorization server is valid for 1 hour. So, if you start to get `401 - Unauthorized` errors after a while, it is probably time to acquire a new access token.

Try a normal request and verify that it returns the HTTP response code `200`:

```
curl -H "Authorization: Bearer $ACCESS_TOKEN" -k https://
localhost:8443/product-composite/1 -w "%{http_code}\n" -o /dev/null -s
```

> The `-w "%{http_code}\n"` switch is used to print the HTTP return status. As long as the command returns `200`, we are not interested in the response body, so we suppress it with the switch `-o /dev/null`.

Verify that the circuit breaker is closed using the `health` API:

```
docker-compose exec product-composite curl -s http://product-
composite:8080/actuator/health | jq -r .components.circuitBreakers.
details.product.details.state
```

We expect it to respond with `CLOSED`.

Forcing the circuit breaker to open when things go wrong

Now, it's time to make things go wrong! By that, I mean it's time to try out some negative tests to verify that the circuit opens up when things start to go wrong. Call the API three times and direct the `product` service to cause a timeout on every call, that is, delay the response by `3` seconds. This should be enough to trip the circuit breaker:

```
curl -H "Authorization: Bearer $ACCESS_TOKEN" -k https://
localhost:8443/product-composite/1?delay=3 -s | jq .
```

We expect a response such as the following each time:

```
{
  "timestamp": "2021-03-12T18:29:01.477+00:00",
  "path": "/product-composite/1",
  "status": 500,
  "error": "Internal Server Error",
  "message": "Did not observe any item or terminal signal within
2000ms in 'onErrorResume' (and no fallback has been configured)",
  "requestId": "641e019c-136"
}
```

Figure 13.3: Response after a timeout

The circuit breaker is now open, so if you make a fourth attempt (within `waitInterval`, that is, `10` seconds), you will see fail-fast behavior and the `fallback` method in action. You will get a response back immediately, instead of an error message once the time limiter kicks in after `2` seconds:

```
{
  "productId": 1,
  "name": "Fallback product1",
  ...
}
```

Figure 13.4: Response when the circuit breaker is open

The response will come from the fallback method. This can be recognized by looking at the value in the name field, `Fallback product1`.

> Fail-fast and fallback methods are key capabilities of a circuit breaker. A configuration with a wait time set to only 10 seconds in the open state requires you to be rather quick to be able to see fail-fast logic and fallback methods in action! Once in a half-open state, you can always submit three new requests that cause a timeout, forcing the circuit breaker back to the open state, and then quickly try the fourth request. Then, you should get a fail-fast response from the fallback method. You can also increase the wait time to a minute or two, but it can be rather boring to wait that amount of time before the circuit switches to the half-open state.

Wait 10 seconds for the circuit breaker to transition to half-open, and then run the following command to verify that the circuit is now in a half-open state:

```
docker-compose exec product-composite curl -s http://product-composite:8080/actuator/health | jq -r .components.circuitBreakers.details.product.details.state
```

Expect it to respond with `HALF_OPEN`.

Closing the circuit breaker again

Once the circuit breaker is in a half-open state, it waits for three calls to see whether it should open the circuit again or go back to normal by closing it.

Let's submit three normal requests to close the circuit breaker:

```
curl -H "Authorization: Bearer $ACCESS_TOKEN" -k https://
localhost:8443/product-composite/1 -w "%{http_code}\n" -o /dev/null -s
```

They should all respond with `200`. Verify that the circuit is closed again by using the `health` API:

```
docker-compose exec product-composite curl -s http://product-
composite:8080/actuator/health | jq -r .components.circuitBreakers.
details.product.details.state
```

We expect it to respond with `CLOSED`.

Wrap this up by listing the last three state transitions using the following command:

```
docker-compose exec product-composite curl -s http://product-
composite:8080/actuator/circuitbreakerevents/product/STATE_
TRANSITION | jq -r '.circuitBreakerEvents[-3].stateTransition,
.circuitBreakerEvents[-2].stateTransition, .circuitBreakerEvents[-1].
stateTransition'
```

Expect it to respond with the following:

Figure 13.5: Circuit breaker state changes

This response tells us that we have taken our circuit breaker through a full lap of its state diagram:

- From closed to open when the timeout errors start to prevent requests from succeeding
- From open to half-open to see whether the error is gone
- From half-open to closed when the error is gone, that is, when we are back to normal operation

With that, we are done with testing the circuit breaker; let's move on and see the retry mechanism in play.

Trying out retries caused by random errors

Let's simulate that there is a - hopefully temporary - random issue with our `product` service or the communication with it.

We can do this by using the `faultPercent` parameter. If we set it to `25`, we expect every fourth request on average to fail. We hope that the retry mechanism will kick in to help us by automatically retrying failed requests. One way of noticing that the retry mechanism has kicked in is to measure the response time of the `curl` command. A normal response should take around 100 ms. Since we have configured the retry mechanism to wait 1 second (see the `waitDuration` parameter in the section on the configuration of the retry mechanism), we expect the response time to increase by 1 second per retry attempt. To force a random error to occur, run the following command a couple of times:

```
time curl -H "Authorization: Bearer $ACCESS_TOKEN" -k https://
localhost:8443/product-composite/1?faultPercent=25 -w "%{http_code}\n"
-o /dev/null -s
```

The command should respond with `200`, indicating that the request succeeded. A response time prefixed with `real`, for example, `real 0m0.078s`, means that the response time was 0.078 s, or 78 ms. A normal response, that is, without any retries, should report a response time of around 100 ms as follows:

Figure 13.6: Elapsed time for a request without a retry

A response after one retry should take a little over 1 second and look as follows:

Figure 13.7: Elapsed time for a request with one retry

The HTTP status code `200` indicates that the request has succeeded, even though it required one retry before succeeding!

After you have noticed a response time of 1 second, indicating that the request required one retry to succeed, run the following command to see the last two retry events:

```
docker-compose exec product-composite curl -s http://product-
composite:8080/actuator/retryevents | jq '.retryEvents[-2],
.retryEvents[-1]'
```

You should be able to see the failed request and the next successful attempt. The `creationTime` timestamps are expected to differ by 1 second. Expect a response such as the following:

```
{
  "retryName": "product",
  "type": "RETRY",
  "creationTime": "2021-03-12T13:31:30.462655100Z[GMT]",
  "errorMessage": "org.springframework.web.reactive.function.client.WebCl
ientResponseException$InternalServerError: 500 Internal Server Error from
 GET http://de68d277780d:8080/product/1?delay=0&faultPercent=25",
  "numberOfAttempts": 1
}
{
  "retryName": "product",
  "type": "SUCCESS",
  "creationTime": "2021-03-12T13:31:31.475549100Z[GMT]",
  "errorMessage": "org.springframework.web.reactive.function.client.WebCl
ientResponseException$InternalServerError: 500 Internal Server Error from
 GET http://de68d277780d:8080/product/1?delay=0&faultPercent=25",
  "numberOfAttempts": 1
}
```

Figure 13.8: Retry events captured after a request with one retry

If you are really unlucky, you will get two faults in a row, and then you will get a response time of 2 seconds instead of 1. If you repeat the preceding command, you will be able to see that the `numberOfAttempts` field is counted for each retry attempt, which is set to `1` in this case: `"numberOfAttempts": 1`. If calls continue to fail, the circuit breaker will kick in and open its circuit, that is, subsequent calls will apply fail-fast logic and the fallback method will be applied!

This concludes the chapter. Feel free to experiment with the parameters in the configuration to learn the resilience mechanisms better.

Don't forget to shut down the system landscape:

```
docker-compose down
```

Summary

In this chapter, we have seen Resilience4j and its circuit breaker, time limiter, and retry mechanism in action.

A circuit breaker can, using fail-fast logic and fallback methods when it is open, prevent a microservice from becoming unresponsive if the synchronous services it depends on stop responding normally. A circuit breaker can also make a microservice resilient by allowing requests when it is half-open to see whether the failing service is operating normally again, and close the circuit if so. To support a circuit breaker in handling unresponsive services, a time limiter can be used to maximize the time a circuit breaker waits before it kicks in.

A retry mechanism can retry requests that randomly fail from time to time, for example, due to temporary network problems. It is very important to only apply retry requests on idempotent services, that is, services that can handle the same request being sent two or more times.

Circuit breakers and retry mechanisms are implemented by following Spring Boot conventions: declaring dependencies and adding annotations and configuration. Resilience4j exposes information about its circuit breakers and retry mechanisms at runtime, using `actuator` endpoints. For circuit breakers, information regarding health, events, and metrics is available. For retries, information regarding events and metrics is available.

We have seen the usage of both endpoints for health and events in this chapter, but we will have to wait until *Chapter 20, Monitoring Microservices*, before we use any of the metrics.

In the next chapter, we will cover the last part of using Spring Cloud, where we will learn how to trace call chains through a set of cooperating microservices using Spring Cloud Sleuth and Zipkin. Head over to *Chapter 14, Understanding Distributed Tracing*, to get started!

Questions

1. What are the states of a circuit breaker and how are they used?
2. How can we handle timeout errors in the circuit breaker?
3. How can we apply fallback logic when a circuit breaker fails fast?
4. How can a retry mechanism and a circuit breaker interfere with each other?
5. Provide an example of a service that you can't apply a retry mechanism to.

14
Understanding Distributed Tracing

In this chapter, we will learn how to use distributed tracing to better understand how our microservices cooperate, for example, in fulfilling a request sent to the external API. Being able to utilize distributed tracing is essential for being able to manage a system landscape of cooperating microservices. As already described in *Chapter 8, Introduction to Spring Cloud*, Spring Cloud Sleuth will be used to collect trace information, and Zipkin will be used for the storage and visualization of said trace information.

In this chapter, we will learn about the following topics:

- Introducing distributed tracing with Spring Cloud Sleuth and Zipkin.
- How to add distributed tracing to the source code.
- How to perform distributed tracing, visualizing both successful and unsuccessful API requests. We will see how both synchronous and asynchronous processing can be visualized.
- How to use either RabbitMQ or Kafka to send trace events from our microservices to the Zipkin server.

Technical requirements

For instructions on how to install the tools used in this book and how to access the source code for this book, see:

- *Chapter 21* for macOS
- *Chapter 22* for Windows

The code examples in this chapter all come from the source code in `$BOOK_HOME/Chapter14`.

If you want to view the changes applied to the source code in this chapter, that is, see what it took to add distributed tracing using Spring Cloud Sleuth and Zipkin, you can compare it with the source code for *Chapter 13, Improving Resilience Using Resilience4j*. You can use your favorite `diff` tool and compare the two folders, `$BOOK_HOME/Chapter13` and `$BOOK_HOME/Chapter14`.

Introducing distributed tracing with Spring Cloud Sleuth and Zipkin

To recapitulate *Chapter 8, Introduction to Spring Cloud*, in reference to the *Using Spring Cloud Sleuth and Zipkin for distributed tracing* section, the tracing information from a complete workflow is called a **trace** or a **trace tree**, and sub-parts of the tree, for example, the basic units of work, are called **spans**. Spans can consist of sub-spans forming the trace tree. The Zipkin UI can visualize a trace tree and its spans as follows:

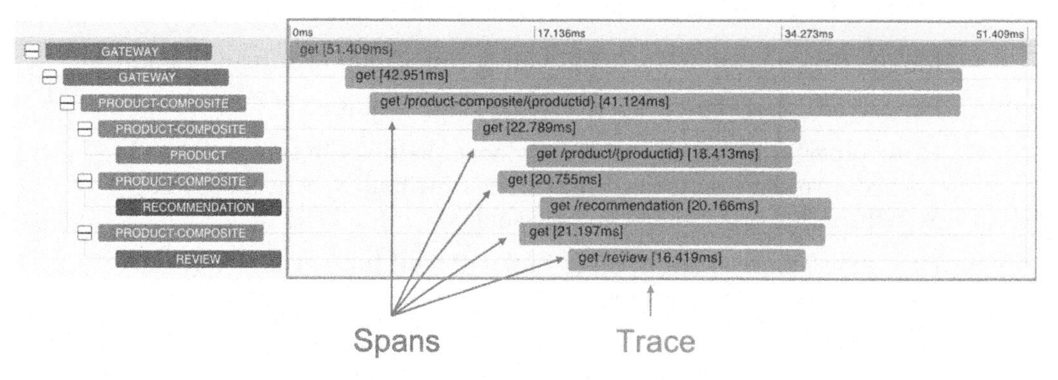

Figure 14.1: Example of a trace with its spans

Spring Cloud Sleuth can send trace information to Zipkin either synchronously over HTTP, or asynchronously using a message broker such as RabbitMQ or Kafka. To avoid creating runtime dependencies on the Zipkin server from the microservices, it is preferable to send trace information to Zipkin asynchronously using either RabbitMQ or Kafka. This is illustrated in the following diagram:

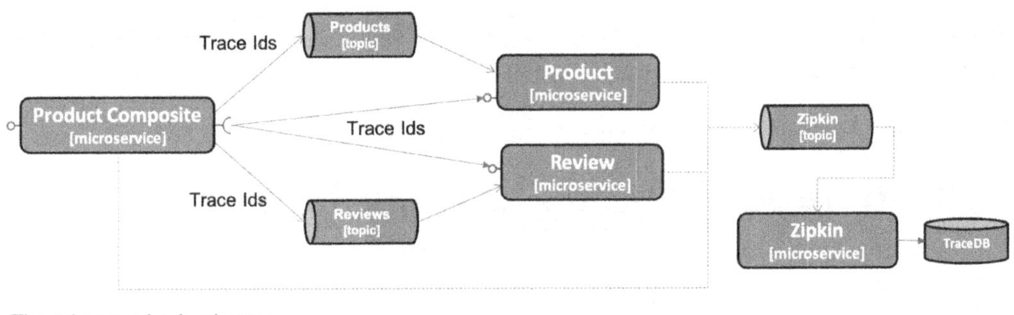

Figure 14.2: Sending trace information to Zipkin using a message broker

Zipkin comes with native support for storing trace information either in memory, or in a database such as Apache Cassandra, Elasticsearch, or MySQL. Added to this, a number of extensions are available. For details, refer to `https://zipkin.io/pages/extensions_choices.html`. In this chapter, we will store the trace information in memory.

With Zipkin introduced and placed in the system landscape, let's see what changes are required in the source code to enable distributed tracing.

Adding distributed tracing to the source code

In this section, we will learn how to update the source code to enable distributed tracing using Spring Cloud Sleuth and Zipkin. This can be done with the following steps:

1. Add dependencies to the build files to bring in Spring Cloud Sleuth and the capability of sending trace information to Zipkin
2. Add dependencies on RabbitMQ and Kafka for the projects that haven't used them before, that is, the Spring Cloud projects `authorization-server`, `eureka-server`, and `gateway`

3. Configure the microservices to send trace information to Zipkin using either RabbitMQ or Kafka
4. Add a Zipkin server to the Docker Compose files
5. Add the `kafka` Spring profile in `docker-compose-kafka.yml` to the Spring Cloud projects `authorization-server`, `eureka-server`, and `gateway`

To run the Zipkin server as a Docker container, we will use a Docker image published by the Zipkin project. Refer to `https://hub.docker.com/r/openzipkin/zipkin` for details.

Adding dependencies to build files

To be able to utilize Spring Cloud Sleuth and the ability to send trace information to Zipkin, we need to add a couple of dependencies to the Gradle project build files, `build.gradle`.

This is accomplished by adding the following two lines:

```
implementation 'org.springframework.cloud:spring-cloud-starter-sleuth'
implementation 'org.springframework.cloud:spring-cloud-sleuth-zipkin'
```

For the Gradle projects that haven't used RabbitMQ and Kafka before, that is, the Spring Cloud projects `authorization-server`, `eureka-server`, and `gateway`, the following dependencies have also been added:

```
implementation 'org.springframework.cloud:spring-cloud-starter-stream-
rabbit'
implementation 'org.springframework.cloud:spring-cloud-starter-stream-
kafka'
```

Adding configuration for Spring Cloud Sleuth and Zipkin

Configuration for using Spring Cloud Sleuth and Zipkin is added to the common configuration file, `config-repo/application.yml`. In the default profile, it is specified that trace information will be sent to Zipkin using RabbitMQ:

```
spring.zipkin.sender.type: rabbit
```

By default, Spring Cloud Sleuth only sends 10% of the traces to Zipkin. To ensure that all traces are sent to Zipkin, the following property is added in the default profile:

```
spring.sleuth.sampler.probability: 1.0
```

When sending traces to Zipkin using Kafka, the Spring profile `kafka` will be used. In the `kafka` profile, we override the setting in the default profile so that trace information is sent to Zipkin using Kafka:

```
---
spring.config.activate.on-profile: kafka

spring.zipkin.sender.type: kafka
```

Finally, the Gateway service needs a parameter in the configuration file `config-repo/gateway.yml` to enable Sleuth to track trace IDs correctly:

```
spring.sleuth.reactor.instrumentation-type: decorate-on-last
```

For details, see: `https://docs.spring.io/spring-cloud-sleuth/docs/3.0.1/reference/html/integrations.html#sleuth-reactor-integration`.

Adding Zipkin to the Docker Compose files

As we mentioned previously, the Zipkin server is added to the Docker Compose files using an already existing Docker image, `openzipkin/zipkin`, published by the Zipkin project. In `docker-compose.yml` and `docker-compose-partitions.yml`, where RabbitMQ is used, the definition of the Zipkin server appears as follows:

```
zipkin:
  image: openzipkin/zipkin:2.23.2
  mem_limit: 1024m
  environment:
    - RABBIT_ADDRESSES=rabbitmq
    - STORAGE_TYPE=mem
  ports:
    - 9411:9411
  depends_on:
    rabbitmq:
      condition: service_healthy
```

Let's explain the preceding source code:

- The version of the Docker image, `openzipkin/zipkin`, is specified to be version `2.23.2`.
- The `RABBIT_ADDRESSES=rabbitmq` environment variable is used to specify that Zipkin will receive trace information using RabbitMQ and that Zipkin will connect to RabbitMQ using the hostname `rabbitmq`.
- The `STORAGE_TYPE=mem` environment variable is used to specify that Zipkin will keep all trace information in memory.
- The memory limit for Zipkin is increased to 1,024 MB, compared to 512 MB for all other containers. The reason for this is that since Zipkin is configured to keep all trace information in memory, it will consume more memory than the other containers after a while.
- Zipkin exposes the HTTP port `9411` for web browsers to access its web user interface.
- Docker will wait to start up the Zipkin server until the RabbitMQ service reports being healthy to Docker.

While it is OK to store the trace information in Zipkin in memory for development and test activities, Zipkin should be configured to store trace information in a database such as Apache Cassandra, Elasticsearch, or MySQL in a production environment.

In `docker-compose-kafka.yml`, where Kafka is used, the definition of the Zipkin server appears as follows:

```
zipkin:
  image: openzipkin/zipkin:2.23.2
  mem_limit: 1024m
  environment:
    - STORAGE_TYPE=mem
    - KAFKA_BOOTSTRAP_SERVERS=kafka:9092
  ports:
    - 9411:9411
  depends_on:
    - kafka
```

Let's explain the preceding source code in detail:

- The configuration for using Zipkin together with Kafka is similar to the configuration we just saw for using Zipkin with RabbitMQ.
- The main difference is the use of the `KAFKA_BOOTSTRAP_SERVERS=kafka:9092` environment variable, which is used to specify that Zipkin will use Kafka to receive trace information and that Zipkin will connect to Kafka using the hostname `kafka` and the port `9092`.
- Docker will wait to start up the Zipkin server until the Kafka service has been started.

In `docker-compose-kafka.yml`, the `kafka` Spring profile is added to the Spring Cloud services `eureka`, `gateway`, and `auth-server`:

```
environment:
  - SPRING_PROFILES_ACTIVE=docker,kafka
```

That's what it takes to add distributed tracing using Spring Cloud Sleuth and Zipkin, so let's try it out in the next section!

Trying out distributed tracing

With the necessary changes to the source code in place, we can try out distributed tracing. We will do this by performing the following steps:

1. Build, start, and verify the system landscape with RabbitMQ as the queue manager.
2. Send a successful API request and see what trace information we can find in Zipkin related to this API request.
3. Send an unsuccessful API request and see what error information we can find.
4. Send a successful API request that triggers asynchronous processing and see how its trace information is represented.
5. Investigate how we can monitor trace information that's passed to Zipkin in RabbitMQ.
6. Switch the queue manager to Kafka and repeat the preceding steps.

We will discuss these steps in detail in the upcoming sections.

Starting up the system landscape with RabbitMQ as the queue manager

Let's start up the system landscape. Build the Docker images with the following commands:

```
cd $BOOK_HOME/Chapter14
./gradlew build && docker-compose build
```

Start the system landscape in Docker and run the usual tests with the following command:

```
./test-em-all.bash start
```

Before we can call the API, we need an access token. Run the following commands to acquire an access token:

```
unset ACCESS_TOKEN
ACCESS_TOKEN=$(curl -k https://writer:secret@localhost:8443/oauth2/
token -d grant_type=client_credentials -s | jq -r .access_token)
echo $ACCESS_TOKEN
```

As noticed in previous chapters, an access token issued by the authorization server is valid for one hour. So, if you start to get `401 Unauthorized` errors after a while, it is probably time to acquire a new access token.

Sending a successful API request

Now, we are ready to send a normal request to the API. Run the following command:

```
curl -H "Authorization: Bearer $ACCESS_TOKEN" -k https://
localhost:8443/product-composite/1 -w "%{http_code}\n" -o /dev/null -s
```

Expect the command to return the HTTP status code for success, `200`.

We can now launch the Zipkin UI to look into what trace information has been sent to Zipkin:

1. Open the following URL in your web browser: `http://localhost:9411/zipkin/`.
2. To find the trace information for our request, we can search for traces that have passed through the `gateway` service. Perform the following steps:
    a. Click on the large plus sign (white **+** sign on red background) and select **serviceName** and then **gateway**.
    b. Click on the **RUN QUERY** button.
    c. Click on the **Start Time** header to see the results ordered by latest first (a down arrow should be visible to the left of the **Start Time** header).

The response from finding traces should look like the following screenshot:

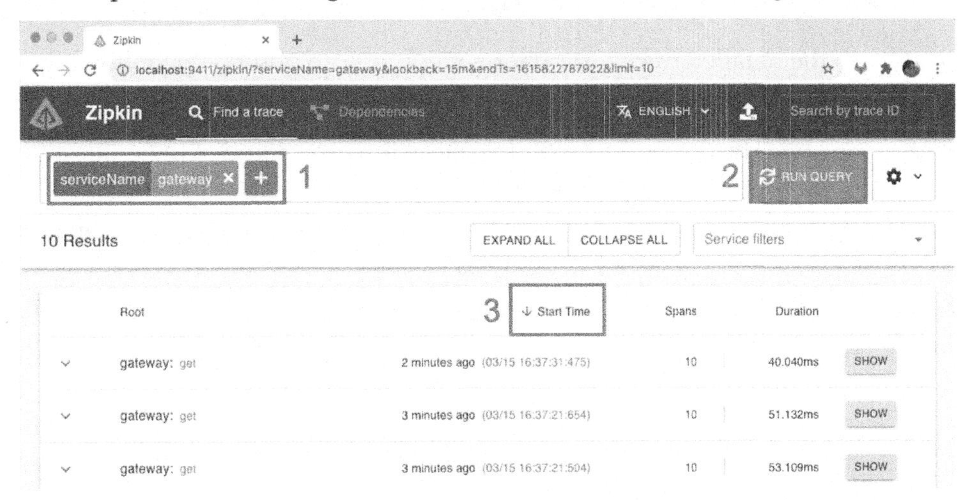

Figure 14.3: Searching for distributed traces using Zipkin

3. The trace information from our preceding API request is the first one in the list. Click on its **SHOW** button to see details pertaining to the trace:

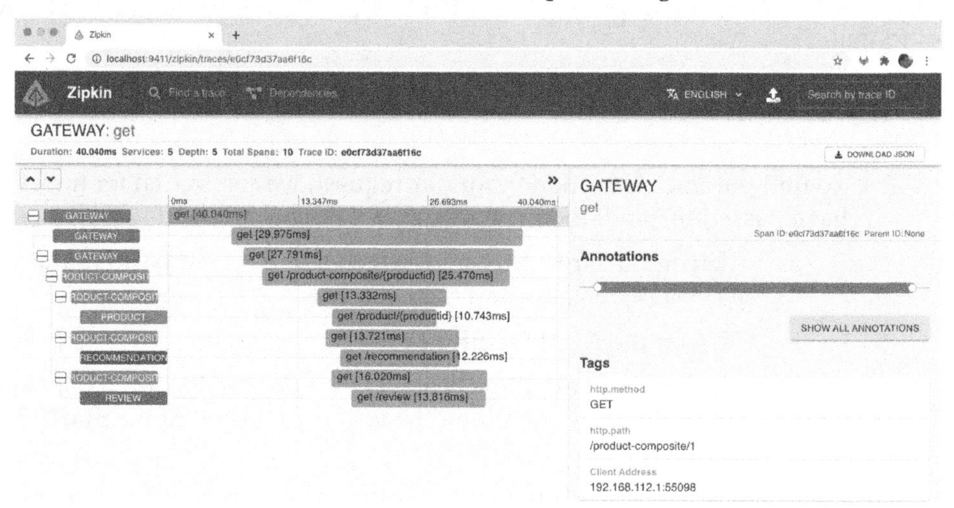

Figure 14.4: Sample distributed trace visualized in Zipkin

In the detailed trace information view, we can observe the following:

a. The request was received by the `gateway` service.

b. The `gateway` service delegated the processing of the request to the `product-composite` service.

c. The `product-composite` service, in turn, sent three parallel requests to the core services: `product`, `recommendation`, and `review`.

d. Once the `product-composite` service received the response from all three core services, it created a composite response and sent it back to the caller through the `gateway` service.

e. In the details view to the right, we can see the HTTP path of the actual request we sent: **/product-composite/1**.

Sending an unsuccessful API request

Let's see what the trace information looks like if we make an unsuccessful API request; for example, searching for a product that does not exist:

1. Send an API request for product ID `12345` and verify that it returns the HTTP status code for `Not Found, 404`:

```
curl -H "Authorization: Bearer $ACCESS_TOKEN" -k https://
localhost:8443/product-composite/12345 -w "%{http_code}\n" -o /
dev/null -s
```

2. In the Zipkin UI, go back to the search page (use the back button in the web browser) and click on the **RUN QUERY** button again. To see the results ordered by latest first, click on the **Start Time** header. Expect a result similar to the following screenshot:

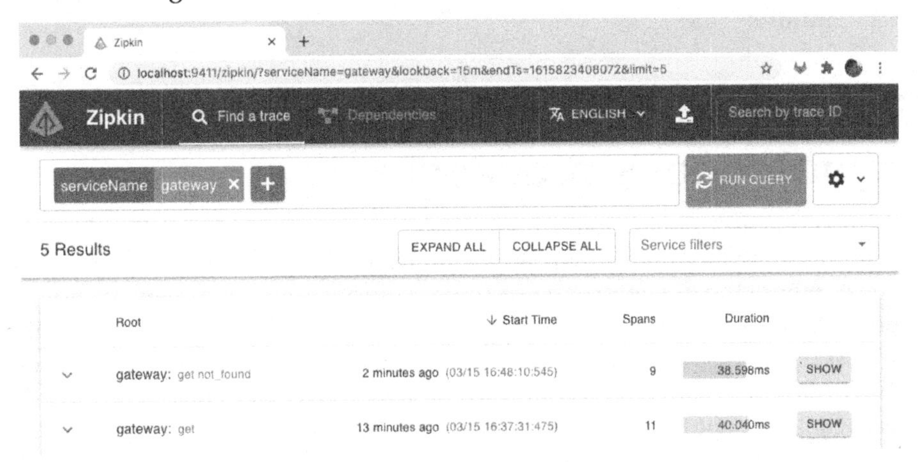

Figure 14.5: Finding a failed request using Zipkin

3. You should see the failed request at the top of the returned list. Note that its duration bar is red, indicating that an error has occurred. Click on its **SHOW** button to see details:

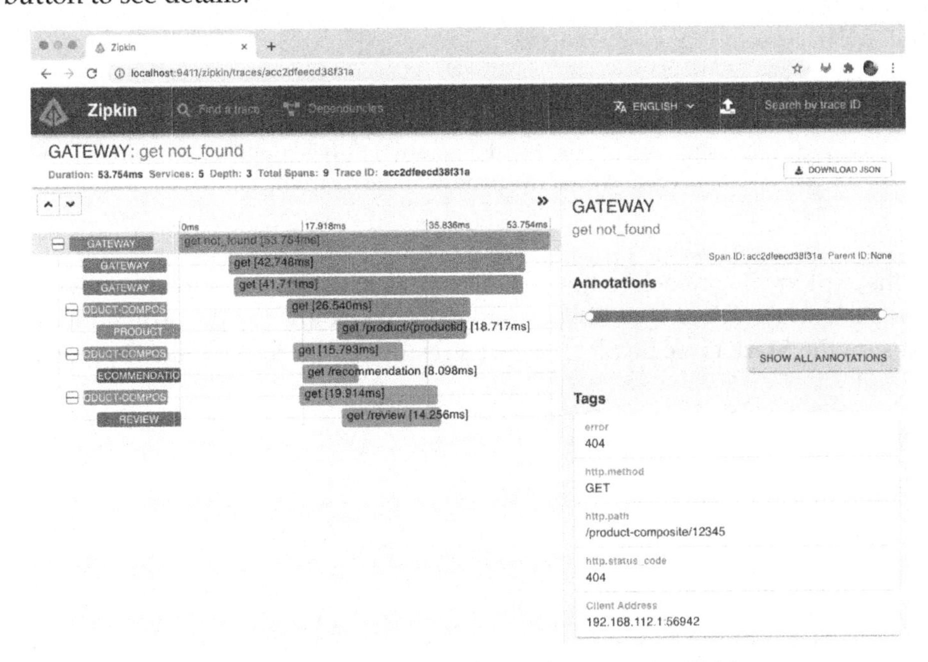

Figure 14.6: Viewing a trace of a failed request using Zipkin

Here, we can see the request path that caused the error, **/product-composite/12345**, as well as the error code: **404** (Not Found). The color coding in red indicates that it is the request to the `product` service that caused the error. This is very useful information when analyzing the root cause of a failure!

Sending an API request that triggers asynchronous processing

The third type of request that is interesting to see represented in the Zipkin UI is a request where parts of its processing are done asynchronously. Let's try a delete request, where the delete process in the core services is done asynchronously. The `product-composite` service sends a delete event to each of the three core services over the message broker and each core service picks up the delete event and processes it asynchronously. Thanks to Spring Cloud Sleuth, trace information is added to the events that are sent to the message broker, resulting in a coherent view of the total processing of the delete request.

Run the following command to delete the product with a product ID of `12345` and verify that it returns the HTTP status code for success, `200`:

```
curl -X DELETE -H "Authorization: Bearer $ACCESS_TOKEN" -k https://
localhost:8443/product-composite/12345 -w "%{http_code}\n" -o /dev/null -s
```

Remember that the delete operation is idempotent, that is, it will succeed even if the product doesn't exist!

In the Zipkin UI, go back to the search page (use the back button in the web browser) and click on the **RUN QUERY** button again. To see the results ordered by latest first, click on the **Start Time** header. Expect a result similar to the following screenshot:

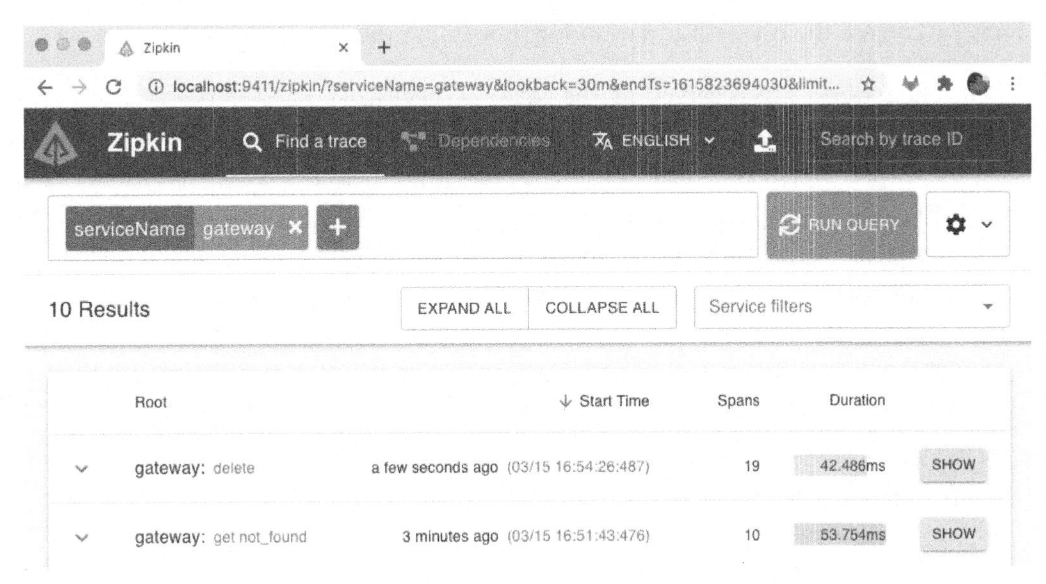

Figure 14.7: Finding a delete request using Zipkin

You should see the delete request at the top of the returned list. Note that the root service name, **gateway**, is suffixed by the HTTP method used, **delete**. Click on its **SHOW** button to see details:

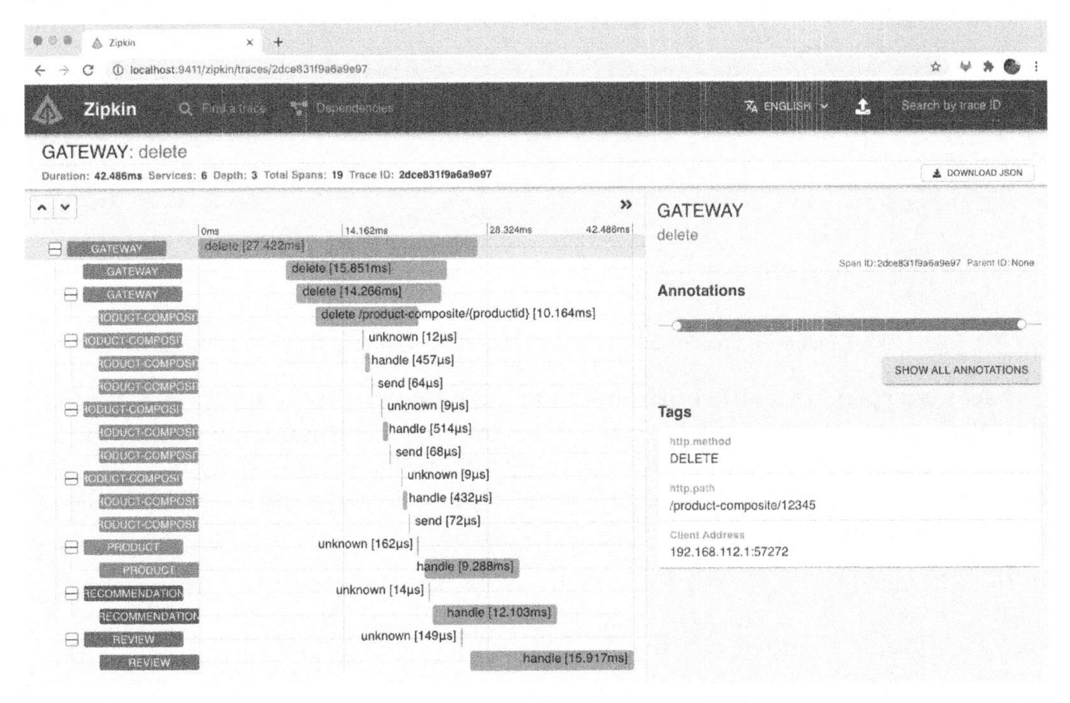

Figure 14.8: Viewing a delete request using Zipkin

Here, we can see the trace information for processing the delete request:

1. The request was received by the `gateway` service.
2. The `gateway` service delegated the processing of the request to the `product-composite` service.
3. The `product-composite` service, in turn, published three events on the message broker (RabbitMQ, in this case).
4. The `product-composite` service is now done and returns a success HTTP status code, `200`, through the `gateway` service back to the caller.
5. The core services (`product`, `recommendation`, and `review`) receive the delete events and start to process them asynchronously, that is, independently of one another.

To confirm the involvement of the message broker, click on the first product span:

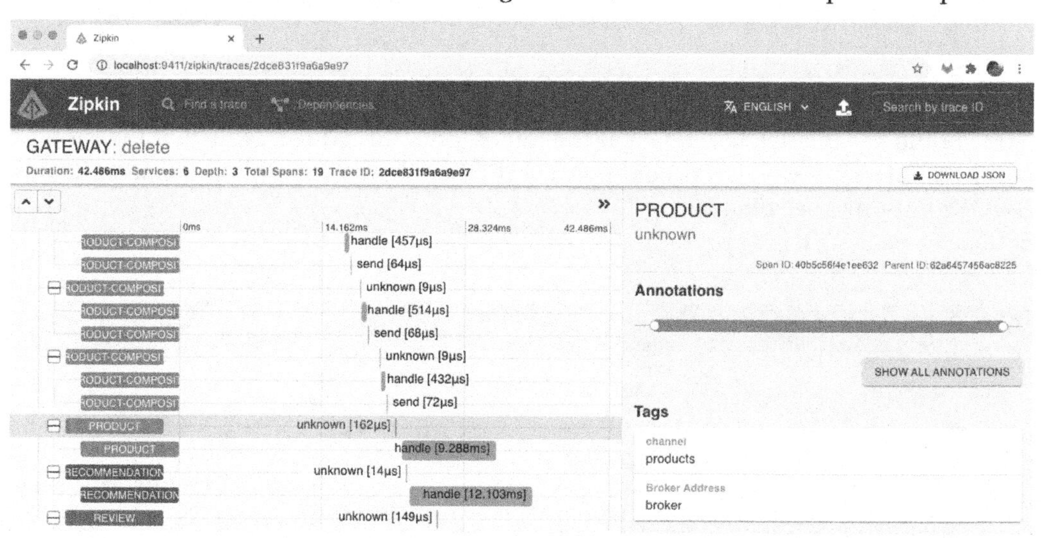

Figure 14.9: Viewing information about the asynchronous processing of an event using Zipkin

The selected span has a rather unhelpful name, **unknown**. But in the **Tags** section of the selected span, to the right, we can see information that is more interesting. Here, we can see that the `product` service was triggered by a message delivered on its input channel, **products**. We can also see the name of the message broker, **broker**, in the field **Broker Address**.

The Zipkin UI contains much more functionality for finding traces of interest!

To get more accustomed to the Zipkin UI, try out the query functionality by clicking on the plus sign and selecting **tagQuery**. For example, to find requests that failed on a `404 - not found` error, set its value to `tagQuery=error and http.status_code=404`, searching for traces that failed on a Not Found (`404`) error. Also, try setting limits for lookback range (start and end time) and the maximum number of hits by clicking on the gear icon to the right of the **RUN QUERY** button.

Monitoring trace information passed to Zipkin in RabbitMQ

To monitor trace information sent to Zipkin over RabbitMQ, we can use the RabbitMQ management Web UI. Trace messages are sent to Zipkin using a queue named `zipkin`. To monitor messages sent through this queue, open the following URL in your web browser: `http://localhost:15672/#/queues/%2F/zipkin`. If required, log in using the username "guest" and the password "guest". Expect a web page that looks like the following:

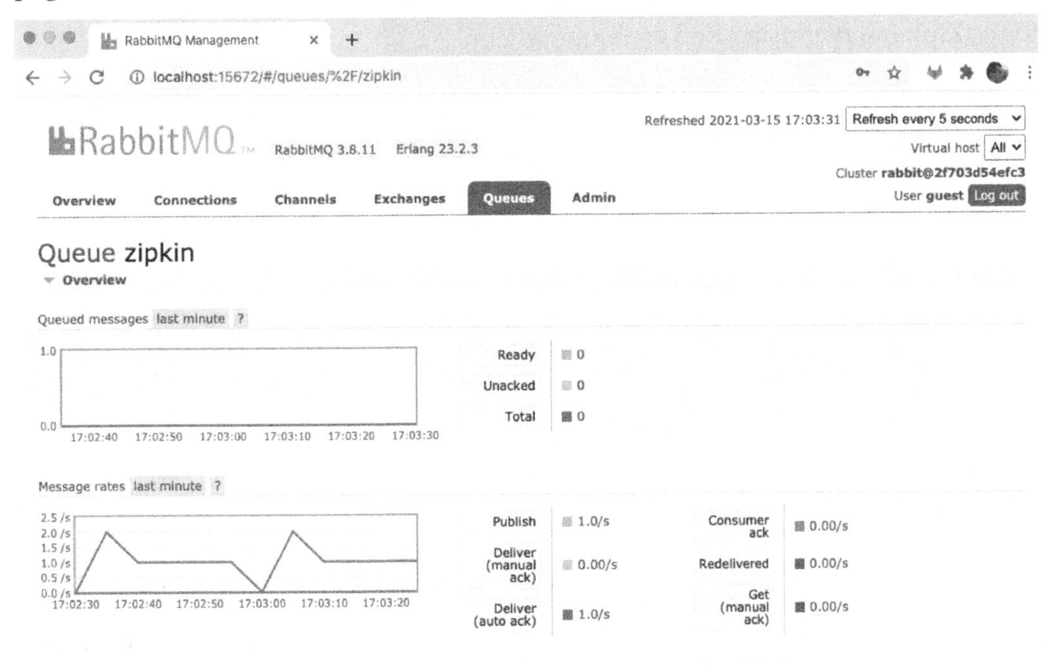

Figure 14.10: Trace records sent through RabbitMQ

In the graph named **Message rates**, we can see that trace messages are sent to Zipkin, currently at an average rate of 1 message per second.

Wrap up the tests of distributed tracing using RabbitMQ by bringing down the system landscape. Run the following command:

```
docker-compose down
```

Using Kafka as a message broker

Let's also verify that we can send trace information to Zipkin using Kafka instead of RabbitMQ!

Start up the system landscape using the following commands:

```
export COMPOSE_FILE=docker-compose-kafka.yml
./test-em-all.bash start
```

Repeat the commands we performed in the previous sections, where we used RabbitMQ, and verify that you can see the same trace information in the Zipkin UI when using Kafka.

Kafka doesn't come with a management web UI like RabbitMQ. Therefore, we need to run a few Kafka commands to be able to verify that the trace events were passed to the Zipkin server using Kafka:

For a recap on how to run Kafka commands when running Kafka as a Docker container, refer to the *Using Kafka with two partitions per topic* section in *Chapter 7, Developing Reactive Microservices*.

1. First, list the available topics in Kafka:

   ```
   docker-compose exec kafka /opt/kafka/bin/kafka-topics.sh
   --zookeeper zookeeper --list
   ```

   Expect to find a topic named `zipkin`:

Figure 14.11: Finding the Zipkin topic in Kafka

2. Next, ask for trace events that were sent to the `zipkin` topic:

```
docker-compose exec kafka /opt/kafka/bin/kafka-console-consumer.
sh --bootstrap-server localhost:9092 --topic zipkin --from-
beginning --timeout-ms 1000
```

Expect a lot of events similar to the following:

Figure 14.12: Viewing a lot of trace events in the Zipkin topic in Kafka

The details of a trace event are not important. The Zipkin server sorts that out for us and makes the information presentable in the Zipkin UI. The important point here is that we can see that the trace events actually were sent to the Zipkin server using Kafka.

Now, bring down the system landscape and unset the `COMPOSE_FILE` environment variable:

```
docker-compose down
unset COMPOSE_FILE
```

That concludes this chapter on distributed tracing!

Summary

In this chapter, we have learned how to use distributed tracing to understand how our microservices cooperate. We have learned how to use Spring Cloud Sleuth to collect trace information, and Zipkin to store and visualize the trace information.

To promote the decoupling of runtime components, we have learned how to configure microservices to send trace information to the Zipkin server asynchronously while using RabbitMQ and Kafka as message brokers. We have seen how adding Spring Cloud Sleuth to microservices is effected by adding a couple of dependencies to the build files and setting up a few configuration parameters. We have also seen how the Zipkin UI makes it very easy to identify which part of a complex workflow caused either an unexpectedly long response time or an error. Both synchronous and asynchronous workflows can be visualized with the Zipkin UI.

In the next chapter, we will learn about container orchestrators, specifically Kubernetes. We will learn how to use Kubernetes to deploy and manage microservices, while also improving important runtime characteristics such as scalability, high availability, and resilience.

Questions

1. What configuration parameter is used to control how trace information is sent to Zipkin?
2. What is the purpose of the `spring.sleuth.sampler.probability` configuration parameter?
3. How can you identify the longest-running request after executing the `test-em-all.bash` test script?

4. How can we find requests that have been interrupted by the timeout introduced in *Chapter 13, Improving Resilience Using Resilience4j*?
5. What does the trace look like for an API request when the circuit breaker introduced in *Chapter 13, Improving Resilience Using Resilience4j*, is open?
6. How can we locate APIs that failed on the caller not being authorized to perform the request?

Part III

Developing Lightweight Microservices Using Kubernetes

This part will help you to understand the importance of Kubernetes as a runtime platform for containerized workloads. You will learn how to set up Kubernetes in a local development environment and deploy microservices on Kubernetes. Finally, you will learn how to use some of the most important features in Kubernetes instead of the corresponding Spring Cloud features to provide a more lightweight microservice system landscape (in other words, one that is easier to maintain and manage).

This part includes the following chapters:

- *Chapter 15, Introduction to Kubernetes*
- *Chapter 16, Deploying Our Microservices in Kubernetes*
- *Chapter 17, Implementing Kubernetes Features to Simplify the System Landscape*
- *Chapter 18, Using a Service Mesh to Improve Observability and Management*
- *Chapter 19, Centralized Logging with the EFK Stack*
- *Chapter 20, Monitoring Microservices*

15

Introduction to Kubernetes

In this chapter, we will start to learn about Kubernetes, the most popular and widely used container orchestrator at the time of writing this book. Since the subjects on container orchestrators in general and Kubernetes itself are too big to be covered in one chapter, I will focus on introducing the areas that I have found to be the most important in my use of Kubernetes over the last few years.

The following topics will be covered in this chapter:

- Introducing Kubernetes concepts
- Introducing Kubernetes API objects
- Introducing Kubernetes runtime components
- Creating a local Kubernetes cluster
- Trying out a sample deployment and getting used to the `kubectl` Kubernetes CLI tool
- Managing a local Kubernetes cluster

Technical requirements

For instructions on how to install the tools used in this book and how to access the source code for this book, see:

- *Chapter 21* for macOS
- *Chapter 22* for Windows

The code examples in this chapter all come from the source code in `$BOOK_HOME/Chapter15`. The source code for the sample deployment on Kubernetes that will be performed in this chapter can be found in the folder `$BOOK_HOME/Chapter15/kubernetes/first-attempts`.

Introducing Kubernetes concepts

At a high level, as a container orchestrator, Kubernetes makes a cluster of (physical or virtual) servers that run containers appear as one big logical server running containers. As an operator, we declare a **desired state** to the Kubernetes cluster by creating objects using the Kubernetes API. Kubernetes continuously compares the desired state with the current state. If it detects differences, it takes action to ensure that the current state is the same as the desired state.

One of the main purposes of a Kubernetes cluster is to deploy and run containers, but also to support zero-downtime rolling upgrades using techniques such as green/blue and canary deployments. Kubernetes can schedule containers, that is, **Pods** that contain one or more co-located containers, to the available nodes in the cluster. To be able to monitor the health of running containers, Kubernetes assumes that containers implement a **liveness probe**. If a liveness probe reports an unhealthy container, Kubernetes will restart the container. Containers can be scaled in the cluster manually or automatically using a horizontal autoscaler. To optimize the use of the available hardware resources in a cluster, for example, memory and CPU, containers can be configured with **quotas** that specify the amount of resources a container needs. On the other hand, limits regarding how much a container is allowed to consume can be specified on the Pod or for a group of Pods on the **namespace** level. Namespaces will be introduced as we proceed through this chapter. This is of extra importance if several teams share a common Kubernetes cluster.

Another main purpose of Kubernetes is to provide service discovery of the running Pods and their containers. Kubernetes **Service** objects can be defined for service discovery and will also load balance incoming requests over the available Pods. Service objects can be exposed to the outside of a Kubernetes cluster. However, as we will see, an **Ingress** object is, in many cases, better suited to handling externally incoming traffic to a group of services. To help Kubernetes find out whether a container is ready to accept incoming requests, a container can implement a **readiness probe**.

Internally, a Kubernetes cluster provides one big flat IP network where each Pod gets its own IP address and can reach all the other Pods, independent of which node they run on. To support multiple network vendors, Kubernetes allows the use of network plugins that comply with the **Container Network Interface** (**CNI**) specification (`https://github.com/containernetworking/cni`). Pods are not isolated by default; they accept all incoming requests. CNI plugins that support the use of network policy definitions can be used to lock down access to Pods, for example, only allowing traffic from Pods in the same namespace.

To allow multiple teams to work on the same Kubernetes cluster in a safe way, **Role-Based Access Control** (**RBAC**, `https://kubernetes.io/docs/reference/access-authn-authz/rbac/`) can be applied. For example, administrators can be authorized to access resources on a cluster level, while the access of team members can be locked down to resources that are created in a namespace owned by the teams.

In total, these concepts provide a platform for running containers that is scalable, secure, highly available, and resilient.

Let's look a bit more into API objects that are available in Kubernetes and, after that, the runtime components that make up a Kubernetes cluster.

Introducing Kubernetes API objects

Kubernetes defines an API that is used to manage different types of *objects* or *resources*, as they are also known. Some of the most commonly used types, or *kinds*, as referred to in the API, are as follows:

- **Node**: A node represents a server, virtual or physical, in the cluster.
- **Pod**: A Pod represents the smallest possible deployable component in Kubernetes, consisting of one or more co-located containers. The containers share the same IP address and port range. This means that containers in the same Pod instance can talk to each other over localhost, but need to be aware of potential port collisions. Typically, a Pod consists of one container, but there are use cases for extending the functionality of the main container by running the second container in a Pod. In *Chapter 18, Using a Service Mesh to Improve Observability and Management*, a second container will be used in the Pods, running a sidecar that makes the main container join the service mesh.
- **Deployment**: A Deployment is used to deploy and upgrade Pods. The Deployment objects hand over the responsibility of creating and monitoring the Pods to a ReplicaSet. When creating a Deployment for the first time, the work performed by the Deployment object is not much more than creating the ReplicaSet object. When performing a rolling upgrade of a Deployment, the role of the Deployment object is more involved.

- **ReplicaSet**: A ReplicaSet is used to ensure that a specified number of Pods are running at all times. If a Pod is deleted, it will be replaced with a new Pod by the ReplicaSet.
- **Service**: A Service is a stable network endpoint that you can use to connect to one or multiple Pods. A Service is assigned an IP address and a DNS name in the internal network of the Kubernetes cluster. The IP address of the Service will stay the same for the lifetime of the Service. Requests that are sent to a Service will be forwarded to one of the available Pods using round robin-based load balancing. By default, a Service is only exposed inside the cluster using a cluster IP address. It is also possible to expose a Service outside the cluster, either on a dedicated port on each node in the cluster or - even better - through an external load balancer that is aware of Kubernetes; that is, it can automatically provision a public IP address and/or DNS name for the Service. Cloud providers that offer Kubernetes as a service, in general, support this type of load balancer.
- **Ingress**: Ingress can manage external access to Services in a Kubernetes cluster, typically using HTTP or HTTPS. For example, it can route traffic to the underlying Services based on URL paths or HTTP headers such as the hostname. Instead of exposing a number of Services externally, either using node ports or through load balancers, it is, in general, more convenient to set up an Ingress in front of the Services. To handle the actual communication defined by the Ingress objects, an Ingress controller must be running in the cluster. We will see an example of an Ingress controller as we proceed.
- **Namespace**: A namespace is used to group and, on some levels, isolate resources in a Kubernetes cluster. The names of resources must be unique in their namespaces, but not between namespaces.
- **ConfigMap**: A ConfigMap is used to store configuration that's used by containers. ConfigMaps can be mapped into a running container as environment variables or files.
- **Secret**: This is used to store sensitive data used by containers, such as credentials. Secrets can be made available to containers in the same way as ConfigMaps. Anyone with full read access to the API server can access the values of created secrets, so they are not as safe as the name might imply.
- **DaemonSet**: This ensures that one Pod is running on each node in a set of nodes in the cluster. In *Chapter 19, Centralized Logging with the EFK Stack*, we will see an example of a log collector, Fluentd, that will run on each worker node as a DaemonSet.

For a full list of resource objects that the Kubernetes API covers in v1.20, see `https://kubernetes.io/docs/reference/generated/kubernetes-api/v1.20/`.

The following diagram summarizes the Kubernetes resources that are involved in handling incoming requests:

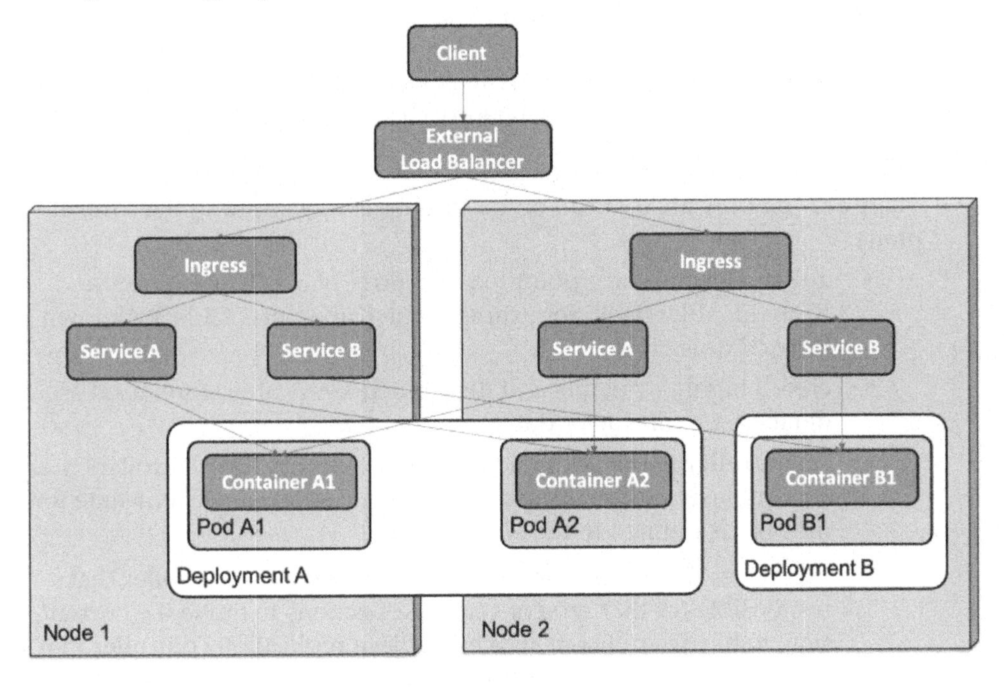

Figure 15.1: Overview of Kubernetes resources

In the preceding diagram, we can see the following:

- Two deployments, **Deployment A** and **Deployment B**, have been deployed to a cluster with two nodes, **Node 1** and **Node 2**
- **Deployment A** contains two Pods, **Pod A1** and **Pod A2**
- **Deployment B** contains one Pod, **Pod B1**
- **Pod A1** is scheduled to **Node 1**
- **Pod A2** and **Pod B1** are scheduled to **Node 2**
- Each Deployment has a corresponding Service deployed, **Service A** and **Service B**, and they are available on all nodes
- An **Ingress** is defined to route incoming requests to the two Services
- A client typically sends requests to the cluster via an **External Load Balancer**

These objects are not, by themselves, running components; instead, they are definitions of different types of desired states. To reflect the desired state in the cluster's current state, Kubernetes comes with an architecture consisting of a number of runtime components, as described in the next section.

Introducing Kubernetes runtime components

A Kubernetes cluster contains two types of nodes: **master nodes** and **worker nodes**. Master nodes manage the cluster, while the main purpose of worker nodes is to run the actual workload, for example, the containers we deploy in the cluster. Kubernetes is built up by a number of runtime components. The most important components are as follows:

- There are components that run on master nodes, constituting the **control plane**:
    - **api-server**, the entry point to the control plane. This exposes a RESTful API, which, for example, the Kubernetes CLI tool known as **kubectl** uses.
    - **etcd**, a highly available and distributed key/value store, used as a database for all cluster data.
    - A **controller manager**, which contains a number of controllers that continuously evaluate the desired state versus the current state for the objects defined in the etcd database.

      Whenever the desired or current state changes, a controller that's responsible for that type of state takes actions to move the current state to the desired state. For example, a replication controller that's responsible for managing Pods will react if a new Pod is added through the API server or a running Pod is deleted and ensures that new pods are started. Another example of a controller is the node controller. It is responsible for acting if a node becomes unavailable, ensuring that Pods running on a failing node are rescheduled on other nodes in the cluster.
    - A **scheduler**, which is responsible for assigning newly created Pods to a node with available capacity, for example, in terms of memory and CPU. **Affinity rules** can be used to control how Pods are assigned to nodes. For example, Pods that perform a lot of disk I/O operations can be assigned to a group of worker nodes that have fast SSD disks. Anti-affinity rules can be defined to separate Pods, for example, to avoid scheduling Pods from the same Deployment to the same worker node.
- Components that run on all the nodes, constituting the **data plane**:
    - **kubelet**, a node agent that executes as a process directly in the nodes' operating system and not as a container. A kubelet ensures that the Pods that are scheduled to its node have their containers up and running and that they are healthy. It acts as a conduit between the api-server and the container runtime on its node.

- **kube-proxy**, a network proxy that enables the Service concept in Kubernetes and is capable of forwarding requests to the appropriate Pods, typically in a round-robin fashion if more than one Pod is available for the specific Service. kube-proxy is deployed as a DaemonSet.
- **Container runtime**, which is the software that runs the containers on a node. Historically, Kubernetes used Docker, but today any implementation of the Kubernetes **Container Runtime Interface** (**CRI**) can be used, for example, **cri-o** (`https://cri-o.io`) and **containerd** (`https://containerd.io/`).

containerd is actually the container engine of Docker. It was separated from Docker back in 2017 and is today a graduated CNCF project.

- **Kubernetes DNS**, which is a DNS server that's used in the cluster's internal network. Services and Pods are assigned a DNS name, and Pods are configured to use this DNS server to resolve the internal DNS names. The DNS server is deployed as a Deployment object and a Service object.

The following diagram summarizes the Kubernetes runtime components described above:

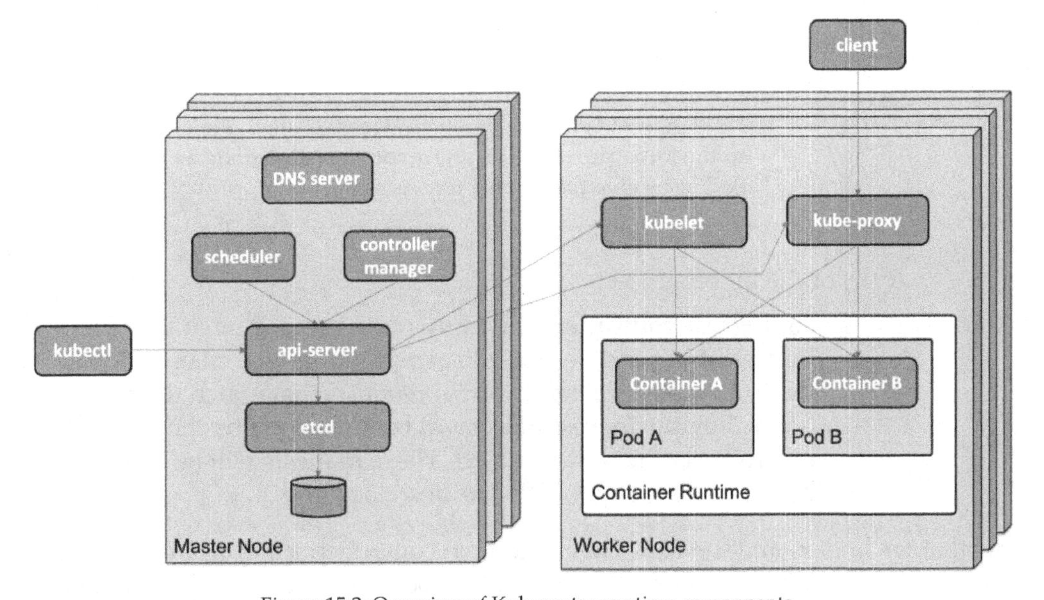

Figure 15.2: Overview of Kubernetes runtime components

Based on the diagram, we can imagine the following sequence of events:

1. An operator uses **kubectl** to send in a new desired state to Kubernetes, containing manifests declaring a new **Deployment**, **Service**, and **Ingress** object. The Ingress defines a route to the Service object and the Service object is defined to select Pods that are configured by the Deployment object.
2. **kubectl** talks to the **api-server** and it stores the new desired state as objects in the **etcd** database.
3. Various **controllers** will react on the creation of the new objects and take the following actions:
    a. For the Deployment object:
        i. New **ReplicaSet** and **Pod** objects will be registered in the api-server.
        ii. The **scheduler** will see the new Pod(s) and schedule them to appropriate worker nodes.
        iii. On each worker node, the **kubelet** agent will launch containers as described by the Pods. The kubelet will use the **container runtime** on the worker node to manage the containers.
    b. For the Service object:
        i. A DNS name will be registered in the internal DNS server for the Service object and the **kube-proxies** will be able to route requests that use the DNS name to one of the available Pods.

Note that Pods are reachable from any node in the cluster, so the kube-proxy must not run on the same node as the Pod to be able to forward requests to it.

    c. For the Ingress object:
        i. An **Ingress controller** will set up routes according to the Ingress object and be ready to accept requests from outside of the Kubernetes cluster. External requests that match the routes defined by the Ingress object will be forwarded by the Ingress controller to the Service object. These requests will be forwarded by the kube-proxy to a Pod as described above.

Now that we understand the Kubernetes runtime components and what they support and run on, let's move on to creating a Kubernetes cluster with Minikube.

Creating a Kubernetes cluster using Minikube

Now, we are ready to create a Kubernetes cluster! We will use Minikube to create a local single-node cluster.

On macOS, we will use **HyperKit** (`https://minikube.sigs.k8s.io/docs/drivers/hyperkit/`) to run a lightweight Linux VM. HyperKit uses the macOS built-in **Hypervisor** framework and is installed by Docker Desktop for Mac, so we don't need to install it separately.

On Windows, we will run Minikube in a Linux server running on **WSL 2** (Windows Subsystem for Linux, v2). The easiest way to run Minikube in WSL 2 is to run Minikube as a Docker container.

Docker and its containers are already running in a separate WSL 2 instance; see the *Installing Docker Desktop for Windows* section in *Chapter 22, Installation Instructions for Microsoft Windows with WSL 2 and Ubuntu.*

One drawback of running Minikube as a container on Docker is that ports exposed by Minikube are only accessible in the host that runs Docker. To make the ports available to Docker clients, for example the Linux server we will use on WSL 2, we can specify port mappings when creating the Minikube cluster.

Before creating the Kubernetes cluster, we need to learn a bit about Minikube profiles, the Kubernetes CLI tool known as `kubectl`, and its use of contexts.

Working with Minikube profiles

In order to run multiple Kubernetes clusters locally, Minikube comes with the concept of **profiles**. For example, if you want to work with multiple versions of Kubernetes, you can create multiple Kubernetes clusters using Minikube. Each cluster will be assigned a separate Minikube profile. Most of the Minikube commands accept a `--profile` flag (or `-p` for short) that can be used to specify which of the Kubernetes clusters the command will be applied to. If you plan to work with one specific profile for a while, a more convenient alternative exists, where you specify the current profile with the following command:

```
minikube profile my-profile
```

This command will set the `my-profile` profile as the current profile.

To get the current profile, run the following command:

```
minikube config get profile
```

If no profile is specified, either using the `minikube profile` command or the `--profile` switch, a default profile named `minikube` will be used.

Information regarding existing profiles can be found with the command `minikube profile list`.

Working with the Kubernetes CLI, kubectl

`kubectl` is the Kubernetes CLI tool. Once a cluster has been set up, this is usually the only tool you need to manage the cluster!

For managing the API objects, as we described earlier in this chapter, the `kubectl apply` command is the only command you need to know about. It is a **declarative command**; that is, as an operator, we ask Kubernetes to apply the object definition we give to the command. It is then up to Kubernetes to figure out what actually needs to be done.

Another example of a declarative command that's hopefully familiar to many readers of this book is a `SQL SELECT` statement, which can join information from several database tables. We only declare the expected result in the SQL query, and it is up to the database query optimizer to figure out in what order the tables should be accessed and what indexes to use to retrieve the data in the most efficient way.

In some cases, **imperative statements** that explicitly tell Kubernetes what to do are preferred. One example is the `kubectl delete` command, where we explicitly tell Kubernetes to delete some API objects. Creating a namespace object can also be conveniently done with an explicit `kubectl create namespace` command.

Repetitive usage of the imperative statements will make them fail, for example, deleting the same API object twice using `kubectl delete` or creating the same namespace twice using `kubectl create`. A declarative command, that is, using `kubectl apply`, will not fail on repetitive usage – it will simply state that there is no change and exit without taking any action.

Some commonly used commands for retrieving information about a Kubernetes cluster are as follows:

- `kubectl get` shows information about the specified API object
- `kubectl describe` gives more detail about the specified API object
- `kubectl logs` displays log output from containers

We will see a lot of examples of these and other `kubectl` commands in this and the upcoming chapters!

If in doubt about how to use the `kubectl` tool, the `kubectl help` and `kubectl <command> --help` commands are always available and provide very useful information. Another helpful command is `kubectl explain`, which can be used to show what fields are available when declaring a Kubernetes object. For example, run the following command if you need to look up the fields available to describe a container in the template of a Deployment object:

```
kubectl explain deployment.spec.template.spec.containers
```

Working with kubectl contexts

To be able to work with more than one Kubernetes cluster, using either Minikube locally or Kubernetes clusters set up on on-premises servers or in the cloud, `kubectl` comes with the concept of **contexts**. A context is a combination of the following:

- A Kubernetes cluster
- Authentication information for a user
- A default namespace

By default, contexts are saved in the `~/.kube/config` file, but the file can be changed using the `KUBECONFIG` environment variable. In this book, we will use the default location, so we will unset `KUBECONFIG` using the `unset KUBECONFIG` command.

When a Kubernetes cluster is created in Minikube, a context is created with the same name as the Minikube profile and is then set as the current context. So, `kubectl` commands that are issued after the cluster is created in Minikube will be sent to that cluster.

To list the available contexts, run the following command:

```
kubectl config get-contexts
```

The following is a sample response:

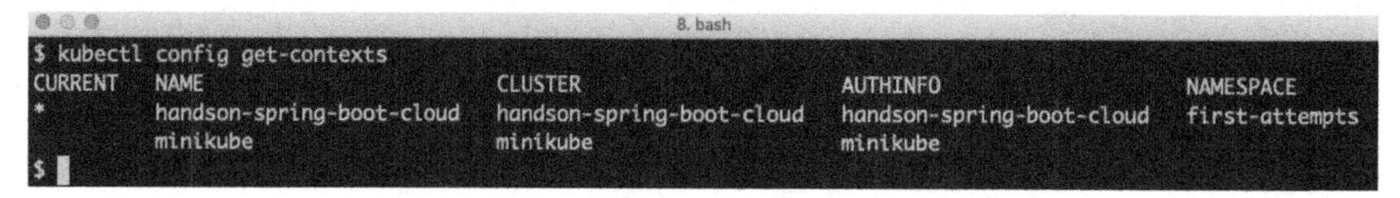
```
$ kubectl config get-contexts
CURRENT   NAME                          CLUSTER                       AUTHINFO                      NAMESPACE
*         handson-spring-boot-cloud     handson-spring-boot-cloud     handson-spring-boot-cloud     first-attempts
          minikube                      minikube                      minikube
$
```

Figure 15.3: List of kubectl contexts

The wildcard, *, in the first column marks the current context.

You will only see the `handson-spring-boot-cloud` context in the preceding response once the cluster has been created, the process for which we will describe shortly.

If you want to switch the current context to another context, that is, work with another Kubernetes cluster, run the following command:

```
kubectl config use-context my-cluster
```

In this example, the current context will be changed to `my-cluster`.

To update a context, for example, switching the default namespace used by `kubectl`, use the `kubectl config set-context` command.

For example, to change the default namespace of the current context to `my-namespace`, use the following command:

```
kubectl config set-context $(kubectl config current-context)
--namespace my-namespace
```

In this command, `kubectl config current-context` is used to get the name of the current context.

Creating a Kubernetes cluster

To create a Kubernetes cluster using Minikube, we need to run a few commands:

- Unset the `KUBECONFIG` environment variable to ensure that the `kubectl` context is created in the default config file, `~/.kube/config`.

- Create the cluster using the `minikube start` command, where we can also specify what version of Kubernetes to use and the amount of hardware resources we want to allocate to the cluster:
    - To be able to complete the examples in the remaining chapters of this book, allocate 10 GB of memory, that is, 10,240 MB, to the cluster. The samples should also work if only 6 GB (6,144 MB) are allocated to the Minikube cluster, albeit more slowly.
    - Allocate the number of CPU cores and disk space you find suitable; 4 CPU cores and 30 GB of disk space are used in the following example.
    - Finally, specify what version of Kubernetes will be used. In this book, we will use v1.20.5.
- Specify the Minikube profile to be used for the coming `minikube` commands. We will use `handson-spring-boot-cloud` as the profile name.
- After the cluster has been created, we will use the add-on manager in Minikube to enable an Ingress controller and a metrics server that comes out of the box with Minikube. The Ingress controller and the metrics server will be used in the next chapters.

Run the following commands to create the Kubernetes cluster on macOS:

```
unset KUBECONFIG

minikube start \
 --profile=handson-spring-boot-cloud \
 --memory=10240 \
 --cpus=4 \
 --disk-size=30g \
 --kubernetes-version=v1.20.5 \
 --driver=hyperkit

minikube profile handson-spring-boot-cloud

minikube addons enable ingress
minikube addons enable metrics-server
```

In WSL 2 on Windows, we need to replace the HyperKit driver with the Docker driver and specify the ports we will need access to in the coming chapters. Run the following commands in WSL 2:

```
unset KUBECONFIG

minikube start \
 --profile=handson-spring-boot-cloud \
 --memory=10240 \
 --cpus=4 \
 --disk-size=30g \
 --kubernetes-version=v1.20.5 \
 --driver=docker \
 --ports=8080:80 --ports=8443:443 \
 --ports=30080:30080 --ports=30443:30443

minikube profile handson-spring-boot-cloud

minikube addons enable ingress
minikube addons enable metrics-server
```

The ports `8080` and `8443` will be used by the Ingress controller and the ports `30080` and `30443` will be used by Services of type `NodePort`.

After the preceding commands complete, you should be able to communicate with the cluster. Try the `kubectl get nodes` command. It should respond with something that looks similar to the following:

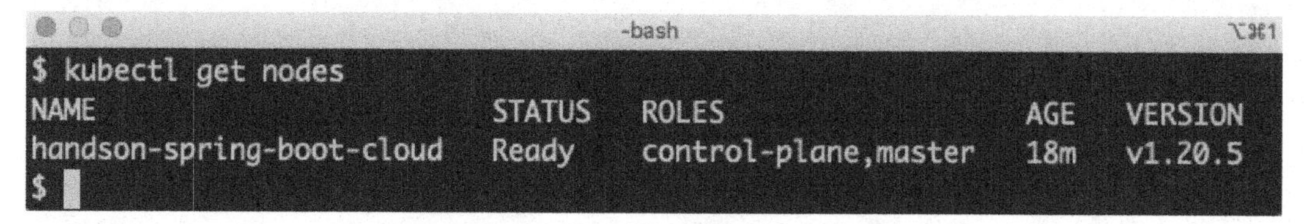

-bash
$ kubectl get nodes
NAME STATUS ROLES AGE VERSION
handson-spring-boot-cloud Ready control-plane,master 18m v1.20.5
$

Figure 15.4: List of nodes in the Kubernetes cluster

Once created, the cluster will initialize itself in the background, starting up a number of system Pods in the `kube-system` namespace. We can monitor its progress by issuing the following command:

```
kubectl get pods --namespace=kube-system
```

Once the startup is complete, the preceding command should report the status for all Pods as **Running** and the **READY** count should be **1/1**, meaning that a single container in each Pod is up and running:

```
$ kubectl get pods --namespace=kube-system
NAME                                              READY   STATUS      RESTARTS   AGE
coredns-74ff55c5b-96zrd                           1/1     Running     0          19m
etcd-handson-spring-boot-cloud                    1/1     Running     0          19m
ingress-nginx-admission-create-kphht              0/1     Completed   0          8m27s
ingress-nginx-admission-patch-qxpts               0/1     Completed   0          8m15s
ingress-nginx-controller-65cf89dc4f-7nls7         1/1     Running     0          6m30s
kube-apiserver-handson-spring-boot-cloud          1/1     Running     0          19m
kube-controller-manager-handson-spring-boot-cloud 1/1     Running     0          19m
kube-proxy-r2cg5                                  1/1     Running     0          19m
kube-scheduler-handson-spring-boot-cloud          1/1     Running     0          19m
metrics-server-56c4f8c9d6-slb7d                   1/1     Running     0          12m
storage-provisioner                               1/1     Running     1          19m
$
```

Figure 15.5: List of running system Pods

Note that two Pods are reported as **Completed**, and not **Running**. They are Pods created by **Job** objects, used to execute a container a fixed number of times like a batch job. Run the command `kubectl get jobs --namespace=kube-system` to reveal the two Job objects.

We are now ready for some action!

Trying out a sample deployment

Let's see how we can do the following:

- Deploy a simple web server based on NGINX in our Kubernetes cluster
- Apply some changes to the deployment:
    - Change the current state by deleting the Pod and verify that the ReplicaSet creates a new one
    - Change the desired state by scaling the web server to three Pods and verify that the ReplicaSet fills the gap by starting up two new Pods
- Route external traffic to the web server using a Service with a node port

First, create a namespace, `first-attempts`, and update the `kubectl` context to use this namespace by default:

```
kubectl create namespace first-attempts
kubectl config set-context $(kubectl config current-context)
--namespace=first-attempts
```

We can now create a deployment of NGINX in the namespace using the `kubernetes/first-attempts/nginx-deployment.yaml` file. This file looks as follows:

```
apiVersion: apps/v1
kind: Deployment
metadata:
  name: nginx-deploy
spec:
  replicas: 1
  selector:
    matchLabels:
      app: nginx-app
  template:
    metadata:
      labels:
        app: nginx-app
    spec:
      containers:
      - name: nginx-container
        image: nginx:latest
        ports:
        - containerPort: 80
```

Let's explain this source code in more detail:

- The `kind` and `apiVersion` attributes are used to specify that we are declaring a Deployment object.
- The `metadata` section is used to describe the Deployment object. For example, we give it the name `nginx-deploy`.

Other commonly used metadata for a Kubernetes object include the name of the `namespace` it belongs to, `labels`, and `annotations`. We will see them used in this chapter and the following chapters.

- Next comes a `spec` section that defines our desired state for the Deployment object:
    - `replicas: 1` specifies we want to have one Pod up and running.
    - A `selector` section that specifies how the Deployment will find the Pods it manages. In this case, the Deployment will look for Pods that have the `app` label set to `nginx-app`.
    - The `template` section is used to specify how Pods will be created:
        - The `metadata` section specifies the `label`, `app: nginx-app`, which is used to identify the Pods, thereby matching the selector.
        - The `spec` section specifies details for the creation of the single container in the Pod, that is, `name`, `image`, and what `ports` it uses.

Create the Deployment with the following commands:

```
cd $BOOK_HOME/Chapter15
kubectl apply -f kubernetes/first-attempts/nginx-deployment.yaml
```

Let's see what we got with the `kubectl get all` command:

```
8. bash
$ kubectl get all
NAME                                READY   STATUS    RESTARTS   AGE
pod/nginx-deploy-59b8c5f7cd-mt6pg   1/1     Running   0          8s

NAME                           READY   UP-TO-DATE   AVAILABLE   AGE
deployment.apps/nginx-deploy   1/1     1            1           8s

NAME                                      DESIRED   CURRENT   READY   AGE
replicaset.apps/nginx-deploy-59b8c5f7cd   1         1         1       8s
$
```

Figure 15.6: Kubernetes objects created by the sample deployment

As expected, we got a Deployment, ReplicaSet, and Pod object. After a short while, which mainly depends on the time it takes to download the NGINX Docker image, the Pod will be up and running, reported as **1/1** in the **READY** column, meaning that the desired state is equal to the current state!

Now, we will change the current state by deleting the Pod. Before deleting the Pod, run the command `kubectl get pod --watch` in another terminal. The use of the `--watch` option makes the command hang, waiting for state changes of Pods in the current namespace. Delete the Pod using the following command:

```
kubectl delete pod --selector app=nginx-app
```

Since the Pod has a random name (`nginx-deploy-59b8c5f7cd-mt6pg` in the preceding example), the Pod is selected based on the `app` label, which is set to `nginx-app` in the Pod.

Note how `kubectl get pod --watch` reports how the current Pod is terminated and at the same time a new Pod is started up. It is the ReplicaSet that detects the difference between the desired and current state and almost immediately starts up a new Pod to compensate for the deviation. The reported events should look like the following screenshot:

```
$ kubectl get pod --watch
NAME                            READY   STATUS              RESTARTS   AGE
nginx-deploy-684c7956fd-d69ln   1/1     Running             0          3m32s
nginx-deploy-684c7956fd-d69ln   1/1     Terminating         0          3m47s
nginx-deploy-684c7956fd-ptbkf   0/1     Pending             0          0s
nginx-deploy-684c7956fd-ptbkf   0/1     Pending             0          0s
nginx-deploy-684c7956fd-ptbkf   0/1     ContainerCreating   0          0s
nginx-deploy-684c7956fd-d69ln   0/1     Terminating         0          3m48s
nginx-deploy-684c7956fd-ptbkf   1/1     Running             0          5s
nginx-deploy-684c7956fd-d69ln   0/1     Terminating         0          4m
$
```

Figure 15.7: kubectl get pod –watch reporting changes to the Pods

In the screenshot, we can see that the Pod with a name ending with `d69ln` was stopped by the `delete` command and that the ReplicaSet immediately started up a new Pod with a name ending with `ptbkf`.

Change the desired state by setting the number of desired Pods to three replicas in the `kubernetes/first-attempts/nginx-deployment.yaml` deployment file. Apply the change in the desired state by simply repeating the `kubectl apply` command, as we mentioned previously.

Again, note that the `kubectl get pod --watch` command reports new Pods being launched by the ReplicaSet to get the current state equivalent to the new desired state, that is, three Pods. After a few seconds, two new NGINX Pods will be reported as up and running. Stop the command with *Ctrl* + *C*.

Run the `kubectl get all` command and expect a response that looks similar to the following:

```
$ kubectl get all
NAME                                READY   STATUS    RESTARTS   AGE
pod/nginx-deploy-59b8c5f7cd-mt6pg   1/1     Running   0          46s
pod/nginx-deploy-59b8c5f7cd-pmns9   1/1     Running   0          12s
pod/nginx-deploy-59b8c5f7cd-vtstj   1/1     Running   0          12s

NAME                           READY   UP-TO-DATE   AVAILABLE   AGE
deployment.apps/nginx-deploy   3/3     3            3           46s

NAME                                      DESIRED   CURRENT   READY   AGE
replicaset.apps/nginx-deploy-59b8c5f7cd   3         3         3       46s
$
```

Figure 15.8: New Pods started up by Kubernetes to meet the desired state

Note the three Pods and that the Deployment object reports **3/3**. This is interpreted as 3 ready and 3 desired Pods, meaning that all desired Pods are ready to be used.

To enable external communication with the web servers, create a Service using the `kubernetes/first-attempts/nginx-service.yaml` file:

```
apiVersion: v1
kind: Service
metadata:
  name: nginx-service
spec:
  type: NodePort
  selector:
    app: nginx-app
  ports:
    - targetPort: 80
      port: 80
      nodePort: 30080
```

The `kind` and `apiVersion` attributes are used to specify that we are declaring a `Service` object.

The `metadata` section is used to describe the `Service` object, for example, to give it a name: `nginx-service`.

Next comes a `spec` section, which defines the desired state of the `Service` object:

- With the `type` field, we specify that we want `NodePort`, that is, a Service that is accessible externally on a dedicated port on each node in the cluster. This means that an external caller can reach the Pods behind this Service using this port on any of the nodes in the cluster, independent of which nodes the Pods actually run on.
- The selector is used by the Service to find available Pods, which, in our case, are Pods labeled with `app: nginx-app`.
- Finally, `ports` are declared as follows:
    - `port: 80` specifies which port the Service will be accessible on, that is, internally in the cluster.
    - `targetPort: 80` specifies the port in the Pod where the requests will be forwarded to.
    - `nodePort: 30080` specifies which port the Service will be externally accessible on using any of the nodes in the cluster. By default, a node port must be in the range of `30000` to `32767`.

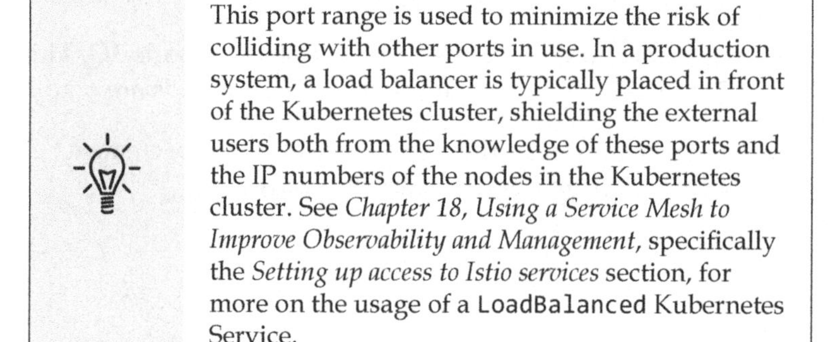

This port range is used to minimize the risk of colliding with other ports in use. In a production system, a load balancer is typically placed in front of the Kubernetes cluster, shielding the external users both from the knowledge of these ports and the IP numbers of the nodes in the Kubernetes cluster. See *Chapter 18, Using a Service Mesh to Improve Observability and Management*, specifically the *Setting up access to Istio services* section, for more on the usage of a `LoadBalanced` Kubernetes Service.

Create the Service with the following command:

```
kubectl apply -f kubernetes/first-attempts/nginx-service.yaml
```

To see what we got, run the `kubectl get svc` command. Expect a response like the following:

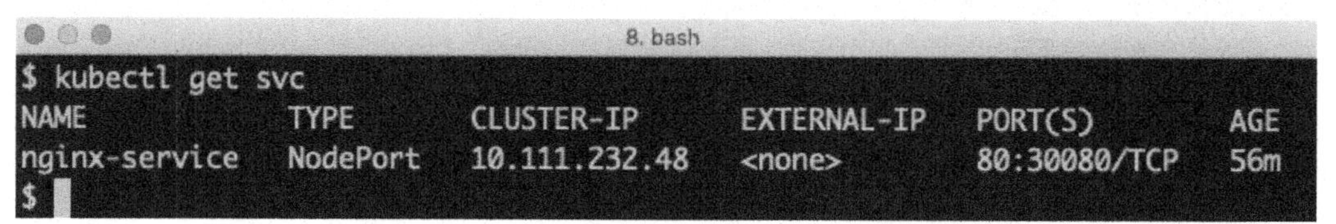

8. bash
$ kubectl get svc
NAME TYPE CLUSTER-IP EXTERNAL-IP PORT(S) AGE
nginx-service NodePort 10.111.232.48 <none> 80:30080/TCP 56m
$

Figure 15.9: NodePort Service for our deployment

`kubectl` supports short names for many of the API objects as an alternative to their full name. For example, `svc` was used in the preceding command instead of the full name, `service`. Run the command `kubectl api-resources` to see all available short names.

To access the web server through the Service's node port, we need to know the IP address or hostname of the single node in our cluster.

On macOS, where we run the Minikube cluster in a VM managed by HyperKit, we can ask Minikube for the IP address of the VM with the `minikube ip` command. In my case, it is `192.168.99.116`.

On Windows, we run the Minikube cluster as a Docker container. The node port, `30080`, is forwarded from the Docker engine to our Linux server in WSL 2 by the `-ports` option in the `minikube start` command. See the *Creating a Kubernetes cluster* section above for details. This means that we can reach the node port using `localhost` in WSL 2. What is even better is that the same goes for Windows, meaning that we can also reach the node port from a web browser running in Windows using `localhost` and port `30080`.

With this information, we can direct our web browser to the deployed web server. On macOS the address is, in my case, `http://192.168.99.116:30080`. On Windows the address is `http://localhost:30080`. Expect a response such as the following:

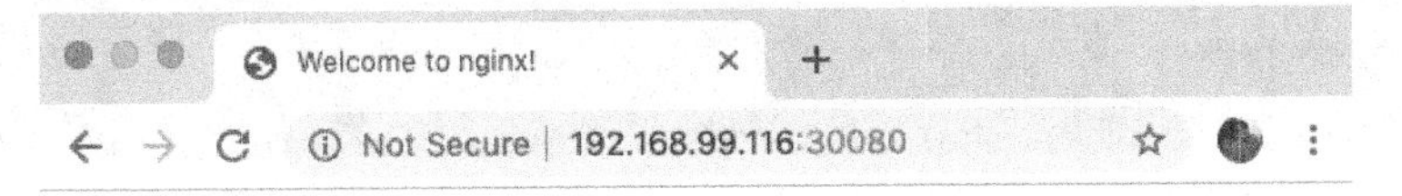

Figure 15.10: NGINX default web page

Great! But what about the internal cluster IP address and port?

One way to verify that the web server is also reachable internally in the cluster is to launch a small Pod that we can use to run `curl` from the inside. The `curl` command will use the internal cluster IP address and port. We don't need to use the internal IP address; instead, we can use a DNS name that is created for the Service in the internal DNS server. The short name of the DNS name is the same as the name of the Service, that is, `nginx-service`.

Run the following command:

```
kubectl run -i --rm --restart=Never curl-client --image=curlimages/curl
--command -- curl -s 'http://nginx-service:80'
```

The command looks a bit complex, but it will do the following:

1. Create a Pod with a small container based on the Docker image `curlimages/curl`, which contains the `curl` command
2. Run the `curl -s 'http://nginx-service:80'` command inside the container and redirect the output to the Terminal using the `-i` option
3. Delete the Pod using the `--rm` option

Expect the output from the preceding command to contain the following information (we are only showing parts of the response here):

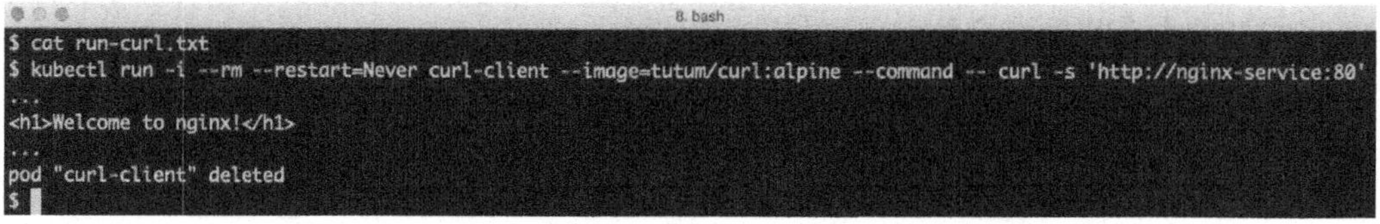

```
$ cat run-curl.txt
$ kubectl run -i --rm --restart=Never curl-client --image=tutum/curl:alpine --command -- curl -s 'http://nginx-service:80'
...
<h1>Welcome to nginx!</h1>
...
pod "curl-client" deleted
$
```

Figure 15.11: Accessing NGINX inside the Kubernetes cluster

This means that the web server is also accessible internally in the cluster!

This is basically all we need to know to be able to deploy our system landscape.

Wrap this up by removing the namespace containing the `nginx` deployment:

```
kubectl delete namespace first-attempts
```

Before we end this introductory chapter on Kubernetes, we need to learn how to manage our Kubernetes cluster.

Managing a local Kubernetes cluster

A running Kubernetes cluster consumes a lot of resources, mostly memory. So, when we are done working with a Kubernetes cluster in Minikube, we must be able to hibernate it in order to release the resources allocated to it. We also need to know how to resume the cluster when we want to continue working with it. Eventually, we must also be able to permanently remove the cluster when we don't want to keep it on disk anymore.

Minikube comes with a `stop` command that can be used to hibernate a Kubernetes cluster. The `start` command we used to initially create the Kubernetes cluster can also be used to resume the cluster from its hibernated state. To permanently remove a cluster, we can use the `delete` command from Minikube.

Hibernating and resuming a Kubernetes cluster

Run the following command to hibernate (that is, `stop`) the Kubernetes cluster:

```
minikube stop
```

Run the following command to resume (that is, `start`) the Kubernetes cluster again:

```
minikube start
```

When resuming an already existing cluster, the `start` command ignores switches that were used when you were creating the cluster.

After resuming the Kubernetes cluster, the `kubectl` context will be updated to use this cluster with the currently used namespace set to `default`. If you are working with another namespace, for example, the `hands-on` namespace that we will use in the upcoming chapter, *Chapter 16, Deploying Our Microservices to Kubernetes*, you can update the `kubectl` context with the following command:

```
kubectl config set-context $(kubectl config current-context)
--namespace=hands-on
```

Subsequent `kubectl` commands will be applied to the `hands-on` namespace when applicable.

Minikube also comes with a more lightweight and faster alternative to the `stop` and `start` commands: the `pause` and `unpause` commands. In this case, the components in the control plane are paused, not stopped, reducing the CPU consumption of the cluster to a minimum. I have, however, seen issues with the these commands when used in the recent chapters, so I recommend using the `start` and `stop` commands.

Terminating a Kubernetes cluster

If you later want to terminate the Kubernetes cluster, you can run the following command:

```
minikube delete --profile handson-spring-boot-cloud
```

You can actually run the `delete` command without specifying the profile, but I find it safer to be explicit about the profile. Otherwise, you may accidentally delete the wrong Kubernetes cluster!

We've successfully learned how to manage a Kubernetes cluster that runs in Minikube. We now know how to suspend and resume a cluster and, when no longer needed, we know how to permanently remove it.

Summary

In this chapter, we have been introduced to Kubernetes as a container orchestrator.

Using Kubernetes, we can handle a cluster of servers as one big logical server that runs our containers. We declare a desired state for the Kubernetes cluster, and it ensures that the actual state is the same as the desired state at all times, provided that enough hardware resources are available in the cluster.

The desired state is declared by creating resources using the Kubernetes API server. The controller manager in Kubernetes and its controllers react to the various resources that were created by the API server and take actions to ensure that the current state meets the new desired state. The scheduler assigns nodes to newly created containers, that is, Pods that contain one or more containers. On each node, an agent, a kubelet, runs and ensures that the Pods that were scheduled to its node are up and running. The kube-proxy acts as a network proxy, enabling a Service abstraction by forwarding requests that are sent to the Service to available Pods in the cluster. External requests can be handled either by a Kubernetes-aware load balancer that can provision a public IP address and/or DNS name for the Service, a node port that's available on all of the nodes in the cluster, or through a dedicated Ingress resource.

We have also tried out Kubernetes by creating a local single-node cluster using Minikube. The Minikube cluster runs on macOS using HyperKit and runs as a Docker container in WSL 2 on Windows. Using the Kubernetes CLI tool known as `kubectl`, we deployed a simple web server based on NGINX. We tried out resilience capabilities by deleting the web server, and we observed it being recreated automatically. We learned how to manually scale it by requesting that three Pods run on the web server. We created a Service with a node port and verified that we could access it both externally and from the inside of the cluster.

Finally, we learned how to manage a Kubernetes cluster running in Minikube in terms of how to hibernate, resume, and terminate the cluster.

We are now ready to deploy our system landscape from the earlier chapters in Kubernetes. Head over to the next chapter to find out how to do this!

Questions

1. What happens if you run the same `kubectl create` command twice?
2. What happens if you run the same `kubectl apply` command twice?
3. In terms of questions 1 and 2, why do they act differently the second time they are run?
4. What is the purpose of a ReplicaSet, and what other resource creates a ReplicaSet?
5. What is the purpose of `etcd` in a Kubernetes cluster?
6. How can a container find out the IP address of another container that runs in the same Pod?
7. What happens if you create two Deployments with the same name but in different namespaces?
8. What configuration of two Services with the same name can make them fail, even if they are created in two different namespaces?

16

Deploying Our Microservices to Kubernetes

In this chapter, we will deploy the microservices in this book to Kubernetes. To bundle and configure the microservices for deployments in different runtime environments, **Helm**, a package manager for Kubernetes, will be used. Before doing that, we need to review how service discovery is used. Since Kubernetes comes with built-in support for service discovery, it seems unnecessary to deploy Netflix Eureka for that purpose. Finally, we will also try out some Spring Boot features that facilitate the deployment of microservices in Kubernetes.

The following topics will be covered in this chapter:

- Replacing Netflix Eureka with Kubernetes Service objects and `kube-proxy` for service discovery
- Introducing how Kubernetes will be used
- Using Spring Boot's support for graceful shutdown and probes for liveness and readiness
- Using Helm to package, configure, and deploy the microservices in different environments
- Verifying the deployments with the test script, `test-em-all.bash`

Technical requirements

For instructions on how to install tools used in this book and how to access the source code for this book, see:

- *Chapter 21* for macOS
- *Chapter 22* for Windows

The code examples in this chapter all come from the source code in `$BOOK_HOME/Chapter16`.

If you want to view the changes applied to the source code in this chapter, that is, see what it took to deploy the microservices on Kubernetes, you can compare it with the source code for *Chapter 15, Introduction to Kubernetes*. You can use your favorite `diff` tool and compare the two folders, `$BOOK_HOME/Chapter15` and `$BOOK_HOME/Chapter16`.

Replacing Netflix Eureka with Kubernetes Services

As shown in the previous chapter, *Chapter 15, Introduction to Kubernetes*, Kubernetes comes with a built-in discovery service based on Kubernetes `Service` objects and the `kube-proxy` runtime component. This makes it unnecessary to deploy a separate discovery service such as Netflix Eureka, which we used in the previous chapters.

An advantage of using the Kubernetes discovery service is that it doesn't require a client library such as Spring Cloud LoadBalancer, which we have been using together with Netflix Eureka. This makes the Kubernetes discovery service easy to use, independent of which language or framework a microservice is based on.

A drawback of using the Kubernetes discovery service is that it only works in a Kubernetes environment. However, since the discovery service is based on `kube-proxy`, which accepts requests to the DNS name or IP address of a Service object, it should be fairly simple to replace it with a similar discovery service, for example, one that comes bundled with another container orchestrator.

To summarize this, we will remove the discovery server based on Netflix Eureka from our microservice landscape, as illustrated in the following diagram:

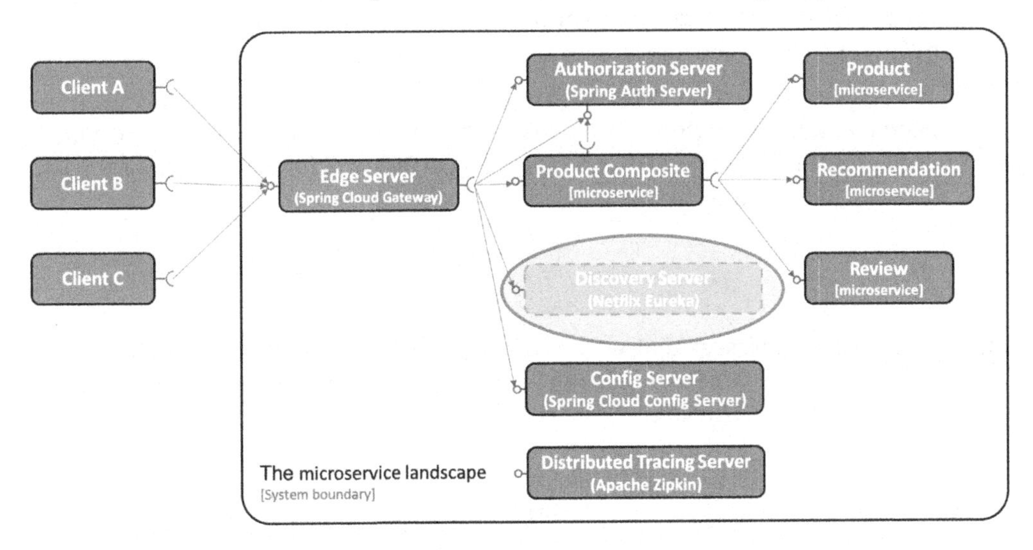

Figure 16.1: Replacing Netflix Eureka with the Kubernetes built-in discovery service

To replace the discovery server based on Netflix Eureka with the built-in discovery service in Kubernetes, we need to make some changes in our build and configuration files. We do not need to make any changes in the Java source code, except for some of the test classes, where a property is no longer required and therefore will be removed. The following changes have been applied to the source code:

- Netflix Eureka and the Spring Cloud LoadBalancer-specific configuration (client and server) have been removed from the configuration repository, `config-repo`.
- Routing rules in the gateway service to the Eureka server have been removed from the `config-repo/gateway.yml` file.
- The Eureka server project, in the `spring-cloud/eureka-server` folder, has been removed.
- The Eureka server has been removed from the Docker Compose files and the `settings.gradle` Gradle file.
- The dependency on `spring-cloud-starter-netflix-eureka-client` has been removed in all of Eureka's client build files, `build.gradle`.
- The property setting `eureka.client.enabled=false` has been removed from all integration tests of former Eureka clients.

- The gateway service no longer uses routing based on the client-side load balancer in Spring Cloud LoadBalancer using the `lb` protocol. For example, the `lb://product-composite` routing destination has been replaced with `http://product-composite` in the `config-repo/gateway.yml` file.
- The HTTP port used by the microservices and the authorization server has been changed from port `8080` (`9999` in the case of the authorization server) to the default HTTP port `80`. This has been configured in `config-repo` for each affected service like so:

```
spring.config.activate.on-profile: docker
server.port: 80
```

None of the HTTP addresses that we are using are affected by the replacement of Netflix Eureka with Kubernetes Services. For example, addresses used by the composite service are unaffected:

```
private final String productServiceUrl = "http://product";
private final String recommendationServiceUrl = "http://recommendation";
private final String reviewServiceUrl = "http://review";
```

This is because we changed the HTTP port used by the microservices and the authorization server to the default HTTP port, `80`, as described previously.

Using Docker Compose still works, even though Netflix Eureka has been removed. This can be used for running functional tests of the microservices without deploying them to Kubernetes, for example, running `test-em-all.bash` together with Docker Desktop in the same way as in the previous chapters. Removing Netflix Eureka, however, means that we no longer have a discovery service in place when using plain Docker and Docker Compose. Therefore, scaling microservices will only work when deploying to Kubernetes.

In *Chapter 17, Implementing Kubernetes Features to Simplify the System Landscape*, in the section *Verifying that microservices work without Kubernetes*, we will discuss the importance of avoiding the source code of the microservices being dependent on the Kubernetes platform, thus avoiding vendor lock-in. We will also use the test script `test-em-all.bash` together with Docker Compose to verify that the microservices don't require Kubernetes from a functional perspective.

Now that we've familiarized ourselves with how Netflix Eureka will be replaced with Kubernetes Services, let's introduce the other Kubernetes objects we will use.

Introducing how Kubernetes will be used

Later on in the chapter, we will see in detail how the various Kubernetes objects are used to deploy the microservices and the resource managers they depend on, like databases and queue managers. Before delving into all the details, let's get an overview of the Kubernetes objects that will be used:

- For each microservice, database, and queue manager that will be deployed in Kubernetes, one Deployment object and one Service object will be created. For all components, except for the edge server named `gateway`, the Service object will be of type `ClusterIP`. For the gateway, the Service object will be of type `NodePort` accepting external HTTPS requests on port `30433`.
- The config server will use a ConfigMap, containing the configuration files in the `config-repo`.
- To hold credentials for the config server and its clients, two Secrets will be created: one for the config server and one for its clients.

Now that we've seen what Kubernetes objects will be created, let's learn about the Spring Boot features that facilitate deployment to Kubernetes.

Using Spring Boot's support for graceful shutdown and probes for liveness and readiness

In Spring Boot v2.3, a couple of useful features were added to support deployments to Kubernetes:

- **Graceful shutdown**

  Whenever a microservice instance needs to be stopped, for example in a rolling upgrade scenario, there is a risk that active requests are affected when the instance is stopped. To minimize this risk, Spring Boot has added support for graceful shutdown. When applying graceful shutdown, a microservice stops accepting new requests and waits for a configurable time for active requests to complete before it shuts down the application. Requests that take a longer time to complete than the shutdown wait period will be aborted. These requests will be seen as exceptional cases that a shutdown procedure can't wait for before it stops the application.

Graceful shutdown has been enabled with a wait period of 10 seconds for all microservices by adding the following to the common file `application.yml` in the `config-repo` folder:

```
server.shutdown: graceful
spring.lifecycle.timeout-per-shutdown-phase: 10s
```

For more information, see `https://docs.spring.io/spring-boot/docs/2.5.2/reference/htmlsingle/#features.graceful-shutdown`.

- **Liveness and readiness probes**

  As described in *Chapter 15, Introduction to Kubernetes*, proper implementations of liveness and readiness probes are essential for Kubernetes to be able to manage our Pods. To briefly recap, a liveness probe tells Kubernetes if a Pod needs to be replaced and a readiness probe tells Kubernetes if its Pod is ready to accept requests. To simplify this work, Spring Boot has added support for implementing liveness and readiness probes. The probes are exposed on the URLs `/actuator/health/liveness` and `/actuator/health/readiness`. They can either be declared by configuration or implementation in source code, if increased control is required compared to what configuration gives. When declaring the probes by configuration, a **health group** can be declared for each probe specifying what existing health indicators it should include. For example, a readiness probe should report `DOWN` if a microservice can't access its MongoDB database. In this case, the health group for the readiness probe should include the `mongo` health indicator. For available health indicators, see `https://docs.spring.io/spring-boot/docs/2.5.2/reference/htmlsingle/#actuator.endpoints.health.auto-configured-health-indicators`.

  In this chapter, we will declare the probes using the following configuration in the common file `application.yml` in the `config-repo` folder:

```
management.endpoint.health.probes.enabled: true
management.endpoint.health.group.readiness.include: rabbit, db, mongo
```

  The first line of the configuration enables the liveness and readiness probes. The second line declares that readiness probes will include health indicators for RabbitMQ, MongoDB, and SQL databases, if available. For the liveness probe, we don't need to add any extra health indicators. For the scope of this chapter, it is sufficient that the liveness probe reports `UP` given that the Spring Boot application is up and running.

  For more information, see `https://docs.spring.io/spring-boot/docs/2.5.2/reference/htmlsingle/#actuator.endpoints.kubernetes-probes`.

We will try out these features once we have deployed our microservices in Kubernetes. Before we do that, we need to learn about Helm and see how it helps us bundle, configure, and deploy microservices to Kubernetes.

Introducing Helm

As described above, deploying a microservice to Kubernetes requires writing manifest files that declare the desired state of a Deployment object and a Service object. If we also need to add some configuration for the microservices, manifests for ConfigMaps and Secrets must be added. The approach of declaring a desired state and handing over the responsibility to Kubernetes to ensure that the actual state is always as close as possible to the desired state is very useful.

But writing and maintaining these manifest files can become a significant maintenance overhead. The files will contain a lot of boilerplate code, meaning duplicated manifests that will look the same for all microservices. It is also cumbersome to handle environment-specific settings without duplicating the whole set of manifest files, even though only a fraction of the content needs to be updated.

In the case of a few microservices that will only be deployed to a few environments, like a test, QA, and production environment, this might not be a major issue to handle. When the number of microservices grows to tens and hundreds and it must be possible to deploy different groups of microservices to different test, QA, and production environments, this quickly becomes an unmanageable maintenance problem.

To address these shortcomings, we will use Helm (`https://helm.sh`), an open source-based package manager for Kubernetes. With Helm comes a templating language that can be used to extract settings specific to a microservice or an environment from generic definitions of the various Kubernetes objects used.

For smaller system landscapes with only a few Deployment objects, simpler templating tools can be sufficient. For example, if you are already familiar with **Ansible** and its **Jinja2** templates, they can be used instead. Also, `kubectl` itself comes with built-in support for **Kustomize**, offering a template-free alternative for customizing Kubernetes manifest files.

A package is known as a **chart** in Helm. A chart contains templates, default values for the templates, and optional dependencies on definitions in other charts. Each component that needs to be deployed, meaning the microservices and the resource managers they depend on like databases and queue managers, will have its own chart describing how to deploy it.

To extract boilerplate definitions from the components' charts, a special type of chart, a **library chart**, will be used. A library chart doesn't contain any deployable definitions but only templates expected to be used by other charts for Kubernetes manifests, in our case for Deployment, Service, ConfigMap, and Secret objects.

Finally, to be able to describe how to deploy all components into different types of environments, for example, for development and test or staging and production, the concept of **parent charts** and **subcharts** will be used. We will define two types of environments, `dev-env` and `prod-env`. Each environment will be implemented as a parent chart that depends on different sets of subcharts, for example the microservice charts. The environment charts will also provide environment-specific default values, such as for the requested number of Pods, Docker image versions, credentials, and resource requests and limits.

In summary, we will have one reusable library chart, named `common`, a set of microservice- and resource manager-specific charts, placed in the `components` folder, and two environment-specific parent charts, placed in the `environments` folder. This file structure looks like:

```
|-- common
|   |-- Chart.yaml
|   |-- templates
|   |-- templates_org
|   `-- values.yaml
|-- components
|   |-- auth-server
|   |-- config-server
|   |-- gateway
|   |-- mongodb
|   |-- mysql
|   |-- product
|   |-- product-composite
|   |-- rabbitmq
|   |-- recommendation
|   |-- review
|   `-- zipkin-server
`-- environments
    |-- dev-env
    `-- prod-env
```

The files can be found in the folder `$BOOK_HOME/Chapter16/kubernetes/helm`.

To share Helm charts with others, they can be published to a Helm **chart repository**. In this book we will not publish any charts, but in *Chapter 17, Implementing Kubernetes Features to Simplify the System Landscape*, we will install a component named **cert-manager** using a Helm chart from a chart repository.

Before we learn about how charts are constructed, let's learn about the most frequently used Helm commands and how to run them.

Running Helm commands

To make Helm do something for us, we will use its CLI tool, `helm`.

Some of the most frequently used Helm commands are:

- `create`: used to create new charts.
- `dependency update` (`dep up` for short): resolves dependencies on other charts. Charts are placed in the `charts` folder and the file `Chart.lock` is updated.
- `dependency build`: rebuilds the dependencies based on the content in the file `Chart.lock`.
- `template`: renders the definitions files created by the templates.
- `install`: installs a chart. This command can override the values supplied by a chart, either using the `--set` flag to override a single value or using the `--values` flag to supply its own `yaml` file with values.
- `install --dry-run`: simulates a deployment without performing it; useful for verifying a deployment before executing it.
- `list`: lists installations in the current Namespace.
- `upgrade`: updates an existing installation.
- `uninstall`: removes an installation.

For full documentation of the commands that Helm provides, see `https://helm.sh/docs/helm/`.

Let's put these Helm commands in context and see what files a chart consists of.

Looking into a Helm chart

A Helm chart has a predefined structure of files. We will use the following files:

- `Chart.yaml`, which contains general information about the chart and a list of other charts it might depend on.
- `templates`, a folder that contains the templates that will be used to deploy the chart.
- `values.yaml`, which contains default values for the variables used by the templates.
- `Chart.lock`, a file created by Helm when resolving the dependencies described in the `Chart.yaml` file. This information describes in more detail what dependencies are actually used. It is used by Helm to track the entire dependency tree, making it possible to recreate the dependency tree exactly as it looked the last time the chart worked.
- `charts`, a folder that will contain the charts this chart depends on after Helm has resolved the dependencies.
- `.helmignore`, an ignore file similar to `.gitignore`. It can be used to list files that should be excluded when building the chart.

Now we understand the structure inside a Helm chart, let's learn about one of the core features of Helm: its template mechanism, and how to pass values to it.

Helm templates and values

Helm templates are used to parameterize Kubernetes manifest files. Using templates, we no longer need to maintain long-winded Deployment manifests for each microservice. Instead, we can define a common template that contains placeholders for where microservice-specific values will be placed in the template, when a manifest is rendered for a specific microservice. Let's see an example, extracted from `kubernetes/helm/common/templates/_deployment.yaml`:

```
apiVersion: apps/v1
kind: Deployment
metadata:
  name: {{ include "common.fullname" . }}
spec:
  replicas: {{ .Values.replicaCount }}
  template:
    spec:
      containers:
        - name: {{ .Chart.Name }}
```

It looks very similar to the Deployment manifest we saw in *Chapter 15, Introduction to Kubernetes*, with the exception of the use of the `{{ ... }}` constructs, used to insert microservice-specific values in the template. The construct `{{ include "common.fullname" . }}` is used to invoke other templates, as explained below. The other two constructs are used to insert values using one of the **built-in objects** in Helm. The most frequently used parts of the built-in objects are:

- `Values`: used to refer to values in the chart's `values.yaml` file or values supplied when running a Helm command like `install`.
- `Release`: used to provide metadata regarding the current release that is installed. It contains fields like:
    - `Name`: name of the release
    - `Namespace`: name of the Namespace where the installation is performed
    - `Service`: name of the installation service, always returning `Helm`
- `Chart`: used to access information from the `Chart.yaml` file. Examples of fields that can be useful for providing metadata for a deployment are:
    - `Name`: name of the chart
    - `Version`: the chart's version number
- `Files`: containing functions for accessing chart-specific files. In this chapter we will use the following two functions in the `Files` object:
    - `Glob`: returns files in a chart based on a **glob pattern**. For example, the pattern `"config-repo/*"` will return all files found in the folder `config-repo`
    - `AsConfig`: returns the content of files as a YAML map appropriate for declaring values in a `ConfigMap`
- `Capabilities`: can be used to find information regarding the capabilities of the Kubernetes cluster that the installation is performed on. For example, a template can use information in this object to adopt a manifest based on what API versions the actual Kubernetes cluster supports. We will not use this object in this chapter, but I think it is of interest to know about for more advanced use cases.

For further details on built-in objects, see `https://helm.sh/docs/chart_template_guide/builtin_objects`.

All objects are accessible in a tree where the root context, in most cases, can be addressed using the current scope, represented by a period, ".", also known as the **dot**. From the examples above we can see the use of the dot, for example in `.Values.replicaCount` and `.Chart.Name`, where we can see that the built-in objects `Values` and `Chart` are accessible directly under the current scope. In the `include` directive above, we can also see the dot being used as a parameter sent to the template named `common.fullname`, meaning the whole tree is sent to the template. Instead of sending the whole tree to a template, a sub-tree can be passed.

When using some of the Helm functions, the current scope will be changed and no longer point to the root context. We will, for example, meet the `range` function later on, which can be used to iterate through collections of values. If we need to access the root context inside the scope of a `range` function, we can use the predefined variable `$`.

Helm templates also support the declaration of variables to reference other objects. For example:

```
$name := .Release.Name
```

In this example, a variable, `name`, has been declared to hold the value of the Helm release that is currently being processed. We will see later on how variables are used in more advanced constructs.

If you recognize the format of using the `{{ ... }}` constructs from using `kubectl`, you are right. They are in both cases based on Go templates. For more information, see `https://golang.org/pkg/text/template/`.

With the templating mechanism introduced, let's learn about how the three types of charts are constructed. We start with the most important chart, the `common` chart, explaining the `components` and `environments` charts after that.

The common library chart

This chart contains reusable templates, also known as **named templates**, for the four types of Kubernetes manifests we will use in this chapter: `Deployment`, `Service`, `ConfigMap`, and `Secret`. The structure and content of the common chart are based on the output from a `helm create` command. Specifically, the template file `_helpers.tpl` has been retained to reuse best practices for naming conventions. It declares the following templates that encapsulate naming conventions:

- `common.name`: based on the chart name.

- `common.fullname`: based on a combination of the name of the release and the chart. In this book, we will override this naming convention and simply use the name of the chart.
- `common.chart`: based on the chart name and version.

For details, see the implementation in the `_helpers.tpl` file.

Named templates, which will only be used by other templates and not used to create manifests themselves, must have a name that starts with an underscore, "_". This is used to prevent Helm from trying to create manifests using them alone.

Since the named templates for the Kubernetes manifests mentioned previously contain the main part of the logic and therefore most of the complexity in the Helm charts, we will go through them one by one.

The ConfigMap template

This template is designed to create ConfigMaps from files in the folder `config-repo`. Each ConfigMap will contain all non-sensitive configuration required by a specific Deployment. The Deployment manifest will map the content of the ConfigMap as a volume in its Pod template. This will result in Pods created by the Deployment being able to access the configuration as files in their local filesystem. See the section *The Deployment template* below for details. The `config-repo` folder needs to be placed in the charts that use the common chart.

In this chapter, this template will be used only by the config server chart in the `components` folder. In the next chapter, all other microservices will also use this template to define their own ConfigMaps, since the config server will be removed.

The templates file is named `_configmap_from_file.yaml` and it looks like:

```
{{- define "common.configmap_from_file" -}}
apiVersion: v1
kind: ConfigMap
metadata:
  name: {{ include "common.fullname" . }}
  labels:
    app.kubernetes.io/name: {{ include "common.name" . }}
    helm.sh/chart: {{ include "common.chart" . }}
    app.kubernetes.io/managed-by: {{ .Release.Service }}
data:
{{ (.Files.Glob "config-repo/*").AsConfig | indent 2 }}
{{- end -}}
```

An explanation of the template is as follows:

- The first line, `{{- define "common.configmap_from_file " -}}`, is used to declare the name of the reusable template. The scope of the template ends with a matching `{{- end -}}`, the last line in this example.
- To set the name of the ConfigMap, the template `common.fullname` from the file `_helpers.tpl` is used.
- Next, a number of labels are defined to make it easier to identify the ConfigMap later on. Again, templates from the `_helpers.tpl` file are used to set the `name` and specify the `chart` used. To mark that this Service has been created using Helm, the label `app.kubernetes.io/managed-by` is set to the value for the field `.Release.Service`. From the earlier description of the `Release` object, we know that it always returns the value `Helm`.
- Next comes the core part of the ConfigMap, its `data` section. To specify the actual configuration in the ConfigMap, the `Glob` function in the `Files` object is used to get all files in the folder `config-repo`. Next, the function `AsConfig` is applied to the content in the files to form a proper YAML map. The result is piped to the `indent` function that ensures a proper indentation is rendered, in this case using two characters.

The hyphens in `{{-` and `-}}` are used to remove preceding and trailing whitespace remaining after the processing of the directive inside the curly braces.

Example of using the ConfigMap template

In this chapter, only the config server will use a ConfigMap. See the section on *The components charts* for a description of how this template is used.

To see the ConfigMap that will be created by Helm using this template, run the following commands:

```
cd $BOOK_HOME/Chapter16/kubernetes/helm/components/config-server
helm dependency update .
helm template . -s templates/configmap_from_file.yaml
```

Expect output from the `helm template` command like the following:

```
---
# Source: config-server/templates/configmap_from_file.yaml
apiVersion: v1
kind: ConfigMap
metadata:
  name: config-server
```

```
  labels:
    app.kubernetes.io/name: config-server
    helm.sh/chart: config-server-1.0.0
    app.kubernetes.io/managed-by: Helm
data:
  application.yml: |-
    app:
      auth-server: localhost
  ...
  auth-server.yml: |-
    server.port: 9999
  ...
```

The `data` field contains the content of all files in the `config-repo` folder.

The Secrets template

This template is designed to create Secrets defined by values like credentials provided by the environments `dev-env` and `prod-env`. The Secrets will be mapped as environment variables in the Pods. See the section *The Deployment template* below for details. Since an environment must be able to define multiple Secrets, this template is designed to create multiple Secret manifests using the `range` function in Helm. The template file is named `_secrets.yaml` and it looks like:

```
{{- define "common.secrets" -}}
{{- range $secretName, $secretMap := .Values.secrets }}
apiVersion: v1
kind: Secret
metadata:
  name: {{ $secretName }}
  labels:
    app.kubernetes.io/name: {{ $secretName }}
    helm.sh/chart: {{ include "common.chart" $ }}
    app.kubernetes.io/managed-by: {{ $.Release.Service }}
type: Opaque
data:
{{- range $key, $val := $secretMap }}
  {{ $key }}: {{ $val | b64enc }}
{{- end }}
---
{{- end -}}
{{- end -}}
```

An explanation of the template is as follows:

- After the declaration of the template in line 1 comes the use of the `range` function in line 2. The function assumes that the field `.Values.secrets` contains a map of Secret names and a map of the Secret's keys/value pairs. A declaration of the Secrets field in one of the environment's `values.yaml` files will look like:

  ```
  secrets:
    a-secret:
      key-1: secret-value-1
      key-2: secret-value-2
    another-secret:
      key-3: secret-value-3
  ```

  This definition will render two Secrets, named `a-secret` and `another-secret`. The `range` function assigns the current Secret name and its map to the variables `$secretName` and `$secretMap`.
- Since the `range` function changes the current scope, we can no longer use the dot notation to pass the root context to the `common.chart` template. Instead, the variable `$` has to be used.
- In the `data` section of the manifest, a second `range` function is applied a second time to traverse the current Secret's key/value pairs. Each key/value pair is assigned by the `range` function to the variables `$key` and `$val`.
- Finally, the Secret's key/value pairs are defined as a map entry in the `data` section. The value in the `$val` variable is piped to the `b64enc` function to get it properly **Base64** encoded as required by a Secret manifest.

The `---` is used to separate the rendered Secret manifests from each other, so that they are processed as separate YAML documents.

Example of using the Secrets template

Secrets are only defined by the environment charts `dev-env` and `prod-env`. They are used to create environment-specific credentials. See the section on *The environment charts* for a description of how this template is used.

To see the Secrets that will be created for the `dev-env` by Helm using this template, run the following commands:

```
cd $BOOK_HOME/Chapter16/kubernetes/helm
for f in components/*; do helm dependency update $f; done
helm dependency update environments/dev-env
helm template environments/dev-env -s templates/secrets.yaml
```

Expect output from the `helm template` command like this:

```
---
# Source: dev-env/templates/secrets.yaml
apiVersion: v1
kind: Secret
metadata:
  name: config-client-credentials
  labels:
    app.kubernetes.io/name: config-client-credentials
    helm.sh/chart: dev-env-1.0.0
    app.kubernetes.io/managed-by: Helm
type: Opaque
data:
  CONFIG_SERVER_PWD: ZGV2LXB3ZA==
  CONFIG_SERVER_USR: ZGV2LXVzcg==
---
# Source: dev-env/templates/secrets.yaml
apiVersion: v1
kind: Secret
metadata:
  name: config-server-secrets
  labels:
    app.kubernetes.io/name: config-server-secrets
    helm.sh/chart: dev-env-1.0.0
    app.kubernetes.io/managed-by: Helm
type: Opaque
data:
  ENCRYPT_KEY: bXktdmVyeS1zZWN1cmUtZW5jcnlwdC1rZXk=
  SPRING_SECURITY_USER_NAME: ZGV2LXVzcg==
  SPRING_SECURITY_USER_PASSWORD: ZGV2LXB3ZA==
```

The Service template

The Service template introduces support for overriding default values from the common chart with values specific to the charts that use the common chart. The common chart will, for example, provide default values for the Service `type` and what `ports` the Service will expose. This will be useful for most of the microservices, but some of them need to be able to override these default values in their own `values.yaml` file.

The template file is named `_service.yaml` and starts like the other named templates with the declaration of its name, followed by the implementation of the override mechanism. It looks like:

```
{{- define "common.service" -}}
{{- $common := dict "Values" .Values.common -}}
{{- $noCommon := omit .Values "common" -}}
{{- $overrides := dict "Values" $noCommon -}}
{{- $noValues := omit . "Values" -}}
{{- with merge $noValues $overrides $common -}}
```

This construct can be explained in the following way:

- When the `_service.yaml` template is used by a microservice to render its Service manifest, the values from the microservice `values.yaml` file will be available in the `.Values` object and the common chart's values will be available under the field `.Values.common`.
- So, the variable `$common` will refer to a dictionary, created by the `dict` function, with one key, `Values`, and its value will be the default values from the common chart. These values are taken from the key `common` key in the `.Values` object.
- The `$noCommon` variable will hold all values from the microservice except values under the `common` key, specified using the `omit` function.
- The `$overrides` variable will refer to a dictionary, also with one key, `Values`, but its value will be the values from the microservice's values, except the `common` values. It gets the values from the `$noCommon` variable declared on the previous line.
- The `$noValues` variable will hold all other built-in objects, except for the `Values` object.
- Now, and here is where the override will happen, the `merge` function will create one dictionary based on the dictionaries referred to by the variables `$noValues`, `$overrides`, and `$common`. In this case, values found in the `$overrides` dictionary will take precedence over values in the `$common` dictionary, thereby overriding its values.
- Finally, the `with` function will change the scope for the template code that follows until its `{{- end -}}` definition is reached. So, the current scope, `"."`, will now refer to the merged dictionary.

Let's take an example to see how this will work out. The common chart's `values.yaml` file contains the following default settings for the Service type and exposed ports:

```
service:
 type: ClusterIP
 ports:
 - port: 80
   targetPort: http
   protocol: TCP
   name: http
```

This setting will render Service objects that are of type `ClusterIP`. The Service objects will expose port `80` and forward requests to the Pods on their port named `http`.

The gateway service needs to expose a `NodePort` and use other port settings. To override the above default values, it declares the following in its chart's `values.yaml` file:

```
service:
  type: NodePort
  ports:
  - port: 443
    targetPort: 8443
    nodePort: 30443
```

The gateway's `values.yaml` file can be found in the folder `$BOOK_HOME/Chapter16/kubernetes/helm/components/gateway/values.yaml`.

The rest of the Service template file looks like:

```
apiVersion: v1
kind: Service
metadata:
  name: {{ include "common.fullname" . }}
  labels:
    app.kubernetes.io/name: {{ include "common.name" . }}
    helm.sh/chart: {{ include "common.chart" . }}
    app.kubernetes.io/managed-by: {{ .Release.Service }}
spec:
  type: {{ .Values.service.type }}
  ports:
```

```
{{ toYaml .Values.service.ports | indent 4 }}
  selector:
    app.kubernetes.io/name: {{ include "common.name" . }}
{{- end -}}
{{- end -}}
```

An explanation of the template is as follows:

- The metadata fields for `name` and `labels` are defined in the same way as already seen for the previous templates.
- The `type` of the Service is set by the field `.Values.service.type`.
- The `ports` exposed by the Service are specified using the field `.Values.service.ports`. The built-in function `toYaml` is used to format its value as `yaml` and the result is piped to the `indent` function, which ensures a proper indentation is rendered, in this case `4` characters.
- Finally, the Pod `selector` is defined. It is based on the label `app.kubernetes.io/name` and is given the name using the template `common.name`.

Example of using the Service template

The Service template is used by each component to create its Service manifest. As described above, the core microservices reuse the configuration in the common chart's `values.yaml` file, while the other components override these values in their own `values.yaml` file.

To see the Service manifest generated for a core component, for the `product` microservice, run the following commands:

```
cd $BOOK_HOME/Chapter16/kubernetes/helm
helm dependency update components/product
helm template components/product -s templates/service.yaml
```

Expect output from the `helm template` command like this:

```
# Source: product/templates/service.yaml
apiVersion: v1
kind: Service
metadata:
  name: product
  labels:
```

```
    app.kubernetes.io/name: product
    helm.sh/chart: product-1.0.0
    app.kubernetes.io/managed-by: Helm
spec:
  type: ClusterIP
  ports:
    - name: http
      port: 80
      protocol: TCP
      targetPort: http
  selector:
    app.kubernetes.io/name: product
```

To see the Service manifest generated for a component that overrides the settings in the common chart, for the `gateway` component, run the following commands:

```
cd $BOOK_HOME/Chapter16/kubernetes/helm
helm dependency update components/gateway
helm template components/gateway -s templates/service.yaml
```

Expect output from the `helm template` command like:

```
---
# Source: gateway/templates/service.yaml
apiVersion: v1
kind: Service
metadata:
  name: gateway
  labels:
    app.kubernetes.io/name: gateway
    helm.sh/chart: gateway-1.0.0
    app.kubernetes.io/managed-by: Helm
spec:
  type: NodePort
  ports:
    - nodePort: 30443
      port: 443
      targetPort: 8443
  selector:
    app.kubernetes.io/name: gateway
```

The Deployment template

Finally, the template for rendering Deployment manifests. This is the most complex template since it must handle many parts of the Deployment manifest as optional. Different components will use different parts of a Deployment manifest. The common charts `values.yaml` file contains default values for these settings that are applicable to most of the components, minimizing the need to override these settings in each component's own chart's `values.yaml` file. The following parts of the Deployment manifest are optional to use by the components:

- Arguments given to the container when it starts up
- Environment variables
- Environment variables from Secrets
- Liveness probe
- Readiness probe
- A ConfigMap and a corresponding volume

The template file is named `_deployment.yaml` and its first lines look very similar to the Service template, utilizing the same type of override mechanism:

```
{{- define "common.deployment" -}}
{{- $common := dict "Values" .Values.common -}}
{{- $noCommon := omit .Values "common" -}}
{{- $overrides := dict "Values" $noCommon -}}
{{- $noValues := omit . "Values" -}}
{{- with merge $noValues $overrides $common -}}
apiVersion: apps/v1
kind: Deployment
metadata:
  name: {{ include "common.fullname" . }}
  labels:
    app.kubernetes.io/name: {{ include "common.name" . }}
    helm.sh/chart: {{ include "common.chart" . }}
    app.kubernetes.io/managed-by: {{ .Release.Service }}
```

For an explanation of this part of the template, see the description of the Service template above.

When it comes to the spec part of the manifest, it starts with:

```
spec:
  replicas: {{ .Values.replicaCount }}
  selector:
    matchLabels:
      app.kubernetes.io/name: {{ include "common.name" . }}
  template:
    metadata:
      labels:
        app.kubernetes.io/name: {{ include "common.name" . }}
    spec:
      containers:
        - name: {{ .Chart.Name }}
          image: "{{ .Values.image.repository }}/{{ .Values.image.name
}}:{{ .Values.image.tag }}"
          imagePullPolicy: {{ .Values.image.pullPolicy }}
```

Here we can see how the core parts of the spec are defined: the requested number of `replicas`, the `selector` for the Pods, and the `template` used to create new Pods. The template defines `labels` that match the selector and defines the `name`, Docker `image`, and the `imagePullPolicy` to use when starting a container.

Next comes the various optional parts of the manifest, as described above:

```
          args:
            {{- toYaml . | nindent 12 }}
          {{- end }}
          {{- if .Values.env }}
          env:
          {{- range $key, $val := .Values.env }}
          - name: {{ $key }}
            value: {{ $val }}
          {{- end }}
          {{- end }}
          {{- if .Values.envFromSecretRefs }}
          envFrom:
          {{- range .Values.envFromSecretRefs }}
          - secretRef:
```

```
                name: {{ . }}
            {{- end }}
            {{- end }}
            {{- if .Values.livenessProbe_enabled }}
            livenessProbe:
{{ toYaml .Values.livenessProbe | indent 12 }}
            {{- end }}
            {{- if .Values.readinessProbe_enabled }}
            readinessProbe:
{{ toYaml .Values.readinessProbe | indent 12 }}
            {{- end }}
```

For the environment variables and Secrets that are mapped to environment variables, the `range` function has been used in the same way as the `secrets` template uses it. The environment variables can either be specified on a component or environment level, depending on their use case. Secrets are always specified by an environment chart. See the following sections regarding the component and environment charts.

The manifest is concluded by the declaration of the `ports` the container exposes, `resource` requests and limits, and finally, the optional declaration of a ConfigMap and a corresponding volume to map the files in the ConfigMap into:

```
            ports:
{{ toYaml .Values.ports | indent 12 }}
            resources:
{{ toYaml .Values.resources | indent 12 }}
        {{- if .Values.configmap.enabled }}
            volumeMounts:
            - name: {{ include "common.fullname" . }}
              mountPath: {{ .Values.configmap.volumeMounts.mountPath }}
        volumes:
          - name: {{ include "common.fullname" . }}
            configMap:
              name: {{ include "common.fullname" . }}
        {{- end }}
{{- end -}}
{{- end -}}
```

From the common chart's `values.yaml` file we can find some default values of interest, for example how default values for the liveness and readiness probes are defined:

```
livenessProbe_enabled: false
livenessProbe:
  httpGet:
    scheme: HTTP
    path: /actuator/health/liveness
    port: 80
  initialDelaySeconds: 10
  periodSeconds: 10
  timeoutSeconds: 2
  failureThreshold: 20
  successThreshold: 1

readinessProbe_enabled: false
readinessProbe:
  httpGet:
    scheme: HTTP
    path: /actuator/health/readiness
    port: 80
  initialDelaySeconds: 10
  periodSeconds: 10
  timeoutSeconds: 2
  failureThreshold: 3
  successThreshold: 1
```

From these declarations, we can see that:

- The probes are by default disabled, since not all deployments are using probes.
- The probes are based on HTTP GET requests sent to the endpoints exposed by Spring Boot, as described in the section *Using Spring Boot's support for graceful shutdown and probes for liveness and readiness* above.
    - As long as the endpoint responds with a `2xx` or a `3xx` response code, the probe is considered to be successful

- The probes can be configured using the following parameters:
  - `initialDelaySeconds` specifies how long Kubernetes waits to probe a container after it's started up.
  - `periodSeconds` specifies the time between probe requests sent by Kubernetes.
  - `timeoutSeconds` specifies how long Kubernetes waits on a response before it treats the probe as failed.
  - `failureThreshold` specifies how many failed attempts Kubernetes makes before giving up. In the case of a liveness probe, this means restarting the Pod. In the case of a readiness probe, it means that Kubernetes will not send any more requests to the container until the readiness probes are successful again.
  - `successThreshold` specifies the number of successful attempts that are required for a probe to be considered successful again after a failure. This only applies to readiness probes, since it must be set to `1` if specified for liveness probes.

Finding optimal settings for the probes can be challenging, that is, finding a proper balance between getting a swift reaction from Kubernetes when the availability of a Pod changes and not overloading the Pods with probe requests.

Specifically, configuring a liveness probe with values that are too low can result in Kubernetes restarting Pods that don't need to be restarted; they just need some extra time to start up. Starting a large number of Pods at the same time, also resulting in extra-long startup times, can in the same way result in a lot of unnecessary restarts.

Setting the configuration values too high on the probes (except for the `successThreshold` value) makes Kubernetes react more slowly, which can be annoying in a development environment. Proper values also depend on the available hardware, which affects the startup times for the Pods. For the scope of this book, `failureThreshold` for the liveness probes is set to a high value, `20`, to avoid unnecessary restarts on computers with limited hardware resources.

Example of using the Deployment template

The Deployment template is used by each component to create its Deployment manifest. The core microservices reuse most of the configuration in the common chart's `values.yaml` file, minimizing the need for component-specific configuration, while the other components override more of these values in their own `values.yaml` file.

To see the Deployment manifest generated for a core component, for the `product` microservice, run the following commands:

```
cd $BOOK_HOME/Chapter16/kubernetes/helm
helm dependency update components/product
helm template components/product -s templates/deployment.yaml
```

To see the Deployment manifest generated for a component that overrides the settings in the common chart, for the MongoDB component, run the following commands:

```
cd $BOOK_HOME/Chapter16/kubernetes/helm
helm dependency update components/mongodb
helm template components/mongodb -s templates/deployment.yaml
```

Expect output from the `helm template` command like:

```
---
# Source: mongodb/templates/deployment.yaml
apiVersion: apps/v1
kind: Deployment
metadata:
  name: mongodb
  labels:
    app.kubernetes.io/name: mongodb
    helm.sh/chart: mongodb-1.0.0
    app.kubernetes.io/managed-by: Helm
spec:
  replicas: 1
  selector:
    matchLabels:
      app.kubernetes.io/name: mongodb
```

```
  template:
    metadata:
      labels:
        app.kubernetes.io/name: mongodb
    spec:
      containers:
        - name: mongodb
          image: "registry.hub.docker.com/library/mongo:4.4.2"
          imagePullPolicy: IfNotPresent
          ports:
            - containerPort: 27017
          resources:
            limits:
              memory: 350Mi
```

This concludes the walkthrough of the reusable named templates in the common chart. The files can be found in the folder `$BOOK_HOME/Chapter16/kubernetes/helm/common`.

Next, let's see how the component-specific charts are defined.

The components charts

The charts for the microservices and the resource managers are stored in the `components` folder and they all share the same file structure:

- `Chart.yaml` expresses a dependency on the `common` library chart.
- The `template` folder contains two templates, `deployment.yaml` and `service.yaml`. Both templates apply the corresponding named template from the common chart. For example, the `service.yaml` template looks like:

  ```
  {{- template "common.service" . -}}
  ```

- The `values.yaml` file contains settings specific to the microservice. For example, the values file for the `auth-server` chart looks like:

  ```
  fullnameOverride: auth-server

  image:
    name: auth-server

  env:
  ```

```
  SPRING_PROFILES_ACTIVE: "docker"
livenessProbe_enabled: true

readinessProbe_enabled: true
```

The `auth-server` only needs to declare its name, Docker image, Spring profile, and that it wants to use the default configuration of the liveness and readiness probes.

The config server differs from the other charts in that it uses a ConfigMap to store the `config-repo` containing the configuration files for all the other microservices. In its `template` folder, it defines a template for a ConfigMap that is based on the named template in the common chart for ConfigMaps that we have already been introduced to:

```
{{- template "common.configmap_from_file" . -}}
```

The template expects to find the property files in the charts folder `config-repo`. To avoid duplicating the `config-repo` from `$BOOK_HOME/Chapter16/config-repo`, a **soft link**, also known as a **symbolic link**, has been created with the command:

```
cd $BOOK_HOME/Chapter16/kubernetes/helm/components/config-server
ln -s ../../../../config-repo config-repo
```

Since Git preserves soft links, you don't need to recreate the soft link - the `git clone` command makes it for you!

As already mentioned in the walkthrough of the common chart, the gateway service differs from the other microservices since it needs to expose a Service of type `NodePort`.

Besides the charts for the microservices, the `components` folder also contains charts for the databases, message broker, and Zipkin server we use. They are structured in the same way as for the microservices. Since the common templates have been designed to streamline the charts for the microservices, the other charts need to override more default values in `values.yaml` files compared to the microservices. For details, look into the `values.yaml` file in the following folders: `mongodb`, `mysql`, `rabbitmq`, and `zipkin-server`.

The environment charts

Finally, the dev-env and prod-env charts in the environments folder tie everything together to complete installation packages for a typical dev/test or staging/prod environment. Their Charts.yaml file contains dependencies on both the common chart and the charts in the components folder, and the template folder contains a secrets.yaml template for creating environment-specific credentials as Secrets. It is based on the named template for Secrets from the common chart as:

```
{{- template "common.secrets" . -}}
```

Looking into the dev-env charts values.yaml file, we can find the following Secret values being defined for the Secret config-server-secrets:

```
secrets:

  config-server-secrets:
    ENCRYPT_KEY: my-very-secure-encrypt-key
    SPRING_SECURITY_USER_NAME: dev-usr
    SPRING_SECURITY_USER_PASSWORD: dev-pwd
```

This will result in the Secret config-server-secrets containing three Secret values, all Base64 encoded. Its manifest will look like:

```
apiVersion: v1
kind: Secret
metadata:
  name: config-server-secrets
  labels:
    ...
type: Opaque
data:
  ENCRYPT_KEY: bXktdmVyeS1zZWN1cmUtZW5jcnlwdC1rZXk=
  SPRING_SECURITY_USER_NAME: ZGV2LXVzcg==
  SPRING_SECURITY_USER_PASSWORD: ZGV2LXB3ZA==
```

Note that this values.yaml file contains sensitive information, for example the encrypt key used by the config server and the password used to access the config server. This file must be stored in a secure way. An alternative, if it is inappropriate to store this file securely, is to remove the sensitive information from this file and supply the sensitive information when the helm install command is executed.

To use the Secret in the Deployment manifest for the config server, the following is defined in the `dev-env` charts `values.yaml` file:

```
config-server:
  envFromSecretRefs:
    - config-server-secrets
```

This will be used by the Deployment template described above to add the Secret as environment variables in the Deployment manifest for the config server.

The `prod-env` chart overrides more values than the `dev-env` chart. For example, the `values.yaml` file in the `prod-env` chart specifies that an extra Spring profile, `prod`, should be used and what version to use for the Docker images. This looks like the following for the `product` microservice:

```
product:
  image:
    tag: v1
  env:
    SPRING_PROFILES_ACTIVE: "docker,prod"
```

With this introduction to what the various types of charts contain, let's move on and use them together with the Helm commands we learned about to deploy our microservices in Kubernetes!

Deploying to Kubernetes for development and test

In this section, we will deploy the microservices in an environment to be used for development and test activities, for example, system integration tests. This type of environment is used primarily for functional tests and is therefore configured to use minimal system resources and the latest available versions of the microservices' Docker images.

To be able to run functional tests, we will deploy the microservices together with the resource managers they require in the same Namespace, which we will call `hands-on`. This makes it easy to set up a test environment, but also to remove it once we are done with it. We can simply delete the Namespace to get rid of all resources used by the test environment. This deployment scenario is illustrated by the following diagram:

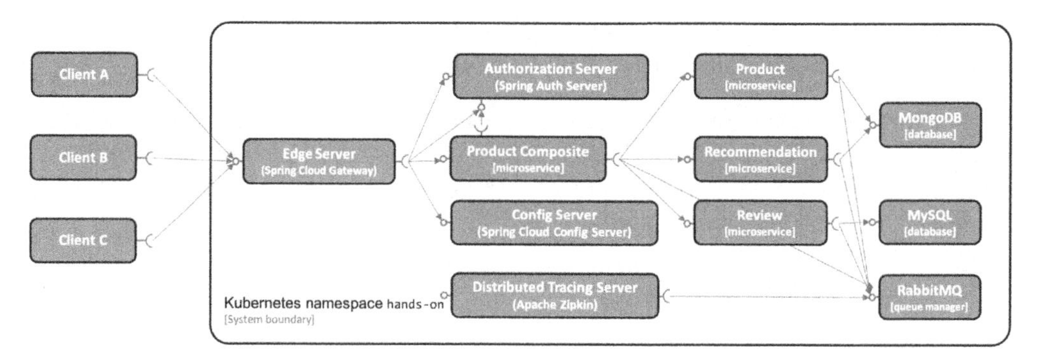

Figure 16.2: Resource managers deployed in the same Kubernetes Namespace as the microservices in the dev environment

Before we can deploy the system landscape, we need to build our Docker images and resolve the dependencies for our Helm charts.

Building Docker images

Normally, we have to push images to a Docker registry and configure Kubernetes to pull images from the registry. In our case, where we have a local single Node cluster, we can shortcut this process by pointing our Docker client to the Docker engine in Minikube and then running the `docker-compose build` command. This will result in the Docker images being immediately available to Kubernetes. For development, we will be using `latest` as the Docker image version for the microservices.

You can build Docker images from source as follows:

```
cd $BOOK_HOME/Chapter16
eval $(minikube docker-env)
./gradlew build && docker-compose build
```

The `eval $(minikube docker-env)` command directs the local Docker client to communicate with the Docker engine in Minikube.

The `docker-compose.yml` file has been updated to specify a name for the Docker images it builds. For example, for the `product` service, we have the following:

```
product:
  build: microservices/product-service
  image: hands-on/product-service
```

`latest` is the default tag for a Docker image name, so it is not specified.

With the Docker images built, it's time to build the Helm charts.

Resolving Helm chart dependencies

First, we update the dependencies in the `components` folder:

```
for f in kubernetes/helm/components/*; do helm dep up $f; done
```

Next, we update the dependencies in the `environments` folder:

```
for f in kubernetes/helm/environments/*; do helm dep up $f; done
```

Finally, we verify that the dependencies for the `dev-env` folder look good:

```
helm dep ls kubernetes/helm/environments/dev-env/
```

Expect the command to respond with:

```
NAME                 VERSION REPOSITORY                                    STATUS
common               1.0.0 file://../../common                             ok
rabbitmq             1.0.0 file://../../components/rabbitmq                ok
mongodb              1.0.0 file://../../components/mongodb                 ok
mysql                1.0.0 file://../../components/mysql                   ok
config-server        1.0.0 file://../../components/config-server           ok
gateway              1.0.0 file://../../components/gateway                 ok
auth-server          1.0.0 file://../../components/auth-server             ok
product              1.0.0 file://../../components/product                 ok
recommendation       1.0.0 file://../../components/recommendation          ok
review               1.0.0 file://../../components/review                  ok
product-composite 1.0.0 file://../../components/product-composite ok
zipkin-server        1.0.0 file://../../components/zipkin-server           ok
$
```

Figure 16.3: Helm chart dependencies resolved

With both Docker images built and Helm dependencies resolved, we can start deploying to Kubernetes!

Deploying to Kubernetes

A deploy to Kubernetes means creating or updating Kubernetes objects. We will use Helm to perform the deployment, per the following steps:

1. To avoid a slow deployment process due to Kubernetes downloading Docker images (potentially causing the liveness probes we described previously to restart our Pods), run the following `docker pull` commands to download the images in advance:

```
eval $(minikube docker-env)
docker pull mysql:5.7.32
docker pull mongo:4.4.2
docker pull rabbitmq:3.8.11-management
docker pull openzipkin/zipkin:2.23.2
```

2. Before using the Helm charts, render the templates using the `helm template` command to see what the manifests will look like:

```
helm template kubernetes/helm/environments/dev-env
```

Note that no interaction was performed with the Kubernetes cluster, so cluster information will be faked, and no tests are run to verify whether the rendered manifest will be accepted by the cluster.

3. To also verify that the Kubernetes cluster will actually accept the rendered manifest, a **dry run** of the installation can be performed by passing `--dry-run` to the `helm install` command. Passing the `--debug` flag will also show which user-supplied and calculated values Helm will use when rendering the manifests. Run the following command to perform a dry run:

```
helm install --dry-run --debug hands-on-dev-env \
 kubernetes/helm/environments/dev-env
```

4. To initiate the deployment of the complete system landscape including creating the Namespace, `hands-on`, run the following command:

```
helm install hands-on-dev-env \
  kubernetes/helm/environments/dev-env \
  -n hands-on \
  --create-namespace
```

Note that here is where the Helm machinery kicks in. It will use the charts we walked through in the *Introducing Helm* section above to render and apply the Kubernetes manifests, resulting in the required Kubernetes objects for the deployment being created.

5. Set the newly created Namespace as the default Namespace for `kubectl`:

```
kubectl config set-context $(kubectl config current-context)
--namespace=hands-on
```

6. To see the Pods starting up, run the command:

```
kubectl get pods --watch
```

This command will continuously report when new Pods are **Running**, and if something goes wrong it will report the status, for example **Error** and **CrashLoopBackOff**. After a while, you will probably see that errors are reported for the **gateway**, **product-composite**, and **zipkin-server** Pods. The reason for this is that they all depend on external resources that they require to be accessible during the startup. If not, they will crash. The gateway and product composite service depend on the auth server, and the Zipkin server depends on access to RabbitMQ. Typically, they start up faster than the resources they rely on, causing this situation. However, Kubernetes will detect the crashed Pods and they will be restarted. Once the resources are up and running, all Pods will start up and be reported as ready, showing **1/1** in the **READY** column. A typical output from the command looks like:

```
product-composite-58744db6d4-2scsf   0/1   Error              0   69s
product-composite-58744db6d4-2scsf   0/1   Running            1   70s
gateway-768df96dcb-56qdq             0/1   Error              1   87s
gateway-768df96dcb-56qdq             0/1   CrashLoopBackOff   1   89s
auth-server-75bdb6949c-9mjkr         1/1   Running            0   99s
gateway-768df96dcb-56qdq             1/1   Running            2   113s
product-composite-58744db6d4-2scsf   1/1   Running            2   2m13s
```

Figure 16.4: Pods restarted until external dependencies are ready

After seeing some output like the above, interrupt the command with *Ctrl*+*C*.

7. Wait for all the Pods in the Namespace to be ready with the command:

```
kubectl wait --timeout=600s --for=condition=ready pod --all
```

Expect the command to respond with eleven log lines like `pod/... condition met`, where the three dots (`...`) are replaced with the name of the actual Pod that is reported to be ready.

8. To see the Docker images that are used, run the following command:

```
kubectl get pods -o json | jq .items[].spec.containers[].image
```

The response should look like the following:

```
"hands-on/config-server:latest"
"hands-on/gateway:latest"
"hands-on/auth-server:latest"
"registry.hub.docker.com/library/mongo:4.4.2"
"registry.hub.docker.com/library/mysql:5.7.32"
"hands-on/product-service:latest"
"hands-on/product-composite-service:latest"
"registry.hub.docker.com/library/rabbitmq:3.8.11-management"
"hands-on/recommendation-service:latest"
"hands-on/review-service:latest"
"registry.hub.docker.com/openzipkin/zipkin:2.23.2"
$
```

Figure 16.5: Docker images used in a test environment

Note that the Docker images have the version tag set to **latest** for the microservices.

We are now ready to test our deployment! But before we can do that, we need to go through changes that are required in the test script for use with Kubernetes.

Changes in the test script for use with Kubernetes

To verify the deployment, we will, as usual, run the test script, `test-em-all.bash`. To work with Kubernetes, the circuit breaker tests have been slightly modified. The circuit breaker tests call the `actuator` endpoints on the `product-composite` service to check their health state and get access to circuit breaker events. Since this endpoint isn't exposed externally, the previous chapters used the `docker-compose exec` command to run a `curl` command inside of the `product-composite` service to perform the tests.

Starting with this chapter, the test script can either use the `docker-compose exec` command or the corresponding `kubectl` command, `kubectl exec`, depending on if we are running the microservices using Docker Compose or Kubernetes.

To know which command to use, a new parameter has been added to the script, `USE_K8S`. It defaults to `false`. For details, see the `testCircuitBreaker()` function in the test script.

Testing the deployment

When launching the test script, we have to give it the address of the host that runs Kubernetes, that is, our Minikube instance, and the Node port where our gateway service listens for external requests. The gateway is accessible using port `30443`. On a Mac, the `minikube ip` command can be used to find the IP address of the Minikube instance. On Windows running WSL 2, where we run the Minikube instances as a Docker container, the host is always `localhost`.

Start by setting up an environment variable for the hostname to use.

On macOS:

```
MINIKUBE_HOST=$(minikube ip)
```

On WSL2:

```
MINIKUBE_HOST=localhost
```

Then, start the tests with the following command:

```
HOST=$MINIKUBE_HOST PORT=30443 USE_K8S=true ./test-em-all.bash
```

In the output from the script, we see how the IP address of the Minikube instance is used, but besides that everything looks the same as when we used Docker Compose in the previous chapters:

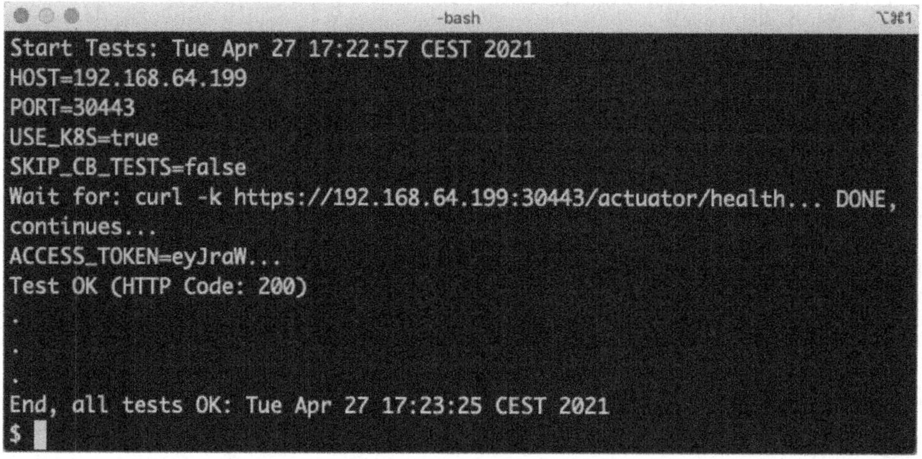

```
Start Tests: Tue Apr 27 17:22:57 CEST 2021
HOST=192.168.64.199
PORT=30443
USE_K8S=true
SKIP_CB_TESTS=false
Wait for: curl -k https://192.168.64.199:30443/actuator/health... DONE,
continues...
ACCESS_TOKEN=eyJraW...
Test OK (HTTP Code: 200)
.
.
.
End, all tests OK: Tue Apr 27 17:23:25 CEST 2021
$
```

Figure 16.6: Output from the automated tests of the system landscape

With the system landscape validations performed, let's see how we can test the new features in Spring Boot, graceful shutdown, and the probes for liveness and readiness.

Testing Spring Boot's support for graceful shutdown and probes for liveness and readiness

In this section, we will test out the new Spring Boot features and see how they interact with other components in Kubernetes.

Let's start with testing Spring Boot's support for graceful shutdown where the application during its shutdown phase will wait a configurable length of time for active requests to complete. Remember that no new requests are allowed during the shutdown phase.

To test the graceful shutdown mechanism, we will run a client that continuously sends requests to the composite service. First, we will use it to send requests that take 5 seconds, a shorter amount of time than the shutdown wait period. The wait period is configured to be 10 seconds. Next, we will use it to send requests that take a longer time, 15 seconds, to see how they are handled. As the test client, we will use **Siege**, a command line-based load test tool.

To be able to test run requests that take this long to complete, we need to temporarily increase the timeout in the `product-composite` service. Otherwise, its circuit breaker will kick in and prevent us from running the long requests. To increase the timeout in the composite service, perform the following steps:

1. Add the following under the `product-composite` section in the values file for the `dev-env`, `kubernetes/helm/environments/dev-env/values.yaml`:

```
    env:
      RESILIENCE4J_TIMELIMITER_INSTANCES_PRODUCT_TIMEOUTDURATION:
  20s
```

   After the change, the configuration file should look like:

```
  product-composite:
    env:
      RESILIENCE4J_TIMELIMITER_INSTANCES_PRODUCT_TIMEOUTDURATION:
  20s
    envFromSecretRefs:
      - config-client-credentials
```

As long as this setting is active, the circuit breaker tests in `test-em-all.bash` will no longer work since they assume a timeout of 2 seconds.

2. Update the Helm installation using Helm's `upgrade` command, using the `--wait` flag to ensure that the update is completed when the command terminates:

```
helm upgrade hands-on-dev-env -n hands-on \
  kubernetes/helm/environments/dev-env --wait
```

Now we can run the tests, proceeding with the following steps to test with requests that are shorter than the shutdown wait period:

1. Get an access token:

```
ACCESS_TOKEN=$(curl -d grant_type=client_credentials \
 -ks https://writer:secret@$MINIKUBE_HOST:30443/oauth2/token \
 | jq .access_token -r)
```

   Ensure you got an access token by issuing the command `echo $ACCESS_TOKEN`. If it's empty, you have to check the `curl` command above and the logs from the gateway and the auth server.

2. Make a test request and ask for a delay of 5 seconds using the `delay` query parameter:

```
time curl -kH "Authorization: Bearer $ACCESS_TOKEN" \
  https://$MINIKUBE_HOST:30443/product-composite/1?delay=5
```

   If you get a normal response and the `time` command reports a 5 second response time, the config changes of the increased timeout worked!

3. Use Siege to start requests that take 5 seconds to complete, with five concurrent users sending requests with a random delay between 0 and 2 seconds to spread the requests a bit:

```
siege -c5 -d2 -v -H "Authorization: Bearer $ACCESS_TOKEN" \
  https://$MINIKUBE_HOST:30443/product-composite/1?delay=5
```

   Expect output from the tool for each completed request like:

```
HTTP/1.1 200 5.04 secs: 771 bytes ==> GET /product-
composite/1?delay=5
```

4. Watch log output from the `product` service in a separate terminal window with the command:

```
kubectl logs -f --tail=0 -l app.kubernetes.io/name=product
```

5. We will now ask Kubernetes to restart the `product` deployment. The restart will first start a new Pod before the old one is shut down, meaning that none of the requests sent by Siege should be affected by the restart. Of specific interest are the few requests that are processed by the old Pod when it starts to shut down. If the graceful shutdown works as expected, none of the active requests should fail. Perform the restart by running the following command in a separate window:

```
kubectl rollout restart deploy/product
```

6. Ensure that there are only successful requests reported in the output from the load test tool, Siege, reporting **200** (OK).

7. In the log output from the now stopped `product` Pod, you should see that all requests were allowed to terminate gracefully before the application was stopped. Expect log output like the following, at the end of the log output:

```
2021-04-26 13:10:07.831  INFO [product,,] 1 ---
[extShutdownHook] o.s.b.w.embedded.netty.GracefulShutdown   :
Commencing graceful shutdown. Waiting for active requests to complete
.
.
.
2021-04-26 13:10:11.694  INFO [product,,] 1 ---
[ netty-shutdown] o.s.b.w.embedded.netty.GracefulShutdown   :
Graceful shutdown complete
```

Figure 16.7: Graceful shutdown where all requests are allowed to complete

Specifically, note the time between the two log messages (4 seconds in this case), indicating that the shutdown procedure actually waited for the last request to complete.

Now let's run the second test, with requests taking a longer time to complete than the shutdown wait period:

1. Restart Siege, requesting longer response times, above the wait limit of 10 seconds. Start five concurrent users asking for a 15 second response time and random delay between the requests of 0-5 seconds. Stop Siege with *Ctrl+C* and run the following command:

```
siege -c5 -d5 -v -H "Authorization: Bearer $ACCESS_TOKEN" \
  https://$MINIKUBE_HOST:30443/product-composite/1?delay=15
```

2. Watch the log output from the `product` Pod with the command:

```
kubectl logs -f --tail=0 -l app.kubernetes.io/name=product
```

3. Restart the `product` deployment:

```
kubectl rollout restart deploy/product
```

4. Follow the log output from the `product` Pod. Once it has shut down, you should be able to see that not all requests were allowed to terminate gracefully before the application was stopped. Expect log output like the following, at the end of the log output:

```
2021-04-26 13:48:59.664  INFO [product,,] 1 ---
[extShutdownHook] o.s.b.w.embedded.netty.GracefulShutdown   :
Commencing graceful shutdown. Waiting for active requests to complete
.
.
.
2021-04-26 13:49:09.672  INFO [product,,] 1 ---
[extShutdownHook] o.s.c.support.DefaultLifecycleProcessor   :
Failed to shut down 1 bean with phase value 2147483647 within timeout
of 10000ms: [webServerGracefulShutdown]
2021-04-26 13:49:09.684  INFO [product,,] 1 ---
[ netty-shutdown] o.s.b.w.embedded.netty.GracefulShutdown   :
Graceful shutdown aborted with one or more requests still active
```

Figure 16.8: Graceful shutdown where some long-running requests are aborted

The log message **Graceful shutdown aborted with one or more requests still active** indicates that at least one request was not allowed to complete before the application was stopped.

5. In the output from the load test tool, Siege, there should now appear one or a few failing requests reporting **500** (Internal Server Error) like:

```
HTTP/1.1 500     12.71 secs:     322 bytes ==> GET  /product-composite/1?delay=15
HTTP/1.1 500     10.72 secs:     322 bytes ==> GET  /product-composite/1?delay=15
```

Figure 16.9: Long-running requests fail during shutdown

This demonstrates how the shutdown procedure proceeds after the configured wait time and that the remaining long-running requests are aborted, as expected.

This completes the tests of Spring Boot's graceful shutdown mechanism, clearly useful to avoid normal client requests being affected by Pods being stopped, for example as a result of scaling down or a rolling upgrade being performed.

Clean up after the tests:

1. Stop the Siege load test tool with *Ctrl+C*
2. Roll back the latest Helm release to get rid of the increased timeout:

```
helm rollback hands-on-dev-env -n hands-on -wait
```

The `helm rollback` command is also useful for rolling back a failed upgrade.

3. Also remove the increased timeout setting in the file `kubernetes/helm/environments/dev-env/values.yaml`
4. Run `test-em-all.bash` to verify that the configuration is rolled back:

```
HOST=$MINIKUBE_HOST PORT=30443 USE_K8S=true ./test-em-all.bash
```

Finally, let's see what information the Spring Boot liveness and readiness probes report. We will use the `product` service, but feel free to also try out the probes for the other services:

1. Run the following command to get the output from the `product` service's liveness probe:

```
kubectl exec -it deploy/product -- \
  curl localhost/actuator/health/liveness -s | jq .
```

Expect it to respond with:

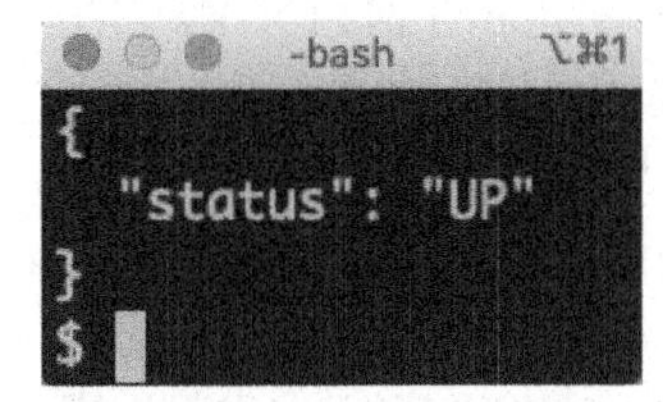

Figure 16.10: Response from a liveness probe

2. Run the following command to get the output from the `product` service's readiness probe:

```
kubectl exec -it deploy/product -- \
  curl localhost/actuator/health/readiness -s | jq .
```

Expect its response to be a bit more extensive:

```
{
  "status": "UP",
  "components": {
    "mongo": {
      "status": "UP",
      "details": {
        "version": "4.4.2"
      }
    },
    "rabbit": {
      "status": "UP",
      "details": {
        "version": "3.8.11"
      }
    }
  }
}
$
```

Figure 16.11: Response from a readiness probe

From the output above, we can confirm that the readiness of the `product` now depends on its access to both MongoDB and RabbitMQ. This is expected, since we configured the readiness health group to include health indicators for RabbitMQ, MongoDB, and SQL databases, if available. See the section *Using Spring Boot's support for graceful shutdown and probes for liveness and readiness* to recap, if required.

Before we move on, let's clean up what we have installed in the development environment. We can do this by simply deleting the Namespace. Deleting the Namespace will recursively delete the resources that exist in the Namespace, including information regarding the Helm installation.

Delete the Namespace with the following command:

```
kubectl delete namespace hands-on
```

If you just want to uninstall what the `helm install` command installed, you can run the command `helm uninstall hands-on-dev-env`.

With the development environment removed, we can move on and set up an environment targeting staging and production.

Deploying to Kubernetes for staging and production

In this section, we will deploy the microservices in an environment for staging and production usage. A staging environment is used for performing **quality assurance** (QA) and **user acceptance tests** (**UATs**) as the last step before taking a new release into production. To be able to verify that the new release not only meets functional requirements but also non-functional requirements, for example, in terms of performance, robustness, scalability, and resilience, a staging environment is configured to be as similar as possible to the production environment.

When deploying to an environment for staging or production, there are a number of changes required compared to when deploying for development or tests:

- **Resource managers should run outside of the Kubernetes cluster**: It is technically feasible to run databases and queue managers for production use on Kubernetes as stateful containers using `StatefulSets` and `PersistentVolumes`. At the time of writing this chapter, I recommend against it, mainly because the support for stateful containers is relatively new and unproven in Kubernetes. Instead, I recommend using the existing database and queue manager services on-premises or as managed services in the cloud, leaving Kubernetes to do what it is best for: running stateless containers. For the scope of this book, to simulate a production environment, we will run MySQL, MongoDB, and RabbitMQ as plain Docker containers outside of Kubernetes using the already existing Docker Compose files.
- **Lockdown**:
    - For security reasons, things like `actuator` endpoints and log levels need to be constrained in a production environment.
    - Externally exposed endpoints should also be reviewed from a security perspective. For example, access to the configuration server should most probably be locked down in a production environment, but we will keep it exposed in this book for convenience.

    - Docker image tags must be specified to be able to track which versions of the microservices have been deployed.

- **Scale up available resources**: To meet the requirements of both high availability and higher load, we need to run at least two Pods per deployment. We might also need to increase the amount of memory and CPU that are allowed to be used per Pod. To avoid running out of memory in the Minikube instance, we will keep one Pod per Deployment but increase the maximum memory allowed in the production environment.
- **Set up a production-ready Kubernetes cluster**: This is outside the scope of this book, but, if feasible, I recommend using one of the managed Kubernetes services provided by the leading cloud providers. For the scope of this book, we will deploy to our local Minikube instance.

This is not meant to be an exhaustive list of things that have to be considered when setting up an environment for production, but it's a good start.

Our simulated production environment will look as follows:

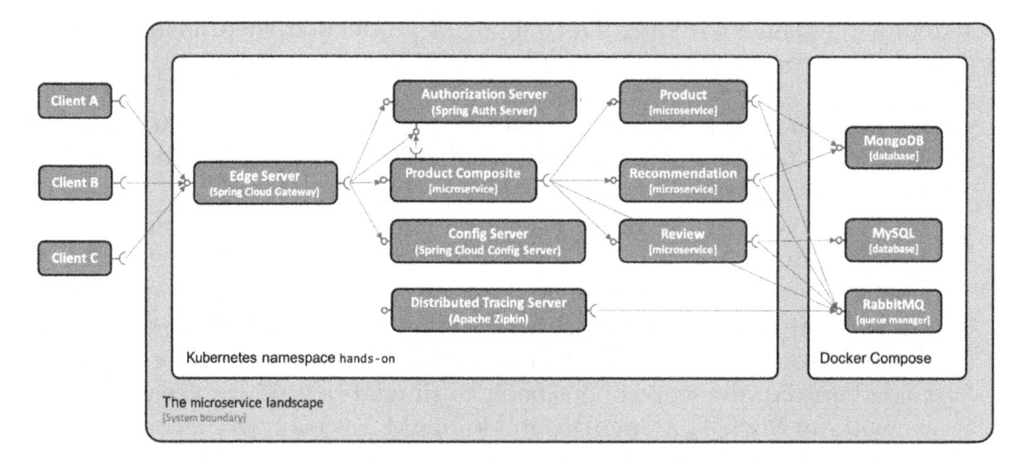

Figure 16.12: Resource managers deployed outside of Kubernetes

Changes in the source code

The following changes have been applied to the source code to prepare for deployment in an environment that's used for staging and production:

- A Spring profile named `prod` has been added to the configuration files in the `config-repo` configuration repository:

  ```
  spring.config.activate.on-profile: prod
  ```

- In the `prod` profiles, the following have been added:
  - URLs to the resource managers that run as plain Docker containers:

    ```
    spring.rabbitmq.host: 172.17.0.1
    spring.data.mongodb.host: 172.17.0.1
    spring.datasource.url: jdbc:mysql://172.17.0.1:3306/review-db
    ```

> We are using the `172.17.0.1` IP address to address the Docker engine in the Minikube instance. This is the default IP address for the Docker engine when creating it with Minikube, at least for Minikube up to version 1.18.
>
> There is work ongoing for establishing a standard DNS name for containers to use if they need to access the Docker host they are running on, but at the time of writing this chapter, this work effort hasn't been completed.

  - Log levels have been set to warning or higher, that is, error or fatal. For example:

    ```
    logging.level.root: WARN
    ```

  - The only `actuator` endpoints that are exposed over HTTP are the `info` and `health` endpoints that are used by the liveness and readiness probes in Kubernetes, as well as the `circuitbreakerevents` endpoint that's used by the test script, `test-em-all.bash`:

    ```
    management.endpoints.web.exposure.include: health,info,
    circuitbreakerevents
    ```

In a real-world production environment, we should also have changed the `imagePullPolicy: Never` setting to `IfNotPresent`, to download Docker images from a Docker registry. But since we will be deploying the production setup to the Minikube instance where we manually build and tag the Docker images, we will not update this setting.

Deploying to Kubernetes

To simulate the use of production-grade resource managers, MySQL, MongoDB, and RabbitMQ will run outside of Kubernetes using Docker Compose. We start them up as we did in the previous chapters:

```
eval $(minikube docker-env)
docker-compose up -d mongodb mysql rabbitmq
```

We also need to tag the existing Docker images with `v1` using the following commands:

```
docker tag hands-on/auth-server hands-on/auth-server:v1
docker tag hands-on/config-server hands-on/config-server:v1
docker tag hands-on/gateway hands-on/gateway:v1
docker tag hands-on/product-composite-service hands-on/product-composite-service:v1
docker tag hands-on/product-service hands-on/product-service:v1
docker tag hands-on/recommendation-service hands-on/recommendation-service:v1
docker tag hands-on/review-service hands-on/review-service:v1
```

From here, the commands are very similar to how we deployed to the development environment.

1. Deploy using Helm:

   ```
   helm install hands-on-prod-env \ kubernetes/helm/environments/prod-env \
   -n hands-on --create-namespace
   ```

2. Wait for the deployments to be up and running:

   ```
   kubectl wait --timeout=600s --for=condition=ready pod --all
   ```

3. To see the Docker images that are currently being used in the production environment, run the following command:

```
kubectl get pods -o json | jq .items[].spec.containers[].image
```

The response should look something like the following:

```
"hands-on/auth-server:v1"
"hands-on/config-server:v1"
"hands-on/gateway:v1"
"hands-on/product-service:v1"
"hands-on/product-composite-service:v1"
"hands-on/recommendation-service:v1"
"hands-on/review-service:v1"
"registry.hub.docker.com/openzipkin/zipkin:2.23.2"
$
```

Figure 16.13: Docker images used in a prod environment

Note the `v1` version of the Docker images!

Also note that the resource manager Pods for MySQL, MongoDB, and RabbitMQ are gone; these can be found with the `docker-compose ps` command.

4. Run the test script, `test-em-all.bash`, to verify the simulated production environment:

```
CONFIG_SERVER_USR=prod-usr \
CONFIG_SERVER_PWD=prod-pwd \
HOST=$MINIKUBE_HOST PORT=30443 USE_K8S=true ./test-em-all.bash
```

Remember that the environment variable, `MINIKUBE_HOST`, must be set for the hostname to use according to the following:

- On macOS: `MINIKUBE_HOST=$(minikube ip)`
- On WSL2: `MINIKUBE_HOST=localhost`

Expect the same type of output that we got when the test script was run against the development environment.

That completes the tests; let's clean up so that the Kubernetes environment is ready for the next chapter.

Cleaning up

To delete the resources that we used, run the following commands:

1. Delete the Namespace:

```
kubectl delete namespace hands-on
```

2. Shut down the resource managers that run outside of Kubernetes:

```
eval $(minikube docker-env)
docker-compose down
```

As already described earlier in this chapter, the `kubectl delete namespace` command will recursively delete all Kubernetes resources that existed in the Namespace, and the `docker-compose down` command will stop MySQL, MongoDB, and RabbitMQ. With the production environment removed, we have reached the end of this chapter.

Summary

In this chapter, we learned how to deploy the microservices in this book on Kubernetes using Helm. We have seen how Helm can be used to create reusable templates minimizing the boilerplate code required to create the Kubernetes manifests. Reusable templates are stored in a common chart, while microservice-specific charts provide values specific to each microservice. At the top level, we have parent charts that describe how a dev/test and stage/production environment should be deployed using the microservice charts, optionally together with charts for resource managers such as databases and queue managers.

We have also seen how we can benefit from using Spring Boot features to facilitate deployments to Kubernetes. Spring Boot's support for graceful shutdown can be used to allow active requests to complete before a Spring Boot-based microservice is stopped, for example during a rolling upgrade. The support for liveness and readiness probes makes it easy to declare probes that are aware of the availability of external resources that a specific microservice depends on.

Finally, to be able to deploy our microservices in Kubernetes, we had to replace Netflix Eureka with the built-in discovery service in Kubernetes. Changing the discovery service was done without any changes in the Java source code – all we had to do was apply changes to the build dependencies and some of the configuration.

In the next chapter, we will see how we can further utilize Kubernetes to reduce the number of supporting services we need to deploy in Kubernetes. Head over to the next chapter to see how we can eliminate the need for the configuration server and how our edge server can be replaced by a Kubernetes Ingress controller.

Questions

1. Why did we remove the Eureka server from the microservice landscape when deploying it on Kubernetes?
2. What did we replace the Eureka server with and how was the source code of the microservices affected by this change?
3. What's the purpose of liveness and readiness probes?
4. How is Spring Boot's mechanism for graceful shutdown useful?
5. What is the purpose of the following Helm template directives?

```
{{- $common := dict "Values" .Values.common -}}
{{- $noCommon := omit .Values "common" -}}
{{- $overrides := dict "Values" $noCommon -}}
{{- $noValues := omit . "Values" -}}
{{- with merge $noValues $overrides $common -}}
```

6. Why would the following named Helm template fail?

```
{{- define "common.secrets" -}}
{{- range $secretName, $secretMap := .Values.secrets }}
apiVersion: v1
kind: Secret
metadata:
  name: {{ $secretName }}
  labels:
    app.kubernetes.io/name: {{ $secretName }}
type: Opaque
data:
{{- range $key, $val := $secretMap }}
  {{ $key }}: {{ $val | b64enc }}
{{- end }}
{{- end -}}
{{- end -}}
```

7. Why would the following manifests not work together?

```
apiVersion: v1
kind: Service
metadata:
  name: review
  labels:
    app.kubernetes.io/name: review
spec:
```

```
  type: ClusterIP
  ports:
    - name: http
      port: 80
      protocol: TCP
      targetPort: http
  selector:
    app.kubernetes.io/pod-name: review
---
apiVersion: apps/v1
kind: Deployment
metadata:
  name: review
  labels:
    app.kubernetes.io/name: review
spec:
  replicas: 1
  selector:
    matchLabels:
      app.kubernetes.io/name: review
  template:
    metadata:
      labels:
        app.kubernetes.io/name: review
    spec:
      containers:
        - name: review
          image: "hands-on/review-service:latest"
          ports:
            - containerPort: 80
              name: http-port
              protocol: TCP
```

8. What is going on here?

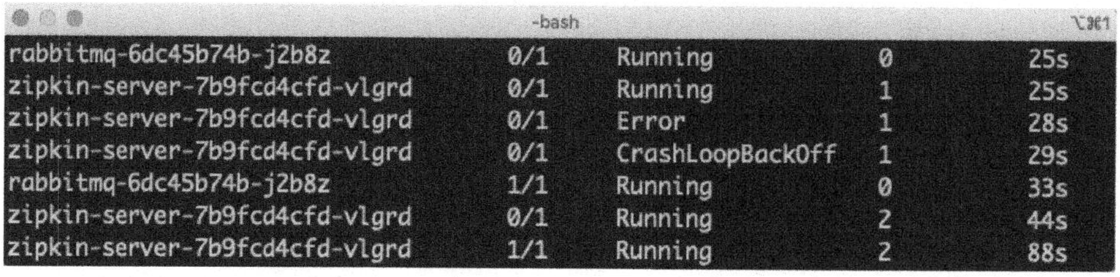

```
-bash
rabbitmq-6dc45b74b-j2b8z             0/1   Running            0   25s
zipkin-server-7b9fcd4cfd-vlgrd       0/1   Running            1   25s
zipkin-server-7b9fcd4cfd-vlgrd       0/1   Error              1   28s
zipkin-server-7b9fcd4cfd-vlgrd       0/1   CrashLoopBackOff   1   29s
rabbitmq-6dc45b74b-j2b8z             1/1   Running            0   33s
zipkin-server-7b9fcd4cfd-vlgrd       0/1   Running            2   44s
zipkin-server-7b9fcd4cfd-vlgrd       1/1   Running            2   88s
```

Figure 16.14: What is going on here?

17

Implementing Kubernetes Features to Simplify the System Landscape

The current microservice landscape contains several supporting services that implement important design patterns required in a large-scale microservice landscape, for example, an edge server, config server, authorization server, and a service for distributed tracing. For a recap, refer to *Chapter 1, Introduction to Microservices*. In the previous chapter, we replaced the implementation of the design pattern for service discovery, based on Netflix Eureka, with the built-in discovery service in Kubernetes. In this chapter, we will further simplify the microservice landscape by reducing the number of supporting services required to be deployed. Instead, the corresponding design patterns will be handled by built-in capabilities in Kubernetes. The Spring Cloud Config Server will be replaced with Kubernetes ConfigMaps and Secrets. The Spring Cloud Gateway will be replaced by a Kubernetes Ingress object, which can act as an edge server in the same way as the Spring Cloud Gateway.

In *Chapter 11*, *Securing Access to APIs*, we introduced the use of certificates to protect the external API. The certificates were provisioned manually, which is both time-consuming and error-prone, specifically when it comes to remembering to rotate the certificates before they expire. In this chapter, we will learn about the **cert-manager** and how it can be used to automate the process of creating, provisioning, and rotating certificates.

When more and more features in a platform such as Kubernetes are being used, it is important to ensure that the source code for the microservices doesn't become dependent on the platform. To ensure that we can still use the microservices without deploying them to Kubernetes, we will conclude the chapter by deploying the microservice landscape using Docker Compose and executing the `test-em-all.bash` test script to verify that the microservices still work from a functional perspective without using Kubernetes.

The following topics will be covered in this chapter:

- Replacing the Spring Cloud Config Server with Kubernetes ConfigMaps and Secrets
- Replacing the Spring Cloud Gateway with a Kubernetes Ingress object
- Using the cert-manager to automatically provision certificates
- Deploying and testing the microservice landscape on Kubernetes
- Deploying and testing the microservice landscape using Docker Compose to ensure that the source code in the microservices isn't locked into Kubernetes

Technical requirements

For instructions on how to install tools used in this book and how to access the source code for this book, see:

- *Chapter 21* for macOS
- *Chapter 22* for Windows

The code examples in this chapter all come from the source code in `$BOOK_HOME/Chapter17`.

If you want to view the changes applied to the source code in this chapter, that is, see what it took to replace the Spring Cloud Config Server and Spring Cloud Gateway with corresponding features in Kubernetes, and use the cert-manager to provision certificates, you can compare it with the source code for *Chapter 16, Deploying Our Microservices to Kubernetes*. You can use your favorite `diff` tool and compare the two folders `$BOOK_HOME/Chapter16` and `$BOOK_HOME/Chapter17`.

Replacing the Spring Cloud Config Server

As we have seen in the previous chapter, ConfigMaps and Secrets can be used to hold configuration information for our microservices. The Spring Cloud Config Server adds features such as keeping all configuration in one place, optional version control using Git, and the ability to encrypt sensitive information on the disk. But it also consumes a non-negligible amount of memory (as with any Java and Spring-based application) and adds significant overhead during startup.

For example, when running automated integration tests such as the test script we are using in this book, `test-em-all.bash`, all microservices are started up at the same time, including the configuration server. Since the other microservices must get their configuration from the configuration server, they all have to wait for the configuration server to be up and running before they can start up themselves. This leads to a significant delay when running integration tests. If we use Kubernetes ConfigMaps and Secrets instead, this delay is eliminated, making automated integration tests run faster. Therefore, it makes sense to use the Spring Cloud Config Server when the underlying platform doesn't provide a similar capability, but when deploying to Kubernetes, it is better to use ConfigMaps and Secrets.

Using Kubernetes ConfigMaps and Secrets instead of the Spring Cloud Config Server will make the microservice landscape start up faster and means it will require less memory. It will also simplify the microservice landscape by eliminating one supporting service, the configuration server. When we perform the replacement, it is important to do it in a way where the source code in the microservices isn't affected, thereby avoiding unnecessary lock-in to Kubernetes.

This change is illustrated by the following diagram:

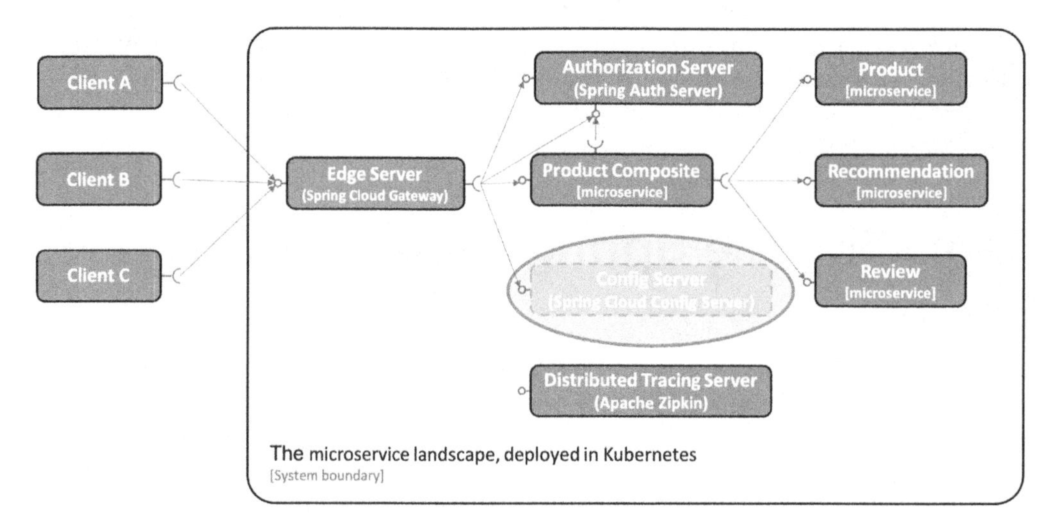

Figure 17.1: Replacing the Spring Cloud Config Server with Kubernetes built-in ConfigMaps and Secrets

Let's see what is required to replace the Spring Cloud Config Server with Kubernetes ConfigMaps and Secrets!

Note especially that we only change the configuration; no changes are required in the Java source code!

Changes required to replace the Spring Cloud Config Server

The following changes have been applied in the configuration of the source code to replace the Spring Cloud Config Server with Kubernetes ConfigMaps and Secrets:

1. We have removed the `spring-cloud/config-server` project and also removed the project in the `settings.gradle` build file.
2. We have removed the Helm chart for the configuration server.
3. We have removed config server-specific tests from the `test-em-all.bash` test script.

4. We have removed the following configuration from all microservices:
    - The `spring-cloud-starter-config` dependency in the `build.gradle` build files
    - The `application.yml` files in the `src/main/resource` folders in each project, which were used to connect to the config server
    - The `spring.cloud.config.enabled=false` property setting in integration tests, since it is no longer required
5. Changes to the configuration files in the `config-repo` folder:
    - We have removed properties with sensitive information, for example, credentials for MongoDB, MySQL, RabbitMQ, and the password for the TLS certificate used by the edge server. Kubernetes Secrets will be used to handle sensitive information.
    - The route to the configuration server API has been removed in the configuration of the edge server.
6. Changes to the microservices' Helm charts in `kubernetes/helm/components`:
    - A `config-repo` folder has been added to each chart. Soft links have been created in Helm chart's `config-repo` folder for the required configuration files from the common `config-repo` folder. For each microservice, a soft link has been created to the commons configuration file, `application.yaml`, and to the microservice-specific configuration file.

For a recap on how soft links are created, refer to the *The components charts* section in *Chapter 16, Deploying Our Microservices to Kubernetes.*

    - The `values.yaml` file has been updated with the following:
        - An environment variable for a Spring property used for pointing out what configuration files to use. For example, the property looks like the following for the `product` microservice:

```
SPRING_CONFIG_LOCATION: file:/config-repo/application.
yml,file:/config-repo/product.yml
```

- A ConfigMap that the microservices will use to find their configuration files. The ConfigMap will be made available inside the container on the `/config-repo` path. The declaration looks like this:

  ```
  configmap:
    enabled: true
    volumeMounts:
      mountPath: /config-repo
  ```

- To create the ConfigMap, a template has been added that is based on the named template, `common.configmap_from_file`, from the common chart.

7. Changes to the environments' Helm charts in `kubernetes/helm/environments`:
   - We have removed the dependency on the config server's chart.
   - The `values.yaml` file has been updated:
     - The Secrets for the config server and its clients have been replaced with Secrets for the resource managers, MongoDB, MySQL, and RabbitMQ, and their clients. For example:

       ```
       rabbitmq-zipkin-credentials:
         RABBIT_USER: rabbit-user-dev
         RABBIT_PASSWORD: rabbit-pwd-dev

       mongodb-credentials:
         SPRING_DATA_MONGODB_AUTHENTICATION_DATABASE: admin
         SPRING_DATA_MONGODB_USERNAME: mongodb-user-dev
         SPRING_DATA_MONGODB_PASSWORD: mongodb-pwd-dev
       ```

Recap from the previous chapter: Note that this `values.yaml` file contains sensitive information, like the passwords from the example above. This file must therefore be stored securely. An alternative, if it is inappropriate to store this file securely, is to remove the sensitive information from this file and supply the sensitive information when the `helm install` command is executed.

- Each component is assigned the Secrets it requires.

Recap from the previous chapter: the Secrets will be mapped into each Pod as environment variables.

For example, the `product` service needs access to both MongoDB and RabbitMQ and is therefore assigned the following two Secrets:

```
product:
  envFromSecretRefs:
    - rabbitmq-credentials
    - mongodb-credentials
```

Most of the changes in the Helm charts' `values.yaml` files end up in Kubernetes manifests for `Deployment` objects. For example, the `product` microservice's `Deployment` object will look like the following:

```
apiVersion: apps/v1
kind: Deployment
metadata:
  name: product
spec:
  template:
    spec:
      containers:
        - name: product
          env:
          - name: SPRING_CONFIG_LOCATION
            value: file:/config-repo/application.yml,file:/config-repo/
product.yml
          - name: SPRING_PROFILES_ACTIVE
            value: docker
          envFrom:
          - secretRef:
              name: rabbitmq-credentials
          - secretRef:
              name: mongodb-credentials
          volumeMounts:
          - name: product
            mountPath: /config-repo
      volumes:
        - name: product
          configMap:
            name: product
```

Note that parts of the manifest that have not been affected by the changes above have been omitted for improved readability.

If you want to render a component's Kubernetes manifest yourself, you can do that by applying Helm's `template` command on the chart of interest. You must also add values from the environment's `values.yaml` file that are applicable for the component to the `template` command. Take the `product` service as an example. The `dev-env` chart's `values.yaml` file contains the following settings that apply to the `product` service:

```
product:
  envFromSecretRefs:
    - rabbitmq-credentials
    - mongodb-credentials
```

To add these settings to the `template` command, we can use the `--set` flag.

There is also a `--values` flag that can be used to add a `values.yaml` file when the command is executed.

When adding values from an environment chart, we must remember that they are parent charts to the component charts. This means that the name of the component chart must be removed from the settings when applied directly to the component chart. In this case, it means that we should add the following values to the `template` command to render the product chart correctly:

```
  envFromSecretRefs:
    - rabbitmq-credentials
    - mongodb-credentials
```

YAML arrays like the one above can be defined using the `--set` flag by listing the elements within curly braces, for example, `"{a,b,c}"`. The `product` chart can be rendered using the following command:

```
helm template kubernetes/helm/components/product \
  --set envFromSecretRefs= \
    "{rabbitmq-credentials, mongodb-credentials}"
```

The result will contain manifests for the `product` microservice, a ConfigMap, a Service, and finally, a Deployment object.

This is what is required to replace the configuration server with Kubernetes ConfigMaps and Secrets. In the next section, we will learn about how we can replace the Spring Cloud Gateway with a Kubernetes Ingress object.

Replacing the Spring Cloud Gateway

In this section, we will further simplify the microservice landscape by replacing the Spring Cloud Gateway using the built-in Ingress object in Kubernetes, reducing the number of supporting services required to be deployed.

As introduced in *Chapter 15, Introduction to Kubernetes*, an Ingress object can be used in Kubernetes to act as an edge server in the same way as a Spring Cloud Gateway. The Spring Cloud Gateway comes with a richer routing functionality compared to an Ingress object. However, the Ingress is part of the Kubernetes platform, requiring no extra deployments, and can also be extended using the cert-manager to automatically provision certificates, as we will see later in this chapter.

We have also used the Spring Cloud Gateway to protect our microservices from unauthenticated requests, by requiring a valid OAuth 2.0/OIDC access token from a trusted OAuth Authorization Server or OIDC Provider. See *Chapter 11, Securing Access to APIs*, if a recap is required. Generally, Kubernetes Ingress objects do not have support for this. Specific implementations of the Ingress controller might, however, support it.

Finally, the composite health check we added to the gateway in *Chapter 10, Using Spring Cloud Gateway to Hide Microservices behind an Edge Server*, can be replaced by the Kubernetes liveness and readiness probes defined in each microservice's deployment manifest.

Therefore, in the same way as for the Spring Cloud Config server, it makes sense to use the Spring Cloud Gateway where the underlying platform doesn't provide a similar capability. When deploying to Kubernetes, it is better to use Ingress objects.

In this chapter, we will delegate the responsibility for validating that the request contains a valid access token to the `product-composite` microservice. The next chapter will introduce the concept of a service mesh, where we will see an alternative implementation of an Ingress that fully supports validating JWT-encoded access tokens.

In the *Verifying that the microservices work without Kubernetes* section, we will still use the Spring Cloud Gateway together with Docker Compose, so we will not remove the project.

The following diagram shows that the Spring Cloud Gateway is removed from the microservice landscape when deploying to Kubernetes:

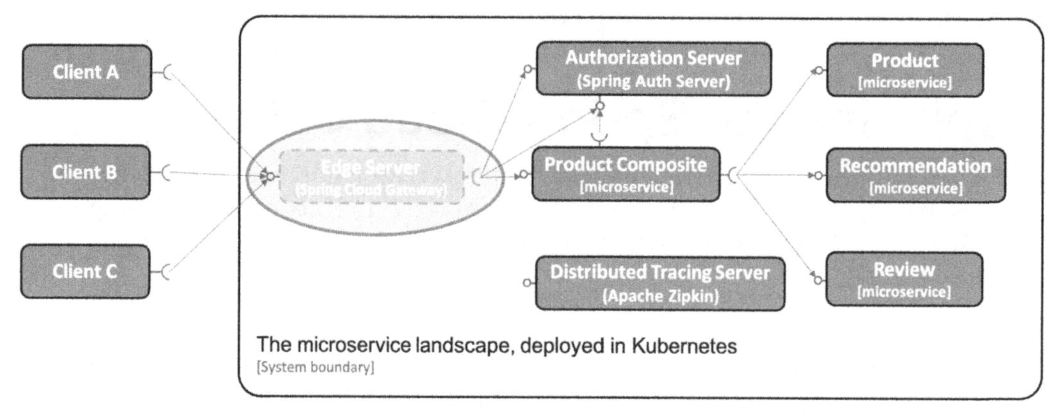

Figure 17.2: Replacing the Spring Cloud Gateway with the Kubernetes built-in Ingress controller

Let's see what is required to replace the Spring Cloud Gateway with a Kubernetes Ingress object!

Note especially that we only change the configuration; that is, no changes are required in the Java source code!

Changes required to replace the Spring Cloud Gateway

The following changes have been applied to the configuration of the source code to replace the Spring Cloud Gateway with a Kubernetes Ingress object:

1. We have removed the Helm chart for the Spring Cloud Gateway.
2. We have added a named template for Ingress manifests and some default values for the Ingress in the `common` chart.

   The named template, `kubernetes/helm/common/templates/_ingress.yaml`, begins with a declaration that we recognize from the previous chapter:

   ```
   {{- define "common.ingress" -}}
   {{- $common := dict "Values" .Values.common -}}
   {{- $noCommon := omit .Values "common" -}}
   {{- $overrides := dict "Values" $noCommon -}}
   {{- $noValues := omit . "Values" -}}
   {{- with merge $noValues $overrides $common -}}
   ```

```
apiVersion: networking.k8s.io/v1
kind: Ingress
metadata:
  name: {{ include "common.fullname" . }}
  labels:
    app.kubernetes.io/name: {{ include "common.name" . }}
    helm.sh/chart: {{ include "common.chart" . }}
    app.kubernetes.io/managed-by: {{ .Release.Service }}
{{- with .Values.ingress.annotations }}
  annotations:
{{ toYaml . | indent 4 }}
{{- end }}
```

The name of the template is `common.ingress`, and the `apiVersion` and `kind` are set to `networking.k8s.io/v1` and `Ingress` to identify it as an Ingress manifest. Most of the remainder of the template above looks the same as seen in other manifests where overriding parameters is required, such as the Deployment or Service template. The only new part is that the template allows the addition of annotations, if required, using the `ingress.annotations` field in the `values.yaml` file.

The rest of the Ingress template contains the main part of the manifest, the `spec` part. It looks like this:

```
spec:
  tls:
    - hosts:
        - {{ .Values.ingress.host | quote }}
      secretName: {{ .Values.ingress.tls.secretName }}
  rules:
    - host: {{ .Values.ingress.host | quote }}
      http:
        paths:
        {{- range .Values.ingress.paths }}
          - path: {{ .path }}
            pathType: Prefix
            backend:
              service:
                name: {{ .service }}
                port:
                  name: http

        {{- end }}
{{- end }}
{{- end -}}
```

First comes a `tls` section where the manifest declares that the Ingress only accepts HTTPS traffic and that the accepted `hostname` will be specified with the key `ingress.host` in the `values.yaml` files. The certificate used for serving HTTPS requests will be stored in a Secret named as specified in the `values.yaml` files using the `ingress.tls.secretName` key.

Next are the routing rules declared in the `rules` section. First is the hostname used for routing. This will be the same hostname as in the `tls` section above. Next comes a list of routes. They will be filled in using the `ingress.paths` section in the `values.yaml` file. Each entry contains a `path` and a name of the `service` that requests to that path will be routed to. Each service is expected to have the name of its port set to `http`.

The common chart's `values.yaml` file provides the following default values for the Ingress manifest:

```
ingress:
  annotations:
    cert-manager.io/issuer: selfsigned
  tls:
    secretName: tls-certificate
```

First is an annotation, `cert-manager.io/issuer`, declared for the Ingress object, indicating that the cert-manager should manage the required certificate for this Ingress object using an issuer named `selfsigned`. More about this below, in the *Automating certificate provisioning* section. Next is the Secret that will hold the certificate, given the default name `tls-certificate`.

3. We have added templates and additional settings in the environment charts, `dev-env` and `prod-env`, for Ingress manifests. The templates are named `ingress.yml` and are based on the named template from the `common` chart described above:

   ```
   {{- template "common.ingress" . -}}
   ```

4. The remaining values required to render an Ingress manifest, a `hostname` and the actual `paths` used for routing, are specified in each environment chart's `values.yaml` files. The declaration looks like this:

   ```
   ingress:
     host: minikube.me
     paths:
       - path: /oauth2
         service: auth-server
       - path: /login
         service: auth-server
       - path: /error
   ```

```
      service: auth-server
    - path: /product-composite
      service: product-composite
    - path: /actuator/health
      service: product-composite
    - path: /openapi
      service: product-composite
    - path: /webjars
      service: product-composite
```

From the configuration, we can see that we will use the hostname `minikube.me` and that three routes are defined for the `auth-server`, while the rest of the declared paths will be routed to the `product-composite` service.

We will register the hostname `minikube.me` in the local `/etc/hosts` file later, in the *Testing with Kubernetes ConfigMaps, Secrets, Ingress, and the cert-manager* section.

The changes above will result in an Ingress manifest being rendered by Helm. Since the Ingress template is only used by the environments charts, we need to render one of the environment charts to see the Ingress manifest.

Run the following command to render manifests using the `dev-env` chart:

```
helm template kubernetes/helm/environments/dev-env
```

Look for `kind: Ingress` in the output and you will find the Ingress manifest. It looks like this:

```
apiVersion: networking.k8s.io/v1
kind: Ingress
metadata:
  name: RELEASE-NAME-dev-env
  labels:
    app.kubernetes.io/name: dev-env
    helm.sh/chart: dev-env-1.0.0
    app.kubernetes.io/managed-by: Helm
  annotations:
    cert-manager.io/issuer: selfsigned
spec:
  tls:
    - hosts:
```

```
      - "minikube.me"
    secretName: tls-certificate
rules:
  - host: "minikube.me"
    http:
      paths:
        - path: /oauth2
          pathType: Prefix
          backend:
            service:
              name: auth-server
              port:
                name: http
        - path: /product-composite
          pathType: Prefix
          backend:
            service:
              name: product-composite
              port:
                name: http
        - path: /actuator/health
          pathType: Prefix
          backend:
            service:
              name: product-composite
              port:
                name: http
```

Note that some of the routing rules have been removed for improved readability.

The final missing piece is how the Secret containing the certificate is created; let's look into that next.

Automating certificate provisioning

The cert-manager (`https://cert-manager.io/docs/`) is a certificate management controller for Kubernetes. It can facilitate the automated creation, provisioning, and rotation of certificates. It supports several sources for the certificates; for example:

- An **RFC8555** (`https://tools.ietf.org/html/rfc8555`)-compliant **ACME server** such as **Let's Encrypt** (`https://letsencrypt.org`)
- **HashiCorp Vault PKI Secrets Engine** (`https://www.vaultproject.io/docs/secrets/pki`)

- Self-signed certificates, issued by the cert-manager itself

For a full list of available issuers, see `https://cert-manager.io/docs/configuration/`.

Since self-signed certificates don't require communication with any external resources, they are a good candidate for use during development. We will use them within the scope of this book.

Using the cert-manager in production typically requires the use of an issuer, such as Let's Encrypt, which can issue certificates for the external APIs that the API clients, for example, web browsers and external systems, will trust.

After installation of the cert-manager in a Kubernetes cluster, at least one `issuer` must be registered. An issuer can either be local to a namespace or accessible cluster-wide. We will use a local issuer that is registered in the existing namespace, `hands-on`.

It will be the responsibility of the environment charts, `dev-env` and `prod-env`, to register a proper issuer. Both environments will use the self-signed issuer. A named template, `_issuer.yaml`, has been added to the `common` chart. It looks like this:

```
{{- define "common.issuer" -}}
apiVersion: cert-manager.io/v1
kind: Issuer
metadata:
  name: selfsigned
spec:
  selfSigned: {}
{{- end -}}
```

The `apiVersion` and `kind` fields specify that this is an issuer defined by the cert-manager. Its name is set to `selfsigned`. In the *Changes required to replace the Spring Cloud Gateway* section above, we saw how this name was used to annotate the Ingress manifest:

```
ingress:
  annotations:
    cert-manager.io/issuer: selfsigned
  tls:
    secretName: tls-certificate
```

This is all that it takes to get the cert-manager to kick in and provide a certificate for the Ingress object. The cert-manager listens for the registration of Ingress objects that are annotated with `cert-manager.io/issuer` and starts to issue certificates using the issuer referenced in the value of the annotation, in this case, `selfsigned`. The cert-manager will use the issuer to create a certificate and will store it in a Secret named by the Ingress object. In our case, the name is set to `tls-certificate`. A `Certificate` object will also be created with the same name, containing administrative information like when it is time for the cert-manager to renew the certificate.

Since the named template, `common.issuer`, does not accept any configuration, all that is required to apply it in the `dev-env` and `prod-env` charts is to add a template in each chart that uses the named template. The template is named `issuer.yaml` and looks like this:

```
{{- template "common.issuer" . -}}
```

With this, we have everything that is required to replace the Spring Cloud Config Server and Gateway with native Kubernetes components and the cert-manager. Let's deploy and run some tests!

Testing with Kubernetes ConfigMaps, Secrets, Ingress, and the cert-manager

With the preceding changes described, we are ready to test the system landscape with the Spring Cloud Config Server and the Spring Cloud Gateway replaced by Kubernetes ConfigMaps, Secrets, an Ingress object, and the cert-manager. As before, when we used the Spring Cloud Gateway as the edge server, the external API will be protected by HTTPS. With this deployment, it will be the Ingress controller that uses the certificate provisioned by the cert-manager to protect the external API with HTTPS. This is illustrated by the following diagram:

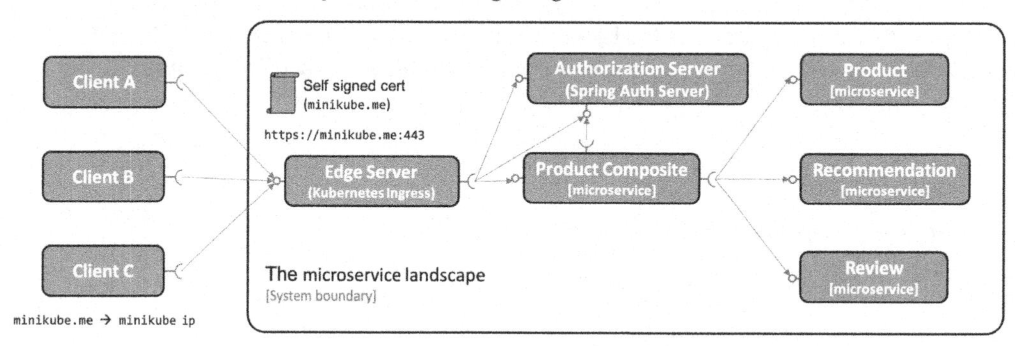

Figure 17.3: Protecting external access using HTTPS

On macOS, the Ingress controller is exposed on the default HTTPS port, `443`, on the Minikube instance. On Windows running WSL 2, where we run the Minikube instance as a Docker container, we communicate with the Minikube instance via `localhost`. When the Minikube instance was created in WSL 2, port forwarding was configured from port `8443` on `localhost` to the `443` port in the Minikube instance. The Ingress controller was installed when we performed the `minikube addons enable ingress` command.

For a recap on the setup of the Minikube instance, see the *Creating a Kubernetes cluster* section in *Chapter 15, Introduction to Kubernetes.*

An interesting question here is how can the Ingress controller use port `443` on the Minikube instance? We have seen the use of services of type `NodePort` that can allocate a port starting from `30000`, so how can the Ingress controller use the standard port for HTTPS, `443`?

The Ingress controller consists of a Deployment, `ingress-nginx-controller`, in the `kube-system` namespace. The answer to the question is that the Deployment configures its Pod using a `hostPort` to map port `443` in the host, that is, the Minikube instance, to port `443` in the container that runs in the Pod. The central parts in the definition of the Deployment look like the following:

```
apiVersion: apps/v1
kind: Deployment
metadata:
  name: ingress-nginx-controller
spec:
  template:
    spec:
      containers:
        image: us.gcr.io/k8s-artifacts-prod/ingress-nginx/
controller:v0.40.2
        ports:
        - containerPort: 443
          hostPort: 443
```

This setup works for a single-node Kubernetes cluster used for development and testing. In a multi-node Kubernetes cluster, external load balancers are used to expose an Ingress controller for high availability and scalability.

The Deployment uses the same type of commands as we used in *Chapter 16, Deploying Our Microservices to Kubernetes*; refer to the *Deploying to Kubernetes for development and test* section. In this section, we will also install the cert-manager and add an entry to the `/etc/hosts` file for the hostname `minikube.me`.

Execute the following steps to deploy the system landscape and verify that it works as expected:

1. Install the cert-manager in the `cert-manager` Namespace and wait for the deployment to complete. Before the cert-manager can be installed, we need to add its Helm repository. Run the following commands:

```
helm repo add jetstack https://charts.jetstack.io
helm repo update
helm install cert-manager jetstack/cert-manager \
  --create-namespace \
  --namespace cert-manager \
  --version v1.3.1 \
  --set installCRDs=true \
  --wait
```

The cert-manager also comes with a set of Kubernetes **Custom Resource Definitions** (**CRDs**), like the `Issuer` object that was introduced above. CRDs are used in Kubernetes to extend its API, that is, to add new objects to its API. The `--set installCRDs=true` flag in the command above ensures that these object definitions are installed when installing the cert-manager.

Verify that three Pods are ready in the `cert-manager` Namespace with the following command:

```
kubectl get pods --namespace cert-manager
```

Expect a response like this:

```
-bash
NAME                                       READY   STATUS    AGE
cert-manager-7998c69865-295wq              1/1     Running   63s
cert-manager-cainjector-7b744d56fb-nb42t   1/1     Running   63s
cert-manager-webhook-7d6d4c78bc-9g47s      1/1     Running   63s
$
```

Figure 17.4: Pods in the cert-manager namespace

2. Map `minikube.me` to the IP address we can use to reach the Minikube instance by adding a line to the `/etc/hosts` file:
    a. On macOS, run the following command to add the line:

    ```
    sudo bash -c "echo $(minikube ip) minikube.me | tee -a /
    etc/hosts"
    ```

    b. On Windows using WSL 2, run the following command to add the line:

    ```
    sudo bash -c "echo 127.0.0.1 minikube.me | tee -a /etc/hosts"
    ```

Note that the `sudo` command will probably ask for your password.

Verify the result with the `cat /etc/hosts` command. Expect a line that contains the IP address described above followed by `minikube.me`; for example, `192.168.64.199 minikube.me`.

If your `/etc/hosts` file contains multiple lines for `minikube.me` (for example, from earlier attempts), you need to remove the old ones manually.

3. You can build Docker images from source as follows:

```
cd $BOOK_HOME/Chapter17
eval $(minikube docker-env)
./gradlew build && docker-compose build
```

4. Pull Docker images to avoid a slow deployment process due to Kubernetes downloading Docker images:

```
eval $(minikube docker-env)
docker pull mysql:5.7.32
docker pull mongo:4.4.2
docker pull rabbitmq:3.8.11-management
docker pull openzipkin/zipkin:2.23.2
```

5. Resolve the Helm chart dependencies:
    a. First, we update the dependencies in the `components` folder:

    ```
    for f in kubernetes/helm/components/*; do helm dep up $f; done
    ```

    b. Next, we update the dependencies in the `environments` folder:

    ```
    for f in kubernetes/helm/environments/*; do helm dep up
    $f; done
    ```

6. Set the `hands-on` namespace as the default namespace for `kubectl`:

```
kubectl config set-context $(kubectl config current-context)
--namespace=hands-on
```

7. In a separate terminal window, run the following command to monitor how certificate objects are created by the cert-manager:

```
kubectl get certificates -w --output-watch-events
```

8. Deploy the system landscape using Helm and wait for all deployments to complete:

```
helm install hands-on-dev-env \
  kubernetes/helm/environments/dev-env \
  -n hands-on \
  --create-namespace \
  --wait
```

9. Note how the certificate is created by the cert-manager during the deployment. Expect the following output from the `kubectl get certificates` command:

```
-bash
EVENT      NAME             READY  SECRET           AGE
ADDED      tls-certificate         tls-certificate  0s
MODIFIED   tls-certificate  False  tls-certificate  0s
...
MODIFIED   tls-certificate  True   tls-certificate  0s
```

Figure 17.5: Events from the cert-manager provisioning a certificate

10. Stop the `kubectl get certificates` command with *Ctrl+C*.
11. Run the test to verify that the system landscape works as expected:
    a. On macOS, run the following command:

    ```
    HOST=minikube.me PORT=443 USE_K8S=true ./test-em-all.bash
    ```

    b. On Windows using WSL 2, run the following command:

    ```
    HOST=minikube.me PORT=8443 USE_K8S=true ./test-em-all.bash
    ```

    Expect output from the tests similar to what we obtained in the previous chapter (in condensed format):

```
Start Tests: Mon May 3 20:57:44 CEST 2021
HOST=minikube.me
PORT=443
USE_K8S=true
SKIP_CB_TESTS=false
Wait for: curl -k https://minikube.me:443/actuator/health... DONE, continues...
ACCESS_TOKEN=eyJra...
Test OK (HTTP Code: 202, )
...
End, all tests OK: Mon May 3 20:58:07 CEST 2021

$
```

Figure 17.6: Verifying the system landscape created by the dev-env Helm chart

Before wrapping up the `dev-env`, let's try out the certificate object that the cert-manager created and see how it can be used to affect the retention time for the certificate.

Rotating certificates

Let's start getting acquainted with the certificate object by issuing the following command:

```
kubectl describe cert tls-certificate
```

At the end of the output from the command, we will find the following information regarding the time that the certificate will be valid for:

```
Not After:           2021-07-31T13:59:26Z
Not Before:          2021-05-02T13:59:26Z
Renewal Time:        2021-07-01T13:59:26Z
```

Figure 17.7: Certificate validation period and renewal time

We can see that the certificate is valid for 90 days (**Not After – Not Before**) and that the cert-manager will try to renew it after 60 days (**Renewal Time – Not Before**). Since the selfsigned issuer we are using doesn't allow any configuration, these are the default values that the cert-manager uses: 90 days lifetime and a renewal process that is initiated after 2/3 of the lifetime.

But we don't want to wait 60 days before we can observe a renewal of the certificate. If we study the API specification for the certificate object at `https://cert-manager.io/docs/reference/api-docs/#cert-manager.io/v1.Certificate`, we will find a field in the `spec` section that is of interest. It is named `renewBefore` and can be used to specify how early the cert-manager should start the renew process. If we want the certificate to be renewed once per minute, we can specify the `renewBefore` to be 90 days - 1 minute = 90*24 hours - 1 minute = 2160 hours - 1 minute = 2159 hours and 59 minutes.

Start the `kubectl get events -w` command in a separate terminal window and run the following `patch` command to add the `renewBefore` field to the certificate:

```
kubectl patch certificate tls-certificate --type=json \
-p='[{"op": "add", "path": "/spec/renewBefore", "value": "2159h59m"}]'
```

Within 1 minute, the `get events` command should start to report on certificate renewals. For each renewal, the following should be printed by the `get events` command:

```
-bash
0s          Normal    Issuing           certificate/tls-certificate
  Renewing certificate as renewal was scheduled at 2021-05-03 14:42:58 +0000 UTC
...
0s          Normal    Issuing           certificate/tls-certificate
  The certificate has been successfully issued
```

Figure 17.8: Events from the cert-manager rotating a certificate

Wait a couple of minutes to verify that the certificate is renewed once per minute. If you are curious about when the next renewal will happen, you can issue the following command:

```
kubectl get cert tls-certificate -o json | jq .status.renewalTime
```

It should respond with a date like **2021-05-02T19:39:06Z**.

If you no longer want to have a custom retention time, you can remove the `renewBefore` field with the following command:

```
kubectl patch certificate tls-certificate --type=json \
  -p='[{"op": "remove", "path": "/spec/renewBefore"}]'
```

This concludes the tests we will do in the system landscape deployed using the `dev-env` chart. We can remove the system landscape with the following command:

```
kubectl delete namespace hands-on
```

Let us also recap how to deploy the system landscape using the `prod-env` chart!

Deploying to Kubernetes for staging and production

Deploying to a staging and production environment using the `prod-env` chart follows the same steps as we used in the *Deploying to Kubernetes for staging and production* section in *Chapter 16, Deploying Our Microservices to Kubernetes*. The steps are recapitulated here in a compact form:

1. Start MySQL, MongoDB, and RabbitMQ outside of Kubernetes:

```
eval $(minikube docker-env)
docker-compose up -d mongodb mysql rabbitmq
```

2. Tag Docker images with `v1` versions:

```
docker tag hands-on/auth-server hands-on/auth-server:v1
docker tag hands-on/product-composite-service hands-on/product-composite-service:v1
docker tag hands-on/product-service hands-on/product-service:v1
docker tag hands-on/recommendation-service hands-on/recommendation-service:v1
docker tag hands-on/review-service hands-on/review-service:v1
```

3. Deploy the microservices using the `prod-env` Helm chart:

```
helm install hands-on-prod-env \
  kubernetes/helm/environments/prod-env \
  -n hands-on --create-namespace \
  --wait
```

4. Run the test to verify that the system landscape works as expected:
   a. On macOS, run the following command:

   ```
   HOST=minikube.me PORT=443 USE_K8S=true ./test-em-all.bash
   ```

   b. On Windows using WSL 2, run the following command:

   ```
   HOST=minikube.me PORT=8443 USE_K8S=true ./test-em-all.bash
   ```

When you are done, clean up the resources created in both Kubernetes and Docker using the following commands:

1. Stop the `kubectl get cert -w` and `kubectl get events -w` commands if they still are running by using *Ctrl* + *C*.

2. Delete the namespace in Kubernetes with the following command:

```
kubectl delete namespace hands-on
```

3. Stop MySQL, MongoDB, and RabbitMQ with the following command:

```
eval $(minikube docker-env)
docker-compose down
```

With this, we are done with all tests running on Kubernetes. Let's see how to verify that the microservices still work *without* Kubernetes.

Verifying that the microservices work without Kubernetes

In this chapter and the previous one, we have seen how features in the Kubernetes platform, such as ConfigMaps, Secrets, Services, and Ingress objects, can simplify the effort of developing a landscape of cooperating microservices. But it is important to ensure that the source code of the microservices doesn't become dependent on the platform from a functional perspective. Avoiding such a lock-in makes it possible to change to another platform in the future, if required, with minimal effort. Changing the platform should not require changes in the source code, but only in the configuration of the microservices.

Testing the microservices using Docker Compose and running the `test-em-all.bash` verification script will ensure that they work from a functional perspective without Kubernetes. When running microservices without Kubernetes, we will lack the non-functional features that Kubernetes provides us with, for example, monitoring, scaling, and restarting containers.

When using Docker Compose, we will replace the following Kubernetes features:

- Instead of ConfigMaps, we use volumes that map the configuration files directly from the host filesystem
- Instead of using Secrets, we keep sensitive information such as credentials in the Docker Compose `.env` file
- Instead of an Ingress, we will use the Spring Cloud Gateway
- Instead of Services, we will map hostnames used by the clients directly to the hostnames of the containers, meaning that we will not have any service discovery in place and will not be able to scale containers

Using Docker Compose this way will result in significant disadvantages from a non-functional perspective compared to using Kubernetes. But this is acceptable, given that Docker Compose will only be used to run functional tests.

Let's go through the changes in the `docker-compose*.yml` files before we run the tests using Docker Compose.

Changes in the Docker Compose files

To run microservices outside Kubernetes, using Docker Compose, the following changes have been applied to the `docker-compose*.yml` files:

- We have removed the configuration server definition
- We have removed the use of the following configuration server environment variables: `CONFIG_SERVER_USR` and `CONFIG_SERVER_PWD`
- We have mapped the `config-repo` folder as a volume in each container that needs to read configuration files from the configuration repository
- We have defined the `SPRING_CONFIG_LOCATION` environment variable to point to the configuration files in the configuration repository
- We have stored sensitive information such as credentials and passwords in TLS certificates in the Docker Compose `.env` file
- We have defined environment variables with credentials for access to resource managers using the variables defined in the `.env` file

For example, the configuration of the `product` microservice looks like the following in `docker-compose.yml`:

```
product:
  build: microservices/product-service
  image: hands-on/product-service
  environment:
    - SPRING_PROFILES_ACTIVE=docker
    - SPRING_CONFIG_LOCATION=file:/config-repo/application.yml,file:/
config-repo/product.yml
    - SPRING_RABBITMQ_USERNAME=${RABBITMQ_USR}
    - SPRING_RABBITMQ_PASSWORD=${RABBITMQ_PWD}
    - SPRING_DATA_MONGODB_AUTHENTICATION_DATABASE=admin
    - SPRING_DATA_MONGODB_USERNAME=${MONGODB_USR}
    - SPRING_DATA_MONGODB_PASSWORD=${MONGODB_PWD}
  volumes:
    - $PWD/config-repo:/config-repo
```

Here is an explanation of the source code:

- The `config-repo` folder is mapped as a volume into the container at `/config-repo`
- The `SPRING_CONFIG_LOCATION` environment variable tells Spring where to find the property files, in this case, the `/config-repo/application.yml` and `/config-repo/product.yml` files
- Credentials for accessing RabbitMQ and MongoDB are set up as environment variables based on the content in the `.env` file

The credentials referred to in the preceding source code are defined in the `.env` file as:

```
RABBITMQ_USR=rabbit-user-prod
RABBITMQ_PWD=rabbit-pwd-prod
MONGODB_USR=mongodb-user-prod
MONGODB_PWD=mongodb-pwd-prod
```

Testing with Docker Compose

To test with Docker Compose, we will use Docker Desktop instead of Minikube. Perform the following steps:

1. To direct the Docker client to use Docker Desktop instead of Minikube, run the following command:
   ```
   eval $(minikube docker-env --unset)
   ```
2. To save memory, you might want to stop the Minikube instance:
   ```
   minikube stop
   ```
3. Start Docker Desktop (if it is not already running).
4. Build the Docker images in Docker Desktop with the following command:
   ```
   docker-compose build
   ```
5. Run the tests using RabbitMQ (with one partition per topic):
   ```
   COMPOSE_FILE=docker-compose.yml ./test-em-all.bash start stop
   ```

6. The tests should begin by starting all the containers, running the tests, and finally stopping all the containers. Expect output similar to what we have seen in the previous chapters (output reduced to improve readability):

```
Start Tests: Mon May 3 19:32:39 CEST 2021
HOST=localhost
PORT=8443
USE_K8S=false
SKIP_CB_TESTS=false
Restarting the test environment...
$ docker-compose down --remove-orphans
$ docker-compose up -d
Creating ..._auth-server_1 ... done
...
Creating ..._zipkin_1             ... done
Wait for: curl -k https://localhost:8443/actuator/health... ,
  retry #1 ... DONE, continues...
ACCESS_TOKEN=eyJra...
Test OK (HTTP Code: 202, )
...
We are done, stopping the test environment...
$ docker-compose down
Stopping ..._zipkin_1             ... done
...
Removing ..._rabbitmq_1           ... done
End, all tests OK: Mon May 3 19:34:34 CEST 2021
$
```

Figure 10.9: Verifying the functionality of the system landscape without using Kubernetes

7. Optionally, run the tests using RabbitMQ with multiple partitions per topic:

```
COMPOSE_FILE=docker-compose-partitions.yml ./test-em-all.bash
start stop
```

   Expect output that's similar to the preceding test.

8. Alternatively, run the test using Kafka with multiple partitions per topic:

```
COMPOSE_FILE=docker-compose-kafka.yml ./test-em-all.bash start
stop
```

   Expect output that's similar to the preceding test.

9. Stop Docker Desktop to save memory, if required.
10. Start the Minikube instance, if it was stopped previously, and set the default namespace to `hands-on`:

```
minikube start
kubectl config set-context $(kubectl config current-context)
--namespace=hands-on
```

11. Point the Docker client back to the Kubernetes cluster in the Minikube instance:

```
eval $(minikube docker-env)
```

With the successful execution of these tests, we have verified that the microservices also work without Kubernetes.

Summary

In this chapter, we have seen how capabilities in Kubernetes can be used to simplify a microservice landscape, meaning that we reduce the number of supporting services to be developed and deployed together with the microservices. We have seen how Kubernetes ConfigMaps and Secrets can be used to replace the Spring Cloud Config Server and how a Kubernetes Ingress object can replace the Spring Cloud Gateway.

Using the cert-manager allowed us to automatically provision certificates for HTTPS endpoints exposed by the Ingress controller, eliminating the need for manual and cumbersome work.

To verify that the source code of the microservices can run on other platforms, that is, isn't locked into Kubernetes, we deployed the microservices using Docker Compose and ran the `test-em-all.bash` test script.

In the next chapter, we will be introduced to the concept of a service mesh and learn how a service mesh product, **Istio**, can be used to improve observability, security, resilience, and routing in a landscape of cooperating microservices that are deployed on Kubernetes.

Head over to the next chapter!

Questions

1. How was the Spring Cloud Config Server replaced by Kubernetes resources?
2. How was the Spring Cloud Gateway replaced by Kubernetes resources?
3. What is required to make the cert-manager automatically provision certificates for an Ingress object?
4. How can the retention time of a certificate be checked and updated?
5. Where is the actual certificate stored?
6. Why did we run the tests using Docker Compose?

18

Using a Service Mesh to Improve Observability and Management

In this chapter, you will be introduced to the concept of a service mesh and see how its capabilities can be used to handle challenges in a system landscape of microservices, in areas including security, policy enforcement, resilience, and traffic management. A service mesh can also be used to provide observability, the capability to visualize how traffic flows between microservices.

A service mesh overlaps partly with the capabilities of Spring Cloud and Kubernetes that we learned about earlier in this book. But most of the functionality in a service mesh complements Spring Cloud and Kubernetes, as we will see in this chapter.

The following topics will be covered in this chapter:

- An introduction to the service mesh concept and Istio, a popular open source implementation
- Deploying Istio in Kubernetes
- Creating, observing, and securing a service mesh
- Ensuring that a service mesh is resilient
- Performing zero-downtime updates
- Testing the microservice landscape using Docker Compose to ensure that the source code in the microservices is not locked into either Kubernetes or Istio

Technical requirements

For instructions on how to install tools used in this book and how to access the source code for this book, see:

- *Chapter 21* for macOS
- *Chapter 22* for Windows

The code examples in this chapter all come from the source code in `$BOOK_HOME/Chapter18`.

If you want to view the changes applied to the source code in this chapter, that is, see what it took to create a service mesh using Istio, you can compare it with the source code for *Chapter 17, Implementing Kubernetes Features to Simplify the System Landscape*. You can use your favorite `diff` tool and compare the two folders, `$BOOK_HOME/Chapter17` and `$BOOK_HOME/Chapter18`.

Introducing service meshes using Istio

A service mesh is an infrastructure layer that controls and observes the communication between services, for example, microservices. The capabilities in a service mesh, for example, observability, security, policy enforcement, resilience, and traffic management, are implemented by controlling and monitoring all internal communication inside the service mesh, that is, between the microservices in the service mesh.

One of the core components in a service mesh is a lightweight **proxy** component that is injected into each microservice that will be part of the service mesh. All traffic in and out of a microservice is configured to go through its proxy component. The proxy components are configured at runtime by a **control plane** in the service mesh, using APIs exposed by the proxy. The control plane also collects telemetry data through these APIs from the proxies to visualize how the traffic flows in the service mesh.

A service mesh also contains a **data plane**, consisting of the proxy components together with separate components for handling external traffic to and from the service mesh, known as an **ingress gateway** and an **egress gateway**. The gateway components also communicate with the control plane using a proxy component. This is illustrated by the following diagram:

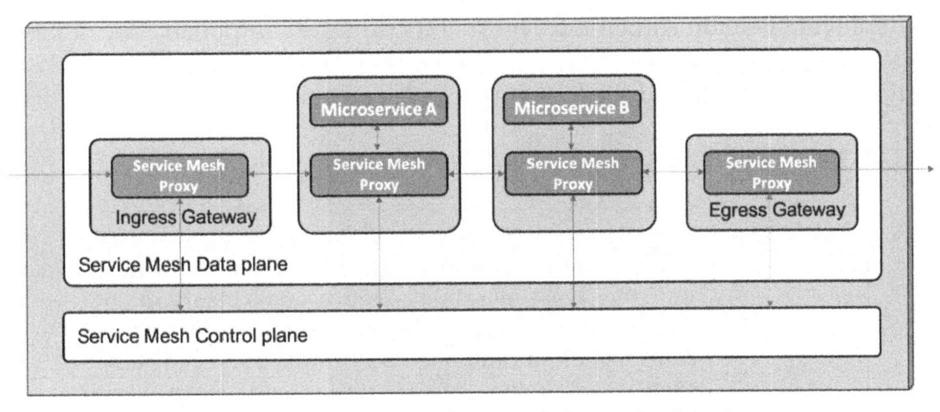

Figure 18.1: Service mesh with a control plane and a data plane

The first publicly available implementation of a service mesh was the open source project **Linkerd**, managed by Buoyant (`https://linkerd.io`), having its origins in Twitter's Finagle project (`http://twitter.github.io/finagle`). It was launched in 2016 and, one year later, in 2017, IBM, Google, and Lyft launched the open source project **Istio** (`https://istio.io`). Since then, several service mesh projects have been launched. For an overview of available implementations, see the service mesh category in CNCF's cloud-native landscape map: `https://landscape.cncf.io/card-mode?category=service-mesh&grouping=category`. In this book, we will use Istio.

Introducing Istio

Istio can be deployed on a number of Kubernetes distributions and platforms using various installation tools as described in `https://istio.io/docs/setup`. We will use Istio's CLI tool, `istioctl`, to install Istio in our Minikube-based, single-node Kubernetes cluster.

Istio is, as explained previously, divided into a control plane and a data plane. As an operator, we will define the desired state by creating Istio objects in the Kubernetes API server, for example, declaring routing rules. The control plane will read these objects and send commands to the proxies in the data plane to take actions according to the desired state, for example, configuring routing rules. The proxies handle the actual communication between the microservices and report back telemetry data to the control plane. The telemetry data is used in the control plane to visualize what's going on in the service mesh.

When deploying Istio on Kubernetes, most of its runtime components are deployed in a separate Kubernetes Namespace, `istio-system`. For the configuration we will use in this book, we will find the following Deployments in this Namespace:

1. `istiod`, Istio's daemon that runs the whole control plane.

Fun fact: Up until Istio v1.4, the control plane was divided into a set of cooperating microservices. Starting with v1.5, they were consolidated into a single binary run by `istiod`, simplifying installation and configuration of the control plane at runtime. Also, runtime characteristics such as startup time, resource usage, and responsiveness improved. This evolution of Istio's control plane is, to me, an interesting lesson learned when it comes to the use of fine-grained microservices.

2. `istio-ingressgateway` and `istio-egressgateway`, Istio's ingress and egress gateway components, are part of the data plane.
3. A number of integrations with other popular open source projects are supported by Istio to bring in extra functionality to the control plane. In this book, we will integrate the following components:
   - **Kiali**: Provides observability to the service mesh, visualizing what is going on in the mesh. For more information, see `https://www.kiali.io`.
   - **Tracing**: Handles and visualizes distributed tracing information, based on either Jaeger or Zipkin. We will use Jaeger. For more information, see `https://www.jaegertracing.io`.
   - **Prometheus**: Performs data ingestion and storage for time series-based data, for example, performance metrics. For more information, see `https://prometheus.io`.
   - **Grafana**: Visualizes performance metrics and other time series-related data collected by Prometheus. For more information, see `https://grafana.com`.

In *Chapter 20, Monitoring Microservices*, we will explore performance monitoring capabilities using Prometheus and Grafana.

4. For more information on available integration in Istio, see `https://istio.io/latest/docs/ops/integrations/`.

The only Istio components that are deployed outside of the `istio-system` Namespace are the proxy components, which are injected into the microservices that are part of the service mesh. The proxy component is based on Lyft's Envoy proxy (`https://www.envoyproxy.io`).

The runtime components in Istio's control plane and data plane are summarized in the following diagram:

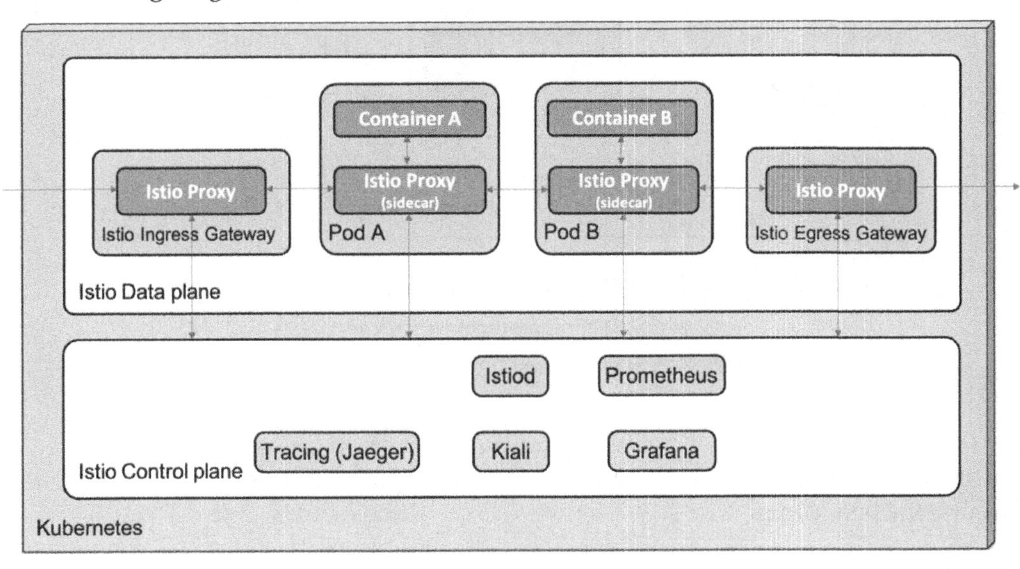

Figure 18.2: Istio runtime components

Now that we've had an introduction, we will look into how these proxy objects can be injected into the microservices.

Injecting Istio proxies into microservices

The microservices we have deployed in Kubernetes in the previous chapters run as a single container in a Kubernetes Pod (refer to the *Introducing Kubernetes API objects* section in *Chapter 15, Introduction to Kubernetes*, for a recap). To make a microservice join an Istio-based service mesh, an Istio proxy is injected into each microservice. This is done by adding an extra container to the Pod that runs the Istio proxy.

A container added to a Pod with the aim of supporting the main container, such as an Istio proxy, is referred to as a **sidecar**.

The following diagram shows how an Istio proxy has been injected into a sample Pod, **Pod A**, as a sidecar:

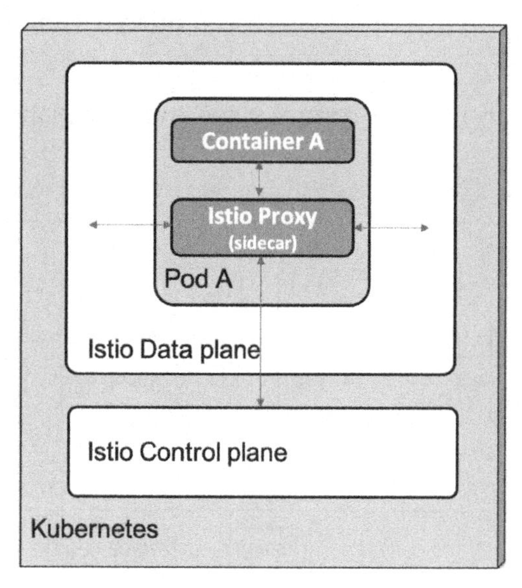

Figure 18.3: Istio proxy injected into Pod A

The main container in the Pod, **Container A**, is configured to route all its traffic through the Istio proxy.

Istio proxies can be injected either automatically when a Pod object is created or manually using the `istioctl` tool. To tell Istio to automatically inject an Istio proxy into new Pods in a Namespace, the Namespace can be labeled with `istio-injection: enabled`. If some Pods in the Namespace are to be excluded from the auto-injection, they can be annotated with `sidecar.istio.io/inject: "false"`.

To inject an Istio proxy manually into the Pods of an existing Deployment object, the following command can be used:

```
kubectl get deployment sample-deployment -o yaml | istioctl kube-inject
-f - | kubectl apply -f -
```

This command may, at first glance, appear somewhat daunting, but it is actually just three separate commands. The previous command sends its output to the next command using pipes, that is, the | character. Let's go through each command:

1. The `kubectl get deployment` command gets the current definition of a Deployment named `sample-deployment` from the Kubernetes API server and returns its definition in the YAML format.
2. The `istioctl kube-inject` command reads the definition from the `kubectl get deployment` command and adds an extra container for an Istio proxy in Pods that the Deployment handles. The configuration for the existing container in the Deployment object is updated so that incoming and outgoing traffic goes through the Istio proxy.

   The `istioctl` command returns the new definition of the Deployment object, including a container for the Istio proxy.
3. The `kubectl apply` command reads the updated configuration from the `istioctl kube-inject` command and applies the updated configuration. An upgrade of the Pods belonging to the Deployment will start up in the same way as we have seen before (refer to the *Trying out a sample deployment* section in *Chapter 15, Introduction to Kubernetes*).

In this book, we will inject the Istio proxies automatically by applying the following definition of the `hands-on` Namespace:

```
apiVersion: v1
kind: Namespace
metadata:
  name: hands-on
  labels:
    istio-injection: enabled
```

From the preceding definition, we can see how the Namespace is given the label `istio-injection` with the value `enabled`.

At the time of writing, Istio is not fully capable of acting as a proxy for MySQL, MongoDB, and RabbitMQ, so they will be excluded from the service mesh by adding the following annotation to their Helm chart's `values.yaml` file:

```
annotations:
  sidecar.istio.io/inject: "false"
```

After this introduction to how Istio proxies can be injected into the Pods, we can now learn about the Istio API objects used in this book.

Introducing Istio API objects

Istio also comes with a set of Kubernetes **Custom Resource Definitions** (**CRDs**). CRDs are used in Kubernetes to extend its API, that is, to add new objects to its API. Refer to the *Introducing Kubernetes API objects* section in *Chapter 15, Introduction to Kubernetes*, for a recap of the Kubernetes API. In this book, we will use the following Istio objects:

- **Gateway** is used to configure how to handle incoming traffic to, and outgoing traffic from, the service mesh. A gateway depends on a virtual service routing the incoming traffic to Kubernetes Services. We will use a gateway object to accept incoming traffic to DNS names ending with `minikube.me`, using HTTPS. The Istio gateway objects will replace the Ingress objects used in the previous chapter. Refer to the *Replacing Kubernetes Ingress controller with Istio ingress gateway* section for details.
- **VirtualService** is used to define routing rules in the service mesh. We will use virtual services to describe how to route incoming traffic from an Istio gateway to the Kubernetes Services and between services. We will also use virtual services to inject faults and delays to test the reliability and resilience capabilities of the service mesh.
- **DestinationRule** is used to define policies and rules for traffic that is routed (using a virtual service) to a specific service (that is, a destination). We will use destination rules to set up encryption policies to encrypt internal HTTP traffic and define service subsets that describe available versions of the services. We will use service subsets when performing zero-downtime (blue/green) deployments from an existing version of a microservice to a new version.

The division of responsibility between `VirtualService` and `DestinationRule` might seem a bit unclear in the beginning. A `VirtualService` object is used to configure routing **to** a service and `DestinationRule` is used to configure how to handle traffic **for** a selected service. So, first are `VirtualService` objects, used to determine where to send a request. Once that is decided, the receiving service's `DestinationRule` is applied.

- **PeerAuthentication** is used to control service-to-service authentication inside the service mesh. Istio can protect communication between services in a service mesh by automatically provisioning **mutual TLS** (**mTLS**) for transport authentication, where client services are authenticated by using a client certificate that is provided by Istio. To allow Kubernetes to call liveness and readiness probes using plain HTTP, we will configure Istio to allow a mix of mTLS and plain HTTP, called `PERMISSIVE` mode.
- **RequestAuthentication** is used to authenticate end users based on credentials provided in a request. Istio supports the use of **JSON Web Tokens** (**JWTs**) in general and specifically when used according to the **OpenID Connect** (**OIDC**) specification. Istio supports the use of the standard discovery endpoint in OIDC to specify where Istio can fetch the public key set (JWKS) to validate signatures of the JWTs. We will configure Istio to authenticate external requests using the auth server by specifying its JWKS discovery endpoint. For a recap, see *Chapter 11, Securing Access to APIs.*
- **AuthorizationPolicy** is used to provide access control in Istio. We will not use Istio's access control in this book. Instead, we will reuse the existing access control implemented in the `product-composite` microservice. We will therefore configure an `AuthorizationPolicy` object that allows access to the `product-composite` microservice for any authenticated user, that is, for requests that contain a valid JWT in the form of an OIDC access token.

For more information on these API objects, see `https://istio.io/v1.9/docs/reference/config/networking/` and `https://istio.io/v1.9/docs/reference/config/security/`.

Now that we have introduced the API object we will use, we will go through the changes applied to the microservice landscape arising from the introduction of Istio.

Simplifying the microservice landscape

As we have seen in the preceding section, Istio comes with components that overlap with components currently used in the microservice landscape in terms of functionality:

- The Istio ingress gateway can act as an edge server, an alternative to a Kubernetes Ingress controller
- The Jaeger component that comes bundled with Istio can be used for distributed tracing instead of the Zipkin server that we deploy together with the microservices

In the following two subsections, we will get an overview of why and how the Kubernetes Ingress controller is replaced with an Istio ingress gateway, and our Zipkin server is replaced with the Jaeger component that comes integrated with Istio.

Replacing Kubernetes Ingress controller with Istio ingress gateway

In the previous chapter, we introduced the Kubernetes Ingress controller as an edge server (refer to the *Replacing the Spring Cloud Gateway* section in *Chapter 17, Implementing Kubernetes Features to Simplify the System Landscape*). An Istio ingress gateway has a number of advantages over a Kubernetes Ingress controller:

- It can report telemetry data to the control plane for the traffic that flows through it
- It can be used for more fine-grained routing
- It can both authenticate and authorize requests before routing them into the service mesh

To benefit from these advantages, we will replace the Kubernetes Ingress controller with the Istio ingress gateway. The Istio ingress gateway is used by creating `Gateway` and `VisualService` objects described previously in the *Introducing Istio API objects* section.

The definition of the previously used Ingress objects has been removed from the `dev-env` and `prod-env` Helm charts in `kubernetes/helm/environments`. Definition files for Istio `Gateway` and `VirtualService` objects will be explained in the *Creating the service mesh* section.

The Istio ingress gateway is reached using a different IP address than the IP address used to access the Kubernetes Ingress controller, so we also need to update the IP address mapped to the hostname, `minikube.me`, which we use when running tests. This is handled in the *Setting up access to Istio services* section.

Replacing the Zipkin server with Istio's Jaeger component

As mentioned in the *Introducing Istio* section, Istio comes with built-in support for distributed tracing using Jaeger. Using Jaeger, we can offload and simplify the microservice landscape by removing the Zipkin server we introduced in *Chapter 14, Understanding Distributed Tracing*.

The following changes have been applied to the source code to remove the Zipkin server:

- The dependency on `org.springframework.cloud:spring-cloud-starter-zipkin` in all microservice build files, `build.gradle`, has been removed
- The definition of the Zipkin server in the three Docker Compose files, `docker-compose.yml`, `docker-compose-partitions.yml`, and `docker-compose-kafka.yml`, has been removed
- The Helm chart for the Zipkin server has been removed
- The Zipkin-specific property, `spring.zipkin.sender.type`, has been removed from the common configuration file, `config-repo/application.yml`

Jaeger will be installed in the *Deploying Istio in a Kubernetes cluster* section coming up.

With these simplifications of the microservice landscape explained, we are ready to deploy Istio in the Kubernetes cluster.

Deploying Istio in a Kubernetes cluster

In this section, we will learn how to deploy Istio in a Kubernetes cluster and how to access the Istio services in it.

We will use Istio's CLI tool, `istioctl`, to install Istio using a `demo` configuration of Istio that is suitable for testing Istio in a development environment, that is, with most features enabled but configured for minimalistic resource usage.

This configuration is unsuitable for production usage and for performance testing.

For other installation options, see `https://istio.io/docs/setup/kubernetes/install`.

To deploy Istio, perform the following steps:

1. Ensure that your Minikube instance from the previous chapter is up and running with the following command:

```
minikube status
```

Expect a response along the lines of the following, provided it is up and running:

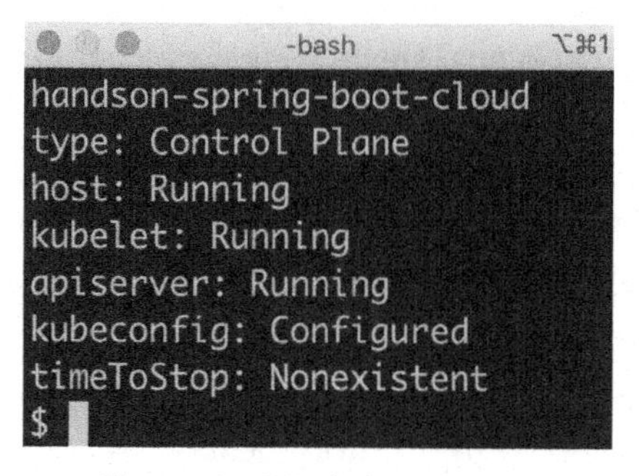

Figure 18.4: Minikube status OK

2. Run a precheck to verify that the Kubernetes cluster is ready for installing Istio in it:

```
istioctl experimental precheck
```

Expect a response including the following headers (details from the output have been removed for clarity):

Figure 18.5: Istio precheck OK

3. Install Istio using the demo profile with the following command:

```
istioctl install --skip-confirmation \
  --set profile=demo \
  --set meshConfig.accessLogFile=/dev/stdout \
  --set meshConfig.accessLogEncoding=JSON
```

The `accessLog` parameters are used to enable the Istio proxies to log requests that are processed. Once Pods are up and running with Istio proxies installed, the access logs can be inspected with the command `kubectl logs <MY-POD> -c istio-proxy`.

4. Wait for the Deployment objects and their Pods to be available with the following command:

```
kubectl -n istio-system wait --timeout=600s
--for=condition=available deployment --all
```

5. Next, install the extra components described in the *Introducing Istio* section – Kiali, Jaeger, Prometheus, and Grafana – with the commands:

```
istio_version=$(istioctl version --short --remote=false)
echo "Installing integrations for Istio v$istio_version"

kubectl apply -n istio-system -f https://raw.githubusercontent.
com/istio/istio/${istio_version}/samples/addons/kiali.yaml

kubectl apply -n istio-system -f https://raw.githubusercontent.
com/istio/istio/${istio_version}/samples/addons/jaeger.yaml

kubectl apply -n istio-system -f https://raw.githubusercontent.
com/istio/istio/${istio_version}/samples/addons/prometheus.yaml

kubectl apply -n istio-system -f https://raw.githubusercontent.
com/istio/istio/${istio_version}/samples/addons/grafana.yaml
```

If any of these commands fail, try rerunning the failing command. Errors can occur due to timing issues, which can be resolved by running commands again. Specifically, the installation of Kiali can result in error messages starting with `unable to recognize`. Rerunning the command makes these error messages go away.

6. Wait a second time for the extra components to be available with the following command:

```
kubectl -n istio-system wait --timeout=600s
--for=condition=available deployment --all
```

7. Finally, run the following command to see what we got installed:

```
kubectl -n istio-system get deploy
```

Expect output similar to this:

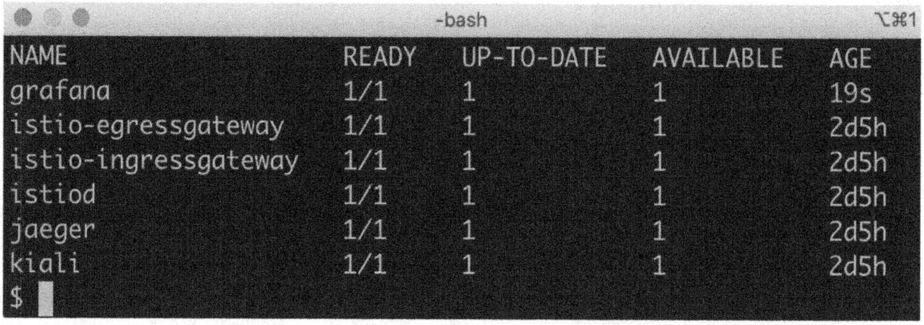

```
NAME                   READY   UP-TO-DATE   AVAILABLE   AGE
grafana                1/1     1            1           19s
istio-egressgateway    1/1     1            1           2d5h
istio-ingressgateway   1/1     1            1           2d5h
istiod                 1/1     1            1           2d5h
jaeger                 1/1     1            1           2d5h
kiali                  1/1     1            1           2d5h
$
```

Figure 18.6: Deployments in the Istio Namespace

Istio is now deployed in Kubernetes, but before we move on and create the service mesh, we need to learn a bit about how to access the Istio services in a Minikube environment.

Setting up access to Istio services

The demo configuration used in the previous section to install Istio comes with a few connectivity-related issues that we need to resolve. The Istio ingress gateway is configured as a load-balanced Kubernetes service; that is, its type is **LoadBalancer**. To be able to access the gateway, we need to run a load balancer in front of the Kubernetes cluster.

Minikube contains a command that can be used to simulate a local load balancer, `minikube tunnel`. This command assigns an external IP address to each load-balanced Kubernetes service, including the Istio ingress gateway. The hostname, `minikube.me`, that we use in our tests needs to be translated to the external IP address of the Istio ingress gateway. To simplify access to the web UIs of components like Kiali and Jaeger, we will also add hostnames dedicated to these services, for example, `kiali.minikube.me`.

We will also register a hostname to the external `health` endpoint as described in the *Observing the service mesh* section. Finally, a few hostnames for services installed and used in subsequent chapters will also be registered so we don't need to add new hostnames in the following chapters. The services that we will install in the next chapters are Kibana, Elasticsearch, and a mail server.

To enable external access using these hostnames to the Istio services, a Helm chart has been created; see `kubernetes/helm/environments/istio-system`. The chart contains a `Gateway`, `VirtualService`, and `DestinationRule` object for each Istio component. To protect requests to these hostnames from eavesdropping, only HTTPS requests are allowed. The `cert-manager`, which was introduced in the previous chapter, is used by the chart to automatically provision a TLS certificate for the hostnames and store it in a Secret named `hands-on-certificate`. All `Gateway` objects are configured to use this Secret in their configuration of the HTTPS protocol. All definition files can be found in the Helm charts `templates` folder.

The use of these API objects will be described in more detail in the *Creating the service mesh* and *Protecting external endpoints with HTTPS and certificates* sections below.

Run the following command to apply the Helm chart:

```
helm upgrade --install istio-hands-on-addons kubernetes/helm/
environments/istio-system -n istio-system --wait
```

This will result in the gateway being able to route requests for the following hostnames to the corresponding Kubernetes Service:

- `kiali.minikube.me` requests are routed to `kiali:20001`
- `tracing.minikube.me` requests are routed to `tracing:80`
- `prometheus.minikube.me` requests are routed to `prometheus:9000`
- `grafana.minikube.me` requests are routed to `grafana:3000`

To verify that the `certificate` and `secret` objects have been created, run the following commands:

```
kubectl -n istio-system get secret hands-on-certificate
kubectl -n istio-system get certificate  hands-on-certificate
```

Expect output like this:

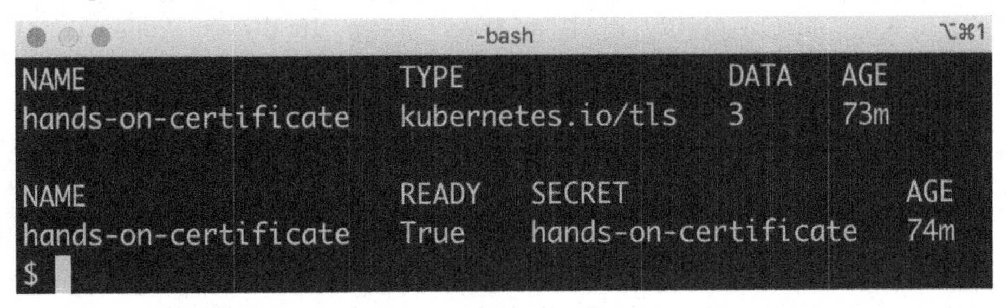
NAME   TYPE   DATA   AGE
hands-on-certificate   kubernetes.io/tls   3   73m

NAME   READY   SECRET   AGE
hands-on-certificate   True   hands-on-certificate   74m
$

Figure 18.7: The cert-manager has delivered both a TLS Secret and a certificate

The following diagram summarizes how the components can be accessed:

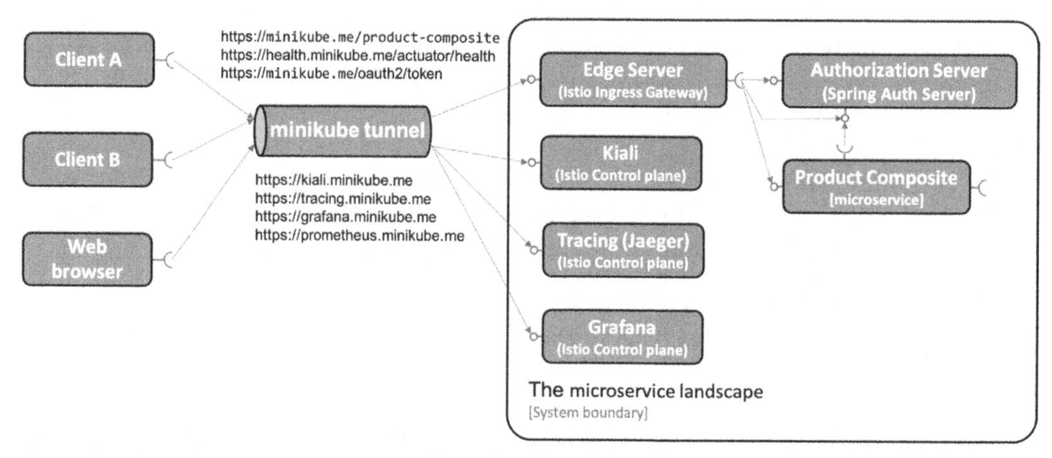

Figure 18.8: Hostnames to be used for accessing components through the Minikube tunnel

Perform the following steps to set up the Minikube tunnel and register the hostnames:

1. Run the following command in a separate terminal window (the command locks the terminal window when the tunnel is up and running):

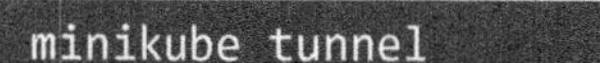

```
minikube tunnel
```

Note that this command requires that your user has `sudo` privileges and that you enter your password during startup and shutdown. It takes a couple of seconds before the command asks for the password, so it is easy to miss!

Once the tunnel is up and running, it will list the `istio-ingressgateway` as one of the services it exposes (the only one in our case).

2. Configure the hostnames to be resolved to the IP address of the Istio ingress gateway. Start by getting the IP address exposed by the `minikube tunnel` command for the Istio ingress gateway and save it in an environment variable named `INGRESS_IP`:

```
INGRESS_IP=$(kubectl -n istio-system get service istio-ingressgateway -o jsonpath='{.status.loadBalancer.ingress[0].ip}')

echo $INGRESS_IP
```

The `echo` command will print an IP address, for example, `10.102.72.36`.

On Windows and WSL 2, this IP address will always be `127.0.0.1` since we are using Minikube's Docker driver.

3. Update `/etc/hosts` so that all `minikube.me` hostnames we will use point to the IP address of the Istio ingress gateway:

```
MINIKUBE_HOSTS="minikube.me grafana.minikube.me kiali.minikube.me prometheus.minikube.me tracing.minikube.me kibana.minikube.me elasticsearch.minikube.me mail.minikube.me health.minikube.me"
echo "$INGRESS_IP $MINIKUBE_HOSTS" | sudo tee -a /etc/hosts
```

4. On Windows, we also need to update the Windows own `hosts` file:
   a. In Windows, open a `PowerShell` terminal.
   b. Open the Windows `hosts` file in Visual Code Studio with the command:

   ```
   code C:\Windows\System32\drivers\etc\hosts
   ```

   c. Add a similar line to the Window `hosts` file:

   ```
   127.0.0.1 minikube.me grafana.minikube.me kiali.minikube.me
   prometheus.minikube.me tracing.minikube.me kibana.minikube.me
   elasticsearch.minikube.me mail.minikube.me health.minikube.me
   ```

   d. When you try to save it, you will get an error regarding `Insufficient permissions`. Click on the **Retry as Admin...** button to update the `hosts` file as an administrator.
   e. Verify the update:

   ```
   cat C:\Windows\System32\drivers\etc\hosts
   ```

By default, the `/etc/hosts` file is overwritten by the content in the Windows `hosts` file when WSL is restarted. Restarting WSL takes a long time as it also restarts Docker. Restarting Docker, in turn, results in the Minikube instance being stopped so it needs to be restarted manually. So, to avoid this slow and tedious restart process, we simply updated both files.

5. Remove the line in `/etc/hosts` where `minikube.me` points to the IP address of the Minikube instance (`minikube ip`). Verify that `/etc/hosts` only contains one line that translates `minikube.me` and that it points to the IP address of the Istio ingress gateway; the value of `$INGRESS_IP`:

```
-bash
$ cat /etc/hosts
...
10.97.25.24 minikube.me grafana.minikube.me kiali.minikube.me
prometheus.minikube.me tracing.minikube.me kibana.minikube.me
elasticsearch.minikube.me mail.minikube.me health.minikube.me
$
```

Figure 18.9: /etc/hosts file updated

6. Verify that Kiali, Jaeger, Grafana, and Prometheus can be reached through the tunnel with the following commands:

```
curl -o /dev/null -sk -L -w "%{http_code}\n" https://kiali.
minikube.me/kiali/
curl -o /dev/null -sk -L -w "%{http_code}\n" https://tracing.
minikube.me
curl -o /dev/null -sk -L -w "%{http_code}\n" https://grafana.
minikube.me
curl -o /dev/null -sk -L -w "%{http_code}\n" https://prometheus.
minikube.me/graph#/
```

Each command should return `200` (OK). If the request sent to Kiali doesn't return 200, it often means that its internal initialization is not complete. Wait a minute and try again in that case.

The `minikube tunnel` command will stop running if, for example, your computer or the Minikube instance are paused or restarted. It needs to be restarted manually in these cases. So, if you fail to call APIs on any of the `minikube.me` hostnames, always check whether the Minikube tunnel is running and restart it if required.

With the Minikube tunnel in place, we are now ready to create the service mesh.

Creating the service mesh

With Istio deployed, we are ready to create the service mesh. The steps required to create the service mesh are basically the same as those we used in *Chapter 17, Implementing Kubernetes Features to Simplify the System Landscape* (refer to the *Testing with Kubernetes ConfigMaps, Secrets, Ingress, and cert-manager* section). Let's first see what additions have been made to the Helm templates to set up the service mesh before we run the commands to create the service mesh.

Source code changes

To be able to run the microservices in a service mesh managed by Istio, the `dev-env` Helm chart brings in two new named templates from the `common` chart, `_istio_base.yaml` and `_istio_dr_mutual_tls.yaml`. Let's go through them one by one.

Content in the _istio_base.yaml template

`_istio_base.yaml` defines a number of Kubernetes manifests that will be used by both environment charts, `dev-env` and `prod-env`. First, it defines three Istio-specific security-related manifests:

- An `AuthorizationPolicy` manifest named `product-composite-require-jwt`
- A `PeerAuthentication` manifest named `default`
- A `RequestAuthentication` manifest named `product-composite-request-authentication`

These three manifests will be explained in the *Securing a service mesh* section below.

The remaining four manifests will be discussed here. They are two pairs of `Gateway` and `VirtualService` manifests that are used to configure access to, and routing from, the hostnames `minikube.me` and `health.minikube.me`. `Gateway` objects will be used to define how to receive external traffic and `VirtualService` objects are used to describe how to route the incoming traffic inside the service mesh.

The `Gateway` manifest for controlling access to `minikube.me` looks like this:

```
apiVersion: networking.istio.io/v1beta1
kind: Gateway
metadata:
  name: hands-on-gw
spec:
  selector:
    istio: ingressgateway
  servers:
  - hosts:
    - minikube.me
    port:
      name: https
      number: 443
      protocol: HTTPS
    tls:
      credentialName: hands-on-certificate
      mode: SIMPLE
```

Here are some explanations for the source code:

- The gateway is named `hands-on-gw`; this name is used by the virtual services underneath.
- The `selector` field specifies that the gateway object will be handled by the default Istio ingress gateway, named `ingressgateway`.
- The `hosts` and `port` fields specify that the gateway will handle incoming requests for the `minikube.me` hostname using HTTPS over port `443`.
- The `tls` field specifies that the Istio ingress gateway can find the certificate and private key used for HTTPS communication in a TLS Secret named `hands-on-certificate`. Refer to the *Protecting external endpoints with HTTPS and certificates* section below for details on how these certificate files are created. The `SIMPLE` mode denotes that normal TLS semantics will be applied.

The `VirtualService` manifest for routing requests sent to `minikube.me` appears as follows:

```
apiVersion: networking.istio.io/v1beta1
kind: VirtualService
metadata:
  name: hands-on-vs
spec:
  gateways:
  - hands-on-gw
```

```
hosts:
- minikube.me
http:
- match:
  - uri:
      prefix: /oauth2
  route:
  - destination:
      host: auth-server
- match:
  ...
```

Explanations for the preceding manifest are as follows:

- The `gateways` and `hosts` fields specify that the virtual service will route requests that are sent to the `minikube.me` hostname through the `hands-on-gw` gateway.
- Under the `http` element follows an array of `match` and `route` blocks that specify how URL paths will be forwarded to the associated Kubernetes service. In the manifest above, only the first pair of `match` and `route` elements is shown. They map requests sent to `minikube.me` using the path `/oauth2` to the `auth-server` service. This mapping should be familiar from how we specified routing rules in both the Spring Cloud Gateway and Ingress objects in the previous chapters. The remaining pairs of `match` and `route` elements configure the same routing rules as we have seen for the Spring Cloud Gateway and Ingress objects:

    - `/login → auth-server`
    - `/error → auth-server`
    - `/product-composite → product-composite`
    - `/openapi → product-composite`
    - `/webjars → product-composite`

  For details, see `kubernetes/helm/common/templates/_istio_base.yaml`.

In the preceding source code, the destination host is specified using its short name, in other words, `product-composite`. This works, since the example is based on Kubernetes definitions from the same Namespace, `hands-on`. If that is not the case, it is recommended in the Istio documentation to use the host's **fully qualified domain name** (**FQDN**) instead. In this case, it is `product-composite.hands-on.svc.cluster.local`.

Content in the _istio_dr_mutual_tls.yaml template

`_istio_dr_mutual_tls.yaml` defines a template for specifying a number of `DestinationRule` objects. It is used to specify that mutual TLS should be used when routing a request to its corresponding service. It can also be used optionally to specify `subsets`, something that we will use in the `prod-env` chart in the *Performing zero-downtime updates* section below. The template looks like this:

```
{{- define "common.istio_dr_mutual_tls" -}}
{{- range $idx, $dr := .Values.destinationRules }}
apiVersion: networking.istio.io/v1beta1
kind: DestinationRule
metadata:
  name: {{ $dr.name }}
spec:
  host: {{ $dr.name }}
{{- if $dr.subsets }}
{{- with $dr.subsets }}
  subsets:
{{ toYaml . | indent 2 }}
{{- end }}
{{- end }}
  trafficPolicy:
    tls:
      mode: ISTIO_MUTUAL
---
{{- end -}}
{{- end -}}
```

Here are some comments about the preceding template:

- The `range` directive loops over the elements defined in the `destinationRules` variable
- The `host` field in the `spec` part of the manifest is used to specify the name of the Kubernetes Service that this `DestinationRule` applies to
- A `subsets` section is only defined if a corresponding element is found in the current element, `$dr`, in the `destinationRules` list
- A `trafficPolicy` is always used to require mutual TLS

The template is used in the `dev-end` Helm chart by specifying the `destinationRules` variable in the `values.yaml` file as follows:

```
destinationRules:
  - name: product-composite
  - name: auth-server
  - name: product
  - name: recommendation
  - name: review
```

The files can be found at `kubernetes/helm/common/templates/_istio_dr_mutual_tls.yaml` and `kubernetes/helm/environments/dev-env/values.yaml`.

With these changes in the source code in place, we are now ready to create the service mesh.

Running commands to create the service mesh

Create the service mesh by running the following commands:

1. Build Docker images from source with the following commands:

   ```
   cd $BOOK_HOME/Chapter18
   eval $(minikube docker-env)
   ./gradlew build && docker-compose build
   ```

2. Recreate the `hands-on` Namespace, and set it as the default Namespace:

   ```
   kubectl delete namespace hands-on
   kubectl apply -f kubernetes/hands-on-namespace.yml
   kubectl config set-context $(kubectl config current-context)
   --namespace=hands-on
   ```

   Note that the `hands-on-namespace.yml` file creates the `hands-on` Namespace labeled with `istio-injection: enabled`. This means that Pods created in this Namespace will get `istio-proxy` containers injected as sidecars automatically.

3. Resolve the Helm chart dependencies with the following commands:

   a. First, we update the dependencies in the `components` folder:

      ```
      for f in kubernetes/helm/components/*; do helm dep up $f;
      done
      ```

b. Next, we update the dependencies in the `environments` folder:

```
for f in kubernetes/helm/environments/*; do helm dep up $f;
done
```

4. Deploy the system landscape using Helm and wait for all Deployments to complete:

```
helm install hands-on-dev-env \
  kubernetes/helm/environments/dev-env \
  -n hands-on --wait
```

5. Once the Deployment is complete, verify that we have two containers in each of the microservice Pods:

```
kubectl get pods
```

Expect a response along the lines of the following:

```
4. bash
$ kubectl get pods
NAME                                  READY   STATUS    RESTARTS   AGE
auth-server-78c9b85c9b-9sjs4          2/2     Running   0          8m4s
mongodb-75d7df8bd7-7s9f6              1/1     Running   0          9m33s
mysql-754d8f7584-26lxd                1/1     Running   0          9m33s
product-8695c57758-64q7x              2/2     Running   0          8m4s
product-composite-74f4dc9b4f-vkvbd    2/2     Running   0          8m4s
rabbitmq-855fb78bcc-5mcq7             1/1     Running   0          9m33s
recommendation-7bc5446b4c-btpqx       2/2     Running   0          8m4s
review-546bb44f8d-hpll7               2/2     Running   0          8m4s$
$ 
```

Figure 18.10: Pods up and running

Note that the Pods that run our microservices report two containers per Pod; that is, they have the Istio proxy injected as a sidecar!

6. Run the usual tests with the following command:

```
./test-em-all.bash
```

The default values for the `test-em-all.bash` script have been updated from previous chapters to accommodate Kubernetes running in Minikube.

Expect the output to be similar to what we have seen in previous chapters:

```
$ ./test-em-all.bash
...
Wait for: curl -k https://health.minikube.me/actuator/health... DONE, continues...
...
Test OK (HTTP Code: 200)
...
End, all tests OK: Thu May 20 12:37:18 CEST 2021
$
```

Figure 18.11: Tests running successfully

7. You can try out the APIs manually by running the following commands:

```
ACCESS_TOKEN=$(curl -k https://writer:secret@minikube.me/oauth2/
token -d grant_type=client_credentials -s | jq .access_token -r)

echo ACCESS_TOKEN=$ACCESS_TOKEN

curl -ks https://minikube.me/product-composite/1 -H
"Authorization: Bearer $ACCESS_TOKEN" | jq .productId
```

   Expect the requested product ID, `1`, in the response.

With the service mesh up and running, let's see how we can observe what's going on in it using Kiali!

Observing the service mesh

In this section, we will use Kiali together with Jaeger to observe what's going on in the service mesh.

Before we do that, we need to understand how to get rid of some noise created by the health checks performed by Kubernetes' liveness and readiness probes. In the previous chapters, they have been using the same port as the API requests. This means that Istio will collect metrics for the usage of both health checks and requests sent to the API. This will cause the graphs shown by Kiali to become unnecessarily cluttered. Kiali can filter out traffic that we are not interested in, but a simpler solution is to use a different port for the health checks.

Microservices can be configured to use a separate port for requests sent to the actuator endpoints, for example, health checks sent to the `/actuator/health` endpoint. The following line has been added to the common configuration file for all microservices, `config-repo/application.yml`:

```
management.server.port: 4004
```

This will make all microservices use port `4004` to expose the health endpoints. The `values.yaml` file in the `common` Helm chart has been updated to use port `4004` in the default liveness and readiness probes. See `kubernetes/helm/common/values.yaml`.

The `product-composite` microservice exposes its management port, not only to the Kubernetes probes, but also externally for health checks, for example, performed by `test-em-all.bash`. This is done through Istio's ingress gateway, and therefore port `4004` is added to the `product-composite` microservice Deployment and Service manifests. See the `ports` and `service.ports` definitions in `kubernetes/helm/components/product-composite/values.yaml`.

The Spring Cloud Gateway (which is retained so we can run tests in Docker Compose) will continue to use the same port for requests to the API and the `health` endpoint. In the `config-repo/gateway.yml` configuration file, the management port is reverted to the port used for the API:

```
management.server.port: 8443
```

To simplify external access to the health check exposed by the `product-composite` microservice, a route is configured for the `health.minikube.me` hostname to the management port on the `product-composite` microservice. Refer to the explanation of the `_istio_base.yaml` template above.

With the requests sent to the health endpoint out of the way, we can start to send some requests through the service mesh.

We will start a low-volume load test using `siege`, which we learned about in *Chapter 16, Deploying Our Microservices to Kubernetes*. After that, we will go through some of the most important parts of Kiali to see how it can be used to observe a service mesh in a web browser. We will also see how Jaeger is used for distributed tracing.

Since the certificate we use is self-signed, web browsers will not rely on it automatically. Most web browsers let you visit the web page if you assure them that you understand the security risks. If the web browser refuses, opening a private window helps in some cases.

Specifically, regarding Chrome, if it does not let you visit the web page, you can use a hidden feature by clicking anywhere on the error page and then typing one of the following words:

- "`thisisunsafe`" for version 65 or newer
- "`badidea`" for versions 62-64
- "`danger`" for earlier versions

At the time of writing, the source code handling this in Chrome can be found at `https://chromium.googlesource.com/chromium/src/+/refs/heads/main/components/security_interstitials/core/browser/resources/interstitial_large.js`. The value of the `BYPASS_SEQUENCE` field is set to the Base64-encoded value `'dGhpc2lzdW5zYWZl'`. Running the following command:

```
echo dGhpc2lzdW5zYWZl | base64 -d
```

reveals the bypass code for the current version of Chrome: `thisisunsafe`.

Start the test client with the following commands:

```
ACCESS_TOKEN=$(curl -k https://writer:secret@minikube.me/oauth2/token
-d grant_type=client_credentials -s | jq .access_token -r)

echo ACCESS_TOKEN=$ACCESS_TOKEN

siege https://minikube.me/product-composite/1 -H "Authorization: Bearer
$ACCESS_TOKEN" -c1 -d1 -v
```

The first command will get an OAuth 2.0/OIDC access token that will be used in the next command, where `siege` is used to submit one HTTP request per second to the `product-composite` API.

Expect output from the `siege` command as follows:

```
-bash
$ siege https://minikube.me/product-composite/1 -H "Authorization: Bearer
 $ACCESS_TOKEN" -c1 -d1 -v
...
The server is now under siege...
HTTP/1.1 200     0.08 secs:     770 bytes ==> GET  /product-composite/1
HTTP/1.1 200     0.09 secs:     770 bytes ==> GET  /product-composite/1
HTTP/1.1 200     0.08 secs:     770 bytes ==> GET  /product-composite/1
$
```

Figure 18.12: System landscape under siege

Use a web browser of your choice that accepts self-signed certificates and proceed with the following steps:

1. Open Kiali's web UI using the `https://kiali.minikube.me` URL and, if asked to log in, use the following username and password: `admin` and `admin`. Expect a web page similar to the following:

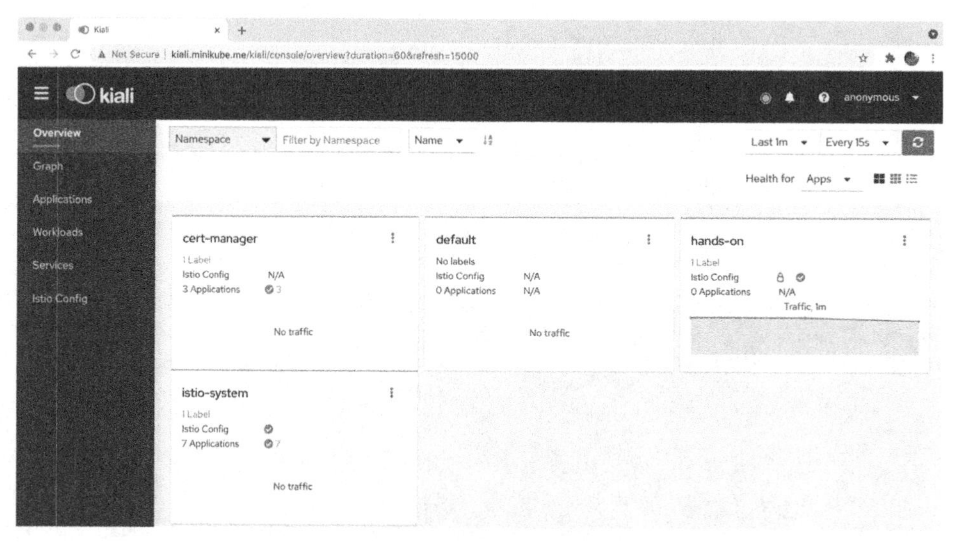

Figure 18.13: Kiali web UI

2. Click on the **Overview** tab, if not already active.

3. Click on the menu in the box named **hands-on** (three vertical dots in the top-right corner) and select **Graph**. Expect a graph to be shown, representing the current traffic flowing through the service mesh, as follows:

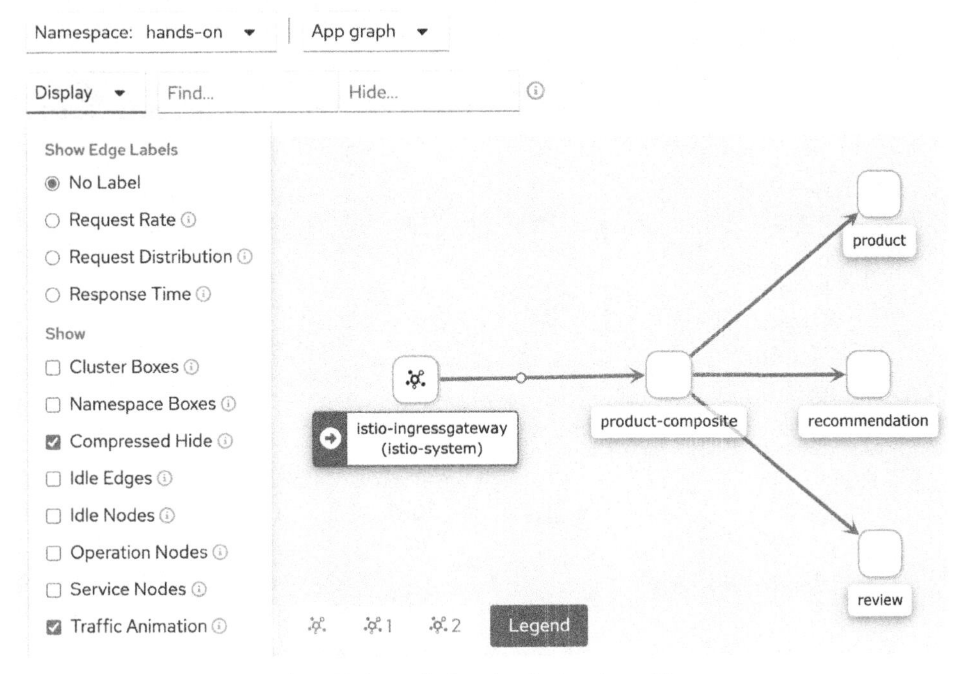

Figure 18.14: Kiali graph showing the hands-on Namespace

4. Click on the **Display** button, unselect **Service Nodes**, and select **Traffic Animation**.

   Kiali displays a graph representing requests that are currently sent through the service mesh, where active requests are represented by small moving circles along the arrows.

   This gives a pretty good initial overview of what's going on in the service mesh!

5. Let's now look at some distributed tracing using Jaeger. Open the web UI using the `https://tracing.minikube.me` URL. Click on the **Service** dropdown in the menu to the left and select the **product-composite** service. Click on the **Find Trace** button and you should see a result like this:

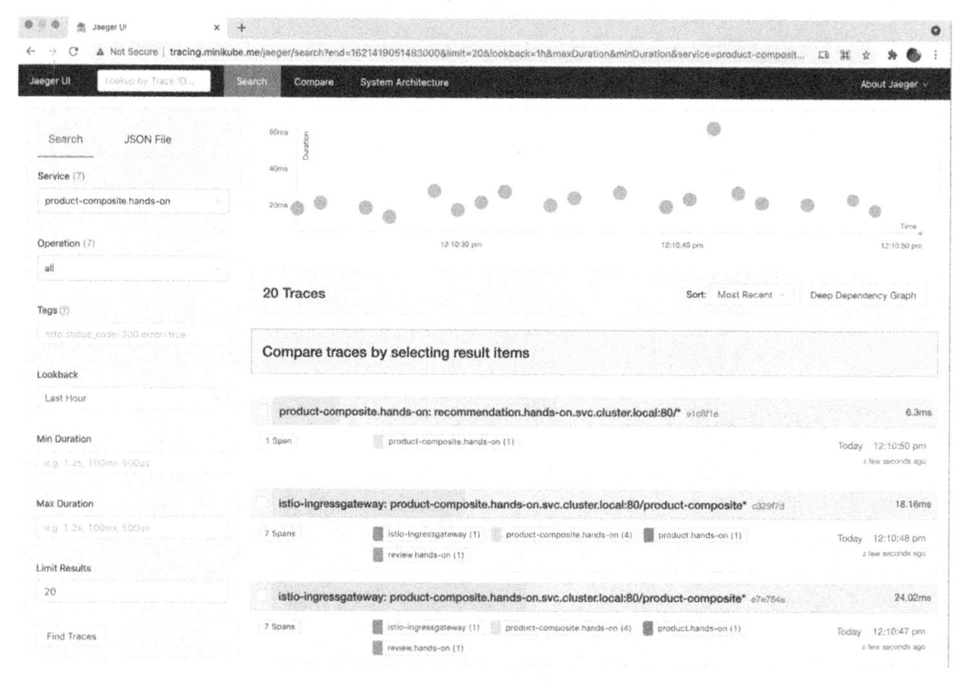

Figure 18.15: Distributed traces visualized by Jaeger

6. Click on one of the traces that is reported to contain **8 Spans** to examine it. Expect a web page such as the following:

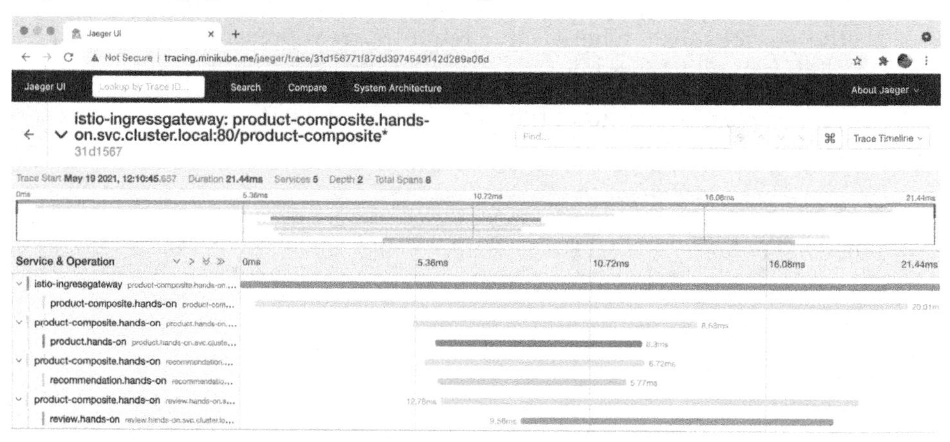

Figure 18.16: View a full trace call tree in Jaeger

This is basically the same tracing information as Zipkin made available in *Chapter 14, Understanding Distributed Tracing*.

There is much more to explore, but this is enough by way of an introduction. Feel free to explore the web UI in Kiali and Jaeger on your own.

Be aware that the access token acquired for the test client, `siege`, is only valid for an hour. If the traffic drops unexpectedly, check the output from `siege`; if it reports `4XX` instead of `200`, it's time to renew the access token!

Let's move on and learn how Istio can be used to improve security in the service mesh!

Securing a service mesh

In this section, we will learn how to use Istio to improve the security of a service mesh. We will cover the following topics:

- How to protect external endpoints with HTTPS and certificates
- How to require that external requests are authenticated using OAuth 2.0/ OIDC access tokens
- How to protect internal communication using mutual authentication (mTLS)

Let's now understand each of these in the following sections.

Protecting external endpoints with HTTPS and certificates

From the *Setting up access to Istio services* and *Content in the _istio_base.yaml template* sections, we learned that the `Gateway` objects use a TLS certificate stored in a Secret named `hands-on-certificate` for its HTTPS endpoints.

The Secret is created by the cert-manager based on the configuration in the `istio-system` Helm chart. The chart's template, `selfsigned-issuer.yaml`, is used to define an internal self-signed CA and has the following content:

```
apiVersion: cert-manager.io/v1
kind: Issuer
metadata:
  name: selfsigned-issuer
```

```
spec:
  selfSigned: {}
---
apiVersion: cert-manager.io/v1
kind: Certificate
metadata:
  name: ca-cert
spec:
  isCA: true
  commonName: hands-on-ca
  secretName: ca-secret
  issuerRef:
    name: selfsigned-issuer
---
apiVersion: cert-manager.io/v1
kind: Issuer
metadata:
  name: ca-issuer
spec:
  ca:
    secretName: ca-secret
```

From the preceding manifests, we can see the following:

- A self-signed issuer named `selfsigned-issuer`.
- This issuer is used to create a self-signed certificate, named `ca-cert`.
- The certificate is given the common name `hands-on-ca`.
- Finally, a self-signed CA, `ca-issuer`, is defined using the certificate, `ca-cert`, as its root certificate. This CA will be used to issue the certificate used by the gateway objects.

The chart's template, `hands-on-certificate.yaml`, defines this certificate as:

```
apiVersion: cert-manager.io/v1
kind: Certificate
metadata:
  name: hands-on-certificate
spec:
  commonName: minikube.me
```

```
subject:
  ...
dnsNames:
- minikube.me
- health.minikube.m
- dashboard.minikube.me
- kiali.minikube.me
- tracing.minikube.me
- prometheus.minikube.me
- grafana.minikube.me
- kibana.minikube.me
- elasticsearch.minikube.me
- mail.minikube.me
issuerRef:
  name: ca-issuer
secretName: hands-on-certificate
```

From this manifest, we can learn that:

- The certificate is named `hands-on-certificate`
- Its common name is set to `minikube.me`
- It specifies a few optional extra details about its `subject` (left out for clarity)
- All other hostnames are declared as **Subject Alternative Names** in the certificate
- It will use the issuer named `ca-issuer` declared above
- The cert-manager will store the TLS certificate in a Secret named `hands-on-certificate`

When the `istio-system` Helm chart was installed, these templates were used to create the corresponding API objects in Kubernetes. This triggered the cert-manager to create the certificates and Secrets.

The template files can be found in the `kubernetes/helm/environments/istio-system/templates` folder.

To verify that it is these certificates that are used by the Istio ingress gateway, we can run the following command:

```
keytool -printcert -sslserver minikube.me | grep -E "Owner:|Issuer:"
```

Expect the following output:

```
-bash
$ keytool -printcert -sslserver minikube.me | grep -E "Owner:|Issuer:"
Owner: SERIALNUMBER=my-sn, CN=minikube.me, OU=my-ou, O=my-org, OID.2.5.4.17=
my-pc, STREET=my-address, L=my-locality, ST=my-province, C=my-country
Issuer: CN=hands-on-ca
$
```

Figure 18.17: Inspecting the certificate for minikube.me

The output shows that the certificate is issued for the common name `minikube.se` and that it is issued by our own CA, using its root certificate with the common name `hands-on-ca`.

As mentioned in *Chapter 17, Implementing Kubernetes Features to Simplify the System Landscape* (refer to the *Automating certificate provisioning* section), this self-signed CA needs to be replaced for production use cases with, for example, Let's Encrypt or another CA that the cert-manager can use to provision trusted certificates.

With the certificate configuration verified, let's move on to see how the Istio ingress gateway can protect microservices from unauthenticated requests.

Authenticating external requests using OAuth 2.0/OIDC access tokens

Istio Ingress Gateway can require and validate JWT-based OAuth 2.0/OIDC access tokens, in other words, protecting the microservices in the service mesh from external unauthenticated requests. For a recap on JWT, OAuth 2.0, and OIDC, refer to *Chapter 11, Securing Access to APIs* (see the *Protecting APIs using OAuth 2.0 and OpenID Connect* section). Istio can also be configured to perform authorization but, as mentioned in the *Introducing Istio API objects* section, we will not use it.

This is configured in the `common` Helm chart's template, `_istio_base.yaml`. The two manifests look like this:

```
apiVersion: security.istio.io/v1beta1
kind: RequestAuthentication
metadata:
  name: product-composite-request-authentication
spec:
  jwtRules:
  - forwardOriginalToken: true
    issuer: http://auth-server
```

```
    jwksUri: http://auth-server.hands-on.svc.cluster.local/oauth2/jwks
  selector:
    matchLabels:
      app.kubernetes.io/name: product-composite

---

apiVersion: security.istio.io/v1beta1
kind: AuthorizationPolicy
metadata:
  name: product-composite-require-jwt
spec:
  action: ALLOW
  rules:
  - {}
  selector:
    matchLabels:
      app.kubernetes.io/name: product-composite
```

From the manifests, we can see the following:

- The `RequestAuthentication` named `product-composite-request-authentication` requires a valid JWT-encoded access token for requests sent to the `product-composite` service:
  - It selects services that it performs request authentication for based on a label selector, `app.kubernetes.io/name: product-composite`.
  - It allows tokens from the issuer, `http://auth-server`.
  - It will use the `http://auth-server.hands-on.svc.cluster.local/oauth2/jwks` URL to fetch a JSON Web Key Set. The key set is used to validate the digital signature of the access tokens.
  - It will forward the access token to the underlying services, in our case the `product-composite` microservice.
- The `AuthorizationPolicy` named `product-composite-require-jwt` is configured to allow all requests to the `product-composite` service; it will not apply any authorization rules.

It can be a bit hard to understand whether Istio's `RequestAuthentication` is validating the access tokens or whether it is only the `product-composite` service that is performing the validation. One way to ensure that Istio is doing its job is to change the configuration of `RequestAuthentication` so that it always rejects access tokens.

To verify that `RequestAuthentication` is in action, apply the following commands:

1. Make a normal request:

```
ACCESS_TOKEN=$(curl -k https://writer:secret@minikube.me/oauth2/
token -d grant_type=client_credentials -s | jq .access_token -r)

echo ACCESS_TOKEN=$ACCESS_TOKEN

curl -k https://minikube.me/product-composite/1 -H
"Authorization: Bearer $ACCESS_TOKEN" -i
```

   Verify that it returns an HTTP response status code `200` (OK).

2. Edit the `RequestAuthentication` object and temporarily change the issuer, for example, to `http://auth-server-x`:

```
kubectl edit RequestAuthentication product-composite-request-
authentication
```

3. Verify the change:

```
kubectl get RequestAuthentication product-composite-request-
authentication -o yaml
```

   Verify that the issuer has been updated, in my case to `http://auth-server-x`.

4. Make the request again. It should fail with the HTTP response status code `401` (Unauthorized) and the error message `Jwt issuer is not configured`:

```
curl -k https://minikube.me/product-composite/1 -H
"Authorization: Bearer $ACCESS_TOKEN" -i
```

   Since it takes a few seconds for Istio to propagate the change, the new name of the issuer, you might need to repeat the command a couple of times before it fails.

   This proves that Istio is validating the access tokens!

5. Revert the changed name of the issuer back to `http://auth-server`:

```
kubectl edit RequestAuthentication product-composite-request-
authentication
```

6. Verify that the request works again. First, wait a few seconds for the change to be propagated. Then, run the command:

```
curl -k https://minikube.me/product-composite/1 -H
"Authorization: Bearer $ACCESS_TOKEN"
```

Suggested additional exercise: Try out the Auth0 OIDC provider, as described in *Chapter 11, Securing Access to APIs* (refer to the *Testing with an external OpenID Connect provider* section). Add your Auth0 provider to `jwt-authentication-policy.yml`. In my case, it appears as follows:

```
  - jwtRules:
      issuer: "https://dev-magnus.eu.auth0.com/"
      jwksUri: "https://dev-magnus.eu.auth0.com/.
well-known/jwks.json"
```

Now, let's move on to the last security mechanism that we will cover in Istio: the automatic protection of internal communication in the service mesh using mutual authentication, mTLS.

Protecting internal communication using mutual authentication (mTLS)

In this section, we will learn how Istio can be configured to automatically protect internal communication within the service mesh using **mutual authentication (mTLS)**. When using mutual authentication, not only does the service prove its identity by exposing a certificate, but the clients also prove their identity to the service by exposing a client-side certificate. This provides a higher level of security compared to normal TLS/HTTPS usage, where only the identity of the service is proven. Setting up and maintaining mutual authentication, that is, the provisioning of new, and rotating of outdated, certificates to the clients, is known to be complex and is therefore seldom used. Istio fully automates the provisioning and rotation of certificates for mutual authentication used for internal communication inside the service mesh. This makes it much easier to use mutual authentication compared to setting it up manually.

So, why should we use mutual authentication? Isn't it sufficient to protect external APIs with HTTPS and OAuth 2.0/OIDC access tokens?

As long as the attacks come through the external API, it might be sufficient. But what if a Pod inside the Kubernetes cluster becomes compromised? For example, if an attacker gains control over a Pod, they can start listening to traffic between other Pods in the Kubernetes cluster. If the internal communication is sent as plain text, it will be very easy for the attacker to gain access to sensitive information sent between Pods in the cluster. To minimize the damage caused by such an intrusion, mutual authentication can be used to prevent an attacker from eavesdropping on internal network traffic.

To enable the use of mutual authentication managed by Istio, Istio needs to be configured both on the server side, using a policy called `PeerAuthentication`, and on the client side, using a `DestinationRule`.

The policy is configured in the `common` Helm chart's template, `_istio_base.yaml`. The manifest looks like this:

```
apiVersion: security.istio.io/v1beta1
kind: PeerAuthentication
metadata:
  name: default
spec:
  mtls:
    mode: PERMISSIVE
```

As mentioned in the *Introducing Istio API objects* section, the `PeerAuthentication` policy is configured to allow both mTLS and plain HTTP requests using the `PERMISSIVE` mode. This enables Kubernetes to call liveness and readiness probes using plain HTTP.

We have also already met the `DestinationRule` manifests in the *Content in the _istio_dr_mutual_tls.yaml template* section. The central part of the `DestinationRule` manifests for requiring mTLS looks like this:

```
  trafficPolicy:
    tls:
      mode: ISTIO_MUTUAL
```

To verify that the internal communication is protected by mTLS, perform the following steps:

1. Ensure that the load tests started in the preceding *Observing the service mesh* section are still running and report `200` (`OK`).
2. Go to the Kiali graph in a web browser (`https://kiali.minikube.me`).
3. Click on the **Display** button and enable the **Security** label. The graph will show a padlock on all communication links that are protected by Istio's automated mutual authentication, as follows:

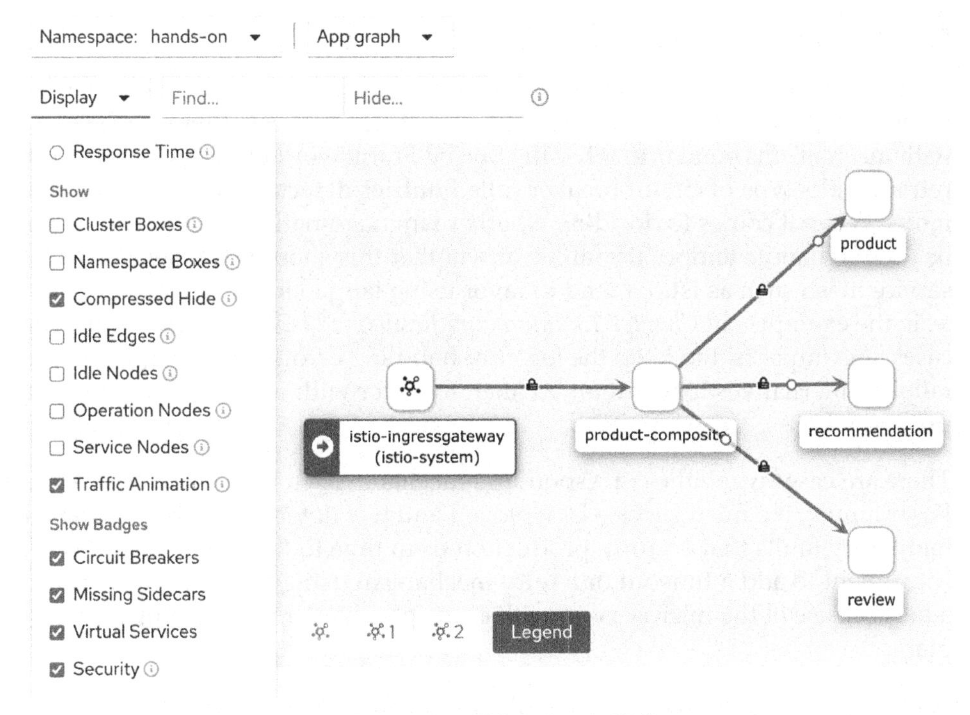

Figure 18.18: Inspecting mTLS settings in Kiali

Expect a padlock on all links.

Calls to RabbitMQ, MySQL, and MongoDB are not handled by Istio proxies, and therefore require manual configuration to be protected using TLS, if required.

With this, we have seen all three security mechanisms in Istio in action, and it is now time to see how Istio can help us to verify that a service mesh is resilient.

Ensuring that a service mesh is resilient

In this section, we will learn how to use Istio to ensure that a service mesh is resilient, that is, that it can handle temporary faults in a service mesh. Istio comes with mechanisms similar to what the Spring Framework offers in terms of timeouts, retries, and a type of circuit breaker called **outlier detection** to handle temporary faults. When it comes to deciding whether language-native mechanisms should be used to handle temporary faults, or whether this should be delegated to a service mesh such as Istio, I tend to favor using language-native mechanisms, as in the examples in *Chapter 13, Improving Resilience Using Resilience4j*. In many cases, it is important to keep the logic for handling errors, for example, handling fallback alternatives for a circuit breaker, together with other business logic for a microservice.

There are cases when the corresponding mechanisms in Istio could be of great help. For example, if a microservice is deployed and it is determined that it can't handle temporary faults that occur in production from time to time, then it can be very convenient to add a timeout or a retry mechanism using Istio instead of waiting for a new release of the microservice with corresponding error handling features put in place.

Another capability in the area of resilience that comes with Istio is the capability to inject faults and delays into an existing service mesh. Why might we want to do that?

Injecting faults and delays in a controlled way is very useful for verifying that the resilient capabilities in the microservices work as expected! We will try them out in this section, verifying that the retry, timeout, and circuit breaker in the `product-composite` microservice work as expected.

In *Chapter 13, Improving Resilience Using Resilience4j* (refer to the *Adding programmable delays and random errors* section), we added support for injecting faults and delays in the microservices source code. That source code should preferably be replaced by using Istio's capabilities for injecting faults and delays at runtime, as demonstrated in the following subsections.

We will begin by injecting faults to see whether the retry mechanisms in the `product-composite` microservice work as expected. After that, we will delay the responses from the `product` service and verify that the circuit breaker handles the delay as expected.

Testing resilience by injecting faults

Let's make the `product` service throw random errors and verify that the microservice landscape handles this correctly. We expect the retry mechanism in the `product-composite` microservice to kick in and retry the request until it succeeds or its limit of the maximum numbers of retries is reached. This will ensure that a short-lived fault does not affect the end user more than the delay introduced by the retry attempts. Refer to the *Adding a retry mechanism* section in *Chapter 13, Improving Resilience Using Resilience4j*, for a recap on the retry mechanism in the `product-composite` microservice.

Faults can be injected using a virtual service like `kubernetes/resilience-tests/product-virtual-service-with-faults.yml`. This appears as follows:

```
apiVersion: networking.istio.io/v1beta1
kind: VirtualService
metadata:
  name: product
spec:
  hosts:
    - product
  http:
  - route:
    - destination:
        host: product
    fault:
      abort:
        httpStatus: 500
        percentage:
          value: 20
```

The definition says that `20`% of the requests sent to the `product` service will be aborted with the HTTP status code `500` (Internal Server Error).

Perform the following steps to test this:

1. Ensure that the load tests using `siege`, as started in the *Observing the service mesh* section, are running.
2. Apply the fault injection with the following command:

```
kubectl apply -f kubernetes/resilience-tests/product-virtual-service-with-faults.yml
```

3. Monitor the output from the `siege` load tests tool. Expect output similar to the following:

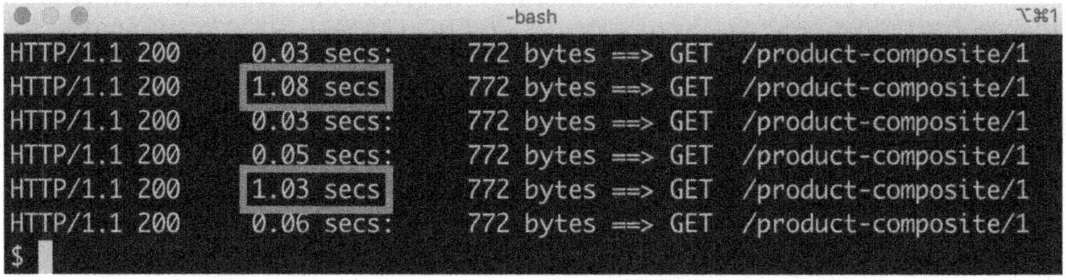

```
-bash
HTTP/1.1 200     0.03 secs:    772 bytes ==> GET  /product-composite/1
HTTP/1.1 200     1.08 secs     772 bytes ==> GET  /product-composite/1
HTTP/1.1 200     0.03 secs:    772 bytes ==> GET  /product-composite/1
HTTP/1.1 200     0.05 secs:    772 bytes ==> GET  /product-composite/1
HTTP/1.1 200     1.03 secs     772 bytes ==> GET  /product-composite/1
HTTP/1.1 200     0.06 secs:    772 bytes ==> GET  /product-composite/1
$
```

Figure 18.19: Observing the retry mechanism in action

From the sample output, we can see that all requests are still successful, in other words, status `200` (OK) is returned; however, some of them (20%) take an extra second to complete. This indicates that the retry mechanism in the `product-composite` microservice has kicked in and has retried a failed request to the `product` service.

4. Conclude the tests by removing the fault injection with the following command:

```
kubectl delete -f kubernetes/resilience-tests/product-virtual-
service-with-faults.yml
```

Let's now move on to the next section, where we will inject delays to trigger the circuit breaker.

Testing resilience by injecting delays

From *Chapter 13, Improving Resilience Using Resilience4j*, we know that a circuit breaker can be used to prevent problems due to the slow or complete lack of response of services after accepting requests.

Let's verify that the circuit breaker in the `product-composite` service works as expected by injecting a delay into the `product` service using Istio. A delay can be injected using a virtual service.

Refer to `kubernetes/resilience-tests/product-virtual-service-with-delay.yml`. Its code appears as follows:

```
apiVersion: networking.istio.io/v1beta1
kind: VirtualService
metadata:
  name: product
spec:
```

```
hosts:
  - product
http:
- route:
  - destination:
      host: product
  fault:
    delay:
      fixedDelay: 3s
      percent: 100
```

This definition says that all requests sent to the `product` service will be delayed by `3` seconds.

Requests sent to the `product` service from the `product-composite` service are configured to time out after 2 seconds. The circuit breaker is configured to open its circuit if 3 consecutive requests fail. When the circuit is open, it will fast-fail; in other words, it will immediately throw an exception, not attempting to call the underlying service. The business logic in the `product-composite` microservice will catch this exception and apply fallback logic. For a recap, see *Chapter 13, Improving Resilience Using Resilience4j* (refer to the *Adding a circuit breaker and a time limiter* section).

Perform the following steps to test the circuit breaker by injecting a delay:

1. Stop the load test by pressing *Ctrl* + *C* in the terminal window where `siege` is running.
2. Create a temporary delay in the `product` service with the following command:

   ```
   kubectl apply -f kubernetes/resilience-tests/product-virtual-service-with-delay.yml
   ```

3. Acquire an access token as follows:

   ```
   ACCESS_TOKEN=$(curl -k https://writer:secret@minikube.me/oauth2/token -d grant_type=client_credentials -s | jq .access_token -r)

   echo ACCESS_TOKEN=$ACCESS_TOKEN
   ```

4. Send six requests in a row:

   ```
   for i in {1..6}; do time curl -k https://minikube.me/product-composite/1 -H "Authorization: Bearer $ACCESS_TOKEN"; done
   ```

Expect the following:

a. The circuit opens up after the first three failed calls
b. The circuit breaker applies fast-fail logic for the last three calls
c. A fallback response is returned for the last three calls

The responses from the first 3 calls are expected to be a timeout-related error message, with a response time of 2 seconds (in other words, the timeout time). Expect responses for the first 3 calls along the lines of the following:

```
{..."message":"Did not observe any item or terminal signal within 2000ms in ..."}
real    0m2.051s
$
```

Figure 18.20: Observing timeouts

The responses from the last 3 calls are expected to come from the fallback logic with a short response time. Expect responses for the last 3 calls as follows:

```
{"productId":1,"name":"Fallback product1"...
real    0m0.011
$
```

Figure 18.21: Fallback method in action

5. Simulate the delay problem being fixed by removing the temporary delay with the following command:

```
kubectl delete -f kubernetes/resilience-tests/product-virtual-
service-with-delay.yml
```

6. Verify that correct answers are returned again, and without any delay, by sending a new request using the `for` loop command in *step 4*.

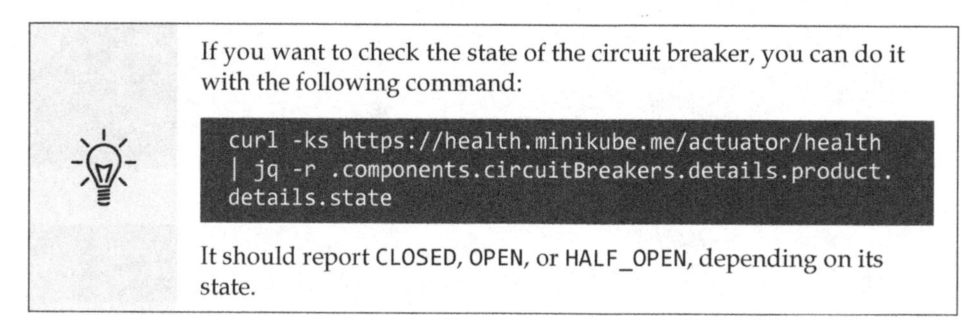

If you want to check the state of the circuit breaker, you can do it with the following command:

```
curl -ks https://health.minikube.me/actuator/health
| jq -r .components.circuitBreakers.details.product.
details.state
```

It should report `CLOSED`, `OPEN`, or `HALF_OPEN`, depending on its state.

This proves that the circuit breaker reacts as expected when we inject a delay using Istio. This concludes testing the features in Istio that can be used to verify that the microservice landscape is resilient. The final feature we will explore in Istio is its support for traffic management; we will see how it can be used to enable deployments with zero downtime.

Performing zero-downtime updates

As mentioned in *Chapter 16, Deploying Our Microservices to Kubernetes*, being able to deploy an update without downtime becomes crucial with a growing number of autonomous microservices that are updated independently of one another.

In this section, we will learn about Istio's traffic management and routing capabilities and how they can be used to perform deployments of new versions of microservices without requiring any downtime. In *Chapter 15, Introduction to Kubernetes*, we learned that Kubernetes can be used to perform a rolling upgrade without requiring any downtime. Using the Kubernetes rolling upgrade mechanism automates the entire process, but unfortunately provides no option to test the new version before all users are routed to it.

Using Istio, we can deploy the new version, but initially route all users to the existing version (called the **old** version in this chapter). After that, we can use Istio's fine-grained routing mechanism to control how users are routed to the new and the old versions. We will see how two popular upgrade strategies can be implemented using Istio:

- **Canary deploys**: When using canary deploys, all users are routed to the old version, except for a group of selected test users who are routed to the new version. When the test users have approved the new version, regular users can be routed to the new version using a blue/green deploy.
- **Blue/green deploys**: Traditionally, a blue/green deploy means that all users are switched to either the blue or the green version, one being the new version and the other being the old version. If something goes wrong when switching over to the new version, it is very simple to switch back to the old version. Using Istio, this strategy can be refined by gradually shifting users over to the new version, for example, starting with 20% of the users and then slowly increasing the percentage. At all times, it is very easy to route all users back to the old version if a fatal error is revealed in the new version.

As already stated in *Chapter 16*, it is important to remember that a prerequisite for these types of upgrade strategies is that the upgrade is **backward-compatible**. Such an upgrade is compatible both in terms of APIs and message formats, which are used to communicate with other services and database structures. If the new version of the microservice requires changes to external APIs, message formats, or database structures that the old version can't handle, these upgrade strategies can't be applied.

We will go through the following deploy scenario:

- We will start by deploying the `v1` and `v2` versions of the microservices, with routing configured to send all requests to the `v1` version of the microservices.
- Next, we will allow a test group to run canary tests; that is, we'll verify the new `v2` versions of the microservices. To simplify the tests somewhat, we will only deploy new versions of the core microservices, that is, the `product`, `recommendation`, and `review` microservices.
- Finally, we will start to move regular users over to the new versions using a blue/green deploy; initially, a small percentage of users and then, over time, more and more users until, eventually, they are all routed to the new version. We will also see how we can quickly switch back to the `v1` version if a fatal error is detected in the new `v2` version.

Let's first see what changes need to be applied to the source code to be able to deploy and route traffic to two concurrent versions, `v1` and `v2`, of the core microservices.

Source code changes

To be able to run multiple versions of a microservice concurrently, the Deployment objects and their corresponding Pods must have different names, for example, `product-v1` and `product-v2`. There must, however, be only one Kubernetes Service object per microservice. All traffic to a specific microservice always goes through the same Service object, irrespective of what version of the Pod the request will be routed to in the end. To configure the actual routing rules for canary tests and blue/green deployment, Istio's `VirtualService` and `DestinationRule` objects are used. Finally, the `values.yaml` file in the `prod-env` Helm chart is used to specify the versions of each microservice that will be used in the production environment.

Let's go through the details for each definition in the following subsections:

- Virtual services and destination rules
- Deployments and services
- Tying things together in the `prod-env` Helm chart

Virtual services and destination rules

To split the traffic between two versions of a microservice, we need to specify the weight distribution between the two versions in a `VirtualService`, on the sender side. The virtual service will spread the traffic between two `Subsets`, called `old` and `new`. The exact meaning of the `new` and `old` subset is defined in a corresponding `DestinationRule`, on the receiver side. It uses `labels` to determine which Pods run the old and new versions of the microservice.

To support canary tests, a routing rule is required in the virtual services that always routes the canary testers to the `new` subset. To identify canary testers, we will assume that requests from a canary tester contain an HTTP header named `X-group` with the value `test`.

A template has been added to the `common` Helm chart for creating a set of virtual services that can split the traffic between two versions of a microservice. The template is named `_istio_vs_green_blue_deploy.yaml` and looks like this:

```
{{- define "common.istio_vs_green_blue_deploy" -}}
{{- range $name := .Values.virtualServices }}
apiVersion: networking.istio.io/v1beta1
kind: VirtualService
metadata:
  name: {{ $name }}
spec:
  hosts:
  - {{ $name }}
  http:
  - match:
    - headers:
        X-group:
          exact: test
    route:
    - destination:
        host: {{ $name }}
        subset: new
  - route:
    - destination:
        host: {{ $name }}
        subset: old
      weight: 100
    - destination:
        host: {{ $name }}
        subset: new
      weight: 0
---
{{- end -}}
{{- end -}}
```

From the template, we can see the following:

- The `range` directive loops over the elements defined in the `virtualServices` variable.
- The `hosts` field in the `spec` part of the manifest is used to specify the names of the Kubernetes service that this `VirtualService` will apply to.
- In the `http` section, three routing destinations are declared:
    - One route matching the canary testers' HTTP header, `X-group`, set to `test`. This route always sends the requests to the `new` subset
    - One route destination for the `old` subset and one for the `new` subset
    - The `weight` is specified as a percentage and the sum of the weights will always be 100
    - All traffic is initially routed to the `old` subset

To be able to route canary testers to the new versions based on header-based routing, the `product-composite` microservice has been updated to forward the HTTP header, `X-group`. Refer to the `getCompositeProduct()` method in the `se.magnus.microservices.composite.product.services.ProductCompositeServiceImpl` class for details.

For the destination rules, we will reuse the template introduced in the *Content in the _istio_dr_mutual_tls.yaml template* section above. This template will be used by the `prod-env` Helm chart to specify the versions of the microservices to be used. This is described in the *Tying things together in the prod-env Helm chart* section below.

Deployments and services

To make it possible for a destination rule to identify the version of a Pod based on its labels, a `version` label has been added in the template for deployments in the `common` Helm chart, `_deployment.yaml`. Its value is set to the `tag` of the Pod's Docker image. We will use the Docker image tags `v1` and `v2`, so that will also be the value of the `version` label. The added line looks like this:

```
version: {{ .Values.image.tag }}
```

To give the Pods and their Deployment objects names that contain their version, their default names have been overridden in the `prod-env` chart. In their `values.yaml` files, the `fullnameOverride` field is used to specify a name that includes version info. This is done for the three core microservices and looks like this:

```
product:
  fullnameOverride: product-v1
```

```
recommendation:
  fullnameOverride: recommendation-v1

review:
  fullnameOverride: review-v1
```

An undesired side effect of this is that the corresponding Service objects will also get a name that includes the version info. As explained above, we need to have one service that can route requests to the different versions of the Pods. To avoid this naming problem, the Service template, `_service.yaml`, in the `common` Helm chart, is updated to use the `common.name` template instead of the `common.fullname` template used previously in *Chapter 17*.

Finally, to be able to deploy multiple versions of the three core microservices, their Helm charts have been duplicated in the `kubernetes/helm/components` folder. The name of the new charts is suffixed with `-green`. The only difference compared to the existing charts is that they don't include the Service template from the `common` chart, avoiding the creation of two Service objects per core microservice. The new charts are named `product-green`, `recommendation-green`, and `review-green`.

Tying things together in the prod-env Helm chart

The `prod-env` Helm chart includes the `_istio_vs_green_blue_deploy.yaml` template from the `common` Helm chart, as well as the templates included by the `dev-env` chart; see the *Creating the service mesh* section.

The three new `*-green` Helm charts for the core microservices are added as dependencies to the `Chart.yaml` file.

In its `values.yaml` file, everything is tied together. From the previous section, we have seen how the `v1` versions of the core microservices are defined with names that include version info.

For the `v2` versions, the three new `*-green` Helm charts are used. The values are the same as for the `v1` versions except for the name and Docker image tag. For example, the configuration of the `v2` version of the `product` microservice looks like this:

```
product-green:
  fullnameOverride: product-v2
  image:
    tag: v2
```

To declare virtual services for the three core microservices, the following declaration is used:

```
virtualServices:
  - product
  - recommendation
  - review
```

Finally, the destination rules are declared in a similar way as in the `dev-env` Helm chart. The main difference is that we now use the subsets to declare the actual versions that should be used when traffic is routed by the virtual services to either the old or the new subset. For example, the destination rule for the `product` microservice is declared like this:

```
destinationRules:
  - ...
  - name: product
    subsets:
    - labels:
        version: v1
      name: old
    - labels:
        version: v2
      name: new
...
```

From the declaration above, we can see that traffic sent to the `old` subset is directed to `v1` Pods of the `product` microservice and to `v2` Pods for the `new` subset.

For details, see the file in the `prod-env` chart available in the `kubernetes/helm/environments/prod-env` folder.

Note that this is where we declare for the production environment what the existing (`old`) and the coming (`new`) versions are, `v1` and `v2` in this scenario. In a future scenario, where it is time to upgrade `v2` to `v3`, the old subset should be updated to use `v2` and the new subset should use `v3`.

Now, we have seen all the changes to the source code and we are ready to deploy `v1` and `v2` versions of the microservices.

Deploying v1 and v2 versions of the microservices with routing to the v1 version

To be able to test the `v1` and `v2` versions of the microservices, we need to remove the development environment we have been using earlier in this chapter and create a production environment where we can deploy the `v1` and `v2` versions of the microservices.

To achieve this, run the following commands:

1. Uninstall the development environment:

```
helm uninstall hands-on-dev-env
```

2. To monitor the termination of Pods in the development environment, run the following command until it reports `No resources found in hands-on namespace.`:

```
kubectl get pods
```

3. Start MySQL, MongoDB, and RabbitMQ outside of Kubernetes:

```
eval $(minikube docker-env)
docker-compose up -d mongodb mysql rabbitmq
```

4. Tag Docker images with `v1` and `v2` versions:

```
docker tag hands-on/auth-server hands-on/auth-server:v1
docker tag hands-on/product-composite-service hands-on/product-composite-service:v1
docker tag hands-on/product-service hands-on/product-service:v1
docker tag hands-on/recommendation-service hands-on/recommendation-service:v1
docker tag hands-on/review-service hands-on/review-service:v1

docker tag hands-on/product-service hands-on/product-service:v2
docker tag hands-on/recommendation-service hands-on/recommendation-service:v2
docker tag hands-on/review-service hands-on/review-service:v2
```

The `v1` and `v2` versions of the microservices will be the same versions of the microservices in this test. But it doesn't matter to Istio, so we can use this simplified approach to test Istio's routing capabilities.

5. Deploy the system landscape using Helm and wait for all deployments to complete:

```
helm install hands-on-prod-env \
  kubernetes/helm/environments/prod-env \
  -n hands-on --wait
```

6. Once the deployment is complete, verify that we have `v1` and `v2` Pods up and running for the three core microservices with the following command:

```
kubectl get pods
```

Expect a response like this:

```
NAME                                   READY   STATUS    RESTARTS
auth-server-7dbbc7d489-mjktc           2/2     Running   0
product-composite-5cd45c94b8-v7qzq     2/2     Running   2
product-v1-5c866949d7-vmlpj            2/2     Running   0
product-v2-567d7bfb78-cmp99            2/2     Running   0
recommendation-v1-5f67c5b75-xk2sb      2/2     Running   0
recommendation-v2-649cf6cf44-xh6pc     2/2     Running   0
review-v1-6489696488-jjr4c             2/2     Running   0
review-v2-547cd7f6bc-zlbl9             2/2     Running   0
$
```

Figure 18.22: v1 and v2 Pods deployed at the same time

7. Run the usual tests to verify that everything works:

```
./test-em-all.bash
```

Unfortunately, the tests will fail initially on an error message like:

```
- Response Body: Jwks doesn't have key to match kid or alg from
Jwt
```

This error is caused by the Istio daemon, `istiod`, caching the JWKS from the auth server in the development environment. The auth server in the production environment will have a new JWKS, but the same identity to `istiod`, so it tries to reuse the old JWKS, causing this failure. Istio caches a JWKS for 20 minutes, so you can simply take a long coffee break and the issue will be gone when you are back. Or you can empty the cache by restarting `istiod` a few times (2 or 3 times should be sufficient). Run the following command to restart the `istiod` Pod:

```
kubectl -n istio-system delete pod -l app=istiod
```

If the tests still fail once the issue with cached JWKS has disappeared, with errors such as this:

```
Test FAILED, EXPECTED VALUE: 3, ACTUAL VALUE: 0, WILL ABORT
```

Then simply rerun the command and it should run fine! These errors are secondary failures caused by the original error caused by the JWKS cache.

Expect output that is similar to what we have seen from the previous chapters:

```
-bash
$ ./test-em-all.bash
...
Wait for: curl -k https://health.minikube.me/actuator/health...
DONE, continues...
...
Test OK (HTTP Code: 200)
...
End, all tests OK: Thu May 20 14:09:30 CEST 2021
$
```

Figure 18.23: Tests run successfully

We are now ready to run some **zero-downtime deploy** tests. Let's begin by verifying that all traffic goes to the `v1` version of the microservices!

Verifying that all traffic initially goes to the v1 version of the microservices

To verify that all requests are routed to the `v1` version of the microservices, we will start up the load test tool, `siege`, and then observe the traffic that flows through the service mesh using Kiali.

Perform the following steps:

1. Get a new access token and start the `siege` load test tool, with the following commands:

```
ACCESS_TOKEN=$(curl -k https://writer:secret@minikube.me/oauth2/
token -d grant_type=client_credentials -s | jq .access_token -r)

echo ACCESS_TOKEN=$ACCESS_TOKEN

siege https://minikube.me/product-composite/1 -H "Authorization:
Bearer $ACCESS_TOKEN" -c1 -d1 -v
```

2. Go to the **Graph** view in Kiali's web UI (`https://kiali.minikube.me`):
    a. Click on the **Display** menu button and deselect **Service Nodes**
    b. Click on the **App graph** menu button and select **Versioned app graph**
    c. Expect only traffic to the **v1** version of the microservices, as follows:

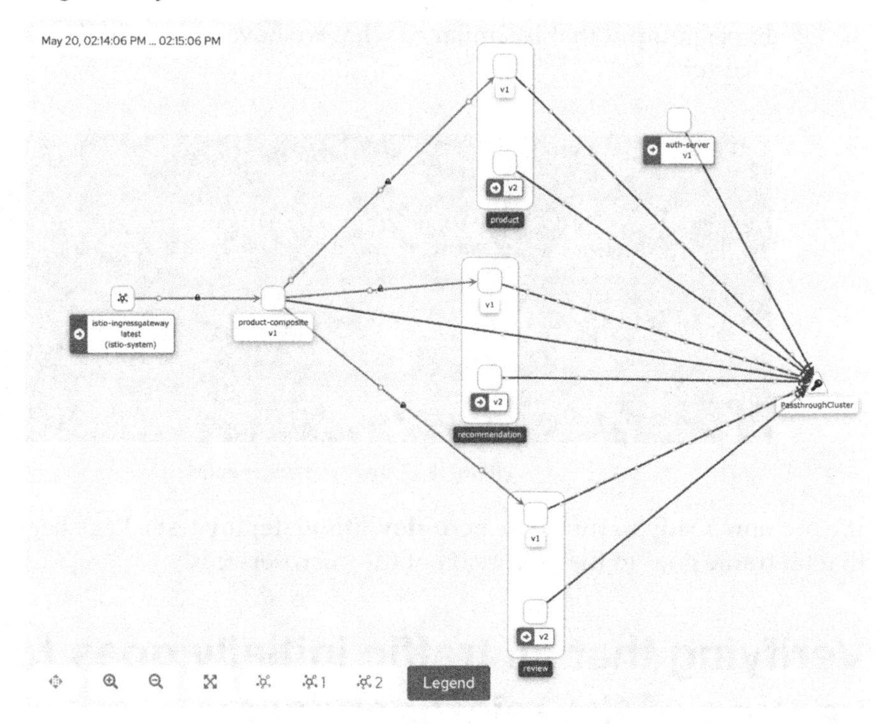

Figure 18.24: All requests go to the v1 Pods

This means that, even though the `v2` versions of the microservices are deployed, they do not get any traffic routed to them. Let's now try out canary tests where selected test users are allowed to try out the `v2` versions of the microservices!

Running canary tests

To run a canary test so that some users are routed to the new versions while all other users are still routed to the old versions of the deployed microservices, we need to add the `X-group` HTTP header set to the value `test` in our requests sent to the external API.

To see which version of a microservice served a request, the `serviceAddresses` field in the response can be inspected. The `serviceAddresses` field contains the hostname of each service that took part in creating the response. The hostname is equal to the name of the Pod, so we can find the version in the hostname; for example, `product-v1-...` for a `product` service of version `v1`, and `product-v2-...` for a `product` service of version `v2`.

Let's begin by sending a normal request and verifying that it is the `v1` versions of the microservices that respond to our request. Next, we'll send a request with the `X-group` HTTP header set to the value `test`, and verify that the new `v2` versions are responding.

To do this, perform the following steps:

1. Perform a normal request to verify that the request is routed to the `v1` version of the microservices by using `jq` to filter out the `serviceAddresses` field in the response:

```
ACCESS_TOKEN=$(curl -k https://writer:secret@minikube.me/oauth2/
token -d grant_type=client_credentials -s | jq .access_token -r)

echo ACCESS_TOKEN=$ACCESS_TOKEN

curl -ks https://minikube.me/product-composite/1 -H
"Authorization: Bearer $ACCESS_TOKEN" | jq .serviceAddresses
```

   Expect a response along the lines of the following:

```
-bash
{
  "cmp": "product-composite-5cd45c94b8-v7qzq/172.17.0.10:80",
  "pro": "product-v1-5c866949d7-vmlpj/172.17.0.16:80",
  "rev": "review-v1-6489696488-jjr4c/172.17.0.11:80",
  "rec": "recommendation-v1-5f67c5b75-xk2sb/172.17.0.12:80"
}
$
```

   Figure 18.25: All requests go to the v1 Pods

   As expected, all three core services are `v1` versions of the microservices.

2. If we add the `X-group=test` header, we expect the request to be served by `v2` versions of the core microservices. Run the following command:

```
curl -ks https://minikube.me/product-composite/1 -H
"Authorization: Bearer $ACCESS_TOKEN" -H "X-group: test" | jq
.serviceAddresses
```

Expect a response similar to the following:

```
{
  "cmp": "product-composite-5cd45c94b8-v7qzq/172.17.0.10:80",
  "pro": "product-v2-567d7bfb78-cmp99/172.17.0.19:80",
  "rev": "review-v2-547cd7f6bc-zlbl9/172.17.0.18:80",
  "rec": "recommendation-v2-649cf6cf44-xh6pc/172.17.0.17:80"
}
$
```

Figure 18.26: Setting HTTP header X-group=test makes the requests go to the v2 Pods

As expected, all three core microservices that respond are now `v2` versions; as a canary tester, we are routed to the new `v2` versions!

Given that the canary tests returned the expected results, we are ready to allow normal users to be routed to the new `v2` versions using blue/green deployment.

Running blue/green deployment

To route a portion of the normal users to the new `v2` versions of the microservices, we need to modify the weight distribution in the virtual services. They are currently 100/0; in other words, all traffic is routed to the old `v1` versions. We can achieve this, as we did before, by editing the manifest files of the virtual services and executing a `kubectl apply` command to make the changes take effect. As an alternative, we can use the `kubectl patch` command to change the weight distribution directly on the virtual service objects in the Kubernetes API server.

I find the `patch` command useful when making a number of changes to the same objects to try something out, for example, to change the weight distribution in the routing rules. In this section, we will use the `kubectl patch` command to quickly change the weight distribution in the routing rules between the `v1` and `v2` versions of the microservices. To get the state of a virtual service after a few `kubectl patch` commands have been executed, a command such as `kubectl get vs NNN -o yaml` can be issued. For example, to get the state of the virtual service of the product microservice, issue the following command: `kubectl get vs product -o yaml`.

Since we haven't used the `kubectl patch` command before and it can be a bit involved to start with, let's undertake a short introduction to see how it works before we perform the green/blue deploy.

A short introduction to the kubectl patch command

The `kubectl patch` command can be used to update specific fields in an existing object in the Kubernetes API server. We will try the patch command on the virtual service for the review microservice, named `review`. The relevant parts of the definition for the virtual service, `review`, appear as follows:

```
spec:
  http:
  - match:
    ...
  - route:
    - destination:
        host: review
        subset: old
      weight: 100
    - destination:
        host: review
        subset: new
      weight: 0
```

A sample patch command that changes the weight distribution of the routing to the `v1` and `v2` Pods in the `review` microservice appears as follows:

```
kubectl patch virtualservice review --type=json -p='[
  {"op": "add", "path": "/spec/http/1/route/0/weight", "value": 80},
  {"op": "add", "path": "/spec/http/1/route/1/weight", "value": 20}
]'
```

The command will configure the routing rules of the `review` microservice to route 80% of the requests to the old version, and 20% of the requests to the new version.

To specify that the `weight` value should be changed in the `review` virtual service, the `/spec/http/1/route/0/weight` path is given for the old version, and `/spec/http/1/route/1/weight` for the new version.

The `0` and `1` in the path are used to specify the index of array elements in the definition of the virtual service. For example, `http/1` means the second element in the array under the `http` element. See the definition of the preceding `review` virtual service.

From the definition, we can see that the first element with index `0` is the `match` element, which we will not change. The second element is the `route` element, which we want to change.

Now that we know a bit more about the `kubectl patch` command, we are ready to test a blue/green deployment.

Performing the blue/green deployment

It is time to gradually move more and more users to the new versions using blue/green deployment. To perform the deployment, run the following steps:

1. Ensure that the load test tool, `siege`, is still running.

   It was started in the preceding *Verifying that all traffic initially goes to the v1 version of the microservices* section.
2. To allow 20% of users to be routed to the new `v2` version of the review microservice, we can patch the virtual service and change weights with the following command:

   ```
   kubectl patch virtualservice review --type=json -p='[
     {"op": "add", "path": "/spec/http/1/route/0/weight", "value":
     80},
     {"op": "add", "path": "/spec/http/1/route/1/weight", "value":
     20}
   ]'
   ```
3. To observe the change in the routing rule, go to the Kiali web UI (`https://kiali.minikube.me`) and select the **Graph** view.
4. Click on the **Display** menu and change the edge labels to **Requests Distribution**.
5. Wait for a minute before the metrics are updated in Kiali so that we can observe the change. Expect the graph in Kiali to show something like the following:

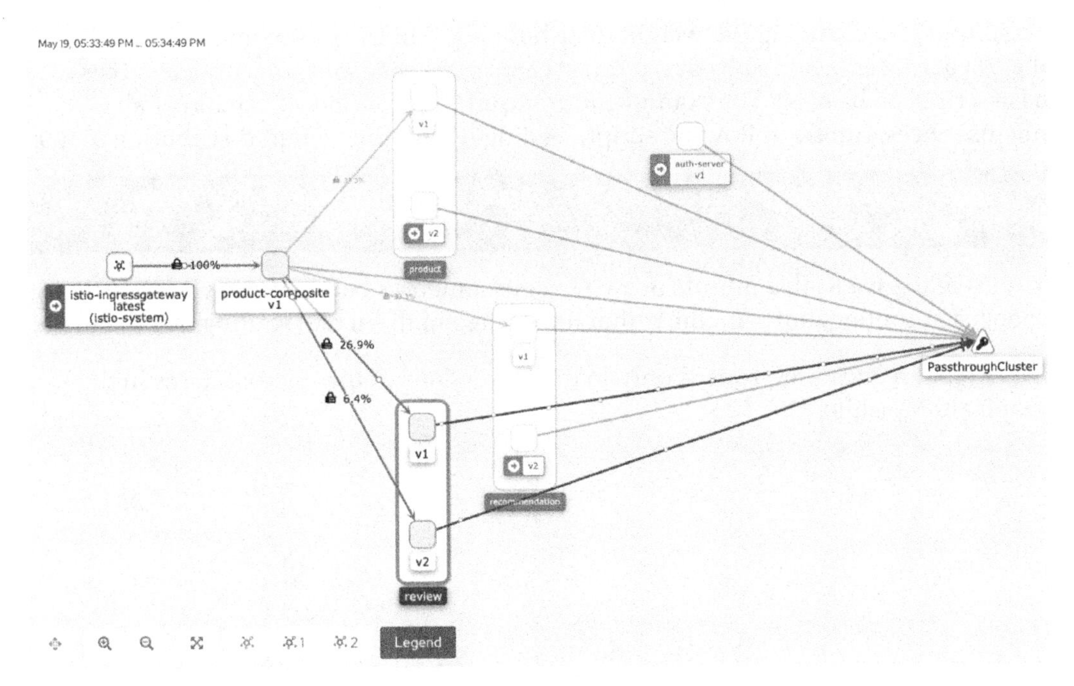

Figure 18.27: 80% goes to v1 services and 20% goes to v2 services

Depending on how long you have waited, the graph might look a bit different! In the screenshot, we can see that Istio now routes traffic to both the `v1` and `v2` versions of the `review` microservice.

Of the 33% of the traffic that is sent to the `review` microservice from the `product-composite` microservice, 6.4% is routed to the new `v2` Pod, and 26.9% to the old `v1` Pod. This means that 6.4/33 = 19% of the requests are routed to the `v2` Pod, and 26.9/33 = 81% to the `v1` Pod. This is in line with the 20/80 distribution we have requested.

Please feel free to try out the preceding `kubectl patch` command to affect the routing rules for the other core microservices, `product` and `recommendation`.

To simplifying changing the weight distribution for all three core microservices, the `./kubernetes/routing-tests/split-traffic-between-old-and-new-services.bash` script can be used. For example, to route all traffic to the `v2` version of all microservices, run the following script, feeding it with the weight distribution `0 100`:

```
./kubernetes/routing-tests/split-traffic-between-old-and-new-services.
bash 0 100
```

You have to give Kiali a minute or two to collect metrics before it can visualize the changes in routing, but remember that the change in the actual routing is immediate!

Expect that requests are routed only to the `v2` versions of the microservices in the graph after a while:

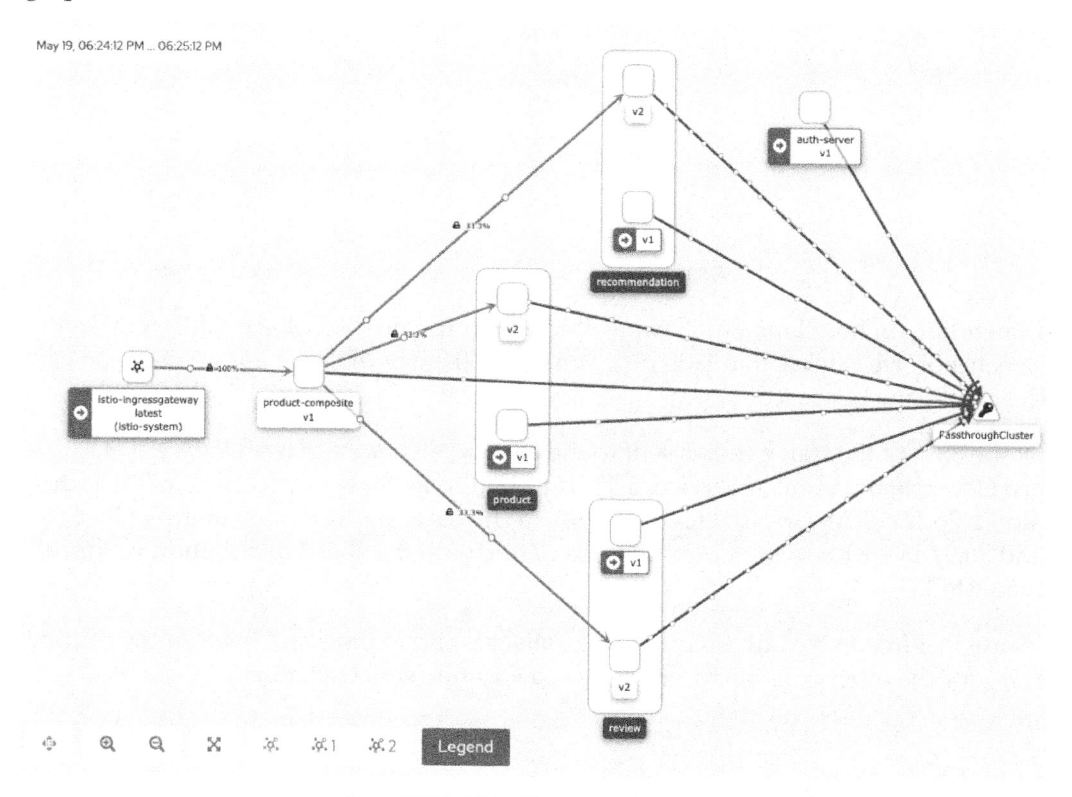

Figure 18.28: All traffic goes to v2 services

Depending on how long you have waited, the graph might look a bit different!

If something goes terribly wrong following the upgrade to `v2`, the following command can be executed to revert all traffic back to the `v1` version of all microservices:

```
./kubernetes/routing-tests/split-traffic-between-old-and-new-services.
bash 100 0
```

After a short while, the graph in Kiali should look like the screenshot in the previous *Verifying that all traffic initially goes to the v1 version of the microservices* section, showing all requests going to the `v1` version of all microservices again.

This concludes the introduction to the service mesh concept and Istio as an implementation of it.

Before we wrap up the chapter, let's recap how we can run tests in Docker Compose to ensure that the source code of our microservices does not rely on either the deployment in Kubernetes or the presence of Istio.

Running tests with Docker Compose

As mentioned a few times now, it is important to ensure that the source code of the microservices doesn't become dependent on a platform such as Kubernetes or Istio from a functional perspective.

To verify that the microservices work as expected without the presence of Kubernetes and Istio, run the tests as described in *Chapter 17* (refer to the *Testing with Docker Compose* section). Since the default values of the test script, `test-em-all.bash`, have been changed, as described previously in the *Running commands to create the service mesh* section, the following parameters must be set when using Docker Compose: `USE_K8S=false HOST=localhost PORT=8443 HEALTH_URL=https://localhost:8443`. For example, to run the tests using the default Docker Compose file, `docker-compose.yml`, run the following command:

```
USE_K8S=false HOST=localhost PORT=8443 HEALTH_URL=https://
localhost:8443 ./test-em-all.bash start stop
```

The test script should, as before, begin by starting all containers; it should then run the tests, and, finally, stop all containers. For details of the expected output, see *Chapter 17* (refer to the *Verifying that the microservices work without Kubernetes* section).

After successfully executing the tests using Docker Compose, we have verified that the microservices are dependent on neither Kubernetes nor Istio from a functional perspective. These tests conclude the chapter on using Istio as a service mesh.

Summary

In this chapter, we learned about the service mesh concept and Istio, an open source implementation of the concept. A service mesh provides capabilities for handling challenges in a system landscape of microservices in areas such as security, policy enforcement, resilience, and traffic management. A service mesh can also be used to make a system landscape of microservices observable by visualizing the traffic that flows through the microservices.

For observability, Istio can be integrated with Kiali, Jaeger, and Grafana (more on Grafana and Prometheus in *Chapter 20, Monitoring Microservices*). When it comes to security, Istio can be configured to use a certificate to protect external APIs with HTTPS and require that external requests contain valid JWT-based OAuth 2.0/OIDC access tokens. Finally, Istio can be configured to automatically protect internal communication using mutual authentication (mTLS).

For resilience and robustness, Istio comes with mechanisms for handling retries, timeouts, and an outlier detection mechanism similar to a circuit breaker. In many cases, it is preferable to implement these resilience capabilities in the source code of the microservices, if possible. The ability in Istio to inject faults and delays is very useful for verifying that the microservices in the service mesh work together as a resilient and robust system landscape. Istio can also be used to handle zero-downtime deployments. Using its fine-grained routing rules, both canary and blue/green deployments can be performed.

One important area that we haven't covered yet is how to collect and analyze log files created by all microservice instances. In the next chapter, we will see how this can be done using a popular stack of tools, known as the EFK stack, based on Elasticsearch, Fluentd, and Kibana.

Questions

1. What is the purpose of a proxy component in a service mesh?
2. What's the difference between a control plane and a data plane in a service mesh?
3. What is the `istioctl kube-inject` command used for?
4. What is the `minikube tunnel` command used for?

5. What tools are Istio integrated with for observability?
6. What configuration is required to make Istio protect communication within the service mesh using mutual authentication?
7. What can the `abort` and `delay` elements in a virtual service be used for?
8. What configuration is required to set up a blue/green deploy scenario?

19

Centralized Logging with the EFK Stack

In this chapter, we will learn how to collect and store log records from microservice instances, as well as how to search and analyze log records. As we mentioned in *Chapter 1, Introduction to Microservices*, it is difficult to get an overview of what is going on in a system landscape of microservices when each microservice instance writes log records to its local filesystem. We need a component that can collect the log records from the microservice's local filesystem and store them in a central database for analysis, search, and visualization. A popular open source-based solution for this is based on the following tools:

- **Elasticsearch**, a distributed database with great capabilities for searching and analyzing large datasets
- **Fluentd**, a data collector that can be used to collect log records from various sources, filter and transform the collected information, and finally send it to various consumers, for example, Elasticsearch
- **Kibana**, a graphical frontend to Elasticsearch that can be used to visualize search results and run analyses of the collected log records

Together, these tools are called the **EFK stack**, named after the initials of each tool.

The following topics will be covered in this chapter:

- Configuring Fluentd
- Deploying the EFK stack on Kubernetes for development and test usage

- Analyzing the collected log records
- Discovering log records from the microservices and finding related log records
- Performing root cause analysis

Technical requirements

For instructions on how to install the tools used in this book and how to access the source code for this book, see:

- *Chapter 21* for macOS
- *Chapter 22* for Windows

The code examples in this chapter all come from the source code in `$BOOK_HOME/Chapter19`.

If you want to view the changes applied to the source code in this chapter, that is, see the changes we made so that we can use the EFK stack for centralized log analysis, you can compare it with the source code for *Chapter 18, Using a Service Mesh to Improve Observability and Management*. You can use your favorite `diff` tool and compare the two folders, `$BOOK_HOME/Chapter18` and `$BOOK_HOME/Chapter19`.

Introducing Fluentd

In this section, we will learn the basics of how to configure Fluentd. Before we do that, let's learn a bit about the background of Fluentd and how it works on a high level.

Overview of Fluentd

Historically, one of the most popular open source stacks for handling log records has been the ELK stack from Elastic (`https://www.elastic.co`), based on Elasticsearch, Logstash (used for log collection and transformation), and Kibana. Since Logstash runs on a Java VM, it requires a relatively large amount of memory. Over the years, a number of open source alternatives have been developed that require significantly less memory than Logstash, one of them being Fluentd (`https://www.fluentd.org`).

Fluentd is managed by the **Cloud Native Computing Foundation** (**CNCF**) (`https://www.cncf.io`), the same organization that manages the Kubernetes project. Therefore, Fluentd has become a natural choice as an open source-based log collector that runs in Kubernetes. Together with Elastic and Kibana, it forms the EFK stack.

CNCF maintains a list of alternative products for several categories, for example for logging. For alternatives to Fluentd listed by CNCF, see `https://landscape.cncf.io/card-mode?category=logging&grouping=category`.

Fluentd is written in a mix of C and Ruby, using C for the performance-critical parts and Ruby where flexibility is of more importance, for example, allowing the simple installation of third-party plugins using Ruby's `gem install` command.

A log record is processed as an event in Fluentd and consists of the following information:

- A `time` field describing when the log record was created
- A `tag` field that identifies what type of log record it is – the tag is used by Fluentd's routing engine to determine how a log record will be processed
- A `record` that contains the actual log information, which is stored as a JSON object

A Fluentd configuration file is used to tell Fluentd how to collect, process, and finally send log records to various targets, such as Elasticsearch. A configuration file consists of the following types of core elements:

- `<source>`: Source elements describe where Fluentd will collect log records, for example, tailing log files that have been written to by Docker containers.

  Tailing a log file means monitoring what is written to a log file. A frequently used Unix/Linux tool for monitoring what is appended to a file is named `tile`.

  Source elements typically tag the log records, describing the type of log record. They could, for example, be used to tag log records to state that they come from containers running in Kubernetes.
- `<filter>`: Filter elements are used to process the log records. For example, a filter element can parse log records that come from Spring Boot-based microservices and extract interesting parts of the log message into separate fields in the log record. Extracting information into separate fields in the log record makes the information searchable by Elasticsearch. A filter element selects the log records to process based on their tags.

- `<match>`: Match elements decide where to send log records, acting as output elements. They are used to perform two main tasks:
  - Sending processed log records to targets such as Elasticsearch.
  - Routing to decide how to process log records. A routing rule can rewrite the tag and re-emit the log record into the Fluentd routing engine for further processing. A routing rule is expressed as an embedded `<rule>` element inside the `<match>` element. Output elements decide what log records to process, in the same way as a filter: based on the tag of the log records.

Fluentd comes with a number of built-in and external third-party plugins that are used by the source, filter, and output elements. We will see some of them in action when we walk through the configuration file in the next section. For more information on the available plugins, see Fluentd's documentation, which is available at `https://docs.fluentd.org`.

With this overview of Fluentd out of the way, we are ready to see how Fluentd can be configured to process the log records from our microservices.

Configuring Fluentd

The configuration of Fluentd is based on the configuration files from a Fluentd project on GitHub, `fluentd-kubernetes-daemonset`. The project contains Fluentd configuration files for how to collect log records from containers that run in Kubernetes and how to send them to Elasticsearch once they have been processed. We will reuse this configuration without changes, and it will simplify our own configuration to a great extent. The Fluentd configuration files can be found at `https://github.com/fluent/fluentd-kubernetes-daemonset/tree/master/archived-image/v1.4/debian-elasticsearch/conf`.

The configuration files that provide this functionality are `kubernetes.conf` and `fluent.conf`. The `kubernetes.conf` configuration file contains the following information:

- Source elements that tail container log files and log files from processes that run outside of Kubernetes, for example, `kubelet` and the Docker daemon. The source elements also tag the log records from Kubernetes with the full name of the log file with "`/`" replaced by "`.`" and prefixed with `kubernetes`. Since the tag is based on the full filename, the name contains the name of the Namespace, Pod, and container, among other things. So, the tag is very useful for finding log records of interest by matching the tag.

For example, the tag from the `product-composite` microservice could be something like `kubernetes.var.log.containers.product-composite-7...s_hands-on_comp-e...b.log`, while the tag for the corresponding `istio-proxy` in the same Pod could be something like `kubernetes.var.log.containers.product-composite-7...s_hands-on_istio-proxy-1...3.log`.

- A filter element that enriches the log records that come from containers running inside Kubernetes, along with Kubernetes-specific fields that contain information such as the names of the containers and the Namespace they run in.

The main configuration file, `fluent.conf`, contains the following information:

- `@include` statements for other configuration files, for example, the `kubernetes.conf` file we described previously. It also includes custom configuration files that are placed in a specific folder, making it very easy for us to reuse these configuration files without any changes and provide our own configuration file that only handles processing related to our own log records. We simply need to place our own configuration file in the folder specified by the `fluent.conf` file.
- An output element that sends log records to Elasticsearch.

As described in the *Deploying Fluentd* section later on, these two configuration files will be packaged into the Docker image we will build for Fluentd.

What's left to cover in our own configuration file is the following:

- Detecting and parsing Spring Boot-formatted log records from our microservices.
- Handling multiline stack traces. Stack traces are written to log files using multiple lines. This makes it hard for Fluentd to handle a stack trace as a single log record.
- Separating log records from the `istio-proxy` sidecars from the log records that were created by the microservices running in the same Pod. The log records that are created by `istio-proxy` don't follow the same pattern as the log patterns that are created by our Spring Boot-based microservices. Therefore, they must be handled separately so that Fluentd doesn't try to parse them as Spring Boot-formatted log records.

To achieve this, the configuration is, to a large extent, based on using the `rewrite_tag_filter` plugin. This plugin can be used for routing log records based on the concept of changing the name of a tag and then re-emitting the log record to the Fluentd routing engine.

This processing is summarized by the following UML activity diagram:

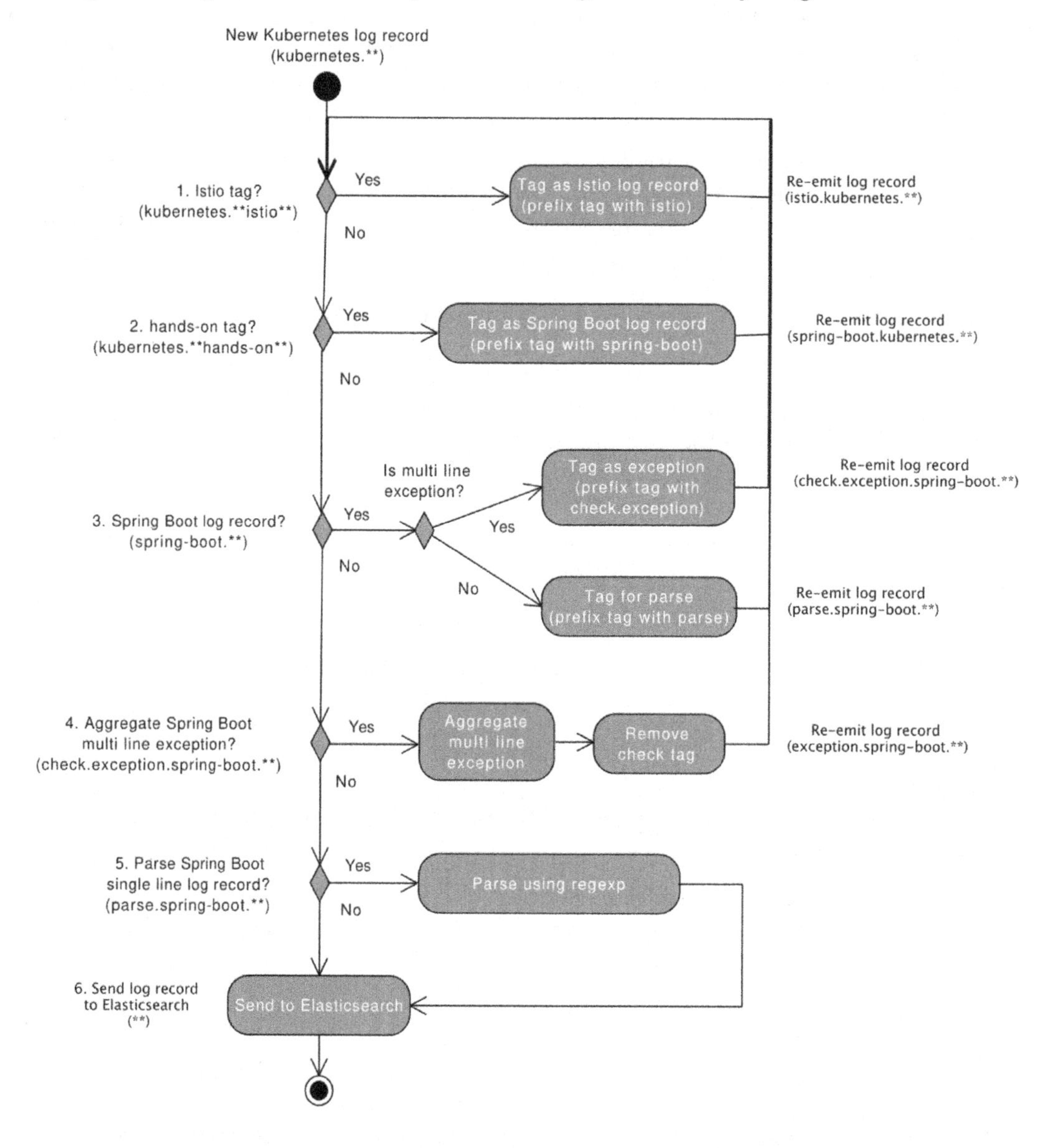

Figure 19.1: Fluentd processing of log records

At a high level, the design of the configuration file looks as follows:

- The tags of all log records from Istio, including `istio-proxy`, are prefixed with `istio` so that they can be separated from the Spring Boot-based log records.

- The tags of all log records from the `hands-on` Namespace (except for the log records from `istio-proxy`) are prefixed with `spring-boot`.
- The log records from Spring Boot are checked for the presence of multiline stack traces. If the log record is part of a multiline stack trace, it is processed by the third-party `detect-exceptions` plugin to recreate the stack trace. Otherwise, it is parsed using a regular expression to extract information of interest. See the *Deploying Fluentd* section for details on this third-party plugin.

The `fluentd-hands-on.conf` configuration file implements this activity diagram. The configuration file is placed inside a Kubernetes ConfigMap (see `kubernetes/efk/fluentd-hands-on-configmap.yml`). Let's go through this step by step, as follows:

1. First comes the definition of the ConfigMap and the filename of the configuration file, `fluentd-hands-on.conf`. It looks as follows:

   ```
   apiVersion: v1
   kind: ConfigMap
   metadata:
     name: fluentd-hands-on-config
     namespace: kube-system
   data:
     fluentd-hands-on.conf: |
   ```

   We can see that the `data` element will contain the configuration of Fluentd. It starts with the filename and uses a vertical bar, `|`, to mark the beginning of the embedded configuration file for Fluentd.

2. The first `<match>` element matches the log records from Istio, that is, tags that are prefixed with `Kubernetes` and contain `istio` as either part of their Namespace or part of their container name. It looks like this:

   ```
       <match kubernetes.**istio**>
         @type rewrite_tag_filter
         <rule>
           key log
           pattern ^(.*)$
           tag istio.${tag}
         </rule>
       </match>
   ```

   Let's explain the preceding source code:

   - The `<match>` element matches any tags that follow the `kubernetes.**istio**` pattern, that is, tags that start with `Kubernetes` and then contain the word `istio` somewhere in the tag name. `istio` can come from the name of either the namespace or the container; both are part of the tag.

- The `<match>` element contains only one `<rule>` element, which prefixes the tag with `istio`. The `${tag}` variable holds the current value of the tag.
- Since this is the only `<rule>` element in the `<match>` element, it is configured to match all log records:
    - Since all log records that come from Kubernetes have a `log` field, the `key` field is set to `log`, that is, the rule looks for a `log` field in the log records.
    - To match any string in the `log` field, the `pattern` field is set to the `^(.*)$` regular expression. `^` marks the beginning of a string, while `$` marks the end of a string. `(.*)` matches any number of characters, except for line breaks.
    - The log records are re-emitted to the Fluentd routing engine. Since no other elements in the configuration file match tags starting with `istio`, the log records will be sent directly to the output element for Elasticsearch, which is defined in the `fluent.conf` file we described previously.

3. The second `<match>` element matches all log records from the `hands-on` Namespace, that is, the log records that are emitted by our microservices. It looks like this:

```
<match kubernetes.**hands-on**>
  @type rewrite_tag_filter
  <rule>
    key log
    pattern ^(.*)$
    tag spring-boot.${tag}
  </rule>
</match>
```

   From the source code, we can see that:

   - The log records emitted by our microservices use formatting rules for the log message defined by Spring Boot, so their tags are prefixed with `spring-boot`. Then, they are re-emitted for further processing.
   - The `<match>` element is configured in the same way as the `<match kubernetes.**istio**>` element we looked at previously, to match all records.

4. The third `<match>` element matches `spring-boot` log records and determines whether they are ordinary Spring Boot log records or part of a multiline stack trace. It looks like this:

```
<match spring-boot.**>
  @type rewrite_tag_filter
  <rule>
    key log
    pattern /^\d{4}-\d{2}-\d{2}\s\d{2}:\d{2}:\d{2}\.\d{3}.*/
    tag parse.${tag}
  </rule>
  <rule>
    key log
    pattern /^.*/
    tag check.exception.${tag}
  </rule>
</match>
```

As seen in the source code, this is determined by using two `<rule>` elements:

- The first uses a regular expression to check whether the `log` field in the log element starts with a timestamp or not.
- If the `log` field starts with a timestamp, the log record is treated as an ordinary Spring Boot log record and its tag is prefixed with `parse`.
- Otherwise, the second `<rule>` element will match, and the log record is handled as a multiline log record. Its tag is prefixed with `check.exception`.
- The log record is re-emitted in either case and its tag will either start with `check.exception.spring-boot.kubernetes` or `parse.spring-boot.kubernetes` after this process.

5. In the fourth `<match>` element, the selected log records have a tag that starts with `check.exception.spring-boot`, that is, log records that are part of a multiline stack trace. It looks like this:

```
<match check.exception.spring-boot.**>
  @type detect_exceptions
  languages java
  remove_tag_prefix check
  message log
  multiline_flush_interval 5
</match>
```

The `detect_exceptions` plugin works like this:

- The `detect_exceptions` plugin is used to combine multiple one-line log records into a single log record that contains a complete stack trace.

- Before a multiline log record is re-emitted into the routing engine, the `check` prefix is removed from the tag to prevent a never-ending processing loop of the log record.

6. Finally, the configuration file consists of a `filter` element that parses Spring Boot log messages using a regular expression, extracting information of interest. It looks like this:

```
<filter parse.spring-boot.**>
  @type parser
  key_name log
  time_key time
  time_format %Y-%m-%d %H:%M:%S.%N
  reserve_data true
  format /^(?<time>\d{4}-\d{2}-
  \d{2}\s\d{2}:\d{2}:\d{2}\.\d{3})\s+
  (?<spring.level>[^\s]+)\s+
  (\[(?<spring.service>[^,]*),(?<spring.trace>[^,]*),(?
  <spring.span>[^\]]*)]*\])\s+
  (?<spring.pid>\d+)\s+---\s+\[\s*(?<spring.thread>[^\]]+)\]\s+
  (?<spring.class>[^\s]+)\s*:\s+
  (?<log>.*)$/
</filter>
```

Note that filter elements don't re-emit log records; instead, they just pass them on to the next element in the configuration file that matches the log record's tag.

The following fields are extracted from the Spring Boot log message that's stored in the `log` field in the log record:

- `<time>`: The timestamp for when the log record was created
- `<spring.level>`: The log level of the log record: `FATAL`, `ERROR`, `WARN`, `INFO`, `DEBUG`, or `TRACE`
- `<spring.service>`: The name of the microservice
- `<spring.trace>`: The trace ID used to perform distributed tracing
- `<spring.span>`: The span ID, the ID of the part of the distributed processing that this microservice executed
- `<spring.pid>`: The process ID
- `<spring.thread>`: The thread ID
- `<spring.class>`: The name of the Java class
- `<log>`: The actual log message

The names of Spring Boot-based microservices are specified using the `spring.application.name` property. This property has been added to each microservice-specific property file in the config repository, in the `config-repo` folder.

Getting regular expressions right can be challenging, to say the least. Thankfully, there are several websites that can help. When it comes to using regular expressions together with Fluentd, I recommend using the following site: `https://fluentular.herokuapp.com/`.

Now that we have been introduced to how Fluentd works and how the configuration file is constructed, we are ready to deploy the EFK stack.

Deploying the EFK stack on Kubernetes

Deploying the EFK stack on Kubernetes will be done in the same way as we have deployed our own microservices: using Kubernetes manifest files for objects such as Deployments, Services, and configuration maps.

The deployment of the EFK stack is divided into three parts:

- Deploying Elasticsearch and Kibana
- Deploying Fluentd
- Setting up access to Elasticsearch and Kibana

But first, we need to build and deploy our own microservices.

Building and deploying our microservices

Building, deploying, and verifying the deployment using the `test-em-all.bash` test script is done in the same way as it was done in *Chapter 18, Using a Service Mesh to Improve Observability and Management*, in the *Running commands to create the service mesh* section. These instructions assume that the cert-manager and Istio are installed as instructed in *Chapters 17* and *18*.

Run the following commands to get started:

1. First, build the Docker images from the source with the following commands:

```
cd $BOOK_HOME/Chapter19
eval $(minikube docker-env)
./gradlew build && docker-compose build
```

Recreate the Namespace, `hands-on`, and set it as the default Namespace:

```
kubectl delete namespace hands-on
kubectl apply -f kubernetes/hands-on-namespace.yml
kubectl config set-context $(kubectl config current-context)
--namespace=hands-on
```

2. Resolve the Helm chart dependencies with the following commands.

   First, we update the dependencies in the `components` folder:

   ```
   for f in kubernetes/helm/components/*; do helm dep up $f; done
   ```

   Next, we update the dependencies in the `environments` folder:

   ```
   for f in kubernetes/helm/environments/*; do helm dep up $f; done
   ```

3. Deploy the system landscape using Helm and wait for all deployments to complete:

   ```
   helm install hands-on-dev-env \
     kubernetes/helm/environments/dev-env \
     -n hands-on --wait
   ```

4. Start the Minikube tunnel in a separate terminal window, if it's not already running (see *Chapter 18*, the *Setting up access to Istio services* section, for a recap, if required):

   ```
   minikube tunnel
   ```

   Remember that this command requires that your user has `sudo` privileges and that you enter your password during startup and shutdown. It takes a couple of seconds before the command asks for the password, so it is easy to miss!

5. Run the normal tests to verify the deployment with the following command:

   ```
   ./test-em-all.bash
   ```

   Expect the output to be similar to what we have seen from the previous chapters:

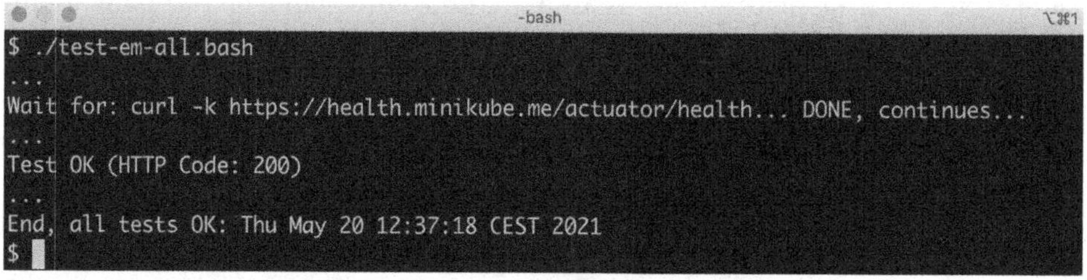

```
-bash
$ ./test-em-all.bash
...
Wait for: curl -k https://health.minikube.me/actuator/health... DONE, continues...
...
Test OK (HTTP Code: 200)
...
End, all tests OK: Thu May 20 12:37:18 CEST 2021
$
```

Figure 19.2: Tests running fine

6. You can also try out the APIs manually by running the following commands:

```
ACCESS_TOKEN=$(curl -k https://writer:secret@minikube.me/oauth2/
token -d grant_type=client_credentials -s | jq .access_token -r)

echo ACCESS_TOKEN=$ACCESS_TOKEN

curl -ks https://minikube.me/product-composite/1 -H
"Authorization: Bearer $ACCESS_TOKEN" | jq .productId
```

   Expect the requested product ID, `1`, in the response.

With the microservices deployed, we can move on and deploy Elasticsearch and Kibana!

Deploying Elasticsearch and Kibana

We will deploy Elasticsearch and Kibana to their own namespace, `logging`. Both Elasticsearch and Kibana will be deployed for development and test usage using a Kubernetes Deployment and Service object. The services will expose the standard ports for Elasticsearch and Kibana internally in the Kubernetes cluster, that is, port `9200` for Elasticsearch and port `5601` for Kibana.

To provide external HTTP access to Elasticsearch and Kibana, we will create Istio objects in the same way as we did in *Chapter 18* for Kiali and Jaeger – see the *Setting up access to Istio services* section for a recap, if required. This will result in Elasticsearch and Kibana being available on `https://elasticsearch.minikube.me` and `https://kibana.minikube.me`.

The manifest files have been packaged in a Helm chart located in the folder `kubernetes/helm/environments/logging`.

For recommended deployment options for Elasticsearch and Kibana in a production environment on Kubernetes, see `https://www.elastic.co/elastic-cloud-kubernetes`.

We will use the versions that were available when this chapter was written:

- Elasticsearch version 7.12.1
- Kibana version 7.12.1

Before we perform the deployments, let's look at the most interesting parts of the manifest files in the Helm chart's `template` folder.

A walkthrough of the manifest files

The manifest file for Elasticsearch, `elasticsearch.yml`, contains a standard Kubernetes Deployment and Service object that we have seen multiple times before, for example, in *Chapter 15, Introduction to Kubernetes*, in the *Trying out a sample deployment* section. The most interesting part of the manifest file is the following:

```
apiVersion: apps/v1
kind: Deployment
...
      containers:
      - name: elasticsearch
        image: docker.elastic.co/elasticsearch/elasticsearch:7.12.1
        resources:
          limits:
            cpu: 500m
            memory: 2Gi
          requests:
            cpu: 500m
            memory: 2Gi
```

Let's explain some of this manifest:

- We use an official Docker image from Elastic that's available at `docker.elastic.co`. The version is set to `7.12.1`.
- The Elasticsearch container is allowed to allocate a relatively large amount of memory – 2 GB – to be able to run queries with good performance. The more memory, the better the performance.

The manifest file for Kibana, `kibana.yml`, also contains a standard Kubernetes Deployment and Service object. The most interesting parts in the manifest file are as follows:

```
apiVersion: apps/v1
kind: Deployment
...
      containers:
      - name: kibana
        image: docker.elastic.co/kibana/kibana:7.12.1
```

```
env:
- name: ELASTICSEARCH_URL
  value: http://elasticsearch:9200
```

Let's explain some of the manifest:

- For Kibana, we also use an official Docker image from Elastic that's available at `docker.elastic.co`. The version is set to `7.12.1`.
- To connect Kibana with the Elasticsearch Pod, an environment variable, `ELASTICSEARCH_URL`, is defined to specify the address to the Elasticsearch service, `http://elasticsearch:9200`.

Finally, the Istio manifests for setting up external access are found in the files `expose-elasticsearch.yml` and `expose-kibana.yml`. For a recap on how the `Gateway`, `VirtualService`, and `DestinationRule` objects are used, see the section *Creating the service mesh* in *Chapter 18*. They will provide the following forwarding of external requests:

- `https://elasticsearch.minikube.me` → `http://elasticsearch:9200`
- `https://kibana.minikube.me` → `http://kibana:5601`

With these insights, we are ready to perform the deployment of Elasticsearch and Kibana.

Running the deploy commands

Deploy Elasticsearch and Kibana by performing the following steps:

1. To make the deploy steps run faster, prefetch the Docker images for Elasticsearch and Kibana with the following commands:

   ```
   eval $(minikube docker-env)
   docker pull docker.elastic.co/elasticsearch/elasticsearch:7.12.1
   docker pull docker.elastic.co/kibana/kibana:7.12.1
   ```

2. Use the Helm chart to create the `logging` namespace, deploy Elasticsearch and Kibana in it, and wait for the Pods to be ready:

   ```
   helm install logging-hands-on-add-on kubernetes/helm/
   environments/logging \
       -n logging --create-namespace --wait
   ```

3. Verify that Elasticsearch is up and running with the following command:

```
curl https://elasticsearch.minikube.me -sk | jq -r .tagline
```

Expect `You Know, for Search` as a response.

Depending on your hardware, you might need to wait for a minute or two before Elasticsearch responds with this message.

4. Verify that Kibana is up and running with the following command:

```
curl https://kibana.minikube.me \
  -kLs -o /dev/null -w "%{http_code}\n"
```

Expect `200` as the response.

Again, you might need to wait for a minute or two before Kibana is initialized and responds with `200`.

With Elasticsearch and Kibana deployed, we can start to deploy Fluentd.

Deploying Fluentd

Deploying Fluentd is a bit more complex compared to deploying Elasticsearch and Kibana. To deploy Fluentd, we will use a Docker image that's been published by the Fluentd project on Docker Hub, `fluent/fluentd-kubernetes-daemonset`, and sample the Kubernetes manifest files from a Fluentd project on GitHub, `fluentd-kubernetes-daemonset`. It is located at `https://github.com/fluent/fluentd-kubernetes-daemonset`. As is implied by the name of the project, Fluentd will be deployed as a DaemonSet, running one Pod per Node in the Kubernetes cluster. Each Fluentd Pod is responsible for collecting log output from processes and containers that run on the same Node as the Pod. Since we are using Minikube with a single Node cluster, we will only have one Fluentd Pod.

To handle multiline log records that contain stack traces from exceptions, we will use a third-party Fluentd plugin provided by Google, `fluent-plugin-detect-exceptions`, which is available at `https://github.com/GoogleCloudPlatform/fluent-plugin-detect-exceptions`. To be able to use this plugin, we will build our own Docker image where the `fluent-plugin-detect-exceptions` plugin will be installed.

Fluentd's Docker image, `fluentd-kubernetes-daemonset`, will be used as the base image.

We will use the following versions:

- Fluentd version 1.4.2
- `fluent-plugin-detect-exceptions` version 0.0.12

Before we perform the deployments, let's look at the most interesting parts of the manifest files.

A walkthrough of the manifest files

The Dockerfile that's used to build the Docker image, `kubernetes/efk/Dockerfile`, looks as follows:

```
FROM fluent/fluentd-kubernetes-daemonset:v1.4.2-debian-
elasticsearch-1.1

RUN gem install fluent-plugin-detect-exceptions -v 0.0.12 \
 && gem sources --clear-all \
 && rm -rf /var/lib/apt/lists/* \
           /home/fluent/.gem/ruby/2.3.0/cache/*.gem
```

Let's explain this in detail:

- The base image is Fluentd's Docker image, `fluentd-kubernetes-daemonset`. The `v1.4.2-debian-elasticsearch-1.1` tag specifies that version 1.4.2 will be used with a package that contains built-in support for sending log records to Elasticsearch. The base Docker image contains the Fluentd configuration files that were mentioned in the *Configuring Fluentd* section.
- The Google plugin, `fluent-plugin-detect-exceptions`, is installed using Ruby's package manager, `gem`.

The manifest file of the DaemonSet, `kubernetes/efk/fluentd-ds.yml`, is based on a sample manifest file in the `fluentd-kubernetes-daemonset` project, which can be found at `https://github.com/fluent/fluentd-kubernetes-daemonset/blob/master/fluentd-daemonset-elasticsearch.yaml`.

This file is a bit complex, so let's go through the most interesting parts separately:

1. First, here's the declaration of the DaemonSet:

```
apiVersion: apps/v1
kind: DaemonSet
metadata:
  name: fluentd
  namespace: kube-system
```

   The `kind` key specifies that this is a DaemonSet. The `namespace` key specifies that the DaemonSet will be created in the `kube-system` namespace and not in the `logging` namespace where Elasticsearch and Kibana are deployed.

2. The next part specifies the template for the Pods that are created by the DaemonSet. The most interesting parts are as follows:

```
spec:
  template:
    spec:
      containers:
      - name: fluentd
        image: hands-on/fluentd:v1
        env:
          - name: FLUENT_ELASTICSEARCH_HOST
            value: "elasticsearch.logging"
          - name: FLUENT_ELASTICSEARCH_PORT
            value: "9200"
```

   The Docker image that's used for the Pods is `hands-on/fluentd:v1`. We will build this Docker image after walking through the manifest files using the Dockerfile we described previously.

   A number of environment variables are supported by the Docker image and are used to customize it. The two most important ones are as follows:

   - `FLUENT_ELASTICSEARCH_HOST`, which specifies the hostname of the Elasticsearch service, `elasticsearch.logging`
   - `FLUENT_ELASTICSEARCH_PORT`, which specifies the port that's used to communicate with Elasticsearch, `9200`

> Since the Fluentd Pod runs in a different namespace to Elasticsearch, the hostname cannot be specified using its short name, that is, `elasticsearch`. Instead, the namespace part of the DNS name must also be specified, that is, `elasticsearch.logging`. As an alternative, the **fully qualified domain name** (**FQDN**), `elasticsearch.logging.svc.cluster.local`, can also be used. But since the last part of the DNS name, `svc.cluster.local`, is shared by all DNS names inside a Kubernetes cluster, it does not need to be specified.

3. Finally, a number of volumes, that is, filesystems, are mapped into the Pod, as follows:

```
volumeMounts:
- name: varlog
  mountPath: /var/log
- name: varlibdockercontainers
  mountPath: /var/lib/docker/containers
  readOnly: true
- name: journal
  mountPath: /var/log/journal
  readOnly: true
- name: fluentd-extra-config
  mountPath: /fluentd/etc/conf.d
volumes:
- name: varlog
  hostPath:
    path: /var/log
- name: varlibdockercontainers
  hostPath:
    path: /var/lib/docker/containers
- name: journal
  hostPath:
    path: /run/log/journal
- name: fluentd-extra-config
  configMap:
    name: "fluentd-hands-on-config"
```

Let's take a look at the source code in detail:

- Three folders on the host (that is, the Node) are mapped into the Fluentd Pod. These folders contain the log files that Fluentd will tail and collect log records from. The folders are `/var/log`, `/var/lib/docker/containers`, and `/run/log/journal`.
- Our own configuration file, which specifies how Fluentd will process log records from our microservices, is mapped using a ConfigMap called `fluentd-hands-on-config` to the `/fluentd/etc/conf.d` folder. The base Docker image configures Fluentd to include any configuration file that's found in the `/fluentd/etc/conf.d` folder. See the *Configuring Fluentd* section for details.

For the full source code of the manifest file for the DaemonSet, see the `kubernetes/efk/fluentd-ds.yml` file.

Now that we've walked through everything, we are ready to perform the deployment of Fluentd.

Running the deploy commands

To deploy Fluentd, we have to build the Docker image, create the ConfigMap, and finally deploy the DaemonSet. Run the following commands to perform these steps:

1. Build the Docker image and tag it with `hands-on/fluentd:v1` using the following command:

```
eval $(minikube docker-env)
docker build -f kubernetes/efk/Dockerfile -t hands-on/fluentd:v1
kubernetes/efk/
```

2. Create the ConfigMap, deploy Fluentd's DaemonSet, and wait for the Pod to be ready with the following commands:

```
kubectl apply -f kubernetes/efk/fluentd-hands-on-configmap.yml
kubectl apply -f kubernetes/efk/fluentd-ds.yml
kubectl wait --timeout=120s --for=condition=Ready pod -l
app=fluentd -n kube-system
```

3. Verify that the Fluentd Pod is healthy with the following command:

```
kubectl logs -n kube-system -l app=fluentd --tail=-1 | grep
"fluentd worker is now running worker"
```

Expect a response of `2021-05-22 14:59:46 +0000 [info]: #0 fluentd worker is now running worker=0`.

As for Elasticsearch and Kibana, you might need to wait for a minute or two before Fluentd responds with this message.

4. Fluentd will start to collect a considerable number of log records from the various containers in the Minikube instance. After a minute or so, you can ask Elasticsearch how many log records have been collected with the following command:

```
curl https://elasticsearch.minikube.me/_all/_count -sk | jq .count
```

5. The command can be a bit slow the first time it is executed but should return a total count of several thousands of log records. In my case, it returned `55607`.

This completes the deployment of the EFK stack. Now, it's time to try it out and find out what all the collected log records are about!

Trying out the EFK stack

The first thing we need to do before we can try out the EFK stack is to initialize Kibana, so it knows what indices to use in Elasticsearch.

An **index** in Elasticsearch corresponds to a **database** in SQL concepts. The SQL concepts **table**, **row**, and **column** correspond to **type**, **document**, and **property** in Elasticsearch.

Once that is done, we will try out the following common tasks:

1. We will start by analyzing what types of log records Fluentd has collected and stored in Elasticsearch. Kibana has a very useful visualization capability that can be used for this.
2. Next, we will learn how to find all related log records created by the microservices while processing an external request. We will use the **trace ID** in the log records as a correlation ID to find related log records.
3. Finally, we will learn how to use Kibana to perform **root cause analysis**, finding the actual reason for an error.

Initializing Kibana

Before we start to use Kibana, we must specify what search indices to use in Elasticsearch and what field in the indices holds the timestamps for the log records.

Just a quick reminder that we are using a certificate created by our own CA, meaning that it is not trusted by web browsers! For a recap on how to make web browsers accept our certificate, see *Chapter 18*, the *Observing the service mesh* section.

Perform the following steps to initialize Kibana:

1. Open Kibana's web UI using the `https://kibana.minikube.me` URL in a web browser.
2. On the welcome page, **Welcome to Kibana**, click on the **Explore on my own** button.
3. If you get a popup saying **Your data is not secure**, you can simply click on **Don't show again** and click on the **Dismiss** button. We don't need to secure the data stored in this book.
4. Click on the "hamburger menu" (three horizontal lines) in the upper-left corner and click on **Visualize Library** in the menu to the left. You will be asked to define an index pattern that's used by Kibana to identify what Elasticsearch indices it should retrieve log records from. Click on the button named **Create index pattern**.
5. Enter `logstash-*` as the index pattern name and click on the **Next Step** button.

   Indices are, by default, named `logstash` for historical reasons, even though it is Fluentd that is used for log collection.

6. On the next page, you will be asked to specify the name of the field that contains the timestamp for the log records. Click on the drop-down list for the **Time** field and select the only available field, **@timestamp**.
7. Click on the **Create index pattern** button.

   Kibana will show a page that summarizes the fields that are available in the selected indices.

With Kibana initialized, we are ready to examine the log records we have collected.

Analyzing the log records

From the deployment of Fluentd, we know that it immediately started to collect a significant number of log records. So, the first thing we need to do is get an understanding of what types of log records Fluentd has collected and stored in Elasticsearch.

We will use Kibana's visualization feature to divide the log records by Kubernetes Namespace and then ask Kibana to show us how the log records are divided by type of container within each Namespace. A pie chart is a suitable chart type for this type of analysis. Perform the following steps to create a pie chart:

1. In Kibana's web UI, click on the hamburger menu again and select **Visualize Library** in the menu.
2. Click on the **Create new visualization** button and select the **Lens** type on the next page. A web page like the following will be displayed:

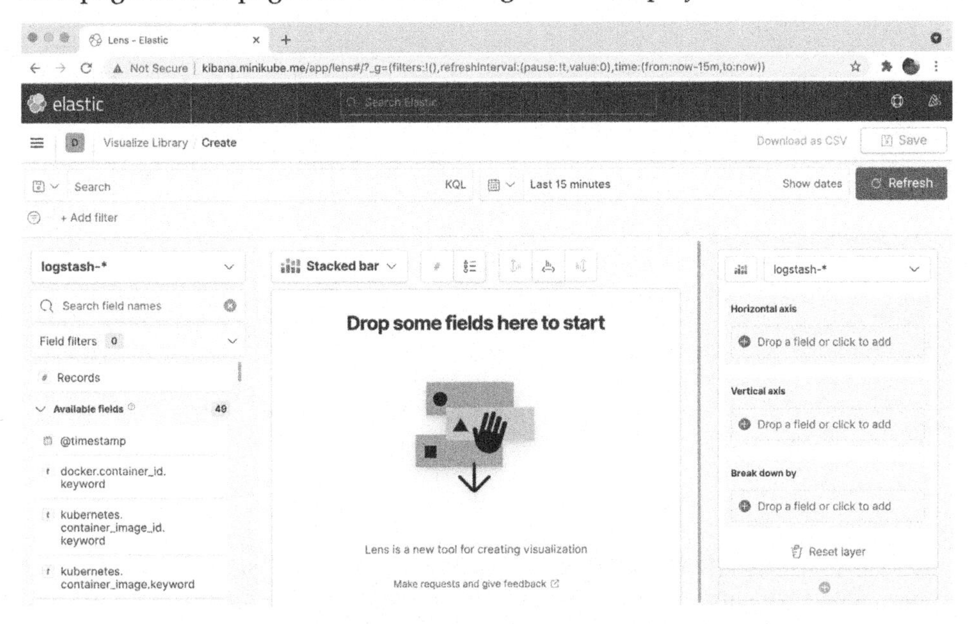

Figure 19.3: Starting to analyze log records in Kibana

3. Verify that **logstash-*** is the selected index pattern in the top-left drop-down menu.
4. In the **Stacked bar** drop-down menu next to the index pattern, select **Pie** as the visualization type.

5. In the time picker (a date interval selector) above the pie chart, set a date interval large enough to cover log records of interest (set to the **Last 15 minutes** in the following screenshot). Click on its calendar icon to adjust the time interval.
6. In the field named **Search field names** below the index pattern, enter `kubernetes.namespace_name.keyword`.
7. Under the **Available fields** list, the field **kubernetes.namespace_name.keyword** is now present. Drag this field into the big box in the middle of the page, named **Drop some fields here to start**. Kibana will immediately start to analyze log records and render a pie chart divided into Kubernetes namespaces. In my case, it looks like:

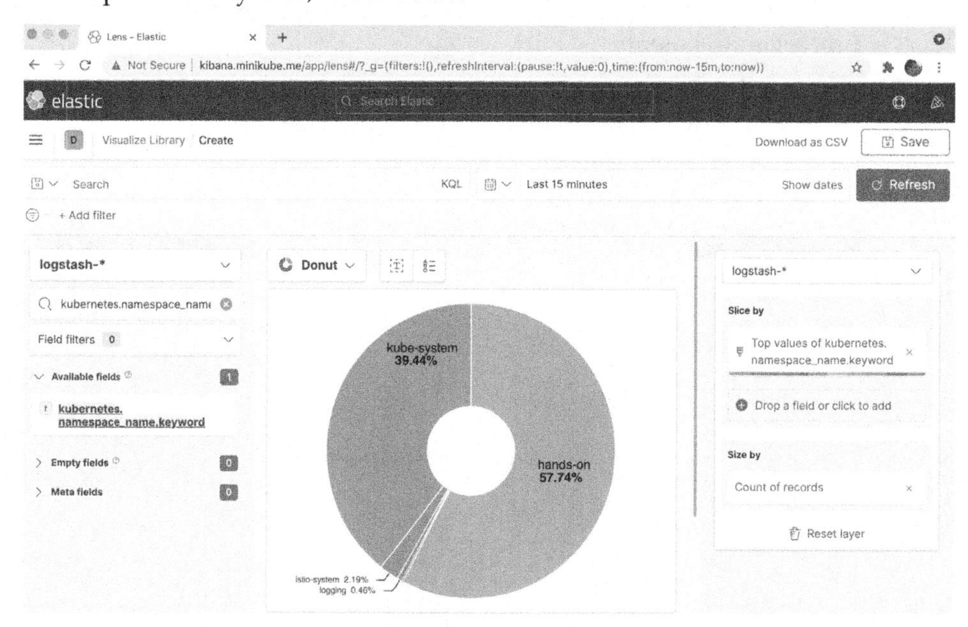

Figure 19.4: Kibana analysis of log records per Kubernetes namespace

We can see that the log records are divided over the Namespaces we have been working with in the previous chapters: `kube-system`, `istio-system`, `logging`, and our own `hands-on` Namespace. To see what containers have created the log records per Namespace, we need to add a second field.

8. In the **Search field names** field, enter `kubernetes.container_name.keyword`.

9. In the **Available fields** list, the field **kubernetes.container_name.keyword** is now present. Drag this field into the big box in the middle of the page showing the pie chart. Kibana will immediately start to analyze log records and render a pie chart divided by Kubernetes namespace and container name. In my case, it looks like:

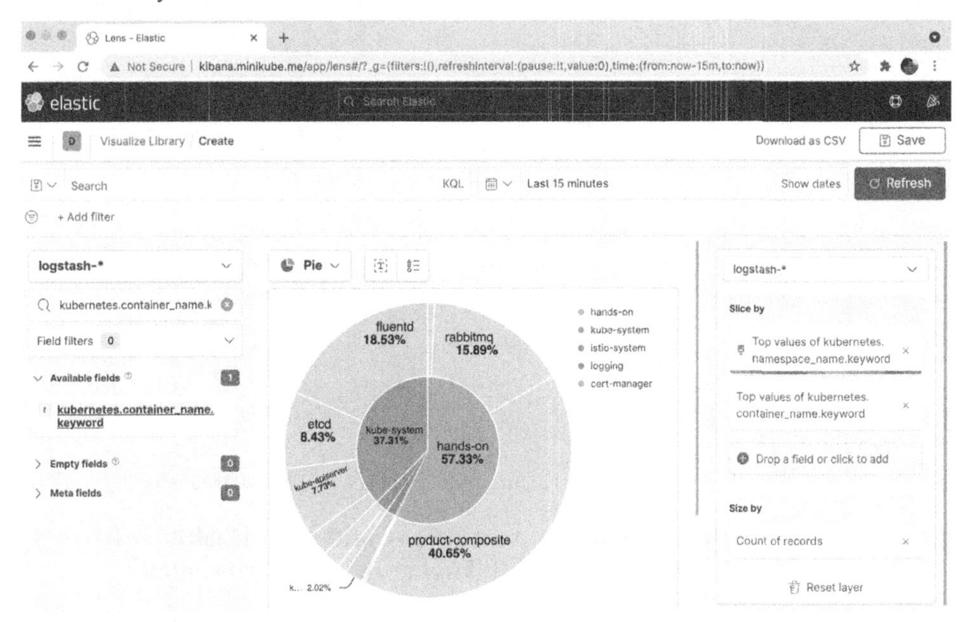

Figure 19.5: Kibana analysis of log records per namespace and container

Here, we can find the log records from our microservices. Most of the log records come from the `product-composite` microservice.

10. Wrap up this introduction to how to analyze what types of log records we have collected by saving this pie chart in a dashboard. Click on the **Save** button in the top-right corner.

11. On the page named **Save Lens visualization**, do the following:

    a. Give it a **Title**, for example, `hands-on-visualization`.

    b. Enter a **Description**, for example, `This is my first visualization in Kibana`.

c. In the **Add to dashboard** box, select **New**. The page should look like this:

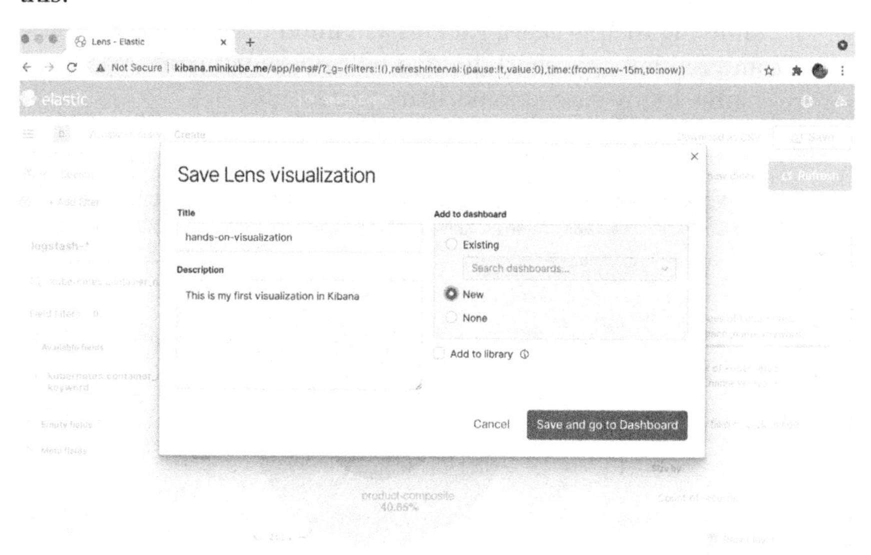

Figure 19.6: Creating a dashboard in Kibana

d. Click on the button named **Save and go to Dashboard**. A dashboard like the following should be presented:

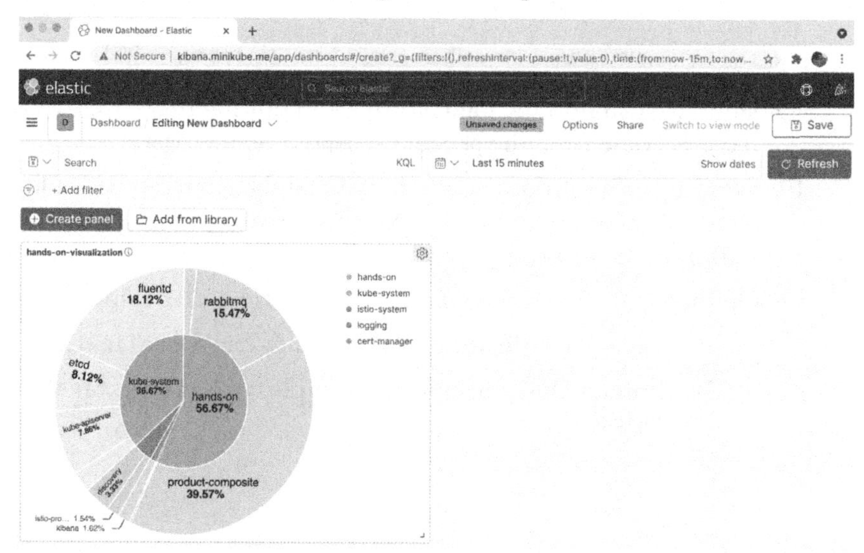

Figure 19.7: The new dashboard in Kibana

12. Click on the **Save** button in the top-right corner, give the dashboard a name, for example, `hands-on-dashboard`, and click on the **Save** button.

    You can now always go back to this dashboard by selecting **Dashboard** from the hamburger menu.

Kibana contains tons of features for analyzing log records - feel free to try them out on your own. For inspiration, see `https://www.elastic.co/guide/en/kibana/7.12/dashboard.html`. We will now move on and start to locate the actual log records from our microservice.

Discovering the log records from microservices

In this section, we will learn how to utilize one of the main features of centralized logging, finding log records from our microservices. We will also learn how to use the trace ID in the log records to find log records from other microservices that belong to the same process, for example, processing an external request sent to the public API.

Let's start by creating some log records that we can look up with the help of Kibana. We will use the API to create a product with a unique product ID and then retrieve information about the product. After that, we can try to find the log records that were created when retrieving the product information.

The creation of log records in the microservices has been updated a bit from the previous chapter so that the `product-composite` and the three core microservices, `product`, `recommendation`, and `review`, all write a log record with the log level set to `INFO` when they begin processing a get request. Let's go over the source code that's been added to each microservice:

- Product composite microservice log creation:

  ```
  LOG.info("Will get composite product info for product.id={}",
  productId);
  ```

- Product microservice log creation:

  ```
  LOG.info("Will get product info for id={}", productId);
  ```

- Recommendation microservice log creation:

  ```
  LOG.info("Will get recommendations for product with id={}",
  productId);
  ```

- Review microservice log creation:

  ```
  LOG.info("Will get reviews for product with id={}", productId);
  ```

For more details, see the source code in the `microservices` folder.

Perform the following steps to use the API to create log records and, after that, use Kibana to look up the log records:

1. Get an access token with the following command:

   ```
   ACCESS_TOKEN=$(curl -k https://writer:secret@minikube.me/oauth2/
   token -d grant_type=client_credentials -s | jq .access_token -r)

   echo ACCESS_TOKEN=$ACCESS_TOKEN
   ```

2. As mentioned in the introduction to this section, we will start by creating a product with a unique product ID. Create a minimalistic product (without recommendations and reviews) for `"productId" :1234` by executing the following command:

   ```
   curl -X POST -k https://minikube.me/product-composite \
     -H "Content-Type: application/json" \
     -H "Authorization: Bearer $ACCESS_TOKEN" \
     --data '{"productId":1234,"name":"product name
   1234","weight":1234}'
   ```

   Read the product with the following command:

   ```
   curl -H "Authorization: Bearer $ACCESS_TOKEN" -k 'https://
   minikube.me/product-composite/1234'
   ```

   Expect a response similar to the following:

   ```
   4. bash
   $ curl -H "Authorization: Bearer $ACCESS_TOKEN" -k 'https://minikube.me/product-composite/1234'
   {"productId":1234,"name":"product name 1234","weight":1234,"recommendations":[],"reviews":[],
   "serviceAddresses":{"cmp":"product-composite-74f4dc9b4f-4s9bk/172.17.0.39:80","pro":"product-869
   5c57758-ttmsg/172.17.0.40:80","rev":"","rec":""}}
   $
   ```

   Figure 19.8: Look up the product with productId = 1234

   Hopefully, we got some log records created by these API calls. Let's jump over to Kibana and find out!

3. On the Kibana web page, click **Discover** from the hamburger menu. You will see something like the following:

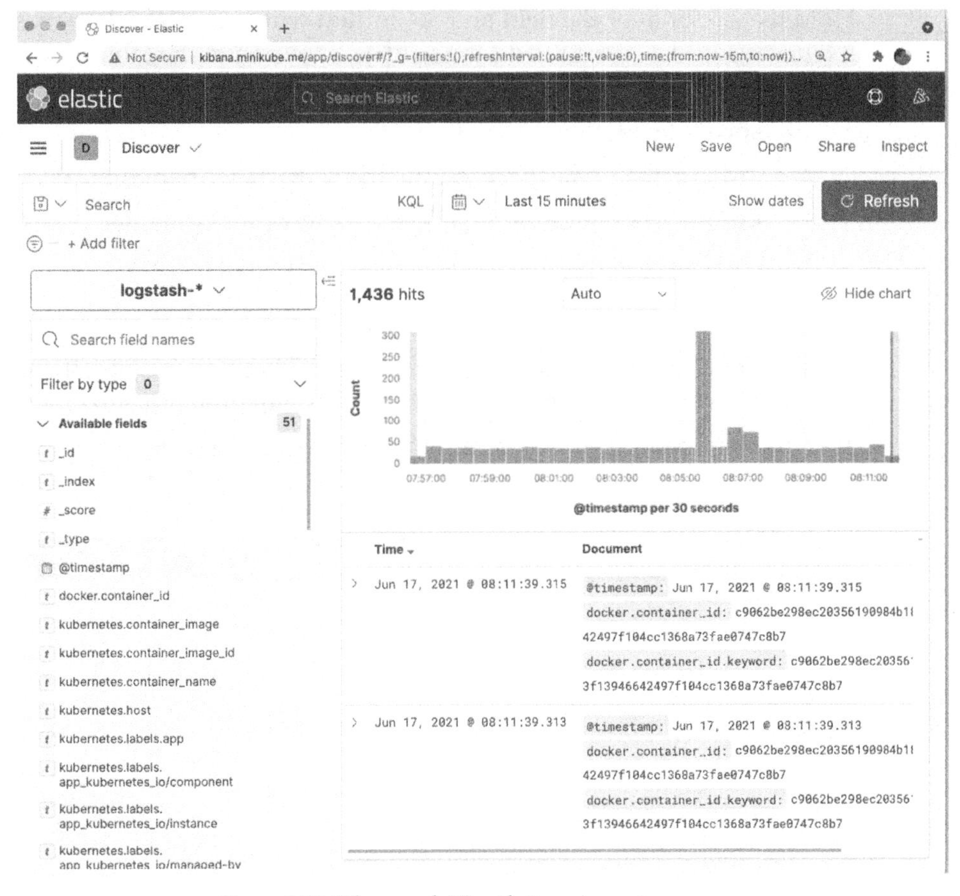

Figure 19.9: Kibana web UI with its major parts

On the left-top corner, we can see that Kibana has found **1,436** log records. The time picker shows that they are from the **Last 15 minutes**. In the histogram, we can see how the log records are spread out over time. Below the histogram is a table showing the most recent log events that were found by the query.

4. If you want to change the time interval, you can use the time picker. Click on its calendar icon to adjust the time interval.
5. To get a better view of the content in the log records, add some fields from the log records as columns in the table under the histogram.
6. Select the fields from the list of **Available fields** to the left. Scroll down until the field is found. To find the fields more easily, use the field named **Search field names** to filter the list of available fields.

Hold the cursor over the field and a **+** button will appear (a white cross in a blue circle); click on it to add the field as a column in the table. Select the following fields, in order:

a. **spring.level**, the log level
b. **kubernetes.namespace_name**, the Kubernetes namespace
c. **kubernetes.container_name**, the name of the container
d. **spring.trace**, the trace ID used for distributed tracing
e. **log**, the actual log message

To save some space, you can hide the list of fields by clicking on the "collapse" icon next to the index pattern field (containing the text **logstash-***).

The web page should look something like the following:

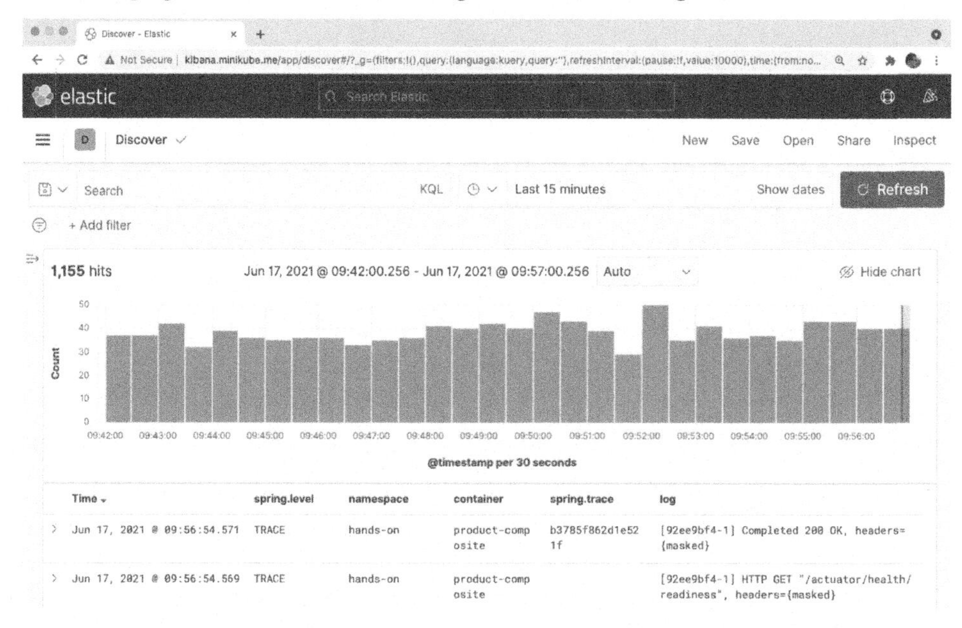

Figure 19.10: Kibana web UI showing log records

The table now contains information that is of interest regarding the log records!

7. To find log records from the call to the `GET` API, we can ask Kibana to find log records where the log field contains the text **product.id=1234**. This matches the log output from the `product-composite` microservice that was shown previously.

This can be done by entering `log:"product.id=1234"` in the top-left **Search** field and clicking on the **Update** button (this button can also be named **Refresh**). Expect one log record to be found:

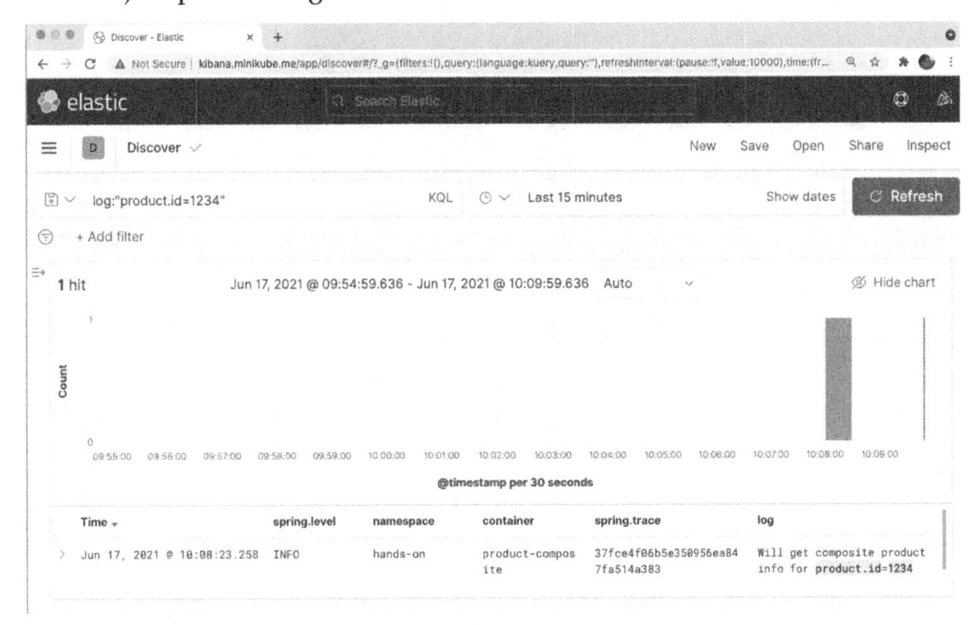

Figure 19.11: Kibana web UI showing a log record for productId = 1234

8. Verify that the timestamp is from when you called the `GET` API and verify that the name of the container that created the log record is **product-composite**, that is, verify that the log record was sent by the product composite microservice.
9. Now, we want to see the related log records from the other microservices that participated in the process of returning information about the product with product ID `1234`. In other words, we want to find log records with the same **trace ID** as that of the log record we found. To do this, place the cursor over the **spring.trace** field for the log record. Two small magnifying glasses will be shown to the right of the field, one with a **+** sign and one with a **-** sign. Click on the magnifying glass with the **+** sign to filter on the trace ID.

10. Clear the **Search** field so that the only search criterion is the filter of the trace field. Then, click on the **Update** button to see the result. Expect a response like the following:

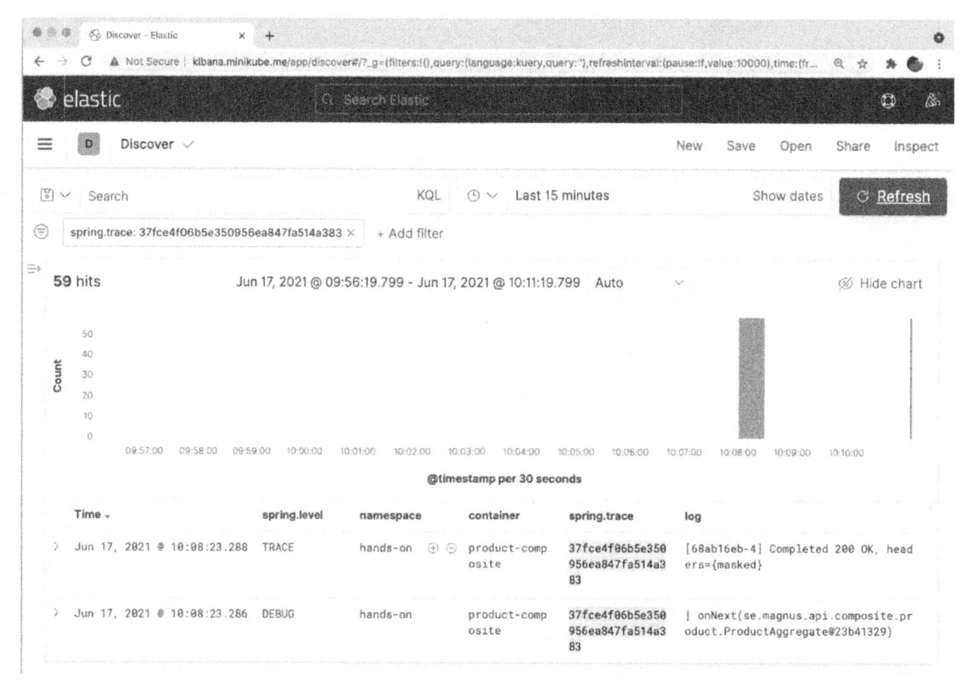

Figure 19.12: Kibana web UI showing log records for a trace ID

We can see a lot of detailed debug and trace messages that clutter the view; let's get rid of them!

11. Place the cursor over a **TRACE** value and click on the magnifying glass with the **-** sign to filter out log records with the log level set to **TRACE**.
12. Repeat the preceding step for the **DEBUG** log record.

    We should now be able to see the four expected log records, one for each microservice involved in the lookup of product information for the product with product ID `1234`:

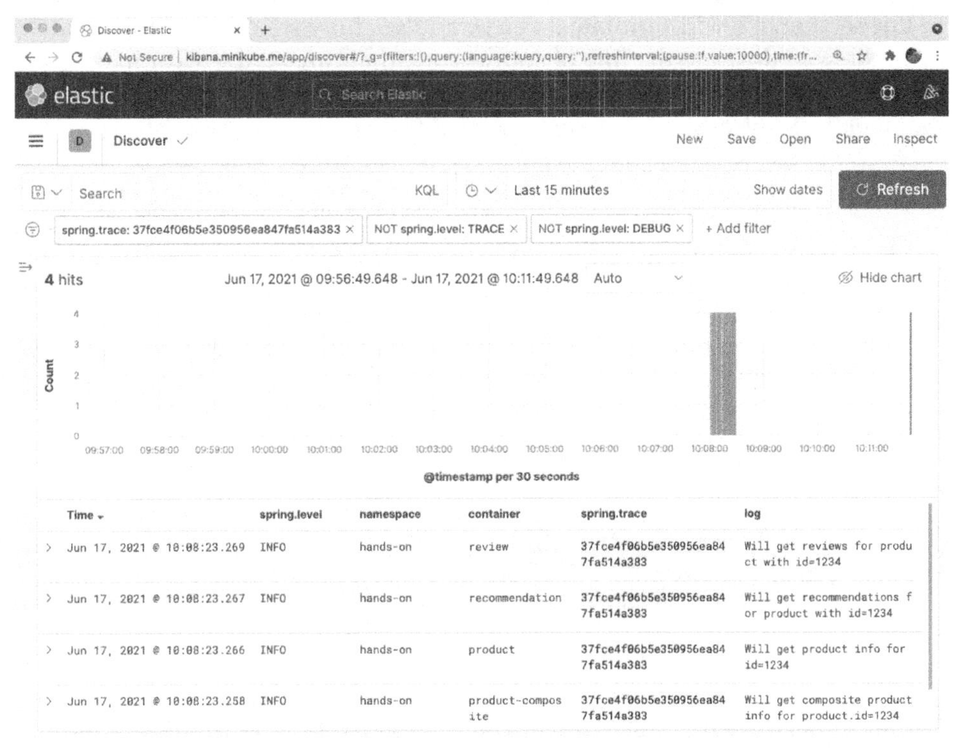

Figure 19.13: Kibana web UI showing log records for a trace ID with log level = INFO

Also, note that the filters that were applied included the trace ID but excluded log records with the log level set to **DEBUG** or **TRACE**.

Now that we know how to find the expected log records, we are ready to take the next step. This will be to learn how to find unexpected log records, that is, error messages, and how to perform root cause analysis to find the reason for these error messages.

Performing root cause analyses

One of the most important features of centralized logging is that it makes it possible to analyze errors using log records from many sources and based on that, perform root cause analysis, finding the actual reason for the error message.

In this section, we will simulate an error and see how we can find information about it, all the way down to the line of source code that caused the error in one of the microservices in the system landscape. To simulate an error, we will reuse the fault parameter we introduced in *Chapter 13, Improving Resilience Using Resilience4j*, in the *Adding programmable delays and random errors* section. We can use this to force the `product` microservice to throw an exception. Perform the following steps:

1. Run the following command to generate a fault in the `product` microservice while searching for product information on the product with product ID `1234`:

   ```
   curl -H "Authorization: Bearer $ACCESS_TOKEN" -k https://
   minikube.me/product-composite/1234?faultPercent=100
   ```

   Expect the following error in response:

   ```
   $ curl -H "Authorization: Bearer $ACCESS_TOKEN" -k https://minikube.me/product-composite/1234?faultPercent=100
   {"timestamp":"2021-05-23T11:03:47.911+00:00","path":"/product-composite/1234","status":500,"error":"Internal Server Error","message":"500 Internal Server Error from GET http://product/product/1234?delay=0&faultPercent=100","requestId":"f21bc7ae-4"}
   $
   ```

   Figure 19.14: A request that caused an error in the processing

   Now, we must pretend that we have no clue about the reason for this error! Otherwise, the root cause analysis wouldn't be very exciting, right?

   Let's assume that we work in a support organization and have been asked to investigate some problems that just occurred while an end user tried to look up information regarding a product with product ID `1234`.

2. Before we start to analyze the problem, let's delete the previous search filters in the Kibana web UI so that we can start from scratch. For each filter we defined in the previous section, click on its close icon (an **x**) to remove it.
3. Start by using the time picker to select a time interval that includes the point in time when the problem occurred. In my case, 15 minutes is sufficient.
4. Next, search for log records with the log level set to **ERROR** within this time frame. This can be done by clicking on the **spring.level** field in the list of selected fields (if you collapsed the field list previously, click on the expand icon to get the list restored). When you click on this field, its most used values will be displayed under it. Filter on the **ERROR** value by clicking on its + sign. Kibana will now show log records within the selected time frame with their log level set to **ERROR**, like this:

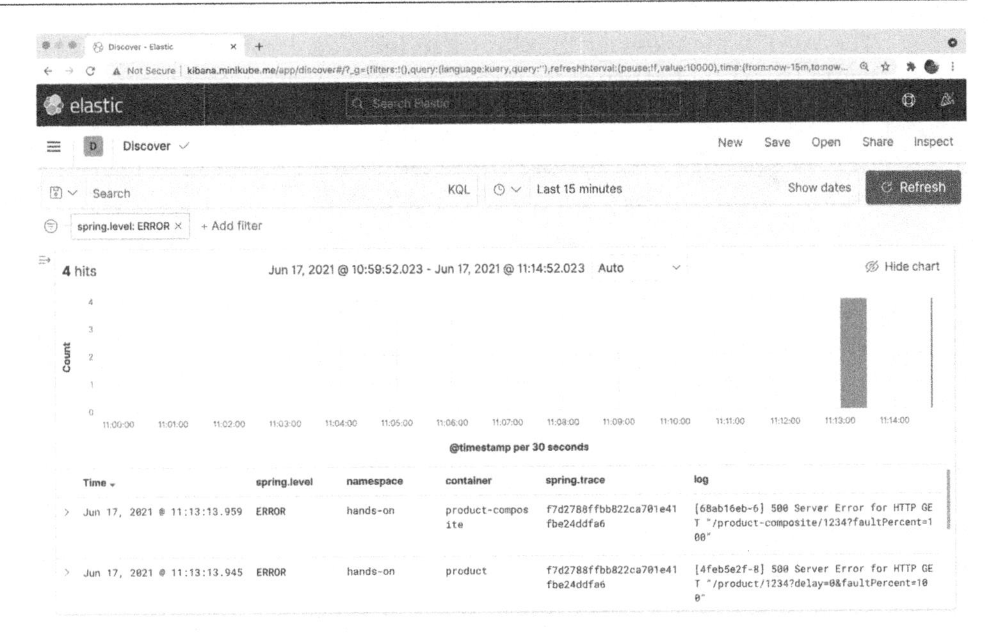

Figure 19.15: Kiali web UI, showing log records that report ERRORs

We can see a number of error messages related to product ID `1234`. The top log entries have the same trace ID, so this seems like a trace ID of interest to use for further investigation.

5. Filter on the trace ID of the first log record in the same way we did in the previous section.
6. Remove the filter of the ERROR log level to be able to see all of the records belonging to this trace ID. Expect Kibana to respond with a lot of log records. Look at the oldest log record that looks suspicious. For example, it may have a WARN or ERROR log level or a strange log message. The default sort order shows the latest log record at the top, so scroll down to the end and search backward (you can also change the sort order to show the oldest log record first by clicking on the small up/down arrow next to the **Time** column header).

The WARN log message that says **Bad luck, an error occurred** looks like it could be the root cause of the problem. Let's investigate it further:

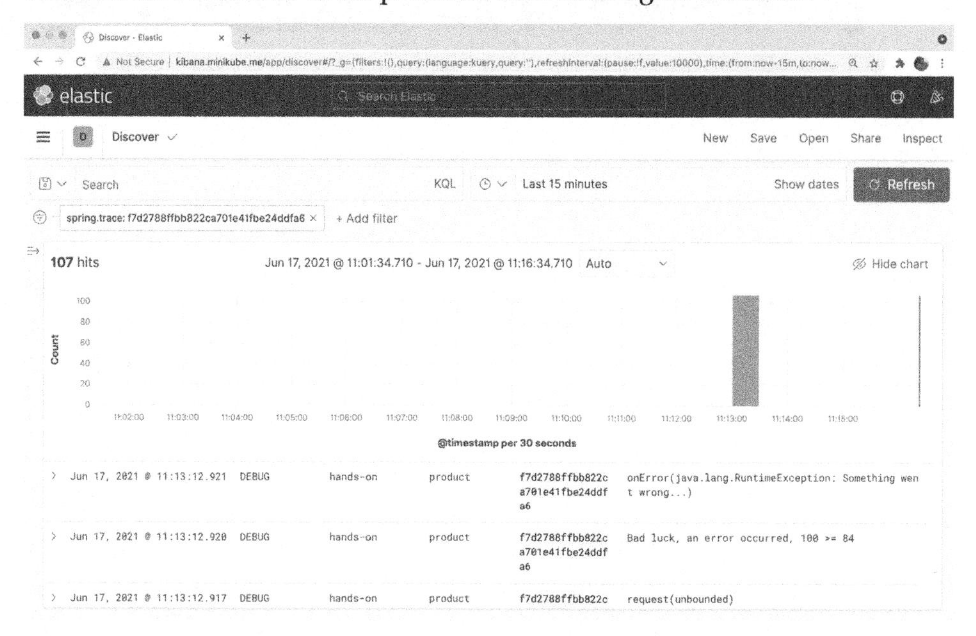

Figure 19.16: Kiali web UI, looking for the root cause

7. Once a log record has been found that might be the root cause of the problem, it is very useful to be able to find the nearby stack trace describing where exceptions were thrown in the source code. Unfortunately, the Fluentd plugin we use for collecting multiline exceptions, `fluent-plugin-detect-exceptions`, is unable to relate stack traces to the trace ID that was used. Therefore, stack traces will not show up in Kibana when we filter on a trace ID. Instead, we can use a feature in Kibana for finding surrounding log records that shows log records that have occurred near in time to a specific log record.
8. Expand the log record that says **Bad luck** using the arrow to the left of the log record. Detailed information about this specific log record will be revealed:

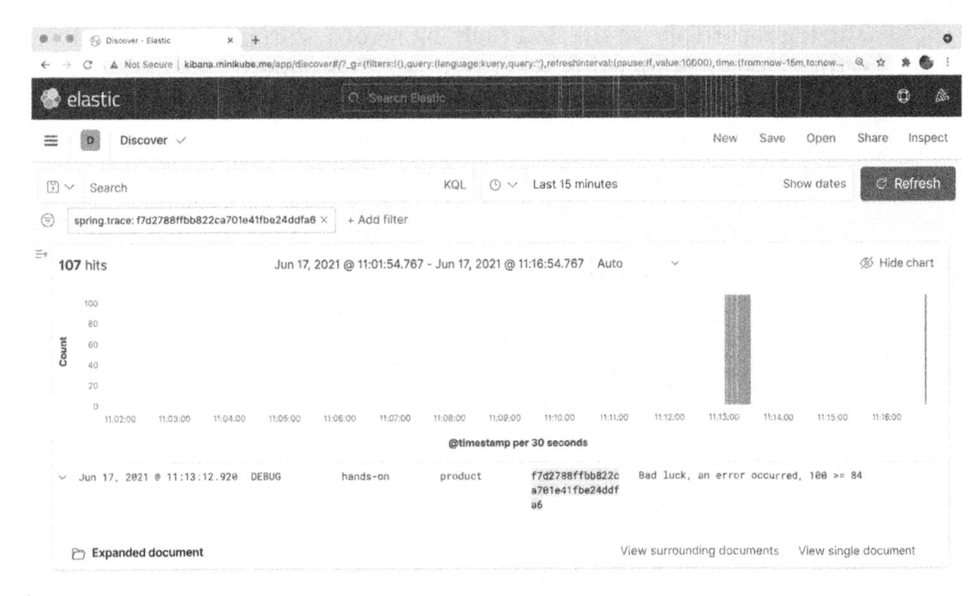

Figure 19.17: Kiali web UI, expanding the log record with the root cause log message

9. There is also a link named **View surrounding documents**; click on it to see nearby log records. Expect a web page like the following:

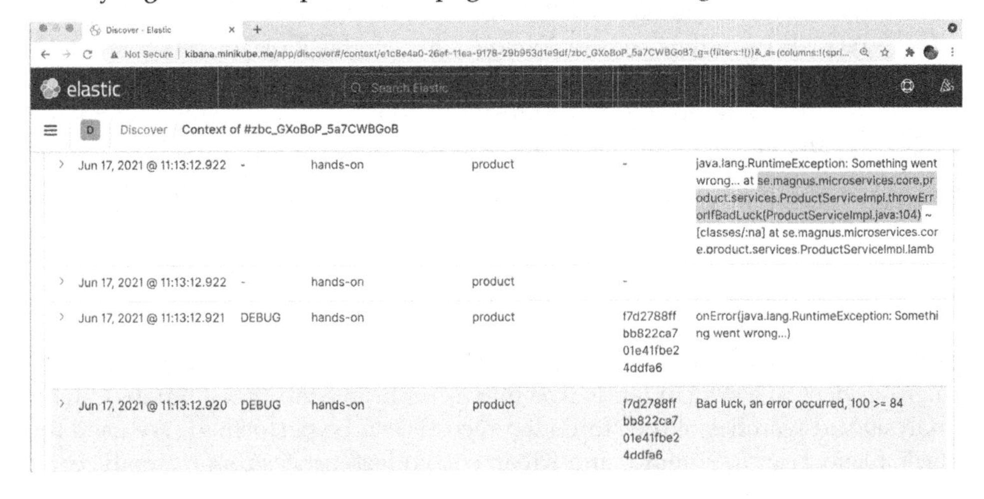

Figure 19.18: Kiali web UI, the root cause found

10. The log record above the **Bad luck** log record with the stack trace for the error message **Something went wrong...** looks interesting and was logged by the `product` microservice just three milliseconds after it logged the **Bad luck** log record. They seem to be related! The stack trace in that log record points to line 104 in `ProductServiceImpl.java`. Looking in the source code (see `microservices/product-service/src/main/java/se/magnus/microservices/core/product/services/ProductServiceImpl.java`), line 104 looks as follows:

    ```
    throw new RuntimeException("Something went wrong...");
    ```

    This is the root cause of the error. We did know this in advance, but now we have seen how we can navigate to it as well.

In this case, the problem is quite simple to resolve: simply omit the `faultPercent` parameter in the request to the API. In other cases, the resolution of the root cause can be much harder to figure out!

11. This concludes the root cause analysis. Click on the back button in the web browser to get back to the main page.
12. To be able to reuse the configuration of the search criteria and table layout, its definition can be saved by Kibana. Select, for example, to filter on log records from the `hands-on` Namespace and click on the **Save** link in the top-right menu. Give the search definition a name and click on the **Save** button. The search definition can be restored when required using the **Open** link in the menu.

This concludes this chapter on using the EFK stack for centralized logging.

Summary

In this chapter, we learned about the importance of collecting log records from microservices in a system landscape into a common centralized database where analysis and searches of the stored log records can be performed. We used the EFK stack, Elasticsearch, Fluentd, and Kibana, to collect, process, store, analyze, and search for log records.

Fluentd was used to collect log records not only from our microservices but also from the various supporting containers in the Kubernetes cluster. Elasticsearch was used as a text search engine. Together with Kibana, we saw how easy it is to get an understanding of what types of log records we have collected.

We also learned how to use Kibana to perform important tasks such as finding related log records from cooperating microservices and how to perform root cause analysis, finding the real problem for an error message.

Being able to collect and analyze log records in this way is an important capability in a production environment, but these types of activities are always done afterward, once the log record has been collected. Another important capability is to be able to monitor the current health of the microservices, collecting and visualizing runtime metrics in terms of the use of hardware resources, response times, and so on. We touched on this subject in the previous chapter, and in the next chapter, we will learn more about monitoring microservices.

Questions

1. A user searched for ERROR log messages in the `hands-on` Namespace for the last 30 days using the search criteria shown in the following screenshot, but none were found. Why?

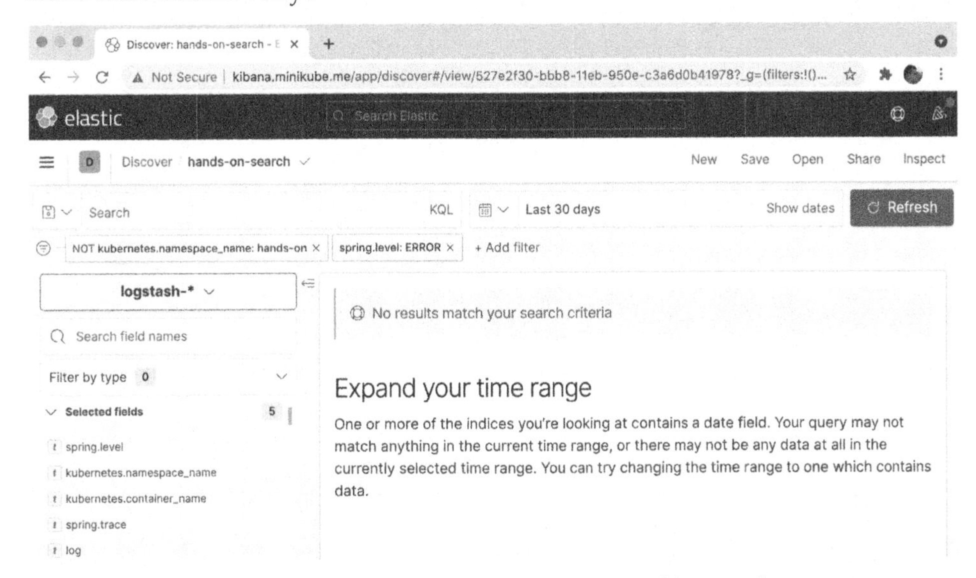

Figure 19.19: Kiali web UI, not showing expected log records

2. A user has found a log record of interest (shown below). How can the user find related log records from this and other microservices, for example, that come from processing an external API request?

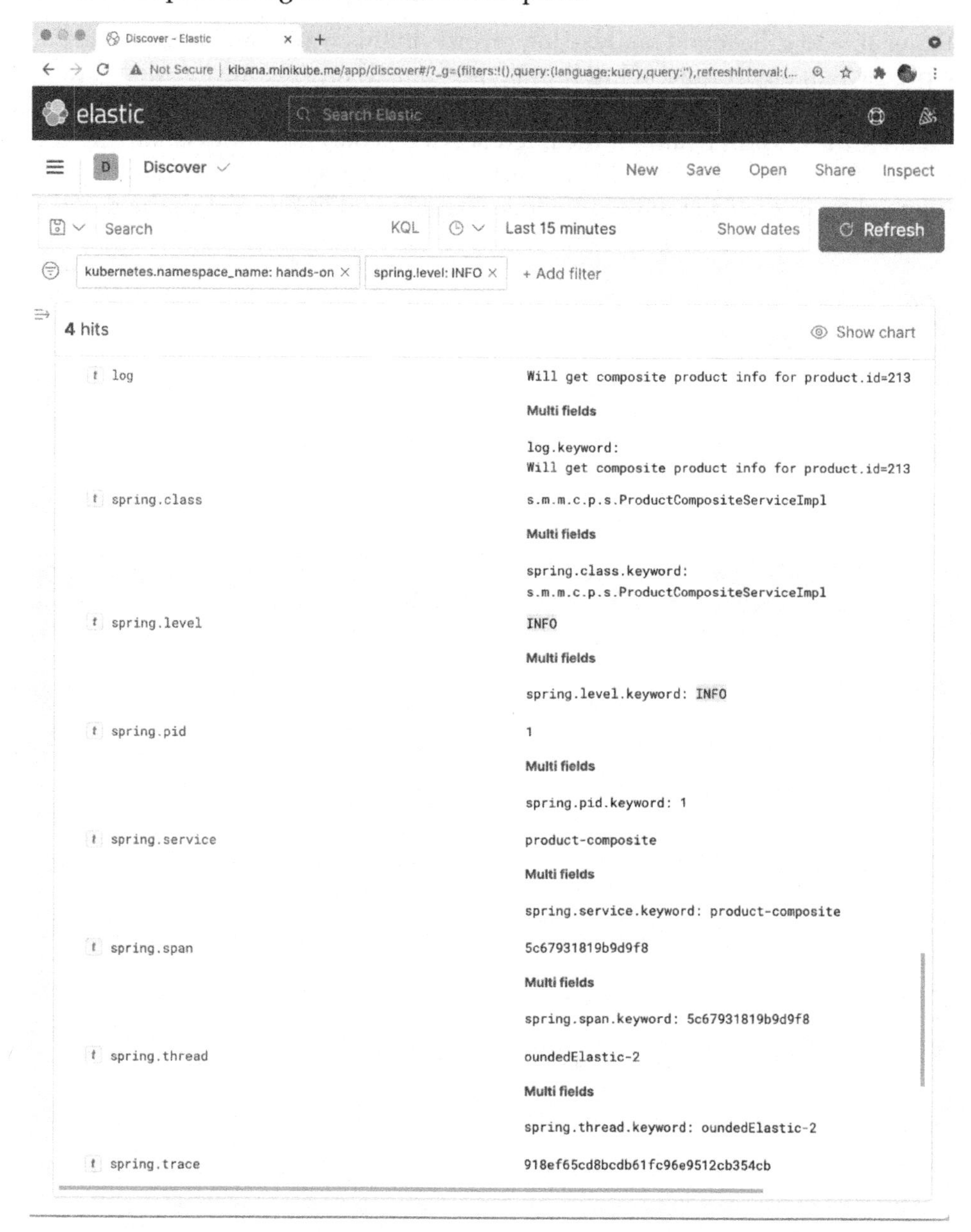

Figure 19.20: Kiali web UI, how do we find related log records?

3. A user has found a log record that seems to indicate the root cause of a problem that was reported by an end user. How can the user find the stack trace that shows where in the source code the error occurred?

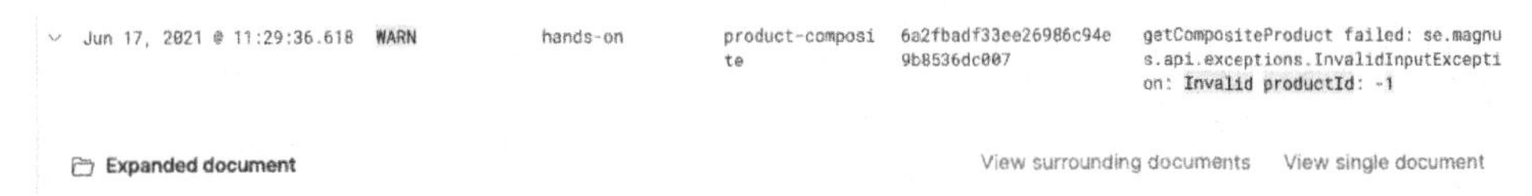

Figure 19.21: Kiali web UI, how do we find the root cause?

4. Why doesn't the following Fluentd configuration element work?

```
<match kubernetes.**hands-on**>
  @type rewrite_tag_filter
  <rule>
    key log
    pattern ^(.*)$
    tag spring-boot.${tag}
  </rule>
</match>
```

5. How can you determine whether Elasticsearch is up and running?
6. You suddenly lose connection to Kibana from your web browser. What could have caused this problem?

20

Monitoring Microservices

In this chapter, we will learn how to use Prometheus and Grafana to collect, monitor, and alert about performance metrics. As we mentioned in *Chapter 1, Introduction to Microservices*, in a production environment it is crucial to be able to collect metrics for application performance and hardware resource usage. Monitoring these metrics is required to avoid long response times or outages for API requests and other processes.

To be able to monitor a system landscape of microservices in a cost-efficient and proactive way, we must also be able to define alarms that are triggered automatically if the metrics exceed the configured limits.

In this chapter, we will cover the following topics:

- Introduction to performance monitoring using Prometheus and Grafana
- Changes in source code for collecting application metrics
- Building and deploying the microservices
- Monitoring microservices using Grafana dashboards
- Setting up alarms in Grafana

Technical requirements

For instructions on how to install the tools used in this book and how to access the source code for this book, see:

- *Chapter 21* for macOS
- *Chapter 22* for Windows

The code examples in this chapter all come from the source code in `$BOOK_HOME/Chapter19`.

If you want to view the changes applied to the source code in this chapter so that you can use Prometheus and Grafana to monitor and alert on performance metrics, you can compare it with the source code for *Chapter 19, Centralized Logging with the EFK Stack*. You can use your favorite diff tool and compare the two folders, `$BOOK_HOME/Chapter19` and `$BOOK_HOME/Chapter20`.

Introduction to performance monitoring using Prometheus and Grafana

In this chapter, we will reuse the deployment of Prometheus and Grafana that we created in *Chapter 18, Using a Service Mesh to Improve Observability and Management*, in the *Deploying Istio in a Kubernetes cluster* section. Also in that chapter, we were briefly introduced to Prometheus, a popular open source database for collecting and storing time series data such as performance metrics. We learned about Grafana, an open source tool for visualizing performance metrics. With the Grafana deployment comes a set of Istio-specific dashboards. Kiali can also render some performance-related graphs without the use of Grafana. In this chapter, we will get some hands-on experience with these tools.

The Istio configuration we deployed in *Chapter 18* includes a configuration of Prometheus, which automatically collects metrics from Pods in Kubernetes. All we need to do is set up an endpoint in our microservice that produces metrics in a format Prometheus can consume. We also need to add annotations to the Kubernetes Pods so that Prometheus can find the address of these endpoints. See the *Changes in source code for collecting application metrics* section of this chapter for details on how to set this up. To demonstrate Grafana's capabilities to raise alerts, we will also deploy a local mail server.

The following diagram illustrates the relationship between the runtime components we just discussed:

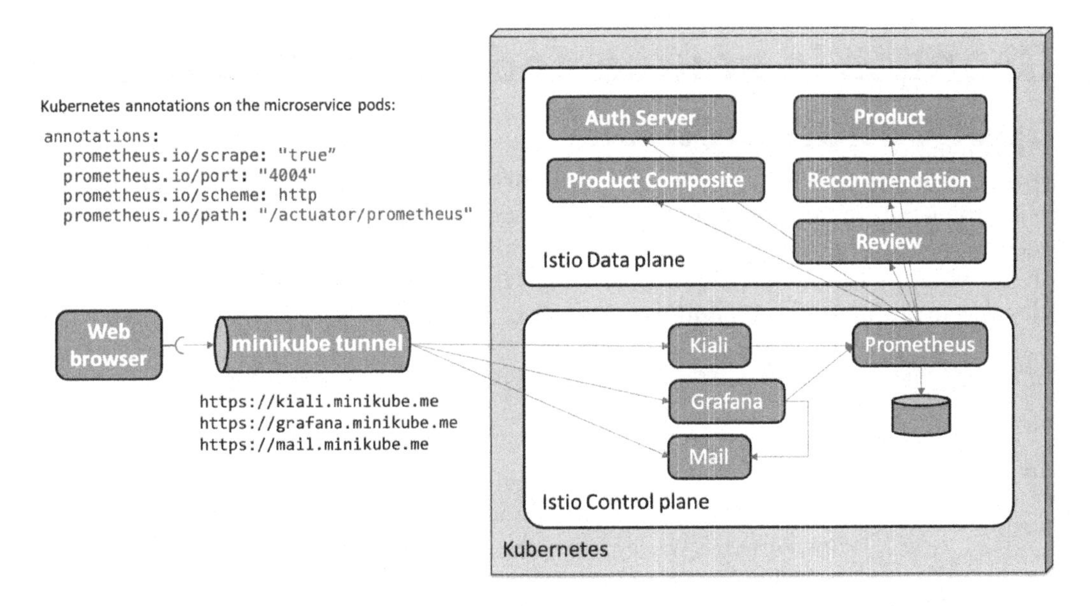

Figure 20.1: Adding Prometheus and Grafana to the system landscape

Here, we can see how Prometheus uses the annotations in the definitions of the Kubernetes Pods to be able to collect metrics from our microservices. It then stores these metrics in its database. A user can access the web UIs of Kiali and Grafana to monitor these metrics in a **Web browser**. The **Web browser** uses the **minikube tunnel** that was introduced in *Chapter 18*, in the *Setting up access to Istio services* section, to access Kiali, Grafana, and also a web page from the mail server to see alerts sent out by Grafana.

Please remember that the configuration that was used for deploying Istio from *Chapter 18* is only intended for development and test, not production. For example, performance metrics stored in the Prometheus database will not survive the Prometheus Pod being restarted!

In the next section, we will look at what changes have been applied to the source code to make the microservices produce performance metrics that Prometheus can collect.

Changes in source code for collecting application metrics

Spring Boot 2 supports producing performance metrics in a Prometheus format using the **Micrometer** library (`https://micrometer.io`). There's only one change we need to make to the source code of the microservices: we need to add a dependency on the Micrometer library, `micrometer-registry-prometheus`, in the Gradle build files, `build.gradle`. The dependency looks like this:

```
implementation 'io.micrometer:micrometer-registry-prometheus'
```

This will make the microservices produce Prometheus metrics on port `4004` using the `/actuator/Prometheus` URI.

In *Chapter 18*, we separated the management port, used by the actuator, from the port serving requests to APIs exposed by a microservice. See the *Observing the service mesh section* for a recap, if required.

To let Prometheus know about these endpoints, each microservice's Pod is annotated with the following code:

```
annotations:
  prometheus.io/scrape: "true"
  prometheus.io/port: "4004"
  prometheus.io/scheme: http
  prometheus.io/path: "/actuator/prometheus"
```

This is added to the `values.yaml` file of each component's Helm chart. See `kubernetes/helm/components`.

To make it easier to identify the source of the metrics once they have been collected by Prometheus, they are tagged with the name of the microservice that produced the metric. This is achieved by adding the following configuration to the common configuration file, `config-repo/application.yml`:

```
management.metrics.tags.application: ${spring.application.name}
```

This will result in each metric that's produced having an extra label named `application`. It will contain the value of the standard Spring property for the name of a microservice, `spring.application.name`.

These are all the changes that are required to prepare the microservices to produce performance metrics and to make Prometheus aware of what endpoints to use to start collecting them. In the next section, we will build and deploy the microservices.

Building and deploying the microservices

Building, deploying, and verifying the deployment using the `test-em-all.bash` test script is done in the same way it was done in *Chapter 19, Centralized Logging with the EFK Stack*, in the *Building and deploying the microservices* section. Run the following commands:

1. Build the Docker images from the source with the following commands:

   ```
   cd $BOOK_HOME/Chapter20
   eval $(minikube docker-env)
   ./gradlew build && docker-compose build
   ```

2. Recreate the Namespace, `hands-on`, and set it as the default Namespace:

   ```
   kubectl delete namespace hands-on
   kubectl apply -f kubernetes/hands-on-namespace.yml
   kubectl config set-context $(kubectl config current-context)
   --namespace=hands-on
   ```

3. Resolve the Helm chart dependencies with the following commands.

   First, we update the dependencies in the `components` folder:

   ```
   for f in kubernetes/helm/components/*; do helm dep up $f; done
   ```

   Next, we update the dependencies in the `environments` folder:

   ```
   for f in kubernetes/helm/environments/*; do helm dep up $f; done
   ```

4. Deploy the system landscape using Helm and wait for all deployments to complete:

   ```
   helm install hands-on-dev-env \
     kubernetes/helm/environments/dev-env \
     -n hands-on --wait
   ```

5. Start the Minikube tunnel, if it's not already running, as follows (see *Chapter 18*, the *Setting up access to Istio services* section, for a recap if you need one):

```
minikube tunnel
```

Remember that this command requires that your user has sudo privileges and that you enter your password during startup and shutdown. It takes a couple of seconds before the command asks for the password, so it is easy to miss!

6. Run the normal tests to verify the deployment with the following command:

```
./test-em-all.bash
```

Expect the output to be similar to what we've seen in the previous chapters:

```
$ ./test-em-all.bash
...
Wait for: curl -k https://health.minikube.me/actuator/health... DONE, continues...
...
Test OK (HTTP Code: 200)
...
End, all tests OK: Thu May 20 12:37:18 CEST 2021
$
```

Figure 20.2: All tests OK

With the microservices deployed, we can move on and start monitoring our microservices using Grafana!

Monitoring microservices using Grafana dashboards

As we already mentioned in the introduction, Kiali provides some very useful dashboards out of the box. In general, they are focused on application-level performance metrics such as requests per second, response times, and fault percentages for processing requests. As we will see shortly, they are very useful on an application level. But if we want to understand the usage of the underlying hardware resources, we need more detailed metrics, for example, Java VM-related metrics.

Grafana has an active community that, among other things, shares reusable dashboards. We will try out a dashboard from the community that's tailored for getting a lot of valuable Java VM-related metrics from a Spring Boot 2 application such as our microservices. Finally, we will see how we can build our own dashboards in Grafana. But let's start by exploring the dashboards that come out of the box in Kiali and Grafana.

Before we do that, we need to make two preparations:

1. Install a local mail server for tests and configure Grafana to be able to send alert emails to it. We will use the mail server in the section *Setting up alarms in Grafana*.
2. To be able to monitor some metrics, we will start the load test tool we used in previous chapters.

Installing a local mail server for tests

In this section, we will set up a local test mail server and configure Grafana to send alert emails to the mail server.

Grafana can send emails to any SMTP mail server but, to keep the tests local, we will deploy a test mail server named `maildev`. Go through the following steps:

1. Install the test mail server in Istio's Namespace with the following commands:

   ```
   kubectl -n istio-system create deployment mail-server --image
   maildev/maildev:1.1.0
   kubectl -n istio-system expose deployment mail-server
   --port=80,25 --type=ClusterIP
   kubectl -n istio-system wait --timeout=60s --for=condition=ready
   pod -l app=mail-server
   ```

2. To make the mail server's web UI available from the outside of Minikube, a set of `Gateway`, `VirtualService`, and `DestinationRule` manifest files has been added for the mail server in Istio's Helm chart. See the template `kubernetes/helm/environments/istio-system/templates/expose-mail.yml`. Run a `helm upgrade` command to apply the new manifest files:

   ```
   helm upgrade istio-hands-on-addons kubernetes/helm/environments/
   istio-system -n istio-system
   ```

3. Verify that the test mail server is up and running by visiting its web page at `https://mail.minikube.me`. Expect a web page such as the following to be rendered:

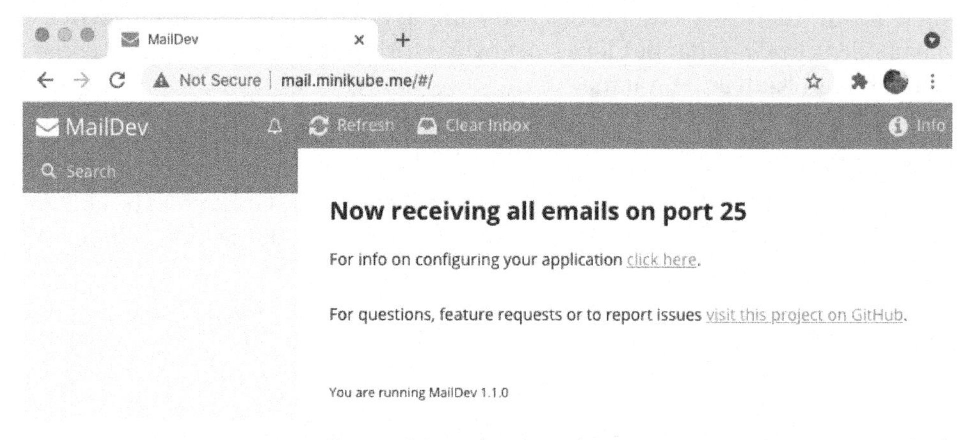

Figure 20.3: Mail server web page

4. Configure Grafana to send emails to the test mail server by setting up a few environment variables. Run the following commands:

```
kubectl -n istio-system set env deployment/grafana \
    GF_SMTP_ENABLED=true \
    GF_SMTP_SKIP_VERIFY=true \
    GF_SMTP_HOST=mail-server:25 \
    GF_SMTP_FROM_ADDRESS=grafana@minikube.me
kubectl -n istio-system wait --timeout=60s --for=condition=ready
pod -l app=Grafana
```

   The `ENABLE` variable is used to allow Grafana to send emails. The `SKIP_VERIFY` variable is used to tell Grafana to skip SSL checks with the test mail server. The `HOST` variable points to our mail server and the `FROM_ADDRESS` variable specifies what "from" address to use in the mail.

For more information on the mail server, see `https://hub.docker.com/r/maildev/maildev`.

Now, we have a test mail server up and running and Grafana has been configured to send emails to it. In the next section, we will start the load test tool.

Starting up the load test

To have something to monitor, let's start up the load test using Siege, which we used in previous chapters. Run the following commands to get an access token and then start up the load test, using the access token for authorization:

```
ACCESS_TOKEN=$(curl -k https://writer:secret@minikube.me/oauth2/token
-d grant_type=client_credentials -s | jq .access_token -r)

echo ACCESS_TOKEN=$ACCESS_TOKEN

siege https://minikube.me/product-composite/1 -H "Authorization: Bearer
$ACCESS_TOKEN" -c1 -d1 -v
```

Remember that an access token is only valid for 1 hour – after that, you need to get a new one.

Now, we are ready to learn about the dashboards in Kiali and Grafana and explore the Grafana dashboards that come with Istio.

Using Kiali's built-in dashboards

In *Chapter 18*, we learned about Kiali, but we skipped the part where Kiali shows performance metrics. Now, it's time to get back to that subject!

Execute the following steps to learn about Kiali's built-in dashboards:

1. Open the Kiali web UI in a web browser using the `https://kiali.minikube.me` URL. Log in with `admin`/`admin` if required.
2. To see our deployments, go to the workloads page by clicking on the **Workloads** tab from the menu on the left-hand side.
3. Select the **product-composite** deployment by clicking on it.

4. On the **product-composite** page, select the **Outbound Metrics** tab. You will see a page like the following screenshot:

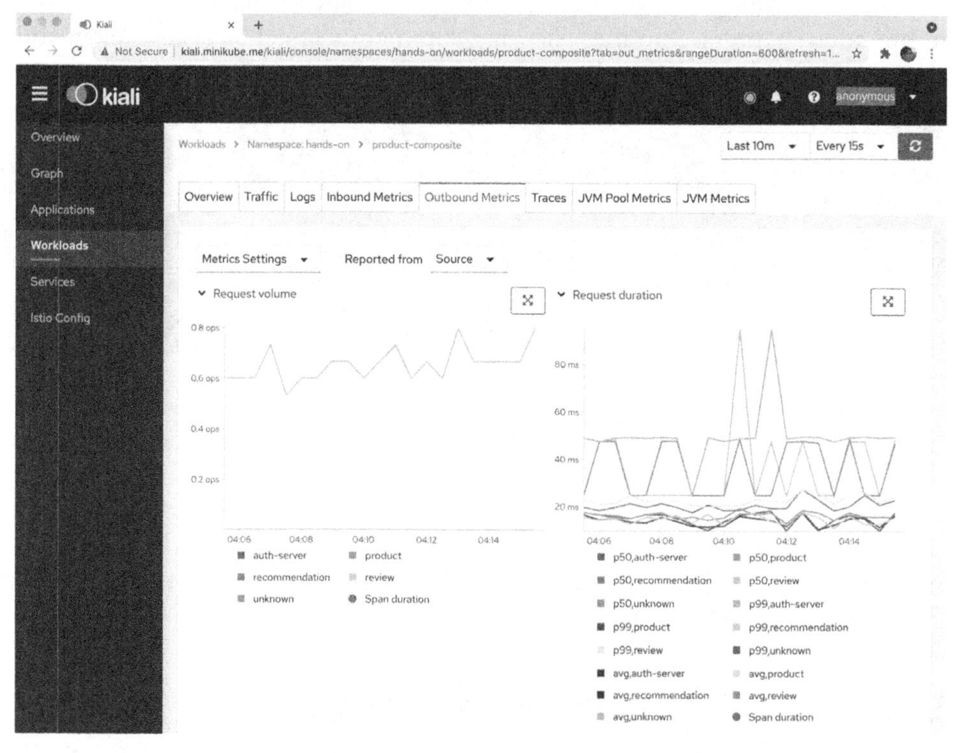

Figure 20.4: Kiali outbound metrics

Kiali will visualize some overall performance graphs that are of great value, and there are more graphs to explore. Feel free to try them out on your own!

5. However, far more detailed performance metrics are available in Grafana. Open the Grafana web UI in a web browser using the `https://grafana.minikube.me` URL.

6. You will be presented with a welcome page with the text **Welcome to Grafana**. Over the welcome text is a **Home** link; click on it and you will be presented with an overview of available dashboards. You will see a folder named **Istio** that contains the dashboards that were installed when Grafana was deployed together with Istio in *Chapter 18*. Click on the folder to expand it and select the dashboard named **Istio Mesh Dashboard**. Expect a web page like the following:

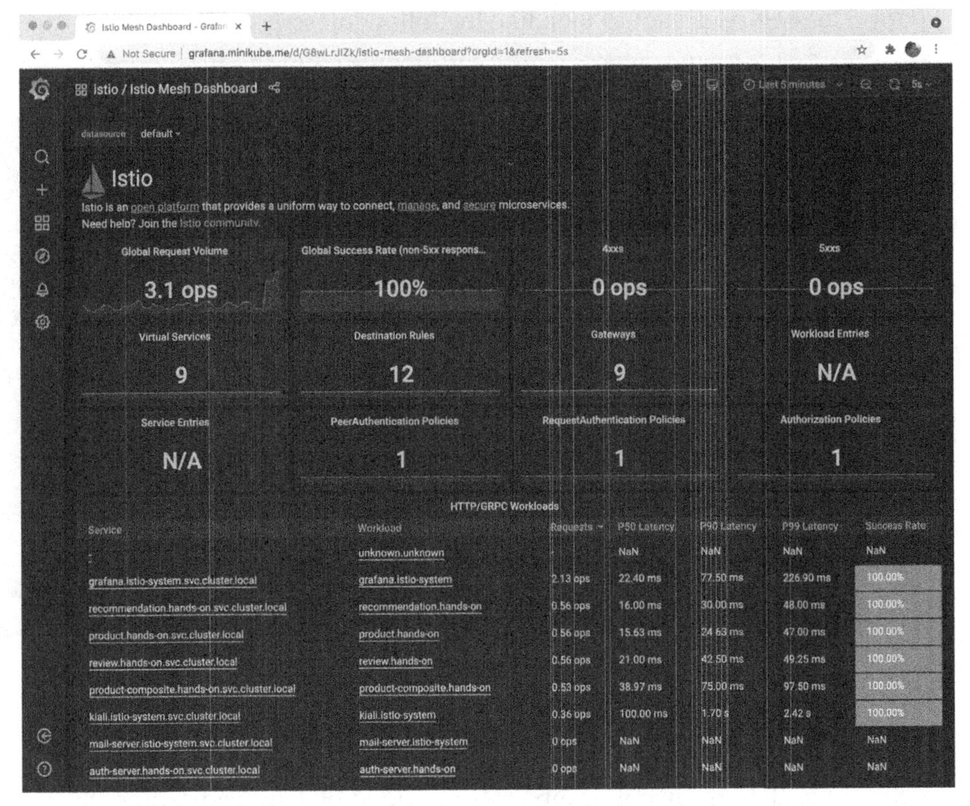

Figure 20.5: Grafana showing Istio Mesh Dashboard

This dashboard gives a very good overview of metrics for the microservices involved in the service mesh, like request rates, response times, and the success rates.

7. There are a lot of detailed performance metrics available; click on the **product-composite** service to see some of them. A dashboard named **Istio Service Dashboard** should be displayed with the product composite service preselected. It contains three rows containing panels with metrics. Expand the first row named **General** to get an overview of the service.

The web page should look like the following screenshot:

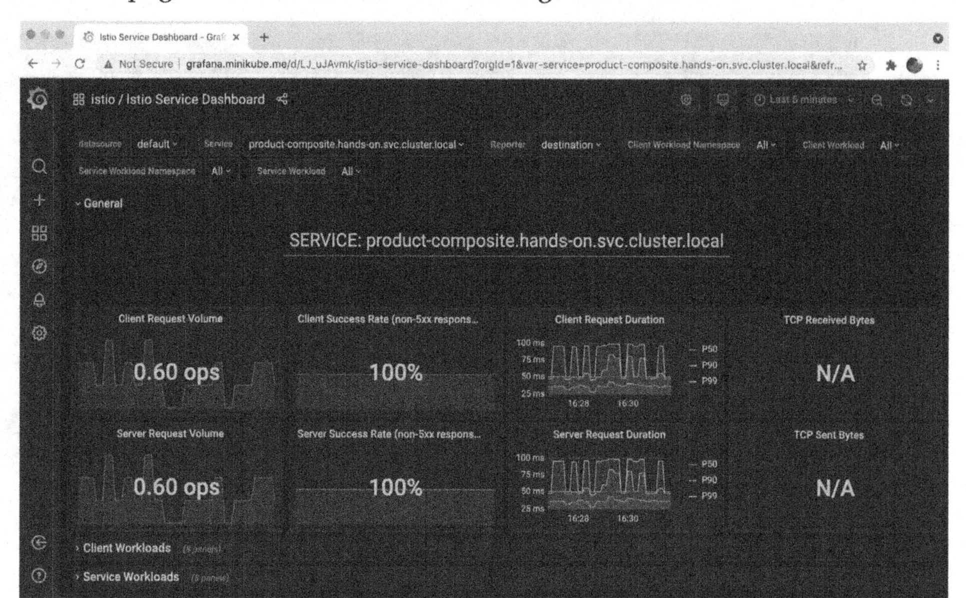

Figure 20.6: Grafana with a lot of metrics for a microservice

Expand the two remaining rows to see more detailed metrics regarding the selected service. Feel free to look around!

8. Go back to the list of dashboards provided by Istio and explore the metrics they provide. To get back to the list of available dashboards, click on the Dashboard icon (four squares) in the menu on the left side.

As we've already mentioned, the Istio dashboards give a very good overview at an application level. But there is also a need for monitoring the metrics for hardware usage per microservice. In the next section, we will learn about how existing dashboards can be imported – specifically, a dashboard showing Java VM metrics for a Spring Boot 2-based application.

Importing existing Grafana dashboards

As we've already mentioned, Grafana has an active community that shares reusable dashboards. They can be explored at `https://grafana.com/grafana/dashboards`. We will try out a dashboard called **JVM (Micrometer) - Kubernetes - Prometheus by Istio** that's tailored for getting a lot of valuable JVM-related metrics from Spring Boot 2 applications in a Kubernetes environment. The link to the dashboard is `https://grafana.com/grafana/dashboards/11955`. Perform the following steps to import this dashboard:

1. Import the dashboard named JVM (Micrometer) by following these steps:
    a. On the Grafana web page, click on the Create icon (a + sign) in the left-hand side menu and then select **Import**.
    b. On the **Import** page, paste the dashboard ID `11955` into the **Import via grafana.com** field and click on the **Load** button next to it.
    c. On the **Import** page that will be displayed, click on the **Prometheus** drop-down menu and select the **Prometheus** data source.
    d. Now, by clicking on the **Import** button, the JVM (Micrometer) dashboard will be imported and rendered.
2. Inspect the **JVM (Micrometer)** dashboard by following these steps:
    a. To get a good view of the metrics, use the time picker (in the top-right corner) to select **Last 5 minutes** and select a refresh rate of **5s** in the dropdown to the right.
    b. In the **Application** drop-down menu, which can be found at the top-left of the page, select the **product-composite** microservice.

c. Since we are running a load test using Siege in the background, we will see a lot of metrics. The following is a sample screenshot:

Figure 20.7: Grafana showing Java VM metrics

In this dashboard, we can find all types of Java VM relevant metrics for, among other things, CPU, memory, heap, and I/O usage, as well as HTTP-related metrics such as requests/second, average duration, and error rates. Feel free to explore these metrics on your own!

Being able to import existing dashboards is of great value when we want to get started quickly. However, what's even more important is to know how to create our own dashboard. We will learn about this in the next section.

Developing your own Grafana dashboards

Getting started with developing Grafana dashboards is straightforward. The important thing for us to understand is what metrics Prometheus makes available for us.

In this section, we will learn how to examine the available metrics. Based on these, we will create a dashboard that can be used to monitor some of the more interesting metrics.

Examining Prometheus metrics

In the *Changes in source code for collecting application metrics* section earlier, we configured Prometheus to collect metrics from our microservices. We can make a call to the same endpoint and see what metrics Prometheus collects. Run the following command:

```
curl https://health.minikube.me/actuator/prometheus -ks
```

Expect a lot of output from the command, as in the following example:

```
-bash
$ curl https://health.minikube.me/actuator/prometheus -ks
...
resilience4j_circuitbreaker_state{... name="product",state="open",} 0.0
resilience4j_circuitbreaker_state{... name="product",state="half_open",} 0.0
resilience4j_circuitbreaker_state{... name="product",state="closed",} 1.0
...
resilience4j_retry_calls_total{... kind="successful_with_retry",name="product",} 0.0
resilience4j_retry_calls_total{... kind="failed_with_retry",name="product",} 0.0
resilience4j_retry_calls_total{... kind="successful_without_retry",name="product",} 10.0
resilience4j_retry_calls_total{... kind="failed_without_retry",name="product",} 6.0
...
$
```

Figure 20.8: Prometheus metrics

Among all of the metrics that are reported, there are two very interesting ones:

- `resilience4j_circuitbreaker_state`: Resilience4j reports on the state of the circuit breaker.
- `resilience4j_retry_calls`: Resilience4j reports on how the retry mechanism operates. It reports four different values for successful and failed requests, combined with and without retries.

Note that the metrics have a label named `application`, which contains the name of the microservice. This field comes from the configuration of the `management.metrics.tags.application` property, which we did in the *Changes in source code for collecting application metrics* section.

These metrics seem interesting to monitor. None of the dashboards we have used so far use metrics from Resilience4j. In the next section, we will create a dashboard for these metrics.

Creating the dashboard

In this section, we will learn how to create a dashboard that visualizes the Resilience4j metrics we described in the previous section.

We will set up the dashboard in the following stages:

- Creating an empty dashboard
- Creating a new panel for the circuit breaker metric
- Creating a new panel for the retry metric
- Arranging the panels

Creating an empty dashboard

Perform the following steps to create an empty dashboard:

1. On the Grafana web page, click on the **+** sign in the left-hand menu and then select **Dashboard**.
2. A web page named **New dashboard** will be displayed:

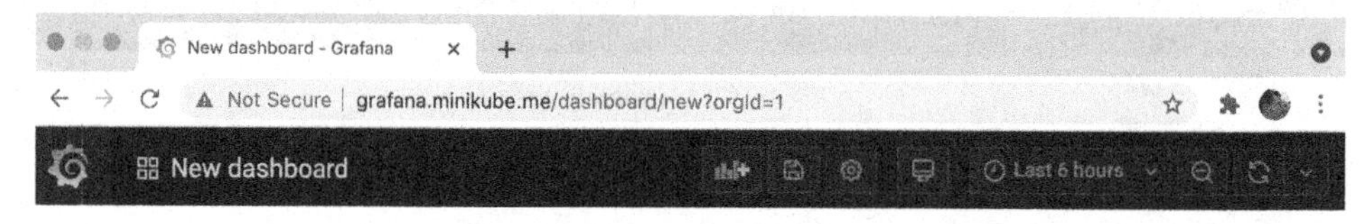

Figure 20.9: Creating a new dashboard in Grafana

3. Click on the Dashboard settings button (it has a gear as its icon), in the menu shown in the preceding screenshot. Then, follow these steps:
    a. Specify the name of the dashboard in the **Name** field and set the value to `Hands-on Dashboard`.
    b. Click on the top-left back button on the web page (not to be mixed up with the web browser's back button).

4. Click on the time picker and select **Last 5 minutes** as the range.
5. Click on the refresh rate icon to the right and specify **5s** as the refresh rate.

Creating a new panel for the circuit breaker metric

Perform the following steps to create a new panel for the circuit breaker metric:

1. Click on the **+ Add new panel** button.

   A page will be displayed where the new panel can be configured.
2. To the right, in the tab named **Panel**, set the **Panel title** to `Circuit Breaker`.
3. In the bottom-left **Query** panel, under the letter **A**, specify the **query** as the name of the circuit breaker metric for the closed state, that is, `resilience4j_circuitbreaker_state{state="closed"}`.
4. In the **Legend** field, specify the value `{{state}}`. This will create a legend in the panel where the involved microservices will be labeled with their name and Namespace.

   The filled-in values should look as follows:

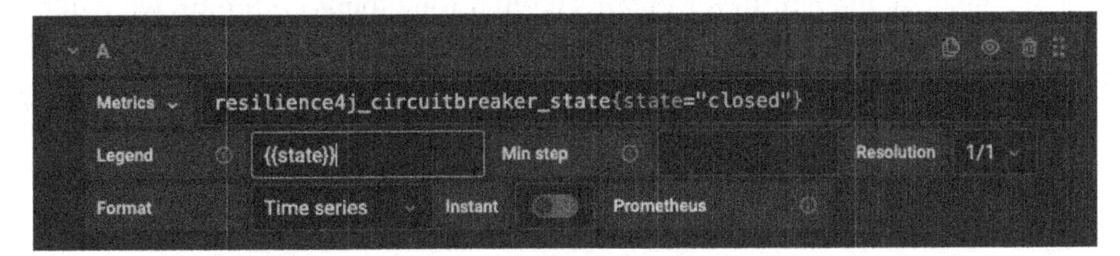

Figure 20.10: Specifying circuit breaker metrics in Grafana

5. Click on the **+ Query** button below to enter a new query under **B** for the **open** state. Set the **query** field to `resilience4j_circuitbreaker_state{state="open"}` and the **Legend** field to `{{state}}`.
6. Click on the **+ Query** button a final time to enter a new query under **C** for the **half_open** state. Set the **query** field to `resilience4j_circuitbreaker_state{state="half_open"}` and the **Legend** field to `{{state}}`.
7. Click on the back button at the top left of the page to get back to the dashboard.

Creating a new panel for the retry metric

Here, we will repeat the same procedure that we went through for adding a panel for the preceding circuit breaker metric, but instead, we will specify the values for the retry metrics:

1. Create a new panel by clicking on the **Add panel** icon (a chart with a plus sign) in the top-level menu and click on **Add new panel** in the new panel.
2. Specify `Retry` as the **Panel title**.
3. In the **query** field, under **A**, specify `rate(resilience4j_retry_calls_total[30s])`.

   Since the retry metric is a counter, its value will only go up. An ever-increasing metric is rather uninteresting to monitor. The **rate** function is used to convert the retry metric into a rate per second metric. The time window specified, that is, `30 s`, is used by the rate function to calculate the average values of the rate.
4. For the **Legend**, specify `{{kind}}`.

   Just like the output for the preceding Prometheus endpoint, we will get four metrics for the retry mechanism. To separate them in the legend, the `kind` attribute needs to be added.
5. Note that Grafana immediately starts to render a graph in the panel editor based on the specified values.
6. Click on the back button to get back to the dashboard.

Arranging the panels

Perform the following steps to arrange the panels on the dashboard:

1. You can resize a panel by dragging its lower right-hand corner to the preferred size.
2. You can also move a panel by dragging its header to the desired position.

   The following is an example layout of the two panels:

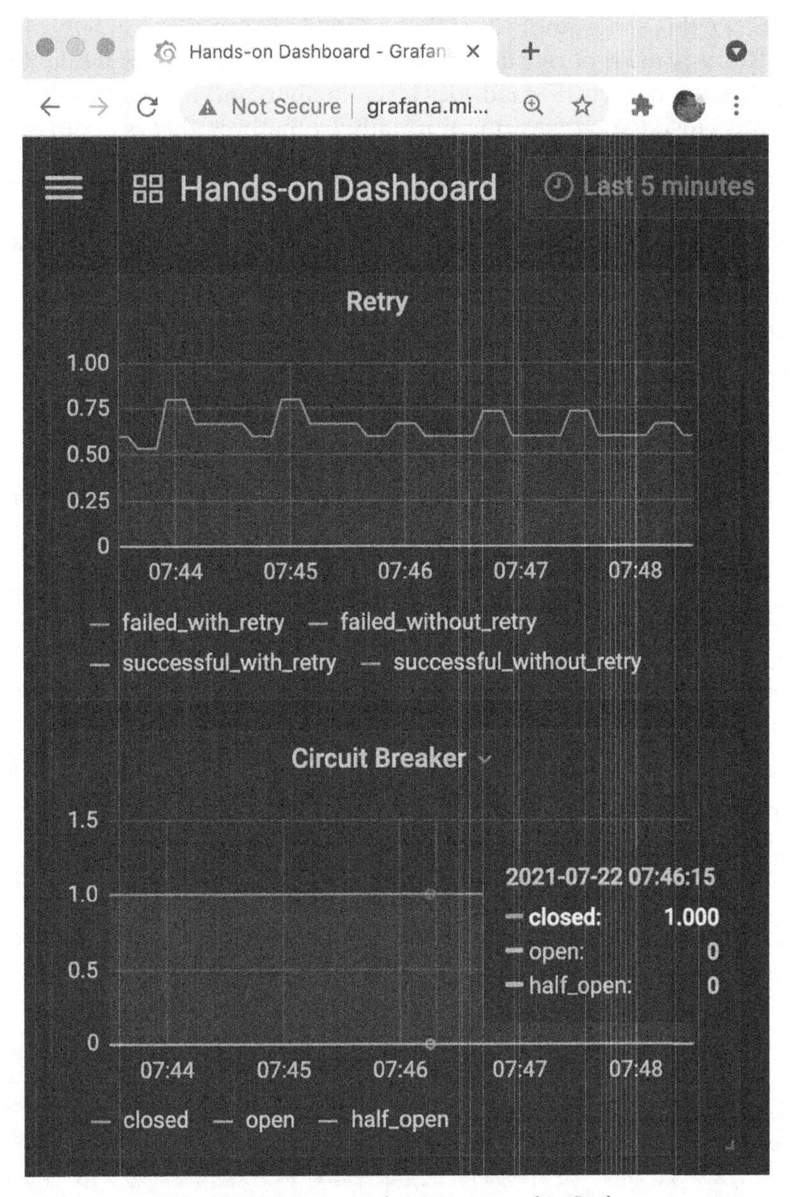

Figure 20.11: Moving and resizing a panel in Grafana

Since this screenshot was taken with Siege running in the background, the **Retry** panel reports **successful_without_retry** metrics while the **Circuit Breaker** reports that **closed=1**, while **open** and **half_open=0**, meaning that it is **closed** and operating normally (something that is about to change in the next section).

3. Finally, click on the **Save** button at the top of the page. A **Save dashboard as...** dialog will show up; ensure that the name is **Hands-on Dashboard** and hit the **Save** button.

With the dashboard created, we are ready to try it out. In the next section, we will try out both metrics.

Trying out the new dashboard

Before we start testing the new dashboard, we must stop the load test tool, Siege. For this, go to the command window where Siege is running and press *Ctrl* + *C* to stop it.

Let's start by testing how to monitor the circuit breaker. Afterward, we will try out the retry metrics.

Testing the circuit breaker metrics

If we force the circuit breaker to open up, its state will change from **closed** to **open**, and then eventually to the **half-open** state. This should be reported in the circuit breaker panel.

Open the circuit, just like we did in *Chapter 13, Improving Resilience Using Resilience4j*, in the *Trying out the circuit breaker and retry mechanism* section; that is, make some requests to the API in a row, all of which will fail. Run the following commands:

```
ACCESS_TOKEN=$(curl -k https://writer:secret@minikube.me/oauth2/token
-d grant_type=client_credentials -s | jq .access_token -r)

echo ACCESS_TOKEN=$ACCESS_TOKEN

for ((n=0; n<4; n++)); do curl -o /dev/null -skL -w "%{http_code}\n"
https://minikube.me/product-composite/1?delay=3 -H "Authorization:
Bearer $ACCESS_TOKEN" -s; done
```

We can expect three `500` responses and a final `200`, indicating three errors in a row, which is what it takes to open the circuit breaker. The last `200` indicates a **fail-fast** response from the `product-composite` microservice when it detects that the circuit is open.

On some rare occasions, I have noticed that the circuit breaker metrics are not reported in Grafana directly after the dashboard is created. If they don't show up after a minute, simply rerun the preceding command to reopen the circuit breaker again.

Expect the value for the **closed** state to drop to **0** and the **open** state to take the value **1**, meaning that the circuit is now open. After 10s, the circuit will turn to the half-open state, indicated by the **half-open** metrics having the value **1** and **open** being set to **0**. This means that the circuit breaker is ready to test some requests to see if the problem that opened the circuit is gone.

Close the circuit breaker again by issuing three successful requests to the API with the following command:

```
for ((n=0; n<4; n++)); do curl -o /dev/null -skL -w "%{http_code}\n"
https://minikube.me/product-composite/1?delay=0 -H "Authorization:
Bearer $ACCESS_TOKEN" -s; done
```

We will get only `200` responses. Note that the circuit breaker metric goes back to normal again, meaning that the **closed** metric goes back to **1**.

After this test, the Grafana dashboard should look as follows:

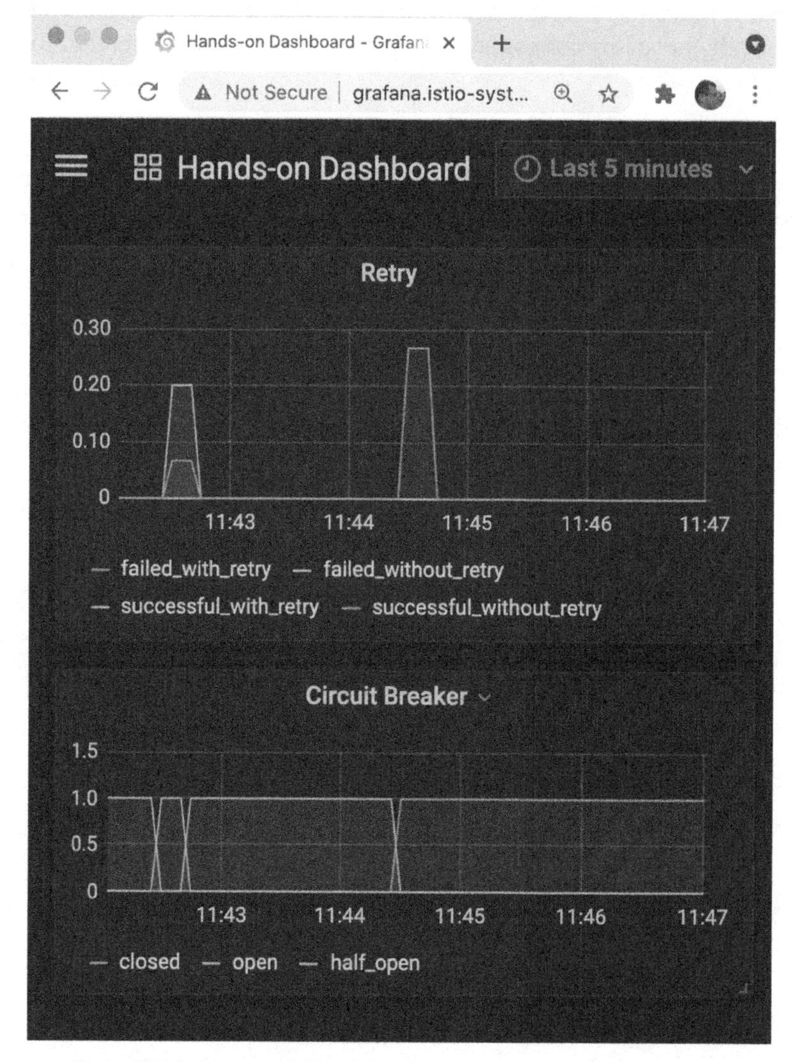

Figure 20.12: Retries and Circuit Breaker in action as viewed in Grafana

From the preceding screenshot, we can see that the retry mechanism also reports metrics that succeeded and failed. When the circuit was opened, all requests failed without retries. When the circuit was closed, all requests were successful without any retries. This is as expected.

Now that we have seen the circuit breaker metrics in action, let's see the retry metrics in action!

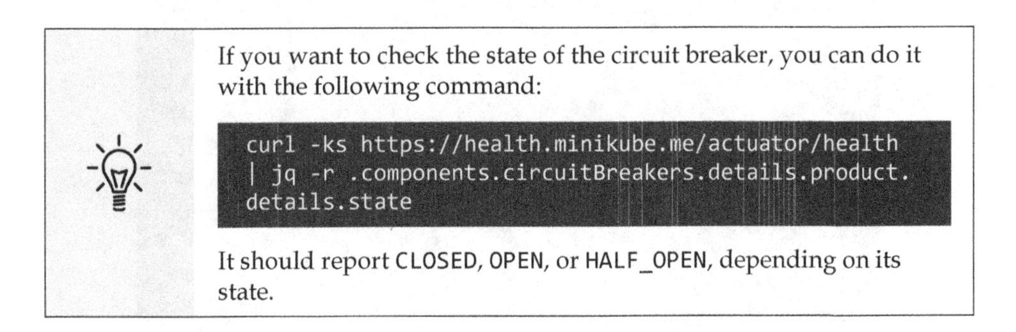

If you want to check the state of the circuit breaker, you can do it with the following command:

```
curl -ks https://health.minikube.me/actuator/health
| jq -r .components.circuitBreakers.details.product.
details.state
```

It should report `CLOSED`, `OPEN`, or `HALF_OPEN`, depending on its state.

Testing the retry metrics

To trigger the retry mechanism, we will use the `faultPercentage` parameter we used in previous chapters. To avoid triggering the circuit breaker, we need to use relatively low values for the parameter. Run the following command:

```
while true; do curl -o /dev/null -s -L -w "%{http_code}\n" -H
"Authorization: Bearer $ACCESS_TOKEN" -k https://minikube.me/product-
composite/1?faultPercent=10; sleep 3; done
```

This command will call the API once every third second. It specifies that 10% of the requests should fail so that the retry mechanism will kick in and retry the failed requests.

After a few minutes, the dashboard should report metrics such as the following:

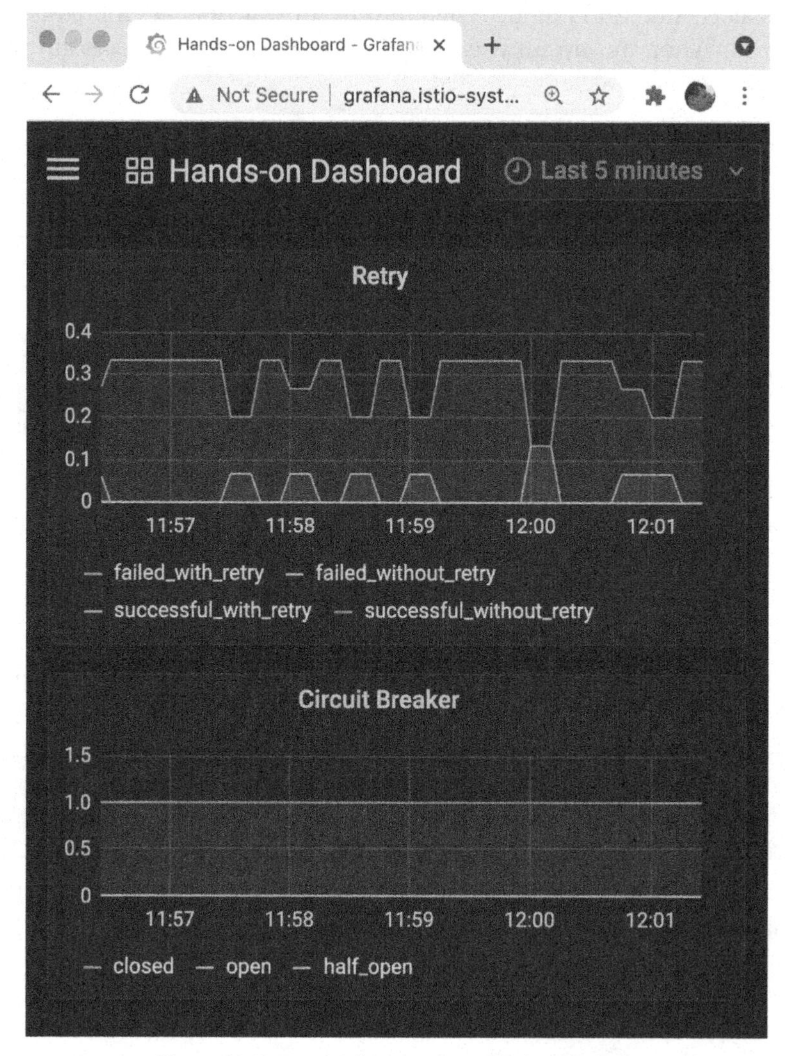

Figure 20.13: Result of retry tests viewed in Grafana

In the preceding screenshot, we can see that most of the requests have been executed successfully, without any retries. Approximately 10% of the requests have been retried by the retry mechanism and successfully executed after the retry.

Before we leave the section on creating dashboards, we will learn how we can export and import dashboards.

Exporting and importing Grafana dashboards

Once a dashboard has been created, we typically want to take two actions:

- Save the definition of the dashboard as source code in a Git repo
- Move the dashboard to other Grafana instances, for example, those used in QA and production environments

To perform these actions, we can use Grafana's API for exporting and importing dashboards. Since we only have one Grafana instance, we will perform the following steps:

1. Export the dashboard to a JSON file
2. Delete the dashboard
3. Import the dashboard from the JSON file

Before we perform these steps, we need to understand the two different types of IDs that a dashboard has:

- `id`, an auto-incremented identifier that is unique only within a Grafana instance.
- `uid`, a unique identifier that can be used in multiple Grafana instances. It is part of the URL when accessing dashboards, meaning that links to a dashboard will stay the same as long as the `uid` of a dashboard remains the same. When a dashboard is created, a random `uid` is created by Grafana.

When we import a dashboard, Grafana will try to update a dashboard if the `id` field is set. To be able to test importing a dashboard in a Grafana instance that doesn't have the dashboard already installed, we need to set the `id` field to `null`.

Perform the following actions to export and then import your dashboard:

1. Identify the `uid` of your dashboard.

   The `uid` value can be found in the URL in the web browser where the dashboard is shown. It will look like this:

   ```
   https://grafana.minikube.me/d/YMcDoBg7k/hands-on-dashboard
   ```

2. The `uid` in the URL above is `YMcDoBg7k`. In a terminal window, create a variable with its value. In my case, it will be:

   ```
   ID=YMcDoBg7k
   ```

3. Export the dashboard to a JSON file with the following command:

   ```
   curl -sk https://grafana.minikube.me/api/dashboards/uid/$ID | jq
   '.dashboard.id=null' > "Hands-on-Dashboard.json"
   ```

   The `curl` command exports the dashboard to JSON format. The `jq` statement sets the `id` field to `null` and the output from the `jq` command is written to a file named `Hands-on-Dashboard.json`.

4. Delete the dashboard.

   In the web browser, select **Dashboards** and **Manage** in the menu to the left. Identify the **Hands-on Dashboard** in the list of dashboards and select it by clicking in the checkbox in front of it. A red **Delete** button will be shown; click on it, and click on the new **Delete** button that is shown in the confirm dialog box that pops up.

5. Recreate the dashboard by importing it from the JSON file with the following command:

   ```
   curl -i -XPOST -H 'Accept: application/json' -H 'Content-Type:
   application/json' -k \
       'https://grafana.minikube.me/api/dashboards/db' \
       -d @Hands-on-Dashboard.json
   ```

   Note that the URL used to access the dashboard is still valid, in my case `https://grafana.minikube.me/d/YMcDoBg7k/hands-on-dashboard`.

6. Verify that the imported dashboard reports metrics in the same way as before it was deleted and reimported. Since the request loop started in the *Testing the retry metrics* section is still running, the same metrics as in that section should be reported.

For more information regarding Grafana's APIs, see `https://grafana.com/docs/grafana/v7.2/http_api/dashboard/#get-dashboard-by-uid`.

Before proceeding to the next section, remember to stop the request loop that we started for the retry test by pressing *Ctrl* + *C* in the terminal window where the request loop executes!

In the next section, we will learn how to set up alarms in Grafana, based on these metrics.

Setting up alarms in Grafana

Being able to monitor the circuit breaker and retry metrics is of great value, but even more important is the capability to define automated alarms on these metrics. Automated alarms relieve us from monitoring the metrics manually.

Grafana comes with built-in support for defining alarms and sending notifications to a number of channels. In this section, we will define alerts on the circuit breaker and configure Grafana to send emails to the test mail server when alerts are raised. The local test mail server was installed in the earlier section *Installing a local mail server for tests*.

For other types of channels supported by the version of Grafana used in this chapter, see `https://grafana.com/docs/grafana/v7.2/alerting/notifications/#list-of-supported-notifiers`.

In the next section, we will define a mail-based notification channel that will be used by the alert in the section after this.

Setting up a mail-based notification channel

To configure a mail-based notification channel in Grafana, perform the following steps:

1. On the Grafana web page, on the menu to the left, click on the Alerting menu choice (with an alarm bell as its icon) and select **Notification channels**.
2. Click on the **Add channel** button.
3. Set the name to `mail`.
4. Select the type as **Email**.
5. Enter an email address of your choice. Emails will only be sent to the local test mail server, independent of the email address that's specified.

6. Expand **Notification settings** and select **Default (Use this notification for all alerts)**.

   The configuration of the notification channel should look as follows:

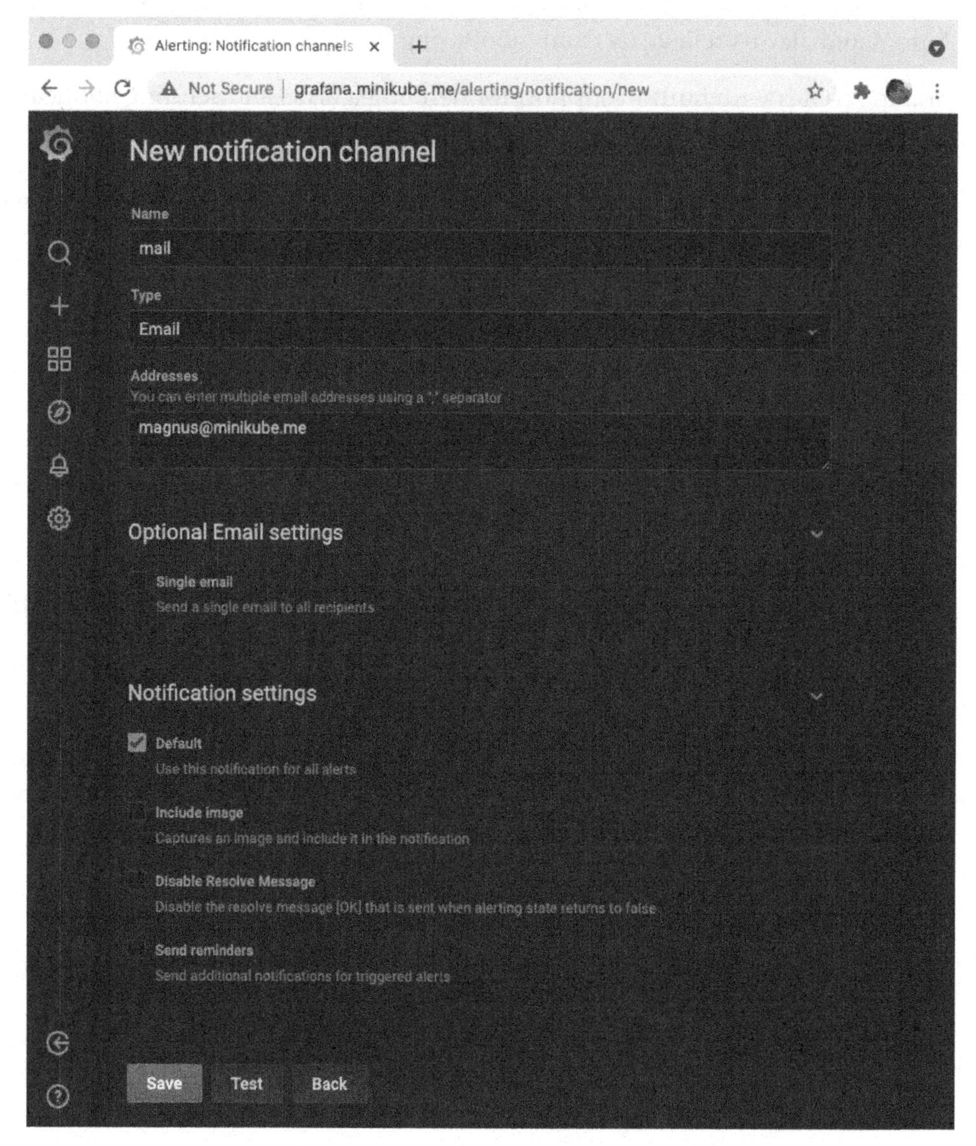

Figure 20.14: Setting up an email-based notification channel

7. Click on the **Test** button to send a test mail.
8. Click on the **Save** button.
9. Click on the **Dashboard** button in the left-hand side menu and then on the **Manage** menu entry.
10. Select **Hands-on Dashboard** from the list to get back to the dashboard.
11. Check the test mail server's web page to ensure that we have received a test email. You should receive the following:

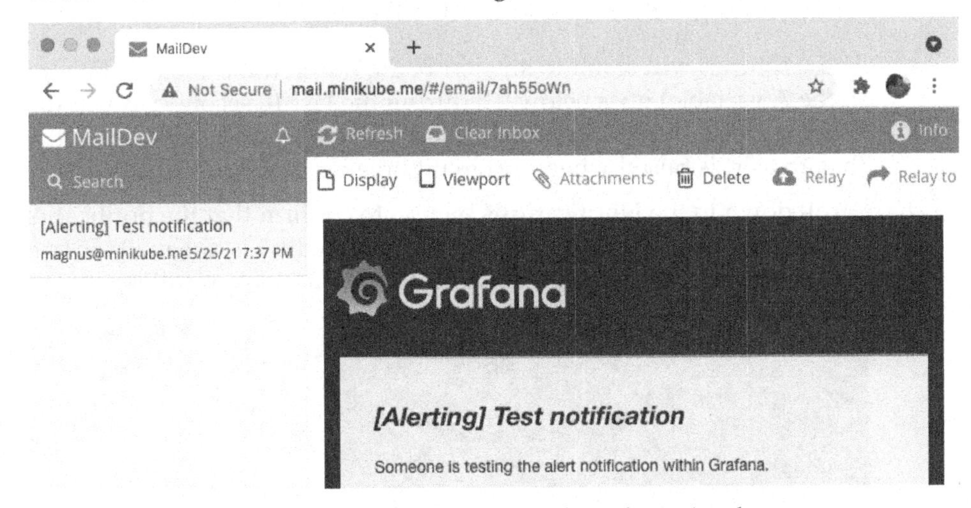

Figure 20.15: Verifying the test mail on the mail server's web page

With a notification channel in place, we are ready to define an alert on the circuit breaker.

Setting up an alarm on the circuit breaker

To create an alarm on the circuit breaker, we need to create the alert and then add an alert list to the dashboard, where we can see what alert events have occurred over time.

Perform the following steps to create an alert for the circuit breaker:

1. In the **Hands-on Dashboard**, click on the header of the **Circuit Breaker** panel. A drop-down menu will appear.
2. Select the **Edit** menu option.
3. Select the **Alert** tab in the tab list (shown as an alarm bell icon).

4. Click on the **Create Alert** button.
5. In the **Evaluate every** field, set the value to `10s`.
6. In the **For** field, set the value to `0m`.
7. In the **Conditions** section, specify the following values:
    - For the **WHEN** field, select `max()`
    - Set the **OF** field to `query(A, 10s, now)`
    - Change **IS ABOVE** to **IS BELOW** and set its value to `0.5`

    These settings will result in an alert being raised if the Closed state (related to the **A** variable) goes below 0.5 during the last 10 seconds. When the circuit breaker is closed, this variable has the value 1, and 0 otherwise. So this means that an alert is raised when the circuit breaker is no longer closed.
8. Scroll down to the **Notifications** section to confirm that the notification will be sent to the default notification channel, that is, the mail channel we defined previously. The alarm definition should look as follows:

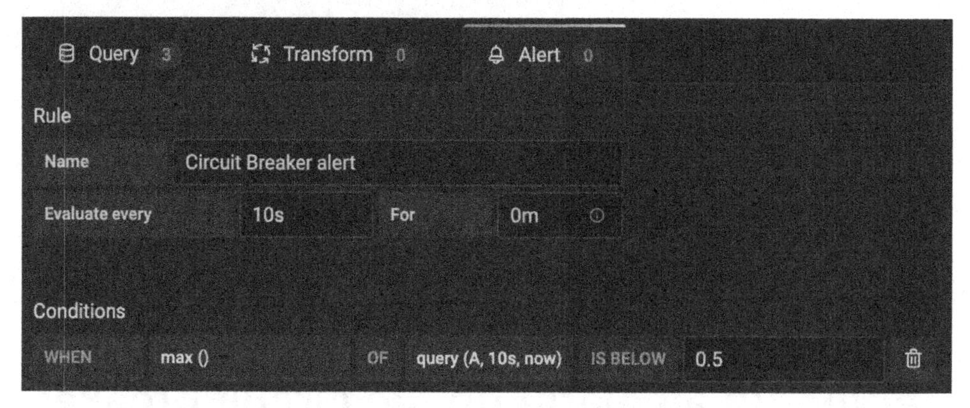

Figure 20.16: Setting up an alarm in Grafana

9. Click on the **Save** button (top right), enter a note like "`Added an alarm`" and then click on the **Save** button.
10. Click on the back button (left arrow) to get back to the dashboard.

Then, we need to perform the following steps to create an alarm list:

1. Click on the **Add panel** button in the top-level menu.
2. Click on the **Add new panel** button in the new panel.
3. In the **Panel** tab to the right, expand the **Settings** row and enter `Circuit Breaker Alerts` as the **Panel title**.

4. Expand the **Visualization** row below the **Settings** row and select **Alert list**.
5. In the **Options** row below, set the **Show** field to **Recent state changes**, set **Max items** to `10`, and enable the option **Alerts from this dashboard**.

   The settings should look as follows (some irrelevant information has been removed):

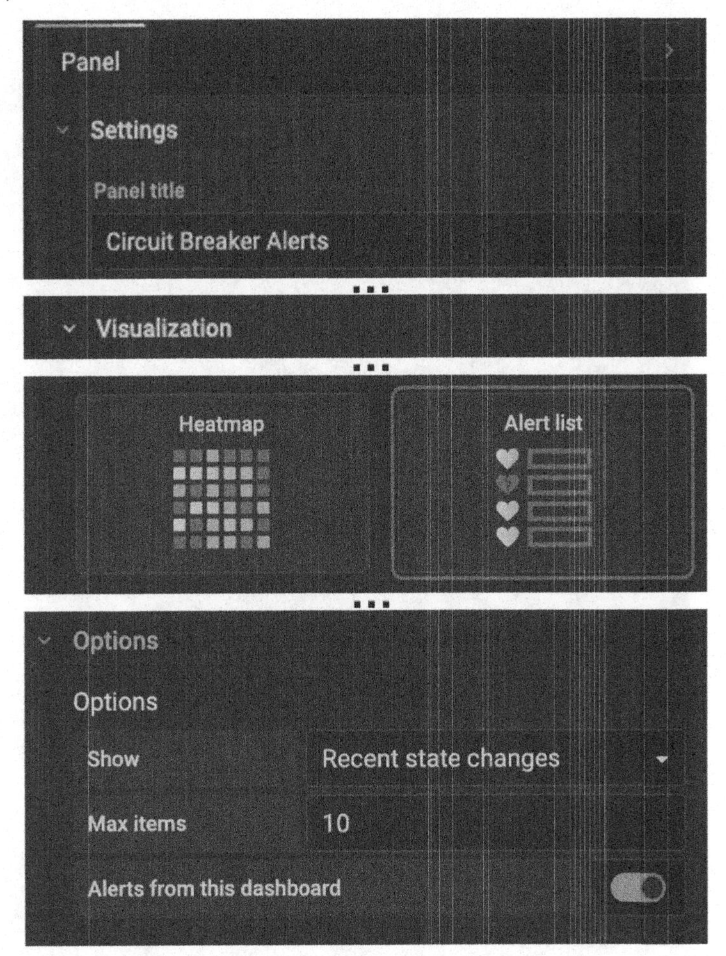

Figure 20.17: Setting up an alarm in Grafana, part 2

6. Click on the back button to get back to the dashboard.
7. Rearrange the panel to suit your needs.

8. Save the changes to the dashboard with a note like "`Added an alert list`".

Here is a sample layout with the alarm list added:

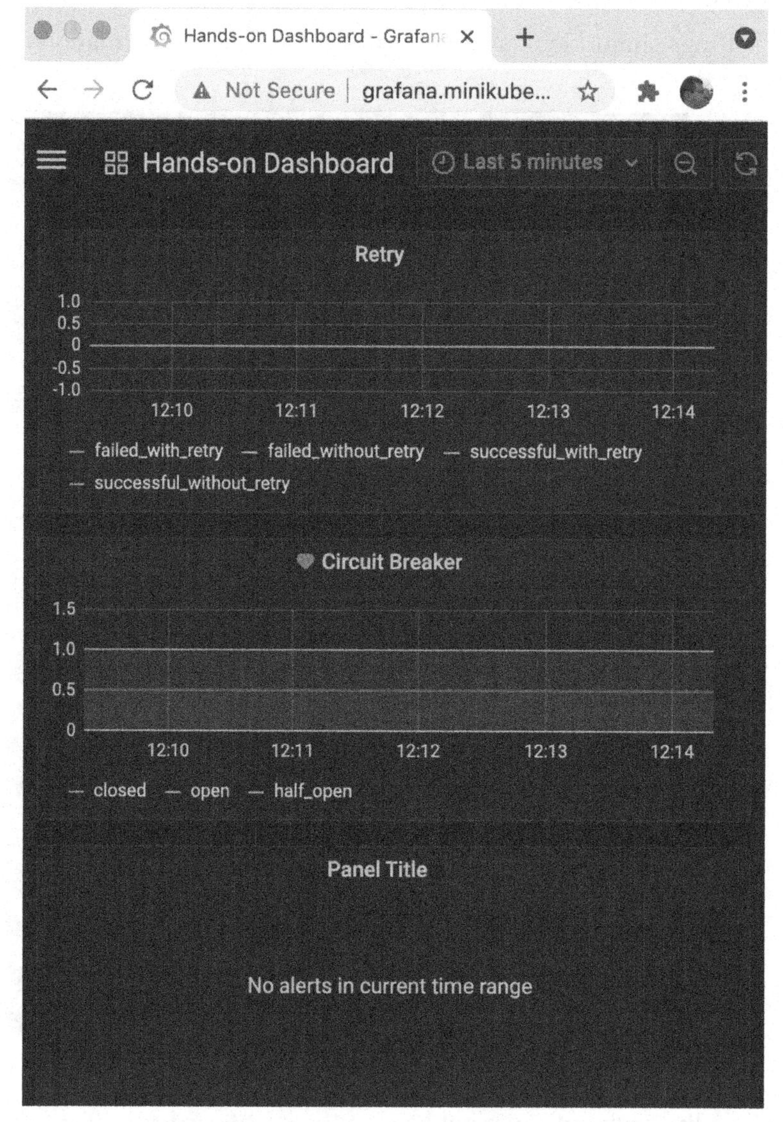

Figure 20.18: Setting up a layout in Grafana with Retry, Circuit Breaker, and alert panels

We can see that the circuit breaker reports the metrics as healthy (with a green heart) and the alert list is currently empty.

Now, it's time to try out the alarm!

Trying out the circuit breaker alarm

Here, we will repeat the tests from the *Testing the circuit breaker metrics* section, but this time, we expect alarms to be raised and emails to be sent as well! Let's get started:

1. Acquire a new access token, if required (valid for 1 hour):

```
ACCESS_TOKEN=$(curl -k https://writer:secret@minikube.me/oauth2/
token -d grant_type=client_credentials -s | jq .access_token -r)

echo ACCESS_TOKEN=$ACCESS_TOKEN
```

2. Open the circuit breaker as we have done before:

```
for ((n=0; n<4; n++)); do curl -o /dev/null -skL -w "%{http_
code}\n" https://minikube.me/product-composite/1?delay=3 -H
"Authorization: Bearer $ACCESS_TOKEN" -s; done
```

The dashboard should report the circuit as open as it did previously. After a few seconds, an alarm should be raised, and an email is also sent. Expect the dashboard to look like the following screenshot:

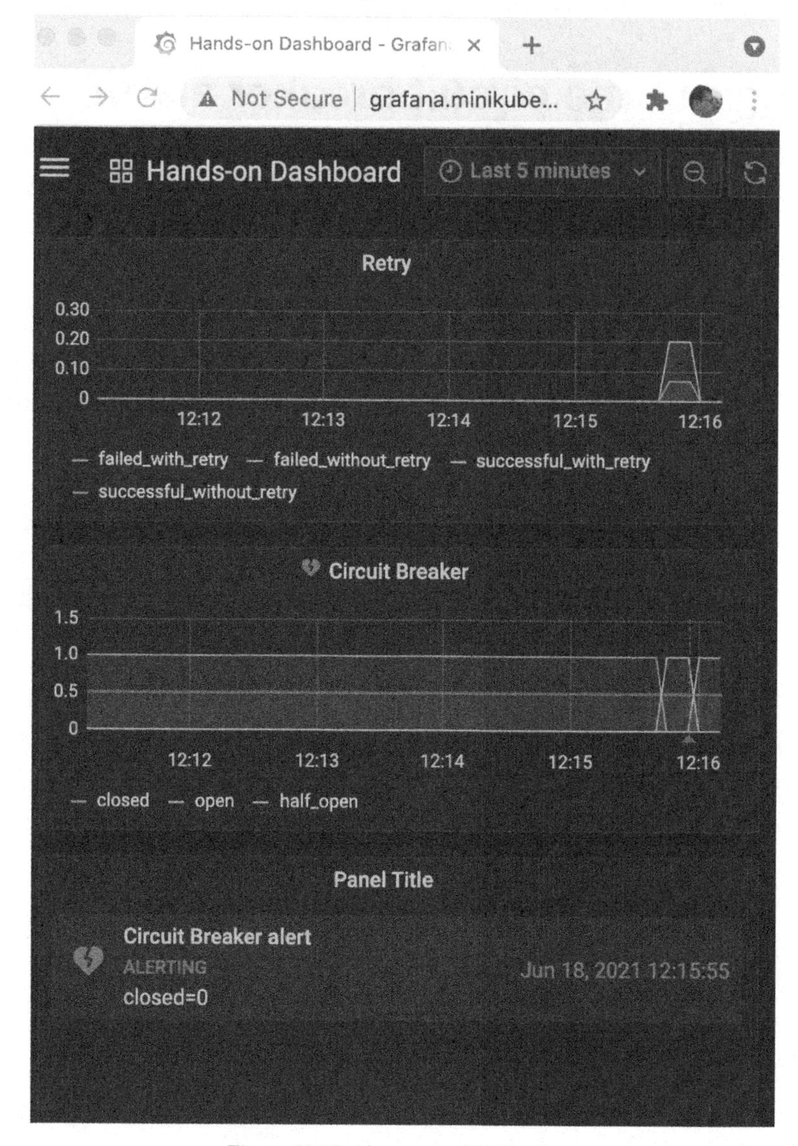

Figure 20.19: Alarm raised in Grafana

Take note of the alarm icon in the header of the circuit breaker panel (a red broken heart). The red line marks the time of the alert event and that an alert has been added to the alert list.

3. In the test mail server, you should see an email, as shown in the following screenshot:

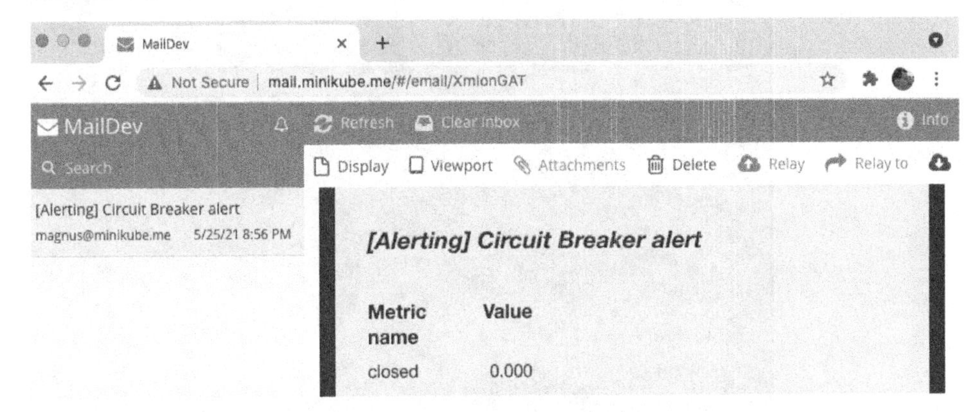

Figure 20.20: Alarm email

4. Great; we got alarms, just like we expected! Now, close the circuit with the following command, simulating that the problem is gone:

```
for ((n=0; n<4; n++)); do curl -o /dev/null -skL -w "%{http_
code}\n" https://minikube.me/product-composite/1?delay=0 -H
"Authorization: Bearer $ACCESS_TOKEN" -s; done
```

The **closed** metric should go back to normal, that is **1**, and the alert should turn green again.

Expect the dashboard to look like the following screenshot:

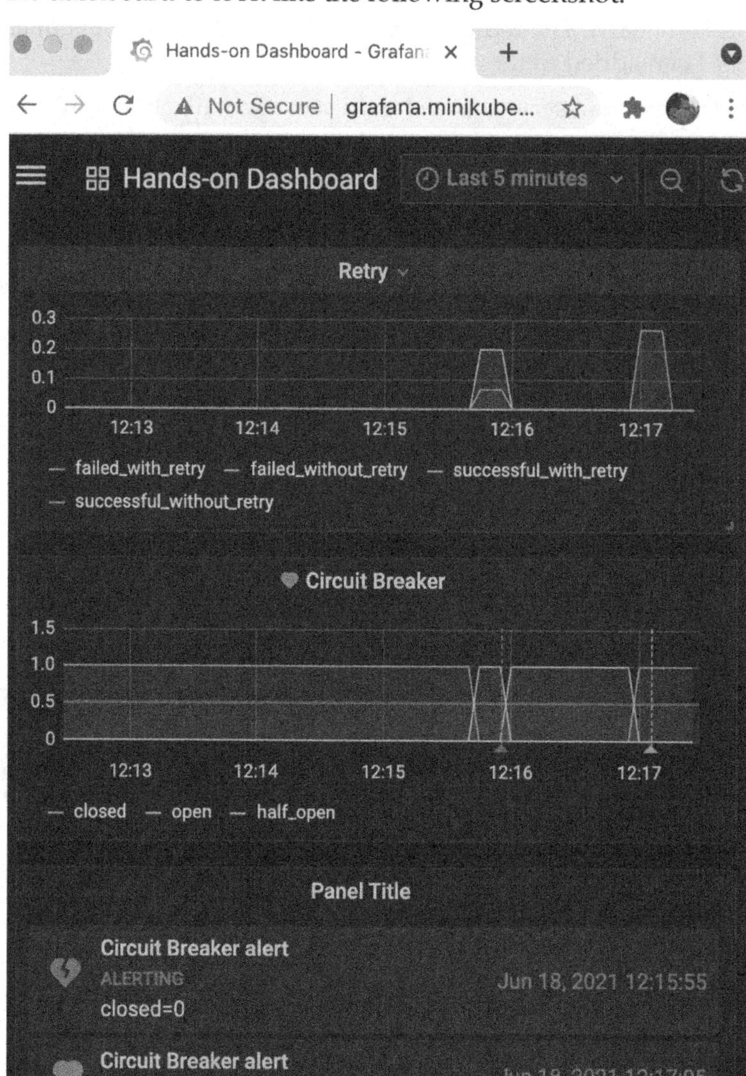

Figure 20.21: Error resolved as reported in Grafana

Note that the alarm icon in the header of the circuit breaker panel is green again; the green line marks the time of the **OK** event and that an **OK** event has been added to the alert list.

5. In the test mail server, you should see an email, as shown in the following screenshot:

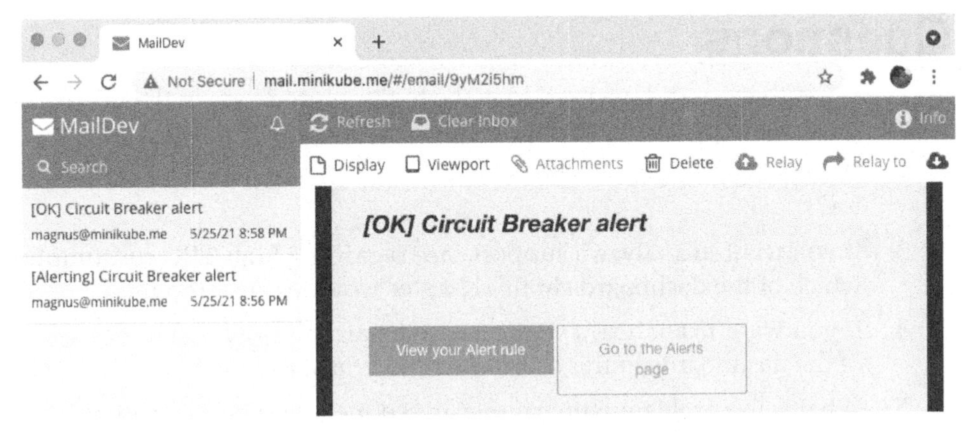

Figure 20.22: Error resolved as reported in an email

That completes how to monitor microservices using Prometheus and Grafana.

Summary

In this chapter, we have learned how to use Prometheus and Grafana to collect and monitor alerts on performance metrics.

We saw that, for collecting performance metrics, we can use Prometheus in a Kubernetes environment. We then learned how Prometheus can automatically collect metrics from a Pod when a few Prometheus annotations are added to the Pod's definition. To produce metrics in our microservices, we used Micrometer.

Then, we saw how we can monitor the collected metrics using dashboards in both Kiali and Grafana, which comes with the installation of Istio. We also experienced how to consume dashboards shared by the Grafana community, and learned how to develop our own dashboards where we used metrics from Resilience4j to monitor the usage of its circuit breaker and retry mechanisms. Using the Grafana API, we can export created dashboards and import them into other Grafana instances.

Finally, we learned how to define alerts on metrics in Grafana and how to use Grafana to send out alert notifications. We used a local test mail server to receive alert notifications from Grafana as emails.

The next two chapters should already be familiar to you, covering the installation of tools on a Mac or Windows PC. Instead, head over to the last chapter in this book, which will introduce how we can compile our Java-based microservices into binary executable files using the brand new, still in beta when writing this book, **Spring Native** project. This will enable the microservices to start up in a fraction of a second, but involves increased complexity and time when it comes to building them.

Questions

1. What changes did we need to make to the source code in the microservices to make them produce metrics that are consumed by Prometheus?
2. What is the `management.metrics.tags.application` config parameter used for?
3. If you want to analyze a support case regarding high CPU consumption, which of the dashboards in this chapter would you start with?
4. If you want to analyze a support case regarding slow API responses, which of the dashboards in this chapter would you start with?
5. What is the problem with counter-based metrics such as Resilience4j's retry metrics and what can be done so that we can monitor them in a useful way?
6. What is going on here?

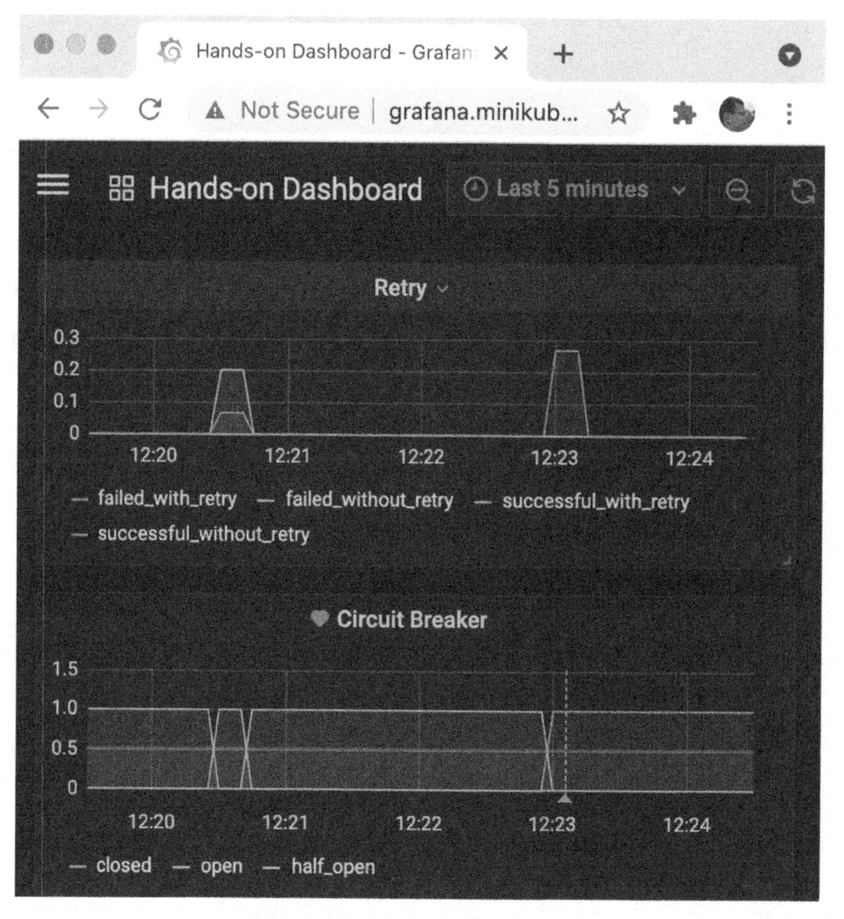

Figure 20.23: What is going on here?

If you are reading this with screenshots rendered in grayscale, it might be hard to figure out what the metrics say. So, here's some help:

a. The state transitions reported by the circuit breaker are, in order:
    1. **half_open → open**
    2. **open → half_open**
    3. **half_open → closed**
b. The retry mechanism reports:
    1. An initial burst of requests, where most of them are reported as **failed_without_retry** and a few are reported as **successful_without_retry**.
    2. A second burst of requests, all reported as **successful_without_retry**.

21

Installation Instructions for macOS

In this chapter, we will learn how to set up the tools required to run the commands described in this book on macOS with an Intel-based CPU. We will also learn how to get access to the source code of the book.

The following topics will be covered in this chapter:

- Technical requirements
- Installing tools
- Accessing the source code

If you are using a Windows PC, you should follow the instructions in *Chapter 22, Installation Instructions for Microsoft Windows with WSL 2 and Ubuntu*.

Technical requirements

All of the commands described in this book are run on a MacBook Pro with macOS Big Sur and use **bash**, a command shell.

If you are using another shell, such as **zsh**, I recommend that you switch to bash before running commands from this book using:

```
/bin/bash
```

If you have a Mac with Apple Silicon, the commands described in this chapter should work. If they don't, please follow the guidance at the provided links for download and installation instructions.

Installing tools

In this section, we will learn how to install and configure the tools. Here is a list of the tools we will install, with a link to more information on downloading and installation, if required:

- **Git**: `https://git-scm.com/downloads`
- **Docker Desktop for Mac**: `https://hub.docker.com/editions/community/docker-ce-desktop-mac/`
- **Java**: `https://adoptopenjdk.net/installation.html`
- **curl**: `https://curl.haxx.se/download.html`
- **jq**: `https://stedolan.github.io/jq/download/`
- **Spring Boot CLI**: `https://docs.spring.io/spring-boot/docs/2.5.2/reference/html/getting-started.html#getting-started.installing.cli`
- **Siege**: `https://github.com/JoeDog/siege#where-is-it`
- **Helm**: `https://helm.sh/docs/intro/install/`
- **kubectl**: `https://kubernetes.io/docs/tasks/tools/install-kubectl-macos/`
- **Minikube**: `https://minikube.sigs.k8s.io/docs/start/`
- **Istioctl**: `https://istio.io/latest/docs/setup/getting-started/#download`

The following versions have been used when writing this book:

- **Git**: v2.24.3
- **Docker Desktop for Mac**: v3.3.1
- **Java**: v16.0.1
- **curl**: v7.64.1
- **jq**: v1.6

- **Spring Boot CLI**: v2.5.2
- **Siege**: 4.0.7
- **Helm**: 3.4.2
- **kubectl**: 1.20.5
- **Minikube**: 1.18.1
- **Istioctl**: 1.9.3

Most of the tools will be installed using the **Homebrew** package manager (`https://brew.sh/`), so we will start by installing Homebrew. After that, we will install most of the tools using Homebrew and wrap up by installing the remaining tools.

For tools where control is required over the version that is installed – not just installing the latest available – I find Homebrew insufficient. When it comes to `minikube`, `kubectl`, and `istioctl`, it is important to install versions that are compatible with each other, specifically when it comes to the versions of Kubernetes that they support. Simply installing and upgrading to the latest versions can lead to situations where incompatible versions of Minikube, Kubernetes, and Istio are used.

For supported Kubernetes versions when it comes to Istio, see `https://istio.io/latest/about/supported-releases/#support-status-of-istio-releases`. For Minikube, see `https://minikube.sigs.k8s.io/docs/handbook/config/#selecting-a-kubernetes-version`.

Installing Homebrew

If you don't have Homebrew installed already, you can install it with the following command:

```
/bin/bash -c "$(curl -fsSL https://raw.githubusercontent.com/Homebrew/
install/master/install.sh)"
```

Installing Homebrew also installs the command-line tools for **Xcode**, if they are not already installed, so it might take a while.

Verify the installation of Homebrew with the following command:

```
brew --version
```

Expect a response such as the following:

```
Homebrew 3.1.1
```

Using Homebrew to install tools

On a macOS, `curl` is already pre-installed and `git` was installed as part of the installation of the command-line tools for Xcode, required by Homebrew. Homebrew can be used to install Docker, Java, jq, Spring Boot CLI, Helm, and Siege with the following commands:

```
brew tap spring-io/tap && \
brew tap AdoptOpenJDK/openjdk && \
brew install --cask adoptopenjdk16 && \
brew install jq && \
brew install spring-boot && \
brew install helm && \
brew install siege && \
brew install --cask docker
```

If you are using an older version of `brew`, older than v2.6, you must replace `brew install --cask` with `brew cask install`.

Install tools without Homebrew

When it comes to installing `minikube`, `kubectl`, and `istioctl`, we will avoid using `brew` for improved control over what versions we install.

To install the kubectl version used in this book, run the following commands:

```
curl -LO "https://dl.k8s.io/release/v1.20.5/bin/darwin/amd64/kubectl"
sudo install kubectl /usr/local/bin/kubectl
rm kubectl
```

To install the Minikube version used in this book, run the following commands:

```
curl -LO https://storage.googleapis.com/minikube/releases/v1.18.1/
minikube-darwin-amd64
sudo install minikube-darwin-amd64 /usr/local/bin/minikube
rm minikube-darwin-amd64
```

To install the Istioctl version used in this book, run the following commands:

```
curl -L https://istio.io/downloadIstio | ISTIO_VERSION=1.9.3 TARGET_
ARCH=x86_64 sh -
sudo install istio-1.9.3/bin/istioctl /usr/local/bin/istioctl
rm -r istio-1.9.3
```

If you want to use the latest versions, with the risk of incompatible versions as describe above, you should be able to install `minikube`, `kubectl`, and `istioctl` with Homebrew using the following commands:

```
brew install kubernetes-cli && \
brew install istioctl && \
brew install minikube
```

With the tools installed, we need to take some post-installation actions before we can verify the installations.

Post-installation actions

We need to take some actions after installing Java and Docker to make them work properly:

1. **Java**

   Add a command to your login script to set up the `JAVA_HOME` environment variable:

   ```
   echo 'export JAVA_HOME=$(/usr/libexec/java_home -v16)' >>
   ~/.bash_profile
   ```

   If you are not using `~/.bash_profile` as your login script, you need to replace it with the login script you use, for example, `~/.zshrc`.

   Apply the settings in your current terminal session:

   ```
   source ~/.bash_profile
   ```

2. **Docker**

To be able to run the examples in this book, it is recommended that you configure Docker so that it can use most of the CPUs except a few (allocating all CPUs to Docker can make the computer unresponsive when tests are running) and 10 GB of memory, if available. The initial chapters will work fine with less memory allocated, for example, 6 GB. But the more features we add later in the book, the more memory will be required by the Docker host to be able to run all the microservices smoothly.

Before we can configure Docker, we must ensure that the Docker daemon is running. You can start Docker as you start any application on a Mac, for example, by using **Spotlight** or opening the `Application` folder in **Finder** and starting it from there.

To configure Docker, click on the Docker icon in the status bar and select **Preferences...**. Go to the **Resources** tab in the **Preferences** settings for Docker and set **CPUs** and **Memory**, as illustrated by the following screenshot:

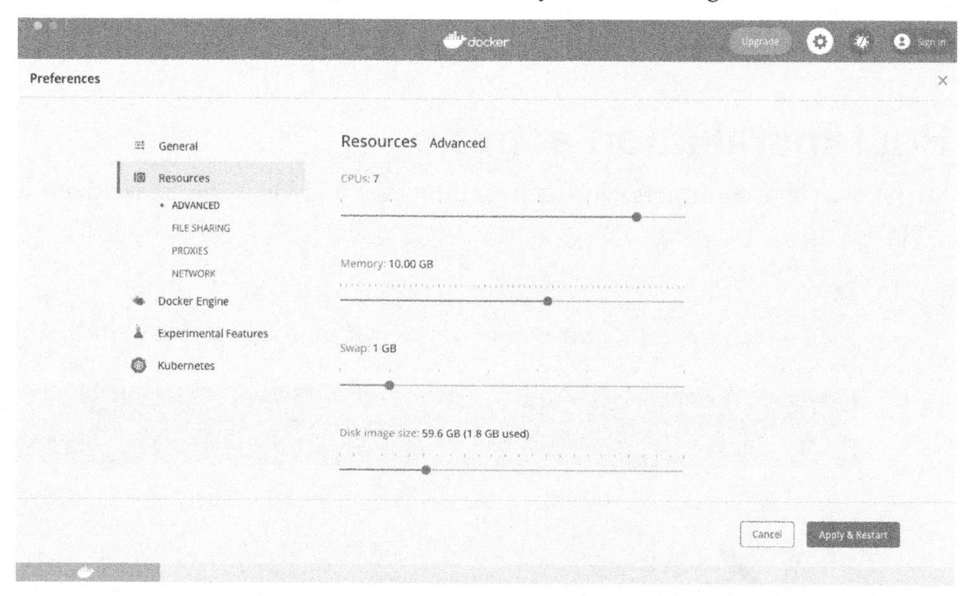

Figure 21.1: Docker Desktop resource configuration

If you don't want to start Docker manually after a system startup, you can go to the **General** tab and select the **Start Docker Desktop when you log in** option, as shown in the screenshot below:

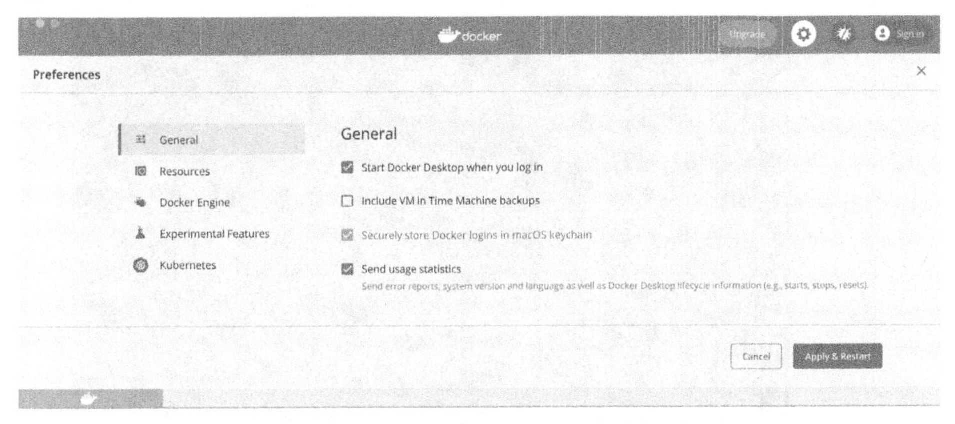

Figure 21.2: Docker Desktop general configuration

Finalize the configuration by clicking on the **Apply & Restart** button.

With the post-installation actions performed, we can verify that the tools are installed as expected.

Verifying the installations

To verify the tool installations, run the following commands to print each tool's version:

```
git version && \
docker version -f json | jq -r .Client.Version && \
java -version 2>&1 | grep "openjdk version" && \
curl --version | grep "curl" && \
jq --version && \
spring --version && \
siege --version 2>&1 | grep SIEGE && \
helm version --short && \
kubectl version --client --short && \
minikube version | grep "minikube" && \
istioctl version --remote=false
```

These commands will return output like the following (some extra version information has been removed for clarity):

```
-bash
git version 2.24.3 (Apple Git-128)
20.10.5
openjdk version "16.0.1" 2021-04-20
curl 7.64.1
jq-1.6
Spring CLI v2.5.2
SIEGE 4.0.7
v3.4.2+g23dd3af
Client Version: v1.20.5
minikube version: v1.18.1
1.9.3
$
```

Figure 21.3: Versions used

With the tools installed and verified, let's see how we can access the source code for this book.

Accessing the source code

The source code for this book can be found in the GitHub repository: `https://github.com/PacktPublishing/Microservices-with-Spring-Boot-and-Spring-Cloud-2E`.

To be able to run the commands that are described in this book, download the source code to a folder and set up an environment variable, `$BOOK_HOME`, that points to that folder. Sample commands are as follows:

```
export BOOK_HOME=~/Documents/Microservices-with-Spring-Boot-and-Spring-Cloud-2E
git clone https://github.com/PacktPublishing/Microservices-with-Spring-Boot-and-Spring-Cloud-2E.git $BOOK_HOME
```

The Java source code is written for Java SE 8 and uses a Java SE 16 JRE when executed in Docker containers. The following versions of Spring are used:

- Spring Framework: 5.3.8
- Spring Boot: 2.5.2
- Spring Cloud: 2020.0.3

The code examples in each chapter all come from the source code in `$BOOK_HOME/ChapterNN`, where `NN` is the number of the chapter. The code examples in the book are in many cases edited to remove irrelevant parts of the source code, such as comments, imports, and log statements.

Using an IDE

I recommend that you work with your Java code using an IDE that supports the development of Spring Boot applications, such as Visual Studio Code, Spring Tool Suite, or IntelliJ IDEA Ultimate Edition. However, you don't need an IDE to be able to follow the instructions in this book.

The structure of the code

Each chapter consists of a number of Java projects, one for each microservice and Spring Cloud service, plus a couple of library projects used by the other projects. *Chapter 14* contains the largest number of projects; its project structure looks like this:

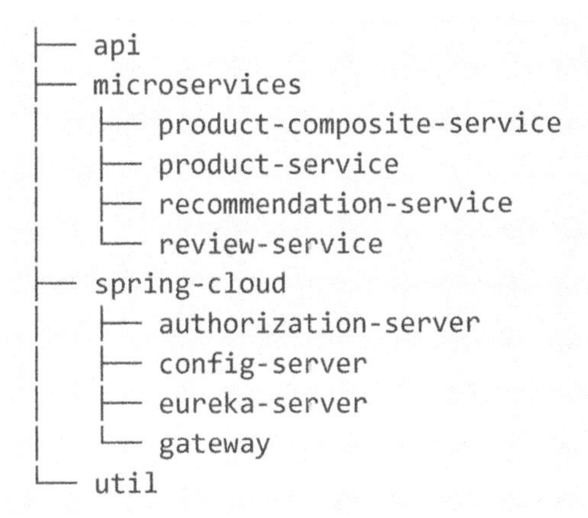

All projects are built using Gradle and have a file structure that follows Gradle's standard conventions:

```
├── build.gradle
├── settings.gradle
└── src
    ├── main
    │   ├── java
    │   └── resources
    └── test
        ├── java
        └── resources
```

For more information on how to organize a Gradle project, see `https://docs.gradle.org/current/userguide/organizing_gradle_projects.html`.

With this, we have the required tools installed for macOS and the source code for the book downloaded. In the next chapter, we will learn how to set up the tools in a Windows environment.

22

Installation Instructions for Microsoft Windows with WSL 2 and Ubuntu

In this chapter, we will learn how to set up the tools required to run the commands described in this book on Microsoft Windows. We will also learn how to get access to the source code of the book.

The following topics will be covered in this chapter:

- Technical requirements
- Installing tools
- Accessing the source code

If you are using a Mac, you should follow the instructions in *Chapter 21, Installation Instructions for macOS*.

Technical requirements

All of the commands described in this book are run on a MacBook Pro using **bash** as the command shell. In this chapter, we will learn how to set up a development environment in Microsoft Windows where the commands in this book can be run without requiring any changes. In a few cases, the commands have to be modified to run in the Windows environment, for example using another host and port for accessing a local Kubernetes cluster. This is clearly pointed out in each chapter and the alternative command to be used in the Windows environment is also specified.

The development environment is based on **Windows Subsystem for Linux v2**, or **WSL 2** for short, which requires **Windows 10, version 1903** or later. We will use WSL 2 to run a Linux server based on **Ubuntu 20.04** where we will run all the commands using bash as the command shell.

Microsoft provides integration between Windows and Linux servers that run in WSL 2. Linux files can be accessed from Windows, and vice versa. We will learn how to access files in the Linux server from Visual Studio Code running in Windows. Ports accessible from localhost in a Linux server are also available on localhost in Windows. We will use this integration to access web pages exposed by web applications running in the Linux server from a web browser running in Windows.

For more information on WSL 2, see `https://docs.microsoft.com/en-us/windows/wsl/`.

Installing tools

In this section, we will learn how to install and configure the tools. Here is a list of the tools we will install, with a link to more information on downloading and installation, if required.

On Windows, we will install the following tools:

- **Windows Subsystem for Linux v2 (WSL 2)**: `https://docs.microsoft.com/en-us/windows/wsl/install-win10`
- **Ubuntu 20.04 in WSL 2**: `https://www.microsoft.com/en-us/p/ubuntu-2004-lts/9n6svws3rx71`
- **Windows Terminal**: `https://www.microsoft.com/en-us/p/windows-terminal/9n0dx20hk701`
- **Docker Desktop for Windows**: `https://hub.docker.com/editions/community/docker-ce-desktop-windows/`

- **Visual Studio Code** and its extension for **Remote WSL**: `https://code.visualstudio.com` and `https://marketplace.visualstudio.com/items?itemName=ms-vscode-remote.remote-wsl`

On the Linux server, we will install the following tools:

- **Git**: `https://git-scm.com/downloads`
- **Java**: `https://adoptopenjdk.net/installation.html`
- **curl**: `https://curl.haxx.se/download.html`
- **jq**: `https://stedolan.github.io/jq/download/`
- **Spring Boot CLI**: `https://docs.spring.io/spring-boot/docs/2.5.2/reference/html/getting-started.html#getting-started.installing.cli`
- **Siege**: `https://github.com/JoeDog/siege#where-is-it`
- **Helm**: `https://helm.sh/docs/intro/install/#from-apt-debianubuntu`
- **kubectl**: `https://kubernetes.io/docs/tasks/tools/install-kubectl-linux/`
- **Minikube**: `https://minikube.sigs.k8s.io/docs/start/`
- **Istioctl**: `https://istio.io/latest/docs/setup/getting-started/#download`

The following versions have been used when writing this book:

- **Windows Terminal**: 1.7.1033
- **Visual Studio Code**: 1.55.0
- **Docker Desktop for Windows**: v3.3.1
- **Git**: v2.25.1
- **Java**: v16
- **curl**: v7.68.0
- **jq**: v1.6
- **Spring Boot CLI**: v2.5.2
- **Siege**: 4.0.4
- **Helm**: 3.5.3
- **kubectl**: 1.20.5
- **Minikube**: 1.18.1
- **Istioctl**: 1.9.3

We will start by installing the tools required on Windows and, after that, we will install the required tools on the Linux server running in WSL 2.

Installing tools on Windows

In the Windows environment, we will install WSL 2 together with a Linux server, Windows Terminal, Docker Desktop, and finally Visual Studio Code with an extension for remote access to files in WSL.

Installing WSL 2 – Windows Subsystem for Linux v2

For more recent versions of Windows 10, WSL 2 can be installed with one command: `wsl -install`. But this description covers older releases back to Windows 10 v1903. These instructions have been tested on a PC with Windows 10 v1909.

Run the following commands to install WSL 2:

1. Enable Windows Subsystem for Linux and the Virtual Machine Platform.

   Open PowerShell as an administrator and run the following two commands:

   ```
   dism.exe /online /enable-feature /featurename:Microsoft-Windows-
   Subsystem-Linux /all /norestart
   dism.exe /online /enable-feature /featurename:VirtualMachinePlat
   form /all /norestart
   ```

2. Restart your PC to complete the installation.
3. Update the WSL 2 Linux kernel:
   i. Download it from `https://wslstorestorage.blob.core.windows.net/wslblob/wsl_update_x64.msi`.
   ii. Execute the downloaded `.msi` file.

4. Set WSL 2 as the default version by opening PowerShell and running the following command:

   ```
   wsl --set-default-version 2
   ```

Installing Ubuntu 20.04 on WSL 2

With WSL 2 in place, we can now install the Linux server. This book uses Ubuntu 20.04, which can be installed from Microsoft Store:

- To select from available Linux distributions for WSL 2, go to `https://aka.ms/wslstore`.
- To go directly to Ubuntu 20.04, visit `https://www.microsoft.com/store/apps/9n6svws3rx71`.

After Ubuntu 20.04 is downloaded, start it to get it installed. A console window will be opened and after a minute or two, you will be asked for a username and password to be used in the Linux server.

Installing Windows Terminal

To simplify access to the Linux server, I strongly recommend installing Windows Terminal. It supports:

- Using multiple tabs
- Using multiple panes within a tab
- Using multiple types of shells, for example: Windows Command Prompt, PowerShell, bash for WSL 2, and Azure CLI
- ...and much more; for more information, see `https://docs.microsoft.com/en-us/windows/terminal/`

Windows Terminal can be installed from Microsoft Store; see `https://aka.ms/terminal`.

When you start Windows Terminal and click on the **down arrow** in the menu, you will find that it is already configured for starting a terminal in the Linux server:

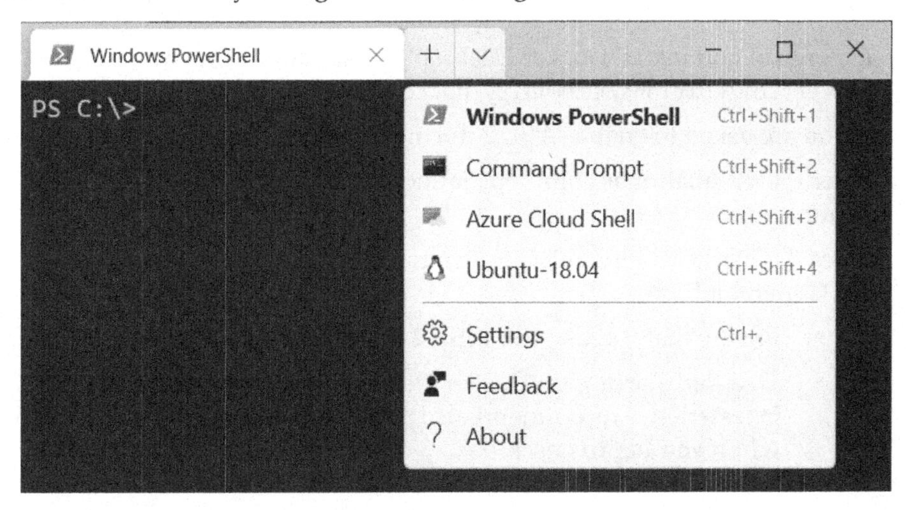

Figure 22.1: Windows Terminal configured for the Linux server in WSL 2

Select **Ubuntu-20.04**, and a bash shell will be started. By default, your working directory will be set to your home folder in Windows, for example `/mnt/c/Users/magnus`. To get to your home folder in the Linux server, simply use the `cd` and `pwd` commands to verify that you are inside your Linux server's filesystem:

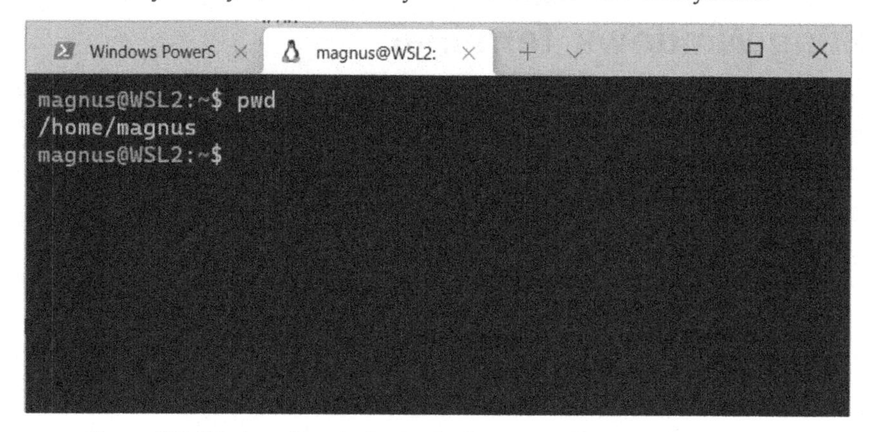

Figure 22.2: Windows Terminal using bash to access files in the Linux server

Installing Docker Desktop for Windows

To install and configure Docker Desktop for Windows, perform the following steps:

1. Download and install Docker Desktop for Windows from `https://hub.docker.com/editions/community/docker-ce-desktop-windows/`.
2. If you are asked to enable WSL 2 during installation, answer **yes**.
3. After the installation is complete, launch **Docker Desktop** from the **Start** menu.
4. From the Docker menu, select **Settings**, and in the Settings window, select the **General** tab:
   - Ensure that the **Use the WSL 2 based engine** check box is selected.
   - To avoid starting up Docker Desktop manually each time the PC is restarted, I recommend also selecting the **Start Docker Desktop when you log in** check box.

The **General** settings should look like the following:

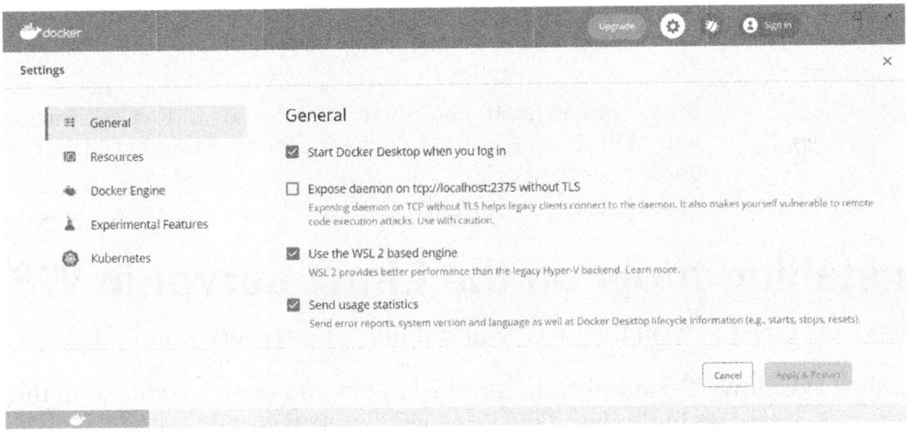

Figure 22.3: Docker Desktop configuration

5. Finalize the configuration by clicking on the **Apply & Restart** button.

Installing Visual Studio Code and its extension for Remote WSL

To simplify editing source code inside the Linux server, I recommend using Visual Studio Code. With its extension for WSL 2, named **Remote WSL**, you can easily work with source code inside the Linux server using Visual Studio Code running in Windows.

To install and configure Visual Studio Code and its extension for Remote WSL, perform the following steps:

1. Visual Studio Code can be downloaded and installed from `https://code.visualstudio.com`:
    - When asked to **Select Additional Tasks**, select the **Add to PATH** option. This will make it possible to open a folder in Visual Studio Code from within the Linux server with the `code` command.
2. After the installation is complete, launch **Visual Studio Code** from the **Start** menu.

3. Install the extension for Remote WSL using the link `https://marketplace.visualstudio.com/items?itemName=ms-vscode-remote.remote-wsl`.

If you want to learn more about how Visual Studio Code integrates with WSL 2, see this article: `https://code.visualstudio.com/docs/remote/wsl`.

Installing tools on the Linux server in WSL 2

Now, it is time to install the tools required in the Linux server in WSL 2.

Launch **Windows Terminal** from the Start menu and open a terminal in the Linux server as described in the *Installing Windows Terminal* section.

The `git` and `curl` tools are already installed in Ubuntu. The remaining tools will be installed using either `apt install`, `sdk install`, or a combination of `curl` and `install`.

Installing tools using apt install

In this section, we will install `java`, `jq`, `siege`, `helm`, and a couple of dependencies required by the other tools.

Install `jq`, `zip`, `unzip`, and `siege` with the following commands:

```
sudo apt update
sudo apt install -y jq
sudo apt install -y zip
sudo apt install -y unzip
sudo apt install -y siege
```

To install Helm, run the following commands:

```
curl https://baltocdn.com/helm/signing.asc | sudo apt-key add -
sudo apt install -y apt-transport-https
echo "deb https://baltocdn.com/helm/stable/debian/ all main" \
  | sudo tee /etc/apt/sources.list.d/helm-stable-debian.list
sudo apt install -y helm
```

To install OpenJDK 16, we will use a distribution named **AdoptOpenJDK**. Run the following commands to install AdoptOpenJDK 16:

```
wget -qO -  https://adoptopenjdk.jfrog.io/adoptopenjdk/api/gpg/key/
public \
  | sudo apt-key add -
sudo add-apt-repository \
  --yes https://adoptopenjdk.jfrog.io/adoptopenjdk/deb/
sudo apt install -y adoptopenjdk-16-hotspot
```

Installing the Spring Boot CLI using sdk install

To install the Spring Boot CLI, we will use **SDKman** (`https://sdkman.io`). Install SDKman with the following commands:

```
curl -s "https://get.sdkman.io" | bash
source "$HOME/.sdkman/bin/sdkman-init.sh"
```

Verify that SDKman was installed correctly with the following command:

```
sdk version
```

Expect it to return something like:

```
SDKMAN5.9.2+613
```

Finally, install the Spring Boot CLI:

```
sdk install springboot 2.5.2
```

Installing the remaining tools using curl and install

Finally, we will install `kubectl`, `minikube`, and `istioctl` using `curl` to download the executable files. Once downloaded, we will use the `install` command to copy the files to the proper places in the filesystem, and also ensure that the `owner` and `access rights` are configured properly. When it comes to these tools, it is important to install versions that are compatible with each other, specifically when it comes to what versions of Kubernetes they support. Simply installing and upgrading to the latest versions can lead to situations where incompatible versions of Minikube, Kubernetes, and Istio are used.

For supported Kubernetes versions when it comes to Istio, see `https://istio.io/latest/about/supported-releases/#support-status-of-istio-releases`. For Minikube, see `https://minikube.sigs.k8s.io/docs/handbook/config/#selecting-a-kubernetes-version`.

To install the kubectl version used in this book, run the following commands:

```
curl -LO "https://dl.k8s.io/release/v1.20.5/bin/linux/amd64/kubectl"
sudo install -o root -g root -m 0755 kubectl /usr/local/bin/kubectl
rm kubectl
```

To install the Minikube version used in this book, run the following commands:

```
curl -LO https://storage.googleapis.com/minikube/releases/v1.18.1/
minikube-linux-amd64
sudo install -o root -g root -m 0755 minikube-linux-amd64 \
  /usr/local/bin/minikube
rm minikube-linux-amd64
```

To install the Istioctl version used in this book, run the following commands:

```
curl -L https://istio.io/downloadIstio | ISTIO_VERSION=1.9.3 TARGET_
ARCH=x86_64 sh -
sudo install -o root -g root -m 0755 istio-1.9.3/bin/istioctl /usr/
local/bin/istioctl
rm -r istio-1.9.3
```

With the tools now installed, we can verify that they have been installed as expected.

Verifying the installations

To verify the tool installations, run the following commands to print each tool's version:

```
git version && \
docker version -f json | jq -r .Client.Version && \
java -version 2>&1 | grep "openjdk version" && \
curl --version | grep "curl" && \
jq --version && \
spring --version && \
siege --version 2>&1 | grep SIEGE && \
helm version --short && \
kubectl version --client --short && \
```

```
minikube version | grep "minikube" && \
istioctl version --remote=false
```

Expect version info like the following:

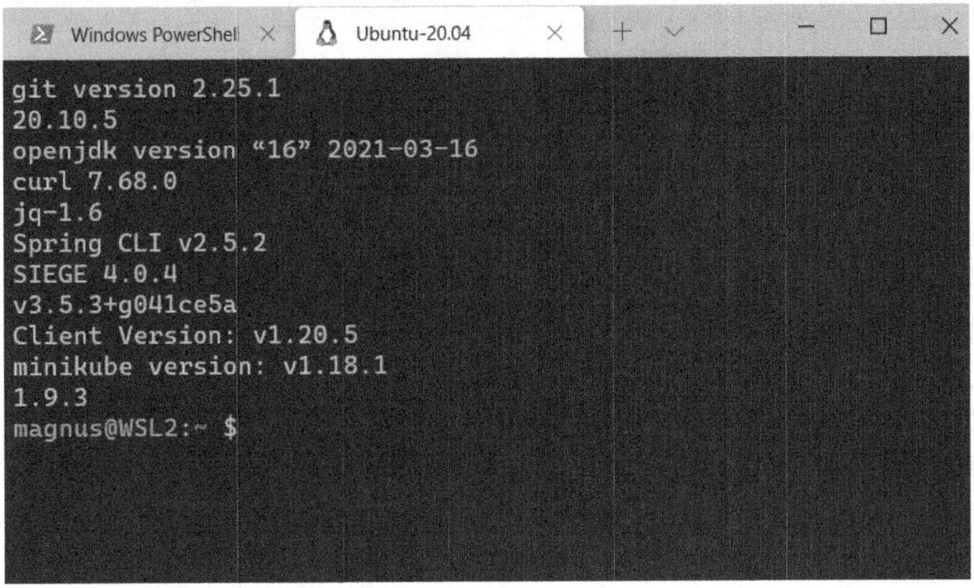
Windows PowerShell
Ubuntu-20.04
git version 2.25.1
20.10.5
openjdk version "16" 2021-03-16
curl 7.68.0
jq-1.6
Spring CLI v2.5.2
SIEGE 4.0.4
v3.5.3+g041ce5a
Client Version: v1.20.5
minikube version: v1.18.1
1.9.3
magnus@WSL2:~ $

Figure 22.4: Versions used on the Linux server in WSL 2

With the tools installed and verified, let's see how we can access the source code for this book.

Accessing the source code

The source code for this book can be found in the GitHub repository at `https://github.com/PacktPublishing/Microservices-with-Spring-Boot-and-Spring-Cloud-2E`.

To be able to run the commands in the Linux server in WSL 2 that are described in this book, download the source code to a folder and set up an environment variable, `$BOOK_HOME`, that points to that folder. Sample commands are as follows:

```
export BOOK_HOME=~/Microservices-with-Spring-Boot-and-Spring-Cloud-2E
git clone https://github.com/PacktPublishing/Microservices-with-Spring-
Boot-and-Spring-Cloud-2E.git $BOOK_HOME
```

To verify access to source code downloaded to the Linux server in WSL 2 from Visual Studio Code, run the following commands:

```
cd $BOOK_HOME
code .
```

Visual Studio Code will open a window from where you can start to inspect the source code. You can also start a Terminal window for running bash commands in the Linux server from the menu selection **Terminal** → **New Terminal**. The Visual Studio Code window should look something like the following:

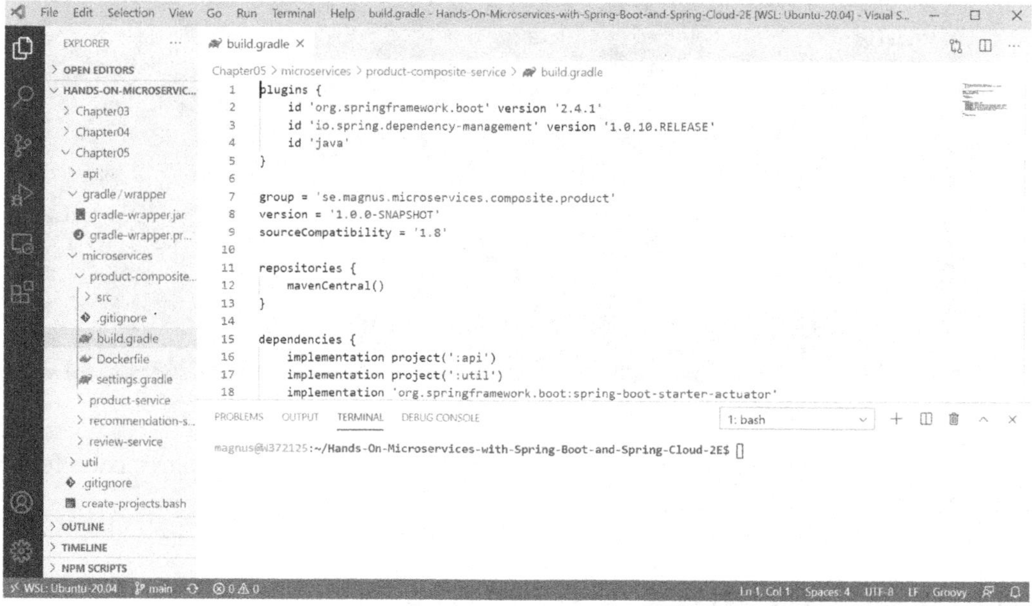

Figure 22.5: Accessing a file in the Linux server from Visual Studio Code

The Java source code is written for Java SE 8 and uses a Java SE 16 JRE when executed in Docker containers. The following versions of Spring are used:

- Spring Framework: 5.3.8
- Spring Boot: 2.5.2
- Spring Cloud: 2020.0.3

The code examples in each chapter all come from the source code in `$BOOK_HOME/ChapterNN`, where `NN` is the number of the chapter. The code examples in the book are in many cases edited to remove irrelevant parts of the source code, such as comments, imports, and log statements.

The structure of the code

Each chapter consists of a number of Java projects, one for each microservice and Spring Cloud service, plus a couple of library projects used by the other projects. *Chapter 14* contains the largest number of projects; its project structure looks like:

```
├── api
├── microservices
│   ├── product-composite-service
│   ├── product-service
│   ├── recommendation-service
│   └── review-service
├── spring-cloud
│   ├── authorization-server
│   ├── config-server
│   ├── eureka-server
│   └── gateway
└── util
```

All projects are built using Gradle and have a file structure according to Gradle standard conventions:

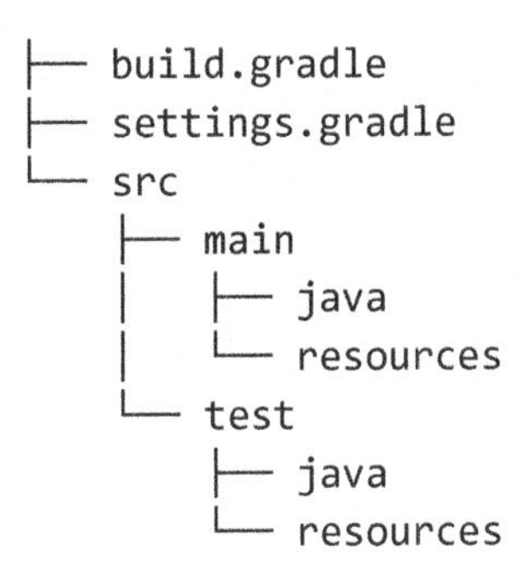

```
├── build.gradle
├── settings.gradle
└── src
    ├── main
    │   ├── java
    │   └── resources
    └── test
        ├── java
        └── resources
```

For more information on how to organize a Gradle project, see `https://docs.gradle.org/current/userguide/organizing_gradle_projects.html`.

With this, we have the required tools installed for WSL 2 and Windows and the source code for the book downloaded. In the next and final chapter, we will learn how to natively compile microservices, reducing their startup time to sub-seconds.

23

Native Compiled Java Microservices

In this chapter, we will learn how to compile the Java source code in our microservices into binary executable files, known as **native images**. A native image starts up significantly faster compared to using a Java VM and is also expected to consume less memory. We will be introduced to the **Spring Native** and **GraalVM** projects and the GraalVM **native-image compiler** and learn how to use them.

We will cover the following topics:

- When to native compile Java source code
- Introducing the Spring Native and GraalVM projects
- Compiling source code to a native image
- Testing with Docker Compose
- Testing with Kubernetes

At the time of writing, the Spring Native project only has beta status and is not ready for production use. As such, certain guidance in this chapter is liable to become outdated as the Spring team improves the project in the future. Native compilation is not required for the microservice landscape we have built in this book, but we intend that this extra chapter gives you an idea about the exciting things it is capable of.

Technical requirements

For instructions on how to install the tools used in this book and how to access the source code for this book, see:

- *Chapter 21* for macOS
- *Chapter 22* for Windows

The code examples in this chapter all come from the source code in `$BOOK_HOME/Chapter23`.

If you want to view the changes applied to the source code in this chapter so you can native compile the microservices, you can compare it with the source code for *Chapter 20, Monitoring Microservices*. You can use your favorite `diff` tool and compare the two folders `$BOOK_HOME/Chapter20` and `$BOOK_HOME/Chapter23`.

When to native compile Java source code

Java has always been known for its **build-once-run-anywhere** capability, providing excellent cross-platform support. The Java source code is compiled once into byte code. At runtime, a Java VM transforms the byte code into executable code for the target platform, using a **Just in Time** compiler, also known as **JIT** compilation. This takes some time, slowing down the startup for Java programs. Before the era of microservices, Java components typically ran on an application server, like a Java EE server. After being deployed, the Java component ran for a long time, making the longer startup time less of a problem.

With the introduction of microservices, this perspective changed. With microservices, there comes the expectation of being able to upgrade them more frequently and being able to quickly scale instances for a microservice up and down, based on its usage. Another expectation is to be able to **scale to zero**, meaning that when a microservice is not used, it should not run any instances at all. An unused microservice should not allocate any hardware resources and, even more importantly, should not create any runtime cost, for example, in a cloud deployment. To be able to meet these expectations, it is important that a microservice instance can be started swiftly. Also, with the use of containers, the importance of cross-platform support has faded so it is not so critical (the requirement still exists since containers can run on different platforms, even though the Linux/x86 platform dominates to a large extent).

Given that the startup time for Java programs can be significantly reduced, other use cases also come to mind; for example, developing Java-based **Function as a Service** (**FaaS**) solutions using AWS Lambda, Azure Functions, or Google Cloud Function, to mention some of the major platforms. Also, developing CLI tools in Java becomes a feasible option.

Together, these lead to a situation where faster startup becomes a more critical requirement than cross-platform support. This requirement can be achieved by compiling the Java source code into the target platform's binary format at build time, in the same way that C or Go programs are compiled. This is known as **Ahead of Time** compilation, or **AOT** compilation. The GraalVM native-image compiler will be used to perform AOT compilation.

As we will see in the next section, the GraalVM native-image compiler comes with a few restrictions, for example, relating to the use of reflection and dynamic proxies. It also takes quite some time to compile Java code to a binary native image. This technology has its strengths and weaknesses.

With a better understanding of when it might be of interest to native compile Java source code, let's learn about the tooling: first, the GraalVM project, and then, the Spring Native project.

Introducing the GraalVM project

Oracle has been working for several years on a high-performance Java VM and associated tools, known together as the **GraalVM** project (`https://www.graalvm.org`). It was launched back in April 2018 (`https://blogs.oracle.com/developers/announcing-graalvm`), but work can be traced back to, for example, a research paper from Oracle Labs in 2013 on the subject: *Maxine: An approachable virtual machine for, and in, java*; see `https://dl.acm.org/doi/10.1145/2400682.2400689`.

Fun Fact: The Maxine VM is known as a **metacircular** Java VM implementation, meaning that it is, itself, written in Java.

GraalVM's virtual machine is polyglot, supporting not only traditional Java VM languages such as Java, Kotlin, and Scala but also languages like JavaScript, C, and C++. The part of GraalVM that we will focus on is its **native-image** compiler, which can be used to compile Java byte code to a native image containing binary executable code for a specific platform.

The native image can run without a Java VM, and it includes binary compiled application classes and other classes required from the application's dependencies. It also includes a runtime system called **Substrate VM** that handles garbage collection, thread scheduling, and more.

The native compiler comes with a few restrictions. For instance, since the native compiler is based on static code analysis, it cannot support the use of **reflection** and **dynamic proxies**. For more information, see `https://www.graalvm.org/reference-manual/native-image/Limitations/`.

To overcome these restrictions, the GraalVM project provides configuration options for the native compiler. To simplify the creation of the configuration information, the GraalVM project provides a tool called a **tracing agent**. It can observe a running Java application's behavior and based on the use of, for example, reflection and dynamic proxies, the tracing agent can create configuration files that help the native compiler generate code that supports the application's use of these features. We will learn how it can be used in the *Running the tracing agent* section. For more information, see `https://www.graalvm.org/reference-manual/native-image/BuildConfiguration/`.

Introducing the Spring Native project

The Spring team has also been working on supporting the native compilation of Spring applications. After 18 months of work, the **Spring Native** project launched a beta release in March 2021; see `https://spring.io/blog/2021/03/11/announcing-spring-native-beta`.

Note that this is currently a **beta** release, not yet ready for production use.

Using Spring Native, we can compile our Spring Boot-based microservices to native images. The Spring Native project comes with a build plugin, **Spring AOT**, that supports both Maven and Gradle, which simplifies the setup required for native compilation. To perform the actual native compilation, Spring Native uses the **GraalVM** native-image compiler under the hood.

The Spring AOT plugin creates a Docker image that contains the native image. To create the Docker image, an existing Spring Boot feature is used by the plugin. For Gradle, it is implemented as a Gradle task named `bootBuildImage`. This task uses **buildpacks**, instead of a Dockerfile, to create the Docker image.

> The concept of buildpacks was introduced by Heroku back in 2011. In 2018, the **Cloud Native Buildpacks** project (`https://buildpacks.io`) was created by Pivotal and Heroku and later that year, it joined CNCF.
>
> To be a bit more formal, a buildpack creates an **OCI image**, according to the OCI Image Format Specification: `https://github.com/opencontainers/image-spec/blob/master/spec.md`. Since the OCI specification is based on Docker's image format, the formats are very similar and are both supported by container engines.

For more information on Spring Boot's usage of buildpacks, see `https://docs.spring.io/spring-boot/docs/2.5.2/reference/html/features.html#features.container-images.building.buildpacks`. To create the OCI images, Spring Boot uses the **Paketo** project; for more information, see `https://paketo.io/docs/builders`.

To simplify the creation of configuration for the GraalVM native compiler, as described above, the Spring AOT plugin generates these configuration files. There are some cases when the Spring AOT plugin can't help, like when serializing JSON documents using reflection and when using a Spring library that is not yet supported by the Spring Native project. In these cases, the Spring Native project provides a set of annotations that can be used for expressing hints to the native compiler. The Spring AOT plugin will use these native hint annotations to refine the configuration it creates for the native compiler. We will see the use of these annotations in the *Providing native hints as annotations* section.

Many of the libraries and frameworks in Spring's ecosystem can be used with the native image compiler, some can't yet be used, and some can be used after using native hints and/or the tracing agent described above. For information on what is currently supported, see `https://docs.spring.io/spring-native/docs/current/reference/htmlsingle/#support`.

With the tooling introduced, let's see how we can use it to native compile our microservices.

Compiling source code to a native image

Before we can compile the Java source code in our microservices to native executable images, the source code needs to be updated a bit. The Spring AOT plugin must be added to the build files, and we also need to add some hints for the native compiler to enable it to compile the source code.

We will start by going through the required code changes. Then, we will learn how to run the GraalVM native image tracing agent to create configuration for libraries and frameworks that are not yet supported by the Spring Native project. After that, we will see how to build native executable images.

Changes in the source code

To be able to native compile the microservices, the following changes have been applied to the source code:

1. The Gradle build files, `build.gradle`, have been updated by adding the Spring AOT plugin and adjusting some dependencies.
2. Hints to the native compiler regarding our own classes have been added as annotations.
3. Configuration to be able to run the GraalVM native image tracing agent has been added.

Let's go through the changes one by one.

Updates to the Gradle build files

The changes described in this section have been applied to the `build.gradle` files in each microservice project, unless stated otherwise.

To enable Spring Native, its Spring AOT plugin has been added as:

```
plugins {
    ...
    id 'org.springframework.experimental.aot' version '0.10.1'
}
```

Since the plugin uses the `bootBuildImage` task to create the Docker image, it is configured together with it. For the `product` microservice, the configuration looks like this:

```
bootBuildImage {
    builder = "paketobuildpacks/builder:tiny"
    imageName = "hands-on/native-product-service"
    environment = [
        "BP_NATIVE_IMAGE" : "true",
        "BP_NATIVE_IMAGE_BUILD_ARGUMENTS" : "--enable-url-
protocols=http,https --initialize-at-build-time=sun.instrument.
InstrumentationImpl"
    ]
}
```

The `builder` and `imageName` properties are used to configure the `bootBuildImage` task, while the settings in the `environment` section configure the Spring AOT plugin. Let's go through each property:

- `builder`: Specifies which of Spring Boot's buildpacks to use. We will use the `tiny` builder, which provides a small footprint and reduced attack surface for security attacks.
- `imageName`: Specifies the name of the Docker image. We will use the same naming conventions as in earlier chapters, but prefix the name of the image with `native-` to separate it from the existing Docker images.
- `"BP_NATIVE_IMAGE" : "true"`: Enables the native image compiler.
- `"BP_NATIVE_IMAGE_BUILD_ARGUMENTS" : "..."`: Gives arguments to the native compiler. For a list of available parameters, see `https://www.graalvm.org/reference-manual/native-image/Options/#options-to-native-image-builder`.

The specific values used for each microservice's `BP_NATIVE_IMAGE_BUILD_ARGUMENTS` parameter come from a trial and error exercise, adding parameter values as required by running the native compiled code. As the Spring Native and GraalVM projects mature over time, I hope that the need for trial and error will vanish.

A few of the libraries used in this book cannot currently be used with Spring Native, and are therefore not used in this chapter:

- `resilience4j`: Affects the use of circuit breakers, retries, and time limiters
- `spring-cloud-binder-stream-rabbit`: We will only use the Kafka binder
- `spring-cloud-sleuth`: We will not be able to create distributed traces

The dependencies on Spring Cloud Sleuth and Spring Cloud Stream's binder for RabbitMQ have been removed from the build files.

Due to the removal of Spring Cloud Stream's binder for RabbitMQ, the default binder property, `spring.cloud.stream.defaultBinder`, has been updated in the property files and test classes to specify `kafka` instead of `rabbit`.

To be able to resolve dependencies for the Spring AOT plugin, the following has been added to the common `settings.gradle` file:

```
pluginManagement {
    repositories {
        maven { url 'https://repo.spring.io/release' }
        gradlePluginPortal()
    }
}
```

These are all the changes required for the build files. In the next section, we will learn about how, in some cases, we need to help the native compiler to compile our source code.

Providing native hints as annotations

There exist a few cases in the source code of this chapter where the GraalVM native compiler needs help from us to be able to compile the source code correctly. The first case is the JSON-based APIs and messages that the microservices use. The JSON parser, Jackson, must be able to create Java objects based on the JSON documents that the microservices receive. Jackson uses reflection to perform this work and we need to tell the native compiler about the classes that Jackson will apply reflection on.

For example, a native hint for the `Product` class looks like this:

```
@TypeHint(types = Product.class, fields = {
  @FieldHint(name = "productId", allowWrite = true),
  @FieldHint(name = "name", allowWrite = true),
  @FieldHint(name = "weight", allowWrite = true),
  @FieldHint(name = "serviceAddress", allowWrite = true)
})
```

To allow the JSON parser to create a `Product` object from a JSON document, we must explicitly allow write access for each field in the class, as seen in the annotation above.

Another corner case we must provide a hint for is when we inject Spring Bean dependencies as classes instead of interfaces. Spring Native supports the injection of Spring Bean dependencies as interfaces, using method parameters. When classes are injected instead of interfaces, we must provide a `ClassProxyHint` annotation. In the source code of this book, we only have one use case of class injection. That is in the `product-composite` microservice, where the class `ProductCompositeServiceImpl` injects an instance of the `ProductCompositeIntegration` class in its constructor. The code looks like this:

```
public ProductCompositeServiceImpl(
  ServiceUtil serviceUtil,
  ProductCompositeIntegration integration) {
```

To allow Spring Native to create the required proxy at build time, the following `ClassProxyHint` is provided:

```
@ClassProxyHint(targetClass = ProductCompositeIntegration.class,
interfaces = {
  ProductService.class,
  RecommendationService.class,
  ReviewService.class,
  org.springframework.aop.SpringProxy.class,
  org.springframework.aop.framework.Advised.class,
  org.springframework.core.DecoratingProxy.class
})
```

All necessary hint annotations have been added to each microservice's main class.

Now that we know how we can provide hints for our own source code, it's time to learn how we can handle cases when libraries we use are not yet supported by the Spring Native project.

When underlying frameworks and libraries don't support native compilation

In the case where frameworks and libraries are not yet supported by the Spring Native project, we can use the GraalVM native image tracing agent. This does not work for all cases, so it must be tested before we're sure it works for a specific use case of a specific library.

As the Spring Native project evolves and begins to support more libraries in the Spring ecosystem, this will become less of a problem.

To enable the tracing agent to observe the execution of JUnit tests, the following `jvmArgs` can be added to the `build.gradle` file in the `test` section:

```
test {
    useJUnitPlatform()
    jvmArgs '-agentlib:native-image-agent=access-filter-file=src/test/
resources/access-filter.json,config-output-dir=native-image-agent-output'
```

The parameter `native-image-agent=access-filter-file` specifies a file listing Java packages and classes that should be excluded by the tracing agent, typically test-related classes that we have no use for at runtime. For example, for the `product` microservice, the file `src/test/resources/access-filter.json` looks like this:

```
{ "rules":
  [
    {"excludeClasses": "org.apache.maven.surefire.**"},
    {"excludeClasses": "net.bytebuddy.**"},
    {"excludeClasses": "org.apiguardian.**"},
    {"excludeClasses": "org.junit.**"},
    {"excludeClasses": "org.gradle.**"},
    {"excludeClasses": "org.mockito.**"},
    {"excludeClasses": "org.springframework.test.**"},
    {"excludeClasses": "org.springframework.boot.test.**"},
    {"excludeClasses": "org.testcontainers.**"},
    {"excludeClasses": "se.magnus.microservices.core.product.
MapperTests"},
    {"excludeClasses": "se.magnus.microservices.core.product.
MongoDbTestBase"},
    {"excludeClasses": "se.magnus.microservices.core.product.
PersistenceTests"},
    {"excludeClasses": "se.magnus.microservices.core.product.
ProductServiceApplicationTests"}
  ]
}
```

The folder specified by the `config-output-dir` parameter will contain the generated configuration files. After reviewing their content, the files should be moved manually to the `src/main/resources/META-INF/native-image` folder, to be picked up by the GraalVM native compiler.

This has already been performed for the core microservices, so they already contain the required configuration files for the native compiler. The `product-composite` microservice doesn't need help from the tracing agent. The `jvmArgs` parameter has therefore been disabled in the build files, retained as a comment like `// jvmArgs ....`

Installing the tracing agent

If you want to try out the tracing agent, you must first install it together with the GraalVM JDK native image compiler. The following subsections walk through the steps required on macOS and Ubuntu under WSL 2 in Microsoft Windows.

Installing the tracing agent on macOS

Install and configure the tracing agent as follows:

1. Install GraalVM JDK using Homebrew with the following command:

   ```
   brew install -cask graalvm/tap/graalvm-ce-java11
   ```

   The GraalVM JDK is installed in the folder `/Library/Java/JavaVirtualMachines`. The installation process will ask for your password to be able to move the files to this folder. At the end, it will report the full path to the GraalVM JDK. In my case, it reported `/Library/Java/JavaVirtualMachines/graalvm-ce-java11-21.1.0`.

2. To be able to use the GraalVM JDK, the environment variables `JAVA_HOME` and `PATH` need to be configured as (using the folder reported by the `brew install` command):

   ```
   export JAVA_HOME=/Library/Java/JavaVirtualMachines/graalvm-ce-java11-21.1.0/Contents/Home
   export PATH=$JAVA_HOME/bin:"$PATH"
   ```

3. Verify that the installation succeeded with the following command:

   ```
   java -version
   ```

Expect it to respond with:

```
openjdk version "11.0.11" 2021-04-20
OpenJDK Runtime Environment GraalVM CE 21.1.0 (build
11.0.11+8-jvmci-21.1-b05)
OpenJDK 64-Bit Server VM GraalVM CE 21.1.0 (build
11.0.11+8-jvmci-21.1-b05, mixed mode, sharing)
```

If macOS refuses to run the `java` command, for example by complaining about a damaged download file or that "*the developer cannot be verified*", you can tell macOS that you trust the installed JDK by running the following command:

```
sudo xattr -r -d com.apple.quarantine /Library/Java/
JavaVirtualMachines/graalvm-ce-java11-21.1.0
```

4. Install the GraalVM native image compiler, including its tracing agent, with the GraalVM updater program, `gu`, and check its version number with the commands:

```
gu install native-image
native-image --version
```

Expect a response like this:

```
GraalVM 21.1.0 Java 11 CE ...
```

5. Configure the Bash startup file for GraalVM and its tracing agent.

   Gradle runs test tasks in a separate process. To make it possible for these test tasks to find the GraalVM tracing agent, we need to configure the Bash startup file, for example, `~/.bash_profile` (depending on what startup file you use in your environment). Add the following to your Bash startup file:

```
export JAVA_HOME=/Library/Java/JavaVirtualMachines/graalvm-ce-
java11-21.1.0/Contents/Home
export PATH=$JAVA_HOME/bin:"$PATH"
```

6. Start a new Terminal window, run the `java -version` command again, and verify that you get the same response as in *step 3*.

The GraalVM tracing agent is now ready to be used by the Gradle test task.

Installing the tracing agent on Ubuntu under WSL 2 in Microsoft Windows

Install and configure the tracing agent as follows:

1. Create a folder, with its full path called `<MY_FOLDER_FULL_PATH>`, where GraalVM will be installed:

   ```
   mkdir -p <MY_FOLDER_FULL_PATH>
   cd <MY_FOLDER_FULL_PATH>
   ```

2. Download and install the GraalVM JDK in the folder with the following commands:

   ```
   graalvm_version=21.1.0
   graalvm_archive=graalvm-ce-java11-linux-amd64-${graalvm_version}
   graalvm_folder=graalvm-ce-java11-${graalvm_version}
   curl -L https://github.com/graalvm/graalvm-ce-builds/releases/
   download/vm-${graalvm_version}/${graalvm_archive}.tar.gz >
   ${graalvm_archive}.tar.gz
   tar -xvf ${graalvm_archive}.tar.gz
   rm ${graalvm_archive}.tar.gz
   ```

3. To be able to install the GraalVM native compiler, the environment variables `JAVA_HOME` and `PATH` need to be configured as:

   ```
   export JAVA_HOME=$PWD/${graalvm_folder}
   export PATH=$JAVA_HOME/bin:$PATH
   ```

4. Install the GraalVM native image compiler, including its tracing agent, with the GraalVM updater program, gu, and check its version number with the following commands:

   ```
   gu install native-image
   native-image --version
   ```

   Expect a response like this:

   ```
   GraalVM 21.1.0 Java 11 CE ...
   ```

5. Configure the Bash startup file for GraalVM and its tracing agent.

   Gradle runs test tasks in a separate process. To make it possible for these test tasks to find the GraalVM tracing agent, we need to configure the Bash startup file, for example, `~/.bash_profile` (depending on what startup file you use in your environment). Add the following to your Bash startup file:

```
export graalvm_version=21.1.0
export graalvm_folder=graalvm-ce-java11-${graalvm_version}
export JAVA_HOME=<MY_FOLDER_FULL_PATH>/${graalvm_folder}
export PATH=$JAVA_HOME/bin:$PATH
```

6. Start a new Terminal window, run the command `java -version`, and verify that the response looks like the following (the output might differ if newer versions are used):

```
openjdk version "11.0.11" 2021-04-20
OpenJDK Runtime Environment GraalVM CE 21.1.0 (build
11.0.11+8-jvmci-21.1-b05)
OpenJDK 64-Bit Server VM GraalVM CE 21.1.0 (build
11.0.11+8-jvmci-21.1-b05, mixed mode, sharing)
```

The GraalVM tracing agent is now ready to be used by the Gradle test task.

Running the tracing agent

If you want to try out the tracing agent, you can do so with the following steps:

1. Activate the `jvmArgs` parameter in the build file for the selected microservice by removing the preceding comment characters `//`.
2. Run a `gradle test` command, in this case for the `product` service:

```
cd $BOOK_HOME/Chapter23
./gradlew :microservices:product-service:test --no-daemon
```

   This is a normal `gradle test` command, but to avoid running out of memory, we disable use of the Gradle daemon. By default, the daemon is limited to use 512 MB for its heap, which is not sufficient for the tracing agent in most cases.

3. After the tests complete, you should find the following files in the `microservices/product-service/native-image-agent-output` folder:

```
jni-config.json
proxy-config.json
reflect-config.json
```

```
resource-config.json
serialization-config.json
```

You can browse through the created files; they should be similar to the files in the folder `microservices/product-service/src/main/resources/META-INF/native-image/`.

Wrap up by adding back the comment before the `jvmArgs` parameter in the build file to disable the tracing agent.

Creating the native images

OK, it is finally time to perform the actual native compilation!

Go through the following steps:

1. This is a very resource-demanding process. Therefore, first ensure that Docker Desktop is allowed to consume at least 10 GB of memory to avoid out-of-memory faults.

If a build fails with an error message that looks like `<container-name> exited with code 137`, you have run out of memory in Docker.

2. If your computer has less than 32 GB of memory, it could be a good idea to stop the Minikube instance at this time, to avoid running out of memory in the computer. Use the following command:

```
minikube stop
```

3. Ensure that the Docker client talks to Docker Desktop and not to the Minikube instance:

```
eval $(minikube docker-env -u)
```

4. Run the following command to compile the `product` service:

```
./gradlew :microservices:product-service:bootBuildImage --no-daemon
```

Expect it to take some time. The command will start up a Docker container that will perform the native compile. The first time it runs, it will also download the GraalVM native compiler to be used in Docker, making the compile time even longer. On my MacBook, the first compile takes 20-30 minutes; after that, it takes around 15 minutes.

Expect a lot of output during the compilation, including all sorts of warning and error messages. A successful compile ends with a log output like this:

```
Successfully built image 'docker.io/hands-on/native-product-service:latest'
```

5. Native compile the three remaining microservices with the following commands:

```
./gradlew :microservices:product-composite-service:bootBuildImage --no-daemon
./gradlew :microservices:recommendation-service:bootBuildImage --no-daemon
./gradlew :microservices:review-service:bootBuildImage --no-daemon
```

6. To verify that the Docker images were successfully built, run the following command:

```
docker images | grep "hands-on/native-.* latest"
```

Expect output like this:

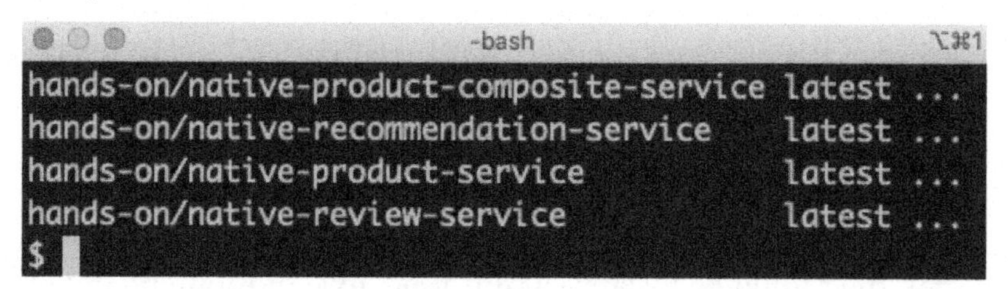
-bash
⌥⌘1
hands-on/native-product-composite-service latest ...
hands-on/native-recommendation-service latest ...
hands-on/native-product-service latest ...
hands-on/native-review-service latest ...
$

Figure 23.1: Docker images containing the native compiled executables

Now that we've created the Docker images containing the native compiled executables, we are ready to try them out! We will start with Docker Compose and, after that, try them out with Kubernetes.

Testing with Docker Compose

We are ready to try out the native compiled microservices.

To use the Docker images that contain the native compiled microservices, a new Docker Compose file has been created, `docker-compose-kafka-native.yml`. It is a copy of `docker-compose-kafka.yml`, where the `build` option has been removed from the definitions of the microservices.

Also, the names of the Docker images to use have been changed, so the ones we created above are used, with names that start with `native-`.

The Docker Compose files are configured to use two partitions per Kafka topic, resulting in two instances for each core microservice. Together with the single `product-composite` instance, this means that seven microservice instances will be started up. For a recap, see *Chapter 7, Developing Reactive Microservices*, the *Running manual tests of the reactive microservice landscape* section.

We'll first get a benchmark using the JVM-based microservices, to compare the startup times and initial memory consumption against. Next, we will repeat this procedure but use the Docker images that contain the native compiled microservices. Run through the following commands to test the JVM-based microservices:

1. Start by compiling the source code and building the JVM-based Docker images in Docker Desktop:

```
cd $BOOK_HOME/Chapter23
eval $(minikube docker-env -u)
./gradlew build -x generateAot -x generateTestAot
docker-compose build
```

Note that we have disabled the new Spring AOT tasks, `generateAot` and `generateTestAot`, in the build command. We don't need them here; they were used in the previous section of this chapter.

2. Use the Docker Compose file for the Java VM-based microservices and Kafka:

```
export COMPOSE_FILE=docker-compose-kafka.yml
```

3. Start all containers, except the microservices' containers:

```
docker-compose up -d mysql mongodb kafka zookeeper auth-server
gateway
```

   Wait for the containers to start up, until the CPU load goes down.

4. Start up the microservices using the Java VM:

```
docker-compose up -d
```

   Wait for the microservices to start up, again monitoring the CPU load.

5. To find out how much time it took to start the microservices, we can look for a log output containing `: Started`. Run the following command:

```
docker-compose logs product-composite product review
recommendation product-p1 review-p1 recommendation-p1 | grep ":
Started"
```

Expect output like this:

```
-bash
product-p1_1          | ... Started ProductServiceApplication in 26.813 seconds
product-composite_1   | ... Started ProductCompositeServiceApplication in 32.124 seconds
recommendation_1      | ... Started RecommendationServiceApplication in 24.416 seconds
product_1             | ... Started ProductServiceApplication in 26.915 seconds
recommendation-p1_1   | ... Started RecommendationServiceApplication in 26.204 seconds
review_1              | ... Started ReviewServiceApplication in 28.651 seconds
review-p1_1           | ... Started ReviewServiceApplication in 27.987 seconds
$
```

Figure 23.2: Startup times for Java VM-based microservices

In the output, we can see startup times varying from 24-32 seconds. Remember that all seven microservice instances were started simultaneously, resulting in longer startup times compared to if they were started up one by one.

6. Run through the tests to verify that the system landscape works as expected:

```
USE_K8S=false HOST=localhost PORT=8443 HEALTH_URL=https://
localhost:8443 ./test-em-all.bash
```

> Sometimes, it takes a minute for the microservices and Kafka to agree on what topics and partitions to use. This will result in various error messages when running the `test-em-all.bash` script during the initialization; for example, `Dispatcher has no subscribers for channel 'unknown.channel.name'`. Simply rerun the test script after a minute.

Note that no circuit breaker-specific tests are executed, since the use of Resilience4j in this chapter currently does not work with Spring Native. Expect the output we have seen in previous chapters from the tests:

```
$ ./test-em-all.bash
...
Wait for: curl -k https://health.minikube.me/actuator/health... DONE, continues...
...
Test OK (HTTP Code: 200)
...
End, all tests OK: Thu May 20 12:37:18 CEST 2021
$
```

Figure 23.3: Output from the test script

7. Finally, to find out how much memory is used after starting up and running the tests, run the following command:

```
docker stats --no-stream
```

Expect a response like this:

```
CONTAINER ID   NAME                                CPU %    MEM USAGE ...
365b171c9c81   chapter23_recommendation-p1_1       0.70%    225.5MiB  ...
c6941fd59a7e   chapter23_product_1                 1.17%    262.8MiB  ...
3e2df5ece813   chapter23_review-p1_1               0.42%    275.6MiB  ...
e884c38b2d8d   chapter23_review_1                  0.57%    278.5MiB  ...
40f2477df35f   chapter23_product-composite_1       1.35%    333.3MiB  ...
7edf6716bd11   chapter23_product-p1_1              0.41%    233.5MiB  ...
608b10241fba   chapter23_recommendation_1          0.84%    258.4MiB  ...
188c00120f13   chapter23_gateway_1                 0.23%    244.4MiB  ...
7306791e33e9   chapter23_kafka_1                   17.74%   357.7MiB  ...
b6040f61fdb6   chapter23_auth-server_1             0.41%    149.7MiB  ...
3a41ba88d826   chapter23_zookeeper_1               0.23%    81.77MiB  ...
def421d686e2   chapter23_mongodb_1                 1.27%    160.6MiB  ...
0c44bfc494a7   chapter23_mysql_1                   4.85%    209MiB    ...
$
```

Figure 23.4: Memory usage for Java VM-based microservices

From the preceding output, we can see that the microservices consume around 220-330 MB.

8. Bring down the system landscape:

```
docker compose down
```

Now, we are ready to repeat the same procedure, but this time using the Docker images with the native compiled microservices:

1. Change to the new Docker Compose file:

   ```
   export COMPOSE_FILE=docker-compose-kafka-native.yml
   ```

2. Start all containers, except for the microservices' containers:

   ```
   docker-compose up -d mysql mongodb kafka zookeeper auth-server
   gateway
   ```

   Wait for the containers to start up, until the CPU load goes down.

3. Start up the microservices using the Java VM:

   ```
   docker-compose up -d
   ```

   Wait for the microservices to start up, again monitoring the CPU load.

4. To find out how much time it took to start the native compiled microservices, run the same command we ran previously:

   ```
   docker-compose logs product-composite product review
   recommendation product-p1 review-p1 recommendation-p1 | grep ":
   Started"
   ```

   Expect output like this:

   ```
   product_1            | ... Started ProductServiceApplication in 0.604 seconds
   review_1             | ... Started ReviewServiceApplication in 0.802 seconds
   review-p1_1          | ... Started ReviewServiceApplication in 0.583 seconds
   product-p1_1         | ... Started ProductServiceApplication in 0.491 seconds
   recommendation_1     | ... Started RecommendationServiceApplication in 0.535 seconds
   product-composite_1  | ... Started ProductCompositeServiceApplication in 0.794 seconds
   recommendation-p1_1  | ... Started RecommendationServiceApplication in 0.736 seconds
   $
   ```

   Figure 23.5: Startup times for native compiled microservices

   In the above output, we can see startup times varying from 0.4-0.8 seconds. Considering that all seven microservices instances were started up at the same time, these are rather impressive figures compared to the 24-32 seconds it took for the Java VM-based tests!

5. Run through the tests to verify that the system landscape works as expected:

   ```
   USE_K8S=false HOST=localhost PORT=8443 HEALTH_URL=https://
   localhost:8443 ./test-em-all.bash
   ```

Expect the same output as from the test above using the Java VM-based Docker images.

6. Finally, to find out how much memory is used after starting up and running the tests, run the following command:

```
docker stats --no-stream
```

Expect a response like this:

```
CONTAINER ID   NAME                               CPU %    MEM USAGE ...
c942bc584d93   chapter23_product_1                0.20%    91.29MiB  ...
77a49dbd6b52   chapter23_product-composite_1      0.24%    89.79MiB  ...
3246d7e78f28   chapter23_recommendation-p1_1      0.19%    87.22MiB  ...
eecdea1dfe19   chapter23_review_1                 0.35%    94.63MiB  ...
b138372f7f1f   chapter23_review-p1_1              0.49%    91.88MiB  ...
893feb3e90c5   chapter23_recommendation_1         0.40%    90MiB     ...
6d2beb891455   chapter23_product-p1_1             0.17%    86.76MiB  ...
098b75bba71f   chapter23_gateway_1                0.30%    252.3MiB  ...
1b44d2d43ea9   chapter23_kafka_1                  5.88%    355.1MiB  ...
e9447a15dbd7   chapter23_auth-server_1            0.42%    152.9MiB  ...
7431969d3264   chapter23_mongodb_1                0.67%    160.9MiB  ...
ac70d72b5086   chapter23_zookeeper_1              0.33%    82.02MiB  ...
d8993843da5f   chapter23_mysql_1                  0.34%    209.5MiB  ...
$
```

Figure 23.6: Memory usage for native compiled microservices

From the preceding output, we can see that the microservices consume around 80-100 MB. Again, this is a noticeable reduction compared to the 220-330 MB that the Java VM containers used!

7. Bring down the system landscape:

```
docker compose down
```

To get a better understanding of both the memory and CPU consumption of the native compiled microservices, a more realistic load test needs to be performed, but that is beyond the scope of this book.

After seeing how much faster and less memory-consuming the native compiled microservices are when starting up compared to Java VM-based alternatives, let's see how we can run them using Kubernetes.

Testing with Kubernetes

Before we can deploy the native compiled microservices in Kubernetes, we need to replace RabbitMQ, which we have been using so far in Kubernetes, with Kafka and Zookeeper. Helm charts have been added for Kafka and Zookeeper in this chapter. Also, a new environment chart has been added, which has been configured to use the Docker images that contain the native compiled microservices. The Helm charts can be found in the following folders:

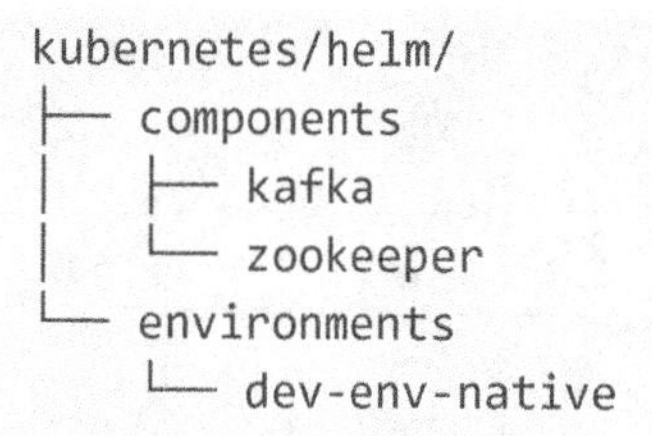

```
kubernetes/helm/
├── components
│   ├── kafka
│   └── zookeeper
└── environments
    └── dev-env-native
```

The Zookeeper chart is based on a `Deployment` and a `Service` object, as we have been using before. But for the Kafka chart, a `StatefulSet` has been used instead of a `Deployment` object. Deploying Kafka on Minikube using a `Deployment` object results in insufficient solutions using services of type `NodePort` and other workarounds.

A `StatefulSet` is similar to a `Deployment` object, since it is used to manage Pods. But it differs in terms of support for **distributed stateful workloads**, where the identity of the Pods is typically of importance. Typical examples of distributed stateful workloads include MongoDB as a distributed database and Kafka as a distributed streaming platform. When using a `StatefulSet`, each Pod gets its own DNS name, and a `Service` object also needs to be created as a **headless** service, meaning that the service itself does not have an IP address. The service's DNS name, instead, translates into the DNS names of the `Pods` managed by the `StatefulSet`.

We will try out the DNS names generated for the Pods of the `StatefulSet` later in this section.

A `Service` object can be marked as headless by setting its `clusterIP` to `None`, like so:

```
apiVersion: v1
kind: Service
metadata:
  name: kafka
```

```
spec:
  clusterIP: None
...
```

We will use a `StatefulSet` to create a three-node Kafka cluster.

There is also a difference, compared to using a `Deployment`, when a disk is attached to the Pods using a `PersistentVolumeClaim` (not covered in this book). When using a `StatefulSet`, a `PersistentVolume` is created for each Pod. This results in each Pod getting its own disk where it can store its own data in a persistent way. This differs from a `Deployment`, where all Pods share the same `PersistentVolume`.

Another thing we need to consider before deploying the native compiled microservices to Kubernetes is how to provision the Docker images. We don't want to run the lengthy native compile commands again to get new Docker images created in the Minikube instance. If we had used a Docker registry in this book, we could have pushed the images to the registry, but we didn't. Instead, we will extract the Docker images from Docker Desktop and import them into the Minikube instance, as a workaround for not using a Docker registry.

Move the Docker images from Docker Desktop to the Minikube instance with the following commands:

1. Export the Docker images from Docker Desktop:

```
docker save hands-on/native-product-composite-service:latest -o native-product-composite.tar

docker save hands-on/native-product-service:latest -o native-product.tar

docker save hands-on/native-recommendation-service:latest -o native-recommendation.tar

docker save hands-on/native-review-service:latest -o native-review.tar
```

2. If you stopped your Minikube instance before building the native images, you need to start it now:

```
minikube start
```

It could also be a good idea to stop Docker Desktop, to preserve memory.

3. Import the Docker images into the Minikube instance:

```
eval $(minikube docker-env)
docker load -i native-product-composite.tar
docker load -i native-product.tar
docker load -i native-recommendation.tar
docker load -i native-review.tar
```

4. Finally, delete the exported `.tar` files:

```
rm native-product-composite.tar native-product.tar native-
recommendation.tar native-review.tar
```

Building, deploying, and verifying the deployment on Kubernetes is done in the same way as in the previous chapters. Run the following commands:

1. Build the Docker image for the auth server with the following command:

```
docker-compose build auth-server
```

2. To make the deploy steps run faster, prefetch the Docker images for Kafka and Zookeeper with the following commands:

```
docker pull zookeeper:3.4.14
docker pull wurstmeister/kafka:2.12-2.5.0
```

3. Recreate the Namespace, `hands-on`, and set it as the default Namespace:

```
kubectl delete namespace hands-on
kubectl apply -f kubernetes/hands-on-namespace.yml
kubectl config set-context $(kubectl config current-context)
--namespace=hands-on
```

4. Resolve the Helm chart dependencies with the following commands.

   First, we update the dependencies in the `components` folder:

```
for f in kubernetes/helm/components/*; do helm dep up $f; done
```

   Next, we update the dependencies in the `environments` folder:

```
for f in kubernetes/helm/environments/*; do helm dep up $f; done
```

5. We are now ready to deploy the system landscape using Helm. Run the following command and wait for all the deployments to complete:

```
helm upgrade -install hands-on-dev-env-native \
  kubernetes/helm/environments/dev-env-native \
  -n hands-on --wait
```

In the previous chapters, we used the `helm install` command. The `helm upgrade -install` command used here is a better alternative for scripting, since it performs an `insert` if the chart is not installed, but an `upgrade` if the chart is already installed. It's a bit like an **upsert** command in the relational database world.

6. Start the Minikube tunnel, if it's not already running (see *Chapter 18, Using a Service Mesh to Improve Observability and Management*, the *Setting up access to Istio services* section, for a recap if required):

```
minikube tunnel
```

Remember that this command requires that your user has `sudo` privileges and that you enter your password during startup and shutdown. It takes a couple of seconds before the command asks for the password, so it is easy to miss!

7. Since it takes some time (maximum 2 minutes on my Mac) for the Kafka cluster to elect leaders for the various partitions used, it can be worth following its progress with the following command:

```
kubectl logs -f -l app=kafka
```

When you have seen output like the following, you can stop the `kubectl logs` command with *Ctrl* + *C*:

```
[2021-06-06 08:48:57,172] INFO [GroupCoordinator 0]: Assignment received from leader for
  group reviewsGroup for generation 1 (kafka.coordinator.group.GroupCoordinator)
[2021-06-06 08:49:00,150] INFO [GroupCoordinator 0]: Assignment received from leader for
  group productsGroup for generation 2 (kafka.coordinator.group.GroupCoordinator)
[2021-06-06 08:49:03,150] INFO [GroupCoordinator 0]: Assignment received from leader for
  group recommendationsGroup for generation 2 (kafka.coordinator.group.GroupCoordinator)
$
```

Figure 23.7: Log output from a Kafka cluster during startup

8. Run the normal tests to verify the deployment with the following command:

```
./test-em-all.bash
```

Expect the output to be like what we've already seen in the previous tests.

9. Check the startup time for one of the Pods:

```
kubectl logs -l app=product-composite --tail=-1 | grep ": Started"
```

Expect a response like this:

```
2021-06-05 15:12:13.849 ... Started ProductCompositeServiceApplication in 0.768 seconds
$
```

Figure 23.8: Startup time when running as a Pod in Kubernetes

Expect a startup time of around what we noticed when using Docker Compose, 0.8 seconds in the example above. Since we also start an Istio proxy as a sidecar, there might be some slight extra delay.

10. Check the Docker images used with the following command:

```
kubectl get pods -o jsonpath="{.items[*].spec.containers[*].image}" | xargs -n1 | grep hands-on
```

Expect the following response:

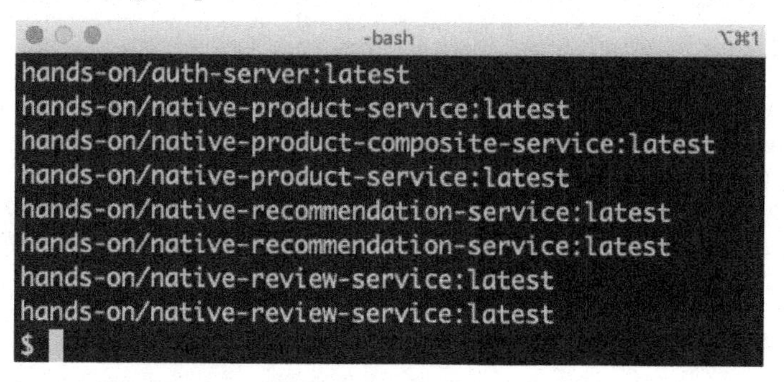

-bash
hands-on/auth-server:latest
hands-on/native-product-service:latest
hands-on/native-product-composite-service:latest
hands-on/native-product-service:latest
hands-on/native-recommendation-service:latest
hands-on/native-recommendation-service:latest
hands-on/native-review-service:latest
hands-on/native-review-service:latest
$

Figure 23.9: Docker images with native compiled code

From the output, we can see that all containers, except the `auth-server`, use Docker images with the name prefix `native`, meaning that we are running native compiled executables inside the Docker containers.

11. To learn a bit more about the difference between a `Deployment` and a `StatefulSet` object, ask one of the Kafka brokers for the address translation of the headless service's DNS name, `kafka.hands-on.svc.cluster.local`. Use the following command:

```
kubectl exec kafka-0 -it -- nslookup kafka.hands-on.svc.cluster.
local
```

Expect it to answer with:

```
-bash
Name:      kafka.hands-on.svc.cluster.local
Address 1: 172.17.0.32 kafka-2.kafka.hands-on.svc.cluster.local
Address 2: 172.17.0.18 kafka-0.kafka.hands-on.svc.cluster.local
Address 3: 172.17.0.31 kafka-1.kafka.hands-on.svc.cluster.local
$
```

Figure 23.10: Resolving the DNS name for a headless service

From the output, we can see that the DNS name is translated into the DNS names of each broker's `Pod` in the cluster, as expected for a headless service.

12. We can also ask for an address translation of the DNS name of one of the broker's `Pods`. We will used the DNS name of the third broker, `kafka-2.kafka.hands-on.svc.cluster.local`:

```
kubectl exec kafka-0 -it -- nslookup kafka-2.kafka.hands-on.svc.
cluster.local
```

Expect it to answer with the IP address of the third broker's `Pod`, like so:

```
-bash
Name:      kafka-2.kafka.hands-on.svc.cluster.local
Address 1: 172.17.0.32 kafka-2.kafka.hands-on.svc.cluster.local
$
```

Figure 23.11: Resolving the DNS name of one of the broker's Pods

This completes this chapter on how to use the Spring Native and GraalVM projects to create native compiled executables for our microservices.

Summary

In this chapter, we were introduced to the Spring Native project and underlying GraalVM project, along with its native image compiler. After declaring Spring Native's plugin in the build file and providing the native image compiler with some hints, it can be used to create native images. These standalone executables files are packaged by the Spring Native plugin into ready-to-use Docker images.

The main benefit of compiling Java-based source code to native images is significantly faster startup time and less memory usage. In a test where we started up seven microservice instances at the same time, we observed sub-second startup times for the native compiled microservices, compared with at least 25 seconds required for the Java VM-based microservices for the same test. Also, the native compiled microservices required half of the memory compared to the Java VM-based microservices after running through the tests in the script, `test-em-all.bash`.

Many of the libraries and frameworks we use in this book are already supported by Spring Native, while some of them are not yet supported. In some cases, the GraalVM native image tracing agent can be used to create configuration to help the native compiler. The tracing agent was configured to run together with our JUnit tests, and it created configuration based on the execution of the tests.

Remember that the Spring Native project has only provided a beta release at the time of writing. A lot of improvements can be expected as the project evolves toward a GA release.

We have also seen how easy it is to replace the Docker images running a Java VM with Docker images containing the native compiled images. We tested the native compiled images, both using Docker Compose and Kubernetes. When used with Kubernetes, we were also introduced to `StatefulSets` as an alternative to `Deployment` objects. `StatefulSets` are specifically useful for stateful workloads, such as a Kafka cluster.

With this, we have reached the end of the book. I hope it has helped you learn how to develop microservices using all the amazing features of Spring Boot, Spring Cloud, Kubernetes, and Istio and that you feel encouraged to try them out!

Questions

1. How are the Spring Native and GraalVM projects related to each other?
2. How is the tracing agent used?
3. What is the difference between JIT and AOT compilation?
4. What is a native hint?
5. How are memory and startup times affected by native compiling Java code?
6. How does a Kubernetes `Deployment` object differ from a `StatefulSet` object?

packt.com

Subscribe to our online digital library for full access to over 7,000 books and videos, as well as industry leading tools to help you plan your personal development and advance your career. For more information, please visit our website.

Why subscribe?

- Spend less time learning and more time coding with practical eBooks and Videos from over 4,000 industry professionals
- Improve your learning with Skill Plans built especially for you
- Get a free eBook or video every month
- Fully searchable for easy access to vital information
- Copy and paste, print, and bookmark content

At www.packt.com, you can also read a collection of free technical articles, sign up for a range of free newsletters, and receive exclusive discounts and offers on Packt books and eBooks.

Other Books You May Enjoy

If you enjoyed this book, you may be interested in these other books by Packt:

Git for Programmers - First Edition

Jesse Liberty

ISBN: 9781801075732

- Create and clone repositories
- Understand the difference between local and remote repositories
- Use, manage, and merge branches back into the main branch
- Utilize tools to manage merge conflicts
- Manage commits on your local machine through interactive rebasing
- Use the log to gain control over all the data in your repository
- Use bisect, blame, and other tools to undo Git mistakes

Mastering TypeScript - Fourth Edition

Nathan Rozentals

ISBN: 9781800564732

- Gain insights into core and advanced TypeScript language features
- Integrate with existing JavaScript libraries and third-party frameworks
- Build full working applications using JavaScript frameworks, such as Angular, React, Vue, and more
- Create test suites for your application with Jest and Selenium
- Apply industry-standard design patterns to build modular code
- Develop web server solutions using NodeJS and Express
- Design and implement serverless API solutions
- Explore micro front-end technologies and techniques

Packt is searching for authors like you

If you're interested in becoming an author for Packt, please visit `authors.packtpub.com` and apply today. We have worked with thousands of developers and tech professionals, just like you, to help them share their insight with the global tech community. You can make a general application, apply for a specific hot topic that we are recruiting an author for, or submit your own idea.

Share your thoughts

Now you've finished *Microservices with Spring Boot and Spring Cloud, Second Edition,* we'd love to hear your thoughts! Scan the QR code below to go straight to the Amazon review page for this book and share your feedback or leave a review on the site that you purchased it from.

https://packt.link/r/1-801-07297-3

Your review is important to us and the tech community and will help us make sure we're delivering excellent quality content.

Index

Symbols

A

B

D

E

F

G

H

I

J

K

N

O

P

Q

R

S

T

Made in the USA
Las Vegas, NV
09 March 2023